COMMUNIST FRONT?

COMMUNIST FRONT?

The Civil Rights Congress, 1946–1956

Gerald Horne

RUTHERFORD ● MADISON ● TEANECK
FAIRLEIGH DICKINSON UNIVERSITY PRESS
LONDON AND TORONTO: ASSOCIATED UNIVERSITY PRESSES

Associated University Presses
440 Forsgate Drive
Cranbury, NJ 08512

Associated University Presses
25 Sicilian Avenue
London WC1A 2QH, England

Associated University Presses
2133 Royal Windsor Drive
Unit 1
Mississauga, Ontario
Canada L5J 1K5

The paper used in this publication meets the requirements
of the American National Standard for Permanence of Paper
for Printed Library Materials Z39.48-1984.

Library of Congress Cataloging-in-Publication Data

Horne, Gerald.
  Communist front?

  Bibliography: p.
  Includes index.
  1. Afro-Americans—Civil rights. 2. Civil Rights
Congress (U.S.) 3. Anti-communist movements—United
States—History—20th century. 4. United States—Race
relations. I. Title.
E185.61.H8 1988   323.1′196073′073   85-45950
ISBN 0-8386-3285-8 (alk. paper)

Printed in the United States of America

Contents

Preface

This book originated in a conversation with the legendary Ernest Kaiser of the Schomburg Library, the most prolific and unsung bibliographer of our era. As my first book was on the way to publication, I was scrounging around for a second topic to pursue and it was Kaiser who brought to my attention the voluminous CRC records at the Schomburg in Harlem. This was the beginning of a trek that took me to libraries at Harvard University, the University of Oregon, the University of Washington, Princeton University, New York University, Columbia University, Howard University—not to mention the Library of Congress, the New York Public Library, the Wisconsin Historical Society, the Southern California Library for Social Studies and Research and Wayne State University. To all of those industrious librarians who lent a hand, allow me to convey my heartfelt thanks. The librarians at the Federal Bureau of Investigation (FBI), as well as the historians there, were helpful. Dorothy Burnham and Esther Jackson were kind enough to open the rich files of the Southern Negro Youth Congress for my perusal; Louise Patterson was similarly gracious in allowing me to examine the fascinating papers of William Patterson, which will one day allow some historian to pen a striking biography. Aubrey Grossman, Ben Margolis, William Mandel, Jess Brown, Henry Kirksey, and John Crawford were helpful in answering inquiries. The law firm of Rabinowitz, Boudin, and Standard, in the midst of litigating against the FBI, on behalf of their client the National Lawyers Guild went beyond the call of duty in allowing me to look at the fruits of their discovery motions; this truck full of documents should keep a future generation of scholars busy. Diana Pandora Houston Peoples was efficient in word processing this manuscript. It is fair to say that this work would have been much more difficult to produce but for the timely assistance of the librarians, staff, and administration of Sarah Lawrence College; they deserve special commendation. Eileen McGann and Regina Cahill provided timely last minute aid, as did Helen Toppins. Two interns who worked closely with me at the headquarters of the National Conference of Black Lawyers—Lisa Donner

9

and Sarah Roff—were quite efficient in performing last-minute research and checking tasks. I should not fail to mention Lottie Gordon and the Reference Center for Marxist Studies, whose growing collection will soon be an essential stop for any researcher interested in the period.

In my first book I attempted, inter alia, to place the Afro-American experience within the international context and tried to explain how the coming to independence of African nations and the competition for their "hearts and minds" between the United States and the Soviet Union helped to bring down the walls of segregation as Jim Crow became a painful Achilles heel in the execution of U.S. foreign policy. Here I elaborate on that theme of why there was a retreat by the racists and expand on the related theme of anticommunism. This book should make clear, but allow me to repeat it here, that I consider anticommunism (along with racism) one of the major scourges of modern times and a major impediment to social progress, as even a cursory examination of the Vietnam War, the Korean War, or Hitler's Germany amply demonstrates. If this modest work contributes a scintilla or iota of understanding of this phenomenon, I will have deemed my labor to have been worthwhile. Moreover, this work should make clear that creative, brilliant lawyers are not sufficient to win progressive law reform and victory; the masses organized, by far, are the decisive factor. This study looks more at how *Communists* functioned within the Civil Rights Congress, rather than how the *Communist Party* functioned. Similarly, the activities of the Civil Rights Congress were so vast and multifaceted that this work can only be considered a beginning; local studies of CRC would no doubt assist a clearer understanding of racism and anticommunism.

Abbreviations

ACLU	American Civil Liberties Union
ALP	American Labor Party
AYD	American Youth for Democracy
CP	Communist Party
CPUSA	Communist Party of the United States of America
CRC	Civil Rights Congress
FEPC	Fair Employment Practices Commission
FIAPP	International Federation of Ex-Political Prisoners
HUAC	House Un-American Activities Committee
ILD	International Labor Defense
ILGWU	International Ladies Garments Workers Union
ILWU	International Longshore & Warehouse Union
IWA	International Woodworkers of America
KKK	Ku Klux Klan
NCFIF	National Committee to Free the Ingram Family
NLG	National Lawyers Guild
NNC	National Negro Congress
OBRC	Ohio Bill of Rights Conference
PP	Progressive Party
SACB	Subversive Activities Control Board
SATR	Smith Act Trial Reports
SCEF	Southern Conference Education Fund
SCLC	Southern Christian Leadership Conference
SFTJ	Sojourners for Truth & Justice
SNCC	Student Non-Violent Coordinating Committee
SNYC	Southern Negro Youth Congress
SWP	Socialist Workers Party
UAW	United Auto Workers
UE	United Electrical, Radio & Machine Workers
WDL	Workers Defense League

Introduction

The House Un-American Activities Committee called them a "Communist front." But, in something of an ecumenical spirit, so did Roger Baldwin of the American Civil Liberties Union. The top "commie hunter" of the now defunct *New York World-Telegram* generously called them the "most successful Commie hoax of all time."[1]

What stirred such passion was the Civil Rights Congress, an organization that undoubtedly included Communists, which was in existence from 1946 to 1956. An amalgamation of the National Negro Congress, the International Labor Defense, and the National Federation for Constitutional Liberties, during its comparatively brief existence CRC and the attorneys who worked with them fought for and established a number of civil liberties rulings that expanded the rights of all in the United States. In state and federal courts they argued landmark cases in areas as disparate as extradition, standing, excessive bail, the right to be silent before a grand jury, and many more. Some of their scores of cases were lost. Others were won. Decades before the issue became a live one in the civil rights movement, CRC and their allies were arguing before the U.S. Supreme Court that an employer had to hire Afro-Americans, as Euro-Americans quit or transferred, until the proportion of Black clerks to white clerks approximated the proportion of Black customers to white customers (about 50%) at this particular store. This "premature antiracism" pushing the controversial issue of quotas—and this is what distinguished CRC from similar organizations that argued cases in the courts—was backed up by spirited mass picketing of Lucky Stores in Contra Costa County, California.[2]

Why, despite their obvious contribution to the ongoing battle for democratic rights, was CRC subjected to such vilification? Why did the FBI break into their offices and bug their phones; why did HUAC frequently call their activists in for grilling; why were their meetings disrupted by young toughs; why did the government send informers and agents provocateurs into their ranks? Can one connect the death of their top leader in San Francisco, Ida

13

Rothstein, to this pattern and practice, or the torching of the CRC office in Philadelphia?[3]

There is no question that the close ties between CRC and the Communist Party engendered bitterness and distortion and misinformation. A number of CRC critics in limning their charge of the organization as no more than a "front" pointed to what they considered to be an undue concentration on cases involving the CP. However, particularly under the leadership of William Patterson, CRC tended to focus heavily on cases of racist repression. For example, when the National Non-Partisan Committee to Defend the Rights of the Twelve Communist Party Leaders held a dinner in the spring of 1950 in honor of "One Hundred Cases In Defense Of Civil Rights," there were at least thirty-eight identifiable cases involving Blacks. In an analysis of the "Bulletin" produced by CRC, in the seventeen issues from 26 December 1950 to 23 April 1951, the case of Willie McGee, a Mississippi Black, received the most attention—forty-four items, 151 inches. Next on the list was the case of the CP leadership, twenty-seven items, 114 inches; next was the case of Patterson himself (fifteen/86), then the Martinsville Seven, Peekskill, and the Trenton Six.[4]

It is more difficult to challenge the CRC's focus on victims of racist repression, yet CRC would have been justified in emphasizing the repression of Communists. In discussing the Smith Act trial of the CP directorate, Arthur Kinoy, Distinguished Professor of Constitutional Law at Rutgers, put it bluntly:

> If the government could win, labor could be devastated. . . . we knew that whatever happened in the Smith Act trial was bound to have a profound effect upon all our work . . . the immediate consequences of the defeat in the Smith Act trial were no less than we had feared. Within a few months after the guilty verdict came in, the Department of Justice, encouraged by the results of the trial, was moving against people's organizations on a hundred different fronts. . . . All our fears that the government's target went far beyond the Smith Act defendants were coming to life.[5]

Defense of the Communists being the first line of defense for all civil liberties generally turned out to be more than an empty slogan. The definition of "communism," which could be as diverse as being against Jim Crow, for recognition of the government in Peking, or against the war in Korea, was tailored not coincidentally to sweep within its ambit just about everyone who was not conservative; the same was true for the term "Communist Front."

Nevertheless, some did challenge CRC's focus on Blacks, e.g., Willie McGee, Rosa Lee Ingram, the Trenton Six, the Martinsville Seven, claiming that CRC had no legitimate interest in them. As shall be seen, this was not the view of the Black defendants themselves. Still, *Time* claimed that for the CRC, the McGee case was simply "surefire propaganda, good for whipping up racial tension . . . and giving U.S. justice a black eye abroad. . . ." Their brother under the skin, *Life,* agreed that but for the CRC's involvement, "There was a bare chance that this sentence might never have been carried out. . . ." (referring to McGee's execution). Putting aside for a moment the salient fact that Black men were being executed steadily on flimsy grounds during this period in cases in which CRC was not involved, it is interesting to examine the record of the NAACP—which tended to play the game "by the rules," bar Communists, etc. Their record in saving Black victims from the gallows was not exactly spectacular, and not the least reason was the bestiality of the Southern authorities.[6] Even when the NAACP won a civil rights victory on behalf of a Black, e.g., *Morgan v. Virginia*[7] involving a Supreme Court ruling in favor of desegregated interstate bus travel in 1946, it required CRC-type tactics brought to the 1960s—"freedom rides"—in order to make this "legal" victory a reality. Moreover, CRC did win cases—the cases of Jerry Newson in Oakland, Rosa Lee Ingram who was eventually freed, Robert Wesley Wells who was eventually freed, etc.. Even when they suffered setbacks, like the Wells case where he was freed after CRC had become defunct, they established important rulings; for example, the Wells litigation established critical rules concerning the insanity defense, legal presumptions, state of mind, etc.[8]

Part of the charge that alleges CRC sectarianism and an undue focus on CP cases involves inevitably their approach to Trotskyists. Specifically, this refers to *Dunn v. U.S.*[9] a case decided by the Supreme Court during the height of World War II. Smith Act violations were charged. This case arose before CRC came into existence, although Corliss Lamont, among others, held CRC's predecessors (ILD, NFCL, NNC) and the CP itself responsible for what was perceived to be a laggard approach in rallying to the defense of the Socialist Workers Party. Most recently, Victor Navasky echoed this charge in reviewing the memoir of former East Bay CRC leader Jessica Mitford. Few acknowledge that the assumed parent, the Communist Party, denounced the charges against the SWP when they were first announced. Later in the *Daily Worker,* in August 1949, after a CRC-endorsed "Bill of Rights Conference" was almost disrupted over the matter, a lengthy letter distinguished the SWP Smith Act case from the Communist Party case because in the former the defendants "admitted from the stand (Record pp. 454, 1015, etc.) to have stored rifles and to holding target practice," and also the "arming of 'military units' " was alleged while the latter were charged simply with advocacy. Still, Red leaders later acknowledged more could have been done. Further, CRC took the position that they could not handle every case—they were not a political legal services office—and that from their political view, SWP's anti-Sovietism only gave succor and strength to the right-wing forces attempting to destabilize CRC, lynch Blacks, and so forth, and that it simply did not make sense to defend those who worked at cross purposes with their goals.[10]

In any case, the many prisoners and soldiers who continually wrote CRC seeking assistance apparently did not accept the notion that they would simply be "used." Mitford addressed this issue directly after the NAACP charged CRC with using a Black family for "ideological purposes" after they had initiated a twenty-four-hour vigil to protect the family's home after a cross had been burned on their lawn. Mitford agreed because, unlike the NAACP, CRC saw such acts not as being "isolated" acts but as "conscious policy . . . to keep the Blacks in a state of subjugation." CRC saw racism itself as having "ideological purposes," not the most negligible of which was making for a cowed underclass of low-paid labor.[11]

Mitford was not the only "celebrity" or person of note to associate with CRC during an era when it was being subjected to excruciating persecution. Dashiell Hammett, the writer, and Fred Field, a Vanderbilt heir, both went to jail as a result of being trustees of CRC's Bail Fund. *Hollywood Life* was not singular in alleging that Hammett was "one of the most dangerous (if not THE) influential communists in America": they accused him of influencing Howard Duff and many others in Hollywood; they went on to charge that Judy Holliday had ties to CRC. This may have been true, but there is little doubt that CRC had influence in Hollywood. After all, during a time when the blacklist was dominating everything and most organizations were running for cover, CRC was not afraid to go at it toe to toe. Thus, John Garfield, Garson Kanin, Oscar Hammerstein II, Gene Kelly, and Katherine Dunham all sponsored CRC's "National Committee to Oust Bilbo." Edward G. Robinson sponsored their founding convention. Elia Kazan, Jerome Robbins, and Arthur Miller were associated with "Veterans Against Discrimination," sponsored by CRC's New York chapter. In the balmy political winds of 1946 Gregory Peck, Dalton Trumbo, Artie Shaw, E. Y. Harburg had no problem working with CRC's Los Angeles chapter; Leonard Bernstein and Clifford Odets apparently felt similarly when they sponsored CRC's 1947 national convention. Of course, this type of support did not survive the onset of the Cold War. The case of actress Kim Hunter is exemplary. According to David Caute, she was "blacklisted" and "offered no more parts" after she had "supported a CRC petition" calling for a new trial for Willie McGee; this after she had won an Academy Award in 1952. Only one slave needed to be beaten to keep the entire plantation in line.[12]

Katherine Dunham was far from being the only prominent Afro-American artist who saw fit to associate with CRC. Given Blacks' generally more progressive political positions (perhaps as a result of their lack of satisfaction with the status quo) and CRC's penchant for vigorously fighting cases of persecution of Blacks, this is not too surprising. Still, it remains remarkable that during a time when ties to the CRC could spell doom for a career, so many of these artists refused to bend. Paul Robeson's close ties to CRC are well known. Canada Lee, his fellow Black actor was also active, particularly in the area of fundraising; so were Alice Childress, Frank Silvera, Charles White, Milt Jackson, Adadata Dafora, Lloyd Richards, W. C. Handy, and

Elizabeth Catlett. Josephine Baker assisted CRC with the McGee case and with the case of Jerry Newson in Oakland. It was not unusual for William Patterson, a prominent Black lawyer during a time when there just were not that many, to send a warm note to "Dear Lena" (Horne) asking to see her "back stage" and reassuring her that "it is not to ask for funds."[13]

CRC was *not* the Communist Party, yet it performed militant and often successful tasks, which helped to attract such luminaries; and herein one begins to comprehend the exegesis of the term "Communist front." Although Americans for Democratic Action would not be tagged a "Democratic Party front" or the *Wall Street Journal* or *New York Herald Tribune* would not be tagged as "G.O.P. fronts," seemingly only organizations that were influenced and led by another political party—the Communist Party—would be subjected to such pejorative designations; and this was done for partisan political reasons, because CRC was clearly competing with these opposing forces for the "hearts and minds" of a considerable segment of the population. Hence, it was not altogether shocking that the *New York World-Telegram* bitterly complained that CRC was "ensnaring and exploiting an astonishing assortment of prominent persons, including Protestant bishops, judges, university professors, movie stars, lawyers and Henry A. Wallace." With undisguised rancor they termed CRC "one of the worst frauds and most mischievous fronts, the Reds ever palmed off on the American public." They scored their apparent success in "tapping rich donors for funds, including the Woolworth 5 and 10 store fortune." This searing criticism had a bipartisan character. *Newsweek* also subjected CRC to crude red-baiting attacks. Ogden Reid, in his notorious "Red Underground" column in the none-too-sober voice of Republicanism, the *New York Herald Tribune,* made CRC a special target. He also attempted to put forward something of a theoretical explanation for the existence of "fronts." According to Lenin, alleged the nonMarxist journalist, the "dictatorship of the proletariat" cannot be realized without these forms, which serve as "transmission belts" to bring forces to the party. J. Edgar Hoover, whose ideas influenced many of those who used the term "Communist front" and whose FBI may have been the source of much of Reid's confidential tidbits, also attempted to underscore the supposed function of "fronts":

Fronts are an integral part of the communist apparatus. . . . To further the cause of communism, noncommunists are relied upon to do the work that communists themselves cannot do. . . . Through their fronts, communists try to enlist the support of and to manipulate a variety of noncommunists. . . . Pains are taken to conceal the communist character of the front organizations. Communists give fronts innocuous names and seemingly orthodox and meritorious programs. . . . Of all the mass techniques which the Reds are using to influence the minds of Americans, the Communist fronts are the most effective. . . . Through "fronts" the Party is able to exert influence on thousands of noncommunists, collect immense sums of money. . . .[14]

While acknowledging the fact and the legitimacy of Communists playing a leading role in CRC, William Patterson angrily rebutted the entire conception of a "Communist front." In terming CRC "the Red Cross of the defenders of peace, constitutional rights, justice and human rights," he noted repeatedly that CRC "is non-partisan, it is controlled by no political party." Later, in responding to an inquiry, he met the matter frontally: "We are a 'front' organization. We front for all that which Jefferson and Lincoln stood for; against the economic royalists Franklin D. Roosevelt fought, against the Jew-baiters, racists and red-baiters who are masters of the Goebbels-Hitler technique." Neither Patterson nor CRC were alone in being subjected to charges of being "fronts" for the Communist Party but Patterson took heart from the word of Elk's leader J. Finley Wilson, who in responding to an anticommunist attack on him by Willard Townsend of the Transport Service Employees union after he had appeared at a CRC rally, made the point that "They would all be smeared as communists." In this regard, the words of James Prickett, cited by Roger Keeran, are still worth pondering:

> non-communists win union elections but Communists "capture" a union. Non-communists join unions; Communists "infiltrate" or "invade" them. A non-communist states his or her position; a Communist "peddles the straight party line." Non-communists influence or lead groups; Communists dominate them. A non-communist political party passes resolutions or makes decisions; but a Communist party invariably issues "directives."

It might have been added here that noncommunists have influence within certain organizations, while communists have "fronts."[15]

Unfortunately, for the most part, the historians—when they have paid attention to the influential CRC at all—have leaned more toward Hoover than Keeran. Philip S. Foner, in his introduction to his edited collection of Robeson's works, scored Richard Kluger's *Simple Justice* in this regard:

> in pages devoted to the campaign against lynching, the poll tax, segregation, to black victims of judicial frame-ups, and other aspects of the civil rights movement, the name of Paul Robeson does not appear once. Nor, for that matter, is there a single mention of the Civil Rights Congress. . . . It would be simple justice if, in a revised edition, the omissions were corrected.

Nevertheless, to his credit David Caute perspicaciously called CRC "most influential," and Michael Belknap noted that the "the organization that protested loudest and did the most to mobilize opposition to the (Communist Party Eleven Smith Act prosecutions) was" CRC; he went on to observe that CRC "set out to broaden support for the campaign . . . by bombarding the public with leaflets, fliers, and speeches, which sought to link the prosecution (of the CP) to abuses of blacks and labor, and thus to convince many non-Communist Americans that they had a stake in the fate of the CPUSA." But Belknap falls into the snare that has caught so many when he makes an apparent reference to CRC as one of the CP's "front groups."[16]

This latter tendency is more typical of the historiographical treatment of CRC. The virulently anticommunist William Nolan, while acknowledging the role of CRC ("It cannot be denied that the (CRC) . . . was effective in securing a reversal of the verdict against the Trenton Six.") accused them of siphoning funds away from such worthy causes for other purposes. Thomas Brooks emulated Nolan's lack of documentation when he charged that the CP "quietly dumped the Congress [National Negro Congress] for a policy of infiltration of the NAACP, . . ." while ignoring the fact that NNC was merged into CRC and that the CP long had looked to work closely with the NAACP. In her new biography of Hammett, Diane Johnson mixes her misinformation when she says that CRC was "dedicated to the civil rights— mainly voting rights—mostly of Communist Party members." In a similar vein, the otherwise estimable Robert Zangrando refers to the "CP–USA's Civil Rights Congress." Ignorance is supposed to be closer to the truth than prejudice, although the writers who have ignored CRC altogether do not necessarily illustrate this bromide. Although they engage in the usual loose talk about fronts and the like, Irving Howe and Lewis Coser in their history of the CP made no reference to CRC in their index; the same holds true for Nathan Glazer's book on the CP, though he includes a chapter on "Negroes and the Party"; Joseph Starobin improves the batting average by mentioning CRC once in passing. While writing a book on a controversy in which CRC played a significant role, Jane Sanders follows the Howe-Coser tendency, as does Mary Sperling McAuliffe.[17]

All this is unfortunate because a critical chapter of U.S. history has been either ignored or reduced to crude simplifications. As Philip S. Foner has observed, it is impossible to write the history of this period of civil rights without reference to CRC. And the point remains that few of these writers actually explore what it means to call an organization a "Communist front." Most implicitly accept the conception of J. Edgar Hoover, and fewer still explore "fronts" tied to other political parties, thus raising the specter of invidious discrimination.

Still, there is no question—and there was no question—that the Communists played a leading role in CRC. Elizabeth Gurley Flynn, future chair of the party and Smith Act defendant, was not alone within the Communist Party in viewing CRC as the penultimate "mass defense organization." This close tie between the CRC and the party was not altogether disastrous, contrary to the conventional wisdom. Jessica Mitford pointed out that the red tag had a differential impact: "If this tended to isolate us in the white community, it had the opposite effect in the black. . . . they empathized with us as members of yet another persecuted minority." This is not surprising; Henry Williams, among others, has noted, "Indeed, of all the groups in the American political spectrum, only the Marxist left paid much heed to the black population. . . ." Steve Nelson, a participant in one of CRC's most celebrated cases, concurred with this analysis, as did Communist Party leader Henry Winston.[18]

The Communists, like the CRC, recognized full well that Jim Crow at home was the Achilles heel for United States policy abroad; and the Congress' constant harping on cases like Willie McGee, Rosa Lee Ingram, et al., dramatized abroad this aching contradiction for all to see. As CP leader Pettis Perry observed, "There is nothing more embarrassing today for U.S. imperialism posing as world 'democrat' than the thorny problem of Jim Crow at home. . . ." His comrade Bob Thompson agreed and added the critical analysis that "the Negro people occupy a unique position in the front of struggle against American imperialism. Everywhere they are the first targets of the growth of fascist reaction and chauvinist nationalism. Everywhere they are resisting and fighting back." However, this too was not a situation without contradiction, according to Perry: "Many Negro reformists, too, are urging: 'Remove the inequalities so the Communists will be left without a propaganda weapon.' " William Z. Foster noted the "anomaly" of the advance of Blacks' rights at the same time that the rights of the people in the country as a whole—particularly with regard to unions and third parties—were being curtailed, thus underscoring the embarrassment of Jim Crow; similarly, he criticized leftist forces for not stressing sufficiently the role of international pressure in bringing about Blacks' gains, thus allowing "Negro reformists" to reap "undeserved prestige."[19]

William Patterson was well aware of all this: "every 'gain'—and American imperialism will in 1952, in my opinion, have a Negro ambassador, perhaps one Negro on the Supreme Court, perhaps a Negro cabinet officer—every gain will come from the fight we have made." This was not hyperbole because CRC's highlighting of the stains on the U.S. escutcheon in the international arena no doubt hastened overdue reform. I. F. Stone put his finger on this point in commenting on the reprieve of twenty-one Nazi war criminals after lack of same for the Martinsville Seven. Because he recognized the necessity of international pressure, Patterson was quite sharp in his response to a Garveyite who he felt was insufficiently sensitive to this. Furthermore, he emphasized the need for "détente" between the United States and the Soviet Union, recognizing that in the period from 1941 to 1945, Black advance was at its zenith.[20]

Unavoidably, such views were not greeted with equanimity by many during the difficult postwar years. Not only did CRC fail to go along with the prevailing anti-Soviet consensus, but it decided to place overt stress on deprivation of Blacks' rights when this was the most obvious embarrassment to the United States abroad. Moreover, a reign of terror was being conducted against Blacks during this era, as a fat file of clippings in the CRC archives demonstrated; lynchings—via "private and public" enterprise—were frequent. A *Madison Capital-Times* reporter could only get one out of one hundred twelve people to sign a petition consisting of excerpts from the Bills of Rights and the Declaration of Independence; reflective of the deleterious impact of "Communist front" ideology on the public was the fact that twenty asked if he were a "Communist." The press was generally hostile to most challenges to the status quo and one could be deemed a "liberal" and still denounce the Montgomery Bus Boycott (viz. Hodding Carter) and call Martin Luther King, Jr. a "troublemaker" (viz. Virginius Dabney). In such a highly charged context, the words of *Pittsburgh Courier* editor P. L. Prattis to Patterson rang even more poignantly.[21]

> I am frightened no end by what I see going on. But I can't relate myself to it as you do. That is why history will recall those like you and forget those like me. Far be it from me to hazard a guess as to what the historian of the future will conclude about these days.

These were indeed bleak times, particularly for reds pressing the rights of Blacks. It was evidence of that bleakness that a noted civil libertarian like Nanette Dembitz, a close relative of Louis Brandeis and then counsel to the New York Civil Liberties Union applauded the witchhunt against organizations like CRC. "The atmosphere of fear that the investigations help create no doubt helps to hinder the Communists from reanimating another round of 'front' organizations. . . . (this) discouragement of 'front' organizations may well be healthy for the body politic." This was not an unusual theme in the supposed bastion of legality and due process, the nation's law reviews.[22]

Alternatively, Patterson and CRC continued to hammer the point home that the government was ultimately responsible for Jim Crow, lynchings, and the like. This partially explained why they tended to gravitate toward cases like the Martinsville Seven. Patterson observed that "the rulers of our country have sought not only to place the brand of criminality upon the colored people but as well the stamp of rapists upon colored men. Colored men are rapists and criminally minded. Colored women are loose and have no moral fiber. . . ." There were other criteria also, according to Patterson:

> It seems to me that the one main question which must be decided first and foremost in all situations of this character is whether the issue or issues that are determined to exist support a program of action, whether limited or on a wide scale. If this question is answered negatively, then a very important reason exists for non-intervention on the part of the organization.[23]

If the case provided a platform for dramatically exploding stereotypes against Blacks and revealing the role of government, CRC would be prone to intervene. Although CRC often found itself involved in cases along with the NAACP and the American Civil Liberties Union, Patterson was quick to note that they were "not a 'left' NAACP"; he went on to underscore that "in all our work our desire is to stimulate greater mass activities and concern for the involvement of masses in what has been for them so long a purely legalistic approach to civil rights." This stress on "mass" action—picketing, demonstrations, petitioning,—was self-consciously the factor that distinguished CRC from its sometime allies. As was stated in their National Board meeting, "It is for CRC to show that the most effective weapon of the people is mass pressure. The two forms of action, legal action and mass pressure, are complementary. The emphasis must be placed upon the mass pressure." Unlike the NAACP and ACLU, CRC was under no illusions about the judiciary: "The courts are not neutral. . . . The courts are agents of reaction." CRC's view was that public pressure could force positive court decisions and that showing that the courts were a mere tool of reaction and not "neutral" was an important factor in radicalizing the population. But for all that, their many court victories demonstrated that they were not indifferent to the issue of excellence of legal skills: "The CRC cannot be without able, the most able, legal forces who know and love the Constitution and are fighters. . . . The more perfect the defense in the courts from a technical point of view, the more quickly and clearly will great masses of the people come to understand that reliance upon the courts alone is a fatal mistake."

This striving for excellence was a hallmark of CRC's work, even in aspects of their work that some might consider trivial. Patterson felt compelled to inform a chapter leader, "your stencils (should) be cut with greater care. The bulletin should always be extremely legible, particularly when it is aimed at activating non-members who will be distracted by a sloppily done job."[24]

It was well that CRC had criteria for the cases they would take on, because, as Patterson alleged, "We would need a fund of million dollars to take up the numerous cases which (we should). . . . our budget is, however, inadequate to even meet our daily needs . . . and it is extremely difficult to take on new issues, as meritorious as they may be." Thus, in addition to their interest in causes—irrespective of their control of a case—they were not afraid to share or even to relinquish leadership: "Many times in the past, CRC has permitted sponsorship of a specific defense activity to pass from its hands to others so that broader forces and more people would become involved in that fight." And unlike those to whom they might relinquish leadership, CRC was not shy about encouraging their forces to lobby the Supreme Court directly. In the 1950 term, CRC had a number of cases, e.g., those of Wesley Robert Wells, Fletcher Mills, Paul Washington, and others coming up and they asserted," the people must not wait until the Supreme Court makes a decision and then express protests." In urging that a deluge of letters be rained down on the justices, they also urged that Justice Robert Jackson be congratulated for his CP-Eleven bail decision: "It is, however, important that other members of the Court, and particularly Chief Justice Vinson should receive carbon copies."[25]

This approach of CRC was deemed unorthodox; but it did provide success. Having many chapters nationally, CRC did have an impact. Still, CRC leaders were often highly critical of their own performance. Membership in the CRC probably never moved beyond ten thousand—although this was no mean figure in such a repressive era and extraordinary factors could have explained what was seen as a lack of growth.[26] Nevertheless, one major self-criticism levelled by the leadership was perceived inability to integrate Red cases with Black cases—Smith Act cases with those of Willie McGee, the Trenton Six, and so forth. At least verbally, CRC seemed to give high priority to the red cases, but it would be hard to deduce this from the frequent self-flagellations voiced. In one early analysis in 1950, Patterson was ringing the changes in this vein, yet in the same speech he was telling about sending Bessie Mitchell, a member of the International Ladies Garment Workers Union and a close relative of one of the Trenton Six, on a crosscountry tour to speak on behalf of the Trenton Six and the CP-Eleven. In 1955, just before the demise of CRC Patterson was advising a member from Southern California that "The Ingram case can break this year. The Parole Board should be deluged with letters. . . . I should also like to see the campaign for 'Wesley Wells' freedom revitalized. Our main job, however, is to bring the Supreme Court to review and reverse the decision of the Subversive Activities Control Board in the case of the Communist Party. . . . There is, of course, also a tremendous job yet to be done on the Steve Nelson case and we are fully responsible for the case of Junius Scales." The many pamphlets that CRC produced seemed to rebut the notion that they neglected unduly Red cases. In any case, one of the many ironies of this alleged "Communist front" is that while they were highly self-critical of their defense of Communists, their detractors saw them as a veritable "legal arm" of the Communists. But the very appellation "Communist front" tends to demonstrate that any understanding of CRC and comprehension of its role was at a premium.[27]

This kind of rhetoric did not just emerge from so-called "conservative" sources. Presumably it was not surprising when George Schuyler alleged that "it was just about as obvious as the Eiffel Tower that (CRC was a) Communist front"; nor should the brow be furrowed in noting that a McCarthyite sympathizer like William O'Neill would speak in a similar vein. But it is symptomatic of the extent to which the right sets the political tone in the United States that an apparently progressive scholar like Mari Jo Buhle could not only use similar language without clarification but, in conjunction with another misguided bias, go further to state (incorrectly) that CRC "was dissolved during the upheaval following the Khruschev report of 1956." It is interesting to compare contemporary views of "fronts" with those of forty years ago. John Loeb, future U.S. ambassador to Peru and Guinea and head of the quintessential cold-war liberal Union for Democratic Action (predecessor of the ADA), claimed in the mid-1940s that "fronts" must be opposed because "Communists are more active, more consecrated, more zealous than their liberal associates"; that is, that liberals must oppose them because they have more energy and are better organizers. Although they understood the contradiction involved in prescribing "uniformity of belief" for a "union for democratic action," Loeb and the UDA leaders glossed over this in their eagerness to fight "communism," as they would subsequently shortchange the battle against racism on the same altar. In his recent look at the "American Left," Bernard Johnpoll returned to the demonology of the past, asserting that "the Communist Party and its innumerable front organizations . . . totally unethical in its behavior to its followers. . . ." Robert Clayton Pierce is not far from the mark in describing the devastating impact of the "front hunt" on the U.S. political scene and on liberalism generally:

> (it) helped unleash attitudes that imperiled all liberals. . . . The projected liberal offensive against racial injustice was sidetracked. . . . The Cold War and fear of Communism became a useful tool to help defeat new social programs. Any proposed social legislation that had any support from radical groups was fair game, no matter how meritorious.

The "front hunt" has larger implications as well. It could be argued that it was little more than a convenient tool to destroy and divert the powerful "popular front" movement that had emerged from the 1930s, in a way analogous to the way Leo K. Adler and Thomas Paterson have shown how the manufactured term "totalitarianism" was used to confuse Nazi Germany with the Soviet Union. Indeed, "communist front" is so ill defined that the World War II Allies, the U.S., U.K.—and the USSR—could easily be termed a "front." An illustrative case study of these trends was the battle in Los Angeles to establish public housing during the height of the red scare; despite support from the CIO, NAACP, Urban League, and others, this effort ran aground on the shoals of red-baiting, including charges of "fronts" involvements. A liberal mayor was defeated by a conservative backed by the *Los Angeles Times* to boot. Setbacks for social progress were the inevitable result of such "front hunts," even though students like Charles Eagles have argued that CRC campaigns only served to "merely stiffen white resistance."[28]

Yet, if African-Americans and their allies were to shrink from pushing for equality every time there was a hint of a "white backlash," there might still be human sales in the free market. CRC, which not only struggled for Black liberation but against political repression as well, certainly was of that opinion. Indeed, they can be given more than a bit of credit for popularizing the term "civil rights" itself as a goal of progressives. The cases they chose to focus on distilled that irreducible human element that served to dramatize their cause and to educate the public. The tactics they developed, many of which were bequeathed to them by their parent organization, the International Labor Defense, are still being used to focus attention on political prisoners not only in the United States but in South Africa, El Salvador, and elsewhere. Many who struggled with CRC went on to play honorable and productive roles in other movements. This is the legacy they have bequeathed to us, the living.[29]

The attack on CRC as a "Communist front" was meant to destabilize a "popular front" of communists and noncommunists and to remove from progressive forces some of their most skilled and energetic organizers. The attack was discriminatory, because similar charges were not hurled at Democratic or Republican "fronts," thus invidiously singling out one particular party—the Communist Party. That attack was harmful to social progress to the extent that it succeeded in destroying effective organizations like the Civil Rights Congress. The attack was spurious to the extent that it signified that CRC was not truly concerned with the plight of Willie McGee, Rosa Lee Ingram, and others, and was just "using them," or that CRC was little more than the legal arm of the Communists. This was even more unfortunate because CRC policy did not always move rigidly in lockstep with that of the CP. The party's slogan of "self-determination for the Black Belt" (i.e., viewing Black Southerners as a "nation," as opposed to a "national minority") was not often employed in the numerous CRC campaigns in the Deep South. Whereas the party subsequently criticized itself for making their campaign against "white chauvinism" much too internal, CRC's campaign in this area was aimed clearly at the real perpetrators of this crime, as their McGee and Martinsville cases demonstrated. Still, the cry of "front" continues to persist.

COMMUNIST FRONT?

1
Germinating and Ripening

The Civil Rights Congress was formed in 1946 as a result of a merger among the National Negro Congress, the Internation Labor Defense, and the National Federation for Constitutional Liberties. Final details were not worked out until 1947. These groups concentrated respectively on Black equality, labor rights, and civil liberties. Without slighting the contributions made by the other two organizations to the combination, it would be hard to dispute that NNC was the heart of CRC. The subsequent addition of William Patterson to the leadership of CRC (though he had served as an ILD official), contributed to their apparent concentration on civil rights questions. Though it was little heralded, it is difficult to overestimate the importance of NNC during their brief ten year history; certainly, Gunnar Myrdal's notion that NNC "local councils . . . were the most important Negro organizations in some Western cities" could easily be given geographic expansion. Despite the ministrations of a number of writers, John Streator is on point when he accords "much of the credit for there being" a March on Washington Movement led by A. Philip Randolph to "NNC activity." Like CRC NNC rarely had a membership roll of more than ten thousand. This still compared favorably to the prewar NAACP roll of fifty thousand. But, as John Loeb may have noted, this low membership was more than compensated for by their energy and zeal.[1]

To stress the role of NNC, however, should not be seen as a slight of ILD; for if NNC was the heart of CRC, then ILD served as the limbs. There was an overlap in the efforts of the three merging organizations in any event; for example, ILD's GI Rights Bureau was concerned with discriminatory discharges from the military, as was NNC and the Veterans Committee Against Discrimination, for that matter. Nevertheless, there was an impressive infusion of skill and talent into CRC from ILD, which not only included their former Vice-President Bill Patterson, but also Max Yergan, Paul Robeson, the excellent civil liberties lawyer Irv Goodman, Herman Rosenfeld, and others. Nor should NCFL be ignored in limning the origins of CRC. Their leader, George Marshall, became chair of CRC's board. A Columbia graduate with a doctorate, Marshall emerged from a highly affluent background: his father was a prominent attorney and a president of the American Jewish Congress. Marshall was not only generous toward CRC but also bankrolled other organizations, e.g., the militant predecessor of SNCC, the Southern Negro Youth Congress. Marshall's highly visible role within CRC (he delivered the keynote address at the Detroit founding convention) probably led to a development that often afflicted CRC leaders struggling on behalf of political prisoners—he became one. He was jailed for not turning over to the House Un-American Activities Committee NCFL records of its contributors. According to CRC, he was placed in a "common jail" in Washington, D.C., accorded "inhuman treatment," given no medication despite a "very bad thyroid condition," allotted one shower per week, "no *New York Times* (sic), no access to Shakespeare," and was fed "miserable" food. Also, like other political prisoners, Marshall lost his case in the U.S. Supreme Court.[2]

Various reasons have been given for the merger of the founding organizations of CRC. Their duplication of effort was just one reason; at other times, this move was ascribed to the "powerful drive" by "reaction," causing a circling of the wagons; at one point it was alleged that the three had "fulfilled their obligations, found themselves no longer relevant." There were also other lesser organizations present at the creation, e.g., the National Committee to Combat Anti-Semitism and the Chicago Civil Liberties Committee, which had abandoned the American Civil Liberties Union. In any case, the founding of CRC in Detroit, 27–28 April 1946 was initiated by twenty-five individuals and sponsored by six hundred; it opened at the First Congregational Church there. The 372 delegates and thirty-eight visitors from twenty-three states were regaled by speeches and papers on the poll tax, peonage, police terror, Jim Crow in Washington, D.C., indemnifying Japanese-Americans, Puerto Rican Independence, a permanent Fair Employment Practices Committee, and many other issues. The Saturday night session was open to the public at the Northern High School Auditorium in the form of a "public hearing" on the Wood-Rankin Committee; the Sunday morning session opened at the Maccabees Auditorium under the chairmanship of Frank Donner, Associate Counsel for the CIO, with Earl Dickerson, president of the predominantly Black National Bar Association giving the main address; finally, and perhaps most importantly, the final afternoon session was chaired by Max Yergan of NNC and focused on organization. The initiating committee of CRC, which included such figures of prominence as John Garfield, Susan B. Anthony, Raymond Pace Alexander, Katherine Dunham, Langston Hughes, Adam Clayton Powell, Arthur M. Schlesinger, and Lulu White (Texas NAACP secretary) were undoubtedly pleased with their handiwork.

They were no doubt less pleased with the critical report issued by HUAC shortly after the convention, which Marshall charged was a form of "intimidation."[3]

Because it could benefit from the infrastructures already established by its parent organizations, it was possible for CRC to hit the ground running; thus, on 11 May 1946, days after the founding, a Continuations Committee met including Louis Burnham, fabled SNYC organizer and journalist, left lawyers like Abraham Isserman and David Scribner, and others. Black woman journalist Charlotta Bass, former Minnesota Farmer-Labor Party Governor Elmer Benson, Frank Donner, Elizabeth Gurley Flynn, Patterson and the lawyers Nathan Witt and Carol King all quickly accepted memberships on the national board. The staff was quickly assembled and consisted of Milton Kaufman as executive director, Milton Kemnitz as field director, and Laurent Frantz (a lawyer and graduate of the University of Tennessee) as field director. What was striking about the assembling of the National Board—given subsequent complaints—was the tremendous outreach made to labor. Scribner was general counsel of the militant United Electrical Workers Union; George Addes was international secretary of the United Auto Workers Union, and Lewis Merrill, president of the progressive United Office and Professional Workers of America, also served. There was "affirmative action" as well, as the board subsequently "resolved to instruct the officers to work as speedily (as possible) to bring a woman into one of the national offices." Female leadership, particularly in the chapters, came to be a hallmark of CRC.[4]

For various reasons, but mainly because of political repression, there was a heavy turnover in the ranks of the top CRC leadership. As early as September 1948, when U.S. Attorney General Tom Clark began to shine his spotlight on CRC, Mary McLeod Bethune beat a speedy retreat from the organization she had helped to bring into being. In his typical philosophical but pointed style, Patterson waxed poetic:

> We know that many are intimidated by the action of the Attorney General. That is as our enemy believed it would be. . . . But there were women like Harriet Tubman and Sojourner Truth who faced just such foes and spat upon them. . . . Yet we say good-by smiling . . . P.S. The NAACP dropped its grand and gallant warrior Dr. Du Bois. You leave our fighting craft. So it is.[5]

Earlier as clouds of reaction were gathering, the President of Morehouse, Benjamin Mays, felt constrained to step down as CRC honorary co-chair. He was blunt about his reason: "since so many persons have said to me that the organization is definitely a communistic one, I thought it was the only fair thing to you—and to myself—to write you and find out at the very source." Kaufman issued an equally blunt denial, but the spindly Black elder who was an early influence on Martin Luther King, Jr., was resolute: "Although I believe in a good many things that the communists do and have supported special projects sponsored by them, I am not a communist and I would not like to be officially connected with an organization that is communistic." Despite his avowed sympathy with CRC aims, Mays fell victim to the ubiquitous "front hunt"—as did those very same aims.[6]

Not long thereafter, Kaufman himself resigned from CRC to be replaced by Joseph Cadden, former executive secretary of the American Youth Congress and political action director of the United Office and Professional Workers Union. Later he was joined by William Lawrence, a former textile worker in Philadelphia, New York state secretary of the ILD, and Communist organizer. Probably the most controversial exit from the CRC staff (although the motion commending Kaufman's work upon his resignation was faint praise indeed), was effected by Len Goldsmith. A journalist, active in the Newspaper Guild, he had been organizer for District Fifty of the United Mine Workers Union; he was also a Columbia University alumnus, a former *New York Times* reporter, the CIO director for New Jersey and education director of the United Office and Professional Workers Union. When he resigned, Patterson pointed a finger at his "factionalism"; two points were clear: he had had many conflicts with other CRC leaders and he eventually became a "friendly witness" in various forums against his former employer. He was replaced by the more reliable Milton Wolff, Abraham Lincoln Brigadista and leader of the Joint Anti-Fascist Refugee Committee, as national organization director. Milt Kaufman, a CIO regional director and oil workers organizer, and executive secretary of the Newspaper Guild and Merchant Marine, Milt Kemnitz, also worked with CRC.[7]

But during its heyday, CRC was led by Aubrey Grossman, Ralph Powe, and William Patterson, who replaced Cadden as executive secretary in 1948 and quickly came to symbolize the very heart of CRC. All three were lawyers, although Grossman had had more experience with the labor movement than the law. Powe, in his thirties while with CRC, was a "son of sharecroppers" from Cheraw, South Carolina, and a Tuskeegee grad who had worked with George Washington Carver. He had taught school in the "Alabama backwoods" before graduating from Howard Law School in 1941. Like so many Black attorneys of that era, he freely acknowledged that one of the "most important influence(s) on my life (was) Charles Houston." Like his confreres, he was a devoted family man and had three sons. Powe served as "special counsel" to CRC and as "secretary to the Legal Committee" and in those posts participated in some of the most important cases of the McCarthy era.[8]

Powe coordinated the work of a diverse and skillful bunch of barristers. In November 1946, months after the founding convention, Powe sat down with Emmanuel Bloch (eventually immortalized as the lawyer for the Rosenbergs), Carol King (perhaps the top immigration lawyer of her day), Abraham Isserman (attorney in the fateful 1949 Smith Act trial of Communists) and

Herman Rosenfeld. They agreed to meet once a week for lunch, in addition to a regular monthly meeting. Powe's role was to investigate all incoming requests for legal assistance, to make a report for the national office and then find an attorney in the field; at that point, the CRC Legal Committee would come in. Powe also traveled frequently across the nation in order to establish lawyers' panels in various cities. The purposes of these striking tours were to stress to lawyers "the need of creative, precedent-breaking legal thinking and acting . . . search out and fight against legalist approaches and methods which are bound to be found not only among lawyers but also chapter leaders . . . meetings on the questions of use and integration of Negro lawyers . . . (and) make a special report on the woman lawyer and CRC (There are many spots where women lawyers play a very leading civil rights role—Los Angeles, Chicago, Cleveland, New York). . . ." One such jaunt involved twenty-three cities and virtually every large one. Its purposes partially exemplified some of CRC's priorities, not only in terms of "affirmative action" but the constant fight they conducted against "legalist" thinking, by which they meant an emphasis on legal advocacy to the detriment of mass organizing. During his tenure with CRC, Powe was quite effective, and not only as a lawyer; he was also an Afro-American and the fact that one of the few of his race to have ascended to so lofty a profession would sacrifice its riches in order to defend victims of racist and political repression had a dramatic impact on CRC's fortunes.[9]

The same held true, perhaps even more so, for William Lorenzo Patterson, a Black man whose picture was to be found in *Time,* who worked with Raymond Pace Alexander, Mary McLeod Bethune, and Thurgood Marshall, and whose personal and political life was virtually larger than life.

His father was from St. Lucia and early in young Bill's life he, the father, was struck by religion, became a Seventh-Day Adventist missionary, moved to Tahiti, then to Panama. Said Patterson, reflecting inferentially on the origins of his materialism, "His religious mania . . . made us doubt religion." Born in the San Francisco Bay Area in the 1890s, he graduated from Tamalpais High School in 1911. His picture at that time reveals a studious-looking, bespectacled gent. His yearbook picture's caption is revealing: "Appearance—Satisfied Eyes—Devilish Ambition—to be a second Booker T. Washington Opinion of Faculty—He's all right when he's there Hobby—Cutting Favorite Song—My Turquoise Lady Nickname—Sweet William." While toiling away at a job, he was able to graduate from the Hastings School of Law of the University of California. He also found time to join the fraternity Omega Psi Phi. Patterson often had occasion to dwell on his fascinating background. And it is not idle speculation to surmise that his interest in such spurious cases of rape as those involving Willie McGee, the Martinsville Seven, and others like them could have been motivated by his family background. His grandmother had been a slave on the Gault plantation near Norfolk. She was "the wife of rape . . . of her white slaveowner . . . and she gave birth to several children." One of those children was his mother; his grandmother was freed in 1851, at which point she married and moved to gold-rush California by ship. Like so many other Black youths, Patterson was raised in a female-headed household as his father found it more necessary to win hearts for Christ abroad than to tend to his children; naturally "Pat," as he came to be called, began work at an early age and his wages from the dining cars of the Southern Pacific funded his higher education.[10]

Patterson's radicalism bloomed early. He was arrested in 1917 for protesting World War I and was defended by the NAACP; around this same time the legendary Communist leader Anita Whitney had recruited him to the Association. Part of the charge against him was that he had called this war to end all war, a "white man's war." The 1919 Big Steel strike in Pittsburgh found attorney Patterson on the case rendering legal assistance. Shortly thereafter, he went to London with the intention of moving to Africa in order to escape the hellish racism so many Afro-Americans have sought to flee. But there he met a Liberian, George Hansbury, founder of the *London Daily Herald,* who convinced him that his fight was in the United States. He came back to New York and became a partner in the law firm of Dyatt, Hall, and Patterson. This leading Black firm was the first to represent a white bank, Chelsea National. It spawned, *inter alia,* Harold Stevens of the New York Court of Appeals, Fritz Alexander and Amos Bowman of the New York State Supreme Court, U.S. Ambassador and future Patterson nemesis, Franklin Williams, and David Dinkins, a leading Black politician. Patterson was making the princely sum of $8,000 in the 1920s (about four times more than he made with CRC in the 1950s), and by his own admission, he was living it up: "I was travelling with the fast set, a clique of young, successful Negroes. There was a constant round of drinking, helling, gambling, big parties and flashy women." It was during this period that he met another young Black lawyer, soon to be disillusioned with the rosy path set out for him while his people remained in virtual bondage—Paul Robeson. Ironically, it was a study by a future Supreme Court justice, whose decisions during the Cold War disappointed him greatly, which helped to turn his life around. Felix Frankfurter's analysis of the Sacco-Vanzetti case "made a deep impression" on Patterson. He immediately set off for Massachusetts where he encountered other leftists like Mother Bloor, John Howard Lawson, Dorothy Parker. He was arrested three times and he was threatened with being sent to an insane asylum; another future antagonist, Arthur Garfield Hays, was his lawyer; Edna St. Vincent Millay, John Dos Passos, and Mike Gold were arrested with him. It was during this tumultuous time, in 1926, that he joined the recently born Communist Party–USA.[11]

He also became a member of the International Labor Defense. Although he led a hunger march to Uniontown, Pennsylvania, in 1931, his most heralded activity during this period was being secretary of ILD during the persecution of the Scottsboro Nine. This was after Louis Engdahl, head of ILD, died of pneumonia in Europe while campaigning against the impending legal lynching of the Scottsboro Nine. Although the nine were ultimately saved, the effort killed one ILD leader and almost killed Patterson. He went to Europe to recuperate.[12]

It was in Germany that Patterson witnessed historical events that were to have profound impact upon him, even greater than those he experienced during his trips to a tense Cuba during this same period: "Twice in the 30's I went into Hitler's Germany—on the first occasion in 1934 to find hundreds of Jewish friends of mine hiding or already entrapped and imprisoned in concentration camps. The last time in 1937, to find many of them dead." In Berlin during that time many were saying "it cannot happen here." Patterson recalled these words ominously in the United States in the 1950s. It was also during the 1930s that Patterson traveled and lived extensively in the USSR and this experience had an equal if not greater impact on his thought. There he "spent a year on his back in a Black Sea sanitarium" and two more years "studying . . . former oppressed nationalities." All was not work and recovery. This former amateur boxer and lifelong baseball fan also found time to pursue his interest in sports; he also married a Soviet woman and fathered children; tragically, "two daughters of mine . . . lost their lives in the war against fascism."[13]

Patterson returned to the United States in better shape physically than he had been when he left, although in late 1950 and early 1951, a Los Angeles physician who was also a CRC member had to nurse him back to health again; ultimately he lived a virtual nine decades. When he worked with the left-wing *Midwest Record* in 1938, he could look back on a decade of labor that had catapulted him into the front ranks of Communist leaders in the United States. It was Patterson who had brought Mother Mooney to meet FDR to plead for freedom for Tom Mooney; it was Patterson who had brought another talented Black lawyer soon to be a Communist, Benjamin Davis, into the Angelo Herndon case as counsel-in-chief. It was Patterson who helped to found the Abraham Lincoln School in Chicago, one of the early experiments in progressive education. And it was Patterson who set up the historic meeting in 1942 between Paul Robeson and Judge Kenesaw Mountain Landis, the commissioner of baseball, which led ultimately to Jackie Robinson breaking down that Jim Crow door and unleashing events that were to change the face of the nation.[14]

The dark-skinned, somewhat stocky, Patterson (he was listed as 5'7" on his passport, although he appeared taller) certainly did not become wealthy working with CRC. For example, in 1950 his total wages before taxes was a meager $2,985; in 1949 the joint income of him and his wife was a still paltry $6,343. Nevertheless, he persisted. Like his contemporaries and friends W. E. B. Du Bois and Paul Robeson, his reduced income did not mean a corresponding reduction in intellectual sustenance. He was a close student of the contemporary political landscape. His files show articles by Thomas Emerson, opinions by Justices Black and Douglas, articles by the U.S. Surgeon General, by Eisenhower, by Dulles. He heaped "the most lavish praise" on Philip Foner's work on Frederick Douglass. All the while, he was performing yeoman duty with CRC. He felt compelled to inform Miriam Schultz, secretary of the Pittsburgh chapter, in late 1953 as the toll of repression deepened, "CRC nationally is little more than one person at the present moment. That one person at the present time is head of the Repeal the McCarran Act Committee, of more than one commission, is concerned with the fight to free Ben Davis, Wesley Robert Wells, and Rosa Lee Ingram, the manner in which the Smith Act is being waged in St. Louis and elsewhere."[15] That one person—Bill Patterson—was obviously one of the most, if not *the most,* important figures of the fightback against Mc-Carthyism.

There are those who might find it surprising that someone with the moneymaking capability of Patterson would subject himself to opprobrium and jail terms on behalf of persecuted racial political minorities. But Harvey Klehr has noted that the path Patterson trod was not that unusual:

> Blacks whose education and occupations should have qualified them for membership in the black bourgeoisie not only joined the CPUSA but did not abandon it even after the party became a negligible force. . . . Undoubtedly, the relative absence of racism in the party and the opportunities it provided for black leadership made it an attractive permanent home for some . . . black party leaders were more likely than white party leaders to have attended college and postgraduate school.

Patterson and the coterie of Black reds of which he was a part were not blasé dilettantes either, as Mark Naison has observed: "James Ford, Benjamin Davis, Merrill Work, and William Patterson were as familiar with the nuance of black organizational life as they were with the political dynamics of the party and were able to interact socially with leaders of the Harlem community without awkwardness or affectation." Moreover, these Black reds, as John Graves has noted, were emerging from a Black community that was less hostile to Communists than other sectors of the population.[16]

Thus, it should not be deemed shocking that even with Patterson's Communist background he would be welcomed in diverse circles. Patterson was viewed as being on the same level as Mary McLeod Bethune, Walter White, and other major Black leaders of the day. He was also helpful to the "up and coming" generation, like future judge Thomas Jones of Brooklyn, for whom he and James Ford helped to generate fees. Patterson was not infrequently found on television or in *Time* magazine, barometers of popularity and name recognition. His disputes with such public figures as Channing Tobias and Walter White were covered widely in the Black press. His celebrity was due not only to Patterson's intellect, to his skill as a lawyer and his organizing ability (not to mention his passionate speaking style), but to his personality as well. The apostate Bella Dodd, while harpooning virtually every red she discussed in her controversial memoir, sheepishly admits that "I liked (Patterson)." Howard Fast, before his apostasy, spoke for many when he unlimbered his rhetorical arm and tossed a bouquet at Patterson: "you are one of the great leaders and heroes of this struggle . . . I am all the richer and better for having known and worked with people like you." A number of CRC "volunteers," who worked closely with him under difficult conditions in an atmosphere that could have generated enmity, spoke similarly: "A kinder, more considerate man never stepped foot into shoe. He carries enough responsibility for three men. . . . he is never too preoccupied to speak the courteous word of greeting to a volunteer." Consequently, his national tours on behalf of CRC were often greeted as if he were a conquering potentate. For example, as a result of his tour to Portland, Oregon, in 1951, "new members" joined "and in the manner that his being here put the CRC on the front pages. . . . The Negro community is still buzzing over the affair."[17]

Naturally, to top it all off, Patterson was the consummate family man, devoted to his wife Louise Thompson—a formidable figure in her own right and a key participant in the Harlem Renaissance—and their daughter Mary. He continually addressed her tenderly, even at an age when other couples had become either jaded or were skidding toward divorce: "My dear wife: what a lucky guy I am to have so inspirational and capable a person as you by my side. . . . your superior talents as a speaker and a leader always are a challenge. Maybe some day I will catch up with you." His passion was not just limited to his wife. During this same period, his brother Bob was on the receiving end of Patterson's verbal efflorescence: "my feeling for Bob transcends anything which I have ever had by way of love for a brother. My love for the rest of the family is of course, as great. That could not be, if it were not for the political affinity which binds us all together."[18]

His oft-expressed feeling for his wife was an extension of his equally strong feelings about equality for women. At a dinner honoring him Patterson took it upon himself to praise the role of women in the struggle, alleging that they "constitute a great reserve for democracy." Patterson was more than slightly ahead of his time in his view of the "woman question." In 1952 he reproved a correspondent for addressing his wife incorrectly: "my own wife goes by her name and is addressed as Louise Thompson as often as Louise Patterson. Frankly I think she should be addressed as Louise Thompson. That is her name." No Mrs. William Patterson for the CRC leader.[19]

Paul Robeson spoke freely in his newspaper *Freedom* of the "great work" done by his close friend and colleague Bill Patterson; inevitably, what he considered "great" was not viewed similarly by those who received the brunt of Patterson's searing attacks. In fact, the CRC office and Patterson's files were burgled so frequently that it probably would have been more efficient to have established their offices in FBI headquarters. These "surreptitious entries" and "black bag jobs" were manifestly illegal, but all was deemed fair when battling the effective CRC, which continually embarrassed the U.S. government in international forums. At the same time, the Canadian government—perhaps out of prompting by their southern neighbor—did not fully appreciate Patterson's "great work" either. The page-one banner headline of the *Toronto Evening Telegram* told the tale: "BAR U.S. 'RIGHTS' OFFICIAL." Patterson was held incommunicado for thirteen hours after he arrived in Toronto in December 1948. He was freed on $500 bond, "on condition" of not speaking at a local meeting nor letting his speech be read. The basis for this exclusion was his alleged Communist ties. He conceded having been vice-chairman of the Illinois Communist Party but he would not say if he was in or out of the party at that moment. Little matter. He was booted out of the Maple Leaf State unceremoniously, with small regard for civil liberties or international human rights.[20]

The atmosphere of terror in which CRC operated probably helps to account for some of the tense relations that existed among certain staff and board members. Patterson was candid in acknowledging this reality: "Some of the members of our Board broke under the weight of terror. . . . threats of character assassination, economic victimization . . . or just common smearing . . . caused some of our Board to waver." Len Goldsmith and Patterson clashed continually; the sharply worded missives that flowed between them were guaranteed to be abrasive. Ineluctably all this proved to be fertile ground for differences about organizational and related matters.[21]

In light of the sharp intellects and well-known personalities among the CRC leadership, combined with a terroristic atmosphere, the clashes among CRC leaders might not be viewed as very significant. Dashiell Hammett, Rev. Charles Hill of Detroit, Dr. Harry Ward, Lee Pressman, Ernest Goodman, Miranda Smith, Aubrey Williams and Arthur Huff Fauset are just a few of those who could claim to be part of the CRC directorate. Fortunately, what John Holton of the Philadelphia chapter felt compelled to tell Aubrey Grossman was more an exception to an overall tone of cooperation than it was the norm:

> I would appreciate it very much if you did not sit up in the national office and tell me that a matter of this nature is a must and I got to do this and that. . . . I know that if you have the patience of a Job it might pay off. . . . Is this the way to work with people . . . I want to cooperate but let's be reasonable.[22]

Grossman in response patiently explained the situation instead of throwing gasoline on the flames and Holton emerged assuaged. The staggering workload faced by CRC national staff exacerbated the conflictual situation, as Patterson had to explain to Detroit chapter leader Arthur McPhaul: "Remember I am alone in the national office and we are getting out a new book on Genocide; preparing to open up the Ingram case, making strenuous efforts to prepare for the McCarran fight . . . It is not an easy job."[23] As this exchange indicates static between the New York office and the branch offices did arise from time to time. Months after the launching of CRC, Louis Colman of the New York branch told Milt Kaufman of the national office: "our national organization has not provided us in New York with organized national campaigns. . . . This lack of national campaign leadership is severely felt in all our work. The second aspect is the direct approach to our own contributors . . . leads to confusion." Even after Patterson came to the national office and gave the chapters more national cases than some wanted to deal with—McGee, Trenton Six, Smith Act cases, Ingram—basic problems continued to exist. Some were endemic; many national organizations have a problem with their affiliates feeling that too much emphasis or power is in the New York or Washington, D.C., national office. Thus, the "Report on Organization" of CRC issued in late 1948 concluded: "I think it is important that we recognize the resistance to 'New York leadership,' that we recognize that it is very difficult to maintain liason [sic] with many scattered CRC chapters. . . ." The solution was to set up regional offices, but money was the usual stumbling block.[24]

This plaint was repeated in a different form by Patterson at the June 1949 Chapter Secretaries Conference in Chicago: "The basic weakness of CRC today is the lack of unity of its national office and its chapters." He went on to call for a break with "all forms of sectarianism and, more particularly, of all racial animosities." This kind of "racial animosity" may have been refracted in the words of the Black Detroit chapter head, Arthur McPhaul, about his co-worker in Motown, Anne Shore, who was Euro-American, and the New York leadership. He remonstrated bitterly that, "I think it is significant that even though I have been the head of the Congress here for two years, most of the people around the country" think Shore is. Acerbically he noted that Blacks are often placed in posts as "window dressing" but "that is not the case here." Showing tact and diplomacy, Patterson demurred and apologized, but this incident showed that operating an interracial organization in a hostile atmosphere in the most racist nation this side of South Africa was not a simple matter. Moreover, CRC was not a monolithic, single-tendency "Communist front," but a grouping of diverse backgrounds and opinions. At their November 1949 "Freedom Crusade" to Washington, D.C., the CRC leadership not only was forced to give delegates a list of non–Jim Crow restaurants and urged "Limit yourself to this list" but also provided a list of issues to raise: "many of us have differing views on foreign and domestic issues. Do not embarrass your fellow delegates by discussing any issues not connected with the above." Again, stirring the pot was the overall atmosphere of repression. Relations of normalcy were difficult during this period. In September 1951 a CRC delegation met with the FBI to complain about the atmosphere of intimidation and "protest against FBI harassment and spying. . . . they specifically demanded an end to the 24-hour vigil being kept outside their houses; being constantly followed by FBI spies; the trailing of their children by agents; and the attempt to extend similar tactics to neighbors and friends. Protest was also made against lewd and insulting remarks made by the men."[25]

Thus as CRC moved its national office from 205 East 42nd Street to 23 West 26th Street to 6 East 17th Street, it was hounded continuously by the FBI and by the repressive apparatus of the state generally. From the state's point of view, this surveillance was understandable, to a limited degree, because CRC was certainly not a negligible organization. The number of chapters varied from forty to seventy, with significant representation in the deep South (higher there than the Communist Party or any other left organization), Puerto Rico, Toronto, etc. Patterson's words in 1952 to Chicago chapter leader Les Davis may have seemed exaggerated to some ("Every 'gain'—and American imperialism will in 1952, in my opinion, have a Negro ambassador, perhaps a Negro on the Supreme Court, perhaps a Negro cabinet officer—every gain will come from the fight we have made"), but he was hardly being outlandish. The year 1952 is a useful benchmark for measuring CRC progress and strength. While a McCarthyite thrall had descended across the nation, the East Bay chapter had 650 dues-paying members, southern California had 464, San Francisco and Marin County 750, Illinois 242. Pueblo, Colorado, CRC reported that a FBI visit "struck fear into our members. We can only meet in small groups quietly. This is a small city, eyes are everywhere." While Spokane with twenty-seven members reported strength among unions, with representation from railway workers, woodworkers, carpenters, and other workers, Pennsylvania reported of its 300 members that they were "influential in Negro Baptist church life . . . weak in trade union life." With all its weaknesses, the CRC in 1952 had come a long way from its early days. True, there was an advantage in some areas. In Michigan, the chapter had inherited the legacy and contacts of the Civil Rights Federation, which had a history of ten years of work for civil rights. In Chicago, the chapter similarly had received an inheritance from the Civil Liberties Committee, which "had broken away from the ACLU over the issue of red-baiting" and had a "membership of 4,000."[26]

For a good part of its existence, CRC had a sliding dues scale of $1 to $100 and a National Board meeting twice yearly; the annual convention was the highest policy-making body. The Resident Board acted between board meetings. At its zenith, there was a staff of ten to eleven people in the national office, including a bookkeeper, a head of prisoners' relief, a secretary, a receptionist, a clerk, two public relations officers, and others, all operating in a seven to eight-room suite. This was a high-powered operation with contacts worldwide. With such labor power available, the national office was able to give sustained support to building chapters. The New York branch at their urging published a pamphlet on this question that remains useful today for organizers trying to build a national organization. They suggest that the executive meet every other week and that members meet regularly; a "special meeting" once a month with films, a speaker, and so forth was deemed a must—along with constant recruiting. Concerning leaflets: "keep in mind your local issues and show how they are related to the state and national issues we fight on." Concerning outdoor meetings: "Take special steps to insure the safety of Negro and Puerto Rican speakers and participants." Concerning meetings with politicians and officials: "Never let an individual or two individuals go in alone. If necessary, it is better to leave without the meeting." Concerning cases of police brutality, they suggest that witnesses be obtained immediately along with "notarized statements from them." And, of course, "In all activities, special attention must be paid to the participation and leadership of Negro people, Puerto Rican people, women, and industrial workers. In addition to this, be alert as to the composition of your particular neighborhood, and see that it is well represented on all occasions."[27]

CRC was continually engaged in membership drives, national conferences, and the like. This was partly plain good sense, since more members meant more dues and the Cold War environment and consequent dropping off of membership meant that continuous recruitment was obligatory. For example, after informing the chapters in mid-1952 that "yesterday our phone was disconnected as to outgoing calls," Aubrey Grossman informed them that recruiting 7,500 new members in an upcoming period was the goal, with a quota for each chapter. Chapters were told to "settle on a concrete plan to visit and win back former members," presumably scared away by the red scare. Reflecting his own background, Grossman insisted "The great bulk of the new membership secured during this drive should come from among union members. . . . we must create chapters in twenty or thirty key industrial cities where they do not exist." There was high praise for Pennsylvania for forming a new chapter in Wilkes-Barre of "100 new members comprised in large part of miners." In addition to appointing a membership director for a chapter, CRC also set up friendly competition between cities, e.g., Los Angeles vs. Detroit, San Diego vs. St. Louis, New Jersey vs. Ohio, etc. to spur recruiting.[28]

CRC publications, and the "Bulletin" in particular, were the glue that held the organization together. The "Bulletin" reported on the organization's activities and its contents were jealously scrutinized by chapter members. At one point Chicago's Les Davis criticized it for not giving enough space to "very important chapters (Michigan, Chicago, etc. and New York State"); he carped about the diffusion he perceived and the lack of stress on key cases along with a "lack of concreteness" and a "lack of graphic materials." This forced the national office to engage in content analysis, which demonstrated that there were eight items on New York comprising twenty inches, three/fourteen for the East Bay, two/nine for New Jersey, two/seven for Wisconsin and two/four for Los Angeles in seventeen issues between December 1950 and April 1951. This refuted partially Davis' démarche, although there was an apparent acquiescence to his other charges.[29]

The "Bulletin" was also used to disseminate current CRC tactical thinking. In September 1951 there was floated the notion of state conferences on "civil rights issues," "under broad sponsorship," but the "response by chapters . . . (was) disheartening." It was emphasized that such conferences should not be "under CRC sponsorship unless impossible in any other way," because CRC can't "move" or "reach" certain groups. National get-togethers were a CRC trademark and even in mid-1954 as the government was bearing down heavily, twenty-one delegates representing thirteen chapters (half the delegates were women) met in St. Louis to discuss the Smith Act, McCarran Act, Ben Davis, Ingram, and related items.[30]

An examination of the "Bulletin" is revealing of the multifaceted activities of the CRC nationally. Lapel buttons were listed for sale ("Repeal McCarran and Taft-Hartley Acts"), as were posters (concerning Willie McGee and publicizing a book on genocide). Although virtually every article in the "Bulletin" concluded with a call for action, and most articles concerned such cases as McGee, the Martinsville Seven, Ingram, or the Smith Act, in the 1950–1954 period, a good deal of attention was paid to campaigning against the film "The Desert Fox" (which they felt was too praiseworthy toward General Rommel, the Nazi) and against the "viciously anti-Semitic" film "Oliver Twist." The Minneapolis chapter forced theater owners to withdraw the latter film before its scheduled screening; similarly, a Chicago chapter protest lead to the cancelling of the play "Little Black Sambo." This kind of chapter activity occurred frequently: The San Francisco chapter was able to stop Kress, Woolworth's, and Newberry from selling "Jim Crow Halloween masks." A national boycott was launched against Florida citrus after the slaying of NAACP official Harry Moore ("if the fruit is marked 'Sunkist' it is definitely Californian"). Protests by the Baltimore chapter led to a commutation of a death sentence for a Black sugar refinery worker. Nine CRC members in Newark were arrested for passing out leaflets against the Korean War. The Tuscon chapter distributed leaflets in the ballpark where the Cleveland Indians played with Jim Crow seating. Chapters of the week were praised in this weekly publication. For example, Harlem in early 1951 in six months went from a "small nucleus to a chapter of 600 members" by recruiting 150 at a time at mass meetings and holding street rallies of 5,000. The national cases, like that of McGee, were continually harped on: "William Faulkner supports McGee defense . . . (Josephine Baker calls) upon her audience from the stage to avenge the death of Willie McGee." Practical hints to chapters were a must: "every chapter should have its finances audited by a certified public accountant. . . . No CRC meeting or affair should take place without a speaker treating of the persecution of the Rosenbergs." And the objective reasons for CRC failures were not ignored:

"The cancellation last week of the meeting of the CRC's National Board was made necessary by the current drive of reaction which makes it impolitic to bring together so large a group of prominent men and women in one place."[31]

Although a lack of funds barred the regular weekly publication of the "Bulletin" from time to time, CRC did not hesitate to urge their readers to support Paul Robeson's new paper: "Chapters are asked to order bundles of papers from *Freedom* . . . each chapter should undertake a mailing of the newspaper with covering letter and sub blank to all its contacts . . . place someone specifically in charge of *Freedom* in your chapter." Along that same line, although CRC meetings were not always well attended, a similar lack of hesitancy was displayed in urging attendance at the founding convention of the National Negro Labor Council, also spurred by Robeson. Strict attention to the question of women was widespread in these pages: "Every possible effort must be made in every chapter not only to advance and bring forward women leaders but to combat every effort to slow the development of women to leadership positions." However, some may have questioned the desire to ensure for prisoners' children that "Every little girl is to have a doll" for Christmas and "for the boys . . . cowboy shirts." On the national question, chapters were reminded that "Negro newspapers are by the far the most sympathetic to CRC's work. . . . Each chapter can and must make contact with the Negro press in its area. . . . Most important: delegations to editors have proven very fruitful (also) local labor, minority and foreign language press." On the ideological level, the "Bulletin" compared the arrest and release of Soviet doctors in 1953 to what happens in the United States: "innocent doctors were released; those who framed them were arrested."[32]

This kaleidoscopic view of the "Bulletin" not only telescopes the multi-faceted activities of CRC but also underscores this publication's value to the organization. It served as a model for chapters to follow in terms of producing local publications. Moreover, it was suggested by the national office that it be viewed as the scaffolding for the erection of a powerful chapter:

the Phoenix chapter reads it from cover to cover at every chapter meeting. The other extreme is the chapter . . . who don't read it at all. . . . Permanently file all copies. . . . Also, we hope that out of careful study of the Bulletin, chapter people will be able to learn the techniques which have been successful (and probably will be again) for doing the various jobs a chapter has to do. . . . the main function of the Bulletin is organizational . . . (it) arrives every Monday (thus schedule meetings with that in mind). . . . There is something wrong if at least one article in each issue does not result in immediate action of one kind or another.

This same report indicated a theme that was ever-present within CRC: "The national office has on occasion managed to force the U.S. commercial press to take notion (sic) of CRC action by creating in the European press news [the] importance of which cannot be ignored." Just as Black artists often had to travel to Europe for recognition in the United States, CRC cases often had to traverse the same path.[33]

CRC complained more than once about the "paper curtain" that barred the U.S. media from reporting on CRC activities and why this forced them to place such emphasis on turning out publications during this era of the red scare. CRC victories during this period were many and varied and helped to set the tone for the post-Montgomery upsurge led by Martin Luther King, Jr. For example, in Louisiana, after a Black trade unionist, Roy Brooks, was shot and killed by police in 1948, after CRC protest "for the first time in the history of the South a policeman was indicted for the murder of a Negro." In Washington, D.C., CRC forced the police to retreat on their policy of breaking up interracial parties and their protest against the intimidation of white families whose homes were for sale to Blacks was equally not without effect. In Houston in 1948 the CRC "won an injunction against the police for interfering with leaflet distribution, after a leaflet distributor had been arrested." In Denver the chapter forced the integration of a bowling alley in Boulder, attacked the University of Denver for not using Black athletes in contests with southern schools and successfully fought frame-ups against Chicanos. Even before Montgomery integration and antiracism were being jammed down the throats of recalcitrants.[34]

Still, despite the victories and the fact that the organization stood tall in the face of intimidation, there was room for improvement within CRC. Mention has already been made of the inevitable "New York–chapter" dichotomy that arose from time to time. There could have been better coordination among the chapters themselves without increasing the burdens of the national office. There could have been better coverage of national conventions of other organizations. All this and more was taken up in the 1952 national meeting of CRC. Patterson pointed to "our failure to give sufficient attention to moving white people in the struggle against white supremacy." He added: "What CRC needs is a trade union backbone, and we don't have it." Complaint was made about not having enough Blacks in the ranks. "Another factor is the tendency to take the Negro people for granted . . . tendency to concentrate all our . . . membership building in Negro neighborhoods." These random but pointed criticisms were developed extensively:

> Our own weaknesses contributed largely to these erroneous views of CRC as a Negro liberation organization. The intensity of our drive for Negro rights obscured its breadth. We did not see how to link up the Christoffel case on the labor front and the anti-Semitic frame-up of Ethel and Julius Rosenberg with the sharpening attacks upon the Negro people. . . . worst of all, we did not immediately link the fight against the Smith Act and the fight for Negro rights.

Patterson placed further stress on a perceived failure of "organizational consolidation" after the publication of the genocide book, and a perceived failure to link the Smith Act defenses to the erosion of civil liberties generally. The West Coast CRC branches were contrasted favorably with the others on this latter point. But even in this almost hypercritical report, rays of sunshine could not help but shine through. Patterson gave high praise for their efforts in publicity and public relations ("No other people's organization has surpassed CRC in this field.") And he expressed hope for the viability of a special appeal: "CRC should have special appeal to working-class white women. Through its channels the moral conscience of progressive white America can be awakened."[35]

This 1952 Chicago gathering took place at the midpoint in CRC's history and after the repression had heightened as a result of the unpopular war in Korea. Patterson's report here was critical; the report of the National Organizational Secretary Aubrey Grossman might be considered withering by comparison:

> the movement we created on these cases was created at the expense of neglect of almost all other CRC issues and cases. . . . A stronger organization would have made this neglect unnecessary. And did not our weakness in organization cause a relapse after the execution of Willie McGee similar to that which is suffered by the individual who strains his body beyond its normal strength?

In Grossman's view, CRC had "strong" chapters in Los Angeles, San Francisco, Oakland, Seattle, Chicago, Milwaukee, Detroit, Philadelphia, and New York, and chapters with "promise" in Denver, Cleveland, Pittsburgh, Honolulu, but there were "no chapters" in Washington, D.C., New Orleans, Birmingham, Memphis, Atlanta, Richmond, Buffalo, Youngstown, Cincinnati, Kansas City, Indianapolis, and many other places. (Note the disproportionate number in this last listing from southern and border states, where the red scare took its greatest toll.) There were "beginnings of chapters" in Baltimore and Boston: "in total we have chapters in thirty-three cities" with a "total membership" of seven thousand. Though seemingly not that large, it is difficult to think of another avowedly left-wing group with such an extensive membership and such a diversity of activities during this period. In a manner familiar during this era, however, Grossman was not swayed: "the basic fact is that we have failed to grow. . . . (it) cannot be blamed on the 'red scare' or any other objective conditions." Apparent evidence of this was that the "strong" Los Angeles chapter recruited more than two hundred people per month. The reason then? CRC "failed to appreciate the mass appeal of our CRC program. We underestimated the people . . . underestimated the understanding of white workers. . . . we did not have the organizational set-up nationally to create or service chapters." Grossman did not stop there:

> Sometimes there is a tendency on the part of CRC people to condemn progressive organizations or people because they do not react so quickly

to the CRC campaigns as we would wish, because they do not permit us to coordinate them and their activities. . . . A few of our chapters, limited by their lack of a mass base, conceive it to be their function simply to take over the mass base of other progressive organizations to carry out a campaign.

He went on to blast "one man" or "one woman" leadership, although he had more to say generally about the issues presented by this latter question: "How does it happen that women who have been the backbone of chapter leadership in many key chapters from the beginning have not been represented in the top national leadership of CRC since its formation." He cited Ida Rothstein in San Francisco, Decca Treuhaft (Jessica Mitford) in Oakland, Anne Shore in Detroit, Frieda Katz in Cleveland, and Elaine Ross in Brooklyn.[36]

A number of points stand out in this analysis. First of all, there is the tendency to downplay the "objective conditions." For the historian it is much easier to measure such things (the number of wiretaps, mail openings, losses of employment, etc.) than it is to gauge an "underestimation" of the masses. Still, one is hard-pressed to enthusiastically concur with Grossman's position on this question. Then, there is the recurrent theme of fighting "male supremacy." This may seem a bit mundane nowadays, but it must not be forgotten that this dialogue was taking place years before any kind of mass feminist consciousness had emerged. CRC's role as a trailblazer for the civil rights movement is fairly clear; the role it played in generating and creating feminist consciousness should not be ignored either.

Grossman's stinging rebukes aside, CRC's accomplishments under exceedingly difficult conditions cannot be gainsaid. Unfortunately, because of the "paper curtain," it was and has been difficult for the public to know about their contribution to human rights. CRC members were well-aware of this obstacle, which is one reason why they poured so much money and energy into turning out publications like the "Bulletin." Yet, CRC did not stop just with this weekly mimeographed newsletter. National and local publications were put out on all of the scores of cases they handled; many in the form of thin pamphlets costing 5¢ or 15¢. From the Washington, D.C., chapter there emerged a "Legislative Bulletin." The organizational secretary put out an "Organizational Letter" aimed at chapter secretaries. "Censored News" was a highly popular, professionally done magazine, approximately thirty pages in length, published regularly in 1948–1949, replete with graphics done imaginatively and catchy headlines. In the final year of its existence, the national office published the "Civil Rights Law Letter," which was aimed at attorneys and was a compendium of up-to-date briefs and analyses of current cases. They published a pamphlet called "Civil Rights Congress Tells What to Do if Approached by FBI Agent." There was one called "People's Champion" about the Patterson indictment, one called "Pittsburgh Freedom News," about the Pittsburg Six, and one called "Voices for Freedom." The Philadelphia chapter published the visually attractive publication called "Let Freedom Ring," while Detroit weighed in with the "Labor Defender." The earliest publication of CRC was the "Action Letter." These publications had a circulation beyond the membership and some had highly respectable sales. Richard Boyer's booklet on the Rosenbergs ("The Cold War Murder") sold at least fifteen thousand copies, while Sender Garlin's "Red Tape and Barbed Wire" sold five thousand copies in one month. The CRC book *We Charge Genocide!* is still selling briskly. Yale University, West Point, the New York Public Library, and the University of Chicago were just a few of the institutions that requested their products. Their law letter was subscribed to by libraries, "prominent law firms . . . government agencies . . . bar associations." A number of their publications were bilingual, again placing them slightly ahead of their time.[37]

This flood of publications was simply an extension of CRC's considerable efforts in the cultural field in general. It is even possible to speak of a "CRC culture" when one considers not only the artistic aspects of their endeavors but the totality of existence they presented. Picnics, rallies, parties, demonstrations, concerts, barbecues, plays, songs, all were conducted under the CRC imprimatur. At the anniversary dinner of CRC in 1954, "The Ballad of CRC" was sung. There were "CRC Folk Singers" in southern California. In Seattle many rallies were begun with songs sung collectively like "If I Had a Hammer." The Detroit chapter favored picnics and carnivals. Beulah Richards, noted Black thespian, performed in a CRC play based on their genocide book. In sum, it was possible to spend most of one's waking time under a CRC umbrella and to live an enriching existence along with it. CRC was also innovative in their presentation of publications. A cartoon format was used frequently, e.g., in the popular "The Plot Against the People." Quite affecting and touching was their pamphlet, "What are They Doing to my Daddy," which tried to show the impact of the Smith Act on children; the children, pictured sympathetically, asked plaintive questions as FBI agents displayed crude brutality. Again, in this area, CRC was a pioneer. Although some might question the Detroit chapter for having a "Miss Civil Rights" pageant in 1948, it was indicative of their attempt to break out of the narrowly constricted bounds into which many left groups too often fell.[38]

Obviously such ambitious efforts produced by CRC could not be accomplished or funded based on airy promises or mere sympathy toward their fiercely antiracist politics. It required the "mother's milk of politics"—money. Lots of it. CRC's unionized staff drew meager salaries of $60 to $90 monthly in 1946; however, CRC went about the task of fundraising the way it did others; that is, it saw it basically as a political question involving organization. Most of their funding came from the chapters, although for the year ending 30 April 1947, their first year of existence, $26,500 from the Robert Marshall Foundation came in handy; $15,218.42 of it went to the "Oust Bilbo" campaign. Despite a total income of $68,976.07 for this year, a

$5,912.94 deficit remained. By late 1948 this deficit had ballooned to $32,960, according to an audited report. Part of this was due to the extraordinary expenses incurred as a result of the indictment of the Communist Party directorate; $10,348 was spent on this case alone, although correspondingly many donors sent funds earmarked specifically for this case. Income that year included $7,238.36 brought in by a Paul Robeson dinner, $5,813.43 from a tag day and $7,063.28 from summer camps; the New York State chapter showed a net worth of $10,383.59. Even in contemporary terms these are not negligible figures and they give an idea of the extent of CRC's work.[39]

But like their political efforts, CRC did much better financially first of all in the pre-1947 period and then in the pre–Korean War period. In any case, chapters were quite innovative in raising funds, from holding auctions in Detroit to selling blood in San Francisco. All this bore fruit. In 1949 New York State provided the national office with $3,872.55, San Francisco with $1,260.50 and Detroit with $1,400. In September 1949, $8,000 was raised at one L. A. fundraiser alone. The efforts of Paul Robeson cannot be overestimated in discussing CRC finances; many of the concerts he gave were on behalf of his favorite organization and he also was not above sending letters to hundreds of people requesting support for CRC. This was necessary partly because chapters were not always resolute in meeting their national financial obligations. In August 1952, for example, Edith Rosenberg, CRC's national finance director sent out a worried note to the chapters requesting per capita dues, but only L. A. complied. The previous year the national office's budget was $75,000. The six-year-long fight to save McGee cost a cool $75,000 alone. Since the May 1950 indictment of Patterson, $10,000 had been spent. Creative writers Howard Fast, Alice Childress, and Lloyd Brown were helping to raise funds, but even their considerable skills were insufficient. Of the twenty New York chapters, the most was turned in by Sunnyside, Queens ($715), while Harlem had donated $207. Still, the situation was serious. A scant year after war had descended on the land of the morning calm, Grossman was writing the chapters even more worriedly about an "emergency situation." Patterson had not been paid in eighteen weeks, the phone was turned off, the rent was past due, and loans were due; besides reliable L. A., only Seattle and Anacortes, Washington, were responding regularly. We are not "crying wolf," Grossman added for dramatic effect, but not to practical effect.[40]

Legal fees were a major part of the CRC debt and was a major element fomenting abrasive relations with aggressive and ambitious attorneys like Bella Abzug. CRC general counsel Samuel Rosenwein was paid the not inconsiderable annual fee of $10,000 at one time. On the other hand, relations with CRC could lead to other fruitful financial avenues. When CRC attorney Robert Truehaft (husband of CRC leader Jessica Mitford) was searching for a lawyer on the Gulf Coast to handle lucrative "oil leases," Grossman referred him to supporters who saw fit to include CRC in their wills. And lawyers were among the legions of CRC creditors often standing in line with hat in hand.

Because of their effort to break through the "paper curtain," publishing bills were heavy and one particularly angry creditor threatened to take CRC to a "collection agency" unless satisfaction was rendered. A clipping service was obligatory for a national organization like CRC and that too proved costly. CRC's list of contributors included United Electrical Workers Local 475, Earl Dickerson, Louise Pettibone Smith, Emmanuel Presbyterian Church and similar reflections of diversity, but their generosity was not always sufficient to keep the wolf from the door. CRC was not some sort of left legal services agency in any case, but these financial difficulties motivated Patterson to say to John Costello of Binghamton, New York, what he had said to others previously: "We, however, are unfortunately burdened down with a number of major cases."[41]

As much as anything else, these economic problems wore down CRC; the lack of a congenial political environment meant that this problem would be exacerbated; their listing by the attorney general as a subversive organization and the constant drumbeat of allegations about their being a "Communist front" ensured that suppliers would be reluctant to handle their accounts, halls would be reluctant to rent to them, their contributors would be harassed. From 1946 to 1956 these problems worsened. Strikingly, right after the beginning of armed conflict in Korea, Grossman sadly informed Detroit chapter leader Anne Shore that the national office was "forced to cut $200 per week from expenditures. . . . The main item is a cut in staff. It will be compensated for by substitution of volunteer help and elimination of non-essential or less essential activities." In other words, CRC's political impact would be lessened. Two years later Grossman was telling their landlord, Vanderbilt heir and CRC Bail Fund trustee, Frederick Field, that they were unable to pay the rent and "a check would only bounce." Understandingly, Field responded that their rent of $115 per month was reasonable: "we have kept the rentals in this building at the lowest possible figure." Rent was scraped up somehow that time, just as the funds for New York Telephone were obtained when they suddenly decided to hike CRC's phone deposit; but shortly thereafter CRC moved again in their nomad trek to 6 East 17th Street where rent was a bit more reasonable at $100 monthly. John Holton discovered months later what had happened to the telephone: "Walter Winchell was absolutely correct when he said that the National Office is in a financial straight [sic]. The realities of life were faced when I tried to reach your office and found the phone temporarily disconnected." Luckily, CRC leaders like Arthur McPhaul of Detroit were not without talent (he was a plasterer by trade) or they had spouses who worked (Mitford's spouse was a successful lawyer, for example), thus certain financial demands could be mitigated.[42]

Finally, in 1956 CRC went out of existence. Although Grossman has expressed the belief that this was unnecessary and that even at this point CRC was as vibrant as its successor (the National Alliance Against Racist and Political Repression) is today, there is little doubt that in its last days

CRC appeared to be spending as much time defending itself from attacks by the government as it was spending on other cases of repression. Grossman has spoken of liquidationist sentiment bobbing to the surface as early as 1953. In any event, at the 1954 CRC Leadership Conference, Patterson freely admitted that "Liquidationism ran amuck in New York and Chicago." This may have been partially generated by the fact that "today there is little more than a series of CRC duchies whose leaders are on speaking acquaintance with the National Office. Sometimes the speaking acquaintance is a very formal one." Even the bellwether Detroit chapter reported at this juncture that "it has no program mounted nor contemplated," despite Patterson's "sharp . . . criticism." Yet, CRC was continuing to juggle popularly received campaigns during these difficult days on behalf of Ben Davis, Wesley Robert Wells, Rosa Lee Ingram—and itself. And despite Patterson's rebukes to New York and Chicago, he conceded that "Now in both of these cities a decidedly strong current moving in the opposite direction is discernible."[43]

These noble sentiments were repeated by Patterson at the 1955 Leadership Conference: "The liquidation of the CRC is a matter that neither life nor history has yet placed on the order of business." Sure, they were forced to liquidate their Political Prisoners Relief Committee, which supplied everything from razors to cigarettes to moral support to prisoners in order to foil the New York Joint Legislative Committee, which hungered for their list of contributors. Sure, on 29 November 1954 the Subversive Activities Control Board opened hearings to label CRC a "Communist front," with the resultant penalties. As was their wont, CRC went on the offensive, charging a frame-up, while issuing the riposte that "This is the only way to fight and fight effectively." Optimistically, plans were made for a tenth-anniversary celebration in 1956 and Patterson bravely stated that "The political climate today is certainly better than at any time since 1948 for the development of such struggles." Yet, on 6 January 1956 a "Resolution on Dissolution of the Civil Rights Congress" was carried eighteen to one, with all except East Side Seattle voting yes. Why the dissolution? The resolution underscored the "rise of new and broad movements and organizations . . . in the defense of the Bill of Rights," (perhaps the Montgomery movement was being pointed to here); "legal persecution" of CRC through the SACB, the Department of Justice, "income tax examinations and grand jury investigations . . . imposing huge tax liabilities under the pretense that all contributions (to CRC) are 'income.' . . . and . . . not 'deductible.' " There was persecution by the N.Y. State Banking Department and the N.Y. attorney general, who tried "to enjoin" CRC "from functioning." In sum, defending CRC "would absorb the efforts, energies and funds of progressives." CRC was not in business just to defend itself, but that was the situation it was evolving toward. Still, these tendencies, as Grossman had cogently observed, did not just arise in 1956 and ending CRC might well be regarded as a gross political error, which probably set back the overall freedom movement, nor can similar liquidationist sentiments in the CP in 1956 be separated. Nonetheless, sympathy toward CRC's plight is not difficult to summon. They carried on in not as organized a form after the dissolution. Mid-1956 found Patterson fighting the government to prevent their taking away Social Security from elderly leftists and Communists like Alexander Bittleman, William Z. Foster, and Jacob Mindel. Nor was it surprising when Leon Katzen, former CRC secretary in Chicago, turned up in March 1956 as leader of the Chicago Joint Defense Committee to Defeat the Smith Act. CRC members and leaders did not simply fold their tents and disappear gently into that good night on 6 January 1956.[44]

CRC was gone, but their voices were not stilled. The kind of drama and innovation they inherited from the International Labor Defense in their campaigns for the Scottsboro Nine and Angelo Herndon was then passed on to those who sought to free Angela Davis, the Soledad Brothers, and many others. The ideology that drove CRC that saw racist and political frame-ups as being a product of a Jim Crow government—a point incessantly stressed by Patterson—was hammered home by those who sought to free the Wilmington Ten and Leonard Peltier. The altered consciousness of those affected and influenced by CRC remained and continued to reverberate in history.

2
Racism and Political Repression

One of the ironies manifestly of the Civil Rights Congress is that while its detractors scored it for being little more than a "Communist front," existing only to defend the Communist Party, to bail its leaders out of jail, internal critics uttered a different critique. Compared to its closest predecessor, the International Labor Defense, they felt that insufficient attention was paid to labor. Although they would not go so far as to say that too much emphasis was placed on Afro-American rights, they felt that those campaigns—for McGee, Ingram, Martinsville, Trenton, Wells, etc.—seemed to receive much of the ink and money; they also felt that more effort could have been devoted to the Smith Act cases—a direct contravention of the notion of CRC's detractors. Arguably, CRC had "civil rights" in its title for a reason. Blacks are predominantly working class and they occupy key stations within the proletariat; hence, focusing on a Black truck driver like McGee does not necessarily neglect the labor link, although CRC propaganda mostly focused on the racist aspects of the case.

In retrospect, given the dynamic impact that the civil rights movement has had on democratic rights generally and the space it has created for struggle by all progressive forces, including labor, CRC's stress on racism against Blacks in particular can be seen as justifiable. The fact that their most important leader, William Patterson, was Black and had a history of struggle around Black rights—and according to Grossman "did not understand" the labor movement (not to mention the racism of the latter, which might make approaches by a Black problematic)—made the CRC's orientation virtually preordained. Let it be said they were pioneers in this area, engaging in tactics and raising questions that most did not see arising until the post-1955 period. Layers of ignorance, bias, and amnesia have covered up much of this rich history. But from this point forward it should not be forgotten that CRC blazed the trail that made the obstacle-strewn path of Dr. King and his hearty band less difficult; by the time that stage of the movement got underway, Euro-Americans had become accustomed to militant anti–Jim Crow protest. Indeed, the post-Montgomery movement may have seemed like a respite in comparison, and Afro-Americans and their allies had received a thorough education in an expertly taught school of struggle.[1]

The watermark of CRC thought on this strategic question was enunciated by Patterson over and over again: that Jim Crow was a policy of the federal government, that it benefited a narrow sector of coupon-clippers who profited from the fact that racism drove down wage levels generally and made for a discrete class of individuals who could be shunted aside to inferior posts. But that was not all. They consistently sought to link the battle for civil rights to the battle for peace (as long as the military budget swelled, how could libraries be built or jobs be created). In a preconvention discussion in May 1950, Patterson, in remarks to chapter secretaries appropriately entitled "The Fight for Civil Rights and the Fight for Peace," called the so-called Negro Question the "Achilles heel" of the warmongers. How could the United States win hearts and minds in a predominantly colored world when people of color in this nation were treated so shabbily? This theme accounts in part not only for CRC's constant stress on breaking into the foreign press but also for the government's unseemly attention to their efforts. Moreover, Blacks were seen by Patterson as a reliable reserve of strength against the Cold War and the red scare: "The Negro people have shown themselves to be the least susceptible to poisoning by cold-war propaganda."[2]

Yet this was only the beginning of their analysis. Patterson, in particular, was well aware that something of a Faustian bargain had been brokered with certain civil rights leaders: that in return for some rights at home, they would engage in anticommunism at home and abroad. This involved battering left forces like CRC, while stroking other antileft forces with sinecures and the like. In mid-1955, while Patterson was seeking to avoid long-term imprisonment and CRC was under siege by a gang of government officials, Patterson outlined to Harry Ward part of this strategy.

> the government is carrying through a twofold program—the one is to make concessions—some of them very astute, as for example the elevation of Benjamin O. Davis to a major Generalship—and then placing him in command of the air force around the Formosa straits. If bombs are to be dropped on colored people the Negro General from America will seemingly be the author of it. (This is the answer to Bandung.)[3]

The other part of this "twofold program" was the iron fist aimed by ruling circles against those with the temerity to refuse such offers. It was not that CRC opposed lofty posts for Blacks; indeed in 1949 at the time their nemesis Tom Clark was being appointed to the Supreme Court, way before other civil rights groups, CRC through a statement by Patterson to the Senate Judiciary

Committee called on the president to "Appoint (a) Negro to (the) Supreme Court"; he suggested William Hastie, Charles Houston, or Charles Howard. What they objected to was going along with the anticommunist drift in order for example, to reach the high court. Patterson was at times brutally frank in assessing this question. In his estimation there were some Blacks who could not be trusted because they were more interested in "securing of judgeships and ambassadorships and positions in the United Nations apparatus. I am not against securing these 'honors' but when they are secured at the expense of the people, then a voice must be raised in protest." At the same time, as Don Carleton noted, the political situation was shifting: "As black Americans began to win new victories . . . the specter of Reds was replaced by the specter of blacks and the civil rights era soon monopolized community fears."[4]

It was this theoretical perspective that drove CRC mercilessly to seek to vindicate the full citizenship rights of Afro-Americans. The need for this heartfelt concern was extraordinary. Just as W. E. B. Du Bois signified his concern for the liberation of Africa in the post–World War II world by using the title of his acclaimed book *Color and Democracy,* which tackled this touchy issue, as the logo on his stationery, so the CRC utilized a special stationery with a seeming inkblot and the words: "An Un-American Product—the Fruit of Jim Crow and Segregation." In 1948 they launched their "I Shall Not Live at Peace with Jim Crow" campaign. Although this campaign was criticized sharply by a number of CRC comrades, it was motivated by fierce antiracist intentions. A pledge, which was supposed to be framed and displayed prominently, announced to all: "As a white American . . . in the spirit of Thomas Jefferson [sic] . . . I pledge eternal hostility against discrimination, segregation and prejudice. . . . I pledge no peace with those who support these alien and abhorrent evils." Perhaps because of internal opposition, this admirable campaign aimed at Euro-Americans did not take flight, but the impact on white workers of entering an office or the shop floor and seeing such a pledge displayed can only be seen as profound.[5]

CRC did not stop with a mere pledge, but, reminiscent of the unjustly condemned Harlem Communist "trials" of the 1930s, they went to some length to ensure that their attack on racism was not just directed at the most egregious southern racists. One example of this laudable self-examination that is still needed today was the 29 June 1952 conference held by the East Hollywood chapter "to examine and study the problem of white chauvinism, to exchange ideas and experiences." CRC was intensely interested in the question of recruiting more Blacks:

The vital necessity for personal friendships with the Negro people stressed—unless we have social relationships, we cannot have successful political relationships, we cannot have successful political relationships. . . . Because of the greater jeopardy to the Negro . . . in speaking out . . . and because of their mistrust of white people due to their being misled and betrayed . . . special emphasis was placed on the oppression of the Negro woman . . . the necessity for every CRC chapter having Negro women on its executive board.

The platform put forward was quite advanced, calling for "ending the practice of Negroes being the last hired and the first fired, hiring Black teachers and librarians, curbing housing discrimination," etc. But, above all, CRC did not hesitate to discipline white members who fell victim to "white chauvinism," which to Blacks was evidence of the organization's sincerity, their good faith, and their sound moral practice. Unfortunately, all chapters were not always so vigorous as were the denizens of East Hollywood. When Grossman wanted to print a cartoon strip on Blacks and the Smith Act, he was forced to complain that "we have practically no orders for it." Finally, he was forced to state the obvious: "because of your present Smith Act trials and your large Negro communities (you) should be able to provide us enough orders to justify the printing." This too demonstrated CRC's attempt to link the "Negro Question" with other significant issues, with little success. Critics might have considered CRC overly sensitive on the "Negro Question," while the CRC were of the opinion that it was difficult to overexert oneself in this area. Soon after arriving at CRC Patterson deemed it meet to rebuke his comrade Abner Berry of the *Daily Worker* staff for alleging that there were "a lot of comfortable Negroes in the South." Depending on what one means by "a lot," there was certainly some truth in Berry's allegation. But Patterson probably felt that it was misleading—particularly for a communist paper seeking class unity—and also that it was dangerously ambiguous, because the lynch laws and the multiclass nature of the "Negro Liberation" movement made it difficult to say that *any* Blacks in the South were "comfortable." In any case, this ultra-"sensitivity" paid off for CRC by attracting not only Afro-American adherents but Euro-Americans in search of antiracism in a society polluted with this noxious brew.[6]

Also evidentiary of this sensitivity was the flap surrounding a white CRC member in Louisiana, Sophie Goff, who hired a Black maid. "Serious objections were raised," she lamented. Her comrades asked, "Is it correct for a white progressive woman to have a Negro domestic worker working for her?" They answered yes, "but only if she paid more than the prevailing wage." Further that a "committee from the CRC will come to my house . . . and inform her as to why she received increase in hourly pay, what the organization stands for, etc." Similarly Patterson rebuked the *National Guardian* for their headline, "Where is Ocie" (referring to a defendant in a CRC case) because "use of the first name should be avoided, since it is common practice in the South not to give Negroes the courtesy of addressing them by their second name."[7]

Proof of CRC's record and its concern for the "Negro Question" was not long in coming. Immediately after their founding they not only publicized and investigated a particularly brutal massacre of Blacks in Columbia, Tennessee, but they also made the Negrophobic Mississippi Senator Theodore Bilbo a household word through their mass "Oust Bilbo" campaign. The Columbia program started with a dispute between a white radio repairman and a Black woman and her nineteen-year-old son, who was a Navy veteran. The white man struck her over a disputed bill and the veteran defended his mother. They were jailed but escaped. A mob attacked the jail. Five hundred state and local police went house to house allegedly searching for them; Black businesses were wrecked and looted; search warrants were absent, naturally; more than a hundred people were arrested, two were killed, and thirty-one were placed on trial; KKK slogans were scrawled everywhere indiscriminately. Eleanor Roosevelt was among those who blasted this treatment. Steven Lawson has noted how CRC, "tainted as a communist front took a leading role in rallying leftist opinion against Bilbo." But it wasn't just "leftist opinion" that harkened to their call. Their National Committee to Oust Bilbo included Adam Clayton Powell, Oscar Hammerstein II, Gene Kelly, Leonard Bernstein, Fannie Hurst, Alain Locke, David O. Selznick, Albert Einstein, Katherine Dunham, John Garfield, and many others, and was chaired by Quentin Reynolds and Vincent Sheehan. Anticipating those who descended into Mississippi twenty years later, CRC sent attorney Emmanuel Bloch— soon to be immortalized as the Rosenbergs' lawyer—to Mississippi to get sworn statements about Bilbo's depredations, his corruption, his warm ties with the Ku Klux Klan and the fiendish tactics he deployed to prevent Blacks from voting. Bloch was just one of a corps of attorneys and investigators sent there. CRC distributed 185,000 petitions in thirty-two states supporting this effort, thus making it a truly national campaign. They published posters, buttons, lithographs, and pamphlets. They provided details for the Senate on his corruption and his role in barring Black voters violently.[8]

This grassroots campaign, which collected 500,000 signatures on petitions presented by Senators Robert Wagner and Styles Bridges, may have been the main factor driving Bilbo to a premature death and from the Senate. In 1946, undermining a racist U.S. Senator was no mean feat. Hate mail rained down on CRC and its supporters in the field were apprehensive. Reverend Charles Hamilton of Aberdeen, Mississippi, wanted to be helpful, but he was reluctant: "I do not want my name circulated about this though, I am willing to furnish information and action at the right moment."[9] A campaign of intimidation and violence was unleashed against identifiable supporters in Mississippi.

The Bilbo campaign was the first major CRC campaign, but it was far from being the only one carried on in their early days, nor was it their swan song in the area of antiracist work. A reign of terror and violence descended ominously on Afro-Americans in the postwar period and CRC attempted to ride to the rescue. For example, after four Blacks were lynched in Monroe,

Georgia, in the summer of 1946, CRC sent at their expense investigators there for two weeks; their report was filed with the U.S. attorney general, who indicated that his hands were tied in such a matter, although clearly no such compunction would have operated if there had been charges of "communist infiltration" being made.[10]

Police terror and brutality remained a major concern for CRC throughout its existence. In early 1948, CRC launched a "Lobby to End Lynching" campaign on Capitol Hill in support of the Wagner-Case AntiLynching Bill. Consistently they prodded the Truman Administration on this issue. In July 1948, as the presidential campaign began to heat up, their press releases asked Attorney General Clark to prosecute the Ku Klux Klan if they held their meeting in Georgia. A week later they forwarded telegrams to Truman, Clark, and Governor Fielding Wright of Mississippi asking for action after the police shot into Blacks' homes and then the Blacks were "jailed indiscriminately"; they accused the authorities of "terrorizing" them. This persistent effort was maintained throughout the Truman Administration. July 1951 found CRC demanding that the White House ensure that every one of the KKK leaders, who had burned fourteen crosses in four southern states on 25 July, be indicted and jailed. After the brutal flogging of a Black man in Swainsboro, Georgia, by two to three hundred Klansmen, CRC again requested that action be taken by Truman. The NAACP and other Blacks, who had avidly backed Truman in 1948, were greatly disappointed by his inaction, which helped to convince him not to seek another term. CRC maintained a large file of clippings and information on KKK activities and monitored their activities closely. Their focus on McGee, Ingram, and other leading southern cases was used as a window to peer in on and to dramatize racist violence. Shortly before becoming defunct, CRC in 1955 campaigned vigorously for passage of antilynching legislation, again in the wake of a racist murder, this time of young Emmett Till. Again, as they had in appealing the sentencing of Communist Party leader Eugene Dennis, they called for a reduction of Mississippi's representation in Congress, pursuant to the Fourteenth Amendment.[11]

Persistently, CRC tried to place their antiracist efforts in the overall context of the fight for democratic rights and a higher standard of living for the poor:

> People who get excited about meat and vegetable and rent prices and taught how to do something can be gotten more easily to fight for poll tax repeal, FEPC, abolition of (HUAC) and the repeal of Taft-Hartley. . . . People who get agitated on these issues can then be counted on in large numbers to defend the rights of Communists and other progressives. . . . Large numbers are needed to affect congressional voting.

Intervention in the congressional process was a trademark of CRC. Frequently they were to be found testifying before national bodies, collecting signatures to deliver to elected officials, and lobbying them. The L.A. chapter was in the forefront of fighting the "loyalty check" in that state. The Michigan chapter obtained 115,000 signatures on petitions to bar passage of the repressive Callahan Act; they sent a delegation of one thousand people to Lansing, registered 155,000 voters within ninety days and distributed 150,000 pamphlets. [12]

CRC's nationally distributed "Action Letter" focused consistently on anti-labor bills, like Taft-Hartley. CRC representatives testified in early 1948 before the U.S. Senate Committee on Rules and Administration on H.R. 29, the bill to ban the poll tax; they worked closely with the National Committee to Abolish the Poll Tax. A major legislative initiative for CRC was the push to pass Fair Employment Practices Committee (FEPC) legislation that would curb job discrimination against Blacks and other national minorities. They had on file a full complement of model pieces of state and federal legislation. They sparked the formation of local and state committees to generate such legislation. The most successful effort in that regard took place in Michigan, where CRC official Rev. Charles Hill played a leading role. When the Civil Rights Act of 1964 was passed, CRC members could take satisfaction in the notion that they had plowed the ground and planted the seeds that eventually bore fruit. Similarly, when the Voting Rights Act of 1965 was passed, CRC workers deserved partial credit. In the spring of 1949 they joined the fur and leather workers and other allies in trying to register Blacks to vote in the virtual feudal duchy of St. Bernard Parish, Louisiana, which a CRC staffer ominously noted was "the home of Leander Perez," the notorious race-baiter: "We expect that not only will they be refused, but that we will be able to lay the basis for a constitutional action to render the state restrictions on registration illegal." [13]

School desegregation was another issue close to CRC's heart. Much of their work was done under the auspices of the Southern Conference Education Fund (SCEF), but their ear was close to the ground also picking up the oncoming hoofbeats. In 1951 CRC member C. H. Talbot of Topeka, Kansas, reported breathlessly to the national office on the progress of the lawsuit that was to become *Brown v. Board of Education* in the U.S. Supreme Court. When the high court upheld segregation in South Carolina schools, no louder opposition was heard than CRC's. When the *Brown* decision was rendered, it was hailed by CRC; Grossman has argued that CRC's efforts, particularly in the international arena, helped to make this decision possible; a United Nations body was just about to release an embarrassing report on this question as the decision came down. The Little Rock incident of 1957 found CRC defunct. But long before this desegregation crisis, CRC had been in close touch with progressive forces there. When Patterson was indicted, the *Arkansas State Press*—which came under severe attack by the racists in 1957—rushed to his defense. From time to time, newspaper officials forwarded to CRC intelligence and political analyses of the situation in the state, similar to this 1951 report:

> Most of the would-be liberals in the state are afraid. . . . Our publication has been boycotted by nearly all of the large department stores in the state because of our fight. But we have the largest circulation of any weekly publication in the state (white or Negro). . . . some of us were even jailed and fined some time ago for "contempt of court." . . . The *State Press,* alone, after bitter fighting is responsible for the hiring of Negro policemen. . . . Every move we make is carefully watched by those who would persecute us.[14]

CRC had more than a theoretical perspective to lend to battles like school desegregation. They had practical experience. They won victories. CRC played a major role in "softening up" the forces of reaction in the postwar, pre-Montgomery era, thereby making a knockout of Jim Crow that much more possible. In the fall of 1949, for example, after holding mass meetings with the NAACP, American Jewish Congress, and other organizations, CRC members in Brooklyn were able to force the Woodward School to admit a six-year-old Black.[15]

Facilitating CRC's antiracist maneuvers was their close tie to the National Lawyers Guild and CRC's own lawyers' panels. The lawyers panel in L.A. was one of the most successful. Established in 1949 with thirty attorneys, by 1950 it had fifty-three; these lawyers took on ninety-eight cases, and by April 1950 they had "favorably terminated" thirty-five, with only three having been settled "unfavorably." Most of these cases, nineteen, involved police brutality against national minorities, with racial discrimination being a close second on the list. Besides improving the atmosphere for the fulfillment of democratic rights, there were other positive byproducts:

> The lawyers who have served on the panel feel that they have learned much . . . it has been possible to fill every request for legal services on a non-fee basis. . . . It should also be noted that during the year the NAACP and the American Jewish Congress have each caused a similar legal panel to be established for the first time. It may not be too farfetched to suggest that the formation of said panels was in part induced by the example set. It appears that there will be collaboration on various cases between the several panels, as occurred in two instances.

This last statement may have been overly optimistic, but there is little doubt that the existence of CRC spurred other civil rights forces on to greater heights and for the larger community served as a benchmark of their progress. The issue of lawyers' panels was seen as essential to CRC victories. Grossman wanted them "on a national scale . . . in all good-sized cities." He added, "I do not feel that CRC can do its job as a defense organization . . .

unless it has hundreds of lawyers throughout the country, organized, and agreed, to work for CRC, and without fee. . . . (there is a) great danger (of) permitting the office counsel to do things that the legal panels should do." Grossman wanted to facilitate this by publicizing "the great tradition . . . of prominent, and often conservative lawyers donating their services. . . . along with this goes . . . the tradition of the militant young lawyer sharpening his spurs." Though these were the dog days of 1950, Grossman had grandiose plans for establishing a national legal committee: "I see an advantage in having big shot lawyers on the Committee but only if they are involved in work. . . . Nothing is worse then the lawyer who conceives his function as 'talking' and not 'doing?' " Their involvement would "assist in helping them grow politically and in stature." Even forming a "Stoolpigeon Information Center" was bruited about.[16]

This was all made easier by CRC's close relationship with the Black press. P. L. Prattis of the *Pittsburgh Courier,* Charolotta Bass of the *California Eagle,* and Nathaniel Sweets of the *St. Louis American* were just a few of the editors and journalists who looked on Patterson as a friend. Patterson received chummy letters from figures like Frank Davis, executive editor of the Associated Negro Press, who shortly after Truman's election offered to provide publicity to CRC's "jim crow drive . . . This presents an excellent opportunity to create interest among the Negro people in CRC."[17]

Unfortunately, this sort of good feeling was not always the norm. In 1952 a Detroit chapter leader, McPhaul, bitterly complained of the formation of the Defense Committee for Negro Leadership, which, in his estimation, "would amount to segregation. . . . while the intent is without a doubt good . . . these things have a way of drifting and becoming what amounts to in fact separation." Doxey Wilkerson responded promptly stressing the "independent" nature of the Black liberation struggle, and McPhaul sheepishly concluded that his earlier information was "incorrect" and his "first conclusions . . . were made on the basis of . . . a misunderstanding."[24] This was something of an internal dispute among comrades, but at times this kind of anger was unleashed externally. After "Burns and Dennis, the two Negro GI's (were) executed by the U.S. government on the island of Guam," McPhaul angrily denounced most Black and other civil rights organizations for not rallying to their defense, initiated by CRC, but for redbaiting them instead; his opinion was that McGee and the Martinsville Seven could have been saved also with more unity.[18]

Still, sometimes with the help of the NAACP and other civil rights forces and sometimes without, CRC kept plugging away—many times successfully. The mass action threatened by CRC in 1948 eventually forced Child's Restaurants, Inc., a national chain, to admit Black customers. A similar protest in 1949 led to similar results at a Boulder, Colorado, cafe; that same year a CRC-sponsored effort got underway in Omaha. But one of the most significant and largest battles in this arena took place in an unlikely place, Des

Moines, Iowa. The result was that the Iowa Supreme Court in its "first civil rights case since 1905" upheld a CRC-sparked lawsuit against Katz's chain of drugstores and restaurants, beginning desegregation. The tactics they used not only mirrored those of the 1960s, but they also paved the way for this later period. In the summer of 1948, John Bibbs, Edna Griffen, and Leonard Hudson, all CRC and Progressive Party members, took seats at the Katz soda fountain and were told, "We don't serve colored." After the lawsuit, and massive sit-ins, picketing, and an effective boycott—the usual CRC approach—they won. But also, somewhat typically, this victory was accompanied by internecine infighting and redbaiting. CRC–Iowa was harsh in its condemnation of the NAACP: "The NAACP had never officially gone on record in support of our battle. . . . We understand that Katz is a ten-dollar member of the NAACP. . . . We sincerely thank the NAACP for whatever it had done besides whisper to the people *not* to join us in our action at Katz." But this was not all. They also accused prominent Black attorney Charles Howard of "redbaiting." They charged that he was allied with a "reactionary" Black attorney who "tried to force" CRC to settle the lawsuit for a measly $150. Howard was also accused of trying to play the NAACP off against CRC and the Progressive Party. Patterson was disturbed by all this, and since Howard was a person whose political role he respected, he was reluctant to echo these allegations, although he admitted that Griffen had made out a "prima facie" case.[19]

Perhaps all the fault was not to found on the side of Howard, despite the chapter's early spectacular victory. By the fall of 1949, Griffen was noting the chapter's "lack of activity" and added the observation that their leaders were "frightened by redbaiting. . . . our forces are extremely few. . . ." One Iowan wrote the national office directly, alleging that CRC was a "Communist front" and adding, "I do not care to be associated with your organization as I believe it is alien to the general welfare." Howard was also adamant. After accusing Griffen of having spread "lies and half-truths" about him, he concluded without equivocation: "under no circumstances nor at any time will I ever work with Edna Griffen." Despite this controversy and the short-lived existence of the Iowa chapter, the legacy left was exceedingly rich. They forced the enforcement of an Iowa civil rights statute that had been adopted in 1884. Yet, typically, one law review's analysis of this matter ignored the role of CRC and the Progressive Party but quoted approvingly Arthur Schlesinger, Jr. and the American Civil Liberties Union. But the record clearly demonstrates that it was the CRC's mass action in the face of the hostility of the county and state governments that forced the state's representatives to troop into court to enforce a statute on the brink of desuetude. Enforcing laws on the books and launching mass actions distinguished SNCC and SCLC in the 1960s from the NAACP, just as it distinguished CRC from them in the pre-1956 period.[20]

CRC also pushed for local legislation when existing laws were deemed inadequate. Again in the heyday of CRC during the pre–Korean War period, CRC was the moving force in Tucson, Arizona, in getting a petition before the governor calling for a special session of the state legislature to enact civil rights legislation. As the *Tucson Daily Citizen* authoritatively intoned "most said they were urged to support the petition by the Tucson Civil Rights Congress." Al Schlackman, "Jewish and a printer," and Flo Mack spoke for CRC. One politico was "particularly interested in discovering whether the Civil Rights Congress was a cover-up name for a Communist Front and drew the wrath of several speakers by refusing to agree fully with them." In another state with a comparatively small number of Blacks, the Civil Rights Congress of Oregon generated a similar campaign. After complaining about the proliferation of confederate caps and flags, they held mass meetings demanding enactment of a city ordinance in Portland calling for an end to Jim Crow in "hotels, skating rinks . . . hospitals . . . restaurants." They met with the mayor and city council to urge passage of the bill. They obtained thousands of signatures on petitions. The mayor in response appointed, in inspired bureaucratic fashion, a committee "to study our proposal." Eventually, they won.[21]

Pressuring employers to hire more Blacks was equally the forté of CRC. The Detroit chapter had forms for the Black public to fill out in order to follow up on various forms of discrimination, but as the effort to establish a FEPC and then an Equal Employment Opportunity Commission demonstrated, discrimination on the job was a constant complaint among Blacks. In early 1949 the Philadelphia–CRC conducted picketing of Woolworth's until they were forced to hire "their first Negro sales girls." During that same year Boston CRC signed an agreement with "Timothy Smith Department (Store)" that provided for hiring of "Negro sales and clerical employees; the first such employees have already been hired." Picketing, neighborhood mass meetings, leaflet distribution, and so forth, characterized this fight, waged "sporadically" since 1940. In an early push for the quotas of the 1970s, CRC joined the Labor Youth League in New York in picketing New York's Parkwest Restaurant because of their lack of Black employees; they demanded that the next person hired be Black. In San Francisco a couple of years later in 1951, CRC forced the California State Employment Service to obligate employers not to inquire concerning the race of job applicants. In 1954 when the Detroit chapter was reeling from the death blows dealt by reaction, they found time to blast the mayor for turning down a Black woman applicant for a high city post because of her ties with unnamed subversive organizations. But as a harbinger of CRC's subsequent demise, the Black woman in question, Beulah Witby, immediately wrote McPhaul demanding that her name be taken off CRC's mailing list.[22]

CRC pioneered particularly in knocking down the walls of segregation above the Mason-Dixon Line, but that was not all. Their maneuvers in the South were particularly noteworthy because of the more hostile environment that greeted them there. It was not an accident that a number of their leading cases—McGee, the Martinsville Seven, Ingram—took place in states like Mississippi, Virginia, and Georgia. In conducting these campaigns CRC was forced to confront directly and indirectly the quaint folkways of the deep South. When three thousand CRC campaigners traveled to Richmond in a vain effort to free the Martinsville defendants, they challenged segregation in buses and eating places. New Orleans, particularly in the pre–Korean War era, was a hotbed of CRC activity. Their chapter was formed in April 1948 in response to a Black male being taken off a bus and shot by police. Oakley Johnson, who was a member of the NAACP and the United Public Workers of America–CIO, was the leading force in the chapter, although the International Longshore and Warehousemen's Union and the furriers were also in on the ground floor there. They went on to make a name for themselves by fighting racist frame-ups all the way up to the Supreme Court. They sponsored voter registration, they defended college youths arrested for participating in interracial parties, they joined with the NAACP in celebrating their fortieth anniversary and maintained fairly close ties contrary to Walter White's démarche. These early premature antiracist efforts caught the eye of the authorities and District Attorney J. Skelly Wright (eventually praised as a progressive federal court judge) called Johnson before a grand jury and grilled him about his ties to the left. Johnson had been a founder of the CP in 1919 and at the University of Michigan had been faculty advisor to the Negro-Caucasian Club, one of the first interracial organizations on a college campus. Because of such pressures, by 1951 Johnson had been ousted from his teaching post at Dillard University and from New Orleans itself and the chapter soon folded. But the legacy left was often quite visible—literally—as Patterson's suggestion to Johnson indicated: "I should like to see a number of streets in white and Negro neighborhoods in New Orleans painted with slogans, with a fast-drying paint, reading 'JIM CROW MUST GO,' 'OUTLAW THE KLAN,' 'LEGAL LYNCHING IS A DISGRACE TO AMERICA,' 'LET'S PRACTICE THE RELIGION WE PREACH.'"[23]

The fact that the most resolute racists—Bilbo, Eastland, McClellan, Stennis, Rankin—were equally the most determined anticommunists guaranteed that repression would hit CRC with both barrels. Nonetheless, the ferocity and the scope of the harassment and terrorism that befell CRC still shocks the conscience in relation to a country that considered itself "democratic." And the fact that CRC refused to flinch but hung in there until forced to dissolve is worthy of comment as well. Courage was not an assumed commodity during those days of darkness. For example, when the West Indian Trotskyite C. L. R. James faced deportation from the United States in 1952, he veritably groveled in order to obtain the good graces of U.S. leaders. He confided to Walter White, whose aid he was seeking, "Any idea that I was a dangerous agitator abroad is entirely ridiculous"—a notion that would have greatly surprised many of his followers. He alleged that his organization, however, was never "larger than 35." He blasted his mentor Trotsky for not being sufficiently anti-Soviet and went so far as to repudiate his major book: "I would get rid of every copy of *World Revolution* that I could, because I no longer believe in it."[24] CRC was forced to liquidate, but it refused to grovel.

The fact that the attacks on CRC were just one more way to disrupt the "popular front" generally should not amaze us. But even granting this basic truism, the lengths to which the authorities went to disrupt CRC's antiracist and antirepression maneuvers is an eye-opener. For example, the atmosphere created generated hate mail unrivaled in nature. The CRC in L.A. was told to "go to your rat holes in Moscow . . . where all you Jew Communists belong . . . hang all Jew communists in L.A." Another correspondent, who was bold enough to include his name, averred, "I hope to see the day when you and your kind of traitors are behind barbed wire." Yet another, similarly motivated by racism, alleged, "What this country needs right now is another Mr. Hitler." "Go back to Russia" was the most frequent allegation.[25] This kind of facist and anticommunist invective was not just found in the City of Angels.

Consequently, the kinds of persecution that hammered at CRC were a given. Patterson was indicted. So was George Marshall. Pressure was placed on other CRC leaders, at times successfully, to become informants. From the time of CRC's origin to their demise in 1956, plotting the level of persecution on a graph would show a steady upward trend, with a jagged acceleration in the post-Korean War period. All kinds of difficulties eventually smothered CRC. Bonding companies were hesitant as early as 1948 to provide bonds for some of the defendants they served. But even before then (and one should note also that another spurt in persecution came after the Progressive Party declared their candidate for president in 1948), harassment was becoming normal. In the allegedly liberal Upper West Side of Manhattan at 85th St. and Broadway, a CRC gathering was broken up violently:

> (it) was disrupted by young hoodlums whose tactics showed not only organization and planning but as well ideological preparation. . . . They heckled and shoved at first, then began more serious physical attacks upon the spectators with concerted efforts to draw the spectators into a violent physical struggle. . . . A member of City Council, who was the principal speaker, had his glasses broken. (The police came and) were in conversation with the leaders of the gangsters.[26]

Throughout the city during the 1948 political campaign for the presidency, not only were Progressive Party meetings disrupted but CRC's as well.

As time passed, things got worse. CRC leader Ida Rothstein was killed by a hit-and-run driver. The Philadelphia headquarters was burned to the ground. Other attacks were a bit more mundane—relatively. In 1952 Patterson informed a couple who were CRC supporters, "I have positive knowledge that the Post Office Department is, for reasons concerning your political beliefs, conducting an investigation of your activities." In 1954 the American Textbook Publishers Institute told Patterson that "under recent legislation in Alabama," a book publisher must "indicate" if "an author mentioned in any textbook is or is not a member or ex-member of any organization listed on the U.S. Attorney-General's" list. CRC was on "that list"; thus the spokesman demanded a "list of all your members, past and present, which we will make available to publishers." Patterson termed this extraordinary demand "incomprehensible" and "vicious," although he probably wondered why they didn't just go to the FBI to get CRC's lists. For as he told Lu Ping of the Peking journal *China Reconstructs,* the government was continually "interfering" with the domestic as well as the foreign mail of CRC. And as he informed a *Daily Worker* reporter in 1955 in utter disgust and perspicacity, "The persecution of CRC has apparently become one of the major projects of the government aparatus."[27]

A familiar, well-practiced tactic of governmental authorities was the infiltration of spies and informants into CRC. Both the revelation of this practice and the practice itself appeared to escalate as 1956 came closer—and indeed, this practice probably brought CRC's demise closer. In August 1953 Nadya Schwartz of the Maryland chapter had to report to Patterson a tendency that was becoming all too common. They had to "expel . . . James Brocton, our former vice-chairman." They discovered that he was at "one time a member of the police force," though he had neglected to inform them of that. "He never participated in any (mass) activity." He said he worked at a tavern, but he could never be reached there. "Yet he attended meetings regularly, asked very specific questions about our plans and . . . members." Naturally, he took a lot of "notes," which he would "surreptitiously" place "in his hip pocket." His name was "Brocton," although he used "Brockington" from time to time. At the meeting to expel him he failed to appear. Concomitant with all this, "agents" began to focus intensely on the chapter. "Our members have been visited and [they] attempted to trail various people. . . . these issues have been taking up all our attention lately." Not only was the pattern of "Brocton" all too typical of an informant, but the last sentence of Schwartz's report was equally the norm: this infiltration hampered and sometimes prevented CRC from aggressively pursuing its antiracist, pro–civil liberties agenda.[28]

March 1954 found the St. Louis chapter enduring a similar travail. The local Black paper, the *Argus* reported "Rev. Obadiah Jones has been ousted from all posts" in the chapter "because of his appearance as a government witness in the trial of the five alleged Communists"; his infiltration was apparently done at the behest of the FBI. They provided him with $10,000 and also asked him to join the CP. He was chair of the chapter and went so far as to advise members of his congregation to join, then reported them to the authorities. This pastor of Mt. Tabor Baptist Church, of African descent, was able to deceive CRC leaders somehow, although he admitted on the stand that he had never heard of Crispus Attucks or Harriet Tubman. His appearance at the trial, needless to say, caused a furor. Black and white pastors of St. Louis filed an *amicus curiae* brief in this Smith Act case condemning the practice of using clerics as spies, but the end result was familiar: the activities of the chapter were disrupted virtually beyond repair and the antiracist and pro–civil liberties movement suffered a damaging setback.[29]

The Wisconsin CRC chapter in 1955 traversed a similar guantlet. They had to expel Keith Fredenberg, "self-confessed informer for the Milwaukee Police Department." A recipient of a government pension and legally blind, in a familiar pattern he was pressured into becoming an agent after having been arrested on a "morals charge" for "molesting young girls." Days later John Gilman, executive director of the chapter and thirteen others, who were mostly leaders of CIO unions, were subpoenaed by the House Un-American Activities Committee. Months later, the chapter was defunct.[30]

Inevitably, one of the strongest chapters, which happened to be located in a land of make-believe, produced one of the strangest tales of CRC infiltration. Early in 1955 Dave Brown, executive secretary of the L.A. chapter, was "kidnapped," allegedly. This act sent shockwaves through the progressive community nationally. But even more seismic reverberations were induced when he confessed that the FBI had helped him invent this story in order "to cover up the fact that he was an undercover agent for the agency." They even went so far as to mail his tie and other effects to the San Francisco office of CRC in order to make his story more plausible. Finally, he came clean to clear his "conscience." Brown had been approached by the FBI in 1950, two years after he had moved to California from New Jersey where he had been an organizer for the Mine, Mill, and Smelter Workers. They paid him $5 a report (which was an incentive to file reports obviously), up to "a high of $250 a month." He had also been active in Labor's League for Peace, the Rosenberg Defense Committee, the Wesley Wells Defense Committee, and many others, that is to say, he filed a lot of reports. Perhaps indicating its importance to the FBI, he was paid an extra $50 to spy on the Rosenberg group. He joined their White House vigil in June 1953, was an honor guard in the chapel after their execution, and saw the bodies buried. This was no low-level left munchkin. Still, this did not prevent him from using dishonestly creative tactics in filing reports. He would simply type in *Peoples World* editorials, then attribute those views to speakers at meetings. Moreover, since the FBI wanted names, he "began to submit fictitious" ones; he would identify persons from picket line pictures, meetings. He disappeared after taking out a double-indemnity insurance policy with the funds to go to his family after he was presumed dead.[31]

Ineluctably, this tale of seduction and betrayal was guaranteed to stoke passions. But particular aspects roiled particularly. At first Brown would meet FBI agents in his car, but then they switched to the Mormon Church in Hollywood. As Patterson angrily told David McKay, leader of the Church of

Jesus Christ of Latter Day Saints, the agent "had a key to the rear door and front door. . . . Several times they came to the church when the pastor was coming in and he greeted Mr. Stewart [the agent] the confession said." All this was too much, even for Brown's wife Sylvia. In no uncertain terms, she denounced the "betrayal perpetrated" by her soon-to-be ex-mate. Ben Margolis, one of the most talented lawyers of his generation and a close confidant of CRC chapter heads Marguerite Robinson and Anne Shore, has spoken informatively about Brown and his escapades:

> I worked very closely with him. His exposure as an agent came as a complete shock. So far as I am aware no one who worked with him had the slightest inkling of what he was doing. To this day I am convinced that he was in fact completely devoted to the Civil Rights Congress and its objectives. His weakness was a need for money, leading to the situation where while he was getting money from the FBI he was working diligently and effectively for and on behalf of the CRC. Of course, when the FBI decided that it wanted to use him as a witness he first ran away and later returned, saying that he would never testify for the FBI and refused at least at that time to testify.

Later, Brown was divorced by his wife, became a taxi driver, and disappeared into the nonpolitical netherworld, but, again, the impact on the theretofore strong L.A. chapter was more than devastating. Confidence in the chapter and its leaders was dealt a maiming body blow from which it too did not recover.[32]

Unfortunately, the type of questionable practices signified by the proliferating deployment of spies and informants was not limited to Maryland or St. Louis or Wisconsin or Los Angeles. It was a national, well-coordinated drive that eroded trust among CRC members and the organization along with it. Syptomatic of its importance was the fact that CRC kept a voluminous file of "Informers," which detailed their practices, their patterns, and their names. Again, strikingly, in 1955, it was discovered that Harry (Dock) Truitt and his wife for the past two years had spied systematically on CRC. Like so many other spies, they had a jail sentence hanging over their heads (involving a labor dispute) and this was used to induce them to spy. The Colorado Committee to Protect Civil Liberties (a CRC affiliate) was spied on by John Lautner, who got $25 per day and $9 daily expenses. The notorious Harvey Matusow, who was reputed to have testified falsely against over two hundred people, who disrupted many lives and organizations and sent scores to jail, also had a role in crucifying CRC. In fact it was the storm generated by the revelations about Matusow that spurred CRC to initiate a petition protesting the use of paid informers, which was signed by Mary McLeod Bethune, George Crockett, Carlton Goodlett, and others. But this heroic riposte proved to be too little, too late, and soon thereafter CRC itself became defunct.[33]

Revelations about spies nesting in CRC may have tumbled out torrentially in 1955, but that does not necessarily show that the practice itself began at that time. If a recounting of investigations of CRC by HUAC and other governmental bodies is any guide, this kind of activity began virtually with the organization's inception. As early as 1947 HUAC termed CRC a "Communist front" and provided an extensive listing of supporters' names and of organizations involved in their campaigns. That same year they produced their tellingly titled *Report on Civil Rights Congress as a Communist Front Organization,* which repeated the charges that have dogged CRC to this day concerning their alleged propensity to defend only Communists, their ties to celebrities (Robeson, Hammett, Langston Hughes, Canada Lee), and detailed lists of their expenditures. At the next session of Congress, then-CRC executive director Joseph Cadden was called in by the Senate Committee on the Judiciary and grilled at length, particularly about the Mundt-Nixon bill. Nevertheless, this negative publicity notwithstanding, the listing by the attorney general of CRC as a "subversive" organization and the constant repetition of this charge in government reports and the news media probably caused the most damage of all.[34]

Along with Harvey Matusow, Matthew Cvetic was one of the most celebrated government spies, the subject of films and reams of articles. In 1950 his testimony before HUAC seared and scored CRC and its leaders. The mass campaign against the anti-communist Mundt-Nixon bill was described by Cvetic as "organized within (CRC)" along with "the Communist Party," ignoring the scores of other groups that opposed this legislative house of horrors. But even here, condemnation was tempered with realism when Congressman Burr Harrison and Cvetic acknowledged that CRC had "been fairly successful." Chimed in Cvetic, "Up until now they have; yes." U.E. was also dragged in; they were accused by the cooperative witness of financing CRC, running off their leaflets, and so forth. Cvetic, who claimed to have been a "member of the (CRC) since its inception in Pittsburgh," offered up hundreds of exhibits, including correspondence and checks; the anticommunist theme was stressed repeatedly, as when Cvetic turned his streaky spotlight on Patterson: "I have attended Communist Party strategy meetings . . . with [Patterson] . . . and [Patterson] has personally acknowledged before four or five people, in my presence, that he was a member of the Communist party." Around this time, the concentrated campaign to place Patterson behind bars accelerated.[35]

Dragging witnesses before HUAC, SACB, and similar forums was a common tactic. Next to the Communist Party, CRC probably received more attention from such bodies than any other organization. Robert Wishart Canon was twisted brutally on the rack by HUAC. He was co-chair of the CRC–Oregon in 1947 and had served as director of admissions at Reed College and dean of students until May 1954; he had worked with the Urban League and was a Communist at the time he was a CRC leader. He was forced in 1954 to squeal on his former comrades. The next year Anita Bell Schneider of San Diego testified before HUAC that she had infiltrated CRC there on behalf of the local police and the FBI. She rose to be corresponding secretary of the Emory Collier Defense Committee, which was organized around a racist frame-up in the area. Like Cvetic, she stressed anticommunism, alleging that the Communist Party "determined . . . the officers" of the chapter and "dictated the program," pointing to the fight to free Wesley Robert Wells. At the same time, Bereneice Baldwin was testifying in Detroit before the SACB that the chapter there was a tool of the party; she pointed to chapter leaders like Jack Raskin, Esther Cooper, and others as card-carrying party members. All the witnesses were not so cooperative. When the Justice Department brought in 1930s hero Angelo Herndon from Chicago to testify in the deportation case of CRC-client Communist leader Claudia Jones, he turned the tables on his questioners by speaking eloquently about Jones and refused to play their game.[36]

Public investigations replete with kleig lights and microphones were not the only form of scrutiny that CRC received. Thanks to a lawsuit filed by the National Lawyers Guild against the FBI and the massive discovery order they obtained, a window has been opened on the agency's illegal activities aimed at CRC. What is surprising about these activities more than anything else is their scope and brazenness. The tapping of CRC telephones was as frequent as the sun setting in the west. Maurice Braverman, a CRC leader in Maryland and a prominent civil liberties lawyer, was bugged repeatedly from 1948 to 1950. This "intercepting (of) the wire or oral communications to which the NLG was a party through the use of electronic or other means" continuously turned up information about CRC. Decca Truehaft and Ida Rothstein in the Bay Area, Jack Zucker and Max Millman of Philadelphia, Frieda Katz and Sam Handelman of Cleveland, Tom Buchanan and Bob Silberstein of Washington, D.C., were among the CRC and NLG members who had their privacy violated. This invasion began as early as 1946, though it certainly increased as time wore on.[37]

The FBI did not just stop with phone-bugging, but used other means—including humans—to intercept CRC communications; opening their mail has been mentioned already. The FBI monitored meetings in their offices. They monitored their rallies and mass meetings. They kept voluminous records on all their activities. They obtained records of their bank accounts. In Philadelphia "through arrangements with . . . and the cooperation of Chief Inspector George Sadler, Postal Inspector's Office . . . photographed the addresses" of a CRC mailing of 2,860. They obtained copies of their mailing lists for purposes of harassment. The Oakland police kept files on CRC and forwarded copies to the FBI. "Surreptitious" entries of CRC offices may have been more frequent than the sun setting in the west. The point is however that what turns up on the record is probably little more than the tip of the proverbial iceberg. Buggings, spies, burglaries, jailings, perhaps murder—no tactic was too crude, no stratagem too unsophisticated to unveil against CRC.[38]

The chapters of CRC had peculiar experiences—in every sense of that term—with the phenomenon of Cold War repression. Seattle and Detroit, where two of the strongest chapters were located, provide microcosmic views of what was happening nationally. Anonymous elements in the former city published a phony though funny anticommunist newsletter entitled the "People's Whirl." Virtually unique in the bulging annals of anticommunist propaganda, this organ, named jocularly after the Communist Party paper *Peoples World,* made a special target of CRC. Some familiar charges were repeated, like CRC diverting funds meant for the McGee campaign. Chapter leader John Daschbach and other members were denounced. Their venom was garnished, however, with poems, songs, humor, all devised to spear CRC and the left. They hit sore spots when they accused CRC and the *Peoples World* of not hiring more Blacks. They accused left leaders of buying new cars, drinking incessantly, womanizing, and other vices. In a gossip column called "We'll Never See," they included a jab at a prominent Puget Sound labor leader: "Karly Larsen out with his wife."[39]

The "People's Whirl," with all of its tongue-not-so-firmly-in-cheek humor was not matched in sophistication by other forms of harassment launched in the direction of the Seattle chapter. Daschbach received post cards in volume guaranteed to hurt a busy political organizer: he was accused of neglecting his children. These unwanted correspondents also asked, "Why don't you get a job?" At one point, a provocateur "came into the CRC office . . . proposing that (CRC) purchase secret information from a Boeing employee." As any other leftist would have done—and that definitely includes the Rosenbergs—the gentleman "was curtly told to beat it." They didn't stop there. Someone sent out post cards with Daschbach's name on them carrying the allegation that the Seattle party was diverting funds. Someone stole CRC envelopes and started a like campaign; someone else started an "anonymous telephone campaign" designed to scare away CRC supporters.[40]

Much of this harassment took place in the last year of CRC's existence, but inevitably there was a spurt of activity around mid-1950. At that point a spate of false ads were placed in local newspapers purportedly, but not actually, put there by CRC. One sought applicants—"white Gentile only"—for a CRC secretarial post. After the ruse was discovered, all the papers were not helpful in repairing the damage done to CRC's reputation. A complaint had to be filed by CRC with the State Board Against Discrimination in Employment after the local *Capitol Hill Times* refused to run CRC's clarification. At another point that year, someone wired the national office alleging that Daschbach had "resigned. All records missing." Again, these are just the actions found in the record. Whispering campaigns, subtle threats, and other methods designed to destabilize the chapter were not necessarily put into the record. Yet the end result was that such tactics played a major role in destroying one of the more important forces for civil rights in the state of Washington.[41]

Detroit's experiences with persecution and harassment may have been even more tumultuous than Seattle's. This grimy midwestern Turin with a history of bitterly recriminative labor relations provided fertile soil for hostile campaigns against CRC. In May 1951 Capt. Charles Hill, Jr., the son of CRC leader Rev. Charles Hill, who had served in World War II as a pilot and received two Bronze Clusters, was finally able to defeat disloyalty charges that would have led to his dismissal from his job. These spurious charges, which were refuted due to the skillful talent of frequent CRC attorney Ernest Goodman, were based solely on his father's ties to the left generally and to CRC in particular. This was not an isolated incident. A number of Michigan cities customarily published the names of those who signed CRC and CP petitions, for the purposes of harassment. Of course, HUAC received one of its more raucous and rough-hewn receptions in Motown; witnesses like Coleman Young and CRC leader Arthur McPhaul demonstratively challenged HUAC in one of this committee's more exciting road shows. This 1952 spectacle was not just challenged by CRC in the hearing room. They set up a "picket line" that was a "tremendous success." They held two mass meetings, one at Rev. Hill's church and another at Ford Local 600 of about five hundred people. They put out tons of literature and a detailed petition. But ominously, as Anne Shore informed Grossman, governmental authorities were not their only opposition: "The Legion says they will counter picket us. The press is having a fine time whipping things up."[42]

As time went on, things got worse. In the steamy, sultry summer of 1953, CRC was holding a party in McPhaul's backyard. Suddenly six police officers appeared, alleged a liquor code violation, and began an exhaustive search. Twenty-six people were arrested, held in jail, and given enormous bonds. Eighteen were convicted; four received one year's probation and a $50 fine, and fourteen received one year's probation and a $10 fine. After the sentencing, the judge floridly commended the jury for their fine work. Within a year the five hundred to a thousand members of the Detroit chapter had dwindled significantly. Even before then, obstacles had been strewn in the path of McPhaul, a longtime autoworker and union official, in his attempts to organize. Paul Robeson wanted to come to one of his favorite cities for a benefit concert, but the Jewish Cultural Center was about the only place progressives could meet. The Detroit City Council was "threatening hall owners . . . with taking away their tax exemption privilege if they permit 'subversive' organizations to meet."[43]

The Detroit chapter probably had closer ties to the industrial working class than any other chapter, which might have spawned even more antagonism toward them. William Hood of the massive Local 600 worked closely with them, as did a number of other locals. There were regular distributions of CRC literature at auto plant gates by fabled organizers like Nelson Davis.

True to form, after the execution of Willie McGee, a decision was made in CRC to bring his widow to Detroit and find her a job in the auto plants; the companies were only hiring white women at this point, but CRC decided to join the effort of the National Negro Labor Council to break down these barriers. In any case, Detroit—a city notorious for its tense relations between the police and Blacks—presented special problems. An all-too-typical case was cited by McPhaul:

> had a big mobilization in the downtown shopping area last Saturday to hand out leaflets and collect petitions. . . . Saul and four Negroes were picked up by the police and intimidated. But quick action of our lawyers, Crockett and Goodman, plus a really militant attitude (freed them).

But what disturbed the police and their patrons most of all most likely was McPhaul's concluding statement: "the Negro people were tremendously impressed with our interracial group in action."[44]

Supporters and those so unlucky as to come into contact with CRC often felt the cold winds of repression blowing on them. The L.A. publisher of the Black weekly *California Eagle,* Charlotta Bass, traditionally stood with CRC in their various campaigns and she paid a price. Jailed CRC leader Emil Freed was told this: "The Eagle is being given a rough time. . . . the South-side is being flooded with free copies of other Negro papers to kill its circulation and advertisers have been approached." Similarly, the printer Jacob Hyams who was so indiscreet as to print a bit of CRC literature was called before the U.S. Senate and examined without mercy. An army physician, in a case that went all the way to the Supreme Court, was ultimately persecuted because, among other things, "I have attended public meetings of the Civil Rights Congress."[45]

In this he found himself in the same boat with Black writer Amiri Baraka, who was bounced out of the U.S. Air Force in the mid-1950s because of a CRC tie. Celebrities were not strangers to CRC. Both Patterson and his wife were celebrities of a sort in any case, his wife being one of the progenitors of the Harlem Renaissance. It was not unusual for Patterson in the early 1940s to go to meet with baseball commissioner Kenesaw Mountain Landis about desegregating the sport, and spend the night in his home. Howard Fast and Paul Robeson were just a couple of the many luminaries who gravitated toward CRC. Breaking this solidarity was a major goal of CRC opponents and a major reason was the fact that these personalities helped to attract people to CRC's banner. Thus José Ferrer was questioned closely about CRC before HUAC in 1951. Lillian Hellman was queried sharply about her knowledge of CRC leader Dashiel Hammett before the same body. Artie Shaw at a 1953 HUAC hearing was raked over the coals about CRC. A similar fate overtook Arthur Miller in 1956. But the infamous 1952 HUAC hearing in Detroit presented the epitome of this trend. Coleman Young was asked by the HUAC interlocutor, "to what extent . . . the (CRC) . . . has assisted the

Communist Party in attainment of any of its objectives?" Said Young without blinking, "I am no stool pigeon."[46]

But as the record shows, "stool pigeons" were all too rife within CRC. This government-induced repression caused a stampede away from CRC, and their controversial antiracist work did not assuage their opponents, especially since much of it was successful. And even when an antiracist campaign of the Civil Rights Congress was not "successful"—after all, Willie McGee was executed—the heightened consciousness, the new members recruited as a result of the effort, and many other results caused by their work were more than sufficient to keep the anticommunist bloodhounds hot on the trail.

3

Against His Will

The fantasy of Afro-American males raping Euro-American women has long agitated certain minds in this nation. Brawny Blacks sating their unquenchable desire by consuming dainty, retiring white damsels animated *Birth of a Nation* and a number of other leading U.S. cultural works. Unfortunately, as Ida B. Wells-Barnett pointed out consistently in the post–Civil War period, the fruit born from this phantasmagoria has been, strangely, Black males swinging from trees. The case of Willie McGee was probably CRC's most well-known case. It involved these Black vs. white controversial elements and took place appropriately in Mississippi. The case came to prominence in 1946 when CRC was born and it ended with McGee's execution in 1951, a time when CRC was reeling from post–Korean War repression. The McGee case no doubt raised national and even international consciousness about race and repression; thus, like Sacco and Vanzetti, McGee did not die in vain, and like those two political prisoners whose case catapulted Patterson into the movement, ironically, his death may have been his triumph. Even today, according to Mississippi State Senator Henry Kirksey, his case continues to be discussed; adds Mississippi's legendary civil rights lawyer Jess Brown, unlike most whites, Blacks in the state rejected the calumny hurled at CRC for defending McGee.

It was far from accidental that the McGee case was chosen by CRC as a high priority. CRC recognized implicitly that dramatic examples like the case of McGee—a Black man, a white woman, the rape issue, and Mississippi—carried all the elements of a tragedy that could illuminate larger issues. The case was a microcosm, a crosssection, a sliver of Americana. Putting the searchlight on McGee brought into sharp relief racism and Afro-America itself. The techniques deployed to try to save McGee, also used in other CRC cases, are still being used to save prisoners in South Africa, Central America,

74

and the United States itself. But the immediate goal was saving McGee and those other Black males marching lockstep to the guillotine. Between 1882 and 1950, according to statistics kept by Tuskeegee Institute, 1,293 whites and 3,436 Blacks were lynched. Next to homicide, rape was the main cause (1,937 v. 910); overwhelmingly, most of those lynched for rape were Black. In Mississippi between 1930 and 1948, 108 people were executed, which included ninety Blacks; six were executed by the state for rape—all Black. Not only did this make out a *prima facie* case for denial of equal protection for McGee but one for African-Americans generally.[1]

This *cause célèbre* of McGee, precisely because it generated massive national and international publicity, generated equally strong anticommunist myths about CRC's motives. As was said so often by so many during this difficult era, race was the "Achilles heel" of the United States. For example, how could hearts and minds be courted in an increasingly colored world when people of color in this country were subjected to such vile brutality. This was a hard question to answer and it was much, much simpler to question the motives of CRC, even if evidence to substantiate such charges was few and far between. CRC was continually accused of not being interested in the fate of McGee—or the Trenton Six or the Martinsville Seven—but were said to be only "using" them. They were accused of diverting funds meant for his defense to other causes. Actually, many of these charges were just echoes from the Scottsboro era and were often stated by those not too active in fighting repression. McGee himself was clear on these issues. He knew that but for CRC he would have been just one more of those thousands of Blacks executed legally or extralegally in this country with little outcry.

In August 1948, he expressed again his thanks and affection for CRC: "I want you to know that I appreciate everything the Congress have did (sic) for me. I hope someday to come face to face and tell you in my own words how much I appreciate what you did for me." Months later this was repeated: "I feel that you all will do everything in your power to set me free." Days before his execution in 1951, in responding to a "false statement" in the *Laurel (Ms.) Daily Leader,* McGee provided his final epitaph to put to rest this shibboleth: "if (it) had not been for you all, my friends, I would not be here. . . . I don't care who helps me fight my enemies." Rationally, McGee did not bother to give an ideological litmus test to the neighbors who were helping him put out a fire at his house, although many—including those who executed him—would have preferred for him to do so.[2]

The fact is that there was substantial mutual affection between McGee, his family, and CRC. Both McGee's mother and his wife continually expressed this affection. As Bessie McGee told Patterson, "I am so thankful for all you have done for us during our troubles. . . . May the Lord bless each of you." Patterson often replied with words of encouragement and advice. A sign of the anticommunist times was the fact that explaining why there should be affection for someone who is trying to save your life or your husband's life or son's life was deemed necessary. In 1950, when McGee's wife was not allowed to visit her husband, she immediately contacted Patterson: "I can't even visit Willie now. . . . I am so worried I don't know what to do." Patterson with like immediacy pressured the prison warden, just as he did when McGee's mail was limited. After his international tour, he peppered McGee with accounts of how he had visited "many countries" about his case. The celebrity of the case, like the Scottsboro case, caused otherwise quiescent individuals and organizations to offer "aid" to McGee, and Patterson subtly warned against these entreaties in communicating with Rosa McGee: "Many people will come to see you now. That is, because we are awakening the whole country in the fight for Willie. . . . Do not promise anyone anything or give anyone anything." Problems persisted, however, as McGee sadly conceded: "I had to slip this letter out to you. The jailer will not give me all my mail from you . . . all and my lawyers won't come when I send for them." Again, CRC quickly responded.[3]

As early as 1946 Milton Kaufman was reassuring Bessie McGee, indicating by way of assurance that reputable Black Mississippians were on board: "Mr. Percy Greene of the *Jackson Advocate* is also helping us and you may be sure that we are doing everything to protect the interests of your son." The correspondence between the McGees and CRC was not only voluminous but at turns touching, affectionate, and directly contradictory to the notion that the Black prisoner was being "used" by CRC. At any rate, those who have made such allegations—strikingly—do not quote the McGees.

Despite this, the charges continued to fly. Days before his execution Patterson had to take time to rebuke *New York Post* columnist Max Lerner for stating that CRC had "used" the Scottsboro Nine. CRC was obviously operating in a difficult environment of racism and bigotry that was not even understood by the presumably well-intentioned. Saving Blacks' lives was not viewed generally as a high priority, just as Black lives were not viewed as valuable, and those who sought to do so were automatically assumed to have ulterior motives—particularly if they were on the left. CRC did have other motives that they were quite open about expressing—seeing the McGee case as a prism through which to view racism in the United States. This was an era when southern "liberals" like Ralph McGill and Hodding Carter were quite open about praising the early KKK; V. O. Key, Jonathan Daniels, Mark Ethridge, and others all opposed federal intervention on race—but backed it for economic development. They were all shameless redbaiters and adamantly fought federal antilynching legislation. Hence the McGee case was guaranteed to ignite their enmity—and it did.[4]

One of McGee's early lawyers, a man of no particular liberal persuasion, also objected to the calumny aimed at CRC. Years later in 1975, Jessica Mitford confidentially informed the Pattersons: "I asked [Dixon] Pyle if he agreed with *Life/Time/Nation* that the Communists and CRC hurt the case? He said absolutely not . . . the Freedom Riders were catylists [sic] for change but 'Laurent Frantz and Jim Dombrowski' laid the foundation." A litmus test for all this is the fact that by and large the Afro-American press— exhibiting once again the yawning gap betweeen the two "nations" inhabiting the United States—did not go along with the "white" line. The *Afro-American,* the *Pittsburgh Courier,* even the conservative *Amsterdam News* generally did not echo the anticommunism of the above-mentioned organs directed at the effort to save McGee's life. Perhaps because they were Black they could better appreciate the value of saving a Black life, irrespective of ideological axes that needed grinding.[5]

Even the moderate Establishment journalist Carl Rowan tended to believe the case was a frame-up: "only the craziest Negro would walk into a white man's house and rape his wife while the white man slept in the next room. . . . And the one thing nobody had accused Willie McGee of was insanity." But symptomatic of his ties, he announced: "Anyone who helps McGee helps the Communists." It may be assumed that the option then was for them to clamor for McGee's execution. Still, Rowan was a bit clearer, symptomatic of his race ties, about the impact of the case:

one thing emerged crystal clear: the Communists were reaping a propaganda bonanza and American democracy was suffering in the court of world opinion. The United States Embassy in Great Britain asked the State Department to send information on the case with which it could counter "propaganda in the London press." The Embassy still was smarting under the applause that went up in Parliament a few days before, when a Member read a letter denouncing the execution, in Martinsville, Virginia, of seven Negroes . . . while . . . the (U.S.) was freeing Nazi war criminals.

Rowan considered himself no novice on the case: "I knew the background of the case, as does almost every Negro boy and girl in America; as do far more citizens of Calcutta, Paris or Shanghai than of Chattanooga, Pittsburgh or St. Paul." This last statement may have been an exaggeration, but the widespread knowledge of McGee abroad was not a chimera and indicates why such a sustained effort to discredit his saviors was launched.[6]

If the Communists "used" this case, which gained worldwide support and sympathy, for their own ends, somehow it did not manifest itself in a membership spurt in Mississippi. Party organizer James Jackson in February 1951 averred, "None of the eleven states of our Party's Southern Region have functioning state organizations. In nine states there are Party clubs or sections in sixty cities and three farm areas. Only in Mississippi and Arkansas are there as yet no clubs of the (Party)." Ironically, the "propaganda" trained on CRC generated hostility that led indirectly to McGee's death and the confusion of his allies. Even Aubrey Williams, usually resolute on such matters, wilted: "Don't send me any more of your material. You people do far more harm than good. The best thing you could do for people like Willie McGee is to go out of existence." Despite it all, CRC kept plugging away.

Contrary to the propaganda, even when McGee requested, "publications . . . for encouraging the reading of the Bible," CRC—led by materialist Communists—dutifully and willingly complied.[7]

So, what were the facts of the McGee case? What about it engendered so much controversy? Dark and handsome, with the typical accent of a Black Mississippian, he was born 4 November 1915 and he married in 1935. He worked at a masonite plant in Laurel, Mississippi, drove a truck and worked in the yard of Mrs. Willett Hawkins, who, according to McGee, "showed a willingness to be familiar and let me have intercourse with her in the back room." He alleged that this began in 1944. After that they allowed their passion to boil over many times. Knowing that carnal knowledge of a Euro-American woman in the deep South by a Black was not guaranteed to win him a life insurance policy, McGee fled to California, but he missed his family and home, so he returned. He and Ms. Hawkins resumed their "criminal conversation." In fact, she began visiting his home and McGee's "wife became suspicious. . . . some words passed between Mrs. Hawkins and my wife." McGee would often slip in the back room while her husband slept in the front room. "I just could not get rid of her at all. . . . I tried everything to get rid of her but she being a white lady I had to do what she said. . . . I was afraid completely to break off." McGee claimed that he had gotten her pregnant, which "had me on the spot." There was also a rumor that McGee and Hawkins had conspired to kill her husband for the insurance money— "Double Indemnity," "The Postman Always Rings Twice," and "Desire Under the Elms" in Black and white. McGee claimed that the night before the rape charge he visited her. The husband saw him (apparently not *in flagrante delicto*), yelled at him, then "grabbed" him. McGee "shoved" back, a mortal sin for a Black at this time. The night the alleged rape took place, he claimed he did not go to her home because of the fracas. One point is irrefutable: McGee was well acquainted with Hawkins for quite a while before the "rape." Rev. G. L. Tucker, her pastor and an avid defender of hers, said as much in an interview with an investigator, who used the ruse that he wanted to talk since his wife was "interested psychologically" in the case. Dixon Pyle, one of McGee's first attorneys, whose racist credentials were burnished by the fact that he used such terms as "n-g-er," shared the view of many that the husband "caught her in the act" and this forced her to yell rape.[8]

McGee's spouse, Rosalee, mirrored her husband's account for the most part. At one point in 1943 when Ms. McGee was with her spouse, Ms. Hawkins asked him to join her immediately and called his wife a "Negro whore" in a rejoinder. That night, she said, he told her the truth about their affair. When he worked at a gas station, Ms. Hawkins would leave notes in the "nozzle of the gas pump" for him. Ms. McGee said her husband had no choice, because "if he said 'no' she'd cry rape anyway." Willie McGee was riding the tiger and it may have been more dangerous to dismount than to continue. "That's why I never got angry at Willie." After he returned from California, Hawkins began lusting after him; she would give notes to a Black girl for McGee. Finally, in 1945 Ms. McGee left her husband as a result of Hawkins' advances. But, like Rev. Tucker, she disputed Hawkins' testimony that she didn't know McGee before the "rape."[9]

This was just one of the peculiarities of Hawkins' argument. She also claimed that McGee raped her while a sick child was in bed with her, while two children were asleep in an adjoining room. She claimed that this "man with kinky hair who wore a T-shirt" who raped her on the night of 3 November 1945 was a total stranger; that she did not cry out although her spouse was in the next room. It was this tissue of Rashomon-like contradiction that drove Willie McGee to the gallows.[10]

Yet it was not without a fight, principally because of CRC. George Marshall, then of NCFL, sent the brilliant journalist and organizer Louis Burnham on a mission to Mississippi to discover the facts. His report dovetailed with that of the McGees and he was struck particularly by the fact that McGee's lawyer "had not conducted an energetic defense and that the jury had deliberated for approximately three minutes."[11] Little wonder. A howling mob surrounded the courthouse for the duration of the trial. When he was arrested in Hattiesburg, thirty miles away, McGee was held incommunicado for two days prior to the indictment, then thirty more days. Attorneys were not allowed to visit. Why did he sign a confession? As he told his mother, "I signed to be living when you got here." He was escorted by beefy state militiamen to the trial in Laurel, where the last lynching had taken place two years earlier. The confession beaten out of him had left him "speechless and helpless," and that is how he was carried into the courthouse on 6 December 1945 as the first trial opened. At his second trial, CRC attorneys were offered a bribe if they'd drop the case; only a change of venue ordered by Judge John Stennis prevented this future U.S. Senator from presiding at this trial. But even here attorney Dixon Pyle conceded that he refused to raise all the evidence for fear of a "riot. . . . We wouldn't have lived to have gotten out of town. . . . Whenever you charge a white woman in the South with having sexual relations with a Nigger in this part of the country, why, you better be god-damn sure." McGee's lawyer in the trial John Poole was "almost disbarred" for pursuing the case too vigorously. Poole too conceded that a thorough job was not done because of fear. A highway patrolman told him, "Poole, I just want to tell you that a group of fellows there are after you. Be on your toes." Compounding the situation was the apparent racism of Pyle meant McGee "didn't [do] too much talking" to his attorney.[12]

The McGee case lanced the ugly sore of U.S. racism and caused the pus of bigotry to flow for all to see. The law firm in his first trial, Koch and Boyd, tried the case in a lightning-fast one day. They did not dare to crossexamine Ms. Hawkins, despite the glaring contradictions in her testimony. According to a McGee lawyer in the second trial, Dan Breland, "they were scared."

Breland's and Pyle's trial did not go much better. Perhaps the machine guns freely brandished, the guns on trucks outside, and the bayonets in the courtroom influenced their behavior. McGee was so weak he had to be placed on the stand bodily. The presiding judge was said to be a friend of Ms. Hawkins. Despite his prodding, McGee wouldn't talk when placed on the witness stand due to his abject fear of the consequences of telling the truth. Breland felt that the defendant and his lawyers would have been lynched if the truth had been told. Hawkins made passes at the district attorney throughout the trial, and given the nature of the charges, this should have impeached her credibility irrevocably in a normal trial, but did not here. Even the district attorney admitted that she had a so-called "loose reputation." They were not able to persuade "colored ministers" to testify on behalf of their brother because of the pervasive air of intimidation. [13]

John Poole was not only "almost disbarred" as a result of defending McGee, but he was virtually ruined economically. At this trial Mr. Hawkins had a pistol in the courtroom and threatened to use it if evidence were introduced concerning the affair between McGee and his wife. He was subsequently disarmed and ejected, but the point had been made. Even the people of Laurel were afraid to talk about the case and CRC operative Laurent Frantz was literally run out of town for trying to get them to act otherwise. As in the second trial, allegations were again raised about Hawkins and her "playing around," this time with "some members of the Laurel police force." At the second trial, Mr. Hawkins had leaped on Pyle and threatened to kill him if he pressed his wife on crossexamination; to that extent, the third trial was not as exciting as the second. One of McGee's lawyers in the third case acknowledged that "we weren't ever prepared to try the case," but the court wouldn't grant a stay; like Pyle, he bared his predilections by freely using the term "n-gg-r." He explained Mr. Hawkins' audacity by way of the "standing joke" in the post office where the cuckold toiled, that his wife was tupping while he worked the night shift; but this "joke" could explain how McGee could visit her under the cover of darkness and then slip home by a respectable hour. [14]

The McGee case resembled something of a pingpong game. CRC lawyers would appeal the obviously tainted trial verdicts to appellate courts, win new trials, be forced to secure local counsel because of archaic Mississippi rules, lose at trial again as a partial result, win again on the appellate level—then lose at trial again. Few cases generated so many appeals, so many innovative legal arguments, and such laborious, determined fighting than McGee's. If CRC was "using" McGee, they certainly went to extraordinary lengths to save his life. They lost the first trial on 6 December 1945, a scant few weeks after his arrest, and he received the death penalty. They appealed to the Supreme Court of Mississippi and on 10 June 1946, in one of the organization's early victories, a new trial was ordered on venue grounds (apparently the howling mob surrounding the courthouse influenced this high court). On

4 November 1946 a new trial opened in Hattiesburg. Again he received the chair. Again CRC appealed. On 9 February 1947 they won again, this time on the grounds of the exclusion of Blacks from the petit and grand juries. In March 1948 the third trial commenced. Again, he was adjudged guilty, but this time the Mississippi Supreme Court would not budge—they upheld the verdict and this was affirmed by the U.S. Supreme Court on 15 May 1950. But the legal beavers of CRC did not stop there. They then filed a *coram nobis* writ in a lower Mississippi court and received a stay of execution before it was overturned. Then, early in 1951, they filed a *habeas corpus* writ in another lower state court, appealed to the state Supreme Court upon losing, then filed in federal district court and lost, then appealed to the U.S. Supreme Court once more.[15]

As the case wore on, the number of ingenious claims by CRC grew correspondingly. Anticipating present-day legal arguments, they raised the issue of the death penalty being reserved for African–Americans. They zeroed in on the prosecution's knowing use of perjured testimony (i.e., that of Ms. Hawkins) and on these additional issues: 1) McGee was denied the right to testify since if he had spoken truthfully, he would have been lynched; 2) under the circumstances, that is, no death penalties for whites committing rape, such a penalty for McGee violated the Eighth Amendment sanction against cruel and unusual punishment; 3) the confession, which was beaten out of him, was obtained in violation of his constitutional rights. Grossman informed his legal consultants—top-flight lawyers all, Richard Gladstein, Ernest Goodman, and Bertram Edises—that this "will be a pioneering project legally" and he was exactly correct, for it certainly was.[16]

This legal labyrinth was not without its suspenseful twists and turns. At one point McGee was scheduled to be executed within hours when he was saved by a reprieve. And even with the terroristic atmosphere prevailing, the case might have been won but for putatively illegal conduct by the state authorities. There was evidence that the state destroyed transcripts of the first and second trials in order to hamper the defense's appeals. Mississippi State Supreme Court Judge W. C. Roberts, who signed a stay of execution, said he felt McGee wasn't guilty. But he didn't write a dissent when the case appeared before him, again out of fear. Allegedly, State Supreme Court Judge Julian P. Alexander felt similarly but didn't act for the same reason. Thus, McGee was marched to the guillotine.[17]

The CRC's defense of McGee was able to draw upon the vast legal wisdom of a network of attorneys that they had helped to organize in the first place. This collective approach to legal strategy and tactics was a useful antidote to the usual overweening individualism that afflicts all too many trial counsel. Hard on the heels of the first trial, Abe Isserman commented on the "entire record and transcript" of the case. He zeroed in immediately on the change of venue issue. Attorney Harriet Bouslog a few years later forwarded a detailed memo to Grossman. She advised him to "be sure . . . your petition meets the requirements of *Snowden v. Hughes,* 88 L.Ed. 497." She reminded him that "re: unlawful administration by state of statute, fair on face, resulting in an unequal application, is no denial of 14th Amendment, unless there is intent." She suggested that he bring in "conspiracy" by the state involving perjured testimony, "Section 47 of Title 8 (*Hardyman v. Collins,* 183 F2d 308," and warned him to "be sure to avoid the pitfalls of *Kentucky v. Powers,* 201 US 1: by noting the test for a civil rights action is different from that in a removal case with reference to *Screws v. U.S.*" Well before *Dombrowski v. Pfister,* the landmark case involving the removal of cases from reactionary state courts to presumably more favorable federal courts, CRC was trying the same tactic twenty years prematurely. All of this sterling legal analysis did not come exclusively from trial lawyers, which of course was symptomatic of CRC's broad approach. The progressive journalist Stetson Kennedy notified the national office that Section 52, Title 18, Chapter 3 of the United States Code could be used for the defense, thereby invoking sanctions against the administration of state law in a racially discriminatory manner.[18]

The excellent legal assistance of the CRC-affiliated attorneys was not rendered without penalty. FBI files reveal an incredible amount of surveillance of McGee attorney Bella Abzug, for example. "Confidential informant C–639" reported faithfully on her movements, just as "Confidential informant CS–NYC–40 furnished bank statements and cancelled checks regarding the bank accounts" of CRC. Apparently, this raw data was insufficient because the Mobile, Alabama, FBI office asked the "New York office to furnish . . . any information it may have as to Communistic connections on the part of Mrs. Bella Abzug." But even with so much unjust scrutiny of the Manhattan-based Abzug, the FBI seemed even more concerned with CRC attorney John Coe of Pensacola, Florida,—a person to whom the charge "outside agitator" just would not stick. As early as 1947, the bureau was begrudgingly describing Coe as "outstanding and brilliant . . . especially good as a defense attorney . . . feared in the courtroom." And they included the all-important intelligence, "He may be a liberal, but I have never heard of him being a radical or a Communist." They concluded that he was not suffering economically since "[he] . . . recently built a $65,000 home on Town Point, Gulf Breeze, Florida."[19]

A few years later the bureau, while acknowledging that "a great deal of information in this report came from New York informants," was arriving at similar conclusions. "[He] speaks very precisely; . . . uses big words and complex language but does it correctly . . . brilliant and keen thinker." They investigated his background: "[his mother] was a member of the Moreno family, one of the old distinguished Spanish first-settler families of Pensacola. . . . family of excellent reputation and high standing in the community." Coe was elected to the state senate. Despite this apparent high regard for Coe's pedigree, the bureau did not hesitate to bug his telephone or contemplate holding him in detention "in the case of an emergency." This bold step was to be taken and was bruited about on the basis of "hearsay, newspaper clippings and super-confidential informants." Later, special note was taken of his sending a postcard to a then-imprisoned William Patterson, but his role in the McGee case—marked "Confidential" by the FBI—attracted most of their attention.[20]

Sterling legal assistance did not come cheaply in this era and the parlous financial state of CRC was far from advantageous. Bella Abzug, a particular victim of the FBI, was quite scrupulous in demanding pay for the work she had done. In February 1951, as the bell began to toll for McGee, she submitted an incredibly detailed bill for $623.04. Five days at $75.00 per diem came to $375.00 alone. In May 1951, after McGee had been laid to rest, she again reached from her office at 205 West 34th Street: "Your failure to meet your commitments has resulted in serious financial hardships to me. I cannot continue to allow myself to be imposed upon in this manner. . . ." In August 1951, another bill for $1,736.36 came to CRC, and September 1951 brought yet another. In December Grossman soothingly admitted that "because of our desperate financial situation . . . I understand that you are desperately in need of money before the first of the year." Still, the wily Californian demurred in part: "We have questions about a portion of the bill. . . . Our question is with reference to the time billed at the rate of $75.00 a day." CRC had been "operating" on the "theory" of $50 per diem—still not a negligible sum in 1951. FBI harassment may have exacerbated the strained personal and political relationships between the Communist Patterson and the non-Communist Abzug, which manifested itself in haggling over dollars. It all steamed to a head in 1951 at a CRC fundraising dinner and sparked a Patterson apology:

> I want to assure you that despite differences we may have had, it was I who proposed your name as a speaker . . . I deplored what happened, particularly in view of the fact that between us there were political differences of a very serious character, and that you may feel in view of that fact I was mean enough to take so unfair an advantage. . . . I deeply appreciate the heroism and the devotion that is inherent in all that you did in the McGee case personally and in the name of the Civil Rights Congress.[21]

This may have assuaged Abzug temporarily, but it did not forestall continuing squalls over financing the McGee defense. Months before his apology, Patterson was irate in sketching the outlines of this matter and he attacked the "terrible callousness and cynicism with which the lawyers have approached the question of fees, jerking them up tens of hundreds of dollars at a moment when a motion or other legal procedure was necessary to save this innocent man's life. . . . already more than $19,500 has been poured into this struggle . . . (mostly) into the maw of these insatiable so-called lawyers there . . . in the past four years."[22]

Raising thousands of dollars for McGee brought to the surface questions

similar to those that arose in the Scottsboro case; i.e., CRC was accused of
the misappropriation of funds. They suspected that this was a FBI-induced
rumor, but even if it were not, the impact was tremendously negative despite
retractions from newspapers that published such charges. For example, in
May 1951 the *Pittsburgh Courier* printed a story wherein the well-known
chanteuse Josephine Baker allegedly accused CRC of using funds meant for
McGee for other illicit purposes. She had given funds to send "two women
South" on a vigil for McGee, but somehow this was transmuted into a more
sinister story. CRC suspected Baker's secretary as a possible source for this
disinformation, while observing "there is probably some connection with
Walter White and this story." Patterson was forced to blast *Courier* Managing
Editor William Nunn for carrying the original falsity but "not . . . a word
concerning the repudiation and the position" by Baker; the whole affair was
termed a "deeply conceived plot," but like an expert cat-burglar, the perpetrator of this rumor had left no fingerprints, yet had done much damage.[23]

Despite such roadblocks, CRC was indefatigable in intensely pursuing
funds for the defense. Oakley Johnson of New Orleans was particularly
helpful here, reaching out to John Dombrowski, Bishop G. Bromley Oxnan,
and others. Black actor Canada Lee sent out a fundraising appeal under his
name, as did Sandy Ray, chair of the Brooklyn Baptist Ministerial Association. Patterson contacted John Garfield and a "few . . . selected people . . .
who are in a position to furnish substantial financial assistance." These
others included Arthur Miller, Lillian Hellman, "Mrs. Marshall Field," and
others. A special appeal was made to fourteen unions and workers' organizations, reaching such figures as Harry Bridges, Ewart Guinier, Ben Gold,
Donald Henderson, and Julius Emspak. As is often the case, all who were
reached were not responsive. Grossman reached Eleanor Roosevelt and
encouraged her with the notion that the NAACP was said to have told its
branches "to take action." But this appeal, shortly before McGee's demise,
was resolutely rebuffed by her; if CRC "would leave these cases" to the
Association she intoned haughtily, McGee and other such defendants
"would not have added suspicions aroused against them."[24]

Aubrey Grossman, an unusually bright attorney of Marxist persuasion and
a key CRC organizer during the McGee controversy, set down in detail weeks
before his client's execution the philosophy of legal defense he and CRC
espoused in defending McGee and others like him. This was at a time when
apparently Abzug and the other attorneys were reluctant to proceed further
for fear of being considered a "laughingstock" because of the alleged wafer-
thin nature of their claims. Not only did Grossman suggest getting other
attorneys if the present attorneys were not compliant, but he went further:

> It is almost never possible to say in advance that a legal proceeding is not
> capable of success, no matter how tenuous the theory upon which it is
> based, if the mass campaign is sufficiently broad and powerful. . . . A legal

proceeding, even if its ultimate result may not be victory, often results in delay.

In suggesting a proceeding pertaining to a federal civil rights act, he was explicit:

It may be that there is no directly relevant case authority for the proposition we will maintain, but this has never been decisive, nor would it be decisive if it were found that requisite legal principles had been decided against us by the U.S. Supreme Court.

Obviously CRC was not running a traditional legal operation, following precedents in lockstep and venturing no further. But, and this was an equivalent value, Grossman and CRC did not waver when it came to innovation in legal thinking:

Some way must be found to get around the latest gadget that the courts have developed which consists of simply not deciding anything against us, but refusing to grant us a hearing, especially on very important constitutional and social questions. Note that in the Martinsville Case, six courts of different judges refused a hearing and in the McGee Case, five. . . . In the civil rights field, it is obvious that we must be trailblazers in the law, as well as in the politics, and often must proceed in a way that no one has ever proceeded before.[25]

Grossman was not engaging in hyperbolic flights of verbiage, for it is certainly the case that in combining mass action in the streets with legal brilliance inside the court, they carried on the tradition set by ILD and distinguished themselves sharply from both the NAACP and the American Civil Liberties Union. In July 1950, on a typical summer evening, they brought one thousand demonstrators, mostly youth, to Times Square to protest the McGee frame-up. Police officers on horses and others with billyclubs rode in and broke up this demonstration. This was a time of conflict over U.S. intervention in Korea and concomitant upset at protest over it. Peace rallies found McGee petitioners present and they were often caught up in ensuing violence. Thus at an August 1950 peace rally of fifteen thousand in Union Square, police and spectators took to heart the *New York Daily News* suggestion that "patriot Americans take violent exception" to the demonstration. One skull was split open and twenty-eight of the demonstrators were arrested, including McGee supporters.[26]

Such ungentlemanly tactics did not deter CRC. Les Davis, the leader of the Chicago chapter, told Grossman about the same time as the Union Square debacle:

One of the things that has detracted from our contribution to the McGee campaign, both in terms of action and original suggestions, has been the tremendous wave of attacks levied at the progressive forces in this city in line with the peace petitions and protests against the Korean War. We have found ourselves enmeshed in a day-by-day struggle to get people out of jail and provide adequate defense.

Nonetheless, these obstacles did not completely block the path of progress. The Chicago chapter was among the many that helped to provide the "ton of money" necessary to defend this case. Nor was the basic political work neglected: "there have been hundreds of letters and telegrams sent. On the Fourth of July alone, more than five hundred postcards were written." Months later the Chicago chapter joined New York in organizing overflow mass meetings in support of McGee. At Harlem's Rockland Palace there were five thousand supporters with Paul Robeson starring on the platform.[27]

CRC's "Program of Action to Save Willie McGee" launched in February 1951 was meant to complement their legal maneuvers in court. By demonstrating mass support for McGee they would in effect shape the decisions of the courts by prevailing in the court of public opinion. If nothing else, this program was certainly ambitious. The goal for their petition campaign was 250,000 signatures, with union- and church committees spearheading the effort. Meetings with elected officials, prayer vigils ("The goal should be 3,000 ministers participating in church committees to defend Willie McGee"), work stoppages, parades, "roving picket lines," sidewalk booths with petitions, "telephone-to-Truman" days, radio programs, newspaper ads, campaigns of letter and phone calls to counterparts in Mississippi (e.g., pastors writing pastors, trade unionists writing trade unionists, etc.) Many of these tactics had already been deployed in the five-year-long struggle to save McGee, but this program was designed to heighten and to escalate this struggle at a crucial moment. Results were not long in coming. In Wisconsin four state legislators took a public position for McGee and significant progress was made in reaching the $12,000 monthly goal for McGee.[28]

The CRC "Bulletin" also became a useful tool for mobilzing the chapters in defense of McGee. They were told of the CRC attorneys (Abzug, Coe, Powe, Grossman, J. P. Coleman, James Wright, George Parker, and Vito Marcantonio) who had met with Justice Hugo Black in a successful effort to obtain a last-minute stay of execution. Similarly, they were informed of the fourteen white women doing "pioneer work" in Mississippi on the case; this was indicative of how CRC tried, judo-style, to use the racial dynamics of the case to their advantage. But most importantly, members were given guidelines on how to organize. In a section entitled "Popularizing CRC Meetings," they were told that the times demanded "popular meetings, not stodgy, cold, politically frightening meetings." Suggested were "use of films, film-strips, recordings . . . Our people are not those who enjoy a day of gossip or card-playing." Equally important, they were given strength in their fundraising efforts: "Never hesitate to ask for money. Never apologize for requesting financial help . . . (don't be) tongue-tied."[29]

This "Bulletin" was supplemented by other sources, e.g., a pamphlet called "Information to Assist Delegates in Seeing Members of Congress," which came in handy during their lobbying ventures in Washington. Such efforts produced results. Congressman Emmanuel Celler of Brooklyn felt compelled to instruct the attorney general of the United States that "A number of important organizations in my district have contacted me regarding this case." He demanded to see a "copy" of any "investigation." But the Denver chapter was forced to sue the school board after they refused to rent space for a Patterson speech on the McGee case. This pattern of peaks and valleys was duplicated nationally.[30]

The same could be said for CRC's effort to attract prominent personalities to the campaign. The reason the record was spotty is exemplified by the experience of Albert Einstein. He protested vigorously the persecution of McGee and this was duly noted by the FBI. Yet all were not intimidated. Chief Justice Allan Crockett of the Utah Supreme Court, the mayor of Berkeley, and the vice-mayor of Oakland all joined the growing protest. So did Clifford Odets, Diego Rivera, David Siquieros, and scores of foreign groups (particularly Australian unions). Walter White asked NAACP chapters to write the governor of Mississippi urging clemency and many of their rank and file joined a fifteen-hundred-strong march on City Hall, just as their chapters joined CRC in sponsoring McGee rallies at City College of New York and New York University.[31]

Patterson was quick to reach out to the community of artists, a carryover from his days with ILD. When CRC sought to produce a "Pageant of the Lynched" at Madison Square Garden in 1948, he reached out to a broad range of artists: "We know that most people are visual minded that . . . it is difficult to bring worn out men and women to a clear appreciation of all of the issues . . . through lectures and discussions alone." But the example of Mississippi writer William Faulkner, hot on the heels of the magnificent triumph of the filmed version of his *Intruder in the Dust,* which also concerned a racist frame-up, was all too common. His words in the *Memphis Commercial Appeal* of 27 March 1951 were quoted far and wide:

> I do not want Willie McGee to be executed because it will make him a martyr and create a long lasting stink in my native state. . . . I have nothing in common with the representatives of the Civil Rights Congress except we both say we want Willie McGee to live. I believe these women who visited in Mississippi recently are being used; that their cause would be best helped with the execution of Willie. I did tell them if they wanted to save Willie they should talk to the women in the kitchen and make their arguments there rather than to the men and the politicians.

This sexist reproach of the historic CRC women's delegation to the Magnolia State demonstrated clearly what McGee's defenders were up against.[32]

Fortunately for CRC, the reception of their message was received with more equanimity abroad. They realized this. They knew that a positive reception abroad would inevitably percolate back home. They recognized that this phenomenon was a reflection of the more positive correlation of political forces abroad in favor of progressives. So just as Faulkner was backward in his approach, the Danish novelist Martin Anderson Nexo was forward-looking when he asked plaintively: "Is it really possible to torture a human being in such a manner in a cultured country?" Cedric Belfrage reported that "Cocteau, Sartre, Camus, expatriate Richard Wright and distinguished Africans sponsored a protest rally in Paris" against the proposed execution of McGee. In the Soviet Union, leading intellectuals and artists like Dmitri Shostakovich and Serge Prokofiev acted similarly. Certainly the White House was not pleased with Patterson's words to the Czechs about *Life* magazine: "Here is another example of how a large American capitalist organ functions. First it broadcasts the 'truth.' . . then hurriedly begins to search for the facts." Nor could they have been satisfied with the international press picking up on Patterson's blast at Eleanor Roosevelt for terming McGee a "bad character." No doubt this is what prompted the State Department to send a representative to Mississippi to get the "full truth," even though, to CRC's dismay, they talked only to the prosecution. They tried to make amends by meeting with a trade union delegation that included William Hood of the gigantic Ford Local 600 and Cleveland Robinson of District 65 of the Distributive Workers of America. Still, this did not prevent CRC from accusing Foggy Bottom of "lying about the case abroad in an effort to quell a rising flood of indignation," nor did it bar Patterson from attacking the U.S. Embassy in London after they had issued a statement on the case.[33]

This "rising flood of indignation" even washed ashore on the banks of other civil rights organizations. Worriedly, Leo Margolin of the American Jewish Committee contacted his counterpart in the ACLU, Alan Reitman, about McGee: "our Paris office keeps abreast of European public opinion. . . . (they) have come across an amazing reaction on the Willie McGee case. . . . The impression abroad that America has a double standard of justice is deplorable because it renders ineffective our efforts to make friends for democracy and influence people in its behalf." No concern was uttered here about the suffering of Blacks in deep South hellholes, just concern about the public relations image of the United States. Reitman concurred with Margolin and suggested to Roger Baldwin that the "stain of McGee case could be erased" by publicizing the Supreme Court reversal of the equally racist Groveland case. In a rare burst of good sense, Baldwin backed off: "nothing can erase (the stain) until black and white are really treated as equals."[34]

The analysis by the AJC Paris office, "European Reaction to Discrimination in America as expressed in Press Comments Following the Execution of Willie McGee," showed clearly why so much concern was displayed by the

State Department. Not only was there a resolute condemnation of the case in the French Parliament, but there was an even sharper rebuff in the French press from right to left—*Le Figaro, Le Monde, L'Aube, Temoignage Chrétien, La Croix, Le Populaire, L'Aurore, Franc Tireur, Combat, Le Matin, L'Observateur.* All joined the chorus of dissent, while *Life* magazine was indicative of the position taken by the U.S. bourgeois media, simply accusing the communists of exploiting the case. Nevertheless, the storm surrounding the McGee case abroad clearly helped to pressure leading circles in the United States to amend the most egregious elements of Jim Crow and it prepared the ground for Montgomery.[35]

Somehow CRC's putative allies in the fight against Jim Crow—the NAACP and ACLU—refused to join with the CRC to save McGee's life. This was possibly explicable in light of the government pressure not to associate with red-tinged groups, but even that misguided pusillanimity couldn't explain ACLU official Herbert Levy's explanation: "I am advised by Thurgood Marshall . . . that there are no civil liberties questions whatsoever in the case. . . . I should think that intervention from English persons would only arouse antagonism . . . and do more harm than good." The future Supreme Court justice even went so far as to say that McGee's "last trial was a fair one," despite overwhelming evidence to the contrary.[36]

Although support from what should have been natural allies was conspicuously lacking, other sectors came through fabulously. There is little doubt that what kept the case before the public eye was the enormous support from African-Americans. The silent demonstration at Dillard University in New Orleans, the rally at a Baptist church in Louisville, the call by the 80,000-strong Packinghouse Workers for a march on Chicago's southside, the countless marches, picketlines, letters, telegrams, petitions, and phone calls were all disproportionately engineered by Blacks, outraged by yet another example of lynch-law and Jim Crow justice. Their nagging suspicions about the phenomenon of white women lusting after Black men then shouting rape propelled their effort.[37]

Even the support generated in the trade union movement was produced primarily by Blacks, as the Communist journal *Political Affairs* observed:

the greatest degree of activity was generated in unions with a large Negro membership, such as in the Packinghouse Union, Marine Cooks and Stewards. . . . in one United Electrical Workers shop in New York, a noon hour action was organized to circulate a petition. . . . demonstrative prayer meeting of 1,000 Chevrolet workers in Flint . . . great demonstration of 8,000 packinghouse workers organized by the Chicago district . . . stoppages that were organized in New York . . . Stoppages (in fur, distributive) . . . (Marine Cooks and Stewards stoppage) . . . involving 300 ships . . . Lithographers Union, which has some 8,000 members (200 Black) . . . adopted a fighting resolution.

This trade union support was generated even though leading anticommunists were not usually found marching under CRC banners; this too shows the influence of Black trade unionists in pushing the leadership. James Carey, secretary-treasurer of the CIO, told the inquiring Isidore Rosenberg of the United Shoe Workers Union that the CIO had "acted on" the McGee case since 1945 and was still working on it, despite a significant caveat: "obviously we are not associating ourselves in this endeavor with those who are exploiting the case merely because of its propaganda value to the Communist Party and the Cominform." Little doubt of who was meant there. Yet Grossman preferred to see the cup as half full and not half empty; he wrote on the top of Rosenberg's copy, "The following letter . . . should open the door for many unions. However you are not authorized to give any publicity of any kind to this and please be sure that no publicity is given to anyone."[38]

As Grossman's note indicated, trade union support for a controversial case challenging Jim Crow during the red scare was not a fortuitous concatenation of circumstances. A special "Program of Action for Trade Unions to Save the Life of Willie McGee" was produced that called for many of the activities that *Political Affairs* observed. Workers were advised to hold shop and office meetings, to distribute literature, to hold discussions at regular meetings, raise funds, order McGee materials—posters, stickers, petitions, fact sheets—to participate in Washington and New York picketlines and vigils, and other related actions. When McGee's wife made a crosscountry tour on behalf of her spouse, Grossman advised Seattle forces, "Be sure that Mrs. McGee (personally) meets some of your key trade union leaders and I would try to get her in to see the president of the IWA" (i.e. lumber workers) This affirmative action to ensure union participation was not a fruitless exertion. The United Office and Professional Workers, and U.E. were just a few of the unions that contributed dollars to the campaign; Shipyard Workers Local 22 was one of the many that forwarded resolutions on the case to Mississippi and Washington; the International Longshore and Warehousemen's Union played a particularly critical role, especially in New Orleans.[39]

Detroit was the site of one of the stronger CRC chapters, the home of the most progressive sector of the industrial proletariat, populated by a large and active Black community; hence, the popular reception here for the McGee campaign was entirely logical. There was in place a Detroit Trade Union Committee to Save Willie McGee with at least fifteen locals participating. The committee claimed that "More than 80% of the UAW Locals in Detroit" were active in the case. A thousand-person-strong prayer meeting was held outside a Chevy plant and this was just one of many events sponsored by the committee, which had fifty to seventy activists working tirelessly on the case. It included "right and center forces . . . Negro and white, predominantly rank and file." Local 600 provided meeting halls, mailing lists, and logistical support; letters were sent to every local in Michigan. Delegations were sent to Washington twice and there were meetings with the governor and state legislature; as a result, pro-McGee resolutions emerged from the Michigan House and Senate. Despite having to contend with the words of *Life* magazine which said that "Willie McGee was an instrument with which to stir hatred of the U.S. abroad and heighten racial tension at home," even the anticommunist Walter Reuther was compelled by pressure from the rank and file to demand that the Mississippi governor grant clemency. Upon McGee's execution, a massive memorial march was held in downtown Detroit. This was part and parcel of a significant trade union movement to save McGee's life, which included five thousand brass workers in Connecticut, the Newspaper Guild, and eight thousand aircraft workers in Paterson, New Jersey, among others, all calling for McGee's freedom.[40]

The entire drive to save McGee's life dovetailed neatly with Patterson's familiar line that Jim Crow was a policy of the federal government engineered for specific reasons. Thus, a major focus was not only on Governor Fielding Wright, Dixiecrat candidate for the vice-presidency in 1948, but on President Truman as well. In the summer of 1950, Grossman floated a proposal with Rev. R. H. Harris of Dallas. He wanted his "reaction, at once" to the idea of Rosalee McGee, William Patterson, and "one or two white people" going to Washington, D.C., and insisting on seeing Truman, and then asking him to phone Wright, demanding clemency. If they were to be refused, the committee would not leave until they had seen him: "This will mean waiting and sleeping either in the White House, or if forcibly removed, then on the steps, or . . . on the sidewalk, until the President sees the committee." The constant democratic process of CRC was displayed once more when this suggestion was sent also to chapter leaders in Seattle, New York, Oakland, Detroit, Los Angeles, Philadelphia, and Chicago—to all the major chapters, with the admonition "let us have your suggestions on dramatic, last-minute actions, either by the National Office or the chapters." Paterson and co. did not wind up snoozing at 1600 Pennsylvania Avenue, but picketlines at the White House were frequent as the time approached for McGee's ultimate doom. But Patterson continued to bombard his foes: "Senator Nixon declared that throughout the world significant sections of the people believe that Willie McGee was a victim of legalized lynching." For one of the few times in his career, he agreed with his fellow Californian, and presaging the vice-president's raucus welcome in Caracas, added: "his parked automobile was plastered with a sticker protesting the legalized lynching of Willie McGee."[41]

One of the most courageous and historic aspects of CRC's work around the McGee case was their repeated forays into the heart of Mississippi, a state where "outside agitators" were treated with less solicitude than roaches. They thus served as a harbinger and indeed laid the foundation for the "Freedom Riders" of the 1960s. Although the Fellowship of Reconciliation had organized the equivalent of freedom rides in the early 1940s, their effort was not as sustained nor was it of the same magnitude as CRC's. But even before these jaunts into a Mississippi-style "heart of darkness" began,

CRC sought valiantly to bolster the morale of the indigenous forces there. They were in close contact with McGee's lawyer after the first trial, Forrest Jackson, who kept them in touch with events, like reports of a prison escape by McGee. Forrest Jackson's role as McGee's lawyer caught the eye of the racists and CRC was forced to approach progressive California attorneys Benjamin Dreyfus and Francis McTernan and ask them to lend support to the Mississippian, since "he and his family have been subjected to considerable pressure because of his successful appeal. Actually I believe that he is being scared out of the case." CRC wanted them and "a few Guild people" to "bolster the guy up" so "he might remain on the case. . . . He probably has all the prejudices of the South but some good instincts notwithstanding." But all the bolstering they could provide could not prevent undue pressure from being placed on a private law practice in a town in the deep South. Jackson left the case.[42]

Similar pressures were placed on all of the local counsel that CRC was forced to hire to handle the case. Dixon Pyles was "inexperienced" and lacked an "adequate theoretical foundation," according to Laurent Frantz, but he was one of the few attorneys willing to stand up to the racists in a case involving the ultimate taboo—a Black man allegedly defiling a white woman. John Poole had his weaknesses and he too was forced from the case, although he went further and issued a parting public blast at CRC as he left. Such a bitterly hostile atmosphere virtually ruled out building even an embryonic CRC chapter there. CRC's southern representative Laurent Frantz was blunt about this as early as January 1947: "You will find seeing people in Laurel a very discouraging business . . . abject terror at the mere mention of the McGee case. . . . My best white contact in the state (is frightened). . . . If you see him, do so quietly and cautiously so as not to cause any talk which might impair his backstage usefulness." Doing political work in Mississippi during this time was worse than the most horrible fantasies imagined in the United States about political life in Eastern Europe at the same period.[43]

Things had not improved measurably as CRC began to organize to send a major delegation of premature antiracist freedom riders to Mississippi. If anything, the war in Korea, then weeks old, had heightened the xenophobia, the racism, the unbridled anticommunism that customarily gripped the mind of Euro-Americans there. Whipping up the hysteria were the newspapers. The *Jackson Daily News* in a scathing editorial actually threatened violence and encouraged it against the CRC caravan to Mississippi, scheduled to arrive 25 July 1950: "A hint to members of the Communistic Civil Rights Congress. . . . 'While this is the closed season for nearly all varmints in Mississippi, we do have people in our midst who are impetuous and act quickly. . . . Why the hell go to Korea to shoot Communists when the hunting is good on home grounds?'" Cars full of CRC supporters were coming from the Bay Area, Detroit, Chicago, New York, New Orleans, Dallas, Washington, D.C., St. Louis, Milwaukee, and Philadelphia; these cars, full of Black and white supporters, snaking their way through apartheid America were an inviting target in any event for those drunk with that strange combination of antiBlack, antiRed bile. Thus, precautions were taken. A number was provided for calling in case of emergency. Patterson suggested strongly to James Wechsler of the *New York Post*, Ralph Matthews of the *Afro-American*, Hodding Carter of the *Delta Democrat*, and the editors of the *Washington Post*, *Pittsburgh Courier*, and *New York Herald Tribune* that they all send reporters there, assuming that this would forestall rampant violence. As was done so often in the 1960s, the attorney general of the United States was asked to "publicly announce" that the Department of Justice would protect pro-McGee activists going to Mississippi. But this was the same Justice Department that was striving mightily to destroy CRC and jail its leaders and, if they were to be there, they would be found on the opposite side of the barricades with the racists.[44]

The results of this action were fairly predictable, although it could have been worse. Grossman was beaten badly, his face "battered and bloody." A FBI agent was ever present there, including being, surreptitiously, one of the eleven who met with the governor. The agent claimed the klan was responsible for the beating; the FBI took down license plates, photos, and signatures of delegates. Police deputized American Legion members; the report on Grossman was so detailed it spoke of "handprints" on his shirt. It was sparked, according to some locals, by the Supreme Court granting yet another stay of execution. Other lawyers were "molested," along with a number of protesters. Still, the governor did grant a "clemency hearing" and the high court did grant a stay, so the protesters left the state feeling their energy had been spent wisely. The *St. Louis American*, a Black paper whose publisher was close to Patterson, was outraged nonetheless. In no uncertain terms he denounced the beating of Grossman, the assault on John Poole and others, and the fact that "one New York newspaper reporter was beaten and chased out of the city." Much of his fire was reserved for the "crypto-liberal" Hodding Carter and the "pro-Dixie *St. Louis Globe-Democrat* and *Chicago Tribune*" and allied forces for ignoring the case.[45]

CRC was not sufficiently intimidated by the terror, beatings, and assaults. Less than a year later in the spring of 1951 they launched a "white women's delegation" to Mississippi. Even before then CRC had sought to dramatize the explosive race-gender issues embodied in the case. They had dispatched Dorothy Bushnell Cole, a "direct descendant of Governor William Bradford" of Mayflower fame and a Vassar graduate to meet with Mississippi's governor and attorney general and other ranking officials. Symptomatic of what she and CRC were up against was the comment attributed to one who was the assumed guardian of law and justice in that benighted state, the chief justice of the state Supreme Court, Harvey McGeehee: "If you believe, or are implying that any white woman in the South, who was not completely down and out, degenerate, degraded and corrupted, could have anything to do with a Negro man, you not only do not know what you are talking about, but you are insulting us, and the whole South." With this tone set at the top, it is little wonder that she found, like the earlier CRC delegation, a tense atmosphere with Blacks and whites reluctant to talk, overweight police officers who compensated for their girth-induced lack of mobility with itchy trigger-fingers, and an apartheid-like array of segregated schools, barbershops, toilets, buses, and virtually everything else necessary to ensure Black inequality.[46]

The "white women's delegation" found the situation little different. They went from door to door in white areas and with scientific precision tabulated the results. They visited forty-four families; twelve were hostile; eight listened but would not discuss the case; seven were convinced of his guilt but deigned to listen. But what made them consider the trip worthwhile was the fact that five had been convinced of his guilt but had a change of mind after the discussion, seven had been convinced of his innocence but were not willing to act or pledge action. The fact that about 40 percent of those surveyed randomly were not unfavorable was considered a heartening sign. They also spent an inordinate amount of time talking with workers, ministers, teachers, and so forth, eighty-five in all, with the "vast Majority" simply paying "lip-service." Although Mayor Allen Thompson of Jackson called them "agitators," the women who had traveled from Richmond, Macon, Winston-Salem, St. Louis, Dallas, Baltimore, and other places (note the heavy representation of southern and border areas) felt that their visit had a positive impact, despite the harassment and arrests they faced.[47]

Decca Truehaft (Jessica Mitford) dissented from this consensus with rancor. "They had no plan of action. . . . There was resistance to efforts to make more definite plans. . . . No apparent anticipation of arrest—no policy . . . No liaison or joint planning with the Negro delegates . . . resistance to any suggestion for such demonstrative action to arrest to attract the attention of passers-by" from jail by singing, shouting, etc.; some thought since the population was "hostile" it would be "provocative, though . . . we finally did sing." Truehaft did not stop there: "no preparation had been made in the South itself for our visit. . . . we were intrusted not to contact the Negro community for fear of running them into trouble after we left" and what was needed was "much more of an effort than we did to contact the working class." Patterson disagreed in part, "important members of the Negro community were informed," though he conceded that unions and sharecroppers were not. Despite weaknesses, the delegation was "positive," he said. He went on to term the South the "soft underbelly of American reaction" and urged them to spend even more time there. Yet an uncharacteristically pessimistic note crept into his reply: "while time in the long run is in our favor, in terms of stopping reaction now, we are operating against time." This proved to be prophetic.[48]

Yet McGee did not die with the world, or Mississippi, in silence. As the day in May 1951 approached on which McGee was to be exterminated, CRC sent yet another bevy of supporters there. Again, the *Jackson Daily News* specifically warned Grossman that if he came to Mississippi "he will do so at his own risk." While connecting again the defense of McGee to U.S. deaths in Korea, they warned pointblank "no personal safety can be guaranteed to Aubrey Grossman." Mississippi Blacks like Percy Green of the *Jackson Advocate* were expressly warned to stay away from CRC. A plethora of hostile articles and editorials streamed from the paper, accurately reflecting the ugly mood of the ultraright racist element.[49]

But CRC was not deterred. CRC activist Anne Braden of Louisville, a participant in the "white women's delegation," was busily organizing among Baptist ministers in Mississippi, but the environment of terror forced her to remind: *"It is important that none of the above be given publicity"* (her emphasis). What she said of one cleric was true for most: "he is working in the very stronghold of Southern reaction . . . the Southern baptists . . . and he knows there is a limit as to how far he can go . . . if he wants to continue working there."[50] Leading Episcopal ministers were also quite helpful, along with the ubiquitous Dr. J. Pius Barbour who facilitated McGee's reading of Bible tracts at CRC's suggestion. This was a truly grassroots effort among the faithful, as two local "Negro ministers" in faraway Tucson asked their people to raise money for the case and well-known Catholics like Dorothy Day contributed publicity.[51]

Up to the very moment when McGee was done away with, CRC was striving to save McGee's life. When Grossman reached out to the ILWU it was on the basis of the same principle that motivated the pulling together of the "white women's" delegation. He inquired of Louis Goldblatt of the ILWU "whether you have an ILWU car going from New Orleans? If you arrange for such a car it may be that CRC can help you fill it if you need help. We want the delegates to be entirely white, to show the support of white people for this case." Some may have quarreled with this principle of (white) race-based organizing, while not denying that it was all important for Euro-Americans to put their bodies on the line. And that they did, along with Blacks, Latinos and others. Forty-one were arrested as they challenged the racists in their own backyard by singing "Hate Jim Crow and Jim Crow hates me and that is why we're fighting for McGee." Most were from Memphis and New York and they focused sharply on the fact that the six different execution dates for McGee in itself constituted cruel and unusual punishment. Meanwhile in Washington, D.C., the *Daily Compass* reported that "100 chained themselves to Lincoln Memorial." These Black and white veterans were joined by two hundred vets chanting "Free Willie McGee"; the White House itself was picketed by three hundred and fifty people. They were outdone by the forces in Jackson, however. Letters from McGee's children sent to Truman graced the front page of the *Peoples World* as two hundred police arrested one hundred people in a prayer vigil; four hundred people had gathered, half of whom were Black. The continuous vigil at the White House included more prominent persons—ninety-three according to CRC figures—including Christopher Morley, Norman Mailer, Donald Ogden Stewart, and Josephine Baker.[52]

Reminiscing, Anne Braden recalled these tumultous times. "Jackson was tense that day. Cops lined the streets everywhere because there was a rumor that the black people were going to march in from all over the countryside, and actually there had been a march organized, which was called off—it was just too dangerous." She was arrested for the first time in her life. She was spokesperson for the group, also a first for the now veteran activist. She also met Bella Abzug and John Coe for the first time. Pregnant, she was placed in prison—the same one as McGee. Again blazing the path for their comrades of the 1960s they began singing freedom songs: "Halleluja I'm a travelin'—Down Freedom's Main Road." She saluted CRC and their Communist allies for pioneering in the notion of stressing whites working in the white community against racism, yet another theme that seemed to emerge full-blown in the 1960s in response to Black nationalist demands, referring here to their "white women's delegation" and like-minded campaigns.[53]

Nevertheless, McGee was murdered, was lynched legally. The actual execution bordered on the grand guignol. It took place outside. McGee, exuding pride and dignity, was marched to the portable gallows as hundreds of racists and Klansmen cheered lustily. Over the radio was playing their response to protesters' freedom songs: "Willie McGee will not be free." But CRC worked on. Josephine Baker stopped her show for ten minutes to discuss the case. The *New York Times* reported that "thousands of letters and telegrams, some from Moscow and Red China. . . . Scores of telephone calls were received all day today by Gov. Fielding Wright." The *Times* added that his "death sentence figured in Chinese Communist propaganda." Wright remained unyielding: his words became the "party line" on the role of the CRC and CP in the case: "The Civil Rights Congress cares nothing for McGee. It has a planned program to destroy the judicial system of every state." At the time, however, the *Times* was compelled to dissent in part: "Although the Communists have been prominent in exploiting the case in their propaganda . . . those who have spoken out in favor of McGee have included many prominent intellectuals and parliamentarians of various shades of opinions." The rhetoric flowed heavy and hot as lava, but McGee was stilled. The *Daily Compass* reported that after the blood ritual, "A path had to be cleared through a crowd of about 500 when his body was brought out and put in a hearse. As the hearse drove away, the crowd cheered loudly. . . . At 2:35 A.M. the news reached 125th Street and Lenox Avenue, Harlem, where several thousand persons were keeping a last-hour vigil. . . . Students at Dillard University, a Negro institution in New Orleans, demonstrated." The Voice of America was obligated to report the fact of McGee's death, thus contributing unintentionally to the darkening of Washington's name abroad, though this hardly required further assistance. At the execution the "Assembly of the French Union halted activity for a minute of silence in his honor." At the same time that millions were rallying across the globe and in Paris, thousands heard Roger Garaudy and anticolonial leader Gabriel d'Arboussier denounce Mississippi's policies.[54]

Like the case of Joe Hill, the case of Willie McGee was one that just would not die. The slatternly "victim" of the alleged rape, Ms. Hawkins, sued the *Daily Worker* after they charged on their "front page" that McGee was murdered because a white woman who "had forced an illicit affair upon him for more than four years suddenly shouted 'rape.'" Dixon Pyles felt that the suit was brought by her lawyer Ross Barnett as a selling point in his race for governor on a racist platform; after all, two district attorneys were defeated because "they were not able to hang Willie." The mood in Mississippi remained sullen a year after the execution, as *Daily Worker* reporter Abner Berry discovered. The locals told him that McGee and the Martinsville seven were murdered to "prove that Negroes couldn't get anywhere with the Communists"; the fact that the seven were defended in part by the NAACP didn't matter, since the Association was seen as subversive and *de facto* "Communists to these white folks." So much for the NAACP separating themselves from CRC for fear of a red taint.[55]

If CRC had been interested in McGee solely for propaganda purposes, as their critics claimed, one would think that his death would have ended their involvement. It was not so. They set up a trust fund for his family with B. F. Logan, religious editor of the *Pittsburgh Courier* as treasurer. The International League Against Anti-Semitism and Racism, in Paris, demonstrated the value of CRC's international connections by kicking in a quick ninety thousand francs; others were equally generous. This probably helped to motivate the police in Jackson who raided his widow's home twice and stole her airline tickets when they knew she was planning to address McGee memorial meetings in New York and elsewhere. CRC did seek to "use" the McGee tragedy in order to prevent future occurrences of this nature. The first anniversary of his lynching marked in May 1952 featured a "Willie McGee Memorial Meeting and Rally Against Genocide" in a host of U.S. cities. The one at Harlem's Golden Gate Ballroom in Harlem called for harsh retribution against a retired white police officer who had killed two Black Yonkers men in cold blood. A letter from the Rosenbergs was read expressing deep sadness at McGee's execution. Other demands called for, "in addition to local demands" put forward, were saving the Groveland, Florida defendants, finding the murderers of NAACP official Harry Moore, saving Louisiana defendants Paul Washington and Ocie Jugger from the death penalty, freeing the remaining Trenton defendants, freeing Rosa Lee Ingram and her sons, freeing Lt. Leon Gilbert, saving the North Carolina four, repealing the Smith

Act—a full plate indeed. Photos and 16mm films were available for such events. McGee's "execution caused protests from every continent on earth" and so did the first anniversary of his execution.[56]

Despite the many attempts to calumniate the role of CRC in a disputatious fashion, Patterson remained resolute over the years. In responding to an inquiring scholar in 1975, he revealed "there was never a moment when Willie McGee wavered in his faith in CRC. . . . Association with a fighting organization raised the morale of Willie McGee. He knew of the case of the 'Scottsboro Boys.' Haywood Patterson wrote him." He went on to discuss the role of NAACP chapters in the struggle and the reluctance of their national office to join it. He also revealed the impact of working with the interracial CRC on McGee and other Mississippi Blacks: "Willie McGee was not, to my knowledge, involved in any political movements before the case. . . . for him, at first, all whites were the enemies of Blacks. That was especially true of all poor whites." Shortly after the execution, Patterson was harshly critical of CRC attorneys involved: "Our lawyers did not accept their responsibility to raise the Civil Rights Statute as sharply and as clearly as they should. In fact, they did not raise it at all. This was a very grievous mistake against which I fought but—not with success." What may have informed this conflict was limned by Patterson in 1975 in commenting to Decca Truehaft about Bella Abzug: "(she) knew her law. She was, however, strong-willed and egotistical. She went to Jackson on her own. . . ."

But the ultimate comment on the aftermath of the McGee case was appropriately enough the resolution of the "Richmond Five" case, five young Blacks charged with raping a white woman, although the doctor who examined her found no evidence of rape. They were arrested. They were jailed for "several weeks." But they were freed eventually. Although it is difficult to prove scientifically that the CRC struggle around McGee or the Martinsville Seven had led directly to this result, it is fair to say that these struggles sensitized and alerted the nation to the nature of racist frame-ups. How many Black youths were saved from the gallows it is difficult to say. But to say there were some may be the ultimate harvest reaped as a result of the fight to save Willie McGee. In 1951 at the age of twenty Lorraine Hansberry was inspired by the call of CRC to travel to Mississippi to save McGee; she also wrote a moving poem about Rosalee McGee. She was simply one of the more notable personalities moved by this moving case and sought mainly to save a life.[57]

4
Defending Communists; Fighting Anticommunism

That the first line of defense for civil liberties in the United States was defending the rights of Communists was repeated so often within and without CRC that after a while it bordered on the trite—but it remained no less true for that. This was true not only because of the CP's pioneering efforts in fighting Jim Crow and its struggling for the right of labor to organize and for its right for Social Security or because of its premature antisexism, but also because reaction's approach was to establish precedent for eliminating civil liberties generally by picking on the reds first. Members of CRC, Communists, and the allies of both warned about this repeatedly, but a major failure of the entire period since encapsulated as "McCarthyism" was that the center and the liberals refused to listen, which rebounded to their own detriment.

Black Communist leader Claude Lightfoot of Chicago pointed out how anti-Communist Party laws "will be an enabling act which reactionary elements can use against all democratic forces." He noted the ruling in Atlanta where a Black teacher had lost her teacher's license because of her NAACP membership, taking the Smith Act one fateful step further. "In the earlier stages . . . we stood alone in forecasting the torrent of reaction that would follow. . . . McCarthyism was jet-propelled into a major force and no one was safe." Days after Lightfoot's prophetic words, Lt. Governor Ernest Hodges of South Carolina put it bluntly, "And if the U.S. Supreme Court can declare certain organizations as subversive, I believe South Carolina can declare the NAACP subversive and illegal." An intimate of Patterson, Earl Dickerson, then president of the National Lawyers Guild, and attorney Richard Westbrooks, another prominent Chicago barrister, saw further dangers for Blacks if the Smith Act were upheld, as recorded in their *amicus* brief to the high court:

> It is inevitable that the decision will inhibit and impair legitimate efforts to extend democratic protections to the Negro people. This is so for two reasons: In the first place advocacy of fundamental changes in government so as to extend democratic protections to the Negro might well be equated, under the broad terms of the Court's decision, with advocacy of the violent overthrow of the government. In the second place, as Justice Black's dissenting opinion points out, the decision imposes a prior restraint upon political expression. If the present decision is permitted to stand, few whether Negro or non-Negro, will undertake to challenge the 'Black Codes' of the South. . . . Only individuals with great courage will vigorously condemn the failure to apprehend and prosecute those who engage in mob violence against Negroes.

Their words proved to be all too prescient.[1]

Assuredly, the cold breath of repression blew over the Communist Party. By 1957, in trials taking place from New York to Hawaii, 107 convictions under the Smith Act had been secured. As David Jacob Group acknowledged, this "had a devastating impact on the Party." This "quasi-fascist repression" caused membership to drop from "an estimated 55 thousand in 1950 to 20 thousand by 1956," then to ten thousand by 1957; partially as a result of events in Hungary and revelations about Stalin. Party members suffered all manner of disabilities, from being ousted from public housing to loss of employment to beatings and death. The First Amendment was ignored when efforts were made to keep the *Daily Worker* off the newstand and the party itself off the ballot. This massive violation of civil liberties had CRC working overtime, particularly in light of the ACLU's failure consistently to uphold their mandate. Since CRC had a number of Communists in their national and local leadership, they were hit doubly hard. Frieda Katz of Cleveland, John Daschbach of Seattle, and Arnold Johnson of New York were among the CRC leaders indicted under the Smith Act. Government organs, like HUAC, continuously sought to link CRC to the so-called Communist menace. When the Hawaii Civil Liberties Committee, a CRC affiliate, was investigated in 1950, HUAC worriedly noted their "cooperation" with CRC, "one of the largest and most active Communist fronts on the United States mainland." In 1953, in an effort to further persecute CRC, HUAC dug up a witness who discussed the suggestion by CRC ("a Communist front organization") to murder Senator Joseph McCarthy himself! Even clearer than the case of the NAACP, when the Communist Party was hit, CRC was more than bruised; defending that party was necessary for their survival, despite the confirmation in the minds of some that this made them a "Communist front."[2]

Thus, though he mouths the conventional undefined wisdom of calling

CRC a "front," Michael Belknap was perceptive in analyzing the role of CRC:

> The organization that protested loudest and did the most to mobilize opposition to the prosecutions (of the CP) was the Civil Rights Congress. . . . the CRC set out to broaden support for the campaign . . . by bombarding the public with leaflets, fliers and speeches, which sought to link the prosecution to abuses of blacks and labor, and thus to convince many non-Communist Americans that they had a stake in the fate of the CPUSA.

Inevitably this approach of seeing the defense of liberty as indivisible was understood imperfectly by some. Alex Deutsch of Deutsch Co. of Los Angeles agreed to donate funds to CRC but only for "Negro rights . . . such as . . . Trenton Six, Willie McGee." Separating Black from red, he added, "I hope none of my money was used in the aid of propaganda for the so-called Communist trials. I consider the book 'We Charge Genocide' propaganda."[3]

Ironically, although CRC critics saw the raison d'etre of CRC as defending Communists, CRC and CP leaders saw this role as insufficient or ineptly performed. Aubrey Grossman, in addition to questioning CRC's campaign in defense of labor rights, felt that CRC was unable to dramatize the Communist cases along the lines of, say, the case of Willie McGee. Patterson himself was scathingly self-critical, perhaps excessively so, in an undated report (probably from 1952) apparently presented to a leading party body. He alleged that "CRC has to a large degree become isolated," and added: "Had the defense commission of the Party remained a functioning body, it is possible that mistakes of which I shall speak might have been avoided." Although Patterson was brought to CRC in 1948 in partial response to the indictment of the CP leadership, he spoke of CRC's "opportunistic deviation" even then. Their "ineffectiveness" then was such that "liquidation was properly on the order of business"; this was because of a "lack of systematic Party attention" and of "weaknesses in CRC leadership." He deplored the failure to produce a literature focusing on the Bill of Rights and the Alien-Sedition laws in the late 1940s (actually this was done, but perhaps the quality of the effort was deemed inadequate). "Persistence in a sectarian course prevented the realization of a united front for defense of constitutional liberties." (Arguably government repression was the most significant factor here.) Other statements Patterson made in this report are tantalizing in their implications: "In fact if the courts can be depended upon, the very establishment of a people's defense organization is an irremediable act of sectarianism." CRC "had been guilty of right opportunism" due to a "failure . . . to clarify these vital questions." Their legendary book, *We Charge Genocide*, had an "impact" that was "terrific," but had a "sale" that was "negligible." "CRC failed to grow in this period. . . . The responsibility is mine. . . . The Party also failed to review the situation, but it was beset with monumental problems and tasks."[4]

This utterly remarkable document conceded the objective factor: "I am not ignoring the weight of ruling class terror," but this was not its import or purpose. Self-criticism was: "failure to develop the struggle against the Smith Act as it smashed forward against the white supremacy line [was due to his] tendency toward one-man leadership [and] failure of collective guidance [because of] self-satisfaction and praise" after the genocide petition. "Giddiness with success was mine." He flayed himself for not defending the party more. Some said CRC "was being made into a Negro national liberation organization." He flayed their inadequate support of labor leaders Harry Bridges and Harold Christoffel and the "tendencies toward Negro nationalism." Stressing Black rights was not wrong, given the centrality of the question, but not backing the party more was: "I hereby helped to isolate the Party. . . . I was guilty of right opportunism as I sought to avoid what seemed to be left sectarianism." He flayed himself for regarding criticism at the time as an "attack upon the work of CRC." Apparently the party assigned Arnold Johnson and another Communist to work with CRC, but Patterson "erred in not really fighting for their integration." Patterson repeated here many of the internal criticisms made of CRC—that they did not put enough emphasis on the party or on labor rights, for example. But what is striking about all this is how it diverges so sharply from the prevailing conception of CRC as a "Communist front" conceived principally to defend the Party's rights.[5]

In a public presentation Communist leader Elizabeth Gurley Glynn issued her own particular criticism. She observed that "Comrade Foster warned us at our 1948 convention not to allow our Party to become a defense organization. . . . A separate permanent nonpartisan organization devoted exclusively to this purpose is required."[14] CRC was to be an essential element of this "mass defense organization." Yet she slammed the mass defense against the Smith Act: "leaflets, pamphlets, ads, mass meetings . . . were excellent but not sustained. It was a mistake that the defendants were not involved more in the mass movement. . . . we cannot farm out the defense of our Party to any other organization and then forget about it and go about our own business as usual." She seemed to feel that that is what the party did to an extent. Patterson was critical of CRC. Flynn was critical of the party. But with 20-20 hindsight one can well wonder at this point whether the correlation of political forces was not such that no other result could have been obtained in the face of such sustained and unscrupulous ruling class pressure? Could the severe repression brought on the party have been mitigated, was it avoidable? Could CRC have done a better job? Maybe.[6]

Stinging self-criticism notwithstanding, the record shows that CRC devoted a substantial amount of their time and resources to defending Communists and fighting anticommunism. Patterson was clear in setting out CRC's particularized role: "We are not defenders of the Communist Party. We are defenders of the rights of the Communist Party to propagate its philosophy. The Communist Party must defend itself and if it does not have the forces with which to do that, forces of the CRC cannot be substituted. This would destroy CRC. . . ." This echoed Flynn's view. He also rebuffed those who would curtail their reaching out to broader forces. When Yetta Land objected to CRC's publication of the pamphlet "Voices for Freedom" on the Communist Party–Eleven case because of the "damaging and untrue" statements in Justice Douglas' dissenting opinion, he denounced her view as simply "asinine." CRC held countless conferences on these questions. In October 1947 they knocked together a conference to ban HUAC that featured Lena Horne. The next year they were holding a conference on getting bail for the Communist Party–Eleven and other Smith Act defendants and had heavy trade union representation; the more than two hundred trade union leaders present resolved to hold "street meetings," distribute two million leaflets in the short term and send delegations to Congress. The next year another major conference, a Bill of Rights Conference was held with wide representation including Clifford Durr, Arthur Miller, Philip Morrison, Du Bois, Roscoe Dunjee, and many others; the repression of free speech was the main question. In the summer of 1950 they held a sizeable rally in Madison Square Garden, focused on the Smith Act cases and other victims of repression. Throughout this period, rallies, conferences, picketlines and the like were generated consistently by CRC, in difficult times.[7]

CRC was also diligent in turning out attractively designed publications to enlighten the public about these cases. Their pamphlet written by Henry Wallace, "America's Thought Police," was well received. Their "Speaker's Outline: The Smith Act" sold for ten cents and was designed to facilitate public presentations on this controversial issue. They even produced a comic book about Smith Act victims that featured Ben Davis. Local and national publications were produced in the thousands on various aspects of the Smith Act.[8]

Most of all, CRC set up committees designed to propagate the cause of Smith Act defendants. There were countless committees. For example, in 1951 there was a Provisional Harlem Committee to Repeal the Smith Act, a California Emergency Defense Committee, a Families of Smith Act Victims Committee, specific committees on the cases of W. A. Hunton, George Crockett, Al Lannon, Louis Weinstock, the Communist Party–Seventeen of New York, and that is just a minor sampling. To maximize this effort and to establish a form broader than CRC itself, the Citizens Emergency Defense Conference was established in 1952. But those who considered CRC a "Communist front," thought of CEDC as a "CRC front." But CEDC, as John Daschbach's lawyer Sarah Lesser noted, may have "drie[d] up most of the sources of funds for CRC." Waldo Salt was treasurer and Clifford McAvoy served as chairman. Their weekly "Smith Act Trial Reports" were usually four pages long, attractively printed and usefully detailed. They cooperated closely with CRC as befitted the fact that a number of CRC warhorses—Angie Dickerson, Paul Robeson, Dashiell Hammett—had had a hand in founding CEDC. Both Patterson and CRC Bail Fund Trustee W. A. Hunton were on their executive committee. When McAvoy was absent, Patterson would generally serve as chair of their meetings. This influence was magnified by the fact that CEDC leaders like Salt and Hugh Mulzac were not very active, and Sam Kantner, executive secretary, and Louis Weinstock made most "decisions and policy." Despite obvious handicaps, CEDC performed yeoman's service. They organized "scores of house parties, socials, mass meetings." Their "high point" was a "picnic in honor of Elizabeth Gurley Flynn (of) 4000 people; this was the first, and . . . the only large mass demonstration" that CEDC organized for the Communist Party-Seventeen. Countless "mailings" and "advertisings" were produced. Their toil led to Guild lawyer Osmond Frankel coming in on the Communist Party–Seventeen case. They established "informal relationships" with the Emergency Civil Liberties Committee. Their many pamphlets were done in runs of five to ten thousand, though their exposé of Louis Budenz went up to sixty-five thousand copies. Their "Smith Act Trial Reports" went to sixty-eight hundred people, including state and federal legislators, trade union leaders, and others. They were proud of SATR, although it was considered "much too narrow . . . like a CP . . . publicity organ." They sent a "World News-Letter every month to newspapers all over the world." Reflecting how enemy propaganda had infected its victims, they worried incessantly that the publication was "very narrow" and "gives the false impression that it is a propaganda organ and CEDC a front for the CP." All this was the "subject of sharp discussion in this office," and caused dissension.[9]

Shortly thereafter, not able to withstand the pressure, Kantner resigned due to the "stress and strain." Shortly after that CEDC was staring in the face "In the Matter of the Proposed Designation of the Citizens Emergency Defense Conference Pursuant to Executive Order No. 10450." The Justice Department, in seeking to show that CEDC was a "Communist front," demanded records, names, minutes, books, everything. Page after page of detailed questions were posed in their interrogatories. They denied the charge, but simply defending Communists in those days ipso facto made out a case for "Communist front" in the eyes of many. CEDC did good work. They polled eight hundred candidates about their views on the Smith Act, they played a pivotal role in the acquittal of Smith Act defendants Simon Gerson and Isidore Begun—a rare occurrence indeed—they helped to coordinate trial strategies and the sharing of information nationally in these cases. They produced publications at minimal prices (eight or ten cents), but none of this was seen as a boon in the government's eyes and they were chased into oblivion with many others.[10]

From the beginning CRC recognized the danger of the anticommunist offensive and some of their initial notorious cases involved victims who were not necessarily card-carrying party members. Carl Marzani had attended Williams College, was a Rhodes scholar, taught economics at New York University, and had worked with the Office of Strategic Services during the war. After resigning from the State Department he was indicted for allegedly denying falsely that in 1940–41 he counseled Communists to sow resentment among Blacks; a Black policeman, Archer Drew, was the principal government witness. CRC "succeeded in arranging bail for Marzani" and they arranged speaking engagements for him; one reason for his persecution was his production of the hard-hitting film "Deadline for Action" for U.E., which explained the workings of capitalism in simple terms. Despite CRC aid, a divided Supreme Court affirmed his conviction and ignored the compelling arguments of his counsel Osmond Fraenkel.[11]

Another early CRC case that marked them as "premature anti-anticommunists" was the case of German artist Gerhart Eisler. He was convicted of contempt of Congress and of having failed to note that he was a Communist on his exit visa. Previously, before these convictions, he had said that he wanted to go home to Germany, but he was labeled "America's number one Communist, atom bomb spy, Soviet agent." He was ordered deported and then the order was cancelled, so he fled to Europe leaving CRC's Bail Fund with a $20,000 loss. From the beginning of CRC they had assisted Eisler, and they continued to fight the case after his departure because the issues involved went beyond him alone. This was no mean feat. Although CRC's reliable ally, Abe Isserman, charged nothing, attorney David Rein wanted a $1000 fee; the cost of the brief and travel was $500. They sought "an attorney of the type of Wilkie" to argue the case in the Supreme Court and to focus on a frequent CRC plaint—the unconstitutionality of HUAC, which had charged Eisler with contempt. They sought to produce *amicus* briefs. All this was expensive.[12]

The Eisler case always had a kind of uniqueness about it. Eisler had landed in the United States as a result of a transit visa; he had wanted to go to Mexico but was denied entry. Some people were being deported who had roots in the United States, while Eisler, who wanted to leave, was prevented from going because of his presumed intelligence connections. Then his confrontation with HUAC did not endear him to government authorities. Like Marzani, CRC sent him on a crosscountry tour, though he was received without much grace in certain areas. The *Detroit Times* of 16 December 1947 reported "Eisler Dodges Eggs . . . 'No. 1 Communist' Cowed by Throng.'" In Ann Arbor he was "prevented" from making a public address in the "wildest (demonstration) on campus in years." Similar events occurred in Trenton. Despite protests by Picasso, Dashiell Hammett, Raymond Pace Alexander, Thomas Mann, Garson Kanin, and others, and despite massive protests in Germany itself, the government would not yield. So he fled, but not because of any perceived wilting of CRC's support for him. On the contrary, as he informed Rein, he held them in the highest esteem: "For Mr.

Patterson's integrity, goodwill and great experience I have nothing but the greatest respect. . . . I cannot agree to your proposal to deal directly with you under the exclusion of the CRC. . . . whatever its weaknesses may be, (CRC) was and is the only organization in the United States which has assisted and is assisting me." He was penniless when he fled to Britain, which would not extradite him. Thus the Supreme Court removed the case from the docket and would not hear the issues CRC wanted to present. But Eisler remained in close contact with Patterson and remained ever grateful for their help in saving him from a jail cell.[13]

The CRC "case load" at this juncture included as well fighting Truman's "loyalty" program and Tom Clark's listing of "subversive" organizations. David Jacob Group has termed the former "one of the most important and effective forms of legal political repression" and termed the president's motivation as almost solely political. Nowhere was "loyalty" or "disloyalty" explicitly defined, although the term was designed to effect thousands of federal employees. Group termed Clark's concoction "an official political blacklist," which "seriously impaired the functioning" of the groups it cited. Many of the cited organizations had their tax exemptions cancelled, "displaced persons" couldn't enter the United States unless they swore they'd never belonged to any organizations on the list; some leaders of organizations on the list were deported, others were denied access to public housing, education benefits, and certain kinds of employment. The loyalty order affected 2.2 million people, even a janitor in a small-town post office, and it required the investigation of all; the FBI, HUAC, local police, schools were all brought into this process. It was not necessary to provide the investigating committees with the names of "confidential informants," which prompted the evening of old scores, while any membership in Clark's "subversive" organizations meant disloyalty.[14]

Immediately CRC marched into court and sought a declaratory judgment challenging the order. They asserted that many would not associate with CRC due to the order and that the application of Executive Order 9835 discriminated. Of those who had been hit by it "in excess of 50% are Negroes, and more than 30% are Jewish; of the thirty-four (34) Post Office employees in Cleveland who have received such notices, twenty-eight (28) are Negro, four (4) are Jewish." They also questioned the constitutionality of Clark's listing, pointing out the due process defect that it did not require a "notice" or hearing. The First, Fifth, Ninth and Tenth Amendments and Article 1–Sec. 9 of the Constitution were invoked against it. But buttressing the government was the "Report on Civil Rights Congress as Communist Front Organization" produced by HUAC. Nixon, Karl Mundt, Parnell Thomas, and other committee members charged that CRC had been established by the party to "(protect) those of its members who run afoul of the law." They listed scores of CRC supporters, often inaccurately, as when Langston Hughes was listed as a party member.[15]

The lawsuit was never the only weapon in CRC's arsenal and this fight was no exception. They sought and obtained a meeting with the attorney general in December 1948 to impress upon him their concern. Unsuccessfully they sought a meeting with Truman, but they continued to blast both of them with heated verbiage. They reached out to prestigious allies like Du Bois for support in their prodigious effort. They worked assiduously at halting the spread of Truman's ideology further by trying to block Clark's appointment to the high court and to obtain his removal as attorney general. Patterson testified before the Judiciary Committee of the U.S. Senate and his reception was not overly friendly:

I was given an hour and ten minutes. There were many brushes with Magnuson, with Donaldson of Missouri, and McCarran, but all of them refrained from showing any open hostility and I was given the opportunity to expand extensively on a number of vital points. Senator Langer went out of his way to demonstratively welcome me when I took the stand and to compliment me after my hearing was over.

Even his eating lunch with Congressman Marcantonio "created quite a bit of concern . . . in the House of Representatives' restaurant." George Marshall expressed well Patterson's and CRC's point of view when he said that the "fundamental rights of the American people are not safe as long as Tom Clark's Attorney General and that he must be removed at once." Clark was such a bête noire in CRC eyes that with unaccustomed ill-humor Patterson demanded that the *Daily Worker* call CRC "to express our point of view" whenever he spoke in New York.[16]

It was understandable why Patterson was so testy. For after a balmy take-off in 1946, CRC found itself repelling a barrage of blows in 1947 that escalated in intensity in the 1948–49 period. It caused membership to level off, funds to be drained, and energy to be sapped. At their Executive Committee emergency meeting, 19 March 1947, CRC decided to "assume responsibility for organizing the campaign to defeat the present legislative drive to outlaw the Communist Party . . . because the drive to outlaw the Communists was in fact one of the worst threats to the American tradition of civil liberties." This measure was adopted unanimously; this meeting was followed up quickly by a 30 June–1 July 1947 Emergency Conference of CRC chapter executives, with fourteen chapters from New York to L. A. repre-sented. Plans were laid for a "Defense Fund Drive" of $150,000 to be raised within the next four months. Quotas were set for seventeen chapters, with New York alone weighing in with $50,000, Los Angeles second at $17,500 and Detroit third at $10,000. In those different days, Katherine Hepburn was listed with Paul Robeson as possible speakers for fundraisers.[17]

CRC warmed up, in a sense, for the Communist Party–Eleven trial by working on the cases of Leon Josephson and Eugene Dennis, the Communist Party general secretary. The cases were similar and involved challenges to the constitutionality of HUAC. Josephson was an attorney who went to Germany in 1934 to work with the underground. He was a Communist. In 1947 HUAC subpoenaed him and he refused to testify. Dennis went to testify before HUAC on 26 March 1947 on the subject of anticommunist legislation. Typically, they tried to browbeat him. More typically, he resisted. He was handed a subpoena to appear at another hearing. He chose not to go and was cited for contempt on 22 April and indicted. CRC hired attorneys Josephy Brodsky and Bernard Jaffe to defend him, and they alleged, among other things that he had been deprived of his First Amendment rights and charged with unconstitutional definitions of "Un-American" and "subversive." Importantly, they went further to challenge the illegitimate purposes of HUAC, i.e., blacklisting, and the very tenure of HUAC members like Congressman Rankin; they claimed that his tenure was illegal because the representation of Mississippi in Congress should have been reduced pursuant to the unenforced Fourteenth Amendment, Section 2. This was a potentially explosive claim because it made clear the link CRC always desired to join—Black and red. On appeal they also raised the issue of the right of government employees to be on juries, thereby linking the interests of labor to the issue and making the political "hat trick."

Although the NAACP's timorousness in the face of government pressure prevented it from joining in on the Fourteenth Amendment question, which was a natural for them, other Blacks were not so cowed. George Crockett argued Dennis' case on appeal and Earl Dickerson assisted on the brief. In a memo to the chapters Patterson noted an *amicus* brief focusing on the Fourteenth Amendment question, which had been signed, by Robeson, Du Bois, and others. This "Brandeis brief," was heavy on history, unlike so many court submissions. Patterson suggested "that it be sent to all progressive lawyers, especially Negro lawyers. . . . it should be used before discussion groups, forums, labor unions . . . state assemblies and city councils can be petitioned to memorialize Congress to end this shame." Again, CRC was not just fighting in court but using a court case for mass education.[18]

The indictment and trial of the Communist Party directorate (known as the trial of the Communist Party-Eleven, it would have been twelve but for William Z. Foster's illness) was an extraordinary occurrence. For one political party in power to put on trial the leadership of a contending party on the translucently spurious Smith Act grounds of, in so many words, teaching Marxism-Leninism, obviously had more to do with politics than with law. It was not accidental that the indictments were floated at the same time that the Progressive Party, then seen as a major challenger to the Democrats' rule and organized in part by Communists, began gathering steam. In their 20 July 1948 statement, CRC hit hard on such points:

The shoddy character of these persecutions is revealed by the suspicious timing of a series of "leaks" to newspapers by this Grand Jury. A close perusal of the record will indicate that whenever the administration was faced with a foreign policy crisis, this Grand Jury and the "leak" technique was used to create a witch hunt atmosphere. . . . It is more than a coincidence that these indictments are handed down on the same day that the State Department accuses the UN of being a transmission belt for Soviet "spies" and on the eve of a special session of Congress which will probably again consider the Mundt-Nixon Bill. . . . this is part of a subversive plot to silence all opposition to the policies of the Democratic and Republican parties.[19]

Without flinching CRC chose to opt for the monumental task, as the *Daily Worker* put it, of undertaking "full responsibility for organizing and conducting the trial and other phases of the defense of the twelve indicted leaders of the Communist Party." This was to be accompanied by a drive to raise $250,000, a decision that was "hailed" by the National Committee of the CP. The Communists also called for maximum assistance to CRC in this dire hour:

> Every Communist has a transcendent responsibility to support, loyally and tirelessly the activities of the CRC. This means active membership in the CRC; this means enlisting your friends and neighbors into the defense organization. This means raising funds for it. For the CRC is heir to a heritage of valiant struggle. For Sacco and Vanzetti; for Tom Mooney, for the Scottsboro boys.[20]

The party was fighting for its life and CRC knew that if it were to go down, CRC would follow quickly. Thus, their fighting words were backed up immediately with fighting actions. In July 1948 an emergency conference was held in the Council of African Affairs library of "200 trade union and community leaders." There were representatives from sixteen American Federation of Labor and forty-four CIO unions plus twenty-six community organizations. The Unions decided to hold "daily" noonday union meetings in plants and shops. The trade unionists then organized full-page advertisements placed in numerous papers across the country signed by over eleven hundred union leaders protesting the indictment; they sought and obtained a meeting with Truman. Ultimately they played a pivotal role in pulling together the National Non-Partisan Committee to Defend the Rights of the Twelve Communist Leaders, with Robeson and Norval Harris as co-chairs, CRC client Harold Christoffel as executive director, and CRC-Chicago leader Father Clarence Parker as vice-chair; another CRC leader, Arnold Johnson, served as secretary.[21]

These forces, spearheaded by CRC, spurred a whirlwind of activity that reached the four corners of the globe. In November 1948, after thanking Dr. K. J. Benes of Prague for his protest regarding the case, Patterson suggested that "copies of all letters which are sent to our organization should be sent to the American Embassy in your country . . . to the President of the United States . . . and to the Attorney General. . . . If it is possible at the same time to release your communications to the American press representatives in your country, this too would be extremely helpful to us in our struggle." Benes's concern was a straw in a gathering wind. Demonstrations in France of thousands protested the trial. George Bernard Shaw was among the luminaries who raised voices. Protests poured in from the Czechoslovak Union of Youth, the World Federation of Democratic Youth, the Free German Youth of Saxony, the China New Democratic Youth League, the Free Youth of Switzerland, the Swiss Workers Party, the Central Board of Polish Trade Unions, the Free German Trade Union Federation, the Argentine League for Human Rights, the Association of Polish War Invalids and hundreds more. One of the most poignant declarations emerged from the "Executive Committee of FIAPP, the international organization representing ten million members of the European underground movement. . . . Members of FIAPP who survived Hitler's concentration camps and prisons have not forgotten the great role played by the leaders of the American Communist Party during the last war. . . ." This International Federation of Ex-Political Prisoners was joined in sentiment by Friedrich Schlotterbeck: "My whole family was exterminated by the Nazis. . . . I myself spent almost ten years in Nazi concentration camps and jails. . . . on October 12th a similar trial was held in Ludwigsburg in the case of trumped-up charges by the American Military Government against my friends van Dyck and Weber, two courageous journalists."[22]

The United States was not ignored in the campaign, though it did appear that a more receptive audience could be found abroad. To break through the "paper curtain," the hostile or nonexistent coverage of the cause in the bourgeois press, CRC strove mightily to produce its own propaganda in a popular form. Their pamphlet "$64 Questions—For All Americans" attempted to capitalize on the popular radio quiz show in exposing the thought control indictment. Eight pages long and prepared in a question-answer format, CRC produced "What Are the Facts in the Case of the Twelve Indicted Communist Leaders"; it included a text of the indictment itself to combat the widespread notion that the Communist Party–Eleven were on trial for attempting to overthrow the U.S. government itself. They collaborated with the CP in producing "Campaign Against the Frame-up of the Communist Leaders—Speaker's Notes." But the "paper curtain" was sufficiently strong to present problems even here. George Marion had written a book *The Communist Trial: An American Crossroads* and had sought CRC's help in getting publicity for it. This former journalist of the *New York Mirror* discovered some cruel facts about the "free press," to his dismay: "The *New York Times*, for instance, has already refused to accept paid advertising for the *Communist Trial*. The fact of publication has not been acknowledged in the columns of major newspapers to which review copies were sent. . . . [There is] nearly uniform press silence." This kind of hostility was encountered at times in CRC's organizing campaign, as when the Board of Governors of Fordham University decided that the First Amendment meant that those gathering signatures on CP-Eleven petitions could be barred from campus.[23]

Although Patterson had stated that the party must defend itself in the final analysis, and this was echoed by Gurley Flynn to some extent, the outside observer could be excused for viewing this as an inconsistently promulgated message. CRC's September 1948 fund-drive for the defendants was deemed the "ONLY" one (CRC's emphasis). Of course, the party continued to provide political direction for the campaign, but the critical political task of fundraising was in theory "farmed-out" to CRC, which underscored Gurley Flynn's admonition in *Political Affairs*. Still, even accepting outright donations could provide problems. Anna Louise Strong on the back of her check to the defense scribbled, "For the American Communists who are getting as raw a deal from American justice as I got from USSR. From a fellow victim of the Cold War." Patterson decided that the check should be refused: "This organization's endorsement under that of Anna Louise Strong's would be, in effect, and particularly so far as the press is concerned, an endorsement of Miss Strong's statement." When this refusal became public, it did not help CRC or the campaign. CRC had a goal of $250,000, but if the fundraising campaign was a barometer for the political effort, things were not going too well. Between 31 July 1948 and 1 February 1949, CRC collected $74,095.45. This was no small amount, but not up to what was required. Moreover, CRC at the same time was raising funds for the Trenton Six, for Willie McGee, and for the usual assortment of cases they handled, which underscored the need for CEDC to be organized. Of that amount, $26,592.05 went for legal defense and the rest for political agitation. That two-to-one ratio signified CRC's unique recipe for fighting cases in the streets as much as the courts. Contrary to Patterson's words quoted above, the CP had its own fundraising campaign because of the burden already on CRC's shoulders. During that same period they raised $86,343.87, of which $64,780 went for legal defense. Attorney's fees were a hefty $2,275 per week, and court records alone weighed in at $1,500 per week. Thus, what is revealed is that the division of labor between CRC and CP was such that the former coordinated the mass defense—as befitted a mass defense organization—and the latter provided legal and political direction.[24]

Whatever the division of labor, CRC definitely did a credible job in bringing the case before the public. It was difficult, however, because they did not have a Black victim of southern lynch law—factors which made McGee's situation so compelling and filled with pathos. Nor did they have a Rosa Lee Ingram, a Black woman resisting the lustful clutches of a white boss. These defendants were eleven men—nine of whom were white—who the public felt were trying to impose some sort of "totalitarian" system viz. Hitlerian, on them. Despite this obvious barrier, CRC proceeded to churn out petitions, telegrams, letters, leaflets, and conferences. They began a film called "The

Investigators," which concerned the case. Their full-page ad in the Black press signed by Du Bois, Robeson, and other Black personalities attracted substantial attention. They responded to hostile articles and editorials across the country. They put a special emphasis on discrete groups, like women. And they had an impact. In an effort to combat the fallacious, silly charge that they were "un-American," CRC was always pleased to hear from a figure like Harrison Parker, chancellor of the Puritan Church of American and "of the 10th generation of his family of Puritan men born on American soil. . . . great-great-grandfther, Isaac Parker, fought along with George Washington at Valley Forge." He told CRC, "You did right in advancing bail for the men convicted in the U.S. Court. . . . they were entitled to the protection of the law."[25]

One reason CRC sought out such influential allies was the increasing isolation that was foisted on them. Page-one headlines terming CRC the "official legal defense arm of the Communist Party" and their headquarters at 23 West 26th Street a "center of Stalinist Organizations" were becoming increasingly common. These distortions did not slow them down and seemed to give them succor. 19 June 1950 found Patterson writing all chapter secretaries and enclosing the national program of action that embodied the "main conclusions" from the National Board meeting held 10–12 June in Chicago. Patterson put forward their political orientation: "All criticism is declared to be Communism. Therefore, the defense of the constitutional rights of the Communists becomes the decisive point in the defense of . . . constitutional liberties. . . . CRC is not defending the Communist Party or any minority party. CRC defends the constitutional right of free speech and assembly of Communists and other political minorities. . . ." Coming after the eleven defendants' convictions, this was still bold talk. Their four-month program aimed at reversing the CP-Eleven and Dennis convictions was equally audacious. Week by week they plotted national activity for the chapters. 21–28 June was to involve pickets and mass meetings. The next week would involve initiating 25,000 letters to Truman demanding amnesty. Then there would be distribution of 250,000 stickers relating to the Dennis case. In addition to raising other cases like Christoffel and Bridges and commemorating Peekskill, they resolved to culminate the effort by sending a delegation to meet with Truman, mostly of non-CRC elements. A united front, consisting of ACLU, NAACP, ADA and other organizations was conceived.[26]

After this period, CRC pressed on and the results flooding in from the chapters were not negligible. In Chicago there was a "chain telephone system" to get wires to Truman, along with "street corner meetings" and "extensive mailings." In Cleveland there were "plant gate distribution of leaflets" and "special attention to unions." "Mass meetings" were occurring in Denver. L. A. saw "emergency conferences on the Right to Bail, petitions, telegrams." Philadelphia found local leaders signing telegrams and petitions. And all this during the midst of an unpopular war in Korea. Patterson, however, saw no need to rest on their laurels: "Special appeals should be made to ministers. . . . If possible they should receive communications not from CRC but from prominent individuals. . . . call upon local newspaper editors." Though it may have been only verbiage, not plans implemented, Patterson's missive of 22 November 1950 contradicted his letter of self-flagellating criticism quoted earlier: "to be effective we must apply the principle of concentration. Therefore, we concentrate as nearly all our forces as is possible on that civil rights case, the decision of which will decide many other cases." What was that case? The CP-Eleven naturally enough.[27]

After the high court upheld, over Justice Black's and Justice Douglas' dissents, the Foley Square convictions, Grossman urged on the chapters a mass campaign forcing a rehearing and a stay of execution: "mass campaign of phone calls, letters, post cards, telegrams and resolutions . . . Special emphasis must be placed here upon labor and Negro organizations." He suggested using "contacts" made "during the McGee campaign." They cobbled together yet another committee—the "Committee for Free Political Advocacy"—with James Wolfe of the Utah Supreme Court, Dickerson, and others demanding that the indictment be dropped. All these memos and committees produced results. Although it may have seemed like small potatoes to some, CRC was ecstatic over the "recently won victory for Henry Winston, the right to travel from Manhattan to Brooklyn." Justice Robert Jackson of the U.S. Supreme Court was highly displeased with CRC's flood of letters and telegrams, on the other hand, and he broadcast to the *New York Times* that it represented the "stupidest kind of tactics." Yet an examination of the papers of Felix Frankfurter indicates that other influences besides the law—after all, this case was an absurdity from a legal viewpoint anyway—played a role in the court's disposition.[28]

As the Truman Administration was being phased out, CRC stepped up its efforts on behalf of the Smith Act defendants. In Harlem at a landmark cultural event, "Charlie (Yardbird) Parker and his Strings" regaled with sweet music those attending the "Free Ben Davis Birthday Ball and Festival" at 217 West 125 Street. Matching their counterpart, the Detroit chapter sought to raise $40,000 to defend Smith Act victims; they also were "planning a large-scale publicity campaign, including radio and television programs, newspaper advertisements and issuance of hundreds of thousands of tabloid newspapers to shop workers." As in most CRC chapter cities, Detroit had its own "little" Smith Act case, with future "liberal" U.S. Senator Philip Hart earning his spurs as the district attorney. Ernest Goodman, longtime CRC attorney, was counsel and he won an immediate victory by reducing bail to a then-meager $5,000. Grossman counselled a tough fight against the practice of the government of "singling out one defendant in each place and fixing a higher bail on him"; it should be fought "because if it can be done in one case it can be done in a dozen." This "pre-trial trial . . . destroys the presumption of innocence" in that the government customarily argued that a clear violation of the Smith Act mandated high bail. Out of Detroit came some of the better coordination of Smith Act counsel across the nation and some of the best defense organization overall, e.g., packing the courtroom, having allies take out loans to raise funds, etc.[29]

Not surprisingly in an organization led by Communists, in their campaigning for Smith Act victims CRC placed emphasis on labor and on Afro-Americans. At CRC's urging they received resolutions of support from Local 121 of the United Gas, Coke, and Chemical Workers—CIO, Local 23 of the International Hod Carriers' Building and Common Laborers Union, the Food, Tobacco, Agriculture, and Allied Workers Union, the National Union of Marine Cooks and Stewards, and many others, as the ad signed by eleven hundred union leaders would demonstrate. "1000 Trade Union Officials" initiated a petition to Truman. They were a principal force in organizing regional meetings in Pittsburgh, Chicago, and L. A. In Chicago, the CRC's "Committee of 100" concentrated on the Foley Square defendants included a representative of the Dining Car and Food Workers. When President Hugo Ernst of the Hotel and Restaurant Employees, "one of the largest in the AFL," assailed the jailing of the Communists in August 1951, CRC deemed it worthy of a press release.[30]

As a persecuted minority themselves, it was felt correctly that Blacks would be more sympathetic to another persecuted minority, the Communist Party. Moreover, the main antagonists of both were right-wing Dixiecrats. So, from the beginning, CRC stressed the issue of "systematic exclusion of Negroes, trade unionists, and other minority groups from federal grand juries." According to CRC, this would open the "way for new attacks on Negro people." They designed many pamphlets and petitions specifically for Black consumption. They suggested that party organizers focus on "Negro papers" in forwarding their releases. Just as foreign support could eventually produce domestic publicity, CRC's close relationship with Black papers like the *Pittsburgh Courier, St. Louis American, California Eagle, Arkansas State Press, Afro-American*, and others could not be ignored forever. CRC trumpeted the fact that prominent Black judge Hubert Delany, who also happened to be a high-level NAACP official, the *Oklahoma Black Dispatch*, the *Philadelphia Tribune* and particularly the *St. Louis American* all denounced the Supreme Court decision upholding the convictions. It probably did not shock Patterson that one of the few bourgeois newspapers that was critical of McCarthyism generally from its inception was the *St. Louis Post-Dispatch* and their editorial page editor Irving Dillard.[31]

This period also saw CRC again trying to break through the "paper curtain" by producing pamphlets by the thousands. In May 1951 there came "The Case of the 11 Communist Leaders" a four-page pamphlet. Probably their most popular and well-known pamphlet was produced by the New York state chapter, called "Deadly Parallel." The "parallel" was with Nazi Germany and their like-minded obsession with Bolshevism; this work featured dramatic photographs, cute rhymes, and gripping language. CRC even went so far as to rent billboard space and put up huge ads about the case. On the individual level, there were countless letters to newspaper editors, appearances on radio, and the like.[32]

Of all of the eleven Communist defendants and the scores of other Smith Act victims nationally, Ben Davis probably received more attention than any other, except possibly Steve Nelson. This was probably not just due to the fact that he was a good friend of Patterson and Robeson. Like both of them he was a lawyer. Davis did present those elements of drama, like the cases of McGee, and Ingram, that CRC deemed necessary for successful defense campaigns. Consider Ben Davis: Here is a rare avis, a Black graduate of Amherst and Harvard Law, a man who came from one of Atlanta's most prominent Black families, who also happened to be Republican leaders. He was a man who came to prominence during the 1930s by participating in one of ILD's most dramatic cases, that of Angelo Herndon. Tall, dark, and handsome with a compelling oratorical style, Davis provided ingredients that were striking: a Black man who relinquished the path to fame and fortune and instead joined with an outlawed political minority. Besides that, he had received notoriety as a member of the New York City Council representing Harlem, which brought him something of a political base.

Although only a few people showed up at the initial meeting, a Ben Davis Freedom Committee was organized and based in Harlem. They held street rallies in Harlem at 118th & Lenox, 115th & Lenox, and 134th & Lenox that "attracted several thousands." Relatively soon they were spreading the fact that a "group of prominent Philadelphia ministers and laymen," in a petition to Truman, announced, "We agree with Walter White when he says 'When Ben Davis goes to jail, a piece of me goes with him.'" Roscoe Dunjee, New York City Councilman Earl Brown, and many others echoed this sentiment. The committee highlighted the fact that in the trial of the eleven, evidence was introduced showing their efforts against Jim Crow. The prosecution said that they were insincere and hypocritical and were only trying to intensify the discontent of Blacks and incite insurrection. Thus, they claimed, Davis' conviction must be reexamined or any fighting for Black rights could be discredited similarly.[33]

Patterson conducted a one-man crusade to free Ben Davis. Often this involved seeking lawyers to assist Davis' attorney, Ralph Powe. The spring of 1954 found the CRC leader in St. Louis. He spoke with the Baptist Ministerial Alliance and "had a long talk with Rev. Johnson of the Third Baptist Church," but a primary part of his mission was meeting with the well-known Black attorney, R. L. Witherspoon. After a bit of cajoling, he agreed to come on board. Patterson also felt that he could garner support in Davis' hometown of Atlanta, but there he found some disappointment. One reason was the configuration of electoral politics, as he confided to Harlem lawyer Hope Stevens. These "southern gentlemen . . . were of the opinion that if such an action were brought by them, it might interfere with their effort to defeat Talmadge's protegy [sic] in the coming elections." But Patterson continued heroically. His peripatetic nature had brought him to an "Elks Convention," where he had met Atlantan Edward D'Antignac who had "expressed sympathy" for Davis. Patterson plucked the strings of sentiment, generating further sympathy for the Black political prisoner. "His face was gaunt. His figure had lost some fifty pounds in weight and his carriage showed definitely the effect that the prison regime was having upon him physically." Yet, said Patterson, his "moral courage, strength and determination dominated the court room." He explained that Davis "came from a relatively secure Negro family. . . but he said, there in that court room, that he was never allowed to forget that he remained a n-gg-r." Then Patterson got quickly to the point: "In short order he will have spent three years in the Jim Crow prison at Terre Haute. . . . It would be a splendid thing if a prominent white Southerner could be secured as a part of . . . a group [to lobby for Davis]. . . . I might add in conclusion that I think Judge Houston or another of the leading Elks might be ready to participate in such a laudable undertaking."[34]

Patterson dug deep into his tactical bag to persuade doubters like D'Antignac and his associates: "It is my feeling if they acted as attorneys in this matter it would not only strengthen their own prestige within that locality but would be nationally and even internationally acclaimed." He added melodrama: "Our situation is not as far removed from that occupied by the Jews of Germany and Poland as some people think." After A. T. Walden announced he could not help with the case, Patterson offered to coordinate all the paperwork in New York so that all he would have to do would be the legal "argument." Patterson was sorrowful about this refusal: "I deeply regret that in my many trips to the South I have generally by-passed Atlanta. The organization of which I am a part has no close contacts in Atlanta and as a consequence we have received no invitations for our leadership to speak there." The Atlantans' decision was not totally inexplicable, as Patterson's own correspondence demonstrated. His letters to them involved widespread use of code language like "W. D." or "Mr. R". Mail-tampering and other bolder forms of harassment were not being sniffed at, particularly in the deep South, and this clearly hindered their efforts.[35]

More success was had by Patterson in encouraging the Black press to focus on Davis. In September 1952 he asked the conservative Dr. C. B. Powell, owner of the *Amsterdam News*, on a "non-partisan basis" to publicize Davis' plight. Again, he appealed to self-interest: "This assertion of independence on your part would only illicit (sic) the admiration of those with whom you are politically associated and would therefore further your own interests." The *Dam News* couldn't help but cover Davis a bit, because he was a former Harlem city councilman, but the same was not necessarily true for the *Afro-American*. Thus, Patterson told editor Carl Murphy that he "noted your news comment . . . with pleasure." The liberal use of praise was not ignored either as Patterson called the *Afro* "the most politically mature of the Negro newspapers. . . ." He reminded Murphy that Davis had worked for the *Afro* after he left school. He contrasted Davis' role in the council with that of his successor, Earl Brown, who "ran away from the fight" over the FBI and the New York Police Department cover-up of New York City police brutality. Patterson's pleas must have been persuasive because the *Afro* did give coverage to Davis' plight and his contemplated lawsuit challenging segregation in federal prisons.[36]

Such a suit was typical of CRC, fighting for progress even when the person bringing suit was jailed. Like his approach to Powell and Murphy, in attempting to involve Harlem lawyer Hope Stevens in the effort, Patterson made both a politician and a personal appeal:

Harlem bears the major responsibility. . . . Hope, these forces only respect strength. . . . True, they make concessions to the reformist Negro leaders. Yet, it is the strength of the left, as weak as it is, that impelled these concessions. Negro lawyers who would really fight simply for respect for human dignity would gain immeasurably more than they are now from the bastards in power. If they would show some respect for Ben and Ben's magnificent courage it would redound to their growth materially in patronage and in legal development and strength. What I should like to see organized is a group that would go to Bennett, head of the Federal Bureau of Prisons in Washington, D.C. and raise the question of Ben's continued imprisonment under these conditions. They could fight to end the Jim Crow system in the federal prisons.

Complaints about the conditions under which Davis was being held were registered as early as October 1951, when his attorney complained about prison segregation and the fact that he was only allowed to write his sister and lawyer. This was followed by the production and heavy promotion of the cartoon strip about Davis, "Now It's Against the Law." The campaign in Philadelphia for Davis was comparable to actions in other cities. They forwarded ten thousand copies of the strip there in June 1953, along with substantial doses of political advice:[37]

. . . link the local situation up with this national campaign. We expect you to visit editors of all the press from right to left, which includes labor, the metropolitan press, the Negro press, the religious press. . . . Much is to be learned about fighting for Amnesty from the steps taken in Cuba, the Argentine, Eastern Europe, China, in granting amnesty to political prisoners and others in the recent period.

CRC organized a deluge of letters to James Bennett of the Federal Bureau of Prisons. A typical missive came from Muriel Symington:

whenever a visitor comes to see Ben Davis . . . his visitor is under the eye and ear observation of a guard. Visitors for every other Smith Act victim are under eye observation only. Mr. Davis' only visitors are his sister and a white woman friend. . . . this gratuitous harassment springs from the fact that one visitor is white.

This highlights another reason why CRC singled out this particular Smith Act defendant for special concern, because he brought the streams of Black and red into a single confluence, thus merging the civil rights and civil liberties fights and dramatizing the racism of those who would prosecute people under the Smith Act. In any case, Bennett claimed that Ben was segregated because he had been threatened by other prisoners and that he was only segregated administratively, along with others who could not go to the mess hall or enter the auditorium. This was labored and spurious, but emblematic of the pressure placed on Bennett. CRC had printed ten thousand cards and twenty thousand brochures about Davis. The committee for Davis was canvassing door to door, setting up tables "in crowded intersections," and holding a "series of house parties for the raising of money." This and Patterson's friendly persuasion encouraged editorial support for the proposed suit on prison segregation, e.g., from the *Afro*. February 1954 saw a delegation headed by Patterson present ten thousand signatures for Davis' amnesty to the attorney general. There were rallies addressed by figures like Robeson, Beaulah Richardson, and Modjeska Simkins, a legendary South Carolina civic and political leader.[38]

Patterson still had difficulty, despite this momentum, in attracting help on behalf of the lawsuit. He forwarded a copy of the *mandamus* petition to Willard Ransom of Indianapolis and asked if it were "adequate. . . . I am not here talking about winning in the court but igniting a broad movement. . . ." This was the watermark of many CRC efforts, for, as he stated, "I think although we might be defeated in the courts, we might win some far-reaching prison reforms." Plaintively, he asked Ransom, "Would you take the case?" He promised him aid and Ransom did issue a statement backing the effort. Patterson was sure that would be helpful. Yet, because of time, although he was "in full accord with the objectives of the case," Ransom was unable to participate in the case. Inevitably, the government sought to dismiss the prison segregation case, because Davis was no longer in federal prison in Terre Haute, but serving a contempt sentence in Pittsburgh. Davis claimed this 1955 transfer was made against his will and that if he had dropped his suit, he would not have been shipped to Pittsburgh. Davis claimed that the Jim Crow he faced in prison—this "badge of inferiority"—continued in Pittsburgh in any case. This suit led directly to desegregation of federal prisons. This assault against Jim Crow was another bazooka in the antiracist arsenal that eventually knocked down the walls of segregation; it was part of an overall offensive. The tactics deployed—mobilizing the press, organizing lawyers, massive propaganda assaults, rallies and canvassing, and so forth—were typical of what CRC did to spur support for some of the most reviled political prisoners in the country. And these tactics ultimately led to freedom for Ben Davis and his co-defendants.[39]

Ben Davis happened to be in another category: an attorney suffering persecution. After the conviction of the Communist Party–Eleven, the court then sought to hold their lawyers in contempt and to jail them; then disbarment proceedings were begun. This was one of the most serious challenges to the bar in U.S. history and, per usual, CRC rushed to the aid of the beleaguered solons, as the organized bar skulked cravenly away. Unfortunately, this experience was nothing new for lawyers involved in CRC cases and it certainly acted as a disincentive for those interested in their cases of racist and political repression. In 1949, in a highly unusual move, a judge sought to bar Patterson and other CRC lawyers from representing the Trenton Six; this case was fought furiously through the federal courts and the streets. When Mississippi lawyer John Poole entered the McGee case, disbarment proceedings were launched against him and were not dropped until he dropped the case. Maryland CRC leader and attorney Maurice Braverman was disbarred. Although he fought the case up to the U.S. Supreme Court, California lawyer and CRC ally Vincent Hallinan was jailed for six months as a result of his vigorous advocacy in the Harry Bridges case. After the effort to disbar and jail the CR–Eleven lawyers had gathered momentum, HUAC subpoenaed twenty L. A. lawyers, most of whom had been active in CRC's most successful lawyers' panel, for intense questioning. One of the more outrageous cases involved CRC–Pittsburgh lawyer Hyman Schlesinger. In the midst of trying a case, Judge Michael Musmanno asked him pointblank, "Are you a member of the Civil Rights Congress. . . . Did you or did you not form the Civil Rights Congress, which is a communist front organization, in your office—the Civil Rights Congress which is part of the movement to overthrow the government of the United States by force and violence." The feisty judge tried to oust him from the case, and when he filed a writ of prohibition, Musmanno met the process server with undisguised contempt. "I am not accepting any service today," he sniffed haughtily and dashed the paper to the street and walked away. He then issued a warrant for Schlesinger's arrest. Before that, he had physically "restrained" the lawyer from leaving the courtroom, thus compounding the transgression. Schlesinger eventually was able to prevail in this particular matter, but only after considerable agony and expense. Still, the shot over the bow had been heard and felt by all lawyers interested in taking on controversial cases.[40]

Thus fusillade aimed at CRC lawyers was designed to have maximum ripple effects. For this network of excellent, diligent lawyers cooperated across state boundaries in efforts of mutual assistance that contradicted the traditional notion of lawyers as egotistical "lone rangers." Louis McCabe of Philadelphia, Richard Gladstein of San Francisco, Harry Sacher of New York, Abe Isserman of New Jersey, and George Crockett of Detroit were the principal CP–Eleven barristers under siege, and they were the ones called upon frequently for consultation on like cases. In mid-1951, as the Smith Act prosecutions esclated, Gladstein was asked to provide guidance on the heart of defending against these thought control attacks: "what is the effective way of presenting Marxist theory in a proceeding under the Smith Act so that it gets across to the jury and the public and . . . how to prevent distortion of theory in such a proceeding by stool pigeons." Concerning self-defense he was asked "what are the problems and what is their suggested solution." These lawyers were not defending activists accused of attempting to overthrow the government by force and violence, as was popularly believed, but rather those charged with teaching Marxism-Leninism. Hence, much of the prosecution involved labored recitations from dusty tomes penned by Marx, Engels, Lenin, Stalin, and others concerning the use of force and related matters, then inquiring if the defendants subscribed to such notions. In an overheated, hysterical, political atmosphere, defending against such charges was no mean feat, but they pressed on and cooperation marked their endeavors. Washington lawyer Joe Forer, involved in similar prosecutions in Baltimore, was supplied with intelligence from other CRC lawyers, with the national office serving as the hub of the wheel from which the spokes emanated. Grossman also forwarded similar information to Pittsburgh–CRC lawyer John McTernan. The national office published a newsletter that summarized "bail activities . . . legal tests, titles and addresses of all committees." A similar letter was sent to Ben Margolis in L. A., Harriet Bouslog of Honolulu, and others defending against such actions.[41]

Despite the overwhelming terror they were faced with, CRC was somewhat optimistic about their ability to mobilize lawyers. Grossman reported enthusiastically in early 1950 that "Initial results in Frisco show that we can really break thru among conservative and reactionary attorneys on this issue. . . . We have a realizable goal of 500 lawyers on the Coast, which I hope we will realize. . . ." Though this was before the Korea freeze, it was still an extraordinary figure, even considering his caveat, "as you know, moving lawyers into action, especially on deadlines is very difficult." Notwithstanding later defections, some of the more significant Smith Act victories were won on the West Coast, even setting aside the *Stack* and *Yates* victories. John Caughlan, attorney for the Seattle defendants, engaged in excellent legal preparation and could draw upon the expertise of those who had passed before him; he obtained research results from New York and L. A. attorneys and held seminars on the issues with other attorneys and defendants. Anticipating much of the pathbreaking work of the 1970s, substantial attention was devoted to the question of jury selection. Typical of CRC efforts nationwide, there was constant attention paid to rallying public opinion, despite pressing financial difficulties. (Their defense committee had a income of $35,808.67, but expenses of $42,308.82 in 1953 for example.) There were emergency conferences with over 250 delegates, there were spirited rallies featuring "group singing" of standards like "If I Had a Hammer," "dramatic reading(s)" by the "Peoples Program Players," satires on McCarthy, and other such cultural events. Seattle had the advantage of having attractive defendants to boot, Bill Pennock had been elected to the state legislature four times, and John Daschbach, a former railroad worker and shipfitter, was popular among workers. But their lawyers had an even larger secret weapon that was often alien to their NAACP and ACLU counterparts: a mass defense committee specializing in shaping public opinion in an era when sequestering juries was not common. They also had the advantage of drawing upon the aggressive and skilled network of the National Lawyers Guild, which their counterparts too shunned generally.[42]

To be sure, it was no easy task to attract lawyers to the banner of the Smith Act defendants and other political detainees. Communist leader Steve Nelson asked seven hundred lawyers to defend him, all of whom refused. In November 1950, when the CP–Eleven were seeking counsel because their lawyers were under siege, they contacted "24 prominent attorneys . . . urging their participation in the case. . . . (finally they) had to appeal to Mr. Herbert Evatt of Australia and Mr. D. M. Pritt of England to participate," since those queried would not. These reluctant lawyers' fear was justified to an extent. Tom Clark, attorney general of the United States, in a widely quoted article in the mass circulation *Look* magazine, which I. F. Stone appropriately termed "extraordinary," demanded that bar associations discipline lawyers who defended political dissidents. Clearly he had CRC in mind and correctly Stone observed that the real issue was whether the "right to counsel" guaranteed by the Sixth Amendment to the U.S. Constitution was "to be destroyed." Fierce retribution faced those who would defy the nation's top law enforcement officer. Even the usually resolute Thomas Emerson of Yale Law School, a Guild leader derisively known as "Tommie the Commie" in unrefined circles, was affected. After speaking before the CRC-initiated Lawyers Defense Committee in early 1950, he worriedly asked, "Would you send me as soon as possible a copy of my statement read at the meeting of February 2. Some of the alumni are howling about it. . . . I would appreciate it also if you would let me know who else spoke." Characteristic of how deeply the roots of persecution had reached was the fact that *New York Post* columnist Leonard Lyons, who customarily was satisfied to report on the doings of the Hollywood hoi polloi, felt compelled to get into the act: "The discredited Civil Rights Congress plans to flood law offices (around) the nation with literature on behalf of the shysters cited for contempt at trials of Commy party leaders." All this is in the midst of reporting breathlessly on the trivialities of the lives of Garbo, Gary Cooper, and Marlon Brando. CRC had surely made it to the big time, but this was not necessarily the kind of publicity they desired.[43]

Their attempt to attract New Deal liberal Harold Ickes to the cause of the persecuted CP–Eleven attorneys showed what they were up against. He explained that he was approaching seventy-seven, had children ten and twelve, and wanted to write a book. Chattily and digressively he recounted his activities on behalf of Indian rights, off-shore oil, and the *New Republic*, then he got to the point:

> I was in full agreement with all of you that non-communist counsel who hate communism but who strongly believe in the First Amendment to the Constitution should enter this case. . . . and try to save what is left of that Amendment since the majority decision in the case of eleven Communists was handed down by the Supreme Court.

But after that big build-up, there came the bigger letdown, as Ickes, like so many others before him, begged out on participation.[44]

Like Ickes, many were concerned with the bizarre behavior of Judge Harold Medina in the Foley Square trial. The courtly Princeton and Columbia Law graduate who had garnered a small fortune before ascending to the bench constantly baited the defendants' counsel, harassed and harangued them, and conducted himself in a literally paranoid manner so bizarre that even the Supreme Court ultimately had to take note and reverse his draconian contempt citations in part, despite pressure to act otherwise. The lawyers before him were not novices, nor was defendant-lawyer Ben Davis. George Crockett was one of the leading lawyers of his generation and so well respected that his defense of reds did not prevent his own rise to the bench, then Congress. Harry Sacher had been a highly successful labor lawyer, his fees reputed to have exceeded a then-healthy $50,000 yearly; McCabe, Gladstein, and Isserman were of similar, if not more, substantive quality. These four were at the pinnacle of their profession, but they chose to do battle within the jaws of the lion. In addition to doing battle in court, miles away from home for months, Crockett had to endure racist insults about the alleged tokenism of his selection as counsel, while some of his compatriots had to deal with frequent anti-Semitic allusions, as illustrated by Leonard Lyons' indelicate comment.[45]

In a sense, this was the least of the lawyers' problems. Isserman was disbarred from New Jersey in 1952. There was a concerted attempt to disbar Isserman and Sacher in New York. Sacher was disbarred from federal court. Charges were brought against Crockett in Michigan and against Gladstein in California. Rapidly, soon after the trial, CRC knocked together the Lawyers Defense Committee. They protested loud and long sentences ranging from thirty days to six months given the lawyers. They avidly gathered endorsements of their efforts from the likes of Einstein, Thomas Mann, Emerson, Robert Lynd, Earl Dickerson, Carey McWilliams, and others. They reprinted Stone's articles on the case and other pamphlets such as the widely circulated "Lawyers Under Fire." They successfully obtained a resolution of support from the Cook County Bar Association (Dickerson's influence here), opposing Crockett's disbarment. They spent untold hours putting together a team of lawyers to fight these cases, as they wound themselves circuitously through the labyrinthal court system. They got unions to file *amicus* briefs stressing all of these lawyers' roles as labor advocates. They tried to convince other lawyers that there was a danger for them if lawyers could be convicted of such serious offenses with lengthy sentences without hearings. With their usual flexible tactics, they abjured splendid but sectarian isolation as they emphasized "how to produce a brief which lawyers who don't agree with us generally will sign." They prevailed upon the Guild leadership to "agree to send copies to its rank and file membership." They planned a dinner in honor of the besieged barristers to raise funds and garner publicity. Naturally, their "Mass Appeal" tried to "include consideration of a section on the special meaning of this struggle to the Negro people, especially in the South, but elsewhere as well."[46]

These moves were worthy, but they were not considered altogether sufficient. The CRC strategy was to try to get chapters to focus on the persecuted lawyer in their area, e.g., Detroit and Crockett, Philadelphia and McCabe. Isserman was hit hard particularly, and he happened to be the lawyer most active previously in CRC matters, which seemed to be a signal to CRC attorneys. Grossman reproved New Jersey–CRC for their alleged lack of effort on behalf of Isserman, who had "been suspended and is, therefore, unable to practice law. This must be attributable to the fact that no campaign was waged around his case and around him." This was a logical, but not necessarily an accurate assumption. Crockett fared a bit better in Detroit, but he too was critical. He wanted to see an "Isserman Defense Committee" and "reviving" of the Sacher Defense Committee but was pessimistic: "All of these are activities for lawyers; and because of that, I have little faith that much will be accomplished. I am not being intentionally pessimistic; instead I am just facing the facts." Facts were not always neutral and objective things, however, and Crockett's approach to the value of legal advocacy, the mass approach, and the value of attracting lawyers like Telford Taylor to their side did not square totally with CRC's: "In the long run the fight for the lawyers will depend upon the argument—written and oral—presented to the Court. And I believe that our present counsel can do the job. I say this now because I anticipate some last-minute suggestion about bringing in 'outstanding' counsel. I want none of that; we have 'outstanding counsel' now." Taylor joined the defense team nonetheless.[47]

Crockett was arguing from a strong position and not just because "prominent" counsel often wanted to dilute, if not contradict, the political thrust of those they were called on to defend. The Detroit chapter, allied with the Black and labor community, organized a militant fightback against the effort to disbar Crockett and won out, although he was forced to cool his heels in federal prison for a few months. When he came home from the grueling trial, he was greeted by a welcome home party organized by his fraternity, Kappa Alpha Psi. His defense committee was incredibly broad and active, including clerics, businessmen, labor leaders, and among others, The *Pittsburgh Courier* of 28 January 1950 headlined, "Hundreds Greet Atty. Crockett at Large Reception." The crowd of five hundred included the head of the predominantly Black Wolverine Bar Association, a striking contrast to Sacher's reception by the Association of the Bar for the City of New York, which sought to have him disbarred. This illustrated once again the differentiated response by Blacks to the red scare, which gave strength to CRC's tendency to stress cases involving Black Equality or the Black angle of anticommunist cases.[48]

The FBI truly took cognizance of the future Congressman's ties to CRC; he was one of the most closely watched of the microscopically scrutinized Lawyers Guild leadership. They were quite concerned with the fact that CRC leader Esther Jackson, wife of leading Black Communist James Jackson, was the major force organizing his defense committee. An informant who had been dispatched to their 31 October 1949 meeting talked to Jackson and Crockett and filched some letters for the FBI's files. Though Crockett repeated tirelessly that he was not a party member, his "Security Index Card" of 5 October 1950, which would have marked him for detention in an "emergency" situation, boldly listed him otherwise. On 22 July 1951 when he spoke at a picnic at "Welcome Park," an informant "reported that Crockett quoted Engels to the effect that when the capitalistic system approached its finale the deepening crisis causes the government to refuse to abide by the law it has itself set up." Another informant reported that on 9 March 1952 he attended a CRC meeting in Detroit; it was added that he "is frequently consulted by CRC functionaries in regard to legal matters." His defense of Patterson at his trial and Detroit CRC functionary Arthur McPhaul before HUAC were duly noted. Clipped and filed away was the *Daily Worker* of 28 September 1952, which displayed a picture of Anne Shore of CRC–Detroit and Crockett in a welcome home reception after his release from prison. His ties with CRC since its inception in 1946 were indicated, his appearances for them in L. A. and elsewhere, and even his attendance at their carnival and picnic at "Brown Derby Park" in September 1950. The FBI's interest in Crockett's relationship with the CRC apparently knew no bounds.[49]

This battle to protect the right of lawyers to engage in vigorous advocacy was a long and bitter one, but like so many others of the CRC, the benefits were reaped by all freedom-loving people. The lawyers suffered. Incomes were slashed. Marital relations were harmed. Time was spent in jail. Yet, but for CRC's Herculean toil, the toll surely would have been much worse. Like so many of their other battles, the precedents they set here—legal and otherwise—amply plowed the ground that allowed a revivified Civil Rights Movement to emerge after CRC's unfortunate demise.

The struggle to rescue the CP–Eleven lawyers from the none-too-tender clutches of prison wardens was not the only ancillary battle that emerged from Foley Square. There was as well the effort to help the families and gain amnesty for the political prisoners themselves. CRC attempted to attend to the children's welfare, to get them to camp, and to attend to the prison needs of the defendants in various ways. Few of the Smith Act defendants were wealthy, and that was putting it mildly; their enforced jail terms only exacerbated their perilous financial states. In 1952 CRC helped to organize the National Meeting of Families—Committee of Smith Act Victims. Participants included mostly CP–Eleven and other Smith Act family members, e.g., Sophie Gerson, Esther Jackson, Helen Winter, Peggy Dennis, Alice Jerome, and Rose Perry, who served as executive secretary. Begun in 1951, they stressed the children's rights to be accepted in "progressive camps," in light of "a number of negative experiences last year"; this and more had placed the youngsters under "great stress." It was not unusual for them to be harassed by FBI agents or ostracized by their classmates. The committee had raised $2,000 from parties, $4,000 from a mailing, $1,000 from a mailing signed by Howard Fast. One mailing went to twenty thousand subscribers of the *Guardian* and what came back were dollar bills, three-fourths from outside of New York. There were expenses not only from sending youngsters to camp, but from visiting prisoners in Kansas, Indiana, and the other far-flung states where the defendants were warehoused. The not unfavorable dollar response was indicative of the chord that had been touched by the families' plight. However, they still felt obligated to add, "We are essentially a group of women, most of us women with children. . . . We are not a Communist Party committee."[50]

Of all the Smith Act victims, all except one had two children or less. Thus, in the summer of 1953, Hammett and Albert Kahn helped to organize the "United Summer Appeal for Children" with Anne Braden, Sidney Gluck, Maurice Sugar, Willard Uphaus, and Patterson joining in. This effort was highly appreciated, although inevitably a number of the children were turned off to radical politics as a result of their harrowing childhood experiences. At the same time, CRC was working tirelessly to win amnesty for the prisoners. W. E. B. Du Bois played a critical role in this. Initially he had been asked to testify in the Foley Square trial, but he demurred on the ground that a slick prosecutor might elicit damaging admissions from him on the need to use violence at times in political struggles. He did petition leaders of the United Nations about violations of the Universal Declaration of Human Rights ("Freedom of thought and conscience and religion" of Article 19, "Freedom of opinion and expression" of Article 20, and "Freedom of peaceful assembly and association" of Article 21) involved in the trial. He ruefully compared in public addresses the amnesty granted to the secessionists of the Civil War. Utilizing his wide net of international contacts that had helped to save him from a jail term in 1951, the NAACP founder sent an urgent letter abroad:

fifteen men and women are now in prison, most of them with five-year terms. Fifty-one others have been convicted, five are now on trial, and others are awaiting trial, making one hundred victims in all . . . (all because) they believe in the doctrines of Karl Marx.

This 1954 appeal was sent to high-ranking personalities in Prague, Belgium, the Soviet Union, China, Cuba (Nicolas Guillen), France (D'Arboussier), London (J. D. Bernal, George Padmore, Sylvia Pankhurst), Japan, Switzerland (Gunnar Myrdal) and World Peace Council leaders (Frederic Joliet-Curie, Jean Laffitte). Although this protest from abroad as usual helped the defendants' case, Du Bois was pessimistic in general:

> I have just received from the Soviet Union by word of mouth an answer to my letter. . . . [They] are considering it with sympathy but they do not think the time now ripe to take any action on the matter in the shape of a reply or protest. . . . I presume this expresses the attitude of a great many of the other persons to whom I addressed these letters.[51]

Apparent setbacks did not slow down CRC. The campaign for amnesty began as early as 1950, when Patterson asked Rev. Sandy Ray of Brooklyn to bring the issue before his convention. Said Patterson, amnesty had "nothing to do with pardon or clemency. It is an expression of dissatisfaction by the people of a policy of government. . . . Fighting for amnesty commits nobody to an ideology or partisan political position. . . . Amnesty does, however, raise sharply the question of the status of political prisoners." Patterson, typically, attempted to tie the issue to the plight of a "vast number of Negroes imprisoned" and "the struggle for the rights of the Negro people." This was followed by a number of concrete actions. Their pamphlet on the question made reference to President Harding's amnesty for Eugene Debs. They printed an amnesty poster, their 1953 calendar highlighted the issue, they drew up petitions, held conferences, published a newsletter, and trumpeted far and wide their endorsements, e.g., from seven members of the Israeli Knesset. The indefatigable activist Marion Bachrach was a driving force of the campaign, along with Carl Marzani. They were able to get sponsorships from the likes of Professor Fred Rodell of Yale, Eleanor Roosevelt, ACLU, etc. The first edition of Bachrach's pamphlet on amnesty in December 1952 sold twenty-five thousand copies. Amnesty committees were organized in Boston, St. Louis, Newark, Chicago, and elsewhere. Dr. Edward Barksy served as chairman of the national organization.[52]

CRC was truly akin to an understaffed fire department in a major metropolis beset by arsonists. As they scurried from one political fire to the next, trying to douse them, still another would break out. As they labored mightily to fight Smith Act prosecutions from New York to Honolulu, then to free those jailed, they had to divert further resources from the battle to fight the passage of anticommunist legislation initiated by Senators Pat McCarran of Nevada and Karl Mundt of North Dakota. Their legislation, eventually subsumed in the Internal Security Act of 1950 that was passed over Truman's veto, was considered a "blueprint for fascism" by many within CRC. As the major organization both spearheading the effort to defeat it and the most likely to be affected by it, this gargantuan battle imposed a heavy burden at a time of already depleted energy.

Some may have considered CRC's fears extravagant, but Thomas Emerson, the leading civil libertarian in the nation, agreed with them: "the McCarran Act establishes the legal foundation upon which a full-fledged police state could be erected." It required the registration of "Communist front" organizations, defined as one "substantially directed, dominated or controlled by a Communist organization" and "primarily operated for the purpose of giving aid and support to a Communist action organization, a Communist foreign government or the world Communist movement." It would establish a government bureaucracy to enforce this measure, which clearly had the extinction of CRC as a direct goal. According to the Yale professor, "None but a few hardy souls dare join or become leaders in an organization dealing with controversial issues." And therein lay the seeds of the "silent fifties." This demonic legislation also authorized the establishment of concentration camps. In essence, if one opposed the war in Korea, atomic weapons, Jim Crow, the persecution of leftists, and other related causes, there was a good chance of falling within the ambit of this broad bill. Political conformity was being legally enforced. Senator McCarran disagreed with this interpretation of the bill, of course. The fact that CRC was targeted however was indicated by his emphasizing Section 31 of his bill, which "takes cognizance of the recent practice employed by Communist party members and sympathizers of parading around and picketing federal courts," thereby targeting one of CRC's favored tactics.[53]

In the months leading up to passage of such bills, CRC was working overtime to defeat it. What was striking about these efforts was the breadth of support they were able to gather. The "Provisional Committee for Democratic Rights to Defeat Thomas-Rankin Committee on Un-American Legislation" was served by Len Goldsmith as executive secretary and CRC Bail Fund Trustee Robert Dunn as treasurer, but the co-chairs included Adam Clayton Powell, Jr., Emmanuel Celler, and Chet Hollified—congressmen all. The National Committee to Defeat the Mundt Bill included the ACLU, the NAACP, the American Jewish Congress, the American Jewish Committee, and many others and included as sponsors Thurman Arnold and Mark Van Doren, among others. There were local committees, particularly in New York. At this time, in 1948, aligning oneself with CRC apparently was not seen as a major faux pas, although there were tensions among the two thousand strong who converged on Washington in May 1948; the crowd indicated what was possible.[54]

Lobbying and testifying before Congress, perhaps because of the influence of their allies, constituted a major part of the CRC attempt to derail this repressive legislation. Goldsmith testified before the Senate Judiciary Committee on 28 May 1948. CRC's Washington representative, Thomas Buchanan, testified before the same committee and urged the chapters to send representatives to do the same. Patterson sought to testify on one configuration of this bill. When Joseph Cadden of the CRC staff testified on the bill before the Senate Judiciary Committee, he wound up apologizing to George Marshall; they asked if he were a Communist and he answered truthfully, then he realized his mistake, since CRC's policy was not to answer at all; then he resigned. During the summer of 1948 CRC went so far as to speak before the Platform Committee of the Democratic Convention on the bill. The bill sailed through Congress nonetheless, and at that point in October 1950 CRC attempted to obtain an injunction restraining the Subversive Activities Control Board from enforcing the final version of this bill, known as the McCarran Act. They sought four kinds of plaintiffs: organizations on the attorney general's subversive list, those not on the list, individuals in such organizations, and individuals not in such organizations. Plaintiffs included Patterson, Gurley Flynn, and trade unionist Hugh Bryson. Attorneys included Powe, John Coe, Clemens France, Charles Howard, F. F. Kane, and Grossman; Ben Margolis of L. A. rendered advice. There were problems, however, in getting this suit off the ground. France, a Rhode Island attorney, expressed misgivings about the suit. He stressed the need for "respectability," reaching out to Harvard's "Prof. Chaffee, et al." and others without "stigma" or CP "affiliation." He noted that the press stressed Flynn's role in the suit in order to "smear" it. CRC's suit was not broader, not for lack of trying, but because of the changing political atmosphere. CRC tried to bring in other counsel—and Abzug, Frank Donner, Arthur Kinoy, and Gloria Agrin joined in, but by the fall of 1950, the backlash of Korea had made many timorous.[55]

CRC's legal campaign was not successful in blocking the implementation of the McCarran Act and preventing its enforcement. But this did not cause them to fold their tents and drift off silently into the night. In 1951 they drew up for mass distribution a list of those who had voted for and against the bill, promising respectively retribution and reward. They set up an "appointment schedule" to press their concerns directly. They published a pamphlet of a speech by progressive attorney John Abt given at an anti-McCarran Act conference in New York in 1953. This was followed up in the spring of 1954 by a "People's Conference in Washington to Repeal the McCarran Act." They proposed local conferences, mass meetings, and lobbying. The statement at the opening session of the conference was made by Doxey Wilkerson, a report was made by Patterson, and the keynote speech was given by Abt. There were panels on youth, Blacks, labor, peace, and so forth. A central resolution concerned "The Negro People and the McCarran Act"; since the NAACP and other Black organizations opposed the act, it was resolved that this community would be a fruitful area for recruiting. This major conference, which took place in Black Washington at 9th and T

Streets, N. W., ignited the publication of fact sheets on right-wing congresspersons like Eastland and McClellan, zeroing in on their racist and anticommunist roles.[56]

Simultaneous with this conference, CRC tried to meet with the attorney general to discuss their concerns, but he refused. They published more literature, this time contrasting the decoration of Senator McCarran by the dictator of Spain, Francisco Franco, with the harsh treatment accorded the Veterans of the Abraham Lincoln Brigade. This offensive signalled that CRC was far from cowed by defeats. The introduction of the Communist Control Act of 1954 found them charging into the fray once more. This time CRC was not allowed to testify, but they pursued other channels of dissent. Quoting an unlikely source, *Life* magazine, one CRC–New Jersey pamphlet blasted the bill in no uncertain terms: "As a weapon against communism the law is somewhere between a mystery and a fraud." This bill, which would basically outlaw the CP, was opposed by the ACLU, the *St. Louis Post Dispatch*, the CIO, *New York Times*, and others. In order to mobilize the opposition, specific instructions were given to the chapters: "Every local civil rights group should have a complete list of every important organization and union in the area. Every local civil rights group should subscribe to the Negro and important trade union papers published in the state." But the correlation of political forces did not favor CRC, as is evidenced by the fact that this bipartisan legislation was pushed most heavily by liberals like Senator Hubert Humphrey, and the bill became law. Apparently, freedom of association pursuant to the First Amendment did not apply to certain sectors of the left.[57]

There were other straws in the wind that showed why CRC faced such an uphill battle. When the leader of the Lawyers Guild, Bob Silberstein, attempted to reach the usually reliable Zachariah Chafee for aid in preparing a brief for the NLG's SACB case, the eminent jurist ducked him: "He has not even acknowledged my communications," Silberstein acknowledged sadly to Patterson. Nonfeasance was bad enough, but the kind of misfeasance engaged in by Len Goldsmith proved to be absolutely debilitating. In late 1954 the *New York Times* reported that the former CRC leader had testified before the SACB. He alleged that twelve congressmen "initiated a coalition of organizations in 1948 that the Communist Party took over that same year under the name of the Civil Rights Congress." This "coalition helped to block the Mundt-Nixon anti-communist bill of 1948." Riddled with informants, besieged by the FBI by means of buggings and burglaries, tied up in protracted legal battles, and turned on by former allies, CRC's problems were compounded by its controversial defense of Communists and attacks against anticommunism. But through it all, CRC persisted, and to understand why, one need not look any further than to the personal example of William Patterson. His coming to the organization in 1948 marked a quantum leap in their productivity. He had the national stature, the passion, and the organizing skill to attract both the press and new adherents. This was positive for CRC, but it seemed to complicate life for their putative competitors, the NAACP and the ACLU, when Patterson helped to bring the case of the Trenton Six to national and international attention in 1949, a scant year after his arrival at the national office.[58]

5

A Northern Scottsboro: CRC, NAACP, and the ACLU in Conflict

The capital city of New Jersey, Trenton, was not as unlikely a place for a "Northern Style Lynching" as some may have imagined. The "Garden State" was one of the last states above the Mason-Dixon line to ban slavery. Nearby Princeton University was long known as the Ivy League school for Euro-Americans from the deep South and it thoughtfully provided dormitories for these gentlemen to house their slaves. Both the Ku Klux Klan and German American Bund had found the state congenial during the first half of the twentieth century. Trenton's Black ghetto was typical of most, with slum-like hovels, dilapidated row houses, garbage-strewn streets garnished with skyrocketing unemployment.

Trenton was the setting for one of the major antiracist battles of both CRC's tenure and U.S. history. It featured an extraordinary attempt to bar CRC lawyers from the defense team, fierce squabbling with the NAACP and the ACLU, and an attempt to turn the defendants against CRC. This dispute with the Association and the Union bubbled over to the Martinsville Seven fight and caused dislocations there as well. It all began on 27 January 1948, when William Horner, a second-hand merchandise dealer and his wife were attacked in their store at 11 A.M. He died without regaining consciousness. His wife spoke of three men who had come into the store, whom she described as white or light-skinned Blacks. Another witness spoke of one light-skinned Black's involvement. This difference was crucial, because after the men who came to be known as the "Trenton Six" were picked up, only one—James Thorpe—was light-skinned and he had only one arm and thereby would have been readily identifiable. These six men were tried by an all-white jury in fifty-five days, the longest trial in the history of New Jersey up to that point. They were given the death penalty. CRC entered the case in September 1948. On 1 August 1949, the New Jersey Supreme Court reversed the original decision and ordered a new trial. On 16 December 1949, CRC lawyers William Patterson, O. John Rogge, and future Rosenberg counsel Emmanuel Bloch were dismissed from the case by the judge, thus leaving the defendants without counsel. The case was fought throughout the state and federal courts on this ground and others and ultimately a number of the six were freed.[1]

But that is only the barest outline of a tangled skein of events. After the slaying of Horner, for weeks a "special fifteen-man motorized bandit squad, armed with tommy guns . . . patrol Negro districts, roughing up, questioning and arresting many Negroes. For two weeks there is a virtual curfew" in Black Trenton. On 6 February police arrested Collis English, twenty-three, a Navy veteran, on the complaint of his stepfather for having used his car without permission; this car was a two-door black sedan made by Ford and it was used to connect him to the killing, even though the getaway car there was a green four-door Plymouth sedan. On 7 February, McKinley Forest went to the police to find out what had happened; he was held. On 8 February, without a warrant, Ralph Cooper, Horace Wilson, and James Thorpe were detained and arrested. On 10 February John MacKenzie, Forest's nephew, was arrested at night at his home without a warrant. The defense alleged that forced confessions were taken. English's sister went to church groups and to the NAACP for help, without success. It seemed like just another frame-up of Black youths. The kind that had blighted Afro-American communities for decades without raising more than a murmur. If history had been a guide, these young Blacks would have been frying in the electric chair within months of their arrest.[2]

On 6 August as the verdict was read, a woman juror fainted, another collapsed. Then CRC entered the case. On 25 October 1949, the recently born *National Guardian*, replete with CRC allies, began an exposé. Then the British and French press picked up the story—a CRC trademark—and began stressing the racist aspects of the case. On 23 December, Dr. J. Minor Sullivan, whose testimony had helped convict the six, claimed that Wilson was innocent. At that juncture, Trenton Public Safety Director Andrew Duch expressed doubt about the convictions and said that the death penalty, in any case, was "extreme."[3]

There were other mysteries and contradictions that emerged in the case. Horace Wilson's boss had a work sheet that showed that he was at work when the incident occurred. The prosecutor, Mario Volpe, who had previously defended a club charged with racial discrimination, shielded exculpatory evidence from the defense. The defense claimed that the real culprit was Jerry Griswold, a colleague of Horner "Who (was) said to have been a lover of the woman who was living with Horner," but he "disappeared" and when he was found the police held him in custody. The twenty-volume record of the case is chock full of other omissions and enigmas, which partially explains why four of the defendants were freed. But Collis English and Ralph Cooper were again found guilty on 14 June 1951. This had been preceded by a trial in February that had been halted because of the sudden illness of the prosecutor. Many had felt that a great part of the defendants' problem was the obstreperous role played by CRC. The CRC had termed the case a "Northern Scottsboro," and perhaps sensing they were right, the judge probably recalled how different that Alabama case would have been if ILD had been ousted early on, so he booted out the CRC lawyers. If the traditional wisdom had held true, all problems should have cleared up when the NAACP-ACLU team headed by Raymond Pace Alexander took over, but their more decorous tactics were no more successful in freeing the defendants than that of CRC had been. The myrmidons of Jersey Justice had other ideas.[4]

But this had been clear from the start. After their first trial, which had been conducted in a conventional way and had culminated in August 1948 with a maximum penalty, was over, CRC lawyers Rogge, Clarence Talisman, Bloch, Patterson, Earl Dickerson, and Solomon Golat moved aggressively into the Supreme Court of New Jersey and won a unanimous reversal. While they geared up for the new trial, the judge ordered them off the case because they did what CRC usually did in cases of this type—they launched a mass campaign to win the case in the court of public opinion. Apparently the judge was unaccustomed to such bold tactics. He charged that they had violated Canons 1, 15, 16, 20, 22, 26, and 32 besides of the Rules Governing the Courts of the State of New Jersey; to wit, by "publicly" discussing the case, terming it a "lynching," and "a Northern Scottsboro case." According to the judge, they "deliberately distorted the facts . . . stirring up unfavorable public opinion." He raised questions, à la Scottsboro, about the funds they had collected for the defense. After observing mysteriously, "I have collected in various ways a large quantity of visual evidence of your activities," he went on to castigate their tactics:

> You have resorted to enormous billboards situated at strategic points on some of the main public highways of this state and in the State of New York . . . perhaps others. . . . You have tried the former case and the appeal in the public press and in every possible way that occurred to you which might serve your purposes, so that these defendants might, in your opinion, receive more favorable consideration than would be uniformly accorded any defendant who is tried in this court.

CRC attorneys could only congratulate the judge at that point in his astuteness in assessing their strategy, but he repaid their compliment by ousting them all from representing their three clients—English, Thorpe and Cooper.[5]

Obviously, as in the defense of Sacher, Crockett and the CP-Eleven counsel, CRC was again faced with one of the more serious threats the bar had encountered in the nation's long history. Would the Sixth Amendment remain a strange combination of hollow words on a scrap of paper if defendants could not choose their counsel of choice? Did lawyers check their First Amendment rights at the door once they joined the bar? In fighting this judicial fiat, CRC was once again not just fighting for their own interests but for the interests of civil liberties generally. With no hearing, and no charge of misconduct, the judge had deprived Rogge, Patterson, and Bloch from appearing in court. Other lawyers correctly saw this as a blow directed against them. The U.E. had an *amicus curiae* brief filed by Morton Stavis; Leonard Boudin filed one for Local 19 of the Social Service Employees Union, Ralph Shapiro did one for the Fur, Dressers, and Dyers Local 140, and in a highly unusual move during these hysterical times, George Gildea petitioned on behalf of the staid Mercer County Bar. They supported an injunction barring the judge from removing Patterson and the others. The federal court agreed. In "shepardizing" this case, one finds that this case continues to be cited and followed for the proposition that defendants should have their lawyer of choice. But that was not all. The court also held that 42 USC §1983 was an explicit statutory exception to the Anti-Injunction Act, 28 USC §2283, a major victory for civil rights forces.[6]

But reminiscent of later times, this time the judge figuratively stood in the courthouse door and still refused to allow CRC lawyers to work on the case. In addition to his other reservations, as CRC explained, he had sought their removal "after they subpoenaed a dissenting police report which would have finally proven the innocence of the six Negro defendants." Two of the other defendants, sensing the publicity and the victories that association with CRC brought, tried to retain these lawyers as well, thus complicating the picture. They said it was because "they brought us out of the death house." A "Northern Scottsboro" was coming closer to reality and the minions of the New Jersey courts were not desirous of such a result. CRC realized this by December 1950 after an involved and protracted struggle:

it became obvious that the strategy of the state of New Jersey was to refuse to let the case come to trail, make the issue the alleged conduct of the lawyers and then blame the CRC because the men remained in jail and the case did not come to trial.

At that point, CRC withdrew, and the second trial began on 5 March 1951. The prosecutor showed that the NAACP–ACLU alliance meant little to him as he "excluded all Jewish and Negro jurors."[7]

Times had changed since Scottsboro. Instead of simply trying to clap the defendants in jail indefinitely or in the grave as had happened in Alabama, the strategy here was more sophisticated, and, in a sense, designed to encompass cold-war liberal tastes. For the longest time the notion had been floated that had it not been for the noisy tactics of CRC, the defendants would have been freed much earlier; if more "civilized" counsel like the Association or Union came onto the scene, then matters could be expeditiously and humanely resolved with justice. Hence, the court ousted CRC and accepted the NAACP-ACLU and set up a laboratory test of the conventional wisdom.

This contretemps involving groups that should have been allies was unfortunate; but there is little doubt that the prevailing McCarthyite atmosphere and the ingrained anticommunism of CRC's would-be allies were the primary causes of the conflict that ensued. Because this triangular relationship was so stormy and so important to the evolution of civil rights and civil liberties during this difficult period, it is worthy of extended examination in order to gain better perspective on the first real explosion of the differences at stake during the Trenton Six case. CRC maintained massive files on the doings of the ACLU and watched their activities closely. Its outlook on both the ACLU and the NAACP was articulated by Patterson's frequent observation, announced for one of the last times at CRC's February 1955 National Leadership Conference: "Many times in the past, CRC has permitted sponsorship of a specific defense activity to pass from its hands to others so that broader forces and more people would become involved in that fight." The Trenton Six exemplified this strategy to an extent. In the halcyon days before the setting in of the political ice age, Donald McCoy and Richard T. Ruteten had been able to write:

> Not only was there considerable cooperation among Jewish and Negro groups, but also a certain amount with Japanese, Catholic and Mexican-American elements as well as with general organizations like the Marxist Civil Rights Congress . . . the ACLU, the American Veterans Committee. . . .[8]

The ACLU did file an *amicus* brief in the CP-Eleven case, pushed principally by NLG stalwart Osmond Fraenkel. But this action was not dispositive of their view on CRC. Time and time again ACLU leaders Clifford Forster and Roger Baldwin employed the imprecise, vague, and basically anti-civil libertarian term "Communist front" when referring to CRC, although they never took the time to define specifically what they meant. In May 1948 Baldwin went so far as to state that, "We are . . . opposed . . . to the concept of civil rights expressed by (CRC). . . . (it takes) the Communist line." Their lack of support for CRC's effort to save the life of Julius and Ethel Rosenberg, among others, showed better than words what that policy meant in practice. Thus, in June 1950 Baldwin told Patterson candidly, "I regret that I cannot make any personal statement concerning the contempt of Congress prisoners since this is a matter on which the ACLU takes an official position with which I believe you are familiar." Baldwin also initiated an unseemly effort to pressure the eminent Black NAACP attorney Charles Houston—who happened to be one of the few in their hierarchy who was anti-anticommunist—to cease working with CRC because that fruitful collaboration "causes confusion" and was "embarrassing." The principled Harvard Law graduate, Houston, was outraged and incensed and promptly resigned from the Union: "I have always had the slightly uncomfortable feeling that the ACLU takes causes only when they are safe, have publicity value and are without risk. Such a cautious role does not suit me." That abrupt departure of one of the few Blacks that the allegedly pro–civil rights ACLU had within its ranks did not shock them into dispensing with their anti-civil libertarian hostility to CRC.[9]

This sort of internal conflict was not unusual for the ACLU. Norman Thomas, while a "socialist" leader, and Corliss Lamont clashed repeatedly. The latter thought it "both unnecessary and undignified for the Civil Liberties Union to keep beating its breast and repeating that it is opposed to Fascist and Communist." Thomas' role was consistently controversial. He backed the government's loyalty program. He opposed the employment of Communist teachers. He supported the ousting of the Communists from the labor movement. This most influential ACLU Board member also would not "tolerate . . . a supporter of Tito on the board of ACLU."[10]

The Union's attitude soured CRC toward their potential ally. When North Carolina lawmakers were about to pass the Shreve-Regan bill in 1949 to outlaw the Communist Party, party leader Junius Scales asked the national office to try to move the Union in New York to action, because, "They seem totally dead around here." Months later Patterson had occasion to go public with their criticism when the ACLU issued their twenty-ninth annual report. In a blistering letter to the editor of the *Daily Compass*, Patterson thundered, "It is the opposite of a true picture that this report paints. . . . The ACLU report conceals the major foe of American democracy. It will but confuse the people further."[11]

But that was a mere tempestuous fancy compared to what erupted in December 1949. It began a month earlier when Elizabeth Allen of Britain's National Council for Civil Liberties informed Patterson that she had received a letter from Baldwin who was highly upset about NCCL, because it "evidently accepts the cooperation of Communists (which) is a position contrary not only to that taken by his own organization but by all agencies in the United States not under Communist control or influence." In justification, Baldwin was alleged to have said, "as Czechoslovakia is now a single party state, denying the basic principle of civil liberties by barring all opposition parties, it could hardly be expected that non-partisan agencies devoted to that principle would attend a conference there." This was in reference to the International Congress on Human Rights in Prague. Patterson was outraged by this protest on the part of Baldwin and pointed out that Baldwin's concern did not extend to taking an interest in his government's rehabilitation of Nazi leaders in the western zone of Germany, contrary to the recently concluded Yalta and Potsdam agreements: "The press, however, stated several days ago that he and Arthur Garfield Hays were reporting to the State Department on the matter of Civil Rights in Germany. I cite this simply to show where he stands. . . . If Baldwin wants to be left behind, so be it." The ACLU leader wound up going to the conference, but this dispute did not improve his relationship with CRC.[12]

As time wore on, the CRC–ACLU tie eroded correspondingly. Patterson sent Patrick Malin of the Union a memo concerning Australian unions and liberals fighting the effort to dissolve the Communist Party of that continental nation; they had proved successful and the general civil liberties atmosphere had improved, according to Patterson, and this was something the ACLU should consider. Apparently, Malin was not interested. In July 1951, as CRC was in the midst of fighting the Smith Act and attempting to liberate the Trenton defendants, Patterson found time to criticize the characterization of CRC in a "directory" that the ACLU had published: "you speak of it as a 'so-called front agency.' . . nowhere else do I find such a characterization, not even where the Workers Defense League is concerned." But the WDL, as Patterson surely realized, was of a quasi-Trotskyite orientation and liberals generally found this anti-Soviet "leftism" more congenial. Finally it seemed that CRC simply wrote off the ACLU. Grossman directed Truehaft, "I would not contact the ACLU for a number of reasons including their inability to be helpful." But this was not a situation that CRC found pleasing, as Grossman glumly informed Anne Shore in mid-1953: ". . . There never were so many forces speaking out against McCarthyism as at the moment, but all are acting more or less individualistically." This was true of the ACLU, which "nationally will not give leadership."[13]

The relationship between CRC and the NAACP was much more complicated and entangled and involved. Walter White of the NAACP served on the board of the ACLU also and reinforced the ACLU predisposition to disregard the branches and affiliates: "[The Board's] position is legally that of the Harvard Board of Overseers or to take a more sublime example, the Supreme Court. . . . (our) final judgments are not subject to amendment or debate"; this after rumblings came in from the ACLU grassroots about the anticommunist tilt of the national leadership. The affluent progressive Corliss Lamont was called by White," our distinguished colleague, the Senator from North Korea," as he sought to oust him from the ACLU board. "The time has come for a crackdown," said White, otherwise "the triumphant fellow-traveller majority will in a few years move to a position indistinguishable from that of the Civil Rights Congress. . . ."[14] Because of CRC's penchant for taking on cases involving brutal racism, it was inevitable that their path would cross that of the NAACP. J. Edgar Hoover had warned about the Communists: "special emphasis is placed by the party on penetrating the major Negro protest and improvement associations." And Communist leaders, many of whom were defended by or were members of CRC, certainly did little to dispel his concern about their intentions of influencing the NAACP.

But over time there was something of an evolution of this conflict between the two organizations. In the late 1940s the party's attack on NAACP leadership was much stronger than it became in subsequent years. In 1949 Communist leader Pettis Perry talked about how "Negro reformist and pro-imperialist elements had to give heed to the rising clamor and demands of the membership for a serious fight for civil rights." He denounced Walter White and his ilk: "Our Negro comrades have a special responsibility to unmask these scoundrels in the eyes of the Negro masses." Still he supported an alliance with the Association irrespective of the posture of the "national leadership" and noted past CRC–NAACP collaborations "in defense of Negro people's rights." In February 1950, while observing approvingly that "between 90 and 95 percent of this [NAACP] membership had been from the Negro workers," Edward Strong pointed out that half that membership had left between 1947–49, which was attributed to their "reformist" leadership and ties to "Wall Street." But he pointed to hopeful signs, like the "refusal of many sections of the (NAACP) to accept the Wilkins edict excluding left progressive unions from the civil rights mobilization," while carping at the "failure of the progressive movement generally to participate sufficiently in the activities undertaken by the NAACP."[15]

By August 1955 Doxey Wilkerson was humming a slightly different tune in his analysis of the forty-sixth NAACP convention. While there was "very little discussion at Atlantic City of the Cold War erosion of the Bill of Rights or of the struggle for peace . . . [and they were] silent . . . on . . . the Smith Act, the McCarran Internal Security Act of 1950, and the Communist Control Act of 1954 . . . [an] anti-communist resolution [was] again adopted." There was hope in the fact that the McCarran-Walter Immigration Act was blasted, along with the use of "paid professional informers and aspects of the Federal Security-Loyalty Program too." Furthermore, "the Proceedings of this convention were markedly free of redbaiting," Bandung was praised, while the militaristic "positions of strength" policy was backed. One of the more perceptive class analyses of the NAACP was done by Frederick Hastings (allegedly the pen name of Henry Winston) in the Communist journal, *Political Affairs.* He spoke of the two-fold nature of the petit-bourgeois NAACP leadership, which needed a movement in order to win concessions for itself. Therefore, "We must therefore think of unity with many forces who for years have been our ideological and even political foes." This mellowing reflected something of an evolution in the Communists' view of the Association, which was reflected to an extent within CRC.[16]

In the early days particularly there was some cooperation between the two civil rights' giants. Len Goldsmith reported in 1948 that "We have succeeded in affiliating NAACP groups to CRC in Louisiana and are in the process in Texas." Lulu White, the head of the NAACP–Houston branch served the CRC branch there in 1946 as co-chair. Evidently, this did not stir much concern in Association offices until 1947, when, after being querried directly by J. Edgar Hoover, Thurgood Marshall sharply inquired about the sharing of offices and leadership between the two organizations. White responded apologetically, but the message was clear and this promising center-left unity dissolved quickly.[17]

This dissolution did not stem the concern about the matter in the NAACP national office. 1949 saw a flap about cooperation between the two in Miami, New Orleans, Philadelphia, and San Francisco. Wilkins claimed that the CRC and CP had "damn near wrecked" the Philadelphia branch and "completely wrecked" the one in San Francisco, although he was not thorough enough to supply details. No doubt the tremendous pressure from the right placed on the Association accelerated their repudiation of CRC. By 1952 NAACP leader Gloster Current was warning the Norfolk branch against sponsoring an affair featuring CRC stalwart Paul Robeson: "Certainly it does not seem wise to sponsor a concert with such a controversial figure."[18]

The CRC–NAACP connection had not always been so star-crossed. They participated together in the meeting on the New York State Law Against Discrimination in Employment, along with the Urban League. When Black leaders were under siege in Cairo, Illinois, after attacking Jim Crow there, CRC was one of the first to come to their defense. But after the passage of the monumental 1950 NAACP resolution on anticommunism, which fundamentally called for a purge, the collaboration between the two groups had to be shrouded. Thus, when Patterson was planning a trip to Richmond in December 1950 to organize against racist repression, he was informed of the necessary confidentiality of the mission by a local supporter: "(we) discussed this with an NAACP board member who has been pretty friendly with us and he said that while he couldn't openly sponsor your visit he would be glad to come to the dinner and the informal house (gathering)."

In 1952 CRC joined the Association in winning support for Thomas Edwards, a Black sugar refinery worker on death row for a "murder frame-up." He won a commutation from the governor after having been convicted of murdering two whites, after having been held "incommunicado" and "beaten repeatedly" to extract a confession. Another successful—and telling—collaboration was the case of Samuel Jordan, a twenty-one-year-old Afro-American from Bayonne, New Jersey, fighting extradition to Georgia. After joint pressure from the sometime allies, for the third time in New Jersey history the governor revoked his scheduled extradition. Jordan, a person with standing and in a position to comment, penned words that could have been the epitaph for CRC–NAACP collaboration. He gave thanks "especially the cooperation of the NAACP and the Civil Rights Congress. If they continue to work together, we can win more such victories."[19]

This kind of center-left unity produced positive results, but, as had happened in relation to the ACLU, the McCarthyite atmosphere and the ingrained anticommunism of the leadership of the NAACP destroyed this favorable eventuality. The fact that the NAACP could have perceived CRC as a "threat" in terms of membership dues, grants, and popularity cannot be discounted either, particularly because for a while CRC was looked on quite favorably by many Blacks. The *Jackson Advocate* truly was not alone when it editorialized, "Most Negroes doubtlessly have developed some feeling of appreciation for the efforts of the Civil Rights Congress." Nor was it surprising that the *Ebony-Jet* magazine empire, when obtaining information on organizations "working to promote the Negro to class 'A' citizenship" would ask CRC to fill out their "questionnaire." But more symptomatic of the developing trend was the fact that after Grossman had worked with a Bob Ellis on an article of interest to CRC, Ellis quickly became "formerly of Ebony magazine," when they "realized it was too hot for them and they refused to print it. Soon after they fired him."[20]

There was most certainly pressure put on the Association to conform to the current fashion, but some of their behavior far exceeded circumspection. After pushing the passage of their anticommunist resolution in 1950, Walter White sent a "Dear Ed" missive to Edward Scheidt, "Special Agent in Charge" of the New York FBI office. He sent copies of articles and letters from Thurgood Marshall to reassure Scheidt that the NAACP "will in no fashion whatever work with the Civil Rights Congress." There was much correspondence and many meetings between White and this agency, but his letter of 13 June 1951 to J. Edgar Hoover represented a zenith—or nadir—of their cooperation. He accused CRC of raising $300,000 for a case, but of spending only half of it; he enclosed what he considered to be documentation of this inflammatory charge, adding conspiratorially, "I ask you to treat (it) as confidential." He linked this accusation to past charges that the *Daily Worker* allegedly ripped off funds from the Scottsboro defendants for "printing presses." White envisioned criminal charges being lodged against CRC. Despite this chummy relationship with the Bureau, by 1953 White was whining about the FBI's treatment of civil rights cases. His limp prostration before the agency did not pay off by lessening FBI aggressiveness towards NAACP interests; indeed by weakening a principal bulwark against the right—CRC—he simply sowed the seeds of his own bitter crop.[21]

The Association was not disillusioned sufficiently to change course, however. After White had agreed to participate in a forum sponsored by the Emergency Civil Liberties Committee, he was forced out after Irving Kristol of the CIA-backed American Committee for Cultural Freedom warned that like CRC, this group, was "an outright Communist front." White meekly withdrew. Not adverse to hitting an opponent when he was down on the canvas, in 1955, Seattle–NAACP leader James McIver testified at a Subversive Activities Control Board hearing denouncing CRC.[22]

As this example showed, there was virtual guerilla warfare taking place across the nation between NAACP and CRC chapters. Wilkins signalled the break-up of their past collaboration by warning the branches not to "cooperate in any movement whatsoever" with CRC or CP. Their anticommunist resolution had caused confusion and had been used to settle old scores by dragging out red charges and conveniently handing a club to Association detractors. The fact that they had to amend the resolution in 1951 to add, "any person excluded from the branch . . . has a right of appeal to the Board and that mere criticism of the local or national officials of the NAACP is not alone and of itself ground for exclusion or rejection," was indicative of the problems encountered.[23]

CRC's relations with the NAACP were difficult and this tendency accelerated after 1950. That year found John Starks of CRC–St. Louis alleging that Stuart Parker, president of the Missouri–NAACP, "connived in the indictment of Jake Bradford," a Black charged with the rape of a white woman. But after CRC sent observers to the scene in Columbia, Missouri, a chagrined Parker "switched his position and declared (Bradford) innocent." Bradford was found guilty, received five years, and CRC set up a defense committee—including Parker. This trend was continued in 1951 in southern California. The CRC there had set up a "Citizens Committee for Defense of Bucky Walker," protesting yet another frame-up and held a large meeting. The NAACP chapter decided to "visit leading Negro people of Riverside, urging them not to attend," since the campaign was "red-inspired." The sabotage did not prevent 750 people from jamming the hall and contributing $500.[24]

Detroit was the home of one of the more vibrant CRC and NAACP chapters, so it should not have been deemed extraordinary that some of the sharpest confrontations took place there. Kindling one hot controversy was a case in the summer of 1951 involving the Brothers Market. They ousted a Black youth from the premises, breaking his hip in the process. Lining up on one side was CRC attorney Ernest Goodman, representing the youth; representing the store was an attorney quite close to the NAACP, Wade McCree. This division was symbolic of what happened during that era. The NAACP, denigrating CRC, announced contrarily that it was "not authorizing pickets, mass meetings or other demonstrations." Strangely, the Association was equally critical of a CRC pledge card stating, "I pledge not to buy anything at Kresge's or Neisner's dime stores as long as they continue to discriminate in the hiring of salesgirls."[25]

San Francisco was the home of a strong CRC chapter and the prospect of the NAACP losing some of its luster in competition with the congress. NAACP operative Franklin Williams, later under fire in the 1960s after having been accused of having had a hand in overthrowing Kwame Nkrumah in Ghana, slyly reported on his disrupting of CRC activities in 1954: "We broke up one such front group here a few months ago by taking the initiative and we shall continue to do so." He attached a flyer they produced: "Keep Your Eyes Wide Open—Don't Get Sucked In! These groups and organizations are attempting to mislead the Negro Community. . . . Double check before you sign petitions, attend meetings, serve on 'Defense' committees. . . ." CRC was displayed prominently on the black-list.[26]

NAACP leaders were not shy about going public with their adverse view of CRC. AT the Forty-Second Annual Convention of the NAACP in Atlanta in July 1951, Walter White at the closing session showed his worry about growing CRC influence, increased by the McGee, Trenton, Ingram, and Martinsville cases, by devoting time to their activity in his address:

> When next Communists or anyone else come to you for funds to "save Willie McGee" ask them these question: Does your organization account to the public through a certified public accountant's audit of all monies raised and expended? What is your record of success of failure in such cases? Is your purpose honestly to save Negroes from injustice or is it to show up and ridicule American judicial processes? Is the master you serve freedom and democracy or some other form of government or ideology.

These were rehashed and unsubstantiated charges traditionally hurled at CRC. But as his book *How Far The Promised Land* showed, the Black masses found it hard to swallow whole White's offering and the growing influence of the left scared him to no end. He was not alone. Herbert Hill, who was at the highest level of the association leadership, was even more harsh. He went so far as to call left organizations like CRC and the CP "one of the Negro's implacable enemies in his fight." They also were hostile to those like Earl Dickerson, who cooperated with CRC; he was not renominated to the NAACP Board. Then they sought, in the words of top NAACP attorney William Ming, to "[win] him away from his present affiliations, a task which has to be undertaken in my judgment." Thurgood Marshall concurred.[27]

The Association carried through on their sectarianism by banning CRC from a number of civil rights mobilizations and related gatherings held in Washington, D.C., in 1950. Kenneth O'Reilly has conceded that Wilkins "red-baited" in barring the Congress; to show his fealty he sent a copy of his angry note to Truman aide Clark Clifford; this was after their friends in the FBI had briefed the White House about an "alleged" CRC and CP plan "to infiltrate" the event. Communist leader Pettis Perry pointed out that "out of 800 people screened, there were probably not over two or three dozen Communist and left forces"; that is to say, in their brisk ferreting process, inevitably the NAACP swept out non-Communist allies with others, to their detriment. And at that the Communist forces still participated; "categorically yes" was Perry's defiant reply. Early on Wilkins had informed Dr. Carlton Goodlett of the NAACP Bay Area leadership and a CRC ally that CRC was "definitely not on [the] list of approved organizations with which [the] Association cooperates." Marshall rationalized this denial of equal protection to CRC by pointing to their "disgusting to say the least" behavior in the Trenton and Martinsville cases; he contended that CRC was "conspicuous by your absence in the fight against segregation, "which revealed either an abominable ignorance or terrible bias. Most of the voluminous correspondence from CRC was marked "file no reply."[28]

Naturally, CRC leaders were none too pleased with this turn of events. Accurately Goldsmith stated that "locally there [was] no problem" in working with the NAACP. . . . Our feeling is that White should be by-passed and that someone like Thurgood Marshall might be (contacted)." This was overly optimistic. Patterson felt compelled to denounce Wilkins' "dogmatic brushing aside of our offers of cooperation." Turning their back on a militant national organization like CRC with one hundred chapters, a national network of more than capable lawyers, and the backing of luminaries like Du Bois and Robeson was somewhat audacious.[29]

The January mobilization had 4,017 delegates, an impressive showing indeed, with the NAACP providing 2,764, the American Jewish Congress 532, and the CIO 380. Patterson tried to be evenhanded in assessing this historic gathering, from which his organization was excluded:

> The Mobilization was characterized by the expressed will of its rank and file for struggle and the contempt which it had for the policy instituted by the NAACP top leadership and carried out by the tools of Murray, Carey and Reuther of the CIO. Greater possibilities than ever now exist of the broadest possible united front with NAACP branches everywhere. In all of our activities they must be specifically invited to participate, and especially where amicus briefs can be filed this matter must be discussed with them.

Cooperation with NAACP chapters continued. It was not unusual when their chapter in Cuthbert, Georgia, sent $5 to CRC "to help you in your fight for the cause of Civil Rights." It was equally typical when in the same year, 1951, Patterson was forced to reprove White for excluding CRC from another event, even though the CRC leader felt that inviting his organization "will fill the enemy with disarray."[30]

Despite these frequent rebuffs, CRC in general and Patterson personally never relented from seeking to unify efforts with the NAACP. When he discovered that they were to be barred from the Washington mobilization, Patterson quickly drafted an "open letter" to the NAACP, extending a "fraternal hand." A failure to invite Robeson, Marcantonio, and the others "would be inconsistent with your own call for unity. In effect, it would hinder the realization of the program your committee has outlined." He sharply questioned their incessant redbaiting. This "open letter" was the first of a number from CRC to the Association. In February 1952 they took out a full-page ad in the *Washington Afro-American* and a number of other papers consisting of an open letter from Patterson to Walter White. Basically it was a call for unity. Patterson desired that this letter be gotten out as a pamphlet in order to popularize the theme. Arthur McPhaul of Detroit echoed many when he said, "It made quite an impact here and I know Chicago felt it, too. In my opinion it has considerable vitality."[31]

This call for unity did not negate in CRC's view the need to criticize when it was necessary. In 1949 Patterson took White to task for his widely circulated statement that changing from black skin to white by chemical means would solve the problem of Jim Crow. "Insulting and degrading . . . laughable . . . a grievous insult" were just a few of the harpoons launched. About that same time CRC again blasted the NAACP leadership, this time about the racist Groveland, Florida, massacre. In a "Dear Henry" letter, Patterson questioned the public relations director of the NAACP for his political analysis, which saw the case as an "accident." Riposted Patterson, "These things do not just happen." With an inflexible upper lip virtually visible, Moon replied cooly, "Dear Pat . . . Thank you for your letter . . . with your interesting—but not unanticipated—commentary on the course of justice in the United States in 1951." Patterson's analysis was shared with the NAACP and it reflected his constant themes:

> What is involved in that case? Jim Crow . . . by government is involved. Will NAACP make that clear? Will they challenge Jim Crow as a policy of government? Will they expose the fascist character of government Jim Crow. . . . I would say imperialism is involved. . . . Will the NAACP top leaders say that?

"We are the only ones who will do that," averred Patterson confidently.[32]

This questioning was not allowed to overshadow the crying need for unity. At the same time that Patterson was scorning their position on Groveland, he sternly told a close ally at the *Arkansas State Press*, "By no stretch of the imagination could I, a Negro, come out in opposition to the NAACP." He told another press critic at the *Denver Star* that he objected to their printing "correspondence between myself and Mr. Roy Wilkins. . . . you quoted his entire letter and carried not even an excerpt from my answer to it." These exchanges may have been considered ambiguous, but that could not have been said after an NAACP leader in Florida, Harry Moore, was slain by assassins, along with his wife. CRC allies like Rev. Kenneth Riply Forbes and Charlotta Bass flew to the funeral; the CRC leadership quickly called for a thorough search for their killers and for speedy justice. Then CRC leader Angie Dickerson met with the governor to press such issues and reportedly was "received most cordially." Similar regret was placed when their longtime antagonist Walter White passed away in 1955. "A great loss to the front of civil rights," was their considered opinion.[33]

Perhaps CRC's position in relation to the NAACP appeared contradictory and ambiguous; if so, it reflected a rapidly shifting situation. For example, one NAACP top lawyer, Charles Houston, before his untimely and premature death, lacked the visceral anticommunism that characterized so many of his colleagues; earlier, he had worked with the ILD on the Scottsboro trial, in contrast to White. In 1950, while these same colleagues were running for cover, he issued a strong statement in support of Harry Sacher in his fight against contempt charges. On the other hand, Patterson judged critically White's lockjaw when it came to speaking out on the "increasing victimization of Negro federal employees" under Truman's loyalty order. Nor was Patterson pleased when Roy Wilkins refused to cooperate with Black labor leader Cleveland Robinson, a future coordinator of the 1963 historic March on Washington, because he was working with CRC.[34]

This checkerboard pattern of both amity and enmity was reflected in their positions on specific questions. CRC was highly critical of the report of the President's Committee on Civil Rights, which they saw correctly as a tool to undermine the Progressive Party and the left generally, including CRC. The Association disagreed. CRC was livid when their ally Du Bois was bounced out of a top NAACP post as the election of 1948 approached. But CRC sympathized with NAACP anger at the scuttling of the Fair Employment Practices Committee, and symbolic of the overall relationship, many NAACP branches helped out with the McGee case and others. Similarly, when the NAACP's Clarendon School case was won at the federal court level in 1951 as a run-up to *Brown v. Board*, Patterson hailed the victory as of "very great importance." He felt that it "blasted to high heaven . . . the theory of gradualism." When *Brown* was won, NAACP attorney George Hays received quick congratulations from Patterson, who expressed the attitude of many toward the NAACP when he claimed, "Our people should act in such a way as to show that we not only have no animosity toward this organization but understand the historic necessity to build it at the moment."[35]

This checkerboard pattern was also evident in CRC's relations with other potential allies. There was a serious clash with Prof. Fred Rodell of Yale, who took an ACLU-style approach toward CRC. He looked askance at their "intellectual dishonesty" and "selectivity" in its defense of civil rights: "you are only for the civil rights of Communists, near-Communists and Negroes." What of the controversial First Amendment Terminiello case, he asked, where was CRC? He claimed that CRC's disagreement with ACLU's "genuine espousal of civil liberties, for all, was the prime reason" for starting CRC. Certainly CRC disagreed with the ACLU posture in such cases as *Beauharnais v. Illinois*, where the latter had submitted a brief on behalf of a white man convicted for distributing on the streets of Chicago "anti-Negro leaflets" of the "White Circle League of America" that called on whites to "preserve and protect white neighborhoods." Patterson did not spare Rodell in responding. Rodell connected his line to defense of the klan and the Nazis, while Patterson countered, "I look forward to the outlawing of . . . malignant racism and anti-Semitism." Engaging in verbal one-upmanship, Rodell in reply modestly accused him of "sheer stupidity" and lashed out: "the greatest threat to liberty . . . comes not from the fascists or Nazis but from their fellow dictators on the so-called Left." Having smoked him out, Patterson charged "your letter exuded not only the odor of white supremacy . . . [but was] blatantly arrogant." This dispute crystallized a lingering fissure between CRC and some of their potential allies in the civil liberties struggle.[36]

Such was the background of CRC's often tempestuous relations with the NAACP and the ACLU. (The fact that the ACLU disagreed with the NAACP's campaign against "Amos 'n' Andy" showed why CRC had to differentiate between the two.) It is necessary to comprehend fully the frequently bitter disagreements between the organizations over the Trenton Six. In November 1948, when Clifford Forster, Acting Director of the ACLU, was contacted by Robert Bush of the local ACLU affiliate over the correct posture to take on this case, he was hesitant: "I don't find that there is any substantial basis to assume that racial prejudice has played any part in this case. . . . it would appear that the authorities have leaned over backwards." Of course he flip-flopped after the case became a cause célèbre, but this initial insouciance CRC considered outrageous. Bush was equally skeptical: "One should take with a grain of salt assertions by the Civil Rights Congress." When a CRC lawyer informed Forster that the "confession (was) secured under . . . duress" and that this was an "important . . . civil rights" issue, Forster still dissented: "no attempt was made to railroad the defendants" was his reassuring reply. Golat was dumbfounded: "even drugs were used to exact the confessions," not to mention the "curfew" and "show of force" by police.[37]

After Baldwin had been deluged with correspondence, early in 1949, the ACLU desired to enter the case on the issues of the state holding back evidence and the due process violation of holding defendants for days before taking them to a judge. But like Judge Hutchinson, ACLU lawyer Herbert Levy objected to the CRC's out-of-court procedures: "public protests of a trial . . . do more harm than good inasmuch as the questions involved are purely legal ones." Patterson was avowedly "amazed" that the Union would claim that "no evidence of racial discrimination appears in the record," and he quoted liberally to prove his point. Levy was unmoved in the face of many inquiries: "I would advise against the making of public protests." Patterson was irate. He castigated Baldwin because of their "attacks" on CRC after they took up an interest in the case, and he alleged that they were claiming undue credit: "it is not enough to say that one has aided a cause because one files a brief." Despite massive evidence to the contrary, Levy was still contending that racism was not involved in the case. Worse, his anti–CRC posture had not receded one iota: "Sometime ago, we did agree to use our best efforts to provide counsel . . . if the Civil Rights Congress and their attorneys withdrew from the case." This was the pressure generated, in league with the judge, on the CRC and the defendants to ensure that a true "Northern Scottsboro" did not ensue.[38]

The defendants' eventual co-counsel in the case, the NAACP, also acted in a manner not inconsistent with their history with CRC. They manifested barely disguised hostility toward CRC, leavened with liberal doses of anti-communism. The NAACP regional conference in the spring of 1949 in South Bend, Indiana was symbolic in a sense, of their relationship to CRC. There was "no support outside one or two on the 12" but the Trenton Six received support; CRC forces in the area disputed Patterson's notion of NAACP "unconscious sabotage" of the Trenton Six effort there, although perhaps what was at issue was not their lack of interest but what kind of interest was being displayed. Unlike the ACLU, however—and this was one reason why CRC found that struggling to cooperate with the NAACP was more fruitful—the association did not have to be convinced that there was racism involved in this case. Thurgood Marshall implicitly recognized this, otherwise they would not have gotten involved. But like the ACLU, their concern was anticommunism. In early 1949 Patterson had to deal with Marshall's contention that at a Newark meeting on the case, the CRC leader had accused the NAACP of not desiring to work with "pink" or "red" groups. There was truth to this, as their history demonstrated, but Patterson moved to allay Marshall's concern so as not to give him a convenient tool of disunity:

I am sincerely sorry to say that your informant was not entirely correct. At the Newark meeting . . . I paid tribute to the NAACP. . . . I paid tribute to Miss Perry. . . . The things I said were neither irresponsible, unwarranted nor unjustified, nor were they in any manner to be construed as an attack upon the NAACP. . . . I am extremely pleased to hear that you will remain in the case of the Trenton Six if only with a brief *amicus curia*.

But this case was getting tons of publicity and the Black masses wanted to know why the NAACP was not playing a leading role; Marshall was searching for larger fish than a mere *amicus* brief. Patterson expressed readiness to work with them on "any case" and added a final sophisticated twist: "Finally, I did not deal with the Trenton Six from the standpoint of any political differences which exist between myself and the leaders of the NAACP. I dealt solely with the attitude of certain leaders of the NAACP towards the Trenton Six."[39]

But after the combined force of the judge, the ACLU, and the NAACP had succeeded in pushing CRC off the case, Patterson was not so charitable:

(NAACP) leadership is making the CRC and its mass activities the main danger rather than the state. . . . Their Clifford Moore, one of the leading attorneys . . . has become a bulwark of strength for the prosecution. His attacks on the CRC in open court are a daily occurrence . . . many of the top leaders of the NAACP (are) agents of the imperialist bourgeoisie and have completely deserted the path of struggle.

"Fierce attacks" by Raymond Pace Alexander were also singled out for criticism. Patterson was not talking behind their back, bringing his accusations directly to James Imbrie, chair of the Joint Committee to Secure a Fair Trial for the Trenton Six, a NAACP–ACLU "front": "You said that your new committee took over the defense of the innocent Trenton Six from a 'communist controlled' organization."

He censured this "red-baiting." Patterson said that he went to Marshall and asked him to bring Raymond Pace Alexander into the case, then he met with Alexander himself: "if attacks have to be made against someone in the case of these innocent men, why can they not be directed against those guilty of that heinous crime of government." Harold Ridenour of the Montana Farmers Union asked the Joint Committee the same question.[40]

This Joint Committee also included Prof. Edward Corwin of Princeton, Bishop Francis McConnell of the Episcopal Church, Thurgood Marshall and Arthur Garfield Hays of the ACLU. Despite the fact that it was expected that their presence would somehow make justice pop up, that was not the case and the controversy dragged on. Patterson remained indignant. He felt that he had left Alexander "with a legal case which a child could win, if that child was desirous of making the fight that is necessary against a government and its agents who have perpetuated one of the most colossal frame-ups." Union leader David Dubinsky sang a different tune. After terming CRC the "legal arm of the Communist Party," he pitched a jeremiad: "The defendants were told 'if you don't take our help, you will burn.' The net result was to discourage all legitimate help from townspeople and interested citizens. . . . After many months of hysterical propagandizing and legal failure, the Communists pulled out of the case." Inevitably, this one-sided view became popular opinion, further undermining CRC's reputation. And like Wilkins, Dubinsky added the familiar point that the six should be freed so that communism could be better fought.[41]

While CRC and their erstwhile allies were engaged in internecine battle, the defendants—young Black workers, some with minimal education—languished in dank prison cells. At the same time, CRC was undergoing its own internal difficulties with the mercurial O. John Rogge, one of their own lawyers assigned to the case. As the political mercury dropped, he was moving on the spectrum from left to right. At first this inter-CRC conflict was clothed in a disagreement over funds: "For some reason or other, I have been unable to get across the idea that a lawyer also has overhead and has to be able to live." He declared that he had spent almost all of his time on CRC matters, like the case of the six and that of Harold Christoffel. But soon after that he was in court testifying as the main government witness in the attempt to convict Du Bois of being agent of an unnamed foreign power.[42]

Naturally Rogge left the case. But that did not halt the stampede of the defendants to CRC. Horace Wilson exclaimed truthfully that "they're the lawyers who brought us out of that death house. We are going to stick together till we're all free." Five of the six were with CRC at this point and they authorized Patterson "to enlist the aid of (your) organization, its friends, and supporters in any steps that it may deem necessary and wise in the conduct of that retrial and (our) defense." Hence, limited education did not prevent them from correctly assessing their interests. Like McGee, the defendants had the benefit of tireless women relatives campaigning on their behalf. In the Mississippian's case, it had been his wife and mother, and the case of the six brought forward Bessie Mitchell, the sister of English, who logged thousands of miles speaking out and galvanizing interest in the case. Coincidentally, English was one of the last defendants freed. With retribution apparently in mind, the state refused to allow him to go out of state for an operation, although it was deemed necessary to do so. English was suffering from a severe heart condition, and actually had had eight heart attacks; the stress of persecution did not ameliorate his condition. Four of the six were freed during the second trial, while he and Ralph Cooper received life terms. Before the third trial was consummated, English died. As Patterson claimed, these cases—even given the adverse conditions of racism and the red scare— could be won. Among other things, the prosecutor had extorted confessions, coached key witnesses, suppressed vital evidence, and made blatant appeals to bigotry and prejudice. The Mayor of Trenton was a "one-time Christian Fronter" and helped to whip up the negative environment. Finally in 1953 Ralph Cooper, the last remaining victim of the frame-up, pleaded "no defense" and was freed; in return he "placed all of the (six) in the store at the time of the alleged murder," although the state's only witness had claimed that "Cooper (himself) was not in the store."[43]

The tactics of winning the case in the court of public opinion were what the judge and the NAACP–ACLU alliance objected to, though light is a disinfectant when it comes to exposing and cleansing a frame-up. They objected as well to the public and visible role of the reviled Communist Party in the case. Henry Winston, organizational secretary of the Communist party, in a widely circulated "Dear Comrades" letter, suggested that they buy CRC literature on the case and spark a "national movement" to free them. The *Daily Worker* covered the case avidly and was not adverse to editorializing for the victims' freedom. Certainly the judge and the "liberal" lawyers must have been disquieted when Patterson reciprocated by sending a "Dear Friend" letter about the Trenton Six that was even more widely circulated:

One political party has openly and clearly expressed itself in reaction to the Trenton Six. . . . The Civil Rights Congress is deeply grateful for this statement issued by the Communist Party. I ask you to utilize it in every possible respect. Particularly must you show the relation of the attack upon the Negro people to the trial of the 12 Communist leaders.

Probably these same forces were not assuaged by the fact that a favorable reference was also made to the role of the Progressive Party. But Patterson remained convinced of the necessity to link Black and red repression for the presumed benefit of both.[44]

Part of the liberals' dismay may have been a competitive disquiet over the publicity and favorable notices that CRC received because of the role they played in the battle. In this sense alone it was Scottsboro all over again. The print media and the budding electronic news media covered the case, although still not to Patterson's satisfaction. Ironically, he expressed these heretical views on "CBS Views the Press" on 19 March 1949, although he sniffed at the fifteen minutes he had been allotted: "For more than a year, there has extended almost complete blackout by the New York papers, and not for lack of its being called to their attention either. . . . For all that has been going on only 60 miles from New York, it might as well be on the moon." He noted the role of Ted Poston of the *New York Post* in exposing the original injustice, but he was scornful of most of the working press and their patrons. Still, there were a respectable number of press notices, particularly when compared with other cases. The U.E. sponsored a "nationwide" ABC program on the six on 14 February 1949. Some of the coverage was negative, though substantial. The flaming anticommunist, Ogden Reid, editor and publisher of the influential *New York Herald Tribune* editorialized against the CRC's view of the case and slanted his coverage in the minds of many; nor would he print Patterson's letters of protest. Naturally, the *Trenton Times* weighed in. Patterson delicately stroked Barry Gray of the powerful WMCA–AM in New York after his program about the six. Diplomatically, he suggested I. F. Stone for a follow-up without tainting him with the red brush: "Mr. Stone has no idea that I am writing this and would perhaps be quite offended if he knew. . . . and yet I regard him as a champion of human rights." Praise was due here to Stone since so much of the case's coverage was biased against the CRC, although the ACLU, typically, found time to give "congratulations on a stimulating presentation" to *The Reporter* after a particularly vile article.[45]

Perhaps part of the publicity generated by the case—eery parallels to Scottsboro aside—was intensified by the open participation of celebrities, a facet usually guaranteed to bring out the paparazzi. The celebrated basso profundo Paul Robeson was chairman of the Committee to Free the Trenton Six and was quite open and candid in campaigning. In words meant to reach deeply, he exclaimed, "My brothers couldn't go to high school in Princeton. They had to go to Trenton, 10 miles away. That's right—Trenton of the 'Trenton Six.' My brother or I could have been one of the Trenton Six." This characterization was repeated frequently by him. The possibility of getting a glimpse of Robeson caused the *Daily Worker* to headline: "1,500 Hail Robeson in Newark: Demand Trenton Six Be Freed." As was customary, a gaggle of members of the Veterans of Foreign Wars were picketing. Dashiell Hammett, chairman of the CRC–NY, joined his proclaimed associate in the Trenton Six effort, principally by raising funds; the popular playwright Clifford Odets was moved to pen a fundraising letter also, then another, and another: "Six innocent men have been sentenced to die. Of what are they guilty. Of being black. . . . This is a Northern Scottsboro case." Enlish's sister, the impressive Bessie Mitchell, played a role in encouraging Odets to speak out when many felt he had been lost to progressive and left politics. She also helped to bring in Eleanor Roosevelt, who told her in 1949, "I am sending your letter to a very influential person in welfare circles in New Jersey asking her to communicate with the Governor concerning the letter which you have written to me."[46]

As was their wont, CRC reached out across the waters for support for the jailed Blacks. Britain's "second largest rank and file trade union body, the Manchester and Salford Trades Council," backed the six, along with a union of Czechoslovakian cinema employees and several Australian unions. Even Therese Thompson was forced to admit to Rogge that her employer, the U.S. State Department, was being deluged at home and abroad: "Due to the interest this case has aroused in India, our United States Information Service representative at Calcutta has requested that the Department furnish him with details." This was not news to Rogge. He found that "the people of Europe know more about the Trenton Six than do the people of America. Protest meetings have been held in many European countries. (Lester Hutchinson, Labor MP) has reported that the frame-up is known to every Englishman."[47]

Characteristically, what made the Trenton Six virtual household names worldwide was the constant labor of CRC members and leadership. A 1951 report circulated internally noted: "Besides affecting broad coalition, broad committees. We must plan the following actions: Delegations, petition campaigns, letters and resolutions to the Governor, local meetings, continuous picketing during trial, parades in Harlem, Monster Rally." Much of this had been fulfulled already; all of it was fulfilled eventually. In generating this torrent of support, Patterson was not alone in stating frankly, "Yes, Bessie Mitchell deserves the greatest credit of all." Her growth during the course of campaign was something that CRC saw as a positive and desired byproduct of being a political "Red Cross." Yet, there was a downside to all this. Patterson remained disturbed about the behavior of his sometime allies:

> It is my belief that the conduct of some of the Negroes who participated in that trial contributed to that criminal act. . . . Mr. Raymond Pace Alexander did not fight for the acquittal of all these innocent men. His summation will forever be a blot upon his record. Nor is that blot cured by any remark that he may now make about the innocence of them all.

Sure, the victory in the case was "as great a morale-builder in the field of civil rights as was the Scottsboro case." Of course there were the resolutions by church groups, unions, and other organizations "influenced by our militancy." But then there were Walter White, Walter Reuther, and others "who hang around the Wilkie Building," who assiduously tried to coopt this sentiment. There was the discomfort caused in U.S. ruling circles as a result of the international uproar that would ultimately lead to the receding of Jim Crow. But there was also the strain on their resources that fighting the Trenton case and so many others had produced: "we are broke." Like a magazine editor paradoxically lamenting an increase in circulation because of the geometric increase in other costs this would cause, Patterson said "Strange as it may seem, while our organizational growth has been splendid indeed, it has only increased our financial burden."[48]

Despite the negativity, it was hard to argue with the growth, particularly when it came in the strategic CRC Youth and Student Division headed by Doris Rashbaum. CRC leaders knew that the energy, commitment, and free time that so often characterized this stratum of society made their aid indispensable. In May 1949 "several score college students" sponsored by CRC "appealed for the intercession by the Human Rights Commission of the United Nations" in the Trenton case. They spoke with Mrs. Roosevelt, who said only member nations could raise the issue, though she had spoken with "influential friends." The *New York Times* reported this and added that CRC had contacted Poland, Yugoslavia, and the USSR in order to fulfill Mrs. Roosevelt's condition. This international thrust was appropriate, because, as Patterson observed, this case "broke first in the British press and was picked up by the Paris paper *Action* before the American metropolitan press took cognizance of it," a typical pattern in CRC cases. Rashbaum followed up on this momentum by contacting about a score of UN missions seeking aid; there was student activity at a number of area campuses, e.g., the City College of New York, Rutgers, and Columbia. Even Princeton University was shaken out of its usual doldrums sufficiently to get involved; a number of students and teachers took up interest in the case and the *Daily Princetonian* did a lengthy series on the case.[49]

Another key link in the chain of resistance was the trade union movement and here Aubrey Grossman played his usual critical role in mobilizing support, along with CRC's Trade Union Director, Charles Doyle. So many unions were helpful here. The Furriers Joint Council sent $50 and joined the United Shoe Workers, the Furniture, Bedding and Allied Trades Joint Council—Metropolitan Council District Three in contributing. The Office Workers, Jewelry Workers, Cooks, Pastry and Cooks Assistants Workers, Hotel and Club Employees, Radio Guild, Department Store Employees, Window Cleaners, Marine Cooks and Stewards, etc., were among the many unions contributing. A sizeable percentage of this aid was given at the behest of Black workers, many of whom were NAACP members as well. Such was the case when CRC received $88.20 from Easton, Pa., raised as the result of an "Easter Cantata."[50]

Equally important was the political protest launched by these unions. It consisted of a steady wave of tsunami proportions. The International Fishermen and Allied Workers Wholesale and Warehouse Workers, the Fur and Leather Workers, were just a few of the many unions who raised their voices on a list too lengthy to recite. Indicative of the era of good feelings in the early days of the case is the fact that Social Service Employees Union #19 of the CIO, employees of the American Jewish Congress, in June 1949 wrote, "Congratulations on the victory of the Trenton Six. Keep up the good work." What is also striking about this list of supporters is the virtual wiping out of almost all of these unions, one way or another, by 1956; aligning with CRC and the left meant paying a heavy price.[51]

The support for the Trenton defendants was diverse. Early in 1949 Grossman reported, "the Elks have given us full support and many NAACP chapters are working very closely together with us in this fight." The support rendered by artists was heartening. Loften Mitchell was inspired to write a play about the case, "The Shame of a Nation." Banned in Trenton was the play about the Scottsboro case, "They Shall Not Die," because of the uncanny resemblance between that case and their controversial local case. The work of an inspired artist was refracted in CRC's pamphlet on the case, "Lynching Northern Style"; illustrated in black and white, 8½" × 14", the last page featured an inventive "CUT THE LYNCH ROPE–CLIP COUPON," featuring a pair of scissors cutting the noose, signifying that one's actions could prevent a lynching.[52]

The response nationwide to a case that CRC made international in scope was equivalently uplifting. Particularly the chapter in New Jersey came forward; as early as January 1949, they plastered the state with over thirty highway billboards. They put out countless pieces of printed matter, including the well-received "Stop Police Brutality," which included a petition to the governor, assembly, and state senate, replete with pictures. The Trenton case propelled but did not create the chapter. Their state conference in November 1947 had 108 delegates and many observers, including many from the unions and the NAACP. With lawyer Solomon Golat in tow, they won many civil rights cases, including one important "test case" against "Monclair Rolling Rink." Their own McCarran Act, the Musto Bill, which would have created a "Subversive Activities Study Commission" met their organized wrath.[53]

The effort in Detroit was as not as significant as it had been during their McGee campaign, perhaps because of the energy devoted to that Mississippi case, but they were able to get union support that proved critical. In Phoenix "an overflow crowd of eight hundred," Black and white, heard Bessie Mitchell tell the story of the six, and hundreds stood outside; more than one hundred people joined CRC as a result. In Tucson, two hundred people stood in the rain in a park to hear Mitchell after the school board cancelled a permit to hold a meeting at school; twenty-five signed up. Mitchell's speech in Sullivan County, New York, led to $574 being raised; despite a "terrific storm raging," and the fact that "half our program was performed by candlelight," the crowd, which also came out to hear Howard Fast, stayed on.[54]

It was this kind of persistence that led to what amounted to a vindication of the Trenton Six. The plusses were many; the development of Bessie Mitchell, the exposing of northern racism and a concomitant raised consciousness, the increased popularity of CRC, and the fact that none of the defendants were executed, as was proposed initially. But the clash with the ACLU and the NAACP and the way a network of forces conspired to forbid CRC from leading the Scottsboro case of the North, demonstrated that some had learned the lessons of the 1930s and would flex every muscle to ensure that the left would not get the credit for beating back racism, even when they deserved credit. Yet these same forces saw that Jim Crow had to recede somewhat, they just wanted it to be done in their way with their allies in the vanguard. One major factor that lifted the scales from their eyes was the fact that racism at home was quickly becoming the aching Achilles heel of U.S. foreign policy abroad, thus harming their ongoing struggle for influence with the USSR. Worse, leading the exposé brigade was, in their mind, the Soviets' main ally in the United States—CRC. It was clear and neat and infuriating all at once. The personal role of William Patterson, a Black lawyer who had forsaken the road to riches, thereby lending saintly status to himself, was galling in particular.

6

The Man Who Cried Genocide: The U.S. Government v. William Patterson et al.

There is little doubt that there were forces in the country that felt that CRC and William L. Patterson in particular were becoming entirely too cheeky and powerful. The machinations that were undertaken to maneuver them out of the Trenton Six case demonstrated the lengths to which some would go in order to prevent them from rising even higher in the pantheon. The coming of the war in Korea was something of a turning point for CRC: it seemed that after the launching of this antipopular war, freedom of speech and other civil liberties had to be repressed as a result. At the same time, Patterson and CRC were taking their fight into international forums, exposing the ugly lesions of racist and political repression to a broader audience. This was taken seriously, quite seriously, in Washington and on Wall Street, insofar as such factors could detrimentally affect the ongoing battle for "hearts and minds" in an increasingly colored world. Eugene Debs was not the first influential leftist to be placed on trial during a time of war. William Patterson was not the last.

His trial was born in a fiery and inflaming incident. The CRC leader was called before Congress to discuss intimate details of his organization's operation. In early August 1950, weeks after the opening of the conflict in Korea, Rep. H. L. Lanham shouted that Patterson was a "Black S.O.B." and a "liar" (he later denied using the term "god-damn," though eyewitnesses disputed this claim) and was held back by police as he attempted to slug the Afro-American leader. Patterson responded in kind. The headline in the *Pittsburgh Courier* cried out in page-one bold headlines, quoting Lanham declaiming, "I Would Have Killed," and this was no exaggeration. Lanham objected to Patterson's attack on his racist practices. The upshot, however, was that Patterson was indicted. After a long and torturous legal battle, he was able to overcome these charges, but not until many dollars and hours had been expended that could have gone to fighting other cases of racist and political repression. Increasingly CRC was becoming an organization that seemed to be in business in order to defend itself.[1]

On 24 July 1950 CRC had been subpoenaed to appear before Congress on 3 August. The two-count indictment of Patterson on charges of contempt of Congress flowed from this appearance. In allegedly trying to ascertain if CRC was engaging in improper lobbying, the committee sought all of their correspondence, records, press releases, articles, statements, cancelled checks, names of contributors, mailing lists, everything. Patterson guessed correctly that the House committee was not composed of dispassionate scholars in search of primary sources in order to write a balanced history, but politicos on a classic fishing expedition in search of damning evidence. Supposedly the House Select Committee on Lobbying Activities was investigating "Lobbying, Direct and Indirect" but Patterson believed otherwise. He began on a conciliatory note, apologizing for his lateness, informing them that he had come to the CRC staff on 19 June 1948. But he denied adamantly that lobbying was the "main aim" of CRC, thus obviating the need to register under the Federal Registration of Lobbying Act. He was forthcoming in sharing certain records, however. He claimed that "We keep no membership files," though he did reveal CRC's income. He also refused to say if he were a member of the Communist Party. Patterson was not altogether surprised by these events, and not only because of the charged political environment. Months after Patterson had come to CRC, their Washington representative, Tom Buchanan, was warning him about filing forms pursuant to the lobbying Act: "I repeat . . . that filing these forms is extremely urgent and that CRC must be particularly careful to comply with such regulations, since we have enemies who are looking for any technicality to prosecute." Prescience was apparently a forté of Mr. Buchanan. He was also fastidious about filing "at the conclusion of each quarter," and he stated that CRC had not been active in lobbying except for the Freedom Crusade of January 1949.[2]

Yet winning this case was not going to be a cakewalk. On 5 January 1951 Abe Isserman informed Patterson that CRC could well be deemed a lobbying group. Nor was he satisfied with the progress of the defense team: "Despite or perhaps because of the relatively large number of lawyers working on various aspects of this case, it is my opinion that there is a lack of a unified, integrated comprehensive approach to this case which will make its successful handling difficult if not impossible." Weeks later he was singing the same aria, this time to Ralph Powe: "We still have not had the necessary initial discussion with Pat on the factual basis of the defense. . . . Time is getting short. . . . It would be most unfortunate if this case goes to trial without the preparation it needs."[3]

Isserman's complaints were echoed somewhat by George Crockett. In the midst of fighting to keep himself out of prison because of his vigorous advocacy during the CP-Eleven trial, he took time out to come to the defense of Patterson. Yet he too was displeased with the defense effort: "Frankly I was beginning to feel that no one was any longer interested in the Patterson case." He was even more dissatisfied with the decision to press the Fourteenth Amendment point, earlier broached by Eugene Dennis and Leon Josephson, that the committee was invalid since Dixiecrats like Lanham were on it, contrary to Section 2 of the Fourteenth Amendment. Crockett expressed "virtually no faith" in this argument and averred that "a lot of useful and valuable time [was] being lost" on it. From his vantage point, he was taking a more hardheaded approach: "Its only value is political. . . . I still believe that our primary object is to secure Bill's freedom and vindication and not to enforce the Fourteenth Amendment by some novel and judicially unsound gimmick." He was desirious of a more "lawyer-like" approach, "divorced of political gimmicks." This dissatisfaction was forcing a difficult decision upon him: "More and more I am coming to the conclusion that this is not a case for me to handle though I want to assist to the fullest extent of my ability. . . . I am suggesting . . . that the Committee look around for other trial counsel." His distance from Washington, D.C., the trial site, and the upcoming court decision on his own case were also stumbling blocks to his participation. Patterson was resolute about not losing the aid of Crockett and not just because of his demonstrated legal skills; there were affirmative action considerations involved in his leaving: "I think I should prefer you be replaced by a Negro lawyer and this is by no means a commentary of any kind on the capabilities of your partner, Ernest Goodman." That was assuredly true, as Goodman was a CRC stalwart in Detroit. But Patterson was engaging in enlightened self-interest here. He was shrewd enough to know that a jury in the nation's capital would probably have Blacks on it and in those times they would no doubt be moved by the sight of a Black lawyer being tried and defended by another Black lawyer; this strategy also dovetailed neatly with CRC's policy of taking affirmative steps to include female and minority lawyers whenever possible. In any case, Crockett was persuaded to stay on board and played a strategic role in the litigation.[4]

Crockett was not alone in questioning of the feasibility of the defense. Laurent Frantz, another attorney involved in this case, was also doubtful: "My feeling is that this is not a favorable period for raising new and exploratory points of constitutional law, if it can be avoided, because the overall atmosphere is not such as to encourage courts to expand the area of constitutional liberty." He suggested the approach employed in *Blau v. U.S.*, 340 US 159. Patterson remained serious about raising the issue, however. Although his own freedom was at stake—he faced a possible two-year sentence—he did not hesitate to use this trial as a forum for raising intractable questions of law and racism in seeking to expose the government's role in supporting and encouraging Jim Crow. Hence, he contacted both Gene Holmes and George Parker of Howard Law School about getting "exact information" on the point of the deprivation of Blacks of the right to vote in Georgia, Lanham's home state. This step proved to be a necessary one on the road to passage of the Voting Rights Act of 1965.[5]

Problems still remained with Crockett. He agreed that it was "most important strategically" to have a Black lawyer on the case, but felt that this would "be satisfied by the participation of our friend, Charlie Howard." Hence, he would only join in if "I am to carry a major share." He was more interested in pressing the point of government employees on the jury panel rather than the Fourteenth Amendment. Although "fully aware" of CRC's "financial situation," he did not hesitate to ask for a fee of not less than $75 per day. CRC wanted Crockett because of his skill and his ethnicity. Earl Dickerson was reluctant to join the defense team due to "years of absence from criminal practice," though he was "deeply interested" in the case since "your constitutional rights have been invaded."[6]

So with much backing and filling, the trial lurched to a commencement in April 1951. An affadavit by Patterson had argued for a sixty-day adjournment, due to the pressures of the McGee case and related matters: "As a result of these efforts, I have had little or no time to work in my defense and to confer with my counsel, nor can this situation be changed without my desertion of the cause of this innocent man." No dice, said the judge. But the defense team persisted by filing a number of motions and affadavits on discrete points. There was a "Motion to compel Government to Elect," a "Motion to Dismiss Indictment," and an "Affadavit of Bias and Prejudice" aimed at the judge, Alexander Holtzoff. Patterson began by listing evidence of the conflict between Patterson and the FBI over the years. Holtzoff, from 1938 to 1945 had been a "Special Assistant to the Attorney General . . . and legal advisor to the FBI." He had co-authored the "Hobbs Concentration Camp Bill." He had been the judge in the Eisler case, where he had come into sharp conflict with CRC. No dice, said the judge. He rejected their argument on the basis of *Eisler v. U.S.*, 83 App.D.C.315. He claimed, "I do not know the defendant personally" and went further to state that "dislike of (the) crime" should not disqualify him, nor should "dislike of Communism." For Patterson to consider himself as being tried by a hanging judge was not an outlandish fear.[7]

The defense had decided on a multifaceted approach. They claimed that the original House subpoena was "defective" in that it was not addressed to Patterson, either as an individual or as an officer; they could argue that this made all events that flowed from this original defect null and void, while the prosecution could argue that his appearance waived any such possible defects. There was also the First Amendment issue, the questioning of the pertinency of the committee's requests, the claim that it was not lobbying by CRC, and the nonexistence of the records desired; Lanham's words were viewed as vitiating the good faith of the request, and, in any case, Patterson had not been allowed a full opportunity to produce the documents requested.

In his opening statement, Crockett stressed that Patterson had not refused to turn over the materials, but the session having terminated in turmoil and confusion, he could not do so. The judge tried to rule out statements by counsel, which included Vito Marcantonio, on the "Negro question." He refused the defense team the opportunity to bring up Lanham's insult. He sought to bar Crockett because of his contempt sentence in the CP–Eleven case. The defense broached the notion that their client had been "framed" after he had objected sharply to the insult given him. Patterson, of course, did not take Lanham's insult in silence, but had read the riot act to him and, fundamentally, he had accused Lanham of having participated in lynching Blacks. Marcantonio's approach to the jury, which had Black representation, stressed the racial elements. He pointed out how the Congressman would only call Patterson "nigra," as he slammed the edge of the jury box.[8]

Their efforts were not futile. The Department of Justice tried to bring another indictment, but federal judge Luther Youngdahl dismissed it on the grounds that the lobbying act was unconstitutional. Friends and critics said that Patterson had been lucky; not only was he able to get Blacks on the jury and then have them bar a verdict of guilty after twenty-five hours of deliberation, but serendipity in the form of the National Association of Manufacturers case intervened as well. The case they fought, which caused the lobbying act to be declared unconstitutional, undoubtedly influenced Judge Youngdahl's decision. Patterson was irate about this contention. He cited the mass pressure that had been generated as the decisive factor. Patterson was able to generate a firestorm of protest in response to his indictment and trial. Even though Patterson thought that his lobbying act failure would lead to his being indicted under the Smith Act, somehow this did not happen, which could also be attributed in part to the pressure he could generate. Patterson avowed that he had not been "lucky" that NAM had defeated the lobbying act just before his second trial. There was merit to his contention that the government had "as good an 'argument'" as they had had at Foley Square. Adding substance to his claim was the fact that the Afro-American press spoke up in virtual unanimity against the attempt to place him behind bars. The *Tulsa Black Dispatch* termed Patterson "bold, courageous" in exposing "Lanham, the lyncher." The *Arizona Sun* generally agreed. Clyde Jackson, city editor of the *Arkansas State Press* in Little Rock forwarded a clipping on the case they had run. After calling Patterson a "great Negro leader," he added, "We hope it will go a little way in showing you there are still some individuals who stand with you in the fight to free our people from bondage."[9]

Equally effusive was Roscoe Dunjee, an NAACP leader and the publisher of the *Oklahoma Black Dispatch*. In one particularly gushing editorial, he compared the CRC leader to Patrick Henry and Frederick Douglass, among others. Personally, he was more pointed in praise: "I think it took a great deal of courage on your part to handle that Georgia thug in the manner you did. . . . What we need more in public life is men who have the courage to stand where and when most of our leadership falters. It is tragic that most of our leadership is selected by our enemies." Patterson also fed Dunjee information on other matters for publicity purposes, e.g., on the case of James Jackson, and on that of Dr. Oakley Johnson, a New Orleans CRC leader, whose teaching contract had not been renewed, perhaps in retaliation for his left ties.[10]

Similar overtures were made to "Dear Friend Murphy" of the *Afro-American* and "Dear Friend Walker" of the *Cleveland Post and Call*. In the latter case, Patterson was diplomatic with the Black Republican: "It was a pleasure to renew my acquaintance with you and although we did not agree on all points . . ." On his crosscountry tour he also spoke out in other media. In Portland he spoke on KPOJ radio; he wagered his host that he "would 'catch hell' " for the program that Patterson was on; the liberal commentator accepted the five-to-one odds. He lost. By this time, Patterson was sophisticated in his dealings with the press. He recognized that there was little need to talk with the monkey when you could talk to the organgrinder: "I am not particularly concerned about press conferences. We do not get very far in working through reporters. I would prefer to sit down with an editor . . . rather than talk for an hour to reporters and the next day see nothing in the press. The reporter can not talk to the editor as I believe I can."[11]

The national buzzing about Patterson's case was not a matter of divine providence or even his widely known reputation. The "Defense Committee for William Patterson" was primarily responsible. Initially Du Bois was chairman, later Bishop J. H. Clayborn of Little Rock. Bishop Hampton Medford was the Washington, D.C., regional chair. The cartoonist Ollie Harrington was secretary, the writer Earl Conrad was treasurer; E. Franklin Frazier and Rev. Leon Sullivan were among the illustrious sponsors. Angie Dickerson was a bulwark of support. Despite this cyclone of activity, they were not always successful in attracting support; for example when they reached the ACLU, they were told, "it was recommended that the ACLU take no action." Herbert Levy of the Union, a lawyer known by some to investigate before making rash declarations, announced, "technically Patterson was guilty as hell."[12]

The Defense Committee was instrumental in organizing Patterson's January 1951 tour of Washington, D.C., Detroit, Chicago, Phoenix, and Los Angeles, and the Pacific Northwest to publicize his plight and that of others, e.g., McGee. The tour was a striking indication of developing trends. In Washington, Mary Church Terrell was notable in her presence, but a *Daily Worker* correspondent was the "only white person present." In Detroit there was a similar situation: "The only white people present however were our own people and I expressed the feeling that we had not had the courage and determination to reach out into new fields." In Chicago the trade unionists were conspicuous by their absence. Phoenix was "magnificent." In this rock-ribbed bastion of the GOP there was a meeting of three hundred people in a Black church, mostly Blacks of course: "it was in a very poor Negro neighborhood without sidewalks or paved roads." As in other meetings, Patterson raised the issue of the Du Bois case. But here too there was a "fear of moving among white Americans. . . . a failure to understand the tremendous moral vitality of our people was reflected." In Los Angeles, despite the fact that a Black reporter at the *Tribune* called him a liar, his press conference was attended by reporters from the *Examiner, Mirror*, and *Times:* "The attitude of the press generally however was extremely objective."[13]

There was a bitter plea from East St. Louis when Patterson could not come there: "This can't be done to us." He managed to squeeze Portland, Oregon, into his itinerary and controversy dogged him there. He told the *Oregon Journal*, "I refused to tell a congressional committee whether I was a Communist. Neither will I tell you." He was heavily redbaited. Many in the press did not seem to be moved by his frequent declaration that he was "the only Negro ever to have been cited for contempt of Congress." But there were contrary trends. Irving Goodman informed Patterson that "your appearance here has given CRC widespread publicity. . . . I heard from an authoritative source that KPOJ announced your broadcast every fifteen minutes between six and eight thirty." This kind of publicity was continued in the state of Washington. The *Spokane Chronicle* carried a lengthy article on the case. One CRC member was especially ebullient, noting Patterson's "skillful linking of the peace and civil rights issues." "The Tacoma meeting was the largest they had since Wallace—about 130 odd. Seattle about 250–60." The Black-white ratio was about thirty to seventy, with a heavy participation of Black ministers. During his visit he had scheduled a luncheon meeting with local attorneys that was sabotaged: "some s.o.b. enemy had called the hotel the night before—pretended to be me—and had the affair called off." The protest to the *Spokane Review* about their failure to mention his press conference was met with the riposte that "they don't publish anything they think might help the Communists." On the whole Patterson gave the trip a balanced evaluation. "Positive" was the reaching out to the Black church and the "strengthened Negro-white unity." "Negative" was the "need (for) more boldness" and the failure "to organize sufficiently." This last point disturbed Patterson deeply. The war and McCarthyism were taking their toll:

> the major characteristic expressing itself everywhere is the lack of sufficient boldness or a lack of understanding of what the principle of the united front demands by way of tactics. We are hesitating to move into new fields and particularly to move among white elements that have not already expressed sympathy and support for the left.

One can detect here the suspicion that what may have been impelling CRC to take on more Black cases as opposed to red ones was the fact that the response was so more substantial with the former. Moreover, Blacks' objective situation similarly impelled them to a kind of radicalism, as was not the case with the Euro-American community. This was the dilemma faced by CRC in the Patterson case and indeed in all of their cases.[14]

The kind of harassment Patterson faced in the West was far from being a regional trend. On 30 December 1951 Walter Winchell, the nationally known commentator, chose to focus on Patterson during his 9:00 P.M. broadcast: "A few months ago I revealed the name of the person now leading the Communist Party in Harlem, New York, the focal point for the American Reds to win over the Harlems from coast to coast. This man's name is William L. Patterson of the West Indies." He congratulated the State Department for snatching his passport. *Life* magazine devoted a major feature to Patterson, replete with pictures and hand-wringing about his impact and influence in Harlem. Close by a big picture of Patterson was the designation, "an old hand in Communist fronts." Even his lawyers were not able to escape the stain. The *Los Angeles Times* said that Marcantonio was "generally considered a party-liner," although he had not been elected to Congress on that ticket.[15]

These vicious attacks did not necessarily deter supporters from flocking to Patterson's banner. Especially was this true of religious elements. He received aid as eighteen Bishops of the AME church, representing 500,000, lent support; so did D. V. Jemison of the powerful National Baptist Convention. Rev. R. L. Turner of San Francisco happily told Patterson that "the sixty-five Baptist Ministers of this city with more than thirty (sic) pastors and their entire membership" were similarly favorable.[34] L. W. Goebel, president of the Evangelical and Reformed Church, was not alone among clerics in writing his Congressperson in protest of Patterson's trial. The Black church particularly was resolute in its support of Patterson, but endorsements of his defense came from diverse circles. Prof. W. J. Fitzpatrick, master of the National Supreme Council of the Masons, offered a letter of support "in the fight you are putting up for your race." Proceeding on a nationalist basis, he cracked irreverently, "if you are interested in making this Georgia cracker out of a lie, please contact me." W. C. Dabney, owner of a publishing house in Cincinnati, was equivalently colorful: "God has granted no greater benefit to our modern America citizens than William L. Patterson and the Civil Rights Congress." Eslanda Goode Robeson forwarded an open letter to the House Investigation Committee. A. J. Elrod, president of the Rutherford Bank in Tennessee, sent $50. Rev. J. Henry Patten of Philadelphia raised the case before five hundred ministers. Arthur Huff Fauset offered aid. Charles White did a drawing of Patterson for a widely produced card and his fellow artist Hugo Gellert did a "Seasons Greetings" card to him; Thomas Mann joined this artistic pantheon. Students at Charles University in Prague were not alone in sending protest letters from abroad.[16]

In addition to the Defense Committee there were other forces mobilizing on his behalf. Patterson's wife Louis Thompson was singularly helpful in galvanizing support within the Black church. When five thousand people rallied in Harlem, Thompson, the national office, and local members were the driving force behind it. All of the chapters were pushed to a new level of effort to save their leader; each was given quotas of phone calls to make to the attorney general and similar tasks. When a delegation of pastors met with an assistant attorney general in New York, the national office deserved major credit for the achievement.[17]

Patterson's legal difficulties did not disappear with the dropping of the lobbying act indictment. Now thoroughly an apostate, John Rogge brought suit against him in 1952 and he was subpoenaed to appear before the House Committee on Education and Labor that same year in order to "finger" the head of the CIO–Rubber Workers and 550 other unions who signed a May 1947 statement attacking redbaiting. Then there were the manifold legal problems that beset him and CRC in 1954, which ultimately led to the liquidation of the organization; the political "Red Cross" was winding up giving as many transfusions to itself as to others wounded. Undoubtedly the impact of CRC in the international arena contributed to this persecution. Whenever U.S. authorities would yelp about deprivation of human rights in the Soviet Union and Eastern Europe generally, Patterson's comrades there could simply point to the names CRC had made prominent—McGee, Ingram, the Trenton Six, the Martinsville Seven—and parry their trust. With the publication of the landmark book, *We Charge Genocide: The Historic Petition to the United Nations for Relief from a Crime of The United States Government Against the Negro People*, Patterson's allies had in one volume a startling indictment of Washington.[18]

This legendary petition was far from being the only démarche by CRC in the international arena, but like so many of their other significant departures, the arrival of William Patterson marked a new level of activity here also. Regular contacts were instituted with the Civil Rights Union, the League for Democratic Rights, and other Canadian groups. This generated a mutually beneficial relationship. Canadians sent money and political support across the border; their U.S. counterparts reciprocated, though more with the latter than the former; they protested the introduction of repressive legislation into Parliament and their neighbors protested the CP-Eleven prosecution, the hounding of Steve Nelson, and similar occurences. But as the cold war hardened, barriers to such contacts were strewn in the path. In October 1950 Thomas Roberts of the League sought a personal consultation, but Grossman reminded him that anyone sent north "would not be permitted to enter Canada . . . [or] would be prevented, as a result of the McCarran Law from leaving the United States."[19]

But it would take more than a simple law to bar intelligence from flowing across the border. Grossman's reply on how to strengthen the League not only aided the civil liberties fight in Canada, but it also provided a glimpse of how CRC viewed their efforts. He suggested that they form lawyers' panels to handle various cases, all "not officially handled" by CRC. Since all attorneys can't do everything well, there should be a division of labor set up, i.e., one does the "court work," another "research," another "analysis of legislation," another "analysis of facts." Because of political persecution, a number of attorneys would not work openly with CRC. Only CRC decided what cases to take, while lawyers "deal only with the legal aspects under fairly close guidance with the officers of the Congress." The coordinating work of the panel was done by an attorney who was secretary of the panel. With "rare exception" there were no fees allotted. In addition to the various local panels, they had a "national panel" that worked on such cases as McGee and Martinsville. They always sought to include "conservative" lawyers and made it clear that attorneys were working for the defendant and not for CRC. It was the giving of this kind of practical aid that the "McCarran Law" had been designed to prevent, but could not stem altogether.[20]

Canada was not the only neighbor attended to by CRC. They carried on a fruitful collaboration with allies in Puerto Rico, the longstanding U.S. colony. This aid took diverse forms. Abraham Pena of the Comite Pro Libertades Civiles was grateful to CRC—during a time when Patterson's organization was under severe siege, they would still forward a "generous contribution" due south. But things were not exactly going swimmingly in Puerto Rico: "Our work here has become increasingly difficult since the Supreme Court decision. The press has been displaying prominently all the redbaiting dished out by the press services." The crackdown on the CP-Eleven had had an impact in Puerto Rico and it was not long before Patterson was asking John Coe to fly to the island at CRC expense to defend Communists arrested there. The shooting at the U.S. House of Representatives had caused an escalation of repression. In October 1954, eleven persons, including two women, were arrested in Puerto Rico, New York, and Texas; this group included Ramon Mirabal Carrion, general secretary of the Communist Party, like Gus Hall kidnapped in Mexico City and turned over to the FBI in Texas. Exorbitant bail had been set and nine months later, four of these people remained in jail. These Smith Act detainees were tried in English, although not all of them understood this alien language. Patterson and U.S. Communist Jesus Colon called for loans to raise bail, which brought in a hefty though insufficient $15,000 and established a "broad" North American Committee to Defend the Puerto Rican Smith Act victims.[21]

CRC also stood in solidarity with their Cuban allies, particularly after the historic attack on the Moncada barracks in 1953 by Fidel Castro and his comrades. Patterson wrote General Batista demanding the "release of all political prisoners" and contacted John Foster Dulles with a similar demand. He urged Robert Woodward, Acting Assistant Secretary of State for Inter-American Affairs, to adopt a list of specific actions that the government should take against Havana; CRC chapters were urged to act likewise. The energetic Black autoworker, Nelson Davis, received special "congratulations" for the "magnificent job" he performed and he wasn't alone. This was just one aspect of a wideranging Caribbean and Latin American outreach managed by CRC, and this was a bilateral process. Saul Cascallar Carrasco, acting secretary of the Argentine League for the Rights of Man, sought in 1949 to launch a "campaign of solidarity with" the Communist Party, "these victims of American reaction"; while Gerardo Pisarello, general secretary of the Comite Pro-Defensa de Obdulio Barthe, sought CRC's aid on behalf of this "Paraguayan patriot." In September 1955, as CRC was winding down, Patterson found time to request that the chapters protest to the recently installed right-wing Guatemalan government against the arrest of Bernardo Alvarado Monzon, a Communist leader. Solidarity between CRC and the region was so firm that even the right-wing Mexican paper *El Universal Grafico* stood with CRC in blasting the execution of Willie McGee. Patterson remained in close contact with these forces. He and Oakley Johnson, late of the CRC–New Orleans chapter, prepared a book-length report on "The Decline of Freedom in the USA" for the Tenth Inter-American Conference at Caracas, Venezuela. These efforts were not without incident. Recently deported to Jamiaca, U.S. Communist leader Ferdinand Smith complained to Patterson about mail tampering, "Maybe you can find a reliable 'cover,' nonpolitical, where I can write to you." They devised an elaborate way of corresponding.[22]

From a certain point of view, the danger of Patterson's contacts undermining U.S. foreign policy in the region justified mail tampering and any other tactic that could derail these plans. If this was the case, these kinds of fears would be magnified when it came to his contacts with Africa, where cases of racist repression were designed to sound loudly. Most of CRC's contact with Africa was effected by CRC Bail Fund Trustee Alphaeus Hunton of the Council on African Affairs, but not always. Inspired by CRC in 1953, a "West African Civil Rights Congress" was organized based in Nigeria and the Gold Coast (Ghana). A number of West Africans like S. T. Addico, Turkson-Ocran, Amaefule Nkoro, and Olatunji A. Fabiyi were in touch with Patterson. His trips to Europe, before his passport was snatched, also provided opportunities for intimate discussions with African students, which may help to explain the snatching. Patterson was naturally attracted to the zenith of oppression on the continent, South Africa. Sam Kahn, formerly that nation's only Communist in the Capetown Parliament until the passing of the Suppression of Communism Act, had read in the *National Guardian* of the case of Patricia Blau and had spoken with British lawyer D. N. Pritt. This led him to Gurley Flynn and CRC:

> I would appreciate your putting me in touch with some lawyer or jurist in New York who might send to me judgments involving questions of civil liberties and constitutional rights arising out of the reactionary laws, suppressive of political and racial organs in the United States and I could reciprocate in respect of South African judicial decisions.[23]

Asia too was part of the CRC purview, particularly after the Korean conflict, and again it was a bilateral tie. Hla Kyway, secretary-general of the Committee for Protection of Democratic rights in Rangoon, Burma, sought advice from CRC, while Patterson reached his Prime Minister for assistance in fighting the denial of Robeson's passport. CRC protested the "anti-labor frame-up" of Amado Hernandez, president of the Phillippines' Congress of Labor and the "death sentence to Mr. Kin Bo Soun by the Li Seung Man Government" in Korea. The Afro-Asian solidarity of CRC reached its high water mark in 1955 during the historic Bandung Conference in Indonesia. Patterson not only castigated Adam Clayton Powell for his trip there and his attempt to inject anticommunism into the meeting; at the same time he tried to place the meeting in context: "Bandung made the meeting at the Summit inevitable. . . . The fight for peace must include and embrace the struggle against white supremacy or it must fail." Seeing the way the war in Korean detrimentally affected U.S. civil liberties, Patterson was not adverse to linking these seemingly disparate questions; nor did the ineffable tie between racism and U.S. foreign policy escape his gaze.[24]

With all this, Patterson and CRC also found time to pay attention to Europe, particularly during the CP-Eleven trial. The International Association of Democratic Lawyers, based in Prague, was contacted about supplying four or five lawyers to come to the trial. Support came from, *inter alia*, Berlin's Verteidgungs Komitee Fur die Opfer der Amerikanischen Reaction, and the Bulgarian National Women's Union. Patterson wrote to D. N. Pritt in England and his secretary replied: With regard to the names of international lawyers who were connected with the Reichstag Fire Enquiry, the only one Mr. Pritt recommends for an invitation now is Mr. George Branting of Stockholm." This kind of communication was also a two-way street. By 1955 Elizabeth Allen, general secretary of CRC's sister organization in England, the National Council for Civil Liberties, was asking Patterson's advice, "we ourselves are now having to do some work to prevent the growth of a colour bar in this country." There were other forms of solidarity. CRC's protest of the jailing of French Communist leader Jacques Duclos included Patterson's picketing of the French consulate in New York. The news agency based in Prague, Telepress, frequently and routinely carried CRC's press releases around the globe.[25]

There were complications. When a U.S. grand jury began poking into the affairs of the American Council for a Democratic Greece, their chairman, Abe Pomerantz, had to pull back from his theretofore close ties with CRC. CRC found handling the so-called doctors' plot in the USSR difficult, but in the end they compared the freeing of the physicians with the continued jailing of Ingram and the Smith Act defendants. More representative of the nature of CRC's foreign policy was Patterson's correspondence with Bea Johnson in West Berlin. For her city and others he suggested a placard "which would have at its top in bold letters: 'AMERICANS GO HOME,'" and

below it pictures of "two lynched Negroes . . . This could be posted anywhere and everywhere Americans could see it."[26]

This solidarity across national borders reached an apogee during the CRC
genocide petition campaigns. This 240-page document hit the Cold War
world like a thunderclap—and that was certainly the intention. In the Communist journal, *Political Affairs*, Harry Haywood laid down the line from the
State Department on the petition: "The existence of discrimination against
minority groups in this country," Dean Acheson wrote on 8 May 1946, "has
an adverse effect upon our relations with other countries." Thus, Anthony
Leviero in the 14 December 1951 *New York Times* told of the State Department's efforts to dispel the world's view of Jim Crow by issuing a pamphlet
entitled "The Negro in American Life," released a few weeks before Patterson's book. The genocide petition whipped up the kind of necessary pressure
that led to the final cracking of the spine of Old Jim Crow.[27]

What was this book that stirred so much contention? There were two
elements that made it important and attention-getting. First of all, presented
in the form of an "Opening Statement," "The Law and Indictment," "The
Evidence," and a "Summary and Prayer," Patterson and his colleagues
presented a devastating argument on the impact of U.S. policies toward
Blacks. The great body of the book consisted of the evidence, and here the
statistics, the cases, and the horrors were astounding. Page after page after
page catalogued lynchings, executions, mutilations, rapes, and just outright
discrimination in areas like housing and employment. The documentation
gathered was voluminous and overwhelming; the material not published in
many instances was more shocking than what went between the covers of the
book. Secondly, this argument reached an international audience in that it
was presented to the United Nations. At a time when Washington was
charging the USSR and its allies with all manner of human rights' depriva-
tions, Patterson's indictment hit with the force of a rifle shot between the eyes
and set U.S. foreign policy back on its heels. No wonder that Patterson's
passport was confiscated upon his return from Paris after having presented
the petition.[28]

The team that was responsible for gathering this material included Patterson, Richard O. Boyer, Howard Fast, Yvonne Gregory, Oakley Johnson, John
Hudson Jones, Ruth Jones, Leon Josephson, Stetson Kennedy, and Elizabeth Lawson. There were scores of petitioners that included a host of CRC
stalwarts (Braverman, Burnham, Bass, Crockett, Du Bois, Fast, Truehaft,
Robeson, and others). Although Patterson was given major responsibility for
producing this document, which came out a year after the Korean conflict
began, he was clear about sharing the accolades. He told Josephson, "without the tremendous effort you put into the writing of this book, it might well
never have appeared. . . . You and Dick (Boyer) and then, lastly, myself,
have, I think, been its major creators." Boyer, a party member from the 1930s
until 1956 was a skilled journalist who had written for the *New Yorker, New*

York Herald Tribune, and others. Patterson communicated similar sentiments as he had done to Josephson: "I want the record to show the tremendous contribution which Dick Boyer put into this, without which it would not
have seen the light of day for months, if ever. Dick Boyer and Leon
Josephson must be noted, together with myself, as responsible for this
work." This stroking was necessary because retribution was so swift. Patterson was forced to protest to President Mordecai Johnson seeking his support
for Oakley Johnson, who had been ousted from Dillard, allegedly because of
his "sterling" research on the petition. He was able to find a post at Houston-
Tillotson. But he was ousted from there in 1952.[29]

Yet it was Patterson who provided the moral force and unalloyed energy
that made the petition possible. It was Patterson who posited the centrality of
the Black question and sought actively to implement this ideological concern. Even after the petition had long been filed and was a dim distant
memory to some, Patterson remained clear about the ideological conviction.
In June 1955 he was urging "white churches" to launch a "holy crusade"
against racism, which "leads directly to events similar to the murderous
campaign of the Nazis against the Jews in Germany, Poland, and elsewhere.
Too few white Americans associate these attacks with the growth of fascism.
They have conditioned themselves to live with the 'occasional' murder of a
Negro and do not see either its moral effect upon them or its physical effect
upon the objective situation." This is what Patterson saw in 1951, and it
contributed to the importance of the petition. Patterson also knew that
internationalizing this struggle was essential. The antilynching movement of
Ida B. Wells had taken off in the 1890s when she internationalized it by
passing out literature at the World Columbian Exposition in Chicago. Her
success in Britain opened doors in the United States ordinarily closed to her.
This was the example that CRC was following. With that, Patterson still felt
that the petition could have stood improvement. He noted "weaknesses,"
e.g., the "absence of an index, failure to deal more exhaustively with the
psychological effects of the manifold forms of Jim Crow, segregation," not
only on Blacks but on whites; thus he wanted to see a second volume.
Nonetheless, he told red patriarch William Z. Foster that "the sale of less
than 100,000 copies would, we believe, be a crime," because of the explosive
and critical character of the material adduced.[30]

Taking such issues before the United Nations was not a new development.
The NAACP had tried it earlier and so had the NNC, but, as Patterson
explained it, their petition "sought redress of the numerous grievances from
which Negroes suffered, while the CRC petition made a specific charge
against the criminal, racist policies of the U.S. government."[31] Earlier, CRC
had gotten Du Bois to do a UN petition on Ingram and had petitioned the UN
about the Trenton Six.

In May 1950 Patterson, Du Bois, Corliss Lamont, I. F. Stone, and others
had submitted another petition to the UN's Commission on Human Rights,

issued by victims of HUAC, like Dalton Trumbo, Lester Cole and John Howard Lawson. The enduring importance of such petitions was shown years later when the Black Panther Party drew up a similar measure, and were assisted by Patterson, in 1970; Shirley Chisholm, Ossie Davis, Dick Gregory, and others joined in this endeavor. Then in 1977 the National Conference of Black Lawyers engaged in a similar maneuver with even more impact than the BPP.[32]

Given the fierce opposition to it, *Genocide* was a runaway bestseller. It sold out in its first week, over five thousand copies, and sold forty-five thousand copies all told, and, according to Patterson, "far beyond that figure" in Europe. This latter point needs to be stressed and mulled over intently in order to savor the full meaning; this petition was a big black eye for the U.S. image abroad. Despite or because of this, Dr. Raphael Lemkin of Yale University, who had formulated the term "genocide," was hostile to CRC's effort. He was anti-Soviet and his views often seemed racist, which no doubt contributed to this bias. Yet, in 1953 he asked the United Nations to find the Soviets guilty of genocide against Jewish people. He conceded that he was "troubled" by CRC's effort and the actual convention that emerged: "there is nothing in the convention which would seriously embarrass the Russians but it could be used to embarrass us," making reference to a "lynch mob in Georgia." This convention was adopted by the General Assembly on 9 December 1948 and it was explicit in noting that genocide did not have to mean extinguishing every member of the group in order for the definition to apply. This is what CRC continually emphasized, to Lemkin's and others dismay. But it was not only Lemkin's footsteps that were being followed. CRC studied the example of Rev. Michael Scott when he came to the UN to petition about conditions in Namibia and the Nurenberg example was also considered as a precedent. The fact that in 1952, fifty-five Senators introduced a constitutional amendment to bar the U.S. Constitution from "being overriden by treaties and executive agreements such as the anti-genocide pact" was indicative of the farreaching effects CRC's efforts were having.[33]

What had moved the U.S. Senate to such rash action was the unprecedented CRC campaign not only to have the genocide pact ratified but to get their book-length petition into as many hands as possible. Special rates were set up of $1.10 for up to one hundred copies and 90¢ for over one hundred copies and the regular price was $1.50. Chapters were given quotas to meet; for example, New York state's was fifty thousand, Chicago's eighteen thousand, and fifteen thousand for Los Angeles. A well-conceived battle plan was drawn up to implement the sales plan. Patterson intended for the book to have the impact of an *Uncle Tom's Cabin* or *The Jungle*, and he did not fall too far short. Angie Dickerson and Bill Mandel were his chief lieutenants, and each county and chapter was asked to assign one person to head sales. They set a meeting of "1500 union officials and shop stewards"; "specific plans" were laid for "sales in large housing projects especially among white tenants." They were to arrange "house parties and book fairs . . . public meetings . . . it should be sold at every type of meeting, affair and demonstration." There was to be "great attention [paid] . . . to such Negro schools as Howard, Lincoln, Tuskeegee, and others." There was to be outreach to "so-called liberals or progressive legislators" and pressure put on them to get them to mention it "on the floor of Congress or on the floor of the city council." The book was to be linked with "concrete cases," e.g., the Smith Act, and Taft-Hartley. "Language groups should everwhere be approached. . . . Book clubs should be approached . . . Street corner sales." They set out to push the book during Negro History Week, have it selected as "gift book of the year." Most of these plans just did not remain on paper but were put into action, which is why an astonishing thirty-five thousand copies were sold in the first six months as the nation reeled in the throes of repression.[34]

Supplementing these aggressive sales efforts were innovative cultural approaches. CRC published a calendar focusing on the petition with pictures of Black and white youths, lynchings, and with fold-outs promoting the book. Albert Wood, a young Black West Indian worker wrote a song, "Genocide," focusing on charges in the book, which was performed far and wide. Similarly, Black actress and playwright Beaulah Richardson wrote a play "Genocide" with a large cast, a chorus of ten voices and children of various ages. Ahead of her time, she included the use of the term "black" in negative contexts, e.g., "black sheep . . . black leg . . . black death" etc., and linked all these notions to genocidal attacks. This analysis was interspersed with speeches by Gene Weltfish, Angie Dickerson, and with much praise for Patterson.[35]

Keep in mind that this beehive of activity was buzzing furiously as Patterson faced the serious threat of being clapped in jail for a few years. If this threat was designed to cow him or CRC into submission, it proved an abject failure, for if anything it seemed to move him and his organization to new heights. Soon "genocide" as a term was on the lips of many and had entered the everyday lexicon, and the book itself was being praised and denounced throughout the nation and world. This was facilitated by the fact that editions were published in French, Spanish, Chinese, Hungarian, Czech, Slovak, and a host of other tongues. The book review editor of the Black weekly *Chicago Enterprise* adopted the view taken by many when he alleged, "We do not agree with them in all things. But it would be foolish to scorn facts simply because they are put forth by that organization." The *New Statesman* of London and the *Nation* both agreed that the evidence cited easily brought the indictment within the definition provided by the Genocide Convention. But the well-known news commentator Drew Pearson speaking on the ABC radio network was more indicative of the mainstream view when he condemned the petition as "Communist propaganda" that would harm the U.S. effort to sway hearts and minds abroad. This view was echoed by the

Chicago Tribune editorially. The *Los Angeles Herald* was cautiously neutral. The *Trenton Times*, under siege by CRC, took pains to focus on such facts as that out of the 105 executions in the United States in 1951 and out of an average of 144 between 1930 and 1950, fifty-seven had been of Euro-Americans and forty-seven had been of Afro-Americans. The "MCS Voice," organ of the Marine Cooks and Stewards union, reflected the progressive labor movement's press when it ran a multipart series on the book and set up a contest with it as a prize.[36]

Patterson also found that he had to respond to negative press directed at the book. The *New York Times* demanded that the UN instead look into allegations of genocide in Eastern Europe. Patterson was dumbfounded: "How strange it seems that the *New York Times* so quickly takes cognizance of the crimes of genocide when it is allegedly committed thousands of miles away but completely ignores it when its commission (sic) here. . . . you took no notice of our terrifying petition . . . [which is] astounding. . . . our fight against Genocide begins at home." Chicago Chapter Secretary Lester Davis had to respond in kind to the *Chicago Tribune*: "Your editorial of Saturday, December 22nd, entitled 'The Genocide Trap' is characteristic of the story told of a man who, after seeing a giraffe for the first time remarked, 'there ain't no such animal.' "[37]

As the thousands of copies sold demonstrated, there was a stunningly favorable and hungry reception of the book. J. Finley Wilson of the Elks wished Patterson "tremendous success" after he bought his copy. Jewish leader Stephen Frichtman called the work "devastating and desperately needed." Naturally, Paul Robeson was expansive in his praise. He had played a pivotal role in preparing and presenting the petition and the finger depicted pointing accusingly on the cover was his. He lauded Patterson for adding "still another contribution to his magnificent record." He was unequivocal in outlining the legal aspects: "from the openly terrorist Ku Klux Klan to the more suave spokesmen of the American Bar Association, there has been a brazenly open recognition of the applicability of the convention to the treatment of the Negro people in the United States." Charles Fielding of Yale Law School, Justices William Douglas and Felix Frankfurter all received copies. "Two Harvard Law Students" called it "historic." It was sent to virtually all independent Third World nations. Pettis Perry was told that "the American Section of the UN sent a courier down for five copies, which we sold." Hugh Bryson of the Marine Cooks reported that "the sales are going fine. . . . The membership are greatly interested." It was not all a downhill ride. The Seattle chapter had to force the library there to take a copy, although they carried *Mein Kampf.* At a Northwestern University debate between Lester Davis and Fraser Lane of the Urban League, the latter started off positively" "I think this is a valuable document and everybody in America ought to have a copy of it." But it suggests how the CRC leader had been demonized in certain circles that Lane opposed the petition "because the name of Patterson is associated with it." Still, it was difficult for any Black to oppose this petition, as evidenced by the support for it from J. A. Rogers.[38]

It was the intention all along of Patterson and CRC to file the petition at the United Nations. They felt that if Robeson were to be the presenter, maximum publicity could be obtained. However, the snatching of Robeson's passport barred this effectively. Du Bois was the next choice, but he had just endured an extremely taxing trial on the charge of being an agent of an unnamed foreign power and just was not up to it. By default the task fell to Patterson. He was to fly to Paris to make the presentation, while Robeson was to go to UN headquarters in New York accompanied by Marcantonio, Ewart Guinier, Howard Fast, Ben Gold, Edward Barsky, and Rev. Mother Lena Stokes. Indicative of how suspicious CRC was of sabotage was the fact that Patterson sent copies to both London and Budapest in case his petitions were confiscated. They were animated by the words often intoned by Patterson: "I am very much of the opinion that if we are going to break this book into the press, it will have to be done in Europe, just as the Trenton Six case was featured in Europe first." Patterson's remarks at the General Assembly in Paris were no less pointed. He declared that "genocide" leads to "fascism" and "another world war." He compared Blacks in the United States to Jews under Hitler and scorned the stereotype of the Afro-American as a "rapist, buffoon, n'er-do-well, petty thief, lazy scoundrel . . . less than human." He rebuffed the American Bar Association and The American Legion for failing to support ratification of the convention.[39]

Patterson had some striking experiences in Europe. His supposition about the importance of "breaking" the book in Europe proved correct as he captured the eye of the press and raised hackles among U.S. officials, especially Black ones. In Budapest he complained about U.S. efforts to muzzle the petition and met with high-ranking officials from both the Peoples Republic of China and the Democratic Peoples Republic of Korea, who informed him of Black-white G.I. clashes and defections to the North. Writing from Paris, Eleanor Roosevelt expressed the concern of U.S. ruling circles when she denounced this trip in a paroxysm of redbaiting in the similarly inclined *New York World Telegram*: "It is prominently featured in the papers over here. . . . one wonders if he has decided to transfer his citizenship to the Soviets." Walter White issued a pamphlet extolling race relations in the United States, which the State Department quickly forwarded to Paris.[40]

Certainly the first half of Roosevelt's statement was accurate, for Patterson's comrades in the French Communist Party were helpful in publicizing the petition. Leading U.S. officials abroad of a darker hue, like Edith Sampson, Ralph Bunche, and Channing Tobias were none-too-pleased with his performance: "Friend Bunche has passed me several times and always avoids me. He ran out of the Polish Embassy when he met me there at a reception." The confrontation with Tobias was tense: "(We) had an extremely interesting talk in which he revealed great fear asking me repeatedly if I was trying to discredit my government and even why I did not leave the country if I hated it so. I said I love the country." Patterson reproved Tobias, a member of the U.S.-United Nations delegation, by informing him that it was "your government" but "my country." At first Tobias "snubbed him," then angrily attacked him: "Why don't you talk about Genocide in the Soviet Union?" was his bitter reproach. He introduced a brochure in French "issued by the U.S. State Department" to refute Patterson. In return Patterson called him an "apologist," and predicted that the United States would "elevate more Negroes to high government positions than ever before" as a result of "left" pressure. Patterson had known Edith Sampson, another member of the UN delegation well. "I have seen the petition and agree with most of it," was her response, and she admitted candidly that it "had very much upset the delegation." She was a mite better than Bunche, who refused to speak to him even though he had known Patterson too for years. Anticipating Nixon, Sampson reminded, " 'You know I'm not a stooge. I told them 16,000,000 Negroes would support that petition. A lot of people won't talk to you but I'm not afraid." Yet all these remarks were only for private consumption and she did not break publicly with her delegation. All prominent Blacks did not snub Patterson in Paris, however, although he felt constrained to try to deflect Richard Wright from emulating Sampson: "Permit me to thank you and Mrs. Wright for your courtesy. I hope you will find time to say publicly the many fine things you said about *Genocide* in private."[41]

The discomfort of the trio of diplomats was indicative of how uncomfortable the rulers of the land of the free felt about CRC's exposé of the dastardly conditions Blacks had been lashed with. J. Saunders Redding, a Black writer, found himself in the difficult position of defending his government against CRC's charges in India:

> Many times I was referred to a pamphlet hysterically titled *We Charge Genocide* published by the American Civil Rights Congress. . . . In Bangalore, after a lecture to the Kannada Writers Association—a lecture, incidentally, that had nothing to do with race relations—a member of the audience rose to read from *We Charge Genocide*. "Is this true?" he challenged. In answer I tried to give a general account of race relations in America. When I had finished, I was told: "What you say does not convince us in the face of this!" He held up the pamphlet.

During his tour, Redding was constantly asked about petitioners Fast and Robeson. There were constant clashes and he took a real beating. In Madras they "were constantly hearing of the low status of American Negroes. . . . They were acquainted with and fully convinced of the frightful truth of the indictments brought against the American society by such an extremist Red publication as *We Charge Genocide*." Repeatedly Indians inquired, ". . . What about the 'Trenton Six,' the 'Martinsville five' (sic) and 'Willie

McGee?'" This was during a meeting with Indian lawyers, indicating that elites abroad were also beginning to be swayed by CRC's charges. U.S. diplomats and elites had to ask themselves if maintaining Jim Crow and rancid racism at home was worth the possibility of diminished influence around the globe.[42]

One of their responses to this question was to snatch Patterson's passport and squelch CRC. If they couldn't kill the message, they assuredly could prevent the messenger from disseminating it widely. An enthusiastic crowd of five thousand greeted Patterson in Harlem after his tour. They were also protesting the harassment of the CRC leader at Idlewild Airport upon his landing in January 1952. Authorities seized copies of *Le Soir, Action* (both from Paris) and *Szabad Nep* of Hungary, all of which carried accounts of Patterson's exploits. He told the clamoring Harlemites of how Europe had been "stirred" by the petition. In his deeply rolling cadences and in an impassioned plea he called for unity with the NAACP. The Rockland Palace audience was told how he had discussed in Paris the idea of a "world conference of colored peoples for human rights and peace this fall" with Egypt, India, Haiti, Kenya, the British West Indies, and others. "All agreed" that the call should be issued by Du Bois. It was conjectured that seizing his passport was designed to prevent such a potentially earthshaking happening, and when such a meeting did occur at Bandung, Patterson was still grounded. After his return he sought the aid of the President of the General Assembly, Luis Padillo Nervo, to intercede to allow him back to Paris, but this attempt proved unsuccessful.[43]

Patteson's forced stay in the United States did have the positive effect of allowing him to concentrate on the petition and draw up more plans for its distribution. There were doubts even among the committed, which drama-tized further the need for Patterson's crucial participation. William Mandel, a key player, was critical at first about the book: "it cannot succeed, because its language and sentence structure are too advanced and complex." He cited words that he felt a working class of limited education would not understand: "warped . . . ethnic . . . commodities . . . negates . . . holocaust . . . iota . . ." About a week later Mandel was retreating rapidly from this under-estimation: "Promoting *Genocide* in the Bay Area has been like breaking through an open door."[44]

At their Chicago convention in August 1952, Patterson was the architect of the plan of work set for the petition's distribution. Again, it was placed in an exceedingly political context: "White salesmen have a special task. . . . A rigid division of labor between white and Negro salesmen and women has to be made. It is not necessary for the white seller to concentrate on Negro communities, as is the actual case. The major weakness in our sales is not there." How true. It was far from being essential to bring coals to Newcastle or to convince Afro-Americans of the dire straits in which they were snared. Thus, Aubrey Grossman stressed another aspect of this approach: "we must make a special appeal to the Jewish organizations that re-Nazification of Germany constitutes a continuation of genocide against the Jews." With other audiences CRC emphasized that the precedents for their petition were other agreements binding on nonsignatories. The Fur and Leather Workers Union had progressive Jewish leadership and Patterson acknowledged that "no union has recognized so quickly and so clearly the value of that historic document." The New York *Yiddish Daily* admitted that the petition "makes a deep and shaking impression." From Chicago Lester Davis reported that "*Genocide* seems to have a strong ready appeal. After showing it around in only a few spots, demands have begun to outnumber our supply." The book also spurred more trade union participation in CRC and caused chapters to emerge in Salt Lake City and elsewhere.[45]

Despite the absolutely critical importance of the genocide petition, Patterson was not satisfied and felt that more could have been done then and later in terms of linking the issues of racism and U.S. foreign policy: "Had there been unified and courageous Left leadership ready, willing, and able to coordinate, clarify, and deepen the struggles of the Negro people around today's issues, these struggles might well have merged organically with those of the Asian-African colonial nations." But there were larger forces at work. Reportedly the State Department had pressured Walter White and other Blacks to attack the petition. Another potential ally who strayed was Roger Baldwin, a member of the official U.S. Committee for a U.S. Genocide Convention. His acerbic comment was that the petition "comes in very ill grace from Communists and fellow-travellers. In Communist countries it is official policy to wipe out entire groups on the basis of race and national origin." He claimed that the "treatment" of Afro-Americans "does not constitute genocide. . . . [it is] pure propaganda . . by the agents of the Soviet Union . . . without basis." This public statement was crafted to destabilize CRC's campaign and Patterson knew it and anticipated it: "I understand that you have been selected to do a hatchet job on *Genocide*. In order that you might be most effective, I am sending you a copy under separate cover." But this sarcasm could not obscure the simple fact that once again the left was experiencing difficulty in attracting center forces in thrall to the right. This was too often the story during CRC's history and it not only spelled doom for the organization and the petition, but soured the overall political atmosphere as well. CRC was bloodied, but remained unbowed. Grossman had the bright idea of a monthly press service to the Black press on genocide. Chapters would send clippings. There would be a yearly summary that could be the basis for another book. There would be a return journey to the UN. But time and events overtook CRC and this notion did not advance beyond the embryo stage. Nevertheless, CRC's genocide petition still stands in hindsight as a major landmark on the path to equality in the United States and sanity in U.S. foreign policy, and it set a precedent still followed regarding the value of internationalizing the struggle against racism.

The effort in Congress to pass the Genocide Convention spurred the near passage of the "Bricker Amendment," which would have restricted the treaty power. The companion drive to make the UN Charter applicable—as it should have been legally in the United States—along with Patterson's efforts, certainly sparked U.S. courts to grant concessions on the civil rights front.[46]

While Patterson was facing down the government in their attempt to jail him and toiling assiduously on the genocide petition, somehow he found the inspiration and energy to throw himself into the battle to halt U.S. foreign aggression in Korea. CRC played a major role in defending those arrested for circulating the antinuclear Stockholm Peace Appeal. CRC chapters were motivated by his important 15 May 1950 memorandum to them entitled ominously "The Fight for Civil Rights and the Fight for Peace." His political science skill had convinced him of the impending conflict that would explode in Korea only weeks later. When this war came, U.S. rulers would have to "gag . . . peace-lovers" and squash civil liberties in order to prosecute it. Thus, CRC had no choice but to fight the warmongers with all the resources they could muster. Weeks after this portentous memo was sent, Patterson was chairing an eighteen-thousand-strong rally in Madison Square Garden that resolutely denounced the U.S. intervention in Korea. Soon after that there were headlines resounding throughout the Afro-American press claiming "The war with Korea is not the Negro's war."[47]

It was not CRC's wont to resort simply to words, no matter how righteous. Patterson quickly reached the American Peace Crusade, which had been pieced together to supplant the government-dissolved Peace Information Center. He suggested the establishment of a "coordinating committee" to find "means by which the educational material and activities of the others may be popularized by each, through their channels." This was a committee of various left organizations that Patterson had pulled together. This "Committee on Organization and Coordination" was designed to harmonize the actions of various groups whose primary missions were not necessarily to act against the Korean War. Patterson suggested a "survey" to "determine every convention of importance to be held anywhere in the country in the next six months." It was his ardent desire to have CRC "drawn into the peace struggle"; he proposed turning the CRC newsletter over to the peace issue for the next issue. Plaintively he implored, "Can there be democracy in the United States if there is not Peace?"[48]

Yet even before the Korean conflict, CRC was waist-deep in the antiwar struggle, as was ILD, which had handled numerous discriminatory army discharges. Unlike many leading capitalist nations, the idea of political organizing in the military had not taken hold firmly in the United States; the promotion of this idea was an ancillary benefit of CRC's work in this field. Hence, when Clyde Harris, who had been bounced from his military job for "attending communist meetings" and "associating with a well-known communist" came to CRC seeking aid, they sprang into action. They worked with

SNYC on courts-martial at the same time. One of their more publicized cases during these early days was the case of Lemas Woods. In March 1946 this Detroiter had accidentally killed another soldier. He was court-martialed and after a three-hour trial, sentenced to death; the third degree was used to force a confession from his lips. After an uproar generated by CRC, he won a stay of execution from Truman and a new trial. The experienced CRC lawyer Ernest Goodman stepped in at this point. At the new trial, Woods was acquitted of murder, convicted of involuntary manslaughter, and received a three-year sentence. This was in August 1947. But CRC did not stop there. They organized a defense committee that included Coleman Young and Carl Winter. Woods had been a member of UAW, Local 208, thus the trade union movement played a large role in his defense. A tidal wave of publicity ensued as a result. And Woods was free by October.[49]

The Woods victory gave CRC the strength to carry on. In late 1947, Ralph Powe was able to get attorney Lee Epstein to take on the case of Robert Johnson, a man facing court-martial by the army. He had been "convicted of rape in Germany. . . . The complete lack of proof of *corpus delecti* . . . [his] conviction is based on his confession." CRC rode to his rescue and Johnson did not pay a cent to Epstein: "In view of the sorry state of the Congress exchequer, I do not feel justified in requesting any fee over and above these expenses."[50] CRC took on the case of Peter Knemp in 1948, an employee at Tinker Field in Oklahoma who was sacked because "you are and have been a member of the Communist Party. . . . you have attended Communist Party meetings." Actually he gave money to and attended meetings of the Progressive Party, but no matter; CRC defended him also. All this was facilitated because Ralph Powe was special counsel to the little-known but important United Negro and Allied Veterans of America. They were then added to the attorney general's subversives' list, which led to their loss of "accreditation as a veterans organization."[51]

All of this was a prelude to CRC's masterful involvement in the defense of soldiers during the conflict in Korea. The *Daily Compass* was candid in assessing the forces at play: "The Army in Korea is prosecuting a greater proportion of Negro soldiers than whites on charges of cowardice, is convicting a greater proportion, and is imposing far heavier sentences on the Negroes, Thurgood Marshall reported on his return here today." What had happened once again was that the NAACP had tailed after CRC, after they had brought the case of Lt. Leon Gilbert before the public's eye. It was Scottsboro and Trenton and Martinsville all over again. Gilbert, thirty-one, had been condemned to death allegedly for refusing to obey an order. His platoon had been in action for thirteen days and he had gone without sleep for six; besides he was ill with dysentery. He claimed that to have obeyed the order would have meant taking his men into certain death. Tried on charges of "misbehaving before the enemy," at an all-white court-martial proceeding and without being allowed to present Black soldiers to testify, he was given a death sentence and stripped of all honors and his commission. After mass protests, Truman was forced to commute the sentence to twenty years of hard labor.[52]

There were other extenuating circumstances in this case. Gilbert had been ordered to advance by a "newly arrived major" and he had refused. Prosecution witnesses were allowed to leave combat to testify, but the defendant's witnesses were not. It was argued that the provision under which he had been convicted was only relevant when a "declaration of war" had ben made, while Korea was touted as a police action. He argued "combat exhaustion" as a defense and submitted a medical examination to document this. The case was fought in the context of the hotly contested charge that Blacks were no more than cannon fodder in this war and were being disproportionately slaughtered. It was charged that Black regiments were not relieved as often as white ones, that they were sent to the front more often. This mass murder was facilitated by the lingering existence of segregation. One Black battalion of 1,500 lost 1,412 men. CRC proclaimed that while the "flying of a jet plane" in Korea by a Black was "ballyhooed," this "same Negro couldn't work in (the) plant where (the) plane is made." These accusations ringing the changes on Jim Crow were all too accurate and therefore even more dangerous. As the United States tried to fight a racist war against a people of color with a Jim Crow army, CRC refused to let anyone forget this and this was bound to incur the wrath of powerful enemies.[53]

This was such a sensitive and volcanic issue that it was veritably unavoidable that the NAACP would be trotted in to defuse the situation; hence, Thurgood Marshall's trip to the Korean peninsula; this was a delicate job, for CRC had a moving case, Gilbert was married and the father of three. His death penalty was given, even though during World War II "not one officer or enlisted man was executed for failure to obey a command." Even Gilbert's "wishy-washy" attorney conceded that the army "wanted to make an example of someone." So here came the NAACP. Their lawyer rejected the assistance of CRC, which had brought the case to light, and claimed that they "solely and exclusively" represented Gilbert.[54] Patterson and Co. were outraged at this case poaching:

> It really seems that if we had not started, they would fall asleep and they only awakened when the Civil Rights Congress started something. . . . It is my opinion that the NAACP is sleeping on this matter, as it slept on the case of the Martinsville 7 in the last days, and the case of Ed Honeycutt. Their lack of faith in the people, without whose support no legal action can be effective, is detrimental to the interests of every defendant whose cause they espouse. It is not true that intervention of the CRC militates against the defendant's chances.[55]

This was a frequent NAACP charge, but Patterson cited the Woods case and the Trenton Six as examples to the contrary. Undaunted, the NAACP organized a "Committee of 100"—a NAACP front—on the Gilbert case. Their speaking of "Soviet and satellite propagandists" was not necessary to Gilbert's freedom, but it did help to stampede support away from his prime base of support, CRC, and thus to delay his getting his freedom. They did ask if a fair trial were possible when a man is tried "200 yards away from the front line." But they had the temerity to speak of "aggression" of the other side, and repeated their frequent bromide that Jim Crow had to be ended in order to better combat communism. Nevertheless, this offensive made CRC circumspect in their approach. In the fall of 1952, Patterson, who earlier had received heartfelt thanks from Kay Gilbert, approached his client's wife warily:

> Mr. John Holton informs me that you contacted him recently with reference to your husband. As you know, our organization has been deeply interested in this case but remained aloof in order that the NAACP would not argue that our "interference" had harmed Leon. I believe, however, that the *amicus* brief of our counsel was one of the most important factors in securing a commutation of the sentence.

He wanted their "full agreement" before CRC reentered the case, since "I would not want to come into conflict with the NAACP in any way." Disorienting pressures had caused the politically inexperienced Gilberts to cave in, on the dubious assumption that he could not be freed because of a CRC taint, even though that same taint had not prevented the voiding of his death sentence. Earlier Gilbert had expressed to CRC attorney Morris Greenbaum his fervent hope: "I do not know what coordination there may be between CRC and NAACP but do hope that such can be made to bring about desired results in my case."[56] But this retrospectively naive hope was drowned in a tide of redbaiting.

Patterson realized that the Gilberts would be subjected to great pressure due to the nature of the case and he moved to augment their backbone with ideological rigor. In the spring of 1951 he told Ms. Gilbert, "He who alleged that the war in Korea is fought to bring democracy to the Korean peoples is a liar. . . . They send black boys from America to fight that war, to enslave others in order that these black boys will not have the opportunity to organize and fight against their own enslavement." Don't place "your reliance on the courts which for centuries have betrayed us." He encouraged her to speak out more in order to win support for her spouse and to bolster her political confidence: "We would like to organize meetings for you." Previously he had told her, "It was this mass pressure that saved your husband's life, as it did before the lives of the Scottsboro Boys, the Martinsville Seven, the Trenton Six, Willie McGee, and others." Valiantly, CRC leader John Holton tried to maintain her spirit: "The only suggestion that I can make is that *you do not give up hope.* . . . there is tremendous hope for your husband." These feelings were reciprocated. "I wish to extend my heartfelt thanks to you and the entire (CRC) for coming to my assistance in my time of need," said Lt. Gilbert.[57]

Gilbert's appreciation was not misplaced, for it was CRC's tireles labor that was responsible for the initial commutation of his sentence and afterward they continued pushing for his freedom. They twisted the arm of the army in order to get the original transcript of the court-martial. CRC chapters, such as the one in St. Louis, distributed leaflets, held meetings, and sent letters to Truman. They encouraged Ben Davis to speak out on the case and got the Marxist-oriented Labor Youth League to take a special interest. This was part of a conscious overall strategy. In August 1951 Patterson told attorney Greenbaum, "I feel . . . that negotiations . . . which have a broad publicity should be immediately conveyed to us in order that we might help develop the mass support, without which no amount of the most excellent legal effort" can succeed. In addition Patterson fought for an elevated status for Gilbert, "as satisfactory a status as was their's in old Europe," in order to engender "a greater respect . . . for political prisoners." Little wonder that Gilbert's wife was thanking CRC profusely in January 1951 for their assistance.[58]

It was CRC's energy that led to angry headlines in the Afro-American press and exclusive interviews with Gilbert himself. "Don't Let My Son Die," "May Carry Case to U.N.," "Spare This Officer's Life!" were words that galvanized Blacks at a time when the administration felt that unblinking unity was all-important. The *Pittsburgh Courier* was not the only newspaper that asked their readers to write to Truman and Black Brigadier General B. O. Davis on Gilbert's behalf. Ultimately Gilbert was able to escape his commuted term of twenty years of hard labor. Yet, Kay Gilbert was not entirely swayed by the anticommunism that had forced them to drop CRC. In 1955, on the eve of CRC's demise, when it was being battered from all sides, she still found time to express her appreciation.[59]

Gilbert was aware that CRC just did not have a narrow-minded interest in his case but was concerned about the scores of Black soldiers they felt had been framed in Korea, a fact confirmed by Thurgood Marshall's report upon his return from Korea. There was also Emil Farig, a Navy man persecuted by loyalty hearings because of his beliefs. In 1954 CRC was campaigning on behalf of Private Ben Phillips, a draftee: "a loyalty oath was placed before him which he refused to sign. . . . He has now been informed that he will be dishonorably discharged." Veiled threats were part of the arsenal tossed at the Pentagon: "I do not think that a matter of this kind should be aired in the Negro or metropolitan press." CRC strove to protect the interests of this N.C.O. adjudged by the army to be both a Communist and CRC member.[60]

Like so many other CRC cases, their demise overtook the effort of CRC to free Phillips. In this sense it was understandable why the U.S. government would spend so much time trying to jail Patterson and to disrupt CRC. It was understandable because CRC was effective. Their genocide petition exposed starkly the hypocrisy of U.S. foreign policy for all to see, with its demanding of human rights and free elections in Eastern Europe when these were not guaranteed for Blacks in the South. Their exposé of the plight of Black soldiers revealed disconcertingly the contradiction of fighting for "democracy" with an army infested by ugly racism. In response, about all the government felt it could do was bludgeon CRC and then bring in the NAACP to place Band-Aids on the bleeding. But at least the end result was that there were some concessions granted and the NAACP was granted an exalted status in higher circles. The specter of the militant CRC made it easier for U.S. rulers to rationalize to their cruder racist colleagues why the excesses of Jim Crow should be eliminated; they needed only to point to the chanting masses mobilized by CRC across the globe. But Patterson and CRC were not finished. They continued to probe mercilessly at the major weakness of "U.S. democracy," the deep South, and thereby hastened the process that made Dr. King and the civil rights laws possible.

7

I Will Not Live in Peace with Jim Crow: CRC in the South

From the beginning, southern solidarity was a trademark of CRC. Their feeling was that the key to social progress in the nation as a whole was the routing of it in the region where the most retrograde, reactionary elements resided. Jim Crow meant among other things that Dixiecrats would have their bloodstained hands on the levers of national power in Washington through the workings of the seniority system. Simultaneously, with the discrediting of Hitlerite racism during World War II, the Dixiecrats and their ilk came to rely more and more on redbaiting; i.e., the proposition that antiracists were subversives. The prominence of CRC in the South both propelled and fed into this distorting analysis. Their "I Will Not Live in Peace with Jim Crow" campaign had an impact in the North, but it was aimed primarily at the South. This analysis and the action that backed it hindered the organizing of CRC chapters and cast much of their work in the form of campaigns around specific incidents. A great deal of the national campaigns and national energy of CRC was devoted to the South: McGee and Bilbo, then Martinsville and Rosa Lee Ingram gripped feverishly their imagination. But these latter two major campaigns were only the most well-known endeavors of the CRC. Before the advent of the Montgomery Bus Boycott, CRC was the leading and the most disciplined force breaking down the walls of Jim Crow. Indeed, their postwar Cold War campaigns were a necessary predicate that lubricated the path for those who came after.

Part of their work involved responding to the recrudescence of nostalgia about the Confederacy that accompanied the resurgence of the Dixiecrats. In a letter to the *New York Times Magazine* Patterson complained about an article about the renewed popularity of the bars and stars, which he consid-

ered not a "fad" but evidence of "mounting fascism." In response a de-
mented critic sent him a note execrating him as a "big ni-g-r pig." But
Patterson was "extremely sorry to hear that no progressive Americans, who
must have read that letter, had the courage to write in a commendatory vein
about it." This spread of Old South cum fascist ideology was a constant
preoccupation of Patterson. Earlier the *Times* had felt his wrath about their
publicizing of Judge George Armstrong, a "millionaire plantation owner,"
who had offered the trustees of Jefferson Military College at Natchez $50
million "to teach and disseminate the superiority of the Anglo-Saxon and
Latin American races."[1]

But writing letters was never the major concern of CRC; organizing against
racist and political repression was. Although the CRC did not have an
organized chapter in Arkansas at that juncture, Patterson was in touch with
sympathizers in the state trying to save Herman Maxwell. Maxwell was a
Black man who had been given the death penalty for the rape of a white
woman. He was facing his third appeal, after the first two had led to reversals
and new trials. It was McGee all over again. Maxwell was twenty, and what
had happened purportedly was, "She then told him that if he didn't consent 'I
will scream and the house will be surrounded.' " It was hard for him to find a
lawyer and CRC helped there as well as drawing out the issue of racism in the
selection of the jury panel. Also like McGee, the U.S. Supreme Court refused
to hear the case and allowed Maxwell to go to his death. Patterson was
personally close to the editors of the *Arkansas State Press*, the leading Black
paper in the state, which facilitated his placing articles supporting this case
and others and making CRC's militance well-known to Black Arkansas.
Daisy Bates of the *Press* was active in the Wallace campaign, and as evidence
of CRC's impact, she went on to play a major role in the epic school
desegregation battle that took place in Little Rock in 1957.[2]

In North Carolina, CRC had similar impact. It was no accident that the sit-
in movement took off in North Carolina in 1960, for CRC had prepared the
ground and plowed the earth years earlier. During the time of their major
campaigns around Major Benton, Clyde Brown, Junius Scales, and the
Daniels case, they were in alliance with the militant tobacco workers, led by
Black women, who were in the throes of a life or death struggle of their own.
The case of Major Benton was a case that CRC took on in its infancy, and its
unsatisfactory settlement definitely affected the way they handled cases
subsequently.

Benton was a World War II veteran with an IQ of sixty-five, i.e., like a nine-
year-old child. He had gone to the courthouse to pay a fine and the police
chose him for interrogation about the rape of a fifty-year-old Euro-American
woman. Four to five police offices questioned him for hours on end, along
with private investigators. They threatened him. They cajoled him. They only
warned him of his rights when he was confessing. The victim failed to identify
him and the only evidence was his "confession." It was this sort of case,

which CRC fought through the highest courts of the state, that paved the way for the U.S. Supreme Court's subsequent promulgation of the *Miranda* warnings.[3]

This case arose in 1946 and was cast by CRC in the context of Blacks fighting abroad for democratic rights they did not enjoy at home, which was a powerful argument at the time. The Black press of the region picked up on the case, which brought CRC much favorable publicity. When a white man who had raped a fifteen-year-old Black girl was freed for the second time, CRC took pains to bring this fact to the attention of the press. Much of their effort here was incited by Laurent Frantz, their principal southern organizer, who maintained the CRC regional office in Nashville, not far from where he had attended college and law school at the University of Tennessee-Knoxville. Frantz knew the region, was a gifted writer and lawyer, and virtually impervious to the charge of being an "outside agitator." Weeks after the birth of CRC he was on the scene in North Carolina busily organizing support and filing reports. Immediately he saw the political and legal benefit of focusing on the "all-white jury question," which had not been raised at the trial, and on the coerced confession.[4]

With the time-tested clockwork that happened so often in the next decade, Frantz helped in organizing a defense committee. It included David Jones, president of predominantly Black Bennett College, members of the Southern Conference for Human Welfare and the Fellowship of Southern Churchmen, Dean James Taylor of North Carolina College for Negroes, the head of the Negro teachers association, and the publisher of the influential *Carolina Times*. A. T. Spaulding of the wealthy Black family that made a small fortune on insurance attended CRC's founding and was helpful. There were problems, however. Most of the people on the committee "will never do anything. . . . [it is] another of those letter-head committees. . . . If we're going to form a mass membership organization on a militant program of fighting Jim Crow, etc., it's not going to be made up of ministers and professors it will have to be made up of people that no one ever heard of. . . . But is that what we want? I don't know." This dilemma was to dog CRC periodically during its history, and certain failures were caused at times by its unsatisfactory resolution. Nonetheless, Frantz strained to sign up Dr. Frank Graham, powerful president of the University of North Carolina: "his name on the Benton defense committee is damn near indispensable. . . . a thing of this kind just isn't considered kosher without his name on it."[5]

But the problems with the defense committee and local counsel led to a settlement that CRC found distasteful. Some of the "ministers and professors," many of whom had petit bourgeois outlooks, had an "unfavorable reaction to the tone of our publicity." Others had a legitimate concern about the local firm that was "anxious to compromise the case and accept a life sentence." At various times Frantz came over from Tennessee in-between traveling to Mississippi for the McGee case and Powe came down from New

York to lend strength to the campaign. Frantz's "hunch was that the local committee would like to get rid of the local attorneys in question but do not have the guts to do so." CRC was having similar difficulties with these lawyers and suggested as an "out" that it take over "hiring and paying for trial counsel." This matter of local counsel was often a difficulty for CRC in the South, where exclusivist bar rules hampered the practices of lawyers with out-of-state licenses. To deal with this problem, they continuously sent lawyers there to monitor the scene. Frantz, Powe, Herman Rosenfeld, and Emmanuel Bloch were frequently found in the Tarheel State during that time. It was Bloch's investigation that propelled CRC into the case and helped to turn up the evidence that revealed the way Benton had been "starved and grilled by seven detectives over a period of twenty-four hours" before confessing and underscored that "witnesses testified that he was far from the scene." It was Frantz who helped lend backbone to the defense committee by helping to involve Local 22 of the United Tobacco Workers in the struggle.[6]

With all that, there were still problems. In a way that was to haunt CRC throughout the years, local counsel "somehow . . . had got the impression that we might be more interested in expanding legal theory through test cases than in saving defendants. I told him we wanted to win in this court if we could, but lay a proper basis for the U.S. Supreme Court in case we lost in this court." Frantz and CRC's Benjamin Goldring backed this up by advising local counsel on all manner of arcane legal points. Although he was offered the opportunity, Frantz refused to participate in oral argument, "because I didn't want to introduce unnecessarily the possible [odium] attaching to an out-of-state attorney."[7] The states' rights barrier of bias did not hurt them this time, insofar as a new trial was won in the North Carolina Supreme Court.

But these buoyant hopes were dashed cruelly. At the trial, the defense decided to throw the case "to the mercy of (the) Judge." Benton received a life sentence with the faint possibility of a pardon "if the occasion warranted it and he conduct himself alright [sic]." reported Rev. L. W. Wertz of the defense committee. R. D. Everett, an attorney on the committee, explained that the prosecution had an "airtight case," and Benton "made a very poor Witness." He threw a bouquet in the direction of CRC, "I am firmly of the opinion that it was only through your interference that the man was not sentenced to death," but they were hardly pleased. It certainly helped that the evidence was on the record and that those without ideological axes to grind had recognized that CRC was helpful and not just trying to expose the capitalist system without considering the defendant involved, but this was a rude awakening in the early history of CRC from which they drew appropriate lessons.[8]

Rev. Wertz agreed with Ralph Powe, who was struck dumb by the outcome. The North Carolina pastor retorted, "I am of the opinion, your attitude in the case was correct. We should have fought it to a finish. Had I known what has been conveyed to me, we would not have listened to what was told on Saturday morning. Jones and Jones seems to think he was rushed by the attorney too much and fast in coming to the terms we did." Powe had spent three weeks in the state working and organizing. He had enlisted Joseph Waddy of the prestigious Black law firm in Washington, D.C., Houston and Houston, and labor lawyer Frank Donner in the case. The lesson he learned here was also one inculcated in CRC itself. Everett tried to console him: "I think our alibi to prove the alibi (sic) in clock-like fashion by witnesses who did not hear each other testify was due to your preparation in advance of the trial. I know we would have acquitted our client if he had been innocent, and I think we did very well for him indeed, after he had advised counsel he was guilty, and we were unable to put him on the stand."[9]

Even though local counsel W. R. Jones felt that Goldring of the national office of CRC "did an excellent piece of work," he was a bit chagrined with the outcome. Perhaps indicative of how busy he and his office were is the fact that the new trial came in April 1947, the North Carolina Supreme Court's reversal of the verdict came in November 1946, but Jones did not read the record until January 1947; this appeared to be a major political error for a CRC lawyer. He conceded that "the sentence came as somewhat of a shock up here"; he thought if the "settlement" came, it would be for fifteen years. Goldring seemed to be nonplussed by it all:

> I understand that the trial judge and even the solicitor for the most part, were scrupulously correct. . . . I have heard high praise of the manner in which the defense was conducted. . . . I have not the slightest hesitation in saying that we did all we possibly knew how: we retained, in my own opinion, by far and away the best counsel in the state. . . . I guess that the chief reason that impelled the taking on of the case was the action of the first trial judge in practically commanding a verdict of guilty. Once that element was removed, the case was hardly too clear-cut at one time for an organization that cannot overtake to handle many cases at one time. But once we get into a case, we prefer to fight for the defendant until the end and even though information turns up, as sometimes happens, which we did not know about at first.

Attorney Everett received $500 from CRC for his labors, but CRC received valuable lessons in return about how to handle such cases. They were not a glorified legal services of the left or even a quasi-law firm, so the way the Benton case was conducted could easily be regarded as improper. Others did not seem to think so. Local counsel W. R. Jones complimented Goldring and the chair of the defense committee. Rev. Wertz earlier had spoken similarly: "We are very thankful to you and your organization for the assistance you are given [sic] and will give. We shall cooperate with you for a full exoneration of this young man."[10]

It was all well and good to have praise on the record, but it did not allay the CRC's concern about botching the Benton case. The composition of the defense committee, the apparent latitude given to local counsel, the inadequacy of preparation in New York, and so forth were all errors made by an organization in its infancy though the lengthy legacy of ILD cannot be discounted. But just as no strike is ever lost, the lessons gained here held CRC in fine stead as they proceeded to tackle other cases, particularly other difficult ones in North Carolina.

A few years later, CRC had an opportunity for redemption when the Clyde Brown case arose. A nineteen-year-old high school student in Winston-Salem, this Black youth was convicted of "beating and raping" a white female. During his trial Afro-Americans were excluded from the jury. An overheated atmosphere of prejudice was created by the local press. There was sharply conflicting testimony by witnesses. By this point William Patterson was the top CRC leader and he did not hesitate to step in. He urged an immediate flow of telegrams and letters to Governor Kerr Scott. He harped on the fact of a coerced confession that elicited admissions about this June 1950 "crime," which called for a penalty of "death by asphyxiation." After the first trial a group of "more than one thousand Negro and white workers held a meeting in Winston-Salem" to protest the verdict.[11]

CRC fought this case up and down the state and federal court system. Ralph Powe was co-counsel on the case, and a number of other CRC lawyers participated. Why this assistance was necessary was revelaed by Velma Hopkins of the defense committee and a local union leader (Brown's mother and aunt were also members of Local 22 of the Tobacco Workers Union). Hopkins reminded Powe of "promises" that they would send "someone down here who could check into the hospital records and do research work which is almost impossible for a local Negro lawyer to do." Not because of concepts of inferiority but for pragmatic reasons she wanted to get "a white attorney in here." Not only was Brown's life at stake but "our security locally will be seriously weakened" if the case is lost. Finally, in April 1952, Brown won a review in the U.S. Supreme Court of his conviction, although they had rejected his previous appeal in June. CRC felt the change was due to their organized pressure and that of the local committee, which was heavily populated with workers, in contrast to the Benton case. But in an opinion of over one hundred pages replete with vehement dissents that raised issues of the meaning of *certiorari* denial, racial exclusion from jury lists, and many others, Brown lost.[12]

There was more of an effort made here to integrate this case within overall CRC efforts. The Peoples Defense Committee in Winston-Salem sold more than twenty-five copies of the genocide book and ordered more. Patterson pointed out that the same two Supreme Court Justices who had voted to review Brown's case (Justices Black and Douglas) "were also paired in the defense of the Bill of Rights in the case of the Communist leaders—an indication of the relationship of the rights of the minority Negro people to those of the minority political party, the Communist Party."[13]

At the same time they were embroiled in the fight to save Brown's life, they took on two other cases that in part raised similar issues. Lloyd and Bennie Daniels were teenagers in Durham facing the gas chamber for allegedly murdering a white cabdriver; they had blood on their clothes from an earlier scrap with other boys; they were arrested without counsel and held incommunicado; they were forced to sign confessions. Raleigh Speller was involved in a rape case of a white female and, like Brown, raised the issue that no white man had ever been executed in North Carolina for the rape of a Black woman. Blacks did not serve on grand or petit juries in the state even though they were 60 percent of the county's population and 35–40 percent of the taxpayers. In Pitt County, where the Speller case arose, Blacks were 44.2 percent of the population over twenty-one years old, and 33 percent of those on the tax list. Their literacy rate was 74.2 percent but no Black had ever served on a grand jury; less than 2 percent of the jury lists were composed of Blacks and less than 1 percent of the petit jurors.[14]

The fact that CRC had access to Euro-American lawyers was helpful to the Carolinians and Patterson in August 1949 encouraged them to take Rogge on the case. Patterson also tried to get the local committee to "affiliate with CRC at the earliest moment," while adding quickly that "whether or not we are formally associated with your committee you can rest assured that in all the publicity which we send out the Daniels case will be mentioned." The Peoples Defense Committee was a juicy prize for CRC. It included the "state organizer for NAACP," the president of the Chapel Hill NAACP, the publisher of the *Carolina Times* (a local Black paper), union leader Moranda Smith (also a member of CRC's board) and the Progressive Party and Furniture Workers Union leader John Hunt. C. A. Simmons, head of the committee, was "one of the original organizers of the Tobacco Workers Union"; as a result of his defense efforts, he lost his job and was out of work for two years.[15]

The committee was seen as the basis for a permanent civil rights organization. They voted to send letters of protest of the CP-Eleven case and another letter to Truman urging the appointment of an African-American to the U.S. Supreme Court. Repeatedly they chided Governor Scott because of his view of these cases. In turn, he redbaited them furiously and castigated their ties to CRC, which he said signified the "inflammatory activity of professional agitators." The committee was not deterred. They put out quite a bit of literature highlighting the most questionable aspects of the Daniels' case, the "extorted confessions." The Daniels were sixteen and seventeen years old. Police found blood on some of their clothing, which was "amply shown by evidence to have been shed in a fight with another Negro in Greenville. No tests were made of this blood to indicate its source." All four defendants were staring at dates with the gas chamber, and the committee sought to place this in a larger context. They observed how after the harvesting season in this agricultural area there was a "typical pattern" of "cracking down" familiar to sharecroppers. "Sheriffs, deputies, constables, and police have their annual 'hunting season' to teach sharecroppers and workers how to step lightly and bow politely." The committee raised money by selling "Daniels Defense Bonds" and they expanded their focus to include police brutality and support for striking fishermen.[16]

As Governor Scott's comment indicated, CRC worked with the committee every step of the way. In August 1949 Patterson told John Hunt, "We have some 75 chapters. . . . You can have the Civil Rights Congress mailing list placed at your disposal. . . ." They were able to get Rogge to work on the case, although this later caused CRC some embarrassment when he requested inflated fees and, worse, testified against Du Bois at his trial. Because of CRC assistance, legal and otherwise, the executions were delayed. Patterson warned the committee against the perils of narrow nationalism: "I note you have mentioned only Negro prisoners in your greetings. I am hoping that you can give consideration to all of the men and women." After the committee decided to dismiss Rogge, CRC aided them in getting Louis Fleischer as a replacement. They got Paul Robeson to raise money and sent out their own national appeal. This was necessary because during the life of the committee, between 1949 and 1954, they took in $8,985.54 and spent $8,964.49.[17]

The legal issues in all these cases were formidable and at the same time trailblazing. The North Carolina Supreme Court refused to review the trial of the Daniels "because attorneys . . . had allegedly been one day late in presenting certain appeal records." *Habeas corpus* was filed in federal district court and they were turned down. This was upheld by the circuit court. The U.S. Supreme Court took up this denial on appeal. The exclusion of Blacks from juries was an issue common to all three cases. Hearing the cases together, the court on 9 February 1953 ruled that the State of North Carolina had lessened its discrimination against Blacks by selecting jurors from tax lists. Justices Black, Frankfurter, and Douglas dissented—Black with a two-thousand-word dissent—and alleged that the decision meant discrimination on the basis of wealth was sanctioned. All the men were executed. When the Daniels cousins were killed, there were "huge crowds" at the funeral. According to the committee, the case "has heightened the organization of other groups in the state devoted to the cause of equal justice and the abolition of unequal punishment." Simultaneously, the North Carolina attorney general moved to designate the committee as "subversive." They continued, "The action of the Attorney General against the Committee indicated to large numbers of people the direct association between 'McCarthyism' and those who would deny equal justice to all citizens." This was all too true, but, like CRC, before long the Peoples Defense Committee was defunct. However the seeds they had planted emerged during the modern civil rights era, as this area became a major battleground. And the legal issues they raised, e.g., exclusion of Blacks from juries, the meaning of *certiorari,* etc., blazed the way for future victories.[18]

CRC also launched a campaign around the Smith Act case of North Carolina Communist leader Junius Scales. From a prominent family and heir to a fortune, Scales was something of an unlikely working class leader. He was indicted under the membership clause of the act and was sentenced to six years, with a denial of bail. CRC also became involved in the highly controversial case of John McCray, editor of the *Columbia Lighthouse and Informer* in South Carolina, a Black weekly. He received sixty days on the chain gang for the alleged libel of the court that sent a Black man, Willie Talbert, to the electric chair on the charge of rape. They pointed him in the direction of CRC attorney John Coe. There were other cases that gripped their attention in this area during the history of CRC indicating beyond a doubt the mark they left.[19]

CRC had a tumultuous time of it in North Carolina, as evidenced by their harassment by the state's attorney general. But this harassment paled into insignificance compared with what they faced in Florida, one of the few southern states where they had organized chapters. As early as the summer of 1948 it was being reported that the Miami chapter was "very disorganized" because of the "transient nature of Miami," but it would be reductionist to point to this transcience as the sole factor causing their troubles there. As in other cities, they shared a small office with allies like the Progressive Party, the Young Progressives of America, and People's Songs, with the party bearing most of the costs. It was not unusual when the police broke up an "interracial" affair sponsored by YPA. As Bella Fisher with gross understatement informed the national office, in the South, "even progressives are more prudent about activities which are accepted in other areas." Shortly thereafter, chapter chairman Victor Emmanuel bolted from CRC and issued a "terrific condemnation" to the press; "it got first page publicity. . . . The Negro press has been playing it up too." The chapter had clashes and encounters with the Ku Klux Klan, "face to face . . . in full dress regalia." Continually there was pressure from the police, some of whom were suspected of being KKK members; they " 'pulled in' . . . one of our Negro boys" and the "first question he was asked" was about CRC. As a result, the chapter opted for a rotating leadership in order to shield their leaders from pressure. Chapter leader Bobby Graff was approached by local Black leaders to speak at an anti-Klan rally. Blacks supported CRC "100%" she said, "but I cannot afford to leave myself open to slander and attack by speaking at a CRC rally." The chapter had been in remission for a while, but in 1954 their old nemesis the *Miami Daily News* was at it again. Max Shlafrock, a CRC member and president and treasurer of M. S. Construction Company, was scored by Damon Runyon, Jr., for having sent greetings to the *Daily Worker* on their thirtieth anniversary. Shlafrock, who had served as CRC treasurer, had received over $600,000 in city contracts. They displayed big pictures of his home and office, perhaps to encourage harassment, and pressured him to leave the left.[20]

Inevitably this compulsion had effect on the chapter. It was feared that conversations from Miami were bugged and the *Daily News* was an ubiquitous menace. In March 1949, again on page one, they focused on CRC, this time on their fund drive. After calling them a "front" for the Communist Party and describing chapter secretary Harriet Feit as a dwarf, they got down to the busines at hand—scurrilous attack. They published pictures of members leaving a CRC meeting with their faces covered, and they noted the participation of the Transport Workers Union, Local 500. Their reporting was striking in another way: "The whole meeting was based on the Negro's plight in the South—with only brief mention of the predicament the twelve Communist leaders face in New York." Apparently, CRC had been leaned on to the point that defending the first line in the fight for civil liberties was being abandoned. Weeks earlier they had decided not to make a big issue of the frequent occurrence of the police breaking up interracial parties and they had dropped a police brutality case on the grounds that it might feed racism, since a Black officer was involved. This last could be seen as admirable, but in toto it seemed that the chapter was bending under the weight of repression.[21]

All the while the national office was warning of the possible adverse consequences of a certain course: "(the chapter) must shift emphasis from the so-called intellectual middle class crowd that has defaulted on the task of winning civil rights to the Negro working people, the young white people, and the white workers." The chapter was castigated for being concerned "with many problems which are not (CRC) problems." It wasn't long before Graff was reporting that "our numbers are decreasing and very few replacements" were arriving. The assassination of NAACP leader Harry Moore and his wife was a signal for the FBI to become "especially busy here hounding progressives and getting them fired." In their defense CRC did have the obstacle of a statute that made integrated meetings illegal. They fought this, of course, but it cost $2000 to begin with, which was "aggravating, especially with several so-called progressive attorneys in town." Even with victories there were problems: "we won the last case of the Negro youth who was shot, but were unable to use the name of the CRC as the organization who fought the case by agreement with the attorney."[22]

The chapter was drifting toward liquidation, but in a pattern repeated elsewhere, CRC cadre—particularly Euro-Americans—joined the NAACP. Graff was elected as a delegate to the national NAACP convention of 1952 and in that same year reported "we have no CRC chapter here"; however, they were able to "set up a local committee for 'Pat's' defense. . . . It was composed of outstanding Negro community leaders in the main." Soon she was on the executive board of the NAACP Miami branch, which facilitated their joining progressive movements. Still, she complained of their failure to push "involvement of the membership or the community." Wistfully, Graff told Grossman, "Remember that even if you don't get a report from us we are still in there with you and doing what we can." Nevertheless, contacts within the NAACP, even in high positions, were not seen as a substitute for an active CRC chapter. The example of Miami showed that with the demise of CRC, cadre did not die with it, but went on to continue the struggle for equality, adding fire to other organizations.[23]

In a sense it was understandable why CRC had so much difficulty keeping a chapter going in the "Sunshine State." During this era Florida was visited with as much violence as any state, including Mississippi. Unlike Mississippi, Blacks there were not hovering on the verge of a majority; the dynamic there seemed to involve white racists reacting to perceived challenges to their diktat. In any case, the Groveland Massacre garnered worldwide headlines and again saw CRC and NAACP working on the same case, but not necessarily together.

This "Little Scottsboro Case" began in 1949 with the rape of a seventeen-year-old Groveland white housewife. Black defendants were sought; in the process, one received a bullet in the head after the sheriff had handcuffed him; another was killed by a posse a few weeks after the attack. The remaining Blacks were beaten until they confessed. The NAACP found "broken teeth . . . dislocated jaw." They never signed a confession; two of them only nodded, the other not even that. An all-white jury convicted two of these men and gave them the death penalty; the other got a life sentence. But that was not all. There was a massive pogrom launched against the Black community of this rural area. Hundreds of people fled. Homes were burned. A nine-year-old Black child was missing and was believed "burned to death." According to CRC investigator Ewart Guinier, "Scarcely a single Negro is left in Groveland." CRC had its own particular view of these events: "At the time, the plantation owners in the area, where poor Negro farm workers [worked] were seeking an excuse for a pogrom against the Negro people in the area." All three defendants were veterans and one had been singled out because of his views on "equal rights." There was resentment of the fact that his father had a "nice house" and property. Due to inflammatory press headlines and articles, the Supreme Court ordered a new trial for the two defendants who appealed, but the press had not learned a lesson. Soon afterward they were up to their old tricks: "There is only one way to act— Take justice into our own hands . . . [Give them] The Supreme Penalty—No Compromise."[24]

In late 1951 the two appellants, Samuel Shepherd and Walter Irvin, were being transported from prison by the authorities en route to the courthouse where hearings on their case were to be held the next morning on their NAACP attorneys' motion for a change of venue. Deputy Jim Yates suggested that the two men had tried to run away. This was after the U.S. Supreme Court had unanimously reversed their conviction, with Justice Robert Jackson calling their first trial "one of the best examples of one of the worst menaces to American justice." Despite this and the possibility they would soon be vindicated, Sheriff Willis McCall said that the men attacked him in an attempt to escape; this after spending two years in a lightless, badly ventilated cell. Irvin was left for dead in a ditch, handcuffed to the slain Shepherd, who had received three blasts in the chest and neck. Earlier Shepherd had claimed that the authorities had tried to entice him to escape. In any case, the police would not allow attorney Robert Carter to speak with the surviving defendant.[25]

The 1949 pogrom guaranteed that the Groveland case would garner national headlines. With the 1951 slaying occurring at the same time CRC was filing their genocide petition and the Truman administration was scoring developments in Eastern Europe, CRC's Soviet allies and others moved to ensure that the case received international headlines. Soviet Foreign Minister Andrei Vishinsky charged that these events were typical of human rights violations in the United States. Canadian External Affairs Minister Lester Pearson charged that "thousands will protest." In response, Patterson asked his northern neighbor to protest the shooting himself by discussing the genocide petition at the UN and raising the question of the sheriff and his deputy not being indicted. But it was Vishinsky's charges to which the press kept returning. As this happened, one could almost see how many people in the United States were coming to take seriously the NAACP allegation that communism could be better fought if Jim Crow were to be curbed. Thurgood Marshall specifically cited Vishinsky in seeking justice for Irvin. Editorially the *New York Post* stated that "it would be sad if Americans responded to the outrage only because of what the Russians say about it." Naturally the *Daily Worker* invoked the name of the Soviet diplomat. Walter Reuther observed in the *New York Times* that the Soviets and Communists at home would make propaganda out of the shooting. In the same paper Vishinsky countered Dean Acheson's charges of the deprivation of human rights in Eastern Europe by citing the slaying: "This is the American way of life. . . . I think some people should look after their own business, before sticking their noses into other people's houses."[26]

What must have been disturbing to U.S. elites was the fact that increasingly Blacks were echoing the Soviet Foreign Minister. Editorially, the Black *St. Louis American* denounced Channing Tobias after he had taken the Soviet leader to task: "he is by no means to be a gauge of what American Negroes are thinking." The CRC ally went on to take on Tobias personally: "Dr. Tobias for years was a top official in the YMCA in its jim crow set-up. He is a . . . middle way leader." They continued, "The point is not that the Russians are right or are without great wrongs and faults. . . . there is no defense to say that the Russians have slave labor. The cold truth is that if these particular prisoners had not been in the world's eyes because of outside forces," the two would have died like so many others.[27]

This editorial byplay was a reflection of an outrage coursing across the nation and the globe. Rev. Paul Moore and Prof. S. Ralph Harlow of Smith College asked why the sheriff was driving alone at night with two prisoners who had been condemned to death. Philip Murray of the CIO wired the President to protest. One commentator called the Lake County tragedy "a stab in the back of the boys fighting in Korea. . . . Stalin couldn't have bought" better propaganda "for a million dollars." The *National Guardian* reported on "worldwide" protests and connected the events to charges of local Blacks becoming "uppity." Stetson Kennedy in the *Compass* disgustedly reported how the sheriff was "treated as guest of honor" at the coroner's jury. A *New York Post* reporter interviewed Florida whites who spoke of keeping Blacks in their place; they also reported Marshall's charge that the defendants were shot to deprive them of a fair trial and asked that their assailants be prosecuted for contempt, citing *U.S. v. Shipp.* In fact the *Post* did special reporting that pointed to the officers' guilt "clearly." *Droit et Liberté* and Telepress reported the international condemnation of U.S. pretensions; the local *St. Petersburg Times* averred that communist "agitators and propagandists were seeking precisely such examples of white injustice to colored races to broadcast to the world. . . . considering that Communist National Headquarters is now located in Harlem, New York's Negro center, it is easy to imagine the capital they will make of the incident."[28]

The NAACP was handling the legal aspects of this case and CRC was handling mass organizing. Although their coordination was not all that it could have been, if the two had been able to agree on such a division of labor during this entire critical era, the entire movement would have been the winner. CRC organized an angry mass rally of one thousand people in New York, sent "carloads of food and clothing" to Groveland, and generated a windstorm of telegrammed protest; all this in the face of what Bobby Graff termed "hysterical baiting" in Florida. The chapter voted "4–2 with still very much hesitancy" to enter the case. They held a mass meeting of over two hundred ("70% Negro"). "The opportunity for organizing a broad committee on Groveland was there. But due to our being afraid to act and our people stopping us at every turn we missed that opportunity too." As had happened in Trenton, the situation operated to limit the role of CRC and expand the role of the NAACP; even CRC members were affected: " 'Our people' have asked that CRC (and PP) stay out so it might be a broad coalition (?) committee." But their timorousness did not prevent their harassment. Two days after their mass meeting a note was placed on their office door saying "stop being anti-American." It was signed by the klan. What followed was a "steady campaign of intimidation" and a great deal of hate mail, some of it signed "The Gremlin from the Kremlin." The press entered the fray, censuring Graff and her "unproletarian house in the southwest section"; the chapter was not moving rapidly on the case and allowed the NAACP to gain a toehold. Still, Patterson was sympathetic to the Floridians' plight: "The signature—'The Gremlin from the Kremlin'—is being used in other sections of the country. . . . The terror there is fierce—perhaps moreso than elsewhere." Graff realized this and reported that "Intimidation of interracial YPA affairs continues." But Patterson reminded her "you must seek to break away from the sole association with the left."[29]

Such factors help to explain why the Groveland case was not settled satisfactorily. There was abject terror, poor coordination with the NAACP, and dwindling funds. These elements played a role in other Florida cases. There was the controversial case of sixteen-year-old Orion Johnson. He was picked up at school for questioning about a bad check. The sheriff drove him home to get his jacket; while there, Johnson allegedly picked up an ice pick. He entered the car and the pick fell. The sheriff reached for his gun, but allegedly Johnson plunged the pick into his skull, snatched the gun, and shot him. During questioning afterward, Johnson was supposed to have said, "under Communism all people are treated right. Everybody is treated equal." This did not endear him to the authorities. He did say that the sheriff had threatened him, and being aware of police community relations, he had decided that the better part of wisdom would be to pack a pick. Others believed that the sheriff had been killed because of his opposition to local gambling and that Johnson was covering up for the real culprit. In neither instance was CRC able to render meaningful assistance. In response to this reign of terror, CRC did try to launch a national boycott of Florida citrus: "The grocer must be made to prove that such produce is not from Florida." But this campaign did not catch fire.[30]

CRC's presence in Alabama was sporadic. Early in their history they joined with SNYC in a peripheral involvement in the case of Peter Paul Hall, a twenty-three-year-old Black man charged with the rape and murder of a seventeen-year-old white girl. In 1950 CRC attorney John Coe joined with Alabama Communist Party leader Sam Hall to bar a Birmingham ordinance that prescribed a penalty of six months in jail and a $100 fine for each day a communist was in the city. This draconian bill, authored by "Bull" Connor, was declared unconstitutional by a federal court; this occurred after CRC had been able to get their ally the *St. Louis American* to blast the bill. In 1952 they intervened in the case of a ten-year-old, allegedly arrested and beaten after stealing. Patterson was in touch with Asbury Howard of the Mine, Mill, and Smelter Workers Union and the Juvenile and Domestic Relations Court of Birmingham to resolve this matter. CRC had contacts there, though they lacked a full, flourishing chapter. The Rev. J. H. Petty, pastor of the Shady Grove Baptist Church in Parrish, Alabama, was their principal contact.[31]

In Mississippi the McGee case certainly made CRC's name well-known statewide, although terror prevented that renown from being translated into booming chapters. At the same time they were pursuing the McGee case they were fighting other cases that raised similar questions, including the difficulty in securing adequate local counsel. Johnny Craft was a twenty-two-year-old Marine veteran who had fought in Okinawa. In August 1946 it was reported that he had fired on a white youth, which precipitated a near massacre of the Black community. A bevy of police officers rushed the home of this son of a tenant farmer and he fired back. A Euro-American landowner had accused Craft of stealing a tire. Like the slave tales of old, Craft fled into the woods with three hundred to five hundred white males nipping at his heels. All this was the culmination of a feud between two white landowners, both seeking to ensure that the Craft family of eleven would remain tenant farmers with them. The Crafts had lived on the same property for almost half a century. CRC's pattern of response was to portray such incidents as being not isolated events but part of a larger scheme. In this instance the beleaguered *Jackson Advocate* agreed: "While Negro citizens of all classes are being subjected to these acts of terrorism and intimidation they appear to be mainly directed against Negro veterans." Veterans, having fought for "democracy," often were less willing to accept the racist status quo. In an atmosphere of sheer horror, all eleven members of the Craft family were arrested, along with thirteen Black witnesses, and Johnny Craft was convicted of assault and battery. There were cross-burnings at Tougaloo. A headline in the *Jackson Clarion-Ledger* read, "Key Negroes Elude Chase—Near War." An editorial in the *Jackson Daily News* read, "White Supremacy in Peril . . . Do you want a white man's government, or will you take the risk of being governed by Negroes."[32] SNYC was involved in posting $11,000 bond and CRC entered the case.

On entering the case, CRC found the facts were much worse than the papers had reported. Craft's father testified that shots had been fired without warning into the house and that fifty cars full of beefy white males had descended on them. They all thought it was the typical Mississippi lynch mob and not a legal lynch mob, i.e., the police; they were all placed under arrest without warrants and his twelve-year-old alone was shot at eight times. A number of the family members had been cuffed and struck.[33]

As had happened in many of their other cases in the South, CRC had incredible difficulties with local counsel, this time the familiar Dixon Pyles. By early in 1947 they had already paid him $2,130 and had agreed to pay him $3,000 more, but they were having trouble with "joint consultation" on the case. Milton Kaufman had to tell Pyles, "Please let me hear from you as soon as possible. I remember that it was in the long silences between us that misunderstandings developed before. We are on too friendly terms now to let any new misunderstandings develop." But Pyles was not being communicative and Ralph Powe a few months later had to repeat these words: "We cannot afford to let the Johnny Craft case go by default. . . . I must again ask why we have not heard from you regarding our request for a rough draft of the *Writ Coram Nobis*. . . . Herman Rosenfeld . . . will personally work with you on the legal aspects of this case even to the point of going to Mississippi to appear as associate counsel during the hearing." When Pyles did contact the national office it was a usual combination of optimism and begging: "the court is going to be forced to reverse this case. . . . Please send me all the money you can. I am constantly in financial distress." There were also differences with him over legal strategy. Despite CRC's dispatching lawyers south to talk with him, he remained reluctant to file the *coram nobis writ*. He felt that this writ was "intended to correct a mistake of fact and not of law"; since there were no new facts in his estimation, no writ would lie.[34]

There were greater differences than those over the writ and money however. Finally, Powe exploded: "Frankly, I am greatly perturbed over our present predicament. . . . I find it hard to accept your suggestion that Craft should be approached with a view to having him 'tell all' and 'come clean.' . . . A Negro has to think a thousand times before giving information that may involve a white person and which, at the same time, may result in his entire family being uprooted and forced to scatter, but quickly." This coincided with Patterson's view that "the percentage of innocence . . . in Southern prisons must go as high as 75% or better. . . . and the 25% who are guilty of crimes of whatever nature or character, the responsibility rests with the state. . . ." It appeared as if Pyles and CRC had irreconcilable differences. Craft was serving a forty-year term in the infamous Parchman prison and CRC was worried that he would not survive there. In all fairness to Pyles it should be pointed out that many of his fellow white Mississippians did not appreciate his aligning himself with a "Communist front" and disbarment was not a farfetched possibility. Still, CRC was not able to get a mass campaign off the ground and Craft had to spend more time than he desired in prison.[35]

In 1955, as CRC was on the way out, they joined with many others in protesting the lynching of the Black youth, Emmett Till. This Mississippian was lynched after allegedly whistling at a white woman. Rarely before had Patterson been so angered. He called unequivocally for the "conviction and execution" of the murderers. Their campaign around the Till case did bring renewed energy to a number of chapters. In October 1955 in Milwaukee, the chapter heard Geraldine Lightfoot and Junius Scales speak before a rally of four hundred people on the Till case. The *Daily Worker* reported that "Although the Armory is far from the Negro community, about two-thirds of the audience were Negroes."[36]

Louisiana was the site of one of the more organized CRC efforts and much of this organization was due to the leadership of Dr. Oakley Johnson, who taught at Dillard University and was a member of the NAACP, the United Public Workers of America, and a number of community organizations. Like Florida, Louisiana was equally the scene of fiercely raging civil rights battles. The CRC chapter there came charging into existence in April 1948 when a Black was taken off a bus in New Orleans and shot by the police. The dispute concerned paying a 5¢ fare. Roy Brooks had been hit "savagely over the head with the butt of his revolver, dragged . . . from the bus, arrested . . . walked . . . at gun point about half a block toward the jail, and then shot . . . twice, once in the back." This incident ignited the CRC's formation and their early leaders included the NAACP, Sleeping Car Porters union, Fur and Leather Workers union, Longshoremen's union leaders, and others. Their pressure led to an indictment, but the white officer was acquitted by an all-white male jury after seven minutes of deliberation. Although the chapter cried "whitewash," this was the "First time . . . ever" that a grand jury in Louisiana indicted a police officer for slaying a Black. Here unions were in on the ground floor, as both the ILWU and the furriers were an integral part of the chapter. CRC was heavily involved in combating the nationwide trend of the police breaking up interracial parties. After a number of people were arrested in 1949 in this way, CRC campaigning led to all of them being discharged. When police disrupted a voter registration effort, also interracial, organized by YPA and involving students from Tulane, Xavier, and Dillard, and they beat another Black youth, CRC was involved.[37]

The chapter's early successes attracted the attention of the authorities. CRC had dug deep roots in the community and had been invited to participate by the NAACP in their fortieth anniversary celebration. FBI agents had a chuckle after NAACP officials subsequently barred Johnson from speaking at one of their events. They also maintained profiles on CRC leaders.

Around that time Johnson was subpoenaed to appear before a grand jury. J. Skelly Wright, who later developed a reputation as something of a liberal, grilled him mercilessly here. Particularly unappreciated was the effort by CRC, YPA, and a number of local unions to protest the CP-Eleven trial. Johnson had been a founder of the party in 1919 and at the University of Michigan had been faculty advisor to the Negro-Caucasian Club, the first interracial organization on campus. Johnson joined the Socialist Party in 1912 and received a doctorate in English from the University of Michigan. He taught in Moscow in 1935 and was with the *Daily Worker* from 1940–44. White-haired and usually wearing a suit and tie draped on his 5'7" frame, he was jolly, smiling, and an asthmatic. This appearance before the grand jury was the beginning of a skein of events that led to the chapter's demise. First of all, YPA backed away, claiming "it is our policy . . . that we shall not seek CRC to represent us officially in local cases." Then when CRC tried to organize a conference locally, "more than thirty persons who were asked to sign the call and endorse the conference refused . . . because they were afraid." CRC was not just protesting police brutality, as important as that was, but making a basic challenge to entrenched political power: When a Black, Samuel Spears, was arrested and beaten in the process of voting, the NAACP would not help until CRC withdrew. Willie Jackson was beaten by police after they found a voter registration card in his pocket. ". . . in cooperation with [others] . . . we are now preparing to lead a delegation of twenty-five leading Negroes to the Parish courthouse to get them registered to vote. We expect not only will they be refused but that we will be able to lay the basis for a constitutional action. . . . This parish is the home of Leander Perez."[38]

Blacks facing capital punishment were the particular specialty of the Louisiana chapter. Even before their forces had congealed into a chapter, they had become involved in 1946 in the case of Milton Harold Wilson. A confession had been beaten out of him to force him to admit to the murder of a white couple; he wound up urinating blood because of a bladder tumor. His first trial was a mistrial. His second found him guilty. In November 1948, the chapter forcefully entered the case, as the state's high court overturned the conviction because of the forced confession. But in his third trial he was found guilty again and received a sentence to the electric chair, despite evidence pointing at others: the father of the slain wife was suspected because he had objected to her prostitution, but this was not allowed in evidence.[39]

All of this was a prelude to the joint case of Paul Washington and Ocie Jugger. In a plot that was becoming all too familiar but actually signified the genocidal conditions that CRC was complaining about, Washington (another war veteran) and Jugger, both in their twenties, were charged with the rape of a white widow. They were represented by a court-appointed white attorney who put up a token defense for his Black clients. They were found guilty and sentenced to death. Then new evidence emerged that allegedly only Jugger had been in the house, not Washington, with the latter claiming that a confession had been beaten out of him. Washington, twenty-five, was a war veteran and unemployed; Jugger was a garbageman, and, like his codefendant, quite handsome; he was small—5'5" and 120 pounds—with distinctive scars on his face and left arm. Originally the alleged rape victim did not identify either man and both said they had been at home at the time of the crime. The "victim," reminiscent of the McGee case, did not cry out and she slept the rest of the night after the rape. Her watch was stolen and when one Vincent North went to pawn it, he was caught, and he accused Washington and Jugger. No defense witnesses were called in their trial and they languished months in jail without bail. This pattern of malfeasance continued when the brother of the victim attended the "Supreme Court hearing and . . . conferred with the justices privately" and allegedly "influenced them against the appeal." Once again, CRC fought this case in the streets and in the courts, through the Louisiana state courts up to the U.S. Supreme Court. Finally in July 1952, Washington and Jugger were executed, when Justices Vinson and Burton refused a stay. A year earlier the state had attempted a "secret execution" without telling CRC, but they discovered the plot at the last moment and received a stay from Justice Douglas: "The undertaker's van, which had already parked at the jail exit, had to drive away empty," Oakley Johnson reported.[40]

With its usual vigor CRC threw itself into this case, organizing delegations to meet with the governor, planting newspaper articles, picketing, sending telegrams. But the atmosphere was a hindrance. Another Black, Edward White, asked for back pay from his boss; he was kidnapped by some men pretending to be police and beaten. They put pornography in his pocket, forced him to call white women, then sought to arrest him for attempting to molest white women. At one point Johnson declared that a demonstration in front of the Louisiana Supreme Court "would be slightly suicidal." Yet they pressed on. Louisiana sought to turn this case into a national one akin to McGee or the CP-Eleven: "the fight for him is a symbol of and a part of the broader struggle for equal rights for all the Negro people and for all people regardless of their color." Ralph Powe of the national office was one of the attorneys involved, along with Ralph Shapiro and Louis Berry, but New Orleans was dissatisfied with the national office's performance. Johnson declaimed that "mistakes of legal character" were made in the case partly due to the national office, and he claimed that they downplayed the "legal" aspects of the case unnecessarily. Truly the defendants' attorney, Jim Mc-Clain, was no fiery militant; he wanted to leave the case because of financial problems. He believed that Jugger was innocent but deemed Washington guilty. Worse, in Patterson's view, he had to be cajoled into raising the point about the exclusion of Blacks from the jury on appeal; the CRC leader denounced these "legalistic conceptions." Most of all they complained that not enough attention was being paid: "Let us get over this national office cliché that 'This is not a national case.' It isn't correct, either, to say merely that this is 'New Orleans' responsibility.' "[41]

Certainly it could not be said that the New Orleans chapter shirked their responsibility. They were striving mightily to make the defendants a symbol of the cause and one way they went about this was by researching the question of rape and race exhaustively. In fact Johnson felt that this research led to his being ousted from Dillard, despite the fact that Judge William Hastie was involved in the study. Later this effort was emulated by John Rousseau, editor of the Louisiana edition of the *Pittsburgh Courier.* In 1892 rape had become a capital crime in the state. The Black Codes had specified the death penalty for slaves for rape exclusively. No Louisiana-born white man had ever been executed for rape, but forty-one Blacks had, including twenty-nine by hanging and twelve by the electric chair, from 1900 through the early fifties. No one at all had been executed for raping a Black woman, and a number of the executed Blacks had been slain not for rape, but for the "intent to commit rape." A number had been found guilty of rape for buying prostitutes; another had been charged with attempted rape for touching a white woman's arm. One Black had been convicted on a Euro-American woman's claim that he "smelled" like a Negro. "To arresting officers, however, it is inconceivable that any white woman would voluntarily engage in an affair with a Negro." On the eve of Washington and Jugger's execution, CRC condemned a North Carolina decision to give eighteen to twenty-four-month sentences to three out of six white paratroopers who had raped a nineteen-year-old Black mother (the other three went scot free) and contrasted that with the treatment of Mack Ingram, a Black tenant farmer, who had been convicted of attempted rape for looking at a seventeen-year-old white girl from 75 feet away and had received a two-year jail term. The term "malicious eyeballing" thus entered the lexicon.[42]

Hundreds gathered as the two were sent to their death, and the local chapter was responsible for that. Although CRC had been criticized for using defendants for their own narrow purposes, Washington's wife thanked them profusely, having recognized that her husband would have gone to his death much earlier, like so many other Blacks, if it had not been for CRC. She had imbibed the militancy of CRC. So had Paul. As he was going to his death, he not only thanked CRC but added "they are taking our people and killing them like dogs. There is got to be a stop to this lynching of our people!"[43]

At the same time that CRC was trying to save the lives of these defendants, the New Orleans chapter found itself attempting to prevent yet another Black from perishing on the gallows. Edward Honeycutt had been convicted of aggravated rape and sentenced to death, allegedly for raping a white woman. The police "beat and whipped him" until he was made deaf, which led to a reversal of the conviction. He had been convicted by an all-white jury in St. Landry's Parish. On appeal CRC had raised their familiar twin issues of the exclusion of Blacks from the jury and a coerced confession. The twenty-seven-year-old Black sharecropper was kidnapped from prison by whites who intended to do away with him; he escaped from them and turned himself back in. The defense, in a maneuver that was eventually successful and heralded in the case of *Dombroski v. Pfister*, had sought the removal of the case to federal court, along with a change of venue. The CRC had entered the case after the NAACP backed out of the legal defense. CRC reached out to the promising Black lawyer, Louis Berry, to work on the case. This was consistent with their affirmative action policy and also motivated by their unhappiness with Jim McClain, who, according to Johnson, was "known as honest, able. . . . But is Southern, conservative, rather unimaginative where new defense links in court may need to be devised." But the U.S. Supreme Court refused to listen, and Honeycutt went to his death, despite the Her-culean efforts of Ralph Powe. Then in late 1954 there arose the tragic case of Clifton Alton Poret, a young Black man convicted of the rape of a white woman and sentenced to death. Johnson had written local attorneys, Jim Dombrowski, and the local editor of the *Pittsburgh Courier*, attempting to get help; since Poret used to live in Los Angeles, the chapter there got involved and they found that the NAACP and ACLU "have no present intentions of moving on the case." They wrote and wired every "big shot" they could think of, including Eleanor Roosevelt and Drew Pearson. They were able to place an ad in the *Los Angeles Daily News* pleading for his life: "Young colored boy, ex-L. A. resident I am sentenced to die. . . . I have no funds to fight for my life. . . . I swear I am not guilty. Won't someone please help me?"[44] Again the U.S. Supreme Court accepted cert but refused to listen.

New Orleans was one of the leading CRC chapters in the deep South and represented in microcosm the problems and prospects they faced. A union leader, A. A. O'Brien, was an early CRC leader there, but soon Johnson was complaining "there is an ugly division in LCRC down here. . . . O'Brien does nothing. . . . doesn't ever open mail." Louis Brown, a Black barber and head of the West Bank NAACP, did not last long as LCRC co-chair either. In fact a number of people who had been energized initially by CRC's militance on the Brooks case defected en masse to the NAACP. By late 1949 CRC had about one hundred members, including students, NAACP members, and longshoremen, although Johnson complained that they had "Few active members." This served to increase the load on Johnson, who was equal to the task. But even when breakthroughs came, like when the "Colored Musicians Local 496" agreed to raise funds for Paul Washington, they insisted that CRC "not (be) mentioned. . . . and it will not be interracial—the night club people have to deal with police, etc." Still when Patterson wanted an ordinance introduced "prohibiting the use of any local station for the purpose of broadcasting anti-Semitic, anti-Negro or any hate propaganda," he turned to New Orleans. The city that time forgot was a useful laboratory, not least of all because of the insensitivity of the government. Mayor de Lesseps Morrison was blunt in justifying police brutality to O'Brien: "a certain amount of coercion above and beyond normalcy is necessary to make persons addicted to criminal tendencies cooperate with officers in their investigations. Otherwise, these reprobates would certainly assume an attitude of innocence and immunity. They would keep their mouths shut."[45] It was difficult to avoid having this backwardness introduce strains into CRC. Johnson felt compelled to remind Patterson to refer to him as "Dr." in printed matter, otherwise "the local press will quickly follow suit, in order to weaken us generally." This was not enough to save him. In 1951 Dillard University chose not to renew his contract, presumably due to his CRC ties, and a student strike arose spontaneously because of his popularity. He moved to stem the strike because he didn't want "to be involved in a struggle against a Negro College" that was "liberal" and one of the "freest and most progressive schools available to Negroes in the Deep South." This, despite the fact that he had "no money saved. My total property consists of a typewriter and some good books." When Johnson left, CRC in New Orleans basically disintegrated, despite the heroic efforts of Lee Brown of ILWU. Johnson's parting words were all too prescient. "Frankly while the people here are loyal and fine, I don't see any likelihood of CRC here holding together after I leave. There is not much of an organization." The CRC "stain" followed him to Houston-Tillotson College, where he was sacked in 1952, because of FBI meddling, according to Johnson.[46]

In Kentucky CRC had many allies but no ongoing organized chapter. Anne Braden, who organized to bring "white women" to Mississippi for the McGee case and who kept other CRC cases before the public in Louisville, explained that this was "because . . . energies are being poured into other organizations," e.g., the Progressive Party, the Negro Labor Council, and so forth. They were able to sell hundreds of copies of the genocide book and "placed (it) on the main libraries of small towns in southern Indiana." Patterson did visit there on occasion and one trip in 1952 caused controversy: "your visit caused a tremendous split in the Baptist Ministers and Deacons dividing it into pro-Patterson and anti-Patterson forces. . . . The effect has been to make the militant people more sure of their ground . . . and to make it clear who is ready to fight and who isn't." Patterson's trip also raised an important ideological question that was to resonate throughout the 1960s and continued to have an impact on Anne Braden, who was one of the more important civil rights activists of that era. Like so many others she was "inspired largely by your observations that we had not done enough to carry such issues to the white community." CRC also had good relations with writers and editors at the local Black paper, the *Defender,* which was distributed in many cities in Kentucky.[47]

At this juncture there was still CRC activity in places like Memphis and Asheville, North Carolina, not to mention Macon. It was from there that Larkin Marshall, who was also a Progressive Party leader of note, reported words that were being mouthed across the nation: "War has dealt our chapter a real blow. . . . we are in the south, fear lurks in every heart when it comes to CRC." CRC had ultimate confidence in Marshall, the first Black to run for the Senate in Georgia since Reconstruction and a newspaper publisher. Milt Wolf felt that in Marshall CRC had a "man who can do just about everything in Ga. . . . he could build us an organization on a state-wide basis . . . of over 12,000. Yes, that is the number of votes he controls down here . . . that is in Bibb County alone." One major problem that their antagonists played on was Marshall's "business jams," one of which was a libel suit he lost.[48]

Another perennial problem faced CRC in Georgia—the NAACP. On one important local case they took the position that they would take over the defense "provided we pull out." Patterson was adamant against that and set down a raison d'etre for the existence of CRC and by implication indicated why their demise was unfortunate for the civil rights movement: "There is only one way to make the NAACP a militant organization, and that lies through the ever increasing militancy of the CRC and the defense organizations created around it. There is no other way, in my opinion."[49]

The situation in Georgia was quite serious, what with the Talmadges and their cronies engaging in massive vote fraud and violence to the point of virtual armed coups in order to maintain power. Maximum unity was essential. But unity could not be forged around the case of a Black private "threatened with serious bodily harm when he refused to leave his seat on a

Greyhound bus." Then there was the case of George Claybon, convicted of the murder of a white pastor in Georgia who spent twelve years in a prison cell there. He was denied parole because he was a "good cook," so he escaped to New York where he was arrested and an extradition battle—a CRC specialty—emerged. He had been accused of having shot the Rev. Charles Lee, relative of Robert E. A woman serving an eight-year burglary term, who had seven other prior convictions, had blamed him. He was held seven days and nights without sleep, threatened with death, and forced to sign a false confession. After his conviction, his accuser was paroled. *Argosy,* a popular magazine of the era, took up the case and found that both the local sheriff and police chief were convinced of his innocence. CRC picketed Governor Thomas Dewey and his party and invoked the strength of the labor movement in Claybon's behalf. Ultimately Claybon received justice, but it would have been expedited if the NAACP had joined in wholeheartedly. The same was true for Ozzie Jones, a Georgian involved in another Black-white rape frame-up case that CRC took the lead on. But the chapter in Georgia was not long for this world. Marshall glumly informed Patterson in mid-1950 that "We are having some hard time in Georgia; they have about run all of my best men out, those that were left, they placed in jail. . . . Wednesday will be election day here. They are making every effort to keep me from voting, but you can just bet I will vote."[50]

Like a scratched record, the case of Rosa Lee Ingram brought up repeated themes. There was conflict with the NAACP, allegations about misuse of funds on the part of CRC, all undergirded by a brutal case of racist exploitation; it could have been Trenton or Groveland all over again. But there were differences, one of the principal ones being the way this case heightened awareness of sexism and brought to the fore even more skilled female leadership. CRC and their allies were well aware of the explosiveness of the case they were handling, which was selected by the *Pittsburgh Courier* as the number one Black news story of 1948. Patterson was of the opinion that "it verges on the woman question to a tremendous degree. . . . [and exposes] the federal government's attitude toward such documents as the Universal Declaration of Human Rights and the Bogota-Colombia Declaration of the Rights and Duties of Man of 1948. . . . It therefore, has within it the possibility of galvanizing into action forces from every stratum of our population including elements considerably to the right of center." The veteran activist Maude Katz held a similar view. Like the Craft and Groveland cases, she attempted to place the Ingram case in a larger political context of landowners trying to keep tenants chained to the soil, the Klan, racist bombings, and the Klan ties of local politicians in Wrightsville and Porterdale, Georgia. The Ingram case, she proclaimed, "symbolizes a society in which womanhood is degraded." In an era when the term "sexual harassment" had not yet been discovered and "woman battering" was not part of many vocabularies, the Ingram case brought to the surface a rage and concern that some did not realize existed. Muriel Symington echoed the sentiments of an even greater number: "One day, the Ingram saga will be cited as one of the glories of Negro history, and be held by us all in prideful remembrance."[51]

What was it that could have stoked passions so furiously? Rosa Ingram was a forty-year-old widowed mother of twelve when she was convicted and two of her sons received the death penalty for the murder of John Stratford on 4 November 1947. Her husband had died four months earlier and two of their brood of fourteen had died in infancy. She was a tenant farmer. Stratford, a white man who also was a tenant, sexually harassed her; he had gotten after her with a rifle. They grappled. He clubbed her. She cried out. One of her sons grabbed the rifle and plunked him on the head. He died. Police arrested her and five of her sons, including James, aged twelve; they were placed in separate jails in different towns and were held incommunicado. They were not told they could have an attorney or of their Fifth Amendment rights. Their one-day trial before an all-white jury took place on 28 January 1948 in Ellaville, Georgia. The prosecution argued that two fights had taken place, the second when Stratford ran; therefore, there was no self-defense involved but rather a conspiracy. In the county where she was tried, Blacks outnumbered whites three-to-two, but whites cast five times more votes; most of the Blacks were sharecroppers, earning less than $200 per year. The state paid $24 per year per capita to school whites and $4 for Blacks. Rosa Lee Ingram and her sons, Wallace and Sammie, were sentenced to die in the electric chair; her son Jackson was sentenced to a year in jail for stealing Stratford's wallet and her son Charlie was set free. After word of the harsh sentence was made known and public opinion reacted sharply, her sentence was changed to life on 6 April 1948. At the hearing after the trial, the judge "a decadent looking man in his eighties, chewed and spit tobacco throughout the hearing with his feet on the desk. . . . Negro reporters and photographers from the *Atlanta World* were forcibly kept from entering into the courtroom by state troopers." Judge William Harper, a reported follower of Governor Talmadge, did not object to the denial to Ingram of the right to counsel, did not allow the defense adequate time to prepare, and sanctioned Black exclusion from the jury. He did bend sufficiently to stay the scheduled 27 February execution. The defense argued that there was a lack of "premeditation" or "intention to kill" necessary for murder. The judge in turn criticized the defense for avoiding the "central issue—the defendants were Negro." Unfortunately, counsel did not raise the jury issue, just the discrepancy between the evidence and the conviction. Although he commuted the death sentence, the judge refused to grant a new trial. The defendants would be eligible for parole in seven years.[52]

The NAACP took over at this point from the court-appointed attorney; they rebuffed aid from CRC. In their motion for a new trial in the State Supreme Court they argued that the verdict was contrary to the evidence, law, and equity. It was denied. This court agreed that two struggles had taken place and that the tenant had died in the second one; whether there was sufficient cooling off time to make the offense a murder was for the jury to decide. A second motion was filed and denied. The NAACP would not take the case to the U.S. Supreme Court because of their analysis that there was no federal question involved; but if the jury issue had been raised, there would have been the requisite jurisdictional basis. All agreed that the defendants had not been served well by their trial attorney, S. Hawkins Dykes, a vice-president of the Georgia Bar Association who had objected to the notion of demonstrations, feeling that they hurt the case. If nothing else, this fiasco showed the value of the CRC lawyers' thinking and fighting politically and not being hamstrung by only fighting by the rules of a racist book.[53]

It was unfortunate that the NAACP refused the hand of cooperation offered by CRC, for the left "Red Cross" had had their operatives on the scene from the inception of the case. A student author in the *Yale Law Journal* was not mistaken in saying that the NAACP did not enter the case at the "outset." But a clash with CRC did develop from the "outset." It did not take too long for angry memos to emerge from both offices. Walter White kicked it off by reviving the age-old charge that CRC was raising money ostensibly for the Ingram defense, but using it for other purposes. But, according to Patterson, this was a classic case of the thief yelling "stop thief": "It has raised some sixty thousand dollars, which are supposedly being held for the benefit of Mrs. Ingram when she gets out. I think that a house has been built for the Ingrams but even the conditions of this new home are primitive, at least this is the manner in which the *Pittsburgh Courier* places the matter. The *Pittsburgh Courier*, while criticizing the NAACP, has itself collected forty-five thousand dollars, and has done nothing." This broadside was launched in 1948 and in 1951 he had more to say: "The house that was built for the Ingrams by the NAACP is jerry built. . . . the contractor made money from the transaction. . . . [it has] no water supply. . . . NAACP in America has given the impression that the Ingrams were 1) literally rolling in money; 2) that they were a lazy, trifling lot." He went on to assess negatively the role of Thurgood Marshall and Robert Carter in this matter, but this was not all part of a plan for destabilizing the Association: "I believe we could launch a well-planned campaign that would shake this thing up without getting into too many of the sordid details of the NAACP's role."[54]

The Ingram case saw as sharp a confrontation with the Association as the Trenton case had presented. William Lawrence as early as May 1948 was explaining to an inquiring correspondent that "the NAACP national leadership was not too anxious and our correspondence and conversations with them on this matter came to naught." A month earlier Patterson was harsher: "The NAACP is seeking to bury it. Their releases now place it among the incidental matters. We must as a consequence find ways and means of lifting it to a higher level politically and organizationally without coming in violent conflict with White et al. . . . . As the NAACP waters the case down generally there will be falling off of its court action. . . . Let us blast white middle-class America out of its complacence."[55]

Ingram continued to languish in prison, along with her sons. Thus in the summer of 1951, her daughter Geneva Ruskin contacted Ralph Powe about freeing her mother: "My mother wants me to get you to be her lawyers she told me Sunday in jail. . . . if you want me to sign any papers I will it [sic] my mother too. . . . But its hard to get any papers in jail—they always stand and watch you. . . ." Apparently the Ingrams had been impressed by CRC's militance and disappointed with the NAACP's buttoned-down lawyering. A day later Rosa Lee Ingram herself told Powe "you can start any kind of action in the court, or out of the court, which you think is alright. I trust your judgement. Any papers you want me to sign I will be glad to sign." But, CRC was leary and in any case was not in the business of lifting clients from the NAACP, no matter how meritorious. Patterson felt that the daughter's word was insufficient. She could sign the proper document, but if the NAACP said that the money raised had to be "cut off unless she repudiates us," she might bend. He remained harsh about the Association and tried to place the case in context: "They dropped the Martinsville 7 at the last moment. We came in and because we are not yet organizationally strong enough, we lost the lives of these men. But I think we exposed the hollowness of the NAACP. . . . [they] are stalling . . . [and won't] appeal to the people to fight for this woman's freedom, which is the only thing that can be effective."[56]

CRC's own role in this struggle was subsumed generally within three organizations led by women. Sojourners for Truth and Justice, the Women's Committee for Equal Justice, and the National Committee to Free the Ingram Family were seen, ironically, by some as CRC "fronts," even though CRC itself through its national office and its chapters performed indefatigably on behalf of the Ingrams. One of their earliest efforts was filing a petition with the United Nations, authored by Du Bois, on the Ingram case. This dramatic action showed that few things were as sensitive for U.S. rulers as having their dirty racist linen displayed before global neighbors. The fact that their Eastern European antagonists welcomed the petition with open arms was even more roiling. Mary Kanable of the Indianapolis CRC put it to Eleanor Roosevelt of the United Nations Human Rights Commission sharply:

> In your letter of 1 December, you told us that "This is a case in which the United Nations has no authority and, therefore, it can take no action. . . ." If the UN can debate the treason trials of central European clergy, why cannot the UN turn its attention to this rank injustice here in the United States?

She claimed that the Ingram case violated the Universal Declaration of Human Rights approved by the General Assembly, including the Preamble and articles 2, 7, 8, and 10. "They would have been freed long ago were they white people." Mrs. Roosevelt was resolute though and adamant: "I know nothing about the Rosa Ingram case nor the brutalities . . . but it certainly is not something which can be discussed in general speeches in the Human Rights Commission." This was surprising, for the press, particularly the Black press, devoted numerous columns to the case. The same was true for the delegation to Georgia in April 1949 to lobby for the Ingrams' freedom.[57]

The National Committee to Free The Ingram Family had chapters nationwide and was formed in New York at Harlem's Hotel Theresa in March 1949. It was virtually all women in leadership and Maude White Katz served as administrative secretary. They issued a newsletter and in a sense served as a miniature CRC. They were also innovative. In April 1950 they appeared at the United Nations in historical costumes dressed like Tubman, Truth, and Stanton protesting the government's treatment of the Ingrams. They also dramatically raised the question of racism, constantly reminding their audience about the near-feudal conditions in rural Georgia. In Shelby County, home of the Ingrams, five hundred Blacks had been lynched in the last sixty years. The income of Blacks was less than $200 per year; of the 750 farms there, 600 were worked by tenants. The Women's Committee for Equal Justice had a broader mission and was not a "membership body," though it did publish a newsletter and played a principal role in disseminating the Du Bois petition. It was served by Halois Robinson as secretary and spokesperson and the legendary Mary Church Terrell as chair. Sojourners for Truth and Justice was initiated by Charlotta Bass, Shirley Graham, Louise Thompson Patterson, Alice Childress, Rosalie McGee—strong CRC supporters; Beulah Richardson served as secretary.[58]

The Ingram case was one of the few that catapulted a woman political prisoner into prominence. It also caused CRC to confront questions of sexism, externally and internally, in a more intense way. In February 1949 Patterson had addressed a letter to Heloise Moorhead, Susan Anthony, Gene Weltfish, and others concerning the setting up of a Women's Committee of CRC to better coordinate work in this field. Weltfish, president of the Congress of American Women and a Columbia anthropologist, was irate: "your letter . . . is so replete with male chauvinism that I waited to count to ten—ten days in fact—before writing you. I think it stinks." She reminded Patterson of a recent occurrence where he spoke on a "platform full of men and an audience full of women." Patterson thanked her for her "candor and criticism," then added: "I, of course, do not control all organizations for which I may have the honor to speak." Then he went on to render a spirited defense: "I should like to inform you that women lead our organizations in Los Angeles, San Francisco, Philadelphia, Denver, Pittsburgh, Miami, New Jersey, Chicago, and in fact, most of CRC chapters throughout the country. . . . the plan that I submitted was not devised by any male committee at all. As a matter of fact, I was the only male on it. It was devised, however, by women who are very active together with you." The two resolved their differences and Patterson continued to work with his female-dominated organization profitably.[59]

Patterson had differences of opinion from time to time with Terrell. She didn't think that "public opinion" would understand his suggestion to push Ingram as Mother of the Year. Nor did she agree with some of his phrasing: "I have never used the word 'Chairlady' in my many years of acting in that capacity for many organizations. . . . I have been 'chairman' of many committees—sex in that case does not matter." The Mother of the Year notion took off. Through their contacts with the *Chicago Defender* and the *Afro-American* chain, CRC was able to launch it. Then there was another flap over Patterson sending out letters under Terrell's name on the Ingram case, linking it with Ben Davis' case, allegedly all without her permission. Patterson demurred, recalling "distinctly" that "in the conversation we had in the Hotel New Yorker in the presence of Mr. Hunton" that this was authorized. He had injected Davis and Wesley Robert Wells into the matter because "these three matters are inseparably related. . . . If I offended in this, I am also extremely sorry." He went on to term her "one of (the) great personalities of my country and my people and every word you say is of concern to me." Later he was more lavish: "I am certain we will work together for a long time with great profit to myself for your inspiration is tremendously helpful." Patterson was equally quick to heap praise on Halois Robinson: "It may seem strange that I would address a letter to you when we see each other more or less regularly. . . . I believe that together with Mrs. Terrell your services as acting secretary for the campaign would guarantee its success. . . . (I will) work side by side with you at all times."[60]

One of the major accomplishments of the Ingram campaign was collecting 100,000 signatures on petitions in support of the family. They kept the question of Ms. Ingram's deteriorating health before the public. They launched a postcard campaign on the case, aimed at "the only woman member of the Georgia Board of Pardon and Parole." When the *New York Times* penned one of their typical editorials, "Toward Human Freedom," Katz was quick to draft an open letter on their "lofty editorial," taking them to task for ignoring Ingram. They received a generally favorable response. One Portland woman wrote, "As a mother, I am deeply concerned over the case of Mrs. Ingram . . . and since Mother's Day is past and gone I feel that I must do something." Ida Henderson, co-chair of the Women's Convention Auxiliary of the National Baptist Convention, announced that "my organization is with you one hundred per cent." They all pushed for pressure to be exerted on the NAACP from the grassroots. They "regularly sent money to" the Ingrams and held four mass demonstrations in Atlanta alone. But the Association continued to scorn WCEJ as "red sponsored," and they accorded CRC and their other allies even worse treatment. Perhaps the Association was reacting to the terror-filled environment. When Patterson contemplated a journey in 1954 to Louisville and points south on behalf of the

Ingrams he was compelled to inquire "is the atmosphere still too hostile for such a project?"[61]

The impact of the various forces campaigning for the Ingrams was significant. Churches were helpful in raising funds. The Committee on Aid to Puerto Rico and the multimillion-member All China Federation of Labor demanded their freedom. But there were contrary trends. K. R. Reid, wife of the anticommunist publisher, Ogden Reid, weaseled when she was asked to aid the Ingrams: "I have made a rule against joining a group unless I can work actively for its objectives." In mid-1954 Patterson was pessimistic: "the Women's Committee for Equal Justice has many supporters but few forces functioning in its leadership. . . . Mrs. Terrell has played a magnificent role but in day-to-day functioning is out of the picture." But WCEJ and their allies had broad reach nonetheless; they were asked to address the National Federation of Negro Women's Clubs of Georgia, and from Louisville it was reported: "We are taking a delegation to the *Louisville Defender,* a Negro newspaper, and the *Courier Journal.* Also, we are getting organizations to send greetings to Mrs. Ingram and protests to Governor Talmadge."[62]

Some of the more heavily publicized events organized by the pro-Ingram forces were the delegations they sent to Georgia, composed mostly of women. Although they were akin to the "white women's delegation" sent to Mississippi, a significant difference was that these delegations were multiracial. There were five in all; in April 1949, December 1952, December 1953, May 1954, and September 1954. The May 1954 delegation was typical. There were seventy-five delegates from eight states, Black and white. New York had the biggest number, twenty-four in all, thirteen Black and eleven white. Georgia was next with fourteen, five white and nine Black. Interestingly, Missouri was next with thirteen, six white and seven Black. Nora Stanton Barney (a descendant of Elizabeth Cady Stanton) and Rosalie McGee participated, along with the Atlanta Council of Negro Women.[63]

All of these delegations received substantial press coverage, more so in the Afro-American press. During the 1952 visit, Talmadge's wife told the white women to wait inside and the Blacks outside. Naturally, they balked. Bitter words were exchanged. An armed confrontation ensued. This was not unexpected, since the delegates had asked President Truman to guarantee their safety during the 1949 visit. Before the 1952 departure, Patterson had sought assurances from Talmadge that "no provocation or incitement" would greet the delegation: "An incident would not only excite a national but an international scandal as well," he warned. Unctously Talmadge replied that "your right of freedom of assembly and freedom of speech will not be abridged" and added ominously, "It is believed that you come for the purpose of violating our laws, disregarding our customs, and seeking to create a riot or disorder." Expect swift retribution if this were to occur, he retorted. The *Atlanta Constitution* was hostile to these jaunts and this did not improve the reception locally. Yet as one Milwaukeean on the 1953 delegation related, this was not a uniform response: "I was agreeably surprised upon my arrival in Atlanta to find that Negro businessmen were not only giving their moral support but that they had as well organized transportation for all the out of town delegates. You know, of course, taxis in Atlanta are Jim Crow and white taxi drivers will not carry Negroes. . . . our meeting with the governor en masse and with the Board of Pardons and Paroles was an unprecedented event." In a sense, this transportation effort was a run-up to a similar effort in Montgomery during the bus boycott of 1955. Their outreach in the "city too busy to hate" was wide. Notices had been "sent to every church to be read" about the case and organizers were "greatly encouraged" by the support of ministers for the event. Radio stations WBGE, "one of the largest," and WERD carried their publicity. During this visit New York sent thirty people and the West Coast managed to send "several." Unsurprisingly it was said "The Ingram case is so well known that the mere mentioning of the name tells the story."[64]

The December 1953 delegation was particularly important. It spurred an increase in contributions to the Ingram family funneled through CRC's Prisoners' Relief Committee. In St. Louis the Ingram forces included an "Urban League group, a group of the NAACP, the Interracial Woman's Committee, a number of churches, the Civil Rights Congress and some labor groups." Allegedly, no one "asked anyone about their political beliefs or convictions." Halois Robinson's decision to have "report back meetings" in Winston-Salem, Chapel Hill, Durham, New Orleans, Birmingham demonstrated the way the Ingram case helped to build CRC and progressive forces generally. The WCEJ in May 1954 launched a "Mother's Day Freedom Appeal" for Ingram; it included another visit to the peach state. The Packinghouse Workers union and the Mine, Mill, and Smelter Workers were among the contributors to the delegation's expenses. This time, in addition to meeting with the Board of Pardons and Paroles, they sang "Oh Freedom" from the steps of the State Capitol. The civil rights movement blossomed in Georgia years before the advent of the turbulent 1960s.[65]

This 1954 push for Ingram's freedom also involved a delegation sent to meet with officials from the Department of Justice and the White House. Terrell headed this group of Black and white people that included Baptist ministers, four Black women trade unionists from North Carolina, representatives of the Emma Lazarus Federation, the American Peace Crusade, and the NAACP. Maxwell Rabb of the president's staff indicated that since the case concerned "state jurisdiction," federal "intervention" would not be "appropriate." Patterson was concerned about the direction of the meeting with the Department of Justice. He told Angie Dickerson that while Terrell "should introduce the subject there will be perhaps lapses in her presentation which you should carefully and with your usual tact fill in. . . . Efforts should be made to see that all the delegates who desire get the opportunity to say something." She was instructed to expose the "demagogy" of Brownell's appearance before the high court on the case of *Brown v. Board of Education*. Patterson was somewhat pleased with the outcome of the meeting, but he lamented the inadequate briefing given the participants before the meeting. He was also displeased with the fact that Justice trotted out a low-level Black official to join the attorneys meeting with them and then insulted him by referring to him as a "good Georgia boy." The official, Maceo Hubbard, showed no resentment, which made Patterson angrier: "I wish that someone had politely asked Mr. Hubart (sic) how old he was, and if he were a family man."[66]

While CRC was working side by side with the women-led committees fighting for the Ingrams' freedom, even Wilson Record's notoriously inaccurate book *The Negro and the Communist Party* noted the protests from abroad, particularly about Ingram, mostly generated by CRC. As a result, "CRC continues to make certain headway among American Negroes." A major responsibility for CRC's own campaign here fell on the shoulders of people in Philadelphia because Ingram's mother, sister, and a large section of her family resided there. They tried to "anchor this campaign in the trade union movement in order to give it some permanency." They did score some gains. The local Black paper, the *Philadelphia Tribune,* covered the case adequately and editorialized for the Ingrams' freedom. Support was sufficiently formidable there that serious thought was given to moving the entire family to that city.[67]

Grounding the Ingram case in the labor movement was a national goal. In 1949 Detroit chapter functionary Esther Jackson forwarded three thousand signatures on petitions gathered not only at "churches and door-to-door" but "at the Ford plant" also. Once more the left unions—Furriers, Mine, Mill, etc. were in the forefront of the campaign. The Food, Tobacco, Agricultural and Allied Workers collected funds for the Ingrams from the Campbell Soup plant in Chicago and elsewhere. CRC's contacts for this case were not just limited to the left; they reached out to predominantly Black sororities like Delta Sigma Theta, the Emma Lazarus Club, and the Junior League.[68]

Still, the assistance from the left should not be downplayed. At Henry Winston's urging, a number of Communist clubs raised funds. The *Daily Worker* provided by far the most consistent and substantial coverage of the case; *Masses and Mainstream* was equally in the forefront of the defense drive. Despite an earlier difficulty, this open Communist role did not present too much of a problem for Terrell and other non-Communist forces; she, for example, was a longtime associate of Ben Davis.[69]

Finally, the Ingrams were freed because of such tireless and selfless efforts, and the NAACP notwithstanding, their prison tenure would have been even lengthier had it not been for this external pressure. In any case, all this was something of a warm-up for future campaigns, as lessons learned here were applicable to other matters. Thus, in 1951 in Richmond, Virginia, the case of the so-called Richmond Five arose: "The white man and woman were on a drinking spree. . . . The man passed out and during his incapacity the woman approached the 5 fellows and as I understand it, she practically seduced them." There was a call for CRC to ride to the rescue: "We hope you can get a lawyer in soon. We'd also like advice about community action." Quickly Patterson replied: "get one or two prominent figures in the community on the committee. . . . a petition should be gotten out raising sharply the question of the murder of the Martinsville 7, that the state not be disgraced again. . . . activities should be organized in a number of churches. From the beginning every possible effort must be made to carry this into the white communities." Make it a "moral issue," he suggested; emphasize the "persecution of the Negro people, its effect upon the moral strength of white America and upon the economic and political status of white America as well. Releases should be gotten out to the Negro press, the labor press and the metropolitan press." Get out a "fact sheet" on the case. "We will move at once to place this before the Youth Festival in Berlin and into the columns of the European press generally." Here connections with the international communist movement proved to be a boon and not a bane. But Patterson's suggestions were a blueprint for fighting virtually any case of this type and his experience with Ingram, Martinsville, and the others proved to be indispensable. The Richmond Five case, still another Black-white rape case, had other elements common to CRC crusades. The locals demanded a CRC lawyer, since "unfortunately, the people still have a great respect, almost unlimited, for lawyers. . . . [besides] we ourselves don't know the legal ins and outs and need advice." Ultimately the case against these Black youths was settled and there was little doubt that the outcome would have been different had it not been for CRC.[70]

Virginia was a southern state where organized CRC activity waxed and waned. Yet there was usually something going on to stoke outrage and generate organizing. In early 1950 there was the case of Samuel Taylor, a thirty-eight-year-old Black man "slashed to death by a lynch gang [of whites] in Ballsville." In Ashland there was a Black man accused of raping a ten-year-old white girl in September 1951. And then there was the strange case of Albert Jackson, who managed to escape execution on 28 July 1952 when an "electrical storm knocked out the power lines." Little publicity had been given to this case by the bourgeois news media up to that time. This twenty-two-year-old Black man had been convicted of raping a white woman. The arresting policeman testified that as he came on the scene, the woman was asking Jackson "Where is my five dollars?" As in Louisiana and other southern states, no white man had ever been executed for rape in the state. The Martinsville case had led to the formation of a nascent CRC chapter in the state and it was revived to save Jackson. This was the pattern in a number of southern states where CRC activity did not occur until emergencies arose.[71]

To save Jackson's life, activists in Richmond put out 15,000 leaflets, held about twelve meetings, including two public meetings, and contacted a number of union leaders, ministers, and rank and filers. "The committee was composed of some of the old members of the Martinsville Seven committee, but we were able to bring in a much broader group." NAACP-affiliated attorneys in the law firm of Hill, Martin, and Robinson were brought in, along with a white Trotskyite lawyer Howard Carwile.

They organized a delegation of twenty-five that met with the governor for three hours after he had first refused them a meeting. Starkly they posed the legal question of "whether a Negro's constitutional rights are violated by a state's reserving the death penalty for Negroes." Telegrams and telephone calls rained down on local officials. But, on 25 August Jackson was executed. Not killed with him was CRC's continuing campaign "against the practice of reserving the death penalty exclusively for Negroes as is done in a number of Southern states."[72]

The drive received perhaps its most severe test in the small Virginia backwater town of Martinsville. A hotbed of racism, this community in 1951 received international notoriety because of the existence of seven of its Black citizens. In 1949 Martinsville was a town of about eighteen thousand people; near the North Carolina border, it was best known for the existence of Bassett Furniture (controlled by the Du Ponts) and the American Furniture Company. It became the scene of another of CRC's harbingers of the 1960s; like Mississippi and Atlanta before it, Martinsville experienced a "freedom ride" before the term became popular. And, like Atlanta, Trenton, and too many other places of CRC cases, Martinsville also was the backdrop of another conflict with the NAACP. The *Morgan* case, which had taken place in Virginia a few years earlier, had not convinced the Association that legal wizardry without mass action was tantamount to the sound of one hand clapping.

The Martinsville case was a Black male-white woman rape case and it was hardly accidental that it arose in Virginia. Prior to 1865, the state required different penalties for whites and Blacks convicted of raping white females; ten to twenty years for white men, five years to death for Black men. The Fourteenth Amendment forced the alteration of this legislation. But the practice continued. Between 1908 and 1951, eight hundred whites had been convicted for rape, but not one had got the chair. From 1885 through 1951, white males had been convicted of having raped a ten-year-old child (a ten-year sentence), a wife's married cousin (three years), a four-and-a-half-year-old girl (three years), an eighty-three-year-old grandmother (five years), a thirty-two-year-old Black woman (seven years), and so forth. In contrast, in *Woodson v. Commonwealth*, the judge spoke of the "black peril" and the necessity to kill Black rapists to prevent mob violence. Similarly, all sixteen of the state's death row inmates in 1950 were African-American, along with a disproportionate percentage of the prison population itself.[73]

The Martinville case involved seven Black males: Francis De Sales

Grayson, thirty-seven, the father of five; John C. Taylor, twenty; James Luther Hairston, twenty; Howard Lee Hairston, nineteen; Frank Hairston, Jr., nineteen; Booker T. Millner, nineteen; Joe Henry Hampton, twenty. All were from the working class in this third largest furniture-producing center in the nation, where Bassett employed 2,500 workers alone, but only 150 Blacks, in an area where Black unemployment was a whopping 20 percent. Their fates were joined on 8 January 1949 when Mrs. Ruby Floyd, a white former mental patient, went to collect a business debt. She alleged that a "squad" of Black men attacked her and raped her. They were arrested. The grand jury was composed of four whites and three Blacks, but the latter were all on the Board of Directors of the American Furniture Company. The judge, Kennon C. Whittle, was a director of six of the town's leading businesses. The prosecutor, W. R. Broaddus, was one of Martinsville's richest men and also a Bassett director. The defendants were saddled with attorneys from the city's power structure and they conducted the trial before the all-white jury with a decided lack of zeal. There were other legal curiosities. The defendants repudiated their extorted confessions, but that cut no ice. Despite the inflamed local atmosphere, the judge refused a change of venue. Two Blacks on the jury panel were stricken because they did not believe in the death penalty for Blacks in such cases. Mrs. Floyd, who disappeared immediately after the conviction, sold the Watchtower magazine and was viewed locally as somewhat eccentric; she was rumored to be a prostitute. One researcher alleged that she "had dated one of the accused men . . . (but no one, except the prosecutors and the police had an opportunity to speak to Mrs. Floyd except during the trial). . . . The boys said she invited the relationship and did not resist." The case raised a smorgasbord of legal questions on appeal, like the change of venue, forced confessions, police misconduct, inadequate cross-examinations, lack of positive identification, the exclusion of Blacks from the jury. Most of these were CRC perennials and when the Supreme Court years later finally reversed field on these issues, CRC's constant prodding over the years was partly responsible. Here they highlighted constantly and incessantly the fact that although one-third of the state's population was Black, there were no Black judges and all forty-four males executed for rape since 1908 had been Black. This case was laborious. Twice the Virginia courts denied their appeals. Twice the U.S. Supreme Court refused the case. In July 1950, forty-eight hours from death, the men got a temporary reprieve. In November 1950, after a delegation from twenty-two states descended on Richmond, a sixty-day stay of execution resulted.[74]

There were other illustrative elements of this case. Just as the McGee case had brought forward the talents of his wife and mother, Josephine Grayson became an accomplished stump speaker and organizer as a result of this case. In turn, CRC's legitimate concern for the welfare of those they defended, which contradicted a somewhat prevalent notion of their "using" these cases for their own narrow ends, was reflected here. Like their treatment of the McGees, after Francis Grayson's death they sought to secure a furnished apartment and income for his family. Josephine Grayson was finding Virginia a "hateful place," while Patterson was ruefully discovering that "money is much more difficult to get than formerly." But this was overcome and CRC was able to assist the family. Indeed some were so impressed with CRC's performance that a fellow death row inmate of Grayson, there for killing a Euro-American woman, urgently reached CRC about displaying their formidable skills on his behalf. Patterson found this appeal "deeply moving" although not a solitary occurence: "The horror of the thing is that from all over the country we are receiving pleas of this character for assistance."[75]

The NAACP did not find "deeply moving" the participation of CRC in this headline-getting case. Robert Harris, who investigated the case years later, put it bluntly and aptly. His summation could have applied to any of their innumerable conflicts:

> The CRC and the NAACP approached the case from two different points of view. The NAACP felt that the state and federal laws and legal procedures were basically just. Therefore, it relied on legal appeals on the hope that somewhere along the line the miscarriage of justice would be rectified. The CRC felt that the fundamental basis of the courts and the laws . . . was to preserve an unjust system of Negro oppression—a system with which the federal courts would not interfere. Thus, its approach was political, to bring the maximum public pressure to bear.

Harris went on to say that "Twice during June 1950, after the first appeal to the U.S. Supreme Court had been turned down, the CRC appealed to the NAACP for a joint campaign." They were refused. But as in other cases, a *de facto* alliance ensued: "Even so, of course, the efforts of the two groups were to a large degree complementary." CRC led the mass political campaign, while the NAACP did most of the legal appeals, initially with the help of CRC lawyers.[76]

As early as mid-1949, Patterson was complaining about a meeting with Thurgood Marshall and other NAACP attorneys. The CRC leader was "calling for cooperation . . . (but) they said that they would not work with us on any basis and if we developed a mass campaign they would publicly declare that it was detrimental to the struggle for these men's lives." Patterson's ire caused him to strike out at one of the least anticommunist NAACP lawyers, Charles Houston: "(he) will waver until such time as he sees a significant broad mass movement as will afford him a protective cloak." Days earlier Patterson had met with local NAACP lawyer M. A. Martin and a NAACP branch leader in Richmond. They had spoken in "glowing terms of . . . joint action" with CRC. They repudiated their words the next day. Indicative of the hamstringing effect of the Attorney General's acts was the fact that Martin, vice-chair of the Association's powerful legal committee, said that the subversive listing barred their working with CRC; this apparently after having received the word from on high. Patterson smoldered indignantly about this rebuff: "I repeat, CRC withdrew from this case upon your insistence that unless our organization did so, you would not proceed. . . . Yours has been a hush-hush policy without regard to the overwhelming strength which derives from the support of the people." This blow-up occurred at a time when Patterson, identified in the local press as the "Scottsboro case lawyer," was in town to file an appeal for Grayson. Ominously the press reported about a "mixed white and Negro meeting" at a local funeral home with Communists, CIO union members and NAACP rank and file present. In any case, the high court of the state refused the NAACP's claim, rejecting the change of venue and inflammatory newspaper publicity grounds; they objected to their point about the trial court judge asking potential jurors if they were anti-death penalty and rejecting them if the answer was yes; they brushed aside questions of the exclusion of Blacks from the jury and the tainted confession; they spurned the notion that only Blacks getting the death penalty for rape was actionable. Similarly, they did not seem to be impressed with the NAACP's sudden rush for ideological purity in disdaining CRC.[77]

Just as the NAACP had taken their scorning of CRC to the public, CRC openly called for a reconciliation. While pricking Wilkins and White about their failure to do mass mobilizing and for having forced out CRC, he extended the olive branch of cooperation. He warned forebodingly, "failure of the NAACP to organize mass action immediately" will doom the seven. He released to the press a telegram to White that called for cooperation beyond Virginia: "Sincerely believe united action our two organizations can secure release of other twenty Negroes facing electrocution frameup charges . . . Extend our hand for joint action."[78]

As in past conflicts, the antagonism toward CRC was expressed more acrimoniously by White, Marshall, and other top NAACP leaders who were more under scrutiny and pressure than by the base of the organization. In late 1950 after the NAACP had made its hostility toward CRC well known, Martin, the law partner of Oliver Hill and future federal judge Spottswood Robinson, was still in touch with Ralph Powe about Martinsville and was still trying to "assist you in your cases." Arguably the official NAACP position was more a product of arm-twisting exerted from the right than profound conviction. In Detroit, Anne Shore told of how local NAACP leaders in their most affluent branch were in a real quandary: "The NAACP has had a hard time of it. We have been trying to get them to work with us. Yesterday, we reached them. The Secretary here, not too bad a guy, sounded desperate. He's had no word from New York and didn't know what to do—but, he's had, he said, a minimum of thirty calls from people asking what to do."[79]

Inevitably in a case of this character—Black/white, male/female, Communist/non-Communist and anticommunist—the press flocked like moths to the light. Most of their reportage was, unfortunately, trash. Occasionally there was an illuminating insight, as when the *Nation* noted a principal difference between the CRC and NAACP efforts: the former insisted that the men were innocent, while the latter conveniently ducked this question and simply focused on such issues as a "fair trial." But even the *Nation* could be derelict, as when Earl Dickerson had to rebuke them for editing one of his articles to make it appear as if he were "red-baiting." Typically, *Time* called the pathbreaking Richmond vigil "517 of the faithful, masterminded by the Communist front Congress of Civil Rights." Both the *New Republic* and *Christian Century* assumed somehow that the defendants were guilty and slanted their articles in that direction. Ignorance was the flip side of the coin of prejudice and CRC had to deal with that tendency also. Patterson found himself reprimanding Whitelaw Reid of the *New York Herald Tribune* weeks before the execution of the seven: "You said that you know little about the facts of the case. . . . How can that be that the publisher of a leading paper . . . can [be] pleading ignorance on cases involving . . . human rights of fifteen million Negroes. . . . I regard the silence of the press as criminal." The prejudice and ignorance of the press shaped public opinion and made CRC's job that much more difficult.[80]

When the U.S. Supreme Court in *Coker v. Georgia* decided finally in 1977 that capital punishment was an improper penalty for rape, in a sense the altruistic labor of CRC had been vindicated. Raising this question during the doldrums of the transition from Truman to Eisenhower was an uphill climb. Yet, they persevered. In early 1951 Patterson launched a petition campaign to save the seven by contacting his numerous allies in the religious community; the goal was to get 50,000 signatures in twenty-five days. Soon petitions were flooding their office from Newark, Florida, Cartersville, Georgia, and elsewhere. Earlier experience also played a role in shaping the crusade for the seven: "During the Scottsboro Case, we issued a bi-weekly bulletin of one page a week, which was distributed in every barbershop, beauty parlor, pool room and candy store on Lenox Avenue. . . . Therefore, I propose that this practice now be used again."[81]

The campaign that gripped Detroit reflected its role as a leading CRC chapter, but at the same time, it was not atypical. They began "hitting the plant gates" with petitions that "paved the way for our appearances before Executive Boards and membership meetings in the shops." Chapter leader Anne Shore was taken aback: "You never saw anything to equal the movement under way here. . . . [we] got money from Cadillac Local UAW. . . . Ministers Conference [Baptist] [is] really moving, with a special petition for circulation in all their churches. . . . we have official delegates from Fur and Leather, three from Dodge 3 (the second biggest in the UAW), Cadillac was sending a minimum of one [to the Virginia freedom ride]." She described the entire organization experience as "wonderful." The "steady stream of little leaflets into the auto plants here" led to the formation of a "newly formed trade union committee" of CRC. As happened so often with CRC mass organizing for defendants, a boom in membership resulted: "we've a couple of chapters started. . . . [We are] recruiting members at mass meetings and such has diminished in the light of the fear and intimidation." This had an impact on the local NAACP secretary, who "said he couldn't move without New York. . . . the NAACP has had a hard time of it."[82]

A major element in generating mass support was a visit to Detroit by Mrs. Grayson. During her sojourn there in the fall of 1950 she had an interview with the *Courier* and spoke at the Baptist Ministers' Conference. The following Sunday, fifteen churches were visited by various speakers:

> We called the churches cold. . . . We were turned down by only one minister, who later relented. . . . The results were magnificent with several hundred dollars being collected. The white speakers were more effective than the Negro, pointing out clearly to us that we must really move the white community actively. . . . Our big weakness in working with the church groups was not to make an effort to break through to the white churches. This indicates the opportunism about which Pat spoke in Chicago.

Triggering this outpouring of activism was not only the usual energy of the chapter, but the special energy of Mrs. Grayson: "Our most significant job was done in relation to the trade unions. . . . we were able to break through several [right wing unions] . . . [with more time] we would have been able to break through into almost every union in the city." The left-led Ford Local 600, the largest in the UAW with over 65,000 members, gave $358.85. Also contributing were Packard Local 190 and Local 208. All this was not greeted with catatonic passivity in the union. The *Beacon,* a local UAW paper, in a hard-hitting editorial accused "the Communist Party and its legal arm—the Civil Rights Congress" of being responsible for the plight of the defendants. Beneath this article was another by Walter White wherein Walter Reuther called on Virginia's governor to grant a stay of execution and not be a "sucker for a left hook."[83]

This outburst of activity was replicated not only across the country, but across the globe. In Harlem there was a massive parade in the fall of 1950 on behalf of the seven. There was also a production of "The Martinsville Chant," a play directed by Ossie Davis and featuring, among others, William Marshall and Vinnie Burrows. But it was the protest from abroad that was most acutely embarrassing during the cold war battle for hearts and minds in an increasingly colored world. CRC drew links between the Martinsville defendants and others similarly situated, which had a dynamic effect on their organizing. In South Africa during the same time, five Black men had been sentenced to death on charges of the rape of a white woman: "As in the U.S., no white man in the Transvaal has ever received the death sentence for rape." The response from abroad was heartening. In London, there were Hyde Park rallies and protests from the Dean of Canterbury, the Caribbean Labour

Congress, and many concerned individuals. According to Patterson, Europeans were "alarmed at the state of democratic procedure" in the United States. A familiar ally in Paris, the Mouvement Contre le Racisme, l'antisemitisme, et pour la Paix, was in the forefront, cobbling together committees of "leading cultural, union, church and governmental figures" for both McGee and the seven. Eastern Europeans, e.g. the Association of Polish Jurists, chimed in. The West Africa Students Union of Charles University in Prague, and individuals from Angola and Lagos were attracted to CRC's cause, as were a number of Latin Americans.[84]

The freedom rides to Virginia were highly publicized. The first was contemplated for the fall of 1950, as the hangman's noose awaited. Howard Fast, Dashiell Hammett, and Earl Conrad were to lead this mass delegation. Patterson had traveled to Europe to rally support and the news trickled back that 1,024 resolutions on the case had been adopted by trade unions, city councils, and organizations in Europe. Apparently this was not an ineffective display of strength, because the governor granted a stay of execution, and in response CRC called off its jaunt to the South.[85]

But the stay was merely a temporary palliative and another date was set for early 1951. CRC quickly got to work. Mass open-air rallies were held in Harlem and tables cluttered their streets and others across the country as petitions were gathered. CRC was not fighting this battle in isolation, but at the same time, it was straining its meager resources to save the life of Willie McGee and to keep both Communists and CRC leaders out of jail. Moreover, as they were struggling to raise funds for the $15 round-trip fare to Virginia and on-site expenses, rumors had begun to percolate about their swindling money from the McGee defense; Rosalee McGee adamantly refuted this in a signed affidavit, but such allegations were not without effects. Undaunted, CRC moved on with its meticulous planning for this landmark event. Mapped out carefully were the "Proposed Rules for the Delegation" that they were instructed to keep with them. It was a broad delegation going beyond the left, so CRC stressed that "whatever differences there may be between people on the delegation [they] must not be allowed to divide us. . . . Spokesmen for the delegation will be selected in an organized and democratic way. Only such spokesmen will speak for it. This of course, will have whatever exceptions the delegation approves." It was to be expected that intimidation would be directed at those assembled, so security was a critical concern: "During the stay in Richmond proceed in groups, not as individuals. Be dignified, orderly and disciplined. Do not give in to any provocation. Avoid arguments with anyone. . . . Put all cars in public garages at all times." Even bombs had to be considered.[86]

The execution dates were set for 2 and 5 February and the delegation was set to go days before to have the maximum impact. Each chapter was given a quota and overall, 250 to 500 people were expected to descend on the state. Painstakingly, Grossman requested reports twice a week from the chapters on how their organizing was proceeding and telegraphic reports in the last ten days; he suggested reading a report on what the Detroit chapter was doing in order to get an idea of how to organize. Detroit's selection as a model was no accident. The plight of the seven had struck a responsive chord in that city of proletarians, increasingly becoming darker in hue and bitten by a recurrent plague of police misconduct aimed precisely at those citizens. About 20 percent of the 500-plus delegation was from this city and its unions were heavily represented. This was done in the face of a NAACP denunciation of the crusade on the eve of its departure. But it was the view of many that if the Association did not want to engage in mass action, that was their lamentable right, but that unity should have precluded them from discouraging others from seeking to save the defendants' lives. The positive response to the delegation showed that the NAACP's maneuver did not destroy the delegation. In fact the "Ford Local voted" the CRC chapter a "commendation for the fine work we have done." All told, representatives of over 160,000 auto workers demanded clemency and freedom for the seven, not to mention the steelworkers, furniture workers, electrical workers, and others who joined in.[87]

As the delegates were reaching Richmond, the voice of protest was becoming more insistent. The head of the Bataka Party of Uganda, sixty-six members of the French Chamber of Deputies, the Zionist Democratic Federation of Israel, seventy thousand Polish youths, the Union of Working Youth of Rumania were among the protesters. The Baptist Morning Minister's Conference of Philadelphia and the president of the National Baptist Convention joined in. But, these U.S. voices were seemingly drowned out by those of Finnish parliamentarians and other groups from West Germany, Tunisia, East Africa and elsewhere. They confronted the embattled Governor John Battle with a five-day vigil at the Richmond capital, accompanied by an all-night vigil at the White House. The thousands of wires and phone calls to the governor from all over the world apparently swayed the governor to meet with the delegation. In solidarity the Afro-Americans of Richmond were sporting black armbands. In solidarity many taxi drivers wouldn't charge them. In solidarity many restaurants supplied free coffee. Other gave the free use of telephones. One local Afro-American echoed the view of many and was all-too-accurate when he commented, "Nothing like this has happened since Grant took Richmond in 1865."[88]

The busload from New York had traveled in Greyhound buses and they were compelled to endure Jim Crow waiting rooms and seating in the South. The others from around the nation that came to bear witness at Thomas Jefferson's state house had similar experiences. Bill Mandel, a Sovietologist, supplied a graphic depiction of the latter-day "vigilantes." There was a sharecropper's daughter descended from President Franklin Pierce who had seen a similar Black-white rape incident in her home of Oklahoma; later she married Henry Winston, Communist chairman. There was a Black ex-Navy man, a young white mother from Colorado, two local white medical students, "a Creole woman from Louisiana whose immensely wealthy tobacco-grower grandfather finally violated the family's deepest secret by telling them they were Blacks when a lynching (burning on tar-soaked ties) took place on their property." There was CRC's principal agent in Richmond, Senora Lawson, who had just barely missed election to the City Council there in 1950. Naturally, there was a FBI plant, whose wages turned out to be a down-payment on college tuition.[89]

As the eleventh hour approached nervously, Supreme Court Justice Fred Vinson turned down a last-minute appeal. A spokesman for President Truman told a group led by Mary Church Terrell that he was "very familiar" with the matter, but "he was not seeing anybody about the case." In Harlem 2,500 gathered at 126th Street and Seventh Avenue to protest; that was followed by a huge demonstration at City Hall. All the while a "Death Watch" bore down on the White House. Richmond was hit by a buzzsaw of protest not seen since Reconstruction, as Mandel ably reported:

> Motion picture theater owners put on the lights after each showing to urge all in the audience to phone or wire the Governor. The white manager of the city-owned segregated dance hall, the Mosque, yielded to the Committee's request to make the same announcement every half hour during the evening. Men grabbed fistfuls of handbills from distributors on the streets to distribute in bars, restaurants and hotel lobbies. Taxi drivers ran out to get five dollar bills changed into nickels for phone campaigners they had never met before. . . . Men stood by to read off numbers into telephone directories. People lined up in mass in front of the telephone booths.

As the execution approached, a mass rally that brought together hundreds was called on four-hours notice in a city not known for its quick responses to organizers' calls. Nine hundred showed up at a church rally, then marched to Capitol Square; a hopeful sign was the fact that 10 percent of the marchers were Euro-Americans: "One of the most encouraging aspects of the whole campaign was the response" of whites. Though they did not possess a parade permit, a police force not known for its sensitivity to civil liberties did not dare to interfere. Fired by the overwhelming response, Mandel offered to cut the power lines into the prison in order to forestall the execution.[90]

This was the first time that Black and white residents of Richmond had joined in such a public protest of Jim-Crow justice. Local power brokers were not pleased and were particularly distraught with the presence of "outside agitators," many of whom were stomp-down, bona fide Communists; their reaction to this helped to set the tone for future invasions by "freedom riders" and the like during the tumultuous 1960s. Yet, all of these marches, protests, and letters did not prevent all seven defendants from being marched to the gallows, strapped down in electric chairs, and juiced tremulously until the breath passed from their bodies. But the protests continued. In San Pedro, California, eighty Black workers at the Western Cotton Compressor Company mill conducted a work stoppage. The "death vigil" at the White House mushroomed to five hundred peoples despite "heckling and harassing" by the police. Their placards reflected a recurrent theme: "Nazis Freed—Negroes Lynched" expressed their disquiet with the speedy rehabilitation of Hitler's henchmen by the United States while they killed their own Black citizens. This disquiet was not eased when it turned out that the "victim" of the alleged crime, Ruby Floyd, was resting in a mental hospital in a neighboring state.[91]

When Josephine Baker, speaking from Havana, announced, "I am absolutely horrified," she synthesized the sentiments of many about the executions. The aftermath of the tragedy saw the *Richmond News Leader* denouncing CRC, accompanied by a concerted campaign of intimidation against Martinsville's Black community; shaken by the brashness of Afro-Americans and their linkage with whites and reds, local elites moved to reassert their hegemony. CRC leaders did not skip a beat in trying to use the energy generated by the crusade to save other political prisoners. Grossman thanked Frank Render of the Richmond YMCA profusely for their "courtesy and friendliness" during their recent stay; but politeness was not his only aim. He reiterated that this gesture was "particularly noted and appreciated . . . because this is a period when those who fight against jim crow are constantly being denied halls, meeting places, the right to speak, jobs and many other rights. . . . it is obvious to us that pressures, small or great, must have been applied to your organization, or you." He tried to lift his colleague's spirit and then rally him to the defense of McGee. Anne Shore was happy about the fact that they had "money coming in from all over the nation . . . enough to finance all 40 people and our campaign for the whole week." But she was sad about the executions and the role of CRC's erstwhile allies: "We decided that we could have saved the men if two things had been done. . . . had NAACP really fought for the seven which they didn't and second had we really been able to move the trade union movement." But their sweat and tears were not totally for naught. After the executions, a Black dentist was murdered. What ensued was singularly uncustomary and the Martinsville episode was seen as being the determinative element. The suspects were arrested promptly and the largest white church in town was offered for the funeral. There was a funeral of 450 Blacks and 150 whites, including the Mayor, two District Attorneys, and a number of police officers. The Mayor went so far as to offer funds to bring in Black attorneys to assist the prosecution.[92]

This was part of the ultimate significance of CRC's work in the South. In order to preempt the drawing power of the left, political elites moved to dispense concessions, principally to NAACP-led forces. This gave the impression that their no-struggle policies had produced fruits, which built them up at the same time. With this in the pocket, they then moved to squash CRC. But CRC's example of militance and mass action was not squashed and when others came around later in the 1960s using the same tactics, they met a community that had received a thorough education in this field. CRC had been an able teacher.

8

Pulling the Worm from the Apple: CRC in New York and the East

Even though it was subject to criticism by CRC leaders such as Aubrey Grossman, the chapter based in the New York metropolitan area and in New York State had a number of signal accomplishments under its belt. They played a pivotal role in the historic U.S. Supreme Court case *Feiner v. New York*. Irving Feiner not only worked with the Progressive Party, but on CRC campaigns as well. Even though his defeat in the high court was a short-term loss, this case established the "fighting words" doctrine as an exception to the First Amendment protection of "free speech" and would be used years later to fight the Ku Klux Klan. This chapter did their part in carrying out the national CRC program against police brutality and helped in the process to alter the texture of police-community relations. Their lawyers, many of whom were also members of the National Lawyers Guild, handled numerous civil rights-civil liberties cases. They formed fruitful ties with the religious community and various political parties. Their exertions on behalf of local Smith Act defendants led to partial acquittals. They fought vigorously to halt deportations to foreign nations and extraditions to southern states, both alien to traditional concepts of justice. The violence in Peekskill that followed from an event they had sponsored splattered their name in headlines across the nation. They pioneered in the defense of the Rosenbergs. All the while they served as a sparkplug for CRC organizing along the entire East Coast.[1]

One facet of CRC's success in what Afro-American and Afro-Caribbean peoples termed the "Big Apple," was their uncanny ability to attract the well-known to their banner. Paul Robeson was one of their prime fundraisers. Du Bois was "honorary" president of the Harlem chapter. They set up an Entertainment and Advertising Arts chapter that included Alice Childress,

Frank Silvera, Charles White, Woodie Guthrie, and many others. Dashiell Hammett who had accumulated a small fortune as a novelist and writer was for a long time head of the chapter. All this explains partially their relative ability to raise money. An audited financial statement in October 1946 showed an income of $10,270.46 and expenditures of $17,134.79. Early in 1951, during the zenith of the red scare, twenty-three city chapters were able to raise $11,159.50. Manhattan raised the most, then Queens. The successful raffles, bazaars, and receptions they held led to the "unanimous agreement of the state leadership that the response of the chapter to this fund drive was an excellent one."[2]

The chapter in New York got off to a quick start. Formed in the spring of 1946, by the summer over four hundred people had joined. They hired an executive secretary at a salary of $100 per month and a number of other employees as well. Their legal staff—David Scribner, Carol King, Nathan Witt, Abe Isserman, David Freedman—was first rate. The Board of Directors included Hulan Jack, Lena Horne, Max Yergan, Howard Melish, Rockwell Kent, and Howard Da Silva; James Egert Allen, a leader of the State NAACP served as vice-president. This abillity to attract prominent personalities was a hallmark. At their 15 May 1946 program the "dramatic presentation (was) written especially for the meeting by Arthur Miller. . . . Josh White of Cafe Downtown Society" sang. At their October 1947 conference, participants included not only trade union leaders like David Livingston and Ewart Guinier, but also Donald Ogden Stewart.[3]

The issues they tackled reflected their strength in the early postwar period. Their Burnside Fordham chapter in the Bronx forced local Grand Union stores to hire Blacks; their Harlem unit served Thanksgiving dinners to over two hundred of the needy. They filed an *amicus curiae* brief in a controversial St. Albans, Queens, restrictive covenant case that involved an effort to prevent the sale of a home to an African-American. They were fighting the extradition of Lorenzo Reed, another Black, to a "Florida chain-gang." CRC stressed "community action in support of the maritime unions and to oppose use of the armed forces for their strike breaking." Their strength was at times expressed ironically. When handling the appeal of thirteen veterans fined for demonstrating against Winston Churchill, the chapter declared "the offer of the American Civil Liberties Union to file a brief *amicus curiae* in this case has been rejected by CRC. Basis for the rejection is that the major activities of ACLU are now antiunion and in defense of fascists." CRC was reasonably strong in New York State, with chapters throughout New York City and also upstate in Rome-Utica, Endicott, and the Mohawk Valley. But by 30 July 1947 they were sadly reporting that their vice-president, Prof. Lyman Bradley, had been "suspended from his chairmanship of the German Department of New York University" because of his conviction of contempt of HUAC.[4]

Traditionally New York had been a bastion of power for the National

Lawyers Guild and this facilitated the functioning of CRC's legal panel. Victor Rabinowitz, Leonard Boudin, William Standard, Sol Cohn were just a few of the top-flight attorneys who allied themselves with CRC and went on to argue scores of cases before the U.S. Supreme Court and to establish priceless reputations as litigators. Hope Stevens, a Harlem lawyer and future chairperson of the National Conference of Black Lawyers, was involved in a not unusual case in 1951. Portnoy Strasser had left her husband and gone with her daughter to live with her parents. Then she moved in with Roy De Carava, a Black photographer then on the path that would lead him to fame. Her parents sought to remove the child from her custody, on the grounds that she was a Communist and he was Black and non-Jewish. Judge Jacob Marks agreed, taking into account the questionably crucial factor that she would leave the child at a day care center.[5]

Another band of professionals that the chapter sought close ties with was the community of pastors and clerics. Like any other major city during this period, this community was often predisposed to opposition to racism and political discrimination. As Patterson told Rev. Eliot White of New York in 1949, "It is my belief that certain sections of the church leadership stand at this moment ahead of all sections of the trade union movement, in the sharpness with which they raise the issue of civil rights." Again, at the CRC National Board meeting in 1950 it was emphasized "Our attitude towards [sic] the church must change. We must have more respect for the church, dress properly, not smoke in church, must work with the people. The world was founded on religion, not Christianity." In the Black community particularly, clerics wielded considerable influence, were often more immune to financial pressures and were subjected to the same racist pressures that propelled many key local CRC cases. Thus, it was not surprising when on 28 October 1951 listeners to WHBI, 1280 on the AM dial, found Louise Patterson discussing the question, "Should a preacher concern himself only with feeding the soul—or the body as well?" The hunters of Communist fronts were not oblivious to CRC's interest. Frederick Woltman of the *New York World Telegram* blasted both Bishop Edward Parsons and Rev. W. Russell Bowie for working with CRC. The CRC in Brooklyn took up the contentious case of Rev. John Howard Melish, who had been removed as rector of the Church of Holy Trinity there after preaching passionately for détente between the United States and the USSR. This extended hand to clerics was not peculiar to New York, however. Because of patient attention and stroking, B. F. Logan, religious editor of the *Pittsburgh Courier*, was "friendly to the efforts of CRC and the various cases" they fought "and was responsible for the good resolution we got out of the AME Bishops on the Patterson case." This was not without toll, as W. J. Walls of the First Episcopal District of the AME Zion Church sought to reassure: "There may be some communists in churches and organizations everywhere, but it does not mean the organization itself is subversive."[6]

Like many national organizations based in New York, CRC at times had the problem of coordinating local and national concerns in Gotham City. The issue of which cases were national and which were local, along with attendant problems, arose starkly around the problem of extraditions and deportations, one of the many unremarked scandals of the red scare. Things had gotten so bad that CRC petitioned certain northern governors to halt all extraditions to the South, because they often resulted in fierce beatings and persecution. One case the local chapter zeroed in on was the case of James Wilson, a twenty-one-year-old Afro-American tried in South Carolina for shooting a white man who had molested his wife and threatened him. The fact that they took on this case was once again illustrative of CRC's penchant for taking on cases that were immediately dramatic. The many rape cases dramatized this as they played on deep-seated feelings and emotions about sex, racism, and injustice; they had to resonate with the common man and woman. Similarly the Wilson case struck those chords. Wilson was tried without an attorney before an all-white jury. CRC rang the changes by charging that he had received a sentence of life on a chain gang "for doing what any decent man would do . . . rising to the defense of his wife." He escaped from the chain gang to the Bronx on the day he was to receive one hundred lashes. The Bronx police found and jailed him. CRC-NY packed the courtroom for his hearing and mobilized mightily to bar him from being sent back to the southern sink of corruption from which he had emerged. Similarly, as Georgians were fighting on their end to prevent George Claybon from being shipped back to their state, in New York, forces were pressuring the governor to assure a like result. When Governor Averill Harriman of New York moved to extradite Willie Reid, "refugee from a Florida chain-gang," he received 3,500 signatures and avid protests from the State NAACP and the American Labor Party as a result of local CRC urging. Their example was taken up by the Los Angeles chapter, which also made extradition a specialty.[7]

In a comparable manner local CRC forces were quite active on the deportation front. Here they worked closely with the unheralded American Committee for Protection of the Foreign Born and had an interlocking directorate with them. Nationally they put out joint pamphlets and collaborated generally. One group of thankful clients was effusive; "(they) were instrumental in our release. They informed and helped mobilize the people; they gave us excellent lawyers; they took care of us; they were in close contact with our families." With the passage of the draconian McCarran and Walter immigration bills, CRC's mission became larger. A joint committee was established with two Afro-Americans in leadership, J. A. Rogers and Richard Moore, signifying the racist character of the legislation and the disparate impact it would have on Afro-Caribbean peoples. But in the summer of 1951, attorneys Carol King and Ann Fagan Ginger brought sad tidings about the "cancellation of [thirty-five] deportees' bail posted by the Bail Fund of the Civil Rights

Congress." The courts objected to CRC's posting bail because of the orgnaization's political stances.[8]

Locally CRC took on cases that had national implications. In mid-1949 the Immigration and Naturalization Service initiated denaturalization proceedings against Hans Friestadt, "recently awarded an Atomic Energy Commission Fellowship in Physics," because he was allegedly a "professed Communist." The national implications of this action were demonstrated when he was invited to speak on "Meet the Press." In late 1951 they rose to the defense of Martin Young, a noncitizen resident of this country for thirty years and a militant union organizer, who was arrested for deportation pursuant to the McCarran Act. CRC-NY was instrumental in organizing the Citiizens Committee to Secure Bail for Martin Young. This native of Russia had been denied bail since his arrest and detained on Ellis Island for ten months in an action upheld by the Circuit Court of Appeals. Nationally, Patterson moved to assist him and finally in October 1952 INS provided him with an "Order of Parole Under Supervision," which dictated that he "terminate and remain disassociated" from Communists or any "affiliate or subdivision of any such group or organization." Presumably that meant CRC-NY and showed how cold war repression hindered CRC's growth, even among those who had benefited from their altruism; just as Friestadt had had his fellowship suspended, Young was signaled to halt his dalliance with the left.[9]

Virtually to the last dying days of CRC-NY they were fighting deportations. One of the most naggingly tendentious involved Claudia Jones, of Trinidadian descent and perhaps the top Black woman Communist in the nation. She had been jailed under the Smith Act and by 1955 was in poor health. Both New York and national CRC forces saw this case as a top priority and a shot over the bow. As Patterson stated, it was an "ominous, vindictive act, designed to silence all outspoken voices against racism. It represents the government's abject fear against all militant Negro Leadership." Local and national CRC forces were involved in a delegation that attempted unsuccessfully to convince Attorney General Brownell not to deport her. They were also unable to prevent the deportation of the Jamaican labor leader, Ferdinand Smith.[10]

Although extradition and deportation cases undoubtedly occupied a large part of their docket, CRC-NY was not limited to these critical fields. Given their base in New York, it was unavoidable that anti-Semitism and anti-Jewish bias would be a concern. In 1950 eight Jewish teachers were suspended by the Board of Education in the midst of a salary fight after 50,000 students had demonstrated in favor of the teachers' goal. Included in this group were a number of CRC supporters, e.g., Abe Lederman, Celia Zitron, and Alice Citron. CRC pressured the board, spoke at the hearing, but were unable to soften appreciably the impact of this decision. The rights of Puerto Ricans and other Latin Americans were of equal concern to this chapter. The

East Harlem CRC organized a giant protest rally "for the freedom of . . . Dr. Pedro Albizo [sic] Campos, Vidal Santiago" at the Club Obrero; as was the practice in California, a bilingual leaflet attracted the crowd. This rally at 102nd Street and Madison Avenue featured Vito Marcantonio and Aubrey Grossman, among others, and also called for "the right to fight for the independence of Puerto Rico" and freedom for Edusdedit Marrero and "all other political prisoners" in Puerto Rico. At their conference for "civil and human rights" in June 1949, sponsored by four hundred people and attended by 1,165, congealed were the chapter's major themes. The "resolutions and proposals . . . unanimously adopted" focused on the CP-Eleven, minority rights, and trade union rights.[11]

As in other CRC centers in diverse metropolitan areas, the rights of African-Americans were a siren difficult to ignore. In the constricted New York housing market, race discrimination was a constant concern. There was Knickerbocker Village, which in its almost twenty years existence had rented to only one Black family; this struggle was taken to the door of the NY State Division of Housing; there was also the campaign against Stuyvesant Town, engaged in a similar pattern of discrimination. Eventually both complexes were opened up and the chapter played a significant role in this process. Another victory involved Godfrey Ferguson, the only Black orderly at Brooklyn Jewish Hospital, fired after being accused of stealing one dollar. In one of their more meaningful labor victories, CRC won this worker "complete exoneration."[12]

The banners carried by the CRC contingent in the May Day parade of 1952 encapsulated neatly their pressing interests during these difficult days. "Defend the Bill of Rights . . . Remember Willie McGee . . . Stop the Government's Attempts to try William L. Patterson Again" were a few of the slogans lofted on high. Those who peered at the banner flapping in the breeze shouting forth "Stop the Government Policy of Lynch Terror and Jim Crow" might have thought immediately of the deep South, but they could not have avoided pondering its applicability to Manhattan itself. As early as August 1946 when they published their "Chapter Guide" the "#1 Issue" listed was "Violence Against the Negro People." In his introduction, Hammett underscored the importance of the question citywide. They saw this in a broad and not a narrow regional scope and they pressed Truman to invoke a federal grand jury after the bloody pogrom against Blacks in Columbia, Tennessee. This detailed how-to guide called for education in chapters, in street and indoor meetings, for mailings, and for collecting signatures at outdoor meetings.[13]

This August 1946 publication was a response to escalating police violence. In June CRC had spearheaded the struggle "against Fascist hoodlums who attacked a Zionist meeting" in the face of police indifference. In between conducting fights like the one against the banning of Fast's *Citizen Tom Paine* from public schools and the barring of Fast and Arnold Johnson from City

College, Queens College, and Columbia, somehow they found the time to make the state-sponsored terror a target. This was consonant with a major theme of CRC and Patterson particularly, that Jim Crow and its related terror was a government-induced policy. Thus in August 1949 a brouhaha erupted when police officers fired bullets into the body of George Westray, a Black truck driver, who had gone to Lincoln Hospital for treatment. He was refused and then the police reappeared and proceeded to beat him; then he was taken to the treatment room, managed to stagger to his feet, at which point the police shot him. CRC's letter campaign to Mayor William O'Dwyer was not successful in bringing justice. This case was a straw in the wind compared to the violence that burst forth at the "Ben Davis Victory Parade" in November 1949. As cold war tensions boiled over, engendered partially by the spectacle of the CP-Eleven trial, the chapter angrily charged "Indiscriminate police clubbing of marchers and spectators alike. . . . Six arrests and six cops injured." The next day, apparently oblivious to the oil on fire provocation involved, the Mayor dispatched 360 more officials to the Harlem site of the incident and adamantly blamed the protesters. Eyewitnesses disagreed, alleging that the police "set out deliberately to break up the demonstration." Already the chapter had been deluged with requests from victims of police brutality and now they found the problem inside their own door. True to their policy of aligning with labor, the chapter launched the most dramatic campaign around Marion Watkins, a Black member of the Paper and Distributive Workers Union, who had been arrested during the fracas. The upshot was that four of those arrested were sentenced to sixty-day workhouse terms by a magistrate who vehemently denounced them as "political lice."[14]

The CRC in New York tried not to simply react to each incident, but to devise a political orientation and strategy on each question as well. They saw the phenomenon as "not merely a question of a lousy cop . . .nor is it a question of isolated incidents." The fact that "9 out of 10 cases" involved Blacks was not seen as accidental, but as part of a concerted policy of racism. One tactic that CRC pushed heavily and that remains on the political agenda was calling for the formation of a "Citizens' Committee to Conduct a Public Hearing on . . . police brutality" and for an independent body to handle such cases. One strategy hailed was building the "broadest united front possible." Such a front factored in their alliances with lawyers, clergy, unions, and the like. The Greenwich Village chapter, always concerned about attacks on racially integrated couples, circulated a petition asking for an "independent" unit within the policy department to investigate police and other forms of racist violence.[15]

The period from 1948 to 1950 was marked by the rise and government-induced fall of the Progressive Party and by the onset of war in Korea, with its concomitant suppression of civil liberties, and this period saw an astonishing rise in politically and racially inspired violence. In 1948 the legal panel's pending cases showed eleven concerned with police brutality, the most in any category. This year also saw a decided spurt in "hoodlum violence" against the Communists and other progressives. Twelve of their clubs in the city "had windows broken and hoodlums coming in and attacking the people. . . . All of the incidents . . . are recorded in the local precinct records." This was combined with "political interference" with meetings: "There have been at least 20 attacks against speakers and campaign workers at street rallies held in Manhattan from January 1948 to November 1948." At one CRC meeting, City Councilman Eugene Connolly was "attacked . . . dragged from the platform and [had] his glasses smashed."[16]

This was not all. There was an uncommon amount of "brutality and stikebreaking police actions against peaceful picket lines" during this period; "another aspect of this disturbing trend is the increasing police harassment and interference with the right of free speech, press and assembly, . . . denial of loud speaker permits, . . . interference with leaflet distribution, petition gathering." Understandably perhaps, a number of CRC leaflets and Communists began to speak darkly of incipient fascist tendencies in a region known widely as a beacon of liberalism. But the beat went on. In August 1950 police officials denied CRC a permit for a rally in Harlem; that same month five Brooklynites got sentences of from four to twelve months for merely painting "Peace-No H Bomb" on a pillar in Prospect Park.[17]

This critical year also saw another case of police violence against a Puerto Rican. There was a rally planned at the office of one of the chapter's key allies, the American Labor Party, at 104th Street and Columbus Avenue. Following their usual tactics, an altercation ensued with the police that led to the arrest of Ray Ramos. As so often happened in such instances, the dialectic of the situation led to CRC's growth: "In our neighborhood the Porto [sic] Rican People have shown their support through signing our petitions and we have gained a number of new members. . . . The response of the Porto Rican people to our appeal for Willie McGee was magnificent." Yet a note of gloom crept in, "But as yet none of the Porto Rican people have taken an active part in our work."[18]

CRC-NY was not without victory in 1950. In May they were able to have a probationary officer dismissed from the police force for having killed an Afro-American. But CRC ire and resources were strained to the limits when the police murdered John Derrick. A seven-year veteran in the armed forces, he had just returned from a tour of duty when they dispensed with him at 119th Street and 8th Avenue in Harlem, even though he was "unarmed" and had his "hands in the air." At this the chapter was absolutely wrathful: "While Negro soldiers die in a so-called 'police action' in Korea, Negro veterans are killed by police action in New York." Linking the slaying of this twenty-four-year-old disabled Black shot down just before Christmas 1950 with the increasingly unpopular conflict in Korea was not going to win CRC many friends in high places. But they were undeterred. Chapter leader Elaine Ross continued the high level of indignation: "Today every policeman on the beat represents an armed threat to the Negro people. To a Negro walking through the streets of Harlem is like walking through territory occupied by the enemy." These military metaphors could not obscure the fact that while McGee, or the Martinsville Seven at least had had the pretense of due process and trials, in ostensibly more "liberal" New York, summary justice without the slightest shred of obeying Fourteenth Amendment rights was becoming the rule—at least for Blacks. It became too much even for the NAACP. Prodded by CRC's Marvel Cooke and "acting in response to hundreds of telephone messages, Lindsay White, president of the New York branch" of the NAACP demanded that the district attorney who had sought to cover up for the officer be ousted. CRC escalated this demand by demanding as well the removal of the mounted police from Harlem, a battalion seen as a gauntlet cast-down to the community at large. This demand was won ultimately, and, in any event, the momentum generated by CRC in New York did lead to advances in curbing this vile misconduct in the future.[19]

The virus of violence afflicting police in the city began to spread northward. CRC forces in Albany were compelled to march to Erastus Corning's City hall during the "evening rush hour" to demand that he investigate the killing of John Ferrell by the police and to demand an end to the Jim Crow police force. Ferrell had been taken to the police station, booked, locked up, and then found "hanged and dead in ten minutes after his arrest." The NAACP, the American Labor Party, and the Communists were also involved in this case. But as horrible as this incident was, many were of the opinion that it paled into significance compared with what happened in Yonkers in 1952. Ex-officer Stanley Labenskey shot and killed two Blacks, James and Wyatt Blacknall, "without provocation," because he objected to "Negroes being served in the same bar as whites." This was admitted by the officer in a sworn statement. Broader forces beyond CRC rose up in response to this atrocity, which the CRC did not oppose. They demanded a special prosecutor. They called for open-air and indoor meetings, petitions, delegations to be sent to politicians, letters and cards to be sent to Governor Thomas Dewey. Finally in the spring of 1952 a mass delegation organized by CRC-NY went to Albany to see the governor. Black and white, they presented him with a petition listing thirty-five instances of police murder and brutality in New York State in the past four years; there had been at least three Black victims of police murder in Yonkers alone in the past few yers. District Attorney George Fanelli of Westchester, who had been so derelict in the face of the Peekskill riot, was assailed vociferously for his continued neglect of his legal duty. They demanded the death penalty on behalf of the murdered, indicative of the fact that they saw the penalty as necessary in certain circumstances, and they demanded the sacking of Fanelli and his replacement by a Black special prosecutor. Once again, the breadth of the coalition and the anger expressed forced the NAACP to join in the campaign directly. Symptomatic of the underlying racism that was engendering such slaughter was the fact that when they came to Dewey's office, his "personal representative" had the gall and temerity to smirkingly grunt, "there is a n-g-er in every wood pile." The coalition, perhaps seeing that a congenial atmosphere was not to be found in Albany, traveled to Washington where they met a similar brick wall within the civil rights section of Eisenhower's Justice Department; the southern refrain of states' rights was now tossed at the New Yorkers. When Labenskey was acquitted despite his open admission of guilt, the committee within CRC realized even more the deleterious effects of anticommunism and political repression on the always tenuous state of race relations. With the political right-wing riding high in the saddle, it was preordained that their racist compatriots—actually they were often the same—would take heart.[20]

Reeling from the shooting of the Blacknalls, the chapter then had to contend with the slaying of Enus L. Christiani, a Black New York University graduate student, by the police. This case was particularly sensitive. The Black community, in an era when higher education for them was at a premium, had to react sharply to the murder of one seen as able to make a valuable contribution and not seen as a rebellious, discontented person. This killing showed the vulnerability of the entire Black populace and sparked concern even among the most recalcitrant middle-class forces. Evidence of this concern was the participation of the NAACP. But what really angered Blacks was that the incident had been kindled by the victim's protest to a white sorority over their use of a "fat mammy as a target for dart throwers in a carnival booth." One thing led to another and before long this veteran and leader of a local committee on FEPC was sprawling in a pool of his own blood. But the results were predictable. A New York County Grand Jury said there was "no basis for an indictment."[21]

With stinging defeat coming after stinging defeat, it would not have been surprising if demoralization had set in. But the chapter persevered. They could continue to point to the dismissal of the probationary officer, James Beaman, after he had killed George West in Harlem; CRC and their attorney Gloria Agrin, who they paid a meager $50, was directly responsible for this. In 1952 the Chelsea CRC won a victory when the judge dismissed charges against an Afro-American framed by the police. Indicative of the way their militance had not waned was the fact that in the year of defeats, 1952, they organized a bristling delegation of Black and white women who invaded the offices of the reactionary *NY World Telegram and Sun* "to protest the 'crime wave' manufactured" by them, "which has resulted in lynch incitement[s] against the Negro and Puerto Rican people of New York." The police had to be called in. But an important milestone was reached nonetheless, and that continues to resonate. The City Council "passed . . . (a) resolution unanimously" asking newspapers "to cease referring to the race and nationality" of crime perpetrators. Observing this principle would help to curb the tendency of the police to see every person of color as a potential robber or mugger and acting accordingly.[22]

One can say the rampant state-sponsored terrorism that gripped New York fed on and fed into the shameful riot at Peekskill in 1949. Having now taken on mythic proportions because of its stunning portrayal in the Hollywood film "Daniel," there is little doubt that it was a planned occurrence designed to frighten masses away from a flourishing CRC and from left forces generally. The slipshod manner in which the culprits were pursued lent credence to the notion that "law and order" was being interpreted, per usual, rather narrowly. The report of the ACLU, backed by Americans for Democratic Action, the American Jewish Congress, and the NAACP was forced to conclude that "there was no Communist provocation at either concern; behind the rioting lay long smoldering anti-Semitism . . ." and anticommunism and racism to boot. Yet the grand jury of Westchester County whitewashed the role of the state troopers and local police, who along with local thugs, had brutally assaulted those attending CRC-sponsored events. Similarly, CRC, Paul Robeson, and a number of others filed suit in December 1949 asking for $2.02 million in damages, but in January 1952 the case was dismissed. In a comparable vein, a letter signed by Charles Chaplin, E.Y. 'Yip' Harburg, and a number of others to Truman demanding that federal action be taken was ignored. Events like these led many to conclude that a whiff of fascism had invaded their nostrils.[23]

It was logical that Paul Robeson would be involved in this tumult. A resident of the metropolitan area, he was one of CRC's staunchest allies and also a close friend of Patterson. They had first encountered each other in the early 1920s in Harlem, both recent law school graduates—Patterson from the University of California and Robeson from Columbia. They married roommates and often had occasion to discuss the future. Robeson freely acknowledged his colleague's influence on him, and vice versa. The internationally renowned thespian recalled that before World War II "Pat and I had long conversations and he was able to point out to me the basic reasons for these things," e.g., colonialism, exploitation. Profusely he thanked his friend "for all the clarity he has brought not only to me but also to the many people with whom he has worked."[24]

Robeson was a major fundraiser for CRC, particularly on cases close to his heart, like the Trenton Six who emerged near his hometown of Princeton. At an early 1949 mass rally for the six at the St. Nicholas Arena in Harlem, not only did he appear with Pete Seeger to sing but he gave a "generous contribution" as well. Later that year in Chicago's Tabernacle Baptist Church he spoke before six thousand people—two thousand outside—and hundreds of dollars were raised. He attracted to CRC's banner prominent celebrities who also contributed materially. And he used his newspaper *Freedom* to highlight CRC cases like those of Willie McGee and Patterson. His early 1951 issues of this paper were typical, featuring front-page editorials on McGee, accompanied by articles by Robeson on the same subject.[25]

Like any sound political tie, this one was reciprocally beneficial, for CRC never hesitated to rise to Robeson's defense when controversy found him. A firestorm was created when at a peace conference in Paris in 1949 he expressed doubts as to whether Blacks would join in a war against the Soviets. Later at a CRC function in Newark, he repeated the substance of these remarks: "American Negroes must not be asked ever again to sacrifice on foreign shores. If we must sacrifice, let it be in Alabama and Mississippi where my race is persecuted." Angry picketers from the Veterans of Foreign Wars circled the site as his supporters cheered him on. Perhaps what stoked such wild fury was the sneaking suspicion that Blacks were not stupid enough to be abused by the same forces who then wanted to send them down the chute of the incinerator. At their Bill of Rights Conference in July 1949, CRC issued a statement of support signed by one hundred Black delegates. When Robeson had to fight John Foster Dulles for the right to obtain a pasport, Patterson and Powe filed a hard-hitting *amicus curiae* brief. Eventually Patterson had to "take over the leadership of Paul Robeson's passport fight."[26]

But even before the Peekskill riot there had been signals that indicated its coming. In 1947 there had been a spate of politically motivated cancellations of contracts at sites where Robeson was scheduled to sing, most notably in Albany and Peoria. In both instances CRC protested vigorously, mobilizing the clergy and trade union allies, e.g., District Council 4A of the United Shoe Workers Union. But their allies in the United Farm Equipment and Metal Workers Union in the rural Illinois metropolis gloomily informed them "we were unable to buy space in the newspapers for an ad and were refused time on the air to give to the public our side of the episode." So much for the free press. Then the irresistible force met the immovable object when Robeson was scheduled to perform in the hotbed of reaction, Miami. The force yielded. Patterson was reluctant to arrange his visit for the chapter there, noting the "tremendous responsibility." Bluntly he asserted, "Reaction wants the murder of Paul Robeson. . . . We must have no political[ly] naive outlook on this question." It was concluded "we feel that Pat should not come to Florida at this time." But this necessary solicitude for Robeson had a downside. Chapter members in Chicago complained of the too-heavy security around Robeson during his trip there; they recognized that it was necessary, but they advised that "less abruptness and more finesse was needed." By forcing CRC to place a shield between Robeson and the masses, reaction was able to lessen his impact and appeal.[27]

Hence trouble was expected when CRC decided to send busloads of their supporters to the rural Westchester community for what was expected to be a successful outing.And trouble stuck at both the first outing in late August 1949 and at the second outing in September, which was designed to show that CRC would not be easily intimidatd. Before the event of 27 August the press whipped up hysteria about Robeson in particular and about his supposed lack of patriotism because of his Paris remarks. The fact that leaders like Du Bois and the boxer Joe Louis backed him somehow got lost. Neither riot was spontaneous, particularly the second one. One teenager said that he and thirty others had been recruited to riot. The *New York Mirror* ran a headline of promise and threat: "Vets Set Huge Rally Against Paul Robeson." As a result over one thousand police were present, but the role they played was basically to stand aside like the matador allowing the bull to charge by, and also to participate. The riot could not have been unexpected, as is evidenced by the presence of a number of television cameras shooting endless reels of film. The state estimated that 15,000 people were at the CRC event; CRC estimated 30,000. In any event a horrible scene of destruction ensued. Pete Seeger, who sang there, saw 4–5″ rocks sailing at them and cracking skulls. In sworn affidavits, Albert Spivey swore he saw "four state troopers beating up two of the concert guards." In his affidavit, Leo Stark, who required stitches in his head, saw 150 police and rowdies go wild. Irving Warman was struck by the women cheering on the thugs and underscored the role the American Legion played. Anita Payne recalled frenzied shouts of "n-g'er" while Dr. Seymour Gladstone heard cries of "kikes . . . n-g-er lovers." Harold Taylor heard "Dirty Jews." Michael Salte saw a burning cross, symbol of the Klan. Nina Phillips had a finger amputated. Esther Marquit had a tooth knocked out by one of those rocks Pete Seeger saw. One member of Local 65 of the Wholesale and Warehouse Workers Union wound up on the "critical list" with a "blood clot on the brain." Starr Koss submitted a drawing of passengers huddling on the floor of the bus as glass splattered around them. It was, in sum, a bloody massacre, lasting over five hours. Twice within the space of days CRC had taken a terrible beating in its home state at the hands of the government and their reactionary allies. Even the delegation from CRC-NY that went to see the Governor about this outrage required an "iron ring of police" to prevent an attack.[28]

The response to Peekskill was swift and immediate. The *Pittsburgh Courier* reflected the view of the Black press by denouncing the rioters and hailing Robeson. The American Jewish Congress demanded the appointment of a special prosecutor. But the Alabama Klan burned an effigy of Robeson and the National Urban League implicitly condemned him at their Denver convention. While Eleanor Roosevelt, Mayor O'Dwyer, and Jackie Robinson blasted the rioters, A. Philip Randolph castigated Robeson, terming him a "Johnny-come-lately to the cause of the Negro." Patterson counterattacked against the increasingly right-leaning labor boss and mobilized his supporters to act similarly. Howard Fast quickly got out a book on Peekskill that Patterson sought to have translated into various languages. To Albert Maltz in Mexico, he suggested that a "boycott of U.S.A. goods" be launched. To comrades in Canada, Britain, and elsewhere he suggested, "I do not see why people should not gather in numbers before the American government's agencies abroad and let them know" their view of U.S. reaction. CRC-NY attempted to capitalize on the publicity generated by the riot—albeit mostly negative—by doing more recruiting.[29]

CRC also launched a multimillion-dollar lawsuit and tried to mobilize around it. Their hopes for the grand jury were dashed cruelly. There were forty-five morning and twenty-two afternoon sessions, resulting in thousands of pages of testimony being heard by twenty-one jurors. But the talk at these sessions of CRC being "a group organized for and serving solely the interests of Communism" was a tip-off that the criminals would not be brought to book. Rogge, Abzug, and Patterson were among the lawyers for twenty-eight plaintiffs suing under federal civil rights laws for $2.02 million, with eighty-four claims in 226 paragraphs. There were urgent meetings at CRC offices and the offices of Bill Standard, but as ever a dearth of funds made it difficult to proceed and the suit came to naught, as did their meeting with the U.S. Attorney General and their petition for dismissal of the police and state officials involved.[30]

One of the hundreds who filed affidavits compared the right wing's slogan at Peekskill, "Wake Up America," to the Nazi slogan, "Deutschland Er-vacht." This whiff of fascism probably led the NAACP and the ACLU to severely condemn the rioters. Roy Wilkins asked Dewey to launch an "immediate investigation," and he joined in the production of CRC's December 1949 report "Violence in Peekskill." But even before they had begun to advance, they were retreating. The grand jury criticized their report harshly and James Wechsler attacked it for being far too sympathetic to the left, CRC, and the Communists. A *Crisis* editorial, while acknowledging accurately that "if hooligans are permitted to crack communist heads today, they will be cracking Catholic or Mormon heads with equal glee on the morrow," still accused the left of "deliberately court(ing) violence" and alleged that they were "arch enemies of civil rights." The Harlem branch of CRC, for which Robeson had been performing at Peekskill, managed to escape their approbation as well. Peekskill was a signal that the left was being isolated from the center as the right marched forward. The indictment and trial of local Communist leaders provided CRC-NY with further evidence, as if any were needed, that the situation was unraveling.[31]

CRC was viewed as a "Communist front," but ironically its most open relationships were with the Progressive Party and the American Labor Party. In many areas they shared office space, e.g., in Detroit and Denver. In 1950, acknowledging CRC as a "non-political organization embracing those of all shades of opinion," the Harlem chapter of CRC went on to "endorse" ALP candidates (Du Bois and others) in local elections, because "the fight for civil rights and the selection of progressive law makers are part of the same struggle." William Patteson did the same in 1952 with regard to the Progressive Party. CRC also defended local Democrats, for instance, when Adam Clayton Powell was attacked physically in Congress. But the main key that was hit by CRC in their dealings with the Democrats and Republicans was slashing attack. It was customary for CRC to submit proposals to the platform committees of both parties on such issues as the Fair Employment Practices Committee, Jim Crow in Washington, the Smith Act. Typical of their proposals to the Democrats was the one they issued in 1948 accusing them of "collusion and conspiracy" with the GOP against the Bill of Rights.[32]

Then after the conviction of the Communist directorate at Foley Square, the so-called "second string" leadership was indicted. And just as CRC-NY had peformed yeoman service in defense of the eleven, most of whom were New York residents, they acted similarly on behalf of what came to be known as the CP-Seventeen, who equally had New York ties. This support was partially a result of enlightened self-interest. Arnold Johnson of the CRC national office, who was coordinating the work on behalf of the eleven and other CP leaders, was indicted with the others in December 1950. When he was arrested in Pittsburgh where he had been organizing, he was "roughed up by federal marshals. . . . [they] twisted [his] arms violently and shoved him." CRC posted bail for all of these defendants. Initially it was $176,000; then it was raised sharply to $875,000. After speaking to the ACLU, bar associations, and lawyers in New York, Chicago, Washington, and elsewhere, they had to fall back on the tight circle of Lawyers Guild members who traditionally handled such cases: "we were frankly advised that retainers would not be accepted nor an assignment welcome because of the risk of injury to the lawyer undertaking this defense." There were victories, however. Marion Bachrach was allowed to be severed from the trial due to information on her health provided by her physician Hugh Auchincloss, Jr. The paid informer, Harvey Matusow, retracted his testimony in his affidavit. Defendants Si Gerson and Isidore Begun had their motion for acquittal accepted—a rare victory during these times that buoyed organizers and defendants alike. But the courageous lawyers in this case—Mary Kaufman, Harry Sacher, A. L. Wirin, Delbert Metzger—had to endure a torturous trial that lasted from 31 March to 23 September 1952, with the guilty verdicts coming down on 21 January 1953. At that point they filed appeals up to the U.S. Supreme Court, but this proved to be futile. Yet CRC's vigorous defense of Communists based on the notion that this was the first line in defense of civil liberties was seen by some as only confirming their role as a "Communist front."[33]

The New York chapter had long been concerned with anticommunist legislation. Many of their publications were devoted to the subject. Their executive secretaries, Wiliam Lawrence and Nat Ross, were personally interested in the subject. When the Mundt bill was being considered, they collected signatures on petitions in the streets every Saturday and Sunday. The Manhattan CRC helped form a Manhattan Citizens Committee to Defeat the Mundt Bill, which was joined by the NAACP and the American Jewish Congress. Special committees were set up around each defendant in the trial of the seventeen and CRC played a leading role in the process. There was a Committee to defend V. J. Jerome, often described in the bourgeois press as the "Communist Cultural Commissar," on which Dashiell Hammett served as chairperson, Du Bois as honorary chairperson, with Hugo Gellert and Waldo Salt as secretaries. It was CRC's view that Jerome had been singled out "because of his exposure of Hollywood's false portrayal of the life of the American Negro." A committee was formed on behalf of Al Lannon, based in the trade union movement, and so on down the line. The Committee to Defend Negro Leadership took a special interest in Claudia Jones, Pettis Perry, and James Jackson and CRC chapter members were instrumental in the organizing of it. They encouraged the NAACP to join them, because the prosecution threatened "Negroes 'right to protest.'" Particularly they knocked the "plaguing" of "Negro communities" by the FBI, "supposedly looking for" Black victims of the Smith Act. They pointed to Jackson whose family was "under virtual house arrest" and were followed to Virginia by the FBI; his parents got calls in the middle of the night. One hundred families near Virginia Union University were visited by the FBI in an attempt to recruit "stool pigeons." Jackson's wife's mother, president of the local NAACP, was "visited and questioned." Scores of members of his family were "questioned" and persecuted, lost their jobs, and suffered other trials. In an effort to track down Jackson all druggists in the area got a letter from J. Edgar Hoover himself listing Jackson's ailments and the drugs he might need; they refused to cooperate. "Every associate" of his in SNYC was questioned along with "100 Negro workers" at a Ford plant in Detroit. This air of intimidation was hotly denounced by the chapter, and the ripple effect of it frightened away potential supporters.[34]

Like the Peekskill riot, the trial of CP-Seventeen and so many other cases that arose in New York, what may have started as a local case became a national case. To an extent this happened with the case at hand because of the high rank of the leaders involved. Thus when U.S. Attorney Myles Lane "provoked" a contempt charge against Flynn, it was Patterson who took the lead in getting Hugh Bryson, Ben Gold, J. Pius Barbour, and others to protest. When he went to the courthouse to confront the prosecution, he was barred by police, who said Lane had ordered them to do so; all this after Lane had tried to coerce Flynn into becoming a "stool pigeon." Many of the local members had a large role in organizing the Committee of the Families of the Seventeen, which directed the energies of the relatives. But all of this activity did not obviate a conviction under the Smith Act with one-to-five year sentences and fines ranging up to $10,000 each. Like the Foley Square trial, the evidence for the convictions was flimsy; for Jones the "sole evidence" against her was an article by her favoring women's rights and attacking the war in Korea.[35]

When the "second string" Communists were arrested, it was the Civil Rights Congress Bail Fund that posted bail. Separate from the CRC, akin to the later evolution of the NAACP and NAACP Legal Defense Fund, it was set up in the 1946–47 period principally because "regular bail bonding companies (had) refused to post bond for Communists" and other dissidents. The procedure was to obtain funds from individuals, give them a certificate of deposit guaranteeing to return the funds within thirty days on surrender of the certificate; they accepted cash or treasury bonds of $100 and over. When Communists were arrested, ruling elites expected to see them stew in jail; after all, the word had been passed to the bail bondsmen. So when the Fund would come along and spring them, indignation waxed. The *Detroit Times* in a large 12″ × 9″ cartoon captured this anger and frustration. It featured laughing "bail jumping U.S. Communists" with a figure in a suit, hat, and glasses in the background holding a lamp with the notation "unlimitd money" and a spade with the notation "bail." Patterson was melodramatically explicit about the necessity of the fund's existence:[36]

> Twice in the thirties I went into Hitler's Germany—on the first occasion in 1934, to find hundreds of Jewish friends of mine hiding or already entrapped and imprisoned in concentration camps. The last time, in 1937, to find many of them dead. . . . (many Germans said) it cannot happen here. . . . I see the same phenomenon here in America. . . . It is not the CRC bail fund which is under attack alone . . . there is no bail fund like it. No other bail fund in America is available to Negro victims of white-supremacist terror.

The beginning of the end for this noble experiment began when the trustees supplied about $250,000 in bail for the Foley Square defendants. By August 1951 they had supplied $650,000 in green for reds and Blacks and others. When the Supreme Court affirmed the conviction of the CP-Eleven, four of them fled. The federal court dragged four trustees—Dashiell Hammett, Frederick Field, Abner Green and Alphaeus Hunton—into a hearing for information on the fugitives. They steadfastly refused to answer questions and refused to produce the books and records of the Fund. They were jailed for contempt and the bail posted by the Fund for them was refused. In January 1952 they resigned as a result and Grace Hutchins, a longtime progressive, accepted the trustee post. In reply the State of New York averred that the trustees "should not be permitted to engineer a liquidation through a substitute trustee of their own choosing. . . . they have breached their fiduciary duties." With that magical incantation, the court set in motion the fund's liquidation, a drawn-out process that lasted until 1960. But with the virtual extinction of the Fund by 1952, there was a quantum drop in CRC's work.[37]

Abner Green was well-known and a leader of the American Committee for Protection of the Foreign Born. Alphaeus Hunton worked closely with Du Bois and Robeson on the Council on African Affairs and was a major intellectual. But the press was attracted inevitably to Frederick Field and to the CRC-NY chairman, Dashiell Hammett. Field was a millionaire many times over and was not hesitant about sharing his bounty with the left. *Newsweek* set the pace for its competitors by asking "What Makes a Millionaire Go Communist?" *Life* and *Saturday Evening Post* followed suit in their coverage of Frederick Vanderbilt Field and others were not far behind. But it was Hammett who made the best copy by their standards. This "creator of (the) modern detective story" had suffered from tuberculosis and alcoholism; early in life he was a Pinkerton detective himself. But by the time of CRC's founding he was a confirmed leftist—a member of the Communist Party according to Albert Maltz—and he applied his time and fortune energetically to the cause. His fortune was harmed grievously as a result. According to Richard Layman, " 'The Adventures of Sam Spade' was forced off the air because of its association with Hammett." Government surveillance on him increased says Layman: "The FBI record of Hammett's activities in the late 1940s is a model of careless reasoning and incomplete investigation, but it indicates the extent of his influence among liberal political groups." How true. The chairman and his close friend Lillian Hellman could open many doors—and pockets—otherwise closed to CRC. So his jailing was sweet revenge for some. Layman has suggested that the "real price of his imprisonment was . . . on his health. When Hammett left prison his health was gone, and he was never a well man again." His Dun and Bradstreet rating also became decidely unhealthy as a consequence. Richard Moody observed that after the jailing the "government discovered that he owed more than $100,000 in back taxes." Even though he had been affluent at one time, he did not die so. If Hellman is correct, this eventuality is even more tragic: "The truth was that Hammett had never been in the office of the Congress, did not know the name of a single contributor." But Hammett himself was charmingly resolute: "if it were more than jail, if it were my life, I would give it for what I think democracy is, and I don't let cops or judges tell me what I think democracy is."[38]

By any measure the Fund was quite a boon for progressives. By 1948 they had $605,000 in par value bonds; they had total assets of $1,016,221.83 and liabilities of $1,936,896.32. The rising level of political and racist repression strained their resources at the seams. The outlay for bail in 1947 was $20,000. By 1948 it had become $88,000, and by the end of the first nine months of 1949, it had reached a total of $120,000. But in his appeal Robert Dunn of the Fund was quick to stress, "As you know, our Bail Fund has never defaulted the return of a loan on request and fully 20% of the Fund has been kept on hand for such returns." CRC-NY lawyer Nathan Witt was one of the largest contributors to this Fund; other claimants included Eleanor Flexner, John Randolph, and Howard Fast. A disproportionate number were Jewish. As of October 1950 they had dispensed funds to forty-one different clients, most of whom were aliens, but the list also included Roosevelt Ward, Fletcher Mills, Harold Christoffel, seven "unemployed youths," Greek sailors, and others.[39]

What complicated the situation was a sudden rush of repression. Judges in immigration cases began to hike bail from $500 to $50,000 on the presumption that they were hastening the riddance of those god-awful outside agitators who had brought the germ of communism to this country. Somehow—probably through a burglary—the FBI obtained a list of those who had given to the fund and began a campaign of harassment. Then, of course, four of the trustees were jailed. But with all this, Grossman felt that other routes could have been taken, as the presumed burglary proved ultimately unnecessary:[40]

> The bail fund records, including the names, were recently turned over to the New York Attorney General and thence to the FBI. The trustees themselves, in July of last year, turned these records over to the New York State Banking Commission. They did this on the theory that the names would not be turned over to the FBI. This was not a decision in which CRC joined and it didn't happen to be one of which I approved.

The sturdy organizer from San Francisco was not the only one who was angry. The jailed Abner Green complained to Patterson about the "complete desertion" of their case, the "complete absence of any public campaign." Patterson agreed that this was outrageous. Patterson did his best to keep up the spirits of the imprisoned. He addressed "Dear Friend Hammett" in the Federal Detention House with a combination of humor and pluck:[41]

> catching guys who are after the Maltese Falcon is an infinitely easier job than catching the guys who are out to destroy constitutional liberties and respect for human rights. . . . I wish to God that some of us on the outside had the great moral reserves that you on the inside have so magnificently displayed.

The disgruntled Green may have been responding to the war hoop of the bourgeois press. Smelling blood, the veteran red hunter Ogden Reid told the readers of the *New York Herald Tribune* in a lengthy dissertation: "Bail Jumpers Stir Resentment and Defections in Party Ranks." If it had not been there originally, it may have been there after the publication of this mixture of half and quarter truths. CRC tried to counterpunch against this barrage of blows. Patterson wrote the editor of the *New York Times* a stern note objecting to the tenor of their coverage. An open letter was placed in the *Washington Star*, the *Afro-American*, the *St. Louis Post Dispatch*, *Compass*, and others. Directed at the U.S. Attorney General, it vociferously protested the jailing of the four trustees and was signed by hundreds of people from labor, the religious, and the Black communities. Finally, the four were freed, but the Fund was liquidated nonetheless.[42]

This liquidation was not simple. Like Grossman, the eagle-eyed lawyer Mary Kaufman objected to the process, fearing that it would lead to the publication of names of CRC contributors, which would set back the movement tremendously. Grace Hutchins was "deeply troubled at the increasing number of persons holding certificates in the Bail Fund, who come in to ask me when they can get back their money. They are hardship cases . . . some are unemployed . . . other have serious illnesses. . . . They made their original [contributions] on the basis, written on the face of the certificate, that they could at most certainly get their money back upon request." But this was no longer certain, for "even if we collect every conceivable asset, there will not be enough on hand to meet all of the claims."[43]

From Dallas, CRC leader and attorney Sam Barbaria objected strongly to the impact of the liquidation on a case he had handled, because it would mean naming names: "I do not stoolpigeon under any circumstances and that receivership up there doesn't have a leg to stand on from what little law I know." He declared that it was "unwise" to proceed in the manner suggested: "Affidavits and court records are evidence in other trials. The police here have a special fund and are currently using hundreds of special agents and spies to run me out of town or at least out of the law business." He went to the heart of the matter as he saw it: "our state has a sharp law designed to prosecute CRC people. . . . the refund can be effected without an affidavit. . . . I am sorry this thing has ended up complicated since none of us have anything to gain personally from participating in matters . . . such as this case." But Robert Dunn was defiant and he prevailed: "I just can't see for the life of me what makes you hesitate. . . . [the] minutes show that we authorized you to put it up. We have your letter. Why hold back from signing a release that merely makes it possible to have us get back the money that was given to you in good faith for this one purpose."[44]

This was not the only problem. After the folding of the Fund, scores of defendants were unable to make bail. Moreover, only 50 percent of claims were to be paid, and there were suits pending against CRC and a number of their clients. The fact that the situation dit not deteriorate further was in large part due to the skill of longtime CRC lawyer Victor Rabinowitz, or so said Dunn: "you have done an extraordinary job of keeping these legalized holdup men from walking off with the entire contents of the bank, including the door of the safe! It would seem that you did at least double the amount of work these 'liquidators' did without any compensation." One of those "holdup men" was the now ubiquitously irritating John Rogge, who brought suit against the Fund on abstruse grounds. David Rein, who handled the case for the fund and CRC, was victorious and he affirmed "the case decided nothing except that Rogge's firm was silly." But all of this cost money to fight and it overstretched to the breaking point the resources of CRC's loyal cadre of litigators. Leo Linder, who worked on the Rogge case, failed on his court claim for attorney's fees; neither he nor Rabinowitz, as of 1954, had been "compensated for the work done by us in the proceeding since it started almost two years ago." Increasingly this was becoming the norm for CRC lawyers, who also had bills to pay and mouths to feed.[45]

This tangled legal web was made more complicated when the Internal Revenue Service asked for an audit, then demanded back taxes and a hefty penalty. After another extended battle, this was disallowed in U.S. Tax Court. Finally, in the fall of 1960, the liquidation of the Fund was completed. By then CRC was long gone and the assault on the Bail Fund had helped to hasten their decline. Principally supported by well-heeled and not-so-affluent contributors, the Fund had been a reliable tool against repression and frame-ups. Yet even a flourishing Bail Fund would not have been that big of a help when CRC in New York faced one of its biggest challenges—saving the lives of Julius and Ethel Rosenberg.[46]

The role of the left generally and CRC in the "Save the Rosenbergs" campaign has been bathed in controversy. In one of the latest expressions of this, Ronald Radosh and Joyce Milton denigrate at every turn the role the Communists played in the case; they barely mention CRC and do not consult their papers. In one of the few references made to CRC, they have Patterson chiding Emily Alman of the Rosenberg Committee "for her efforts to forge a broad-based movement composed of supporters from across the political spectrum. The Right could not save the Rosenbergs, he argued." A comparison of this mangling of the facts with what Patterson actually said provides a microcosmic cross section of the way certain writers have tried to disfigure CRC's and the left's actual role. Concerning the united front. Patterson called for

> that movement of the people which is so undeniably correct that middle class elements would be attracted to it and honest people to the right of center forced to find means of expressing themselves in parallel actions or joining with the left. There can be no united front that excludes the left; that is not a united front. For me it is false to say that the right can save Ethel and Julius Rosenberg, or that the right saw the menace of this case to democracy before the left.

What Patterson was arguing was exactly the opposite of what these authors claimed; he was polemicizing against the notion that the Rosenbergs could be saved only if the committee avoided the taint of the left; he was not arguing that they could be saved only if the left was involved and all others were excluded. But on the sensitive questions of the left and the Communists, anything goes, including ignoring rules of evidence and distorting meanings.[47]

The fact is that CRC could have done more to save the life of the Rosenbergs—and Willie McGee and the Martinsville Seven and Paul Washington and Albert Jackson. It is virtually racist how this latter point is ignored. Of course, complicating the Rosenbergs' situation was the fact that just as Patterson had to respond to those who wanted to ban the left from the coalition, there were many who felt that bringing a "Communist front" into the defense would only confirm the allegations that the committee was comprised of "Soviet spies." Still, it is striking that the sons of the Rosenbergs recall attending their "first Rosenberg meeting" during the summer of

1952: "The major address was delivered by William Patterson." A mass campaign to save the defendants was launched by CRC at a time when they were waging fierce battles on a number of other fronts. Yet when James Ford complained on the eve of a Rosenberg memorial in 1955 that "not enough had been done to save the lives of the Rosenbergs . . . except in Europe" he was not totally off-base. But note that the European effort he praised was sparked primarily by the CRC.[48]

There are the culprits in the search for the truth about who let the Rosenbergs down. There was the ACLU, which refused to intervene because of the influence of Norman Thomas and like-minded right-wing social democrats. Roy Wilkins insisted rigidly that "under no circumstances is the NAACP to be affiliated" with the Rosenbergs' defense. The local NAACP official whose inquiry prompted Wilkins' inflexibility revealed in a damaging admission: "I checked with the FBI prior to writing you." The Association received many mailings from the Rosenberg Committee; most were marked with the notation "file no reply" or "Discard now." Futilely Patterson contacted the union leader, David Dubinsky; even then he was seeking to combat the notion circulated in the *New York Post* that "there are left forces who would want to see the Rosenbergs murdered."[49]

There was constant concern that CRC and the Rosenberg Committee were not doing a sufficient job in reaching the labor movement, although Dubinsky's cold shoulder may indicate that the fault did not rest entirely with CRC. This was Grossman's compalint about numerous CRC efforts and this one was not immune:

> The trouble with the Rosenberg labor leaflets is that the Rosenberg Committee does not consider the labor movement very important. Consequently they have let not very important reasons dictate the continued delays. . . . the world campaign . . . undoubtedly is not yet capable of success because it does not include any substantial participation by unions in the United States.[50]

CRC and the Committee to Secure Justice for the Rosenbergs worked closely most of the time. The situation in San Diego, where they shared the same address and some personnel, was duplicated in a number of areas. Still sometimes there were problems coordinating properly with the leadership of the Rosenberg Committee. After CRC published Richard Boyer's moving pamphlet, "The Cold War Murder: The Frame-up Against Ethel and Julius Rosenberg" (with an equally moving introduction by Patterson), the CRC leader had to tell the committee, "I hope that you will . . . place no difficulty in the way of our reaching these key people with our very important pamphlet. . . . obstacles to this end should be moved out of our path at once." Nonetheless, David Alman of the committee, after a critical midwest conference that discussed the case extensively, informed Patterson thankfully, "It was the feeling of everyone I spoke to after the Conference that the greatest single contribution had been the one that comes with you. . . . The Conference would (not) have been the same without you."[51]

There was no doubt that the Rosenbergs themselves were grateful for CRC's selfless aid. When CRC cried over the death of Willie McGee, Julius Rosenberg cried with them: "My heart is sad, my eyes are filled with tears. My heart hurts at crimes which have been directed so long against the Negro people. . . . I was terribly shocked to read that Willie McGee was executed. . . . I must yell 'Shame America.' " Both were particulary appreciative of the freedom train that came to the gates of Sing Sing, organized by CRC-NY and designed to both protest their jailing and boost their morale. Ethel Rosenberg cooed to her lawyer Emmanuel Bloch, a longtime CRC lawyer from the early days of the Bilbo and McGee battles in Mississippi, her frank appreciation: "And on Sunday, December 21, 1952, I sat quietly in my cell listening to the songs that close to 1,000 people were singing in a heavy rain at Ossining Station . . . and feeling a calm and a safety and a spiritual bond that no deprivation, no loneliness, no danger could shatter!" The CRC rented a special seven-car train, and even though some feared it would result in a "little Peekskill," fortunately no such thing occurred.[52]

CRC was resolute about pointing to anti-Semitism as a prime motivating factor in the execution of the Rosenbergs. Ruefully, CRC-NY member Boyer contrasted the freeing of Ilse Koch, "Nazi Murderess of Buchenwald," by U.S. authorities. When a writer for the *New York World Telegram* sniffed that Julius was one of those "CCNY boys who sold out their country," Patterson angrily assailed their "vicious anti-Semitism." CRC membership was disproportionately Jewish, particularly in New York, and this case brought to the surface fears that had haunted many about the level of anti-Jewish prejudice. Working on this case caused a certain amount of introspection, and then action, among members. This tendency reached even to Minneapolis, where CRC leader Irene Paull discussed how they put on a "cantata . . . in the synagogues. . . . I wrote the words and a progressive inter-racial group of kids accompanied it with Yiddish and Hebrew songs. You have no idea, Pat, what an impact it has made . . . for the Jewish people to hear their songs of sorrow and struggle and hope sung by a chorus . . . of Negroes, Germans, Scandinavians, Irish, Italians and Jews. . . . We put it on over the radio and it made a hit." After engaging in what was then a rare attack on Israeli policies, she pointed out how working with CRC "has done something important for me." Paull was Jewish and she conceded that she hated "gentiles" for their anti-Semitism; they called her grandfather "Greenhorn . . . sheeny." Then she discovered that "the cause of my people was really not a separate thing, but the cause of all people." This same odyssey was undergone by countless CRC cadre and it can be counted as one of their many accomplishments. So puffed up was Paull that she boasted "I don't think I should stay in the background on CRC in order to keep my job. My job isn't that important." But this was not puffery, for so inspired was she that she not only played a leading role in the local Rosenberg Committee, but in 1952 recruited twenty others.[53]

Patterson was disappointed in the response of certain sectors of the Afro-American community to the Rosenbergs' case. He complained that the "Negro press of America is strangely silent" about the Rosenbergs, though he contended that if "rapist" were substituted for "spy," one could more readily demonstrate the implications of the case for Blacks. Even the *National Guardian* rejected the ad for the Sing-Sing demonstration, because they were "advised" that "the Ossining mobilization might work to the detriment of" the Rosenbergs. As noted, the ACLU, like their NAACP allies, was reluctant to join. Herbert Levy, their staff counsel, found "no valid civil liberties points" in the conviction; strangely, he denied that the death penalty was a civil liberties issue and agreed with the bizarre idea that it was "proper" to introduce Communist Party membership as "evidence of motive." The Rosenbergs' murder was an inevitable outcome of viewing Communists as directed by the hand of Moscow.[54]

James Ford was perspicacious in seeing the movement abroad as being essential to the Rosenbergs' defense. Thanks to CRC, the Mouvement Contre Le Racisme, L'Antisemitisme et Pour la Paix of France, the Democratic Rights Council of Australia, Nippon Kokumin Kuyenkai of Tokyo, the Progressive Youth League of New Zealand and many others were among those that raised their voices in protest. CRC had asked the International Association of Democratic Lawyers "to take some action with His Holiness the Pope on behalf of the Rosenbergs." Communist allies were invaluable here. The Party newspaper in France, *L'Humanité*, published Patterson's letter on the case, published "ten articles" of their own, and added, "We want to develop an important and large campaign in France and this is why we are asking you to send us . . . some material to help us." This planting and tending led to the formation of Rosenberg committees worldwide and it produced consistently huge demonstrations, especially in Europe.[55]

Naturally CRC did not ignore the domestic front. The Rosenbergs' presence in New York guaranteed that this area would be a major center of defense activity. Patterson stressed that "in the past period the Rosenberg Case has been consuming a tremendous amount of the time of all of us. There were a number of things that I just could not get around to." Ida Rothstein of CRC-SF added, "the main activities of CRC, as well as of the entire Progressive movement is the Rosenberg case, and rightly so." Consistently he called for demonstrations, parades, and mass delegations; special brochures were formulatd targeted at various communities, e.g., "The Rosenbergs and the Negro People." Requests flooded the national office from the chapters for brochures on the case: eight thousand for Seattle, five thousand for Olympia, three thousand for Tacoma, twenty thousand for Detroit, ten thousand for Oakland, ten thousand to San Francisco, seven thousand for Newark, and so forth. The Rosenberg Committee had in its leadership many CRC stalwarts, like Du Bois and Shirley Graham, which laid a basis for coordination. Fifty thousand people signed an *amicus curiae* brief to the Supreme Court urging a new trial; thousands rang doorbells for six months to get names. Together they assailed the American Jewish Committee, the American Jewish Congress, and the Anti-Defamation League because they called the issue of anti-Semitism in relation to the case "fraudulent" and termed the committee "Communist inspired."[56]

The San Francisco area turned out to be a bastion of pro-Rosenberg sentiment. The chapter gleefully declared, "Sonoma Branch has already bought radio time and will have an ad in the Santa Rosa and Petaluma papers; Marin City [is active]; San Francisco has assigned many of its best forces to the Rosenberg Committee." At a Smith Act rally they allotted time "to the Rosenberg children's plight, with stationery provided for those who wanted to write cards and letters to Mayor Wagner." Not coincidentally, soon a CRC leader was "held by immigration. . . . The one and only charge against him, apparently, is that he was a member of the CRC." But that did not slow down CRC's train of support. Spurred by the case a steelworker from Chicago pledged to "donate $10.00 per payday 'in perpetuity,' as long as there are political prisoners and McCarthyism." From Detroit Anne Shore spoke of "busyness with . . . an all-out mobilization around the Rosenberg case." From Philadelphia, J. S. Zucker told of a "mass leaflet" distribution and delegations to "opinion forming individuals." In Seattle there were pickets at federal facilities. All this activity did not save the defendants. In a retrospective analysis, Patterson was critical of the "tendency to hold that prominent individuals must spearhead the battles. . . . This attitude has not been a major weakness of CRC," as much as it afflicted some of their allies. The policy left the celebrities frequently without a mass base. Nevertheless, CRC—especially the New York cadre—could be proud of their role in one of the more stirring cases of the century. Their example was not only worthy in itself, but it also served to inspire nearby chapters.[57]

For example, because of its proximity to the Big Apple, the New Jersey chapter often looked eastward for resources. With branches in Trenton, New Brunswick, Paterson, Newark, and Union County, they had about three hundred members at its zenith. The chapter was "predominantly" white, "though split evenly" between males and females. In Newark they campaigned successfully, however, against police brutality in Black communities. In Bayonne they successfully stopped the extradition of a Black man, Sam Jordan, to the deep South. In Linden they were able to deflect charges filed against autoworkers who were beaten after passing out antiwar literature. As elsewhere, the NAACP "avoided (the chapter) like the plague" though there was some cooperation on the case of the Trenton Six, where CRC-NJ rose to new heights. Because of the prevailing anticommunism, they could only gain "quiet support" from other Afro-American community leaders. This atmosphere may also help explain why one of their leaders, Martha Stone—

later to be an ACLU leader—wound up destroying most of their records. Chapter leader Lew Moroze trod a different path, going from CRC to teaching, and a court battle he led created added protection for nontenured teachers in a landmark case. Like so many other CRC members, his activism did not die with the liquidation of the organization in 1956, but continued unabated.[58]

New England, even though it was an area replete with the factories and history of progressivism that usually marked CRC strength, was comparatively weak in chapter productivity. The Connecticut Volunteers for Civil Rights was the affiliate in that area; its major mark was done in defending local Smith Act victims. Massachusetts' CRC chapter fought an extremely important state case, which involved an indictment of Communist leader Otis Archer Hood for being in the party in violation of state law. If there was any value to the Smith Act from the party's point of view, at least it was that the act was federal, which nationalized and to an extent simplified defense efforts; if forty-eight different states had started indicting Communists under state laws, multitudinous problems would have been created for the Communists. Hood charged that the state law conflicted with the federal law and was thereby preempted, and that the case involved a bill of attainder, vagueness, and the violation of privileges and immunities. In 1955 this state court agreed, but not until after more funds had been spent and more energy expended did this CP leader and member of the Executive Board of the Massachusetts CRC escape imprisonment.[59]

The Boston chapter had difficulty in taking off. In 1948 their leader, Henry Cooperstock, was complaining that his letters to the future apostate, Len Goldsmith, "go unanswered." In return he apologized for his not "very good alibis" and denied that he had said that the defense of the CP-Eleven should be "soft-pedalled." They were able to set up a tour for Leon Josephson that was "directed to industrial workers . . . student bodies and . . . small meetings of professionals." Similarly their "Greater Boston Committee to Free the Trenton Six" raised a respectable amount of funds. They were not without victories either. In late 1948, one week after their conference to "defeat the discriminatory hiring policies of the Timothy Smith Department Store in Roxbury and . . . other firms," the store capitulated and hired two Blacks and "promised" to hire more; this was "two days after a citizens' delegation" led by CRC met with the store's president; before that a militant picket line had ringed the store, joined by labor and members of religious community.[60]

After that CRC activity ebbed and flowed. By 1954 there was a loosely affiliated Massachusetts Committee for the Bill of Rights in Boston that attained a number of successes. They published a popular newsletter and prepared legislative testimony. The Hood case was their triumph; in addition to the indictment, the state had seized his library and had intended to have "burned or otherwise destroyed" works of Jefferson, Roosevelt, children's

books. This was prevented. CRC protested zealously the formation of the
State Commission on Communism and Subversive Activities, which on the
eve of a strike by insurance agents called hearings on communism in the
union; this led to the breaking of the strike, decertification of the union and a
wage cut.[61]

The Brockton chapter was organized in 1948 with the legendary Bertha
Reynolds playing the leading role. But by late 1950 she was complaining
about the "miserable history of the New England chapter, of which I was
asked to serve as chairman 'until they could get someone else.' . . . I had no
qualifications, contacts or ability to get about. . . . we should have had
aboard [people] from the grassroots [instead] of prominent people or too
busy trade unionists who never showed up." The poignancy of her message
was only exceeded in pathos by the severity of CRC's cadre problems: "I'm
an old lady with some time, but little strength. . . . I do not live in Brockton
and have no car. . . . About all I can do is circulate literature and write
letters. . . .None of our group has connections . . . by which we could win
wider support, or raise money. We tap the same contacts. . . . this is a sad
tale." It certainly was.[62]

Boston and Brockton were part of a wider New England chapter CRC,
which Reynolds served as chairperson. Another problem they had was the
involvement of their members in third party work, as well as lack of "cooperation of the Board and the whole membership." But the internal difficulties
were maddening. Allegations of embezzlement of funds were made, which
was a rarity for CRC. Then Patterson exploded when Cooperstock became
secretary of the chapter: "I did not know you would be the next secretary. . . . your selection was made without any consultation with me whatsoever; I know nothing about your background (or) your qualifications. . . .
This is, of course, no way to work." While observing that "your organization
is an independent one," and underscoring that "any other method of work
only feeds the slander that it is a front for some political party" (an ever-
present concern for CRC), Patterson was upset about the process of selection. P. M. Koritz, the first New England chapter leader, was jailed in North
Carolina for his role in a tobacco strike. In 1949 the FBI alleged that the cast
of "Finian's Rainbow" was working for CRC, but by 1950 their "informants
report[ed] decrease in activities . . . difficulty in meeting financial obligations." Yet this tempest in a teapot was settled and the chapter went on to
score some gains, including a striking "Women Fight Back Rally" cosponsored by the Congress of American Women, the Jewish People's Fraternal
Order, and the Emma Lazarus Club, focusing on Jane Rogers and other
female victims of the Smith Act: "This meeting is not limited to women.
Men, of course, are also urged to attend."[63]

One demographic characteristic that Philadelphia possessed that New
England did not was a large Afro-American population and this may have
accounted for their more flourishing and longer lasting range of activities. At

their founding in 1946, the chapters' sponsors included such luminaries as Raymond Pace Alexander, Arthur Huff Fauset, and Robert Nix; Ashley Montagu was a prominent Euro-American sponsor. But even with that, they got off to a slow start, though what may have been at play was stringent self-criticism more than anything else. For example, the chapter had a sizeable income of $15,075.61 in 1951 and a still respectable $9,270.17 in 1952. At the same time they were using these funds to deluge the area with information on the Smith Act, the McGee case, and local cases. Ringing complaints were heard about the scale and content of their work from the chapter leader, J. S. Zucker:

> We have some 350 members. What do we do with them. . . . there is a great lack of clarity, at least on my part. . . . I think the organization can built [sic] only on the neighborhood issues. . . . (the chapter is not) working in a manner which would lead towards building it as a mass membership organization. . . . we have failed to distinguish between working in a mass way and working to build a mass organization . . . two major weaknesses. . . . every civil rights issue which should have become the property of the progressive movement as a whole became (CRC) property . . . and that we had projected for the CRC campaigns which bore no relationship to the strength of the organization.

Eventually there were CRC branches in north and south Philadelphia, in Germantown, and other places. For CRC to grow in Philadelphia, they proposed a focus on "Negro rights" e.g., the case of Fletcher Mills, and the Smith Act. The chapter was set back when in 1951 Father Kenneth Ripley Forbes, who had rendered great service to Patterson when he was on trial, resigned as chair of the local CRC board and became Chairman of the Social Action Committee of the Episcopalian League; he intended to continue cooperating with CRC, but his loss was a blow.[64]

Despite their self-criticism, CRC in this region was comparatively strong. Their example inspired the formation of a chapter of twenty-one members in Wilkes Barre by 1952, based, like so many other CRC units, in the Black church. But the problems involved in organizing during a period of right-wing ascendancy were summarized neatly by Rev. S. A. Amos of CRC-Scranton: "The people here are perfectly willing to move forward into the field of whatever the organization stands for, if that is not subversive. The Negro people of this country are seeking some way to rid themselves of the continued segregation which is so prevalent and pronounced." The problem was that by the then-prevailing standards, fighting Jim Crow could be presumptively deemed "subversive."[65]

Nevertheless, fight Jim Crow is what CRC in this area did. As in Miami and Washington, D.C., a specialty of this chapter was resisting police efforts to disrupt interracial parties. They came to the aid of Blacks barred from hotels for racial reasons. They pushed for desegregation in the schools and insisted on FEPC clauses in union contracts. At the same time they had to suffer the slings and arrows of a constant nemesis, Walter Annenberg, editor and publisher of the *Philadelphia Inquirer*, who denounced them on more than one occasion and constantly accused them of financial irregularities.[66]

One factor that raised the *Inquirer's* ire was CRC's constant attack on anticommunism and its defense of Communists. The chapter was surveilled closely by the FBI; they listed the background of scores of key members and compared their positions to the reds' to show identity; Holton was listed as a red. This was not due to narrow motivation but was based on broader reasoning. As Fred Richard Zimring noted in his dissertation on the persecuted Temple University academic Barrows Dunham, who CRC defended, "The capitulation of liberal, anti-Communists elites appeared in all segments of American society and was a decisive factor in the destruction of the intellectual left in the academy." Thus it was inevitable that the *Inquirer* would feature a page-one headline on Zucker being subpoenaed by McCarthy and identifying him as "bail bondsman for top Communists." Earlier he had been a reluctant witness before HUAC in October 1951 and had posted $20,000 bail for the Communist leader Steve Nelson. CRC rushed to the assistance of those indicted for distributing the *Daily Worker* and devoted numerous hours to defending Thomas Nabried, Walter Lowenfels, and other top local Communists indicted under the Smith Act.[67]

But it wouldn't be a CRC chapter if questions of Black rights were not in the forefront of their concerns and Philadelphia did not disappoint. Another case concerned Ed Haley, who came to the defense of his sixty-one-year-old father when a white mob attacked him in their home; he killed one white man and the police arrested him, not the mob, and denied him bail. First, CRC won him a manslaughter plea and eventually an unconditional pardon. One of their specialties was fighting racist frame-ups, like the case of Leroy Grice and another concerning Byard Jenkins, who had been accused of the murder of a white woman and whose confession was extracted by force. But their leading case of this genre was the one involving Fletcher Mills. In rural Alabama in 1945 he had had an altercation with the owner of the land he sharecropped. He fled to Detroit, fearing violence. Then he moved to New York and worked there four years as a fur worker. In July 1949 he was arrested in Philadelphia. At that point the chapter went into action, generating a blizzard of petitions, letters, and phone calls designed to prevent his extradition to the south. To work their way through the complicated, Byzantine legal procedures involved, they attracted prominent Black lawyers Charles Roxborough and Theodore Spaulding, who was a GOP candidate for Congress. They also devised the politically and legally innovative tactic of attempting to use the Dred Scott case and the Fugitive Slave Act to save Mills.[68]

Also striking was the reasoning they used to sway the masses on Mills' behalf. In one neighborhood they put out a flyer averring "we who are white have a responsibility to rid ourselves of feeling and acting superior [toward Blacks]. We, white members of the Civil Rights Congress have a special responsibility of bringing to your attention the case of Fletcher Mills." Raising antiracist consciousness among Euro-Americans was an obvious goal here and it also animated the remarks of Aubrey Williams of the *Southern Farmer* who spoke of the "universal rule . . . that no Negro must ever be guilty of striking a white man. . . . White juries simply will not permit a Negro to raise his hand against a white man. . . . police will arrest a Negro for some disturbance which he would never think of arresting a white man for." As in many other parts of the U.S., Blacks were killed by police in Birmingham at the rate of "three or four a month" and "little or no investigation is ever made."[69]

In defending Mills CRC raised the specter of a New Jersey Black man exradited to Georgia in the custody of a deputy sheriff who subsequently became a Ku Klux Klan Imperial Wizard and boasted of how a "large percentage of law enforcement officers" in Georgia and Alabama were Klansmen. Such constant prodding was not without effect. In 1948 CRC was able to get charges dismissed against the nineteen-year-old Black activist, Harold Allen, arrested on a charge of inciting to riot after he was involved in a picket against Woolworth's due to racist hiring practices. CRC attracted funds from a number of progressive trade unions and from organizations as diverse as "the Harriet Beecher Stowe Literary Club." The Black press gave the Mills case publicity and one CRC official claimed "the response is much better from conservative organizations than from the progressive." Such factors led John Holton of CRC to begin "an intensified study of the psychological make-up of the Negro," but all this energy and the legal talent of lawyers like Ralph Shapiro and Ralph Powe did not bar the saving of Mills.[70]

One of the reasons for this may have been the dissension that wracked the defense team. One lawyer, Albert Gerber, threatened that "unless we receive not less than the sum of $500.00 on or before" a date certain he would withdraw; he claimed that despite having put in "hundreds of hours of time," he had not been paid. Another area attorney, David Levinson, was hit with the charge of "white chauvinism," but "he refused to accept it." Zucker "then told him that he will stay in the case only if he follows CRC policy. He told me that he will not make [Powe] counsel of record and that he will not follow CRC policy and that he will get out of the case only if Fletcher Mills asks him to. Mr. Mills has given us a letter addressed to Levinson in which he tells [him] that if it is a choice between him and the CRC, he will take CRC." Lawyers were not the only problem. It was difficult finding witnesses willing to testify about racial conditions in Alabama and there was a decided "inability to develop a sustained program of action around the Mills case."[71]

CRC in Philadelphia performed outstanding work in the national cases, e.g., McGee, the Rosenbergs, the CP-Eleven. When HUAC came to town, it was "forced to leave" because of the "resistance of the unions" and other forces energized by CRC. Although by 1953 a number of CRC chapters were limping or defunct, John Holton was reporting, "Things are improving here. You should begin to feel a change." Patterson frequently tossed bouquets in their direction: "The shifting of sentiment which you note is felt very keenly here. . . . You are really doing an excellent job. . . . You are carrying on in the fashion of a people's leader." In 1953 it was reported, "The movement in Philadelphia is strong. On Italian Day there were 10,000 Italian people devoting the entire day to protests and symposiums [sic] opposing the [Smith] act. . . . All the progressive organizations in our city are opposed to the Act." Patterson went on to tell Holton, "You have done this ever since I have known and worked with you. You have been of inestimable aid to the National Office."[72]

The Baltimore chapter was begun toward the end of 1948; like so many others, its formation was sparked by the prodding of Patterson. A number of its leaders and key functionaries were attorneys and this had both a positive effect and a downside. Patterson felt that their literature was phrased in a stodgy style and was unable to understand the "failure of our CRC in Baltimore to really move." He found it "incomprehensible. . . . You have there police brutality in its most vicious and most inhuman phases, courts that regard the Negro as a sub-human being. . . . And yet there is no action. . . . jim crowism is rampant . . . everywhere—and yet no real action. . . . It is no longer possible to allow the present situation to continue."[73]

Patterson's stern admonitions notwithstanding, the chapter there, though small, had impact. Attorney Maurice Braverman worked closely with NAACP attorneys on police brutality cases and published a well-received pamphlet on the topic. Attorney Harold Buchman, Phil Boyer, and others were among CRC plaintiffs who sued the city for $500,000, claiming that they were denied the right to engage in interracial athletic activities because the local Board of Recreation and Parks would not allow mixed basketball teams in park leagues or mixed tennis. When they tried to violate this law, they were "arrested . . . assaulted, intimidated . . . by police." But what was fascinating about this case was the example of Euro-Americans stating boldly that racism not only chained Blacks but themselves as well. *Boyer, et.al. v. Garrett, et.al* sought damages and an injunction. A claim under the U.N. Charter was raised innovatively. Yet the district court and the circuit court granted defendants' motion for summary judgment and the U.S. Supreme Court denied *certiorari*, denying that this gross human rights violation contravened the First and Fourteenth Amendments.[74]

One of their most stirring battles concerned the so-called Ober Law. Introduced in the state legislature by Frank Ober, a former corporation lawyer, it provided for fines and imprisonment for membership in ill-defined "subversive organizations" and it instituted a loyalty oath. Like so much other repressive legislation during this era, although it was ostensibly aimed at Communists, it would have had an impact on all forward-looking forces. Hence, the Citizens Committee Against the Ober Law not only included CRC but academics from Johns Hopkins University, pastors, rabbis, physicians, and labor leaders. An *amicus curiae* brief was filed by the Marine Cooks Union and they requested a CRC brief, (not the other way around). But also filing were former members of the State Commission on Subversive Activities. They were out-gunned by Thurgood Marshall and Bob Carter for the NAACP, William Murphy for the National Council of Arts, Sciences, and Professions, Lee Pressman for the International Workers Order, John Abt for Maryland's Progressive Party, Nathan Witt for a number of CIO unions and Braverman for the Maryland Communists. These men were not altogether successful in overturning this law, but for years this case, *Lancaster v. Hammond,* set the tone on the state's interpretation of standing taxpayer suits and general rules of equity. And the fears about the law's impact were realized when it was utilized to knock the Progressive Party off the ballot.[75]

Baltimore CRC'ers were also unsuccessful in reversing the loyalty oath requirement for running for public office, despite the efforts of Buchman, Murphy (of the family that owned the *Afro-American*) and Duke Avnet. They were active in the local Smith Act *U.S. v. Philip Frankfeld, et.al.* case. Evidence of their effectiveness was provided by the fact that in a landmark case, Braverman was disbarred and prevented from engaging in law practice. Even though lawyers did play an active role in this case, they were not the sole constituency involved. In 1952, for example, CRC chapter leader Nadya Schwartz was telling Grossman "many of our active members are factory workers on the swing shift." They attracted Blacks when they campaigned "to open up sales employment and fountain service to [them] in a shopping area composed of a majority of Negro shoppers." They badgered the state to take action on this outrage and it did—the state Attorney General ruled that stores that don't serve Blacks did not violate the Fourteenth Amendment provision of equal protection under the law. At this time CRC had eleven "active" members and "regular" meetings. An Afro-American pastor was chairperson and they had prisoners, publicity, fundraising, and entertainment committees. As in other cities, they formed the core of the Rosenberg Committee there. But Patterson was not satisfied: "The Baltimore CRC has heretofore been very slow to react."[76]

Baltimore's neighbor, Washington, D.C., was equally a center of CRC activism. Increasingly Black, the nation's capital was not only a pit of police brutality and Jim Crow, but for a while CRC's National Legislative Bureau was based there and served as the organization's eyes and ears at the apex of political power. After Patterson came on board in 1948, one of this chapter's first endeavors was the launching of a campaign to "Wipe Out Jim Crow in Wasington in 1949." The Justice Department was asked to enforce Reconstruction and antidiscrimination laws. At Truman's inauguration CRC distributed flyers of protest. With Robeson leading the way, three thousand people picketed Truman before his election, demanding action on civil rights. From there en masse they desegregated a number of restaurants, which created a furor. Later they demanded that the Civil Service Commission oust Annabel Matthews because of her attempt to bar Blacks from the American Association of University Women. All this was done despite the fact that "up to now . . . about 10 of us have carried the entire load of CRC activity here, and our link with national CRC has been very slender."[77]

Their grappling with racism included working with Senator Claude Pepper on an extradition case and through Virginia Durr, who "has influence" on Alabama's governor. Like members in Miami and Philadelphia, they faced raids from police at interracial parties. One such raid in the fall of 1948 "was the featured local news account today in all the Washington papers." The police had no warrant, yet they held the guests for four hours because of an alleged "shooting." Twenty officers stormed in at 1:25 AM, snatched a book by Aptheker and an "index file," and peppered their entry with "anti-Semitic" remarks. Their antisexism did not extend to gay rights, however: "While they were waiting two homosexuals were led in. As a result of hearing the detailed description of their indecent and obscene acts, one of the girls became violently nauseated." Fourteen people were arrested. In response CRC picketed the police, distributed ten thousand flyers, and hired crack attorneys Joe Forer and Charles Houston to press their case; they also received editorial support from the *Star*, the *Post*, and the *Afro-American*.[78]

Even though this sort of local activity was a preoccupying concern, it was unavoidable that national issues would be a primary focus here. When Attorney General Tom Clark submitted his "subversive" list, they sprang into action. They distributed fifteen thousand leaflets, arranged for Lawyers Guild speakers, drew up petitions, raised money, and held a mass meeting with Winston. At the same time, they were mobilizing similarly around the Trenton Six. Their picketing of the police was accompanied by a coffin with "death of civil liberties" written on it. It was the "first picket line against police in many years here. . . . police raids stopped, none [have] occurred since." These national concerns were seen by the national office as essential; thus, "CRC was the only progressive organization to fight Forrestal's move to set up a civilian volunteer Red Squad here." They took an "active part" in the Elks convention and helped set up a "local coordinating council" of all antidiscrimination groups. It was claimed that Washington was the city "most directly oposed" to "Red-baiting" because many were subjected to the "loyalty order . . . [hundreds of] local police [and FBI engage in] wire-tapping, spying . . . 'shadowing.' " Not paradoxically, this did not mean more growth for CRC: "no government worker" would "dare join" CRC because of the persecution, though many worked with the Progressiv Party. At picket lines, police photographers snapped pictures. Clergy were reluctant to rent them halls. Even when CRC backed issues the newspapers supported, they still called them "subversive." The business agent of a union who was an officer in the chapter was forced to resign.[79]

But the chapter pushed on. In September 1949 they sponsored a picketing of the Justice Department because of the CP-Eleven case. Another June 1949 rally on the Smith Act "was the best attended meeting any progressive organization has held in Washington since the war." Prematurely they worked "to seat a Negro justice on the Supreme Court." They worked with the GOP, the NAACP and others with the National Committee to Abolish the Poll Tax. Tom Buchanan of CRC's National Legislative Bureau was a frequent witness before congressional committees. On one occasion the Senate Judiciary Committee dismissed him because he would not say if he were a Communist. They labored tirelessly to compel the city government "to enforce 1872–73 laws against Jim Crow." They forced the city commissioners to "test the law in court" as a result of pressures initiated by the CRC sparked "Coordinating Committee for the Enforcement of the D.C. Anti-Discrimination Laws," which encompassed over forty organizations. Earlier they had succeeded in barring Jim Crow at federally administered swimming pools and their test case on restaurants ultimately triumphed. Constantly, they pointed out that loyalty investigations were "aimed chiefly against Negroes and any other persons who favor fair employment practices." For example, at the Post Office, charges had been filed against 130 people, seventy-three Black, forty-five Jewish and the rest white gentiles. This beehive of activity led to CRC-DC raising $2,684 in 1949 while the Progressive Party "five times as large," raised $3,400. But that was hardly sufficient to sustain their Washington office and Buchanan was contemplating leaving.[80]

Buchanan was a Communist and he played a pivotal role in CRC local and national work. The "Washington Legislative Bulletin," homed in on specific Congresspersons and their committees, their bills and their fate; for a while, it came out weekly. When the NAACP barred CRC from their National Mobilization in 1950, Buchanan in turn organized a pilgrimage to Frederick Douglass' home. He followed Patterson's advice that theirs should "be open to all. . . . so much so that the contrast between the invitation to their mobilization and ours to this event, will not be lost. . . . Above all, Carter Woodson should be invited." The formation of the National Committee to Defeat the Mundt Bill was another product of Buchanan's skill as an organizer. The CRC film, "The Investigators," and a regular CRC-Lawyers Guild radio program were too. But there were problems between him and the national office. At one point he denounced Patterson for apparently not having read his mail after the CRC leader had written asking him to help organize a campaign they had launched months ago and that he had informed Patterson about. When financial constraints caused a discussion about shutting down the Washington office, Buchanan juxtaposed the pearls of victory emerging from his shop with what he perceived as waste in the national office, that is, the literature they published that he saw as needlessly expensive, the unnecessary reprinting of legal briefs, and what he viewed as undue orientation toward New York to the detriment of the nation as a whole. Not long thereafter, the Washington office was liquidated and Buchanan departed.[81]

Because of the financial problems that drove out Buchanan in 1950 (Buchanan had been a reporter for the *Washington Star* but was fired for being a red), the chapter's activity dropped off a bit—but it was not extinguished altogether. In a town that had a large Afro-American population they continued to make a link with the church. It was Patterson's feeling that "the ideological level in the struggle for civil rights in the churches today is higher than that in the trade unions. It is closer to the community. . . . If we cannot find a road to these people, then we have some very grave weaknesses in our work." And Patterson followed up on this theoretical conception, particularly in CRC's frequent slashing attacks on police brutality. This appropriate antiracist approach was a hallmark of the chapter and came to the fore dramatically in the case of Marie Richardson. This Afro-American woman was a clerk at the Library of Congress. She was a former Howard student and had attended Terrell Law School. She had worked with the National Council of Negro Women, the Progressive Party, the National Committee to Abolish the Poll Tax, and others. She was one of the first Black women to hold national office in a union when in 1941 she was designated a national representative of the United Federal Workers; she organized workers in Freedman's Hospital. All this was put down on her job application, but she was charged with falsification in any case, and FBI undercover agents testified against her. She was represented by Powe and the two Black law firms of Parker & Parker and Cobb, Howard, and Hayes.[82]

Quickly organized by CRC was the Committee to Defend Marie Richardson Harris. It was believed that the prominent position of her brother, Thomas Richardson, as a leader of the antiwar American Peace Crusade, led to her indictment in late 1951. She was convicted in early 1952 and received a two-to-seven-year sentence and a $2,000 fine, despite CRC's protestations.

This loss notwithstanding, CRC in Washington, as in the rest of the eastern United States, had much to show for its limited tenure. The battles against Jim Crow in Washington were particularly important because the diplomats coming to the nation's capital were increasingly of color and did not appreciate being subjected to inferior treatment. And as Jim Crow cracked there, it was just a matter of time before it cracked in the rest of the United States. This forms part of CRC's legacy. Their "premature antiracism" helped to pave the way for the civil rights movement, just as their "premature anti-anticommunism" created openings and space for not only the civil rights movement to emerge but for other dissenting voices as well. The chapter was monitored closely by the FBI. When 3,500 people arrived for the Freedom

Crusade and met with Gen. Omar Bradley at the Pentagon, and with Democrat and GOP leaders, this was reported by one of their agents. Similarly, they were aware that Buchanan met with Jewish business leaders to raise funds and that they had pledged twenty-five-dollars a month to CRC. After the office at 930 F Street, NW, closed, the CRC file became thinner.[83]

9

Working-Class Heroes and Heroines: CRC in the Midwest

Aubrey Grossman was of the opinion that CRC could have done a much better job of appealing to and organizing among the trade union movement. It is certainly true that the concentration on Black and red cases often meant that cases of labor repression did not receive the attention they should have. The formation of the Negro Labor Council assuaged this to an extent but during an era when the CIO was under siege and progressive unions were under attack, they could have used all the help they could get. It is equally true that CRC did receive a modicum of support from unions for their cases, e.g., from the U.E.; the Furriers Union; Public Workers Union; Teachers Union; Longshoremen's Union; Mine, Mill Workers Union. The Midwest provides a microcosmic view of how well CRC appealed to organized labor and to the working class generally. The industrial heartland, replete with steel mills, auto factories and the like, was the sort of area in which Communists and CRC would expect to receive support. Generally this expectation was confirmed, particularly in Detroit and Chicago.

The home of Westinghouse, U.S. Steel, and the Mellon fortune and close by the coal mines of West Virginia and the rolling farmlands of Ohio, Pittsburgh became a focal point of CRC activity. Much of this had to do with the controversial cases involving the Communist Steve Nelson, but there were other sticky questions. One chapter leader was not far wrong when she alleged, "Pittsburgh is perhaps the city where the most sustained attack by pro-fascist forces has taken place." Certainly the Afro-American leader Nate Albert would have concurred in this assessment. During the summer of 1948, he was jailed after having attempted to integrate a swimming pool, while those who attacked him viciously were set scot free. Dorothy Albert suffered too. She was dismissed from her teaching post because it was alleged she was

a Communist and CRC member. Said one concurring judge, "Every Communist is a potential Russian spy." A similar fate befell Alice Roth, who was
summoned to a grand jury and asked if she were a Communist. Rockwell
Kent was denied a passport and one of the grounds for that was his urging
that Steve Nelson be released on bail. What all these Pittsburgh cases had in
common was that they all involved CRC and their attorneys, Powe, Patterson,
and Hyman Schlesinger.[1]

For a while CRC's offices were in Schlesinger's suite, then they shared
offices with the American Slav Congress. The Pittsburgh lawyer did quite a
bit of legal work for the U.E. and their leader Thomas Quinn was also close to
CRC. This conglomeration of forces was able to achieve victories, such as
pressuring Judge Sam Weiss not to extradite an Afro-American to Georgia in
1947. Even though by 1952 quite a few CRC chapters had been forced down
the tubes as a result of government repression, John Holton was singing that
in Pittsburgh "things are beginning to move in CRC. Material is going out of
the office. . . . They are ready to move. . . . There is life [here]. It is functioning. We have an advisory committee of 10–12 people." In the four weeks after
Holton's arrival from Philadelphia, they had distributed five thousand pieces
of literature and had held a testimonial for Rockwell Kent of three hundred
people: "This was the largest affair held in Pittsburgh for some years." But all
was not sweetness and light. Despite the positive publicity surrounding the
Nate Albert case, "very few Negroes" were reported. Moreover, "Needless
to say, with respect to labor forces, CRC just doesn't have any." Both of these
points were exaggerated, but they did point to a crisis, which Holton claimed,
like a fish, was rotting from the top in the form of chapter leader Evelyn
Abelson: "(she) has hindered the progress of CRC. . . . It's unfortunate that
she held this office so long. . . . Leadership has been suppressed rather than
encouraged. . . . White chauvinism is very much evident here. Collective
decisions meant absolutely nothing. . . . Evelyn has resented my leadership,
my being in Pittsburgh. How such a person remained in leadership so long is
beyond me." As he saw it, there were "three bad things" about the chapter:
"(1) a great deal of gossiping and rumor pedaling [sic]; (2) unilateral action
[being taken] after a collective decision has been made; and (3) white chauvinism." These were inflammatory allegations for this chapter of thirty-five
members to ponder. In Abelson's defense, these problems may not all have
been self-induced. During this same period she was telling Patterson, "The
FBI was hounding my family again yesterday. This is their third visit."[2]

Like other CRC chapters, the FBI monitored the Pittsburgh chapter's local
activities with an overweening thoroughness. They managed to obtain a copy
of their mailing list, which had a substantial labor component by the way, and
added a yes or no notation by each name, "Reported to be a member of CP"
by one of their ubiquitous informants. The Bureau also had a list of those
from Pittsburgh who had attended CRC's critical January 1949 "Freedom
Crusade." When CRC members there held a banquet in September 1949 with

George Crockett speaking, an informant was there. The informant apparently was a chapter member since this person "advised" that Miriam Schultz, the chapter leader, visited "her home" on 16 December 1952. When in July 1953 the chapter had to change the venue of a meeting "caused by refusal of Olivet Baptist Church Board of Trustees to allow meeting in that church," an informant was there to observe the thirty-five in attendance and see $44.50 collected. There were reports on Ingram committee meetings and the Bill of Rights Conference in New York. Even though a chapter of thirty-five members might not have seemed formidable, the FBI certainly thought so. The atmosphere created—or perhaps the Bureau's instigation—led to a number of assassination attempts directed at Steve Nelson. During the second one in late 1953 "a bullet was fired into his house as he sat in his living room with his children. . . . this following the murderous assault on (Communist) Robert Thompson in a New York City jail." The Bureau might have had difficulty establishing a plausible denial, because regularly there were "three cars with two men each" in front of his home who were agents. "They have scrutinized persons walking up and down the street; they have followed the Nelson family, including two young children, to grocery stores, to the public library, or their ordinary daily errands; they have injected into the whole neighborhood an atmosphere of menace and fear."[3]

What had Nelson done that would cause such attention and diversion of the taxpayers' resources? In 1948 this Communist of Yugoslavian descent with close ties to the area's diverse Slavic community was basically called an atom bomb spy at a HUAC hearing, but no formal charges ensued. But then he caught the eye of Judge Musmanno, the chapter's nemesis, who had plagued them on cases involving Roth, Albert, and even Schlesinger, whom he had tried to bar from a case. Appropriately, Musmanno had studied law in fascist Italy. The crusty reactionary bought literature at a Communist bookstore, then swore out an arrest warrant. This was done pursuant to the state's sedition law. Nelson, Andrew Onda, and James Dolsen, in an equally appropriate touch, were all arrested at midnight. The judge in the case was "picked by Musmanno" and was a founding member of "Americans Battling Communism." Of course, he chose not to recuse himself in a case concerning Communists. The prosecutor William Cercone was Musmanno's nephew. The chief witness was Musmanno himself; others were the veteran stool pigeons, Matt Cvetic and Manning Johnson. Nelson had an auto accident and had his case severed; then he was forced to leave his sickbed and act as his own attorney after over seven hundred lawyers were queried and refused the opportunity to defend him. Although CRC was able to get him some legal assistance, the judge would not grant a continuance or a delay. He received a twenty-year term and was denied bail initially, but after mass pressure was generated by CRC, he was granted bail of $20,000. He was sentenced on 26 June 1952 and then had to face a Smith Act trial opening in November. Finally in January 1954 in a critically important decision impinging on "states' rights", the Pennsylvania Supreme Court reversed the conviction. The federal government had occupied the field with their own anticommunist laws; this decision had an impact on a good many stringent anti-civil liberties laws in a number of states. Indicative of its importance was the fact that twenty-six states fielded briefs to overturn the state's high court decision. At the time, forty-three sedition cases were pending in various states—Paul Sweezy in New Hampshire, Dirk Struik and Otis Hood in Massachusetts, Willard Uphaus in Connecticut, Carl Braden and others in Kentucky.[4]

The problem of securing attorneys for this crucial case was of some magnitude. The resources of CRC were stretched tremendously, given their Smith Act defenses, and those of McGee, the Martinsville Seven, the Trenton Six, etc. Abe Isserman, a reliable CRC attorney, captured the tensions of the period in his report from Pittsburgh on the case:

> I had to borrow from McTernan to get out there and from Schlesinger to get back. Neither of them could afford it, and I should not have been put in that position. I have taken care of my debt to them, which amounted to $96. I can only ask that you, without further delay, make good on the promise you made last Sunday. . . . it is useless to talk about compensation for work done. I am very much interested in this case from many angles and will do what I can on a voluntary basis. . . . I am faced with an absolute necessity to do work for which I get some remuneration. I had a sense while in Pittsburgh of a glaring neglect of this case in the months between indictment and trial—a neglect which will detract considerably from the kind of defense that can be interposed.

Another attorney, Basil Pollitt, was similarly pessimistic after the trial got under way:

> The judge consistently rules against us. . . . The atmosphere of the town is more hysterical than any I have yet encountered. . . . We are working very hard here. As you can see from the opening, the outline of the trial shapes up very much like Foley Square. The difference is that there are only two of us working here. As a result we are working about 18 hours a day.

Pollitt reprimanded the "New York office" because much of the work he was doing, e.g., statistical analysis and "factual work," could have been done in New York "months ago." John McTernan, the fabled civil rights lawyer who was persuaded to lend a hand, was pictured as being "particularly under a very heavy strain." Yet the prosecution was portrayed as "quite amatuerish," even though the jury "would have to be a hero to vote for acquittal." Basil Pollitt realized "the heavy stress under which you fellows work and the large demands on your funds" but he needed pay anyway. It wasn't much: $11 per day for ten days for expenses and no legal fee. But he had more complaints. Not only was "stenographic help . . . very short, [but] . . . I seem to have lost the greater part of my already small practice by coming out here."

However, Pollitt did an estimable job of "building . . . a suitable pool of available research lawyers" and he continued to provide graphic accounts of what was going on: "The case itself is degenerating into the customary long parade of stool pigeons sliming their way to the witness stand. . . . The new factor . . . is the movie of Matt Cvetic. . . . We are attempting to prevent the showing of the film."[5]

The Smith Act case was no picnic either. The Philadelphia chapter, recognizing the importance of the case, desired to get involved, but, according to J. S. Zucker, the western Pennsylvanians were reluctant to deal with him. The ACLU agreed to cooperate but would not formally "associate" with CRC. Patterson deemed this unfortunate because he considered this one of the "most important of the Smith Act cases," even though it was difficult to mobilize support for it. For this and related reasons, he counseled that they "fight very hard" for a Black lawyer in the case, "even if it means getting a younger man who does not measure up to the others in terms of experience." In addition to premature affirmative action, he advised that they "bring in [the] peace issue, since if there is peace abroad then" a "corresponding truce in the attack against" civil liberties at home is necessary. A number of publications about this trial were put out and a surprising amount of publicity was produced along with the endorsement of Dorothy Day's *Catholic Worker,* then served by Michael Harrington as associate editor. CRC reproduced in bulk this welcome stamp of approval and printed a number of pamphlets on the case aimed at workers. A controversy arose when Ben Davis came to testify from the prison in Terre Haute but would not answer certain queries, e.g., revealing the names of the party's Negro Commission members. He was held in contempt and sixty more days were added to his jail sentence. But this was not altogether for naught because at the federal level, former NAACP leader Judge William Hastie penned a blistering dissent against the entire Smith Act that provided the legal and intellectual foundation for the eventual overturn of the legislation.[6]

Hastie's famous dissent was a vindication of CRC's tireless toil, and when the Smith Act was finally set back, and though CRC was gone from the scene, it could claim some credit. For they certainly did work toward that day. Miriam Schultz told Patterson in the spring of 1953, "the communication we addressed to the Homestead Local 1397 asking for support in the leaflet distribution hearing was read at the union meeting, and [they] voted to support us. This is one of the large locals of U.S. Steel. . . . It is the first time in some time that a major steel local has supported a CRC action here." Patterson held private meetings with "the editor of the *Pittsburgh Post Gazette,* the editor of the *Pittsburgh Courier* and one of the leading television commentators. Steve [Nelson] accompanied in each case." He also met with "foreign language editors" in this polyglot of a city. Schultz went to the local Baptist conference for support: "I had barely an opportunity to give them my name, and to state why I had come. Rev. Walker immediately took the offensive. . . . Of the two evils, Communism and tuberculosis, Communism was the greater, he said." He topped his bitter jeremiad by repeated stale charges about CRC diversion of Martinsville funds.[7]

The road was not always smooth: "Andy [Onda] is specially burned up since it appears to him that the only time a lawyer will read our record is when he gets cash on the line especially since the record of the first trial was in [Pollitt's] possession for several months. One feels uneasy when you see things like that." Some were not satisfied with the support from labor and Schultz's experience showed that local Black support could have stood improvement. The lamentable role of the Black stool pigeon, Manning Johnson, Patterson wanted to make known to the Black community there. It could also be discussed with *Pittsburgh Courier* editors, with whom Patterson had a longstanding relationship. Even though there were complaints about Pollitt, there was satisfaction with the work of Victor Rabinowitz and the analytical, lengthly brief he authored. At one Nelson rally, I. F. Stone seized the opportunity to endorse Adlai Stevenson and received quite a cool reception, but even this snafu could not dim the critical importance of what was known as the Nelson cases and the work of the Pittsburgh chapter on them, which lasted virtually to the time of CRC's demise.[8]

Pittsburgh's neighbor, Ohio, would have seemed to be a logical place for CRC strength and that proved to be true generally. The FBI reported a September 1948 meeting in Cincinnatti organized by Communists Gus Hall and Phil Parr aimed at forming a chapter there, but it did not get too far. Beginning in 1946 Frieda Katz, another in a long line of CRC leaders who were women, was a principal CRC contact in Cleveland. It was reported in late 1946 that "we have been making efforts, off and on, since the formation of the Civil Rights Congress in April, to get a chapter started in Cleveland. So far, our efforts have been to no avail." The national office wanted Katz's Citizens Council for Equal Rights to form the basis for the Cleveland chapter; Katz did agree to coordinate her local "Oust Bilbo" efforts with those of CRC and when CRC submitted 500,000 signatures on their petitions, a significant percentage were from the Lake Erie metropolis. With the aid of Katz and allies among labor the Executive Board of the Cleveland Industrial Union Council endorsed the entire CRC program in the balmy days of June 1946. Although their critics thought otherwise, they disagreed with the notion that issues like "lack of free elections in Poland" or "Soviet concentration camps" should have been considered before their endorsement, since CRC was a civil rights organization and that's what their program concerned. But the *Cleveland Plain Dealer* dissented and prominently played up the view of the critics.[9]

By March 1947 the Equal Rights committee had voted to affiliate with CRC. Cleveland's role as a steel and auto center with a large Afro-American population helped to prompt the national office to send a field organizer, William Haber, there a few months later. By this time there was a North

Canton CRC with seventy-six members and affiliation by the Stark County Industrial Union Council, both evidence of CRC's ability to attract union support when the heavy hand of the state was not sufficiently interposed. Their innovative flyer at the 1948 Boston-Cleveland World Series baseball game was well-received which linked the CP-Eleven case with the Indians' hiring of their first Black ballplayers, Larry Doby and the immortal Satchel Paige. Entitled "Go to Bat for Freedom," the flyer included a box score and was issued on behalf of their Gus Hall Defense Committee. In 1949, in an attempt to broaden and expand ranks, they organized the Ohio Bill of Rights Conference. Two hundred delegates were present but they were "predominantly middle class . . . very few trade unionists [were] present. . . . Negro representation was weak . . . (however) a number of ministers were present, most of them Negro." In industrial Cleveland this deficiency bordered on being a mortal sin.[10]

When the AF of L met in Cleveland in 1950, Haber was there to lobby for civil rights, even though the local press had called both the Ohio Bill of Rights Conference (OBRC) and their parent, CRC, a "Communist front" and "subversive." Probably they recalled CRC's labor on behalf of Alex Balint, CIO leader and Regional Director of the Mine, Mill workers, who had been deported; Haber had been secretary of his defense committee. In a move that threatened all labor, Balint had been arrested just prior to a contemplated strike against the second largest die casting company in the country, Precision Casting Company. It was similar to what happened to CRC's trade union director, Charles Doyle, the vice president of the Gas, Coke, and Chemical Workers Union who was arrested three days after a strike of 3,500 at Mellon's Carborundum Company in Niagara Falls. The AF of L and the NAACP joined the CRC-led campaign in the face of recriminating redbaiting by the local press. Some sectors of labor appreciated CRC's picketing of a local city councilman's home because of his balking on passage of FEPC legislation, though the *Cleveland Press* assailed their "vicious . . . (and) misguided tactics." At another point the *Press* was forced to give grudging praise to CRC's defense of labor: "It is unfortunate that the only protest against the attempt this week of Georgia's ruthless governor, Herman Talmadge, to lure away Cleveland industries, came from the phony Civil Rights Congress."[11]

Their FEPC enterprise showed that despite the original OBRC conference, CRC was acting to attract the sizeable African-American community; inevitably this breathed new life into the chapter. This success encouraged the national office to request that they extend their tentacles to other cities, but Elsie Zazrivy had to remind them, "at present Cleveland is all that we can possibly handle." There was some growth, but two years later in 1952 Katz could say: "Our local cases have taken up a good deal of time but both of them are being developed on fairly broad lines with [the] participation of ACLU . . . we are taking care of Ohio wives and families of Smith Act victims. . . . We have [the] beginnings of a new chapter in Akron, built around the Hamshall case as well as a defense committee organized in Dayton around the Taft-Harley perjury cases." Grossman was enthusiastic: "Things seem to be popping in Cleveland to the extent that has never before existed in terms of CRC activities."[12]

Police brutality and racist violence were a serious problem in many large U.S. cities and the home of John D. Rockefeller was no exception. In 1952 Nathaniel Wooden, a Black steelworker, was beaten by a racist mob. CRC sparked the formation of a broad defense committee that included clerics, unions, and NAACP, and the Progressive Party. A delegation of twenty-one people visited the mayor to press their concern. The result: the leader of the gang was arrested and tried and Wooden returned to his job: "The case is creating quite a stir in Cleveland . . . although there is some resentment being expressed by the top leadership [of the ACLU, NAACP] . . . in relation to our moving in. . . . [NAACP] attempted to dissuade us from seeing the mayor. . . . a real peoples movement is growing from this work." Some joined CRC as a result. Another CRC victory in Cleveland involved Oscar Smilack, a Columbus businessman called before the Ohio House Un-American Commission who refused to sing. In a move that echoed what they would accuse the USSR of, Smilack was ordered to the state hospital for the criminally insane. Working together, CRC and ACLU obtained his release. In February 1952, at a time when chapters were reeling from war-induced repression, Katz could aver proudly, "Generally this past month has seen more activity on civil rights than we have had for some time in Cleveland."[13]

The FBI was not sitting idly by as their antagonist flourished. April 1952 saw the filing of an incredibly detailed report of a single CRC meeting in Cleveland. Revealingly, it was added, "Care should be used in disseminating the above information to paraphrase it so [as] not to reveal the identity of the informant." There were only ten people at this meeting, which demonstrated the reach of the Bureau. There were fifty-seven women at another meeting where Sojourners for Truth and Justice leaders Angie Dickerson and Beulah Richardson spoke and one of their agents was there as well. Then in 1953 push came to shove. At a meeting to support Steve Nelson, "an organized mob of some 100 Catholic youth organized and briefed by the Cleveland Red squad [created] Real atmosphere of hysteria, they broke a window. . . . In spite of this . . . over 150 people literally fought their way into the hall. . . . We were well prepared on security and our people were really disciplined in a very tense situation. . . . The ACLU here has agreed to an investigation of police harassment." Apparently that was not enough for the disrupters because an attack was launched against one of CRC's key religious support-ers: "Reverend Ware whose home was bombed has told us in very sharp terms that he will have nothing to do with our organization in any way. He has obviously been visited and pressured by FBI and others."[14]

By design or accident there were not that many people courageous enough to run the risk of being killed, even Communists. And those that were were beset by other difficulties. At this same time OBRC was seeking to raise $40,000 for a Smith Act trial involving, *inter alia,* Frieda Katz and Bob Campbell. Twenty-two FBI agents came to arrest Katz on 6 October 1953. They were not impressed by the fact that she had spearheaded the fight against racism in public accommodations, was a longtime member of the NAACP, the ACLU, and the B'nai Brith, and had worked on the Martinsville Seven and McGee cases. Campbell, a Black CRC leader, was from Brooklyn, where he had run for Borough President in 1937 and had got a hefty 34,000 votes and had worked with Ben Davis in Harlem and was regarded highly. He came to Ohio in 1948, where he quickly threw himself into the fight to save McGee and the Martinsville defendants. Like CRC nationally, their Cleveland affiliate was rapidly becoming a Red Cross that spent much of its time supplying itself with blood transfusions. Then they were fighting the case of Frank Hashmall, a blacklisted worker and Communist, who got one to ten years for registering his car under an assumed name; bail was denied and he was jailed. A state judge finally agreed that "a Communist is entitled to evenhanded justice in our courts," but only after the expenditure of mounds of time was he vindicated.[15]

Besieged on all fronts, OBRC then had to devote resources to fight a bill that would have given twenty years and a $20,000 fine to any who tried to alter the Ohio constitution. As Katz informed Patterson, OBRC was not reclining prostrate while reaction whirred:

> There has developed a loose coalition against this legislation. . . . the labor movement, the Jewish community organizations, the NAACP, the churches and the Civil Liberties Union on a statewide basis . . . We have been able to move and speak to many community and labor forces who today at least recognize our role in this fight. We are not bragging . . . [as a result] the whole Democratic minority in the Senate with the exception of Senator Celebrezze voted against.

Ultimately this lobbying led to the reversal of this legislative maneuver, but like a single firefighters' battalion in a major metropolis, OBRC was forced to run hither and yon putting out brushfires. In the spring of 1954 there was another bombing, this time of the Mt. Zion Congregational Church. In a four-month period during this same year there were nine acknowledged incidents of violence and vandalism against CRC and their supporters. They campaigned against "white only" notices in want ads: "Tomorrow they might read . . . No Catholics, No Jews, No Foreign Born." They called for a local FEPC bill and pushed City Hall for hearings. They continued to protest against police brutality and "vandals (throwing) rocks, tar and paint bombs" at the homes of Black families. Yet on 31 October 1955 Katz, the chapter's sparkplug, went on trial pursuant to the Smith Act and not long after the chapter that had done so much to expand civil rights and liberties was no more.[16]

This pattern of concerted harassment against CRC by state and extra-legal organs reached something of an apogee in Indiana, particularly the steeltown of Gary. Named after a steel baron, this town had only been in existence for about forty years when CRC appeared on the scene. It had the combination of proletarians and Blacks and Black proletarians that CRC usually found congenial. Before the arrival of the chapter, Katherine Hyndman—yet another female CRC leader—had made the name of the organization known by selling their materials, circulating their petitions, etc. By the fall of 1949, there was a chapter meeting in a "Negro church" with its major project being desegregation of "parks and beaches." "A Negro steelworker" was president, a "Negro woman steelworker" was vice-president, the "wife of a Negro steelworker" was treasurer: "all the executive committee members are either steelworkers or wives of steelworkers, Negro and white . . ." Continued Hyndman, "I am making it a special point to involve Negro women in the leadership." They had at this point "about 80 members . . . 14 new members this past week."[17]

Concomitant with the rise of CRC was a staggering assault on it: "Then came the assaults on the home of progressives, including my home, after an inter-racial beach party August 28th. The reign of terror went on for a full week and it became necessary for me to get away for a few weeks since I was one of the main targets. We tried to get a meeting organized during that time but one place after another was cancelled." Hyndman termed this "KKK terror." Yet in the midst of this furor, they signed up "52 new members for Gary; 9 from East Chicago." At an October 1949 rally they sold "all the 200 copies" of CRC's incendiary pamphlet on fascist tendencies in the U.S., "Deadly Parallel."[18]

But with every rise in CRC popularity, their antagonists upped the ante. After a meeting with Robeson in March 1950 the "local capitalist newspaper opened a red-baiting barrage, they managed to get the names of people on the executive committee and printed only the names and addresses of the new people; they tried to intimidate the leaders of the church where the meeting was scheduled." Calls came to the church saying "that a mob was on its way to the church to break up the meeting." Unavoidably, all this led to a "let-down." The chapter vice-president "became intimidated" and dropped out. "Other active steelworkers who are shop stewards or planned to run for union office," dropped out. The recording secretary dropped out. But the "continuous red-baiting in Gary's only daily newspaper" did not abate.[19]

Their effort to generate support for the Trenton Six presented the epitome of this trend and a cross section of their frustration. After one meeting with local Baptist ministers, "They said they are willing to help the Trenton Six but couldn't it be arranged somehow to do it thru [sic] the NAACP instead of the CRC?" Wittingly or unwittingly, ruling-class terror aimed at CRC bolstered the role of the NAACP by making work with them seem more respectable and acceptable. Even Hyndman, a staunch comrade if there ever was one, began to have doubts; she questioned her own role since it "calls forth such red-baiting," not to mention the issue of her possible deportation. The *Hammond Times* and other local papers assailed her frequently but since most CRC'ers "prefer not be known publicly" she had little choice but to assume a public role. With studied understatement Hyndman, who was facing imminent deportation to Yugoslavia, concluded, "The building of a mass movement these days is very difficult and presents new problems daily."[20]

As in so many cases, the ruling-class pressure that helped to sink CRC and push the NAACP to the fore weakened the civil rights movement. In Gary, as in so many other cities, the Association's local leadership had "very weak leadership, tied to reactionaries in high places" Hyndman remained optimistic that CRC's "activities will help to prod them to cooperate" and fight back, but this was a bit of wishful thinking. Months later she was conceding, "The NAACP is led by red-baiting Republicans so it's pretty difficult to get a united front." Clearly they were "doing more and conducting more activities than the NAACP." When the local Association chapter called a meeting in preparation for their Washingon, D.C., mobilization, from which CRC was barred on anticommunist grounds, seventeen people came—half of whom were CRC members. CRC's membership locally was about five times larger than the NAACP's twenty-three paid-up members. The NAACP's capitulation to anticommunism removed from the ranks those most resolute in fighting for justice in an age of repression. But the NAACP and their allies had powerful supporters who demanded no less. The editor of the redbaiting *Gary Post-Tribune* was "the chairman of the board of directors of the Urban League."[21]

As Hyndman pondered what moves to make, Patterson illustrated the value of experienced leadership by offering pointed advice on how to proceed. If the ministers wouldn't work with CRC on the Trenton case, then "help them . . . set up an independent committee." Contrary to the ranting of propagandists, CRC's primary goal was justice for the defendants, much more than feathering their own nest. Concerning her role as CRC spokesperson, he stated "I would retreat but I would be constantly behind the person I advance. It is not always necessary that the best speaker, the one best acquainted with the facts, be the spokesman if there are objective conditions which this person cannot at the moment surmount, it might be more profitable to advance one less ably equipped." For one of the leaders in this category, Patterson suggested that remarks might "have to [be] written out for her." After noting how this woman had been very much "frightened" when called on to speak, he observed if she "cannot be helped," then she shouldn't have been a leader in the "first instance." According to Patterson, that only "strengthens . . . reactionaries." Patterson saw this as a process of building cadre, others saw it as opportunism, but there is no doubt that it represented the use of flexible tactics.[22]

This lack of rigidity did not faze CRC's opponents. Weeks after the opening of the war in Korea, when domestic dissent was seen even more as a threat to national unity, the *Gary Post-Tribune* brought tidings of the American Legion opening a "counter drive on Reds." They also promised to "press court action for deportation of Katherine Hyndman, who never has been naturalized." After that, Hyndman was arrested for "disorderly conduct" while circulating a peace petition at Inland Steel's gates. She was tried, fined $100, and received a sixty-day prison term. Said Hyndman, "The so-called trial was so raw and crude that even the Legion had to publicly criticize it." The Legion was forced to complain about the judge conducting the trial without a continuance after her attorney withdrew since it allowed CRC to claim correctly that "Nazi tactics" were being used. The *Post-Tribune* was not impressed. They continued their tom-tom attack against Hyndman and CRC.[23]

By the fall of 1951 Hyndman was relating sadly that the chapter "is inactive . . . [it is] virtually impossible to get a hall or church" for rallies. This was not because she or their other leaders were suddenly found to have halitosis. Hyndman was sufficiently perspicacious to see the "chief" factor as "harassment." In a pattern repeated in pockets of CRC strength across the nation "at times there were more detectives and FBI agents outside the meeting place, in cars, than members inside." Worse, "to top it all the president of the chapter was found to be financially irresponsible and that was the last straw." But the "chief" factor was persecution. When Charlotta Bass of the Progressive Party came to speak in Gary in 1952, the American Legion "openly announced its plans for physical attacks on the meeting" and Bass, as the press howled. As for Hyndman herself, "there has been a lot of FBI cruising around my residence in the last few days." When support against her deportation was rallied, "tremendous pressure on the national group community" by the INS and the FBI ensued. The fuse was lit for the detonation of CRC-Gary by the leaders of the FBI and their patrons.[24]

There were other problems, however, with CRC's work in the state. Hyndman complained of "too much organization looseness. No one is required to give regular reports. . . . there are three chapters in Indiana but no effort has been made to coordinate the work or to establish any contact [with them]." Hyndman may have overstated the case. In early 1950, when they had 130 members in Gary, activity in South Bend and Indianapolis hardly approached this. Still, there were problems keeping up with a far-flung organization that stretched from New York to Honolulu—five thousand miles. CRC Public Relations Director, Will Hayett, related with chagrin in mid-1950 how he heard about a flourishing chapter in Indianapolis, but "the national office knows nothing about this strong chapter. . . . As far as we know they don't exist." Similarly, said Hayett, "Last summer I picked up an Albany paper and read that the CRC there led a protest demonstration against the Peekskill outrage. But we have no CRC chapter in Albany."

Looseness aside, CRC chapters in Indiana faced similar problems. In mid-1951 Josephine Bush was writing from the state's largest city that "because of the Red Scare our membership can only be counted by the names on paper." This was a change from two years previously when there had been "30 paid memberships, regular monthly meetings . . . mostly working class, somewhat over 50% being Negro." In South Bend in 1952 it was related that "due to many difficulties and problems . . . it would be impossible to plan any kind of membership meeting with Mrs. McGee or Mr. Patterson." This inability was symptomatic of their ongoing problems. Matters were not helped when pressure was exerted on a leading CRC member, Willard Ransom, who was also a leader of the NAACP, to choose between the two, or when another CRC leader, Judge Norval Harris, had dragged back into the public eye the fact of his having served a year in federal prison in 1932 for forging veterans' names to bonus certificates. Roosevelt gave him a pardon but CRC opponents used this to bludgeon the organization.[25]

Chicago had one of the stronger CRC chapters, though this was not always the opinion of the national office. Yet this chapter withstood the sternest blows that the McCarthyites could dish out and kept on keeping on. Unsurprisingly, racist violence and police brutality, along with the rights of reds, were some of their major concerns. The fact that Patterson was familiar with the city, having lived there for a number of years, contributed to the chapter's growth, as did the kind of Black and working-class community that CRC usually found congenial.

The origins of the chapter stemmed from the departure of the Chicago Civil Liberties Committee from the ACLU in 1945 over the defense of racists and fascists. Yet, by late 1946 there was a formal break between CCLC and CRC, as the former began to swing back to the right, and by 1950 it began to bar reds, and their leader joined the local Right to Work Committee.

There were also a number of leaders in Chicago who wielded influence. Alfred Wagenknecht's opposition to CRC's "I Shall Not Live at Peace with Jim Crow" pledge was not helpful in getting the chapter off the ground; he objected to the use of the term "white supremacy" and the non-use of the term "Negro." But his influence was not always baneful; he was a primary force behind the move to have unions install civil rights committees in their locals "which would then receive direction from CRC. We already have a few established." This type of action was reflective of the chapter's influence, which was particularly strong in the pre-Korean War period; at CRC's prodding in December 1948 Mayor Martin Kennelly proclaimed a Bill of Rights Week.[26]

Like Boston and Washington, there were certain problems with the leadership of the chapter in Chicago. In mid-1949 the Executive Secretary, Arthur Price, resigned; this "deeply concerned" Patterson and the national office, who suggested Conrad Komorowski and Sylvia Woods to work with the local chapter. But then Patterson alleged that "a number of people here think it would be a mistake to put Conrad on that job. . . . the feeling was that he might lack the drive and was not an organizer." Then Patterson had to deny to Price that he "had suggested that you resign. . . . I did not act in any individual capacity but in an organizational way." The national office was concerned that Chicago allegedly had taken Trenton Six money and used it for their state office, and also about their lack of activity on the CP-Eleven case.[27]

But as the response from the Mayor demonstrated amply, CRC was not bereft of influence. When Gerhart Eisler came to town in 1948, they wangled speaking invitations from the UAW, the Packinghouse Workers Union, Hyde Park Church, and Roosevelt College. When James Montgomery became ensnarled in a rape frame-up in Waukegan, Illinois, they obtained the services of a "wealthy" lawyer and freed him. Chicago has been long known as a big city suffused with provincialism and the CRC docket there showed it; much of their activity was geared toward local cases. But these cases were far from trivial and it could be argued that this local focus helped to account for their longevity insofar as they touched the lives of the local citizenry. In 1949 they mobilized three to four hundred people to picket City Hall after the harassment of a Black family that had moved to a white neighborhood. They had a sizeable bail fund of $87,000. They did send 135 to a mobilization at Foley Square and organized around the Mundt-Nixon bill, but complaints from New York continued. Milt Wolff complained that the chapter "doesn't send in money . . . doesn't respond to a simple request for information regarding membership." Komorowski made a strenuous objection: "I have never met you. . . . I have never had an opportunity to talk to Patterson during this period." He alleged that he couldn't give a membership report because "no proper membership files were maintained." At the time he began there was "one functioning chapter" on the near North Side; now there was one each on the West Side, South Side, Northwest Side, and in Lillydale.[28]

But Wolff was unmoved. Contrary to their relative strength, he averred, "Chicago, Detroit and possibly Philadelphia have been the great desert in the National CRC organization." When Chicago sent in $3 he claimed that it was the "first time" Chicago responded on "organizational matters." Despite these adamant protestations, Chicago continued to make a big issue out of segregated housing and their March 1949 second annual state conference featured ads and greetings from the NAACP, the Shoe Workers Union, the Fur and Leather Workers Union, the Packinghouse Workers Union, UE and others.[29]

When Lester Davis came on board as executive secretary, he helped to set up the Illinois Council to Repeal the McCarran Act, which issued buttons, put five hundred "collection cans . . . in key spots" around town and generally beat the drum about the bill. The case of Robert Kirkendell became an object of their attention. This nineteen-year-old Afro-American received seventy-five years in prison. In July 1949 he was charged with rape of a fifty-two-year-old white "spinster." After a four-day trial, the all-white jury gave him the heavy sentence, despite the fact that the only evidence was supplied by the alleged victim. Six witnesses said he was two miles from the scene of the crime at the time. Before his arrest, the defendant, who was a peddler on the side, refused a five-dollar "shakedown fee." CRC's thrust against police misconduct was so strong that when Oscar Brown, Jr., sought information on the issue for a show he was doing, he came to the chapter's door. But as 1950 progressed, Davis glumly stated, "Many of those who should be among our mainstays are reluctant to cooperate or [are] negative in their attitude toward CRC."[30]

Patterson's response was to remind them, "There are friends of CRC in Chicago who will not take part in its political activities but will devote themselves to the task of raising funds. . . . Above all, let us not forget public relations work." He was right. Gwendolyn Brooks, who had recently been awarded the Pulitzer Prize, consented to allow CRC to sponsor a fundraising affair in her honor. Patterson's advice sometimes seemed contrary to basic organizing principles. He equated CRC with a " 'fire brigade.' . . . If therefore . . . we clog the apparatus with [a] long-range program, it will not be carried out." But his prognostication was affirmed when days after the outbreak of war in Korea, Davis told him, "Each day produces a new emergency requiring quick action and we find ourselves going from one jail to another to bail out and defend victims of police persecution."[31]

The chapter needed help: "Any time 350 letters sent out to a membership produces only seven members and one red squad detective, then the time has come to do some serious thinking." Davis became pessimistic: "Under the present conditions, it seems unrealistic for us to continue operating. Our work is not effective. . . . a poor defense effort is, in many ways, worse than no defense at all. A lad, whose only crime was endeavoring to secure Peace Petitions and, whom we defended, was convicted and fined $200.00 because of an error in strategy which should not have been made and would not have been made had we been able to give the matter more thought and consideration." But unlike other chapters, CRC in Chicago did not fold in the face of war-induced repression but appeared to become stronger. When so-called antisubversive bills were introduced in the state legislature, the local CRC "office [became] a beehive of activity and is the central clearinghouse for mobilizing all of the progressive forces in the city around this issue." Calls, leaflets, telegrams, targeted mailings, street corner meetings, all emerged from their office. But once again this was a local issue. During this same period of euphoria, Davis was also asserting, "On Willie McGee, the Trenton Six, Pat, and other national issues, positively nothing has been done." Arguably this was shortsighted, since the wave of repression was being generated nationally and was simply manifested locally. But Davis did not see this lack of attention as the chapter's fault: "This I attribute to lack of direction from the National Office." Chapter chairperson Father Clarence Parker declared that "up to this point no real action has been taken" on the CP-Eleven case, even though Chicago had been the site for a number of important national rallies and meetings on peace and civil liberties; one with Howard Fast filled a hall with six hundred clamoring protest.[32]

Patterson remained concerned about the local leadership, perhaps stimulated by their seeming inability to galvanize their constituency around national questions. In 1950 he continued to be "intensely dissatisfied with the overall picture and expressed this point of view with extreme sharpness." There were conflicts between him, Arthur Price, and Father Parker that did not totally diminish when Lester Davis, a photojournalist, took over, perhaps because Patterson candidly conceded that he "should be very happy to see a woman among the top leaders." Komorowski, who at that point was secretary of the Executive Board suggested that the national office write Davis regularly, "something [you] did not do in my case . . . and tell him what is expected in the way of reports, and so on." Still, when Parker moved to the South in the summer of 1951, Patterson counted the departure of this progressive cleric with many national ties "an almost irreparable loss."[33]

Possibly as a result of the turmoil at the top, Chicago—its successes notwithstanding—had a "membership situation (that was) not good, because we 1) have not turned victories into organization gain; 2) have not had a consistent policy of re-registering and re-vitalizing expiring memberships." Taken in context, Komorowski's judgment was a bit pessimistic, because compared to other areas CRC was veritably flourishing in Illinois. There was one chapter in the 42nd Ward and one in Waukegan, in addition to those already noted. There were chapters in East St. Louis and Peoria and 676 members statewide in 1949. By the beginning of 1950 there were 922 in Chicago alone and 1,109, almost a 100 percent increase, in the state. This was accompanied by victories. Lillydale won a case against the Chicago Transit Authority, even though it met irregularly. The 42nd Ward Chapter met every Tuesday and like the other chapters, had dues of fifty cents per month; it also included a youth branch. The Southside met every two weeks and had 312 on the rolls and thirty at the core. The Westside had 132 and a core of fifteen. Each chapter had police brutality and job discrimination committees. Peoria was not atypical in having all industrial workers as members, half Black and half white, while the East St. Louis' chapter was entirely working class and 90 percent Black.[34]

With such strength, chalking up gains had to follow, and they did. This same year, 1950, Patterson was informed:

we recently won a victory in discrimination in education in the schools of Argo, Illinois, causing the funds to be cut off, forcing NAACP into the united front which they did not agree to but which the overwhelming mass sentiment of the community forced them to. We initiated this campaign after the NAACP entered the campaign and is presently in a position of moving as we move. Based on this victory East St. Louis has summarily ended discrimination in schools and we expect shortly to be in a position to win any case . . . [in] the state on the question of discrimination in public schools. I need not mention to you the singular contribution the East St. Louis chapter has made to the whole field of mass struggle for job opportunities for the Negro people. . . . Here in Chicago a modest campaign against job discrimination has been initiated with two victories.

The Chicago leadership at this juncture prayed for an end to the "lack of understanding" between the local and national offices and extended a "sincere hand of cooperation." Patterson agreed that the East St. Louis victory was "one of the most important this year," while lamenting that "our role was more or less submerged."[35]

Waukegan was also a site of CRC activity. When repressive legislation came up for a vote in Congress in 1950, their chapter in a three-week period sent about one hundred messages to their Senators and an equal number to Truman. They were not averse to taking the battle in to the streets, and as a result an ordinance was introduced to bar passing out handbills. Meanwhile, back in Chicago, 1951 saw CRC starting a school for struggle that would teach political skills, including "writing press releases and leaflets . . . [and] every phase of activity"; the purpose was "improvement and development of leadership cadre on local levels." Growth continued; a new office was opened on the Southside. Maurice Horowitz, former Progressive Party of Indiana leader and U.E. organizer, became organizational secretary, thus strengthening CRC's links with these important constituencies. Their bail fund sent $7,000 to Pittsburgh for Dolsen's bail and worked to raise more. Since Supreme Court Justice Minton was from Indiana, Patterson suggested, "Someone should meet at once with Dr. Thompson and a number of other prominent people . . . requesting that they immediately begin to pressure Minton." All tactics were being utilized to gain freedom for the CP-Eleven.[36]

"Prominent people" were a special target of CRC in the Second City. Patterson and Robeson met with Earl Dickerson "together and talked into the wee hours of the morning and I believe in this man we have a force deeply nationalistic, tremendously courageous and as well ambitious—all of which makes, under careful direction for the development of a great anti-imperialistic fighter." Less success was had with attorney Belford Lawson and his journalist wife when Patterson met with them: "I tried to bring Belford into the case of the seventeen but his asking price was prohibitive and though we are guaranteeing him $15,000 free of taxes, we could not get him. He is a very mercurial chap, fully understanding what it is all about but not going to take such chances as will harm him. I think she is just as clever, or more so." Still, CRC had uncommon success in attracting leading figures from labor, academia, the professions, and the arts.[37]

But mass support had to be the bulwark of CRC activity and it was. Across the street from the Newberry Library at Clark and Oak Streets at night from 8 to 9:30 P.M. during the summer, CRC had soapbox speakers declaiming on the issues of the day. They were able to get charges dismissed against Tom Jones, an Afro-American attacked by a street car conductor, then charged. They won freedom for Clarence Foster, who had escaped to Chicago from a chain gang in the deep south and was scheduled for extradition. Continuously they protested anti-Black mob violence, like the disturbances in Cicero and the actions of the White Circle League, a protofascist front. They published a newspaper, numerous leaflets, and held many demonstrations. Much of this activity was helped along by Patterson, a former Chicago resident. During one trip there in 1952, he "spoke at U.C., Roosevelt College, met with some UAW people, Fur and Leather, and had several discussions with leading white clergymen." But he remained critical of the chapter in spite of its gains: "Chicago is not close enough to the Negro women. It seems not to be aware of the multitudinous small clubs that are on the South Side. . . . I was disturbed by what I regarded as a tendency to put too much weight upon the decision of lawyers as to the cases we should or should not take up. Lawyers will never determine for us the character of which [cases] we will take up." On another occasion he sharply knocked "liquidationist tendencies" in the chapter.[38]

Nevertheless, compared to other CRC units, Chicago was performing adequately. Patterson's familiarity with the area probably gave him a better sense of the potentiality there, thus, ironically, increasing his frustration. Who could object when in late 1952 in the Windy City CRC conducted a sit-down strike in City Hall after a "Negro mother and 13 children [were] evicted from [a] public housing project. . . . 50 people here are determined to stay until [the] Mayor finds [her a] home." In that same period they were holding a bazaar that "netted $1,700"; they sent a "batch of petitions" to Truman concerning freeing Ben Davis; they sent three hundred cards to Smith Act victims, and they were quite active in the campaign to save the Rosenbergs. All this was nothing to sniff at.[39]

But problems continued to nip at the heels of the chapter. That same year found "hate-crazed white hoodlums" trying to prevent an "inter-racial party" led by CRC from entering a theater. "Police guards and several riot squads" had to intervene. The mob grew to several hundred "maniacs." CRC had been conducting a campaign for over a year to integrate this particular theater. Their action here and in other northern cities shows how CRC, before Montgomery, was demolishing the walls of Jim Crow and indeed creating favorable conditions for the post-1955 movement. But as they were pointing with glee at their accomplishments, they had to soberly assess the fact that Les Davis was devoting less time to CRC because "economic necessity has forced me to give attention to earning money." Jo Granat eventually became executive secretary; she fulfilled Patterson's wish for more women in the leadership and her experience in leading the Rosenberg defense effort in Chicago proved exceedingly helpful. There were other concerns, however; Otto Wangerin, who became administrative secretary, observed that "ever since Lester left the question has been on the agenda of finding a Negro person to become head of the CRC." He reminded Patterson "you raised this matter on a number of occasions." The turnover in leadership did not prevent them from continuing to pile up victories. Patterson gratefully acknowledged that the chapter played a "quite conspicuous role" in the "tremendous victory won" in defeating the virulently anticommunist Broyles bill. And at Patterson's suggestion they protested the repression in Cuba that flowed from the 26 July 1953 attack on the Moncada led by Fidel Castro.[40]

It would not have been CRC if the flames of repression were not lapping at the chapter. Before HUAC, Father Clarence Parker was forced to reconcile his religious beliefs with associating with a so-called "communist front." Milt Wolff called this a "trial by ordeal." Parker was more delicate: "The Un-Americans were painfully polite [though] many traps were spread." The Smith Act also became a factor, even though Chicago's performance on the CP-Eleven case continued to draw fire from Patterson. He tried to convince them that the case would have local manifestation if it were not fought nationally: "The cases of the twelve act as the central point of the attack. Reaction will try to win a victory at the fountainhead and [then] will move into the periphery trying to win victories." Patterson proved prophetic. In the Northern District of Illinois, Eastern Division, U.S. District Court, Max Weiss' Smith Act case was debated. This time the chapter rallied. All who gave twenty dollars to the defense would receive a sculptured head of Harriet Tubman, and there were similar efforts launched to raise funds. Then there was the case of the leading Black Communist, Claude Lightfoot, who had an eagerly active defense committee. They issued many pamphlets and press releases. They juxtaposed the dropping of the indictment against the Cicero rioters of 1951 with the hounding of Lightfoot. They carped incessantly on what they perceived to be extraordinarily high bail. Patterson and Robeson came to Chicago numerous times on Lightfoot's behalf. A crack team of lawyers, composed of George Crockett, John Abt, and Pearl Hart, was put together. CRC leaders Jo Granat and John Bernard were leaders of Lightfoot's defense team, indicative of the interlocking directorate. But Lightfoot's 1955 trial was one of the last official acts of CRC in Illinois, for not long after that they were defunct.[41]

Wisconsin was similar to Illinois and Ohio in that it saw organized CRC activity throughout the history of the national organization. Like Detroit, CIO unions were heavily represented in Wisconsin's CRC ranks. Like Gary, "both major newspapers" attempted to "outdo each other in red-baiting and witch-hunts" in Milwaukee. When the American-German Citizens Committee cosponsored a visit by Eisler to the town that made beer famous, all hell broke loose. Heckling and press baiting were fierce. They issued many bulletins, fought extraditions, and joined with the NAACP in a number of efforts.

The year 1949 was something of a typical year for the Wisconsin chapters. There were four weekly radio programs in Rice Lake. Two thousand open letters were sent to residents of Barron County concerning issues ignored by the press. There were six street corner meetings on the Ingram case, the Trenton Six Case. Bessie Mitchell spoke to 400 in Milwaukee and 150 in Madison about the six. A major issue was supporting migrant laborers, mostly Black, and helping them to "get aid, relief and justice." They were handling a number of deportation cases, and at this time there were chapters in Milwaukee, Madison, Racine, and Barron County. At the same time they were continuing to try to deflect harassment. James Selcraig writes that the conflict in northern Wisconsin between CRC and right-wing priests was bitter: "The priests made plans to pack the CRC meetings and have supporters sing patriotic songs and give anti-Communist speeches." The state leader of CRC, Josephine Norstrand, was a particular target. They complained about how she was usually "smartly dressed," in one tendentious article about an appearance in the state by Katherine Hyndman of CRC-Gary. Threatened violence forced the cancellation of the meeting. But CRC was not deterred. They campaigned against the Klan, which burned crosses in front of members' homes in Barron Country, and they tried to bar Confederate caps from the area. In this predominantly Euro-American state, the chair of CRC, Perry Love, was Black.[42]

In 1953 CRC even went so far as to become involved in a baseball fracas, when Milwaukee Braves hurler Lew Burdette threw at Dodger backstop Roy Campanella, one of the few Black players then playing the game. Patterson was "very much upset by the . . . incident. Personally I regard these attempts at beanballing Negro players as a conscious thing. . . . The racists want riots against the Negro people and this offers a better avenue for perpetrating one than most." In response Norstrand launched a "telephone campaign directed to the manager." Another one of their big issues was fighting the issue of loyalty oaths to secure public housing.[43]

The fact that Norstrand aimed their campaign at the team's manager rather than at one of the higher-ups signaled that her gears were not meshing altogether with those of the rest of CRC. She and Patterson clashed after he expressed his familiar formulation that he loved the country but had "hate" for the government; she felt this was unnecessarily inflammatory. Then Patterson castigated her for not raising the issue, as a white woman, of racists using them to "carry on their lynch program. . . . I did not like your speech." Things got worse when in 1953 Norstrand had to back out of going to Pittsburgh for the Nelson trial: "My first grandson is being christened on the 10th and also, its Mother's Day." Patterson was restrained in response: "I think that your grandchildren will deeply appreciate some day the part his [sic] grandma played in organizing the successful fight for Steve Nelson's defense." Norstrand had a background that should have held her in good stead in the movement. For ten years she had worked with the Wisconsin State Conference on Social Legislation. Moreover, in 1952, when many CRC chapters were being rapidly extinguished, she was able to say that they had "just recruited . . . 300 new members in Milwaukee County—two hundred . . . in other chapters." They went block by block and prizes were given for the most recruits.[44]

In any event, eventually she "was asked to resign." The new leader, John Gilman, asked Patterson to notify all that she was forced out and "cannot be trusted in any way." This incident was only part of a pattern of disruption that beset the chapter. In 1954 Gilman spoke of "great difficulties in rebuilding due to the disruptive elements and also the shape the organization was in when Mrs. Norstrand was asked to resign." The Ingram Committee split from the CRC due to the latter being "tainted." Gilman, a former chair of the Rosenberg Committee in the state, sheepishly conceded to Patterson, "I imagine you are a bit disgusted with Milwaukee. You have reason to be. . . . I have a small business which takes up my entire day and can only give part of my time to CRC activity." But since Patterson felt Norstrand had a "well deserved reputation" for disruption, he was willing to settle for Gilman's schedule.[45]

Norstrand notwithstanding, CRC-Wisconsin was probably riddled with more informers and infiltrators than any other chapter. Not coincidentally, by 1954 there were only twenty-five "paid up" members and 105 "unpaid." That year alone there were "at least four FBI stool pigeons who have attempted to disrupt work in the CRC in the last six months. One was expelled, two were dropped and one remains yet to be eased out. . . . the [latter] carries out [much] work and thus makes it difficult to expose him. The FBI has harassed the members on personal visits." CRC continued to play a "fair role" in the movement to recall McCarthy; they obtained 1,500 signatures with a "mere handful of people," but the Democrats repaid them by broadcasting an "exposé" on CRC over television. The local press remained hostile.[46]

One of those expelled from CRC was Theodore Livingston; he was "disrupting constantly" according to Gilman and was in "contact with the FBI." He was Black and claimed to be a personal friend of Patterson. He was on parole for "post office theft." In a move that recalled the 1930s, Livingston was "given a jury trial made up of seven Negro . . . members and a unanimous vote was cast for expulsion so that the questions of 'white chauvinism' was squashed." Livingston was said to be acting president of the Negro Labor Council chapter [this was denied by CRC] and on the state advisory board of CRC-Wisconsin. Interestingly, before Norstrand was forced out, Livingston and a cabal had tried to oust her. His expulsion followed a *Milwaukee Journal* article concerning her departure; it was assumed that he had leaked the information, since he was always known to be close to Trotskyites; the information in the press about the size of CRC meetings, their sites, and their strength in Barron County was assumed to have come from an inside source. After his ouster, Livingston picketed CRC meetings, passing out leaflets complaining of being railroaded, defending the Trotskyites, and blasting "Moscow." Another "informer" was Keith Fredenberg. Ousted in 1955, he was a "self-confessed informer for Milwaukee Police Department." Like Livingston, he was a criminal—it was easier for police authorities to pressure such men—who had been arrested for "molesting young girls several years ago." In addition he was partially blind. At any rate, after Fredenberg's expulsion in 1955, it was not long before CRC itself had hit the skids and certainly the disruptive activities of government agents there did not prolong their existence.[47]

The signal accomplishment of CRC in the state was the campaign surrounding Harold Christoffel, a leading labor case nationally as well. This effort was evidence of the organization's interest and concern with the labor question, although there were those who felt that much, much more could have been done, especially in comparison to the Black and red cases. Aubrey Grossman was one of the clearest proponents of the view that CRC had a stake in the direction of the labor movement. He didn't feel that the CRC could "survive" without these ties and complained of the "many examples of how we produce insoluble problems and terrific weaknesses where we try to build mainly with middle-class people (however well-intentioned they may be) . . . sooner or later, some top trade unionist must be brought into the National Office, and not necessarily, or even properly, as Trade Union Director." Grossman was arguing for a continuation of the policies of ILD, which had made labor a specialty. In his role as organizational secretary, Grossman counseled constantly that chapters focus "concentration . . . among basic industrial workers." The Midwest, Detroit and Gary particularly, fulfilled his mandate more than other chapters. Still, when William Green, president of the A.F. of L. gave thanks to CRC in 1947 "for the service . . . rendered" in the Taft-Hartley fight, and expressed hope that "we may engage in team work" in the future, it indicated that CRC was making some inroads in this area.[48]

CRC did have a Trade Union Director and a Labor Advisory Committee, chock full of affiliations of CIO unions. As late as 1951 they could muster signatures of 187 trade union leaders on an *amicus curiae* brief on the CP-Eleven case. But their labor supporters were hit as hard, if not more, as their Black and red supporters. Jack Zucker, a CRC-Philadelphia leader, who was a UE member, was hauled before HUAC and grilled about the union and its ties to the left. Supporters like Karley Larson, First Vice-President of District two of the International Woodworkers of America-CIO, and William Sentner, International Representative of UE, "who was conducting a strike," were indicted under the Smith Act. Even CRC's Trade Union Director Charles Doyle, former international vice-president of the Chemical Workers, faced deportation. He charged the police with "abusive" and "unlawful" treatment while he was in detention pending deportation. This was one aspect of a total onslaught against CRC's labor allies.[49]

Michael Francis Urmann has been among those who have underlined that Communists were "an important element in the . . . CIO's rapid growth and was the basis of the strength of the CIO." Given this influence, the alliance between certain CIO unions and the Communist-led CRC should not be shocking. Of course, the Red Scare after the war complicated matters, especially when it led the CIO to become mute as the plight of the Black worker deteriorated. Nonetheless, their ties were striking. Patterson was with Maritime Union leader Ferdinand Smith when he was deported. Asbury Howard, a leader of the Mine, Mill Workers Union and president of the Bessemer, Alabama, NAACP, was also CRC's principal contact in that region. William Hood, the head of the giant Ford Local 600 in Detroit, in his keynote address at the founding of the Negro Labor Council, highlighted CRC cases like the Trenton Six and the Martinsville Seven. The Fur and Leather Workers Union contributed frequently to the coffers of CRC; the Mine, Mill Workers Union earmarked their donation specifically for Patterson's defense and when they held a conference in Charleston, South Carolina, on "The Fight for Civil Rights and Negro Liberation," they were sure to involve CRC; the same happened when they began to establish "civil and minority rights committees in every local." Patterson spoke at their conventions and they went as far as to offer their entire mailing list to CRC, but Grossman refused this because "something could happen." To counter the government's propagandizing, Patterson suggested that they and like-minded unions send Blacks abroad as representatives to counter the influence of Redding, Rowan, White, Tobias. "Who better than such Americans can expose the myth of ruling class morality. . . . It is time the 'left' recognized [this]." The Mine, Mill Workers Union was so steadfast that CRC wanted to give them an award for their successes in the field of "Negro rights."[50]

Other workers' organizations were helped by CRC and they in turn helped CRC. The International Workers Order, which began in the 1930s and offered insurance to Blacks when other companies would not, in the 1950s had assets of $7 million and was assisted by CRC when it came under fire from the government because of its ties to the left. When Julius Emspak was being prosecuted, part of the charge against the UE leader was that he did not answer questions concerning CRC. As UE leaders were being hauled before HUAC and similar bodies, CRC attorneys were defending them. Even the Beauty Culturists Association of New York had CRC attorney Hope Stevens as their "Legal Adviser."[51]

Other than the industrial CIO unions, CRC also rushed to the defense of teachers, postal workers, and other government employees. Ralph Powe was the attorney for a teacher dismissed after it was alleged that she was "mentally deranged," although her politics was suspected to be the real cause; the case went to the U.S. Supreme Court. The anticommunist Feinberg Law was fought to a similar level through the courts of New York, up to the high court. The Cleveland-CRC chapter forced the rehiring of Joseph Bryant, a Black postal worker, after he ran afoul of racists. The loyalty purge hit the postal workers' union hard and CRC was there to help. This brought the thanks of the president of the Cleveland branch of the National Alliance of Postal Employees. Clarence Emery, a meat inspector for seven and a half years with the U.S. Department of Agriculture, said "I know nothing" about Communists, though he admitted to being "liberal and progressive" with an "efficiency rating of 'very good,'" but he was investigated for loyalty anyway. Patterson responded promptly, "You should demand at once an administrative hearing. . . . [and] I shall see that a Washington attorney of the Civil Rights Congress accompanies you." The ACLU, NLG, and others joined CRC in assailing the "terror program which is being carried out against innumerable government employees today." In a comparable manner, CRC advised an employee in the Canal Zone who was asked to sign a no-strike affidavit.[52]

With this background, the development of a national campaign around the Wisconsin labor leader Harold Christoffel should be seen as consistent with their political outlook. Born in 1912 and of Swiss descent, the lean 6'2" 150-pound trade unionist served in the army during World War II and sired nine children. He was a leader of Local 248 of the UAW in Milwaukee. He received a two-to-six-year term for perjury when he denied he was a Communist during a hearing on the Taft-Harley bill. This was the climax of a long battle between the Allis-Chalmers plant and Local 248, which he led from its inception in 1937. This was a time when the traditionally hostile press in Milwaukee was raising the usual furor about CRC and Communists. His first trial was thrown out by the U.S. Supreme Court in yet another high court victory for CRC, because the "perjured" testimony was made before a congressional committee without a quorum. Curious aspects were numerous. At his second trial, thirteen Congressmen swore under oath that they had been present, even though the House of Representatives refused to turn over the minutes of attendance; they were pressed by the court and then claimed that there were no such records. The former secretary of the city's Industrial Union Council, who worked with Christoffel, "secretly" removed files, without authorization, and took them to Chicago. There they were inspected and photographed by a reporter from the Hearst-owned *Milwaukee Sentinel;* the informant's trip was paid for by the paper. When Louis Budenz testified against Christoffel at the trial, the judge allowed his testimony because of past strikes in which he had participated, but he disallowed the testimony of others pointing to management as cause of those same strikes. Thirteen Congressmen testified that they were present on the day in question, Saturday, when members were known rarely to show up; besides it was snowing. Fred Hartley, the Congressman of Taft-Hartley fame, made damaging confessions concerning the keeping of quorum records, and the transacting of other business without a quorum. The ubiquitous Budenz said that he knew the labor leader well, though he mangled the pronunciation of his name. Little wonder that Christoffel's lawyer accused all of them of "wholesale perjury," lamenting that it was his client who had been convicted of that same offense.[53]

After the ouster of Christoffel from Local 248, the union degenerated into a weak, company-dominated union controlled by Walter Reuther's allies. The entire union leadership was fined by the company following the strike in 1947 and all were blacklisted. This was the message CRC took to union halls and unionists across the country, that this would be their fate if they did not align with Christoffel; at the same time they put the spotlight on the sorry state of labor-management relations and the deterioration of workers' living conditions during the Red Scare. In plotting a national tour for Christoffel, the national office reminded the chapters, "I know that you are overloaded with both cases and meetings. . . . We are not asking you to arrange special meetings for him, but to attempt to schedule him into as many trade union meetings and mass organization meetings as possible during his stay in your city. It will also be necessary to provide housing for him. . . . We will also include in his speaking engagements an appeal for support for CRC and its various cases and for membership in CRC."[54]

But complicating the defense of the labor leader was the role of the ever-present O. John Rogge, the attorney. First, Patterson raised an oblique concern about his role. Then the circuit court charged the lawyer with "inexcusable neglect in looking out for the interests of a client under criminal sentence," because he failed "to file certain motions in time." For his part, Rogge complained bitterly about spending so much time on CRC cases, like Christoffel, with only minimal compensation. Apparently his message didn't get across, for in October 1951, as his client's case was reaching a new stage, he announced, "With great reluctance I have been forced to decide to try and impress a lien on the bonds of Civil Rights Congress. . . . I cannot stay in business unless I receive some money for the work I have done." Patterson's view of all this was less charitable: "I have heard by the grapevine that he is trying to 'snatch' the gold. . . . The New York State Insurance and Banking Commission has tied up . . . the bonds and the courts will not deliver them to anybody until the New York State investigation has been completed. The old vulture will not feed off that fund." Rogge wanted $18,000, but the response of his client was to replace him as counsel.[55]

Rogge also caused difficulties with the UAW by pressing them for funds. This caused Emil Mazey, secretary-treasurer, to denounce him: "I think it particularly ungracious that either you or Mr. Christoffel should, at this time, complain about the generosity of the Union in this matter." He said that he had deposited $5,000 for Christoffel's bail in addition to supplying supplementary funds. But a few weeks later in April 1948 Mazey informed that the

UAW International Executive Board "voted unanimously not to appropriate any further funds to the Christoffel case." One UAW member expressed the sentiments of a number of them in opposition: "I as well as many others feel that brother Christoffel, is in this predicament only because he fought for the workers at Allis Chalmers irregardless of what our UAW politics are or have been." There was something to this. In 1946, Allis-Chalmers workers went on strike. Company executives appeared before the congressional committee debating Taft-Hartley, then Christoffel was invited to appear, which helped to spark his legal problems. Then investigators were sent to Milwaukee to quiz and harass strike leaders; and to crown it all, Christoffel was placed on trial, which was seen as a signal during a time of increased labor militancy.[56]

As time wore on, Christoffel increasingly had difficulty attracting support, even from the left-led unions. Early in 1953 he conceded that "the last trip I made to Detroit to speak to the various unions, was not very successful from a financial standpoint." Ben Gold, as usual, had been "very sympathetic." Christoffel asked Patterson, "Would you consider going to see Gold for a contribution to our depleted defense fund. . . . some years ago, the Fur Workers donated $500 to our fund." The other stalwart, "the UE donated $1,000, and, of course, are in a sense furnishing the attorney." But all this aid did not prevent the brave unionist from being trooped off to jail in Lorton, Virginia.[57]

While there, CRC did not desert him. Lottie Gordon, then secretary of their Prisoners Relief Committee made a special appeal for him: "Will you take a 'Loyalty Pledge' to labor's first Taft-Hartley victim. . . . Mr. Christoffel has children. And in keeping with the Prisoners' Relief Committee traditional pledge to frame-up victims, we are undertaking to help Mrs. Christoffel in caring for them. We are anxious to send Mrs. Christoffel a substantial sum of money every week so that neither she nor Mr. Christoffel need worry about the children." She requested a monthly pledge.[58]

It turned out that CRC was not exaggerating in stressing the importance of this case. Not only did it send a clear signal to militant trade unionists seeking better contracts, but it also served as legal precedent. In *U.S. v. Bryan* the executive secretary of the Joint Anti-Fascist Refugee Committee was asked by HUAC to turn over their records, he refused. He was convicted and it was upheld. The *Christoffel* case was distinguished here, but Justice Robert Jackson, concurring, expressed the position of many observers when he commented that he didn't "see how this decision and that in the *Christoffel* case can coexist." *Christoffel* also was an issue in *U.S. v. Fleichman* and a string of other cases following it. As the case wound its way through the courts, Christoffel's new lawyer, David Scribner, was astonished at how the courts handled it: "The court supports practically every legal argument that was advanced by us, but for one reason or another the Court rules against us. . . . Essentially the Court said that the weakness lay in the trial work. I am certainly not ready to agree with the Court on that, though I have very serious criticism of the manner in which the case was tried below," i.e., the finger was being pointed at Rogge in addition to the courts. But whomever was to blame, the fact is that Harold Christoffel, who not only represented CRC's top labor case but who actually became a valued CRC organizer in the trade union movement, became yet another victim of Cold War hysteria.[59]

There were other legal curiosities that Scribner could point to at the circuit court level: "most startling . . . is the fact that two out of the three members of the Court are not sure that they are right: Note the last paragraph in the decision . . . [it] is a wonderful acknowledgment of the weakness of the prosecution's case." What had been said was jarring: "Our conclusion is that a new trial is not warranted. This resolution of our doubts does not entirely remove them from the minds of two of us, who believe that the reviewing authority of the Supreme Court might well be invoked for further consideration of the case." At a time when judges were mostly cowing before the right-wing juggernaut, this was quite an admission.[60]

Minnesota was similar to its neighbor Wisconsin in that labor was a keen concern there. CRC in Minnesota helped the car washers organize a union, and one of their principal cases concerned the attempt to deport Peter Warhol, business agent of Local 61, of the Upholsterers' Union, whose wife was a descendant of U.S. Grant. But, in a sense, the battles fought in Minnesota were qualitatively different from others because they were conducted against the backdrop of routing the left from the Democratic Farmer-Labor Party, which brought to the fore Hubert Humphrey, Walter Mondale, Donald Fraser, and a generation of leading U.S. politicians. Like CRC, the Democratic Farmer-Labor Party was accused of being a "Communist front." Although John Earl Haynes in his overwritten study is highly sympathetic to the anticommunists, even he concedes that the various anticommunists of various stripes had in common "simply gang[ing] up" for "licking the Commies." Once that was over, they suffered splits. CRC leader Irene Paull was a participant in this critical struggle of the late 1940s and thus she brought a particular perspective to her work. At this time in an extremely self-critical analysis she was lamenting that "my weakness is lack of organizational ability. . . . I can't seem to develop a virtue I wasn't born with," though she admitted that her strength was "fighting and public relations work," qualities that came in handy during the epic DFL battles. Judge Edward Totten was chairman of the Minnesota chapter, which had about three hundred members in 1948, with twenty active ones, at least on paper; that has to be said because the fate of this chapter fluctuated. Early in 1950, the St. Paul branch was "temporarily discontinued," yet a month later the chapter was sponsoring "Negro history week . . . a play by Meridel LeSueur as a benefit" for the Trenton Six and Ingram; the chapter "put ourselves on a systematic basis. We meet once a month . . . are alert to all campaigns and put on affairs. . . . We are winning many friends in the Negro community. Half of our board now is Negro." This was even more striking because the main Black paper, the *Minneapolis Spokesman*, a "Humphrey rag" said Paull, constantly warned Afro-Americans against associating with CRC.[61]

As in other areas, the chapter vigorously opposed the Mundt-Nixon bill, but with a caveat: "So many people have taken action but don't want me to publicize it through our channels." Putting pressure on Hubert Humphrey was a primary thrust of the chapter, including picketing his office. After a Robeson rally where this was a major point, "36 members" were recruited. They survived the Korea crunch, but not without difficulty. In June 1951 the chairperson of their chapter was "picked up together with a St. Paul leader and charged with harboring a criminal." The "'criminal . . .' a Negro woman charged in perjury for saying she was not a communist. She washed pots and pans at a veteran's hospital." At this time the chapter had an Executive Board of eight people with the "average attendance" at chapter meetings being fifteen; the chair and vice-chair aside, all the leaders were women. Still, Paull glumly remarked that "intimidation has cost us several officers and left the chapter" in the hands of a few women who did all the basic work. There was frequent "intimidation" about their Martinsville Seven and other petitions. They were able to entice the "largest Negro church in the city, on Easter Sunday" to discuss McGee for "about an hour" with the "entire congregation signing the petition and send wires (about 1,500 altogether)." But this was more the exception than the rule: "Many Negro people are afraid to sign CRC petitions because of the pressure that has been on them from all angles not to sign our petitions, but they sign letters and petitions which we prepare not mentioning CRC."[62]

Paull concluded by telling Grossman, "I am writing this letter on my employer's time and sneak it out of the typewriter the minute he comes by." This was a frequent mode of operating within CRC, because all CRC leaders were not so lucky as to be able to do political work full-time. But this could be a problem, and it was not endemic or peculiar to Minnesota, as Grossman brought sharply to Paull's attention: "you cannot build a CRC in Minneapolis unless three or four of our leading people are spending all their time (apart, of course, from families and jobs) on the CRC." Paull had her own complaints about the national office. After a national meeting in Chicago in 1951, she was irate: "we were talked to death. . . . [we] don't have to be propagandized or convinced. What we want . . . is concrete suggestions, ideas, exchange of experiences. . . . Also it is unforgivable to hold sessions late." Obviously, Paull, because of her many obligations, was stingy with her time and it turned out that this was for good reasons, for before long she had suffered the fate of many CRC cadre: "It was decided that I was to retire from all assignments for a month. . . . that I was to be seen only socially. I was also ordered to have a physical check-up. . . . I'm so tired." Soon thereafter, the new chapter sparkplug, Alma Foley, was admitting, "The state of the organization is not good."[63]

If the typical pattern had held, at this point CRC-Minneapolis would have folded, but this did not occur. In 1953 they had a resurgence and one meeting late that year was said to be the "best attended . . . since we fought in the Willie McGee [case]." At the CRC annual meeting in St. Louis in 1954 this chapter was said to have the "best organization set-up of those in attendance"; they had annual picnics, spring festivals, and Meridel LeSeuer continued to work closely with them, attracting many others. Their protest against the anti-Semitic film "Oliver Twist" was one of the most effective in the country and within the organization. But by 1956 this chapter too had gone the way of others—it was defunct.[64]

Wisconsin and Minnesota had admirable records, but the anchor of CRC activity in the Midwest had to be the Michigan chapter based in Detroit. Its predecessor was formed in 1934 in response to anticommunist legislation, strikes, labor organizing, and the like. It was no accident that that CRC founding conference had been held in Detroit, because that city's pre-1946 civil rights activity presented the sort of militancy and organization the CRC aspired toward. By 1947 Detroit chapter leader Anne Shore was proudly declaring, "We feel like an octopus here, we have so many exciting projects that we can hardly keep track of them all. It would literally take pages and pages to outline all the things that are going on." This was not puffery. At this stage the Greater Detroit and Wayne County Industrial Union Council was affiliated with CRC and this labor tie was to remain the chapter's hallmark throughout its life, more than any other chapter. The chapter was circulating petitions on the Columbia, Tennessee, pogrom, was fighting for a state FEPC, and was contributing greatly to the "Oust Bilbo" campaign. The FEPC effort was typical. It "involved about 3,000 distributors in Detroit and several hundred outstate. . . . A corps of fifteen to twenty people will be found to assume the job of building community chapters. . . . Next week an appointment with the governor—later a hearing before the Senate Labor Committee which is sympathetic." This was done under the auspices of a special CRC-FEPC committee. They had a delegation in early 1947 going to see Philip Murray to "discuss the problem of red-baiting among the progressives" in the CIO. But with all this there was a "very bad . . . financial picture." The wife of executive secretary Jack Raskin, in a spousal pattern repeated elsewhere, supported him, and Shore was living off "money she inherited from her mother."[65]

The financial situation was not all that was awry in the motor city, however. Right after the Korean conflict, Shore set down at length the problems afflicting the chapter:

> There is a fine potential here . . . but is so amorphous that it drives me crazy. The hundreds of contacts we have all seem to be in Jack's head. The office is a mess. The bail fund, what there is of it . . . is mostly in Jack's head. . . . There are no chapters. . . . There is no functioning Board. It's even worse than CRC in L.A. . . . . People are scared here. . . . We are

doing nothing about Dennis. Little about the 11 and little about McGee. . . . We have been doing a minimum on Mundt-Nixon. . . . The middle class here is really frightened. A truly different picture from L.A.

Shore's experience in Southern California, which boasted of one of the strongest CRC chapters, may have colored her perceptions unduly, although there may have been more than a smidgen of truth in them. Jack Raskin was viewed as a problem by more than her. In August 1946 Milt Kaufman told Raskin off: "your seeming inability to write letters becomes more than a mere matter of personal idiosyncracy, Jack. It creates political difficulties." The relationship between Patterson and Raskin also had its rough spots. One particularly nettlesome incident involved a major snafu:

Can you give me some idea as to the significance of (these) remarks? ". . . progressive forces got their signals crossed in fighting the Callahan Act, a [local] Mundt-Nixon type of [law]. . . . first they collected signatures to force a referendum. Then they tried to get an injunction to *prevent* the referendum, fearing it would go against them. There was a different situation, however, in that the Michigan Attorney General said the law was unconstitutional and refused to enforce it."

Raskin reciprocated in criticism. After Patterson was appointed as executive secretary, the Detroit leader objected to the process: "what's the sense in giving an opinion on an accomplished fact?" Patterson demurred, saying that the Executive Board of CRC had made the "recommendation" of his selection; William Lawrence of CRC also objected to Raskin's point.[66]

This auspicious beginning to their relationship was replicated subsequently. First Patterson noted how he was "deeply concerned of [their] failure" to follow up on certain cases and how "worried" he was since Detroit was deemed by CRC to be a "concentration area." Raskin came right back and carped about the sending of Earl Conrad instead of Du Bois to speak there: "it's a continuation of the same policy within the national office which new leadership was suppose[d] to change. . . . [it] creates a sense of distrust on the part of local leadership for national leadership." Then Shore got into the act. She criticized the canceling of the "Chicago staff meeting" in 1949 as "shortsighted." But that was not all: "the decision to have a staff meeting was a collective one. The decision to call it off was not. This sort of thing has taken place many times in the past." Then things came to a head with Patterson calling Raskin to task; he harshly judged Raskin's "silence" and the continuing "unsatisfactory situation," but did not deign to stop there: "I do not understand your attitude at all and am deeply dissatisfied with the relationship which exists between the national office and the Detroit chapter; and I do not believe that the weaknesses of the [national office] are alone the responsible factors. . . . [The national office] has received no letters that I know of from Esther Cooper at all." Patterson said that he was "disturbed" because of the tendency of the chapter to deal with "technical questions," but did "nothing" about "program[s] . . . [the] financial situation."[67]

These problems were abated to some extent when Arthur McPhaul came on board as chapter executive-secretary. An Afro-American, he came to CRC after Raskin resigned for "personal reasons" around 1950. Born in Oklahoma, he was forty at the time, married, and had two children. Though he had skill as a plasterer and did this work to supplement his CRC income, he had been a committeeman of powerful Ford Local 600, where he had been for twenty-two years, and then they fired him allegedly for making "inflammatory speeches in the dining room of the Rouge plant," This charge was upheld, so the union's loss was CRC's gain. McPhaul exemplified militancy and he was a pioneer in fighting for women's rights as well. During the war he had fought successfully for the hiring of Black women in the plant. In June 1952 he ran afoul of the law when he refused to turn over the records of CRC to HUAC when it came to Detroit. Then he was fingered as being a member of the Communist Party. Ernest Goodman and George Crockett handled this case, which ultimately reached the U.S. Supreme Court, but McPhaul had to go to jail. The final verdict was a five-to-four decision, with Justices Warren, Douglas, Black, and Brennan dissenting; Douglas' opinion was bitter and rousing, accusing the majority to no avail of having done away with the presumption of innocence.[68]

McPhaul's arrival lessened but did not extinguish the chapter's problems. Patterson in mid-1951 raised a sensitive point: "Arthur has to learn greater patience than is his now. That is one of his weaknesses. . . . Patience does not mean tolerance. . . . Patience flows from understanding of the degree to which people have been corrupted by their life in society." Shore saw the situation differently. She was of the opinion that national leaders did not always accord McPhaul the proper respect in that too often matters concerning policy went to her and not him, even though he was the top leader. In no equivocal terms she told Grossman, "This too-often-repeated error smacks of white chauvinism. . . . Pat is guilty too."[69]

CRC-Michigan was not unlike the mid-1970s Yankees in that they brawled and quarreled while chalking up gain after gain. During the 1949–50 period, when heated missives were flying back and forth between New York and Detroit, Raskin was still capable of proclaiming:

> We have been busy raising money; we had a very successful Robeson meeting; we are conducting the defense of about 20 deportees; we are at the present time forming a Crockett Defense Committee and fight against discrimination in housing involving Negroes and Mexicans. . . . on the questions of membership we have done a very poor job. . . . [we are] concentrating on four major fronts: [the] Deportation drive . . . We have 40 deportation cases and 4 denaturalization cases; 2) The Mundt-Ferguson Bill . . . 3) police brutality . . . FEPC and housing; 4) major emphasis on the 11 and their attorneys.

Shore had returned to Detroit from L.A., but Esther Cooper had left, which "leaves us without a Negro on our executive staff." This concern for affirmative action was consistent with CRC policy, but Patterson objected specifically to point number one. He didn't feel "deportation cases can be our first point of concentration." He thought that this should be left to the American Committee for the Protection of the Foreign Born. He observed that there should be more emphasis on the rights of third political parties, unions, and Blacks, adding, "The drawing in of a Negro force as a member of the staff is a must." Despite Patterson's admonition, by 1953 Detroit's bail fund had worked for "over fifty deportees free on bail ranging from one to five thousand dollars each." The presence of Saul Grossman in Detroit had much to do with this thrust. He was executive secretary of the Michigan Committee for Protection of the Foreign Born and worked closely with CRC. HUAC asked for their records in 1952. Like McPhaul, Grossman refused and received a one-year sentence and a $1,000 fine. There was a joint McPhaul-Grossman defense committee and such links virtually ensured that deportation would continue to occupy the attention of the Detroit chapter more than it did the others.[70]

Extradition was the flip side of the deportation coin and like other chapters, Detroit did not ignore this issue. Their biggest case involved Haywood Patterson, one of the original Scottsboro Nine. After seventeen years in Alabama prisons, he escaped to Detroit in June 1948 and was arrested by FBI agents in June 1950; *Time* magazine was not alone in noting the role played by the "Communist line" CRC, which initially, through the efforts of Ernest Goodman, fought to have bail reduced from $10,000 to $5,000, then put the money up. They did not stop there; they proceeded to launch a campaign so powerful that Governor G. Mennen Williams dared not extradite him. By this time Patterson had formed a tenuous tie to CRC, and many CRC members did not particularly like him, yet as the progeny of one of the most important ILD cases, Shore conceded "all of us have a responsibility to him." So they persuaded the president of Cadillac Local 22 to give funds for the defense effort. They initiated a campaign of letter writing to the governors of Michigan and Alabama and to Truman as well. CRC attorney Bob Truehaft in California knew the governor from their days in the Office of Price Administration, as did Thomas Emerson, who was OPA's former general counsel, and their contacts proved useful. They wanted Patterson to go to New York for speaking and fundraising purposes, but he declined because he felt he wouldn't be "safe." When he won this fight, in gushing prose he thanked CRC for their aid and struck a familiar chord: "people in the North do not half realize what goes on down South and how Negroes are framed." But this victory did not end Patterson's woes and he was charged with murder and contracted cancer before being slain in prison.[71]

Labor played a substantial role in the Patterson fight and it was a constituency that the Detroit chapter worked closely with. The evidence was abundant. When Rogge came to Detroit in 1948 to speak before one thousand workers on the Christoffel case, Local 208 of the UAW heled to organize the effort and the Wayne County CIO sponsored it. When twenty-eight Black and poor Georgians who were picking pickels in Bay City were stranded, they were "adopted" by CRC; they had come to the state "under conditions like slave labor" and CRC brought them to a Detroit church to reside until they could get on their feet. Ford Local 600 was probably their closest ally and even in 1951 when Robeson and Vito Marcantonio came, though the "weather was bad, it rained . . . and never was warm enough," thousands turned out for their picnic in August; "the conservative *Detroit Times* said 10,000" came to hear the CRC giants.[72]

In the 1953–54 period, McPhaul assessed at length this CRC-labor relationship. "Up until two or three years ago we in Michigan enjoyed a very good working relationship with the trade union movement." Objectively and in a manner that was all to infrequent during this era, he frankly blamed reaction for whatever reversals had been suffered since then. Still on the "Negro question" they continued to make headway. On the McGee case "we were able to move the entire UAW-CIO, including Walter Reuther." Their tactics were striking and are still used to this day. First, they would unleash a "barrage of leaflets" at the "plant gates." Then, they would "work on secondary leaders," e.g., shop stewards. After that they would move to the executive board level after laying this foundation; by this point they would have their issue percolating and bubbling from the bottom up, so that leadership could not ignore it. With such tactics, even "right-led" locals gave funds and supported the Martinsville Seven. When HUAC came to Detroit they distributed 50,000 leaflets and an eighteen-page fact sheet in this manner. The result? Letters and editorials in union papers proliferated against the Un-Americans. Local 600 invited CRC to sit in on a "strategy committee" against HUAC. When the anticommunist Trucks Act was introduced, 35,000 leaflets were passed out; soon, eighty union leaders were signing an *amicus curiae* brief on the bill, with seventy from the right, seven from the center, and only three from the left. McPhaul recognized that even during a period of right-wing terror they could still move unions that had heavy Black membership because they were less anticommunist and more sensitive to race: "The unions are very sensitive on the questions of Genocide against the Negro people."[73]

Many chapters published regular newletters, but Detroit's was called appropriately the "Labor Defender." In 1953, when a number of other chapters were suffering grievously, it was being issued monthly in runs of 50,000 each and was being distributed at "all major plant gates in the city." It was an attractive publication, with cartoons, snappy headlines, and the like. The headline of the April 1954 issue was indicative of the thrust of the paper and the chapter: "Expose Labor Spies Still Operate at Ford." More than other chapters, Detroit linked the issue of political repression with labor. CRC's success in the field of labor meant that they began to have ironic problems that other chapters would have loved to have had: "It's funny about these left unions—they often do less than the others on cases like [Martinsville] and McGee. At least they never come to us and when we go to them it's harder to get in than anything." The left-led unions were more under fire and often felt compelled to more stoutly resist the blandishments of CRC and the Black and progressive workers in their ranks.[74]

One reason that helps to explain CRC's ability to appeal to labor during the darkest days of the red scare was their resolute, unending opposition to racism, racist violence, and police brutality. This was appreciated sincerely among Afro-Americans particularly and this rubbed off on the labor movement. It was not hyperbole when it was said in mid-1952 by one CRC leader, "CRC has tremendous prestige in the community. Officials at City Hall, Lansing, etc. are afraid of our ability to move masses of people." Black workers were appreciative of their efforts to establish a state FEPC. In the early days of CRC, they obtained 180,000 signatures on petitions calling for this, issued weekly bulletins, sponsored statewide conferences in Detroit and Lansing, formed FEPC committees in more than twelve cities and had an extensive hearing with the governor. The year 1947 also saw them join with the NAACP, the Lawyers Guild, the YWCA, the American Jewish Committee and others in the National Emergency Committee Against Mob Violence, pushing antilynching bills. CRC initiated a delegation of twenty-five that included the Wayne County CIO, Packard Local 190, Plymouth Local 51, the National Council of Negro Women, which went to Washington to lobby for anti-poll tax and anti-job discrimination measures. This was a period when Detroit had a reputation for having one of the more brutal police forces in the nation and this problem had to be addressed by the chapter. The police shooting of fifteen-year-old Leon Mosely dramatized this question in the spring of 1948. CRC organized a march of thousands on City Hall and joined with the NAACP in meeting with the mayor. Pressure unleashed by the Committee for Justice for Leon Mosely, which included CRC, CIO, UAW, CP, and their activities led to the firing of the two officers involved and a manslaughter indictment.[75]

One incident of police brutality in the motor city not only catapulted CRC into further local prominence as a fighter against repression but still continues to resonate today. It involved the family of Berry Gordy, owner of the Motown entertainment company and today one of the most affluent Afro-Americans in this country; perhaps his experience in this controversial incident provided him with the organizing skills and incentive to go on and form his pathbreaking record company a scant few years later. It all began in late 1950 when police came to the home of Charles Gordy, Berry's brother, to arrest his seventeen-year-old son. They were asked if they had a warrant and they answered no and tried to push in. A shot was fired at the elder Gordy and he fired back; one officer was killed and another wounded. Scores of police converged on the house. There was machine gun and pistol fire at the fifteen huddled in the house. A crowd estimated by the *Detroit Times* to be over four thousand Blacks (CRC's estimate was six thousand) gathered spontaneously to watch. McPhaul, who was present, said the "police were abusive and threatening . . . they pushed and shoved people at the point of bayonets and butts of rifles." He placed the Gordy case in the context of the rampant job discrimination facing Blacks who encountered "white only" requests for most jobs and hence suffered an inability to obtain skilled jobs. The chapter accused the police officers of terrorizing, beating, cursing, and stealing money: "This was a little piece of Korea in our own backyard." Charles Gordy was arrested finally on charges of first-degree murder, while the original armed robbery charge against his son was dropped.[76]

The bourgeois press and their allies quickly tried to turn a setback into a victory by blaming CRC and the Communist leader Carl Winter and his party; they accused the reds of "attempting to incite a riot," and an editorial in the *Detroit News* charged they were attempting "to divide us" over the case. Another headline read "Reds Use Gordy Case in Racial Propaganda"; yet another blared, "Red Rats at Work." Initially the NAACP joined in this cacophony, as Walter White lavishly praised the role of the police. In return a *Free Press* editorial complimented the NAACP for trying to "checkmate the purposeful breeders of fury." But the Association had to reverse field quickly like a shifty halfback because their view was clearly at odds with the demonstrated sentiment of their primary constituency. Rev. Horace White, one of the more prominent Black pastors, accused the CRC of trying to "create trouble" and "confusion," but Afro-Americans, accustomed to moving monolithically on ticklish questions on race, rejected such assertion. Quickly Edward Turner, president of the local NAACP branch, told Esther Gordy that they had voted to "endorse financially and morally the Gordy Defense Committee." Willis Ward, a Black man who was a former prosecutor, denounced the police action. The leading black newspaper, the *Michigan Chronicle* acted similarly; in their estimation the pictures they ran graphically showed the "plundering" of apartments in the neighborhood and an extraordinary number of bullet holes inflicted by the police. Their coverage provided a blow-by-blow description of the trial, hailing the "new record for attendance" and lamenting the fact that "Gordy's wife is broke." Finally, prominent Black attorney Wade McCree was persuaded to join the defense team, though he had conflicts with CRC throughout as he opposed a mass campaign.[77]

But this opposition did not detain the CRC. Immediately they distributed 50,000 leaflets and circulated a petition. A CRC committee against police brutality was formed involving about sixty people. One of their leaders, Rev. Charles Hill, compared the case to the notorious Sweet incident of thirty years earlier that involved the moving of a Black doctor into a previously all-white area and a subsequent attack on his home. Their tireless organizing led to the formation of a CRC branch in the neighborhood where the Gordy case took place. Once again, they began to distribute leaflets at plant gates. Gordy was an autoworker and a member of the left-led Ford Local 600. Some distributing leaflets at the Ford plant were arrested, but the charges were dropped after "the howl that went up." The police were displeased with the black eye they had received as a result of the case and they retaliated in other ways. CRC proclaimed that "police brutality is at an all-time high." Blacks were being beaten for little or no reason and certain officers were rumored to have alleged that it was a payback for the slaying of their compatriot.[78]

But the chapter was not intimidated; they even reached out to their allies in Czechoslovakia for support. They participated in the delegation of sixty that met with mayor Albert Cobo which demanded an investigation of the police and the freeing of Gordy. Their literature compared Detroit in 1950 to Germany in 1935: "Brutality, murder and frame-ups—this is the official policy toward the Negro community." Appropriately, Berry Gordy, the defendant's brother, was treasurer of the Defense Committee, and CRC helped in the raising of funds. Yet, the effort was wracked with dissension; the attorneys wanted to conduct a traditional defense that abjured mass protest, the NAACP wanted to keep CRC out of the defense effort, and the police and their backers kept up a steady beat of pressure on their opponents. As a result, Gordy was convicted of first-degree murder.[79]

This wasn't the last hurrah for CRC in this area and they continued to cry out against police misconduct and racist practices. In 1952 this meant focusing on the case of James Henderson in Mt. Clemens, Michigan, an Afro-American accused of the rape of a white woman, who under the threat of mob violence was tried and got a life sentence after the jury had deliberated for four hours. Through the good offices of CRC, Ford Local 600 gave money to his defense committee and Rev. Hill, Coleman Young, and Ernest Goodman came to his assistance. In 1953 McPhaul himself was subjected to "brutal treatment" after a "minor auto accident." He demanded an audience with the Police Commissioner to "discuss the whole question of police brutality and especially as it relates to Negro citizens." Throughout CRC's history, this question remained a prime concern and when their ally Coleman Young was finally elected Mayor, he implemented some of their major proposals.[80]

In a sense the Michigan chapter was a model for others to emulate. It did not ignore labor, it did not ignore the Blacks and it did not ignore the reds. This latter issue had to be addressed initially in 1948 when the Communist leaders, including Michigan's Carl Winter, were indicted. After Korea, they had to put out such brushfires as the attempt to bar the *Daily Worker* from newstands; this led to "partial victory" because the paper did return, yet the persecution continued.[81]

But even before these skirmishes, CRC had become involved in the ill-fated effort beginning in 1947 to prevent the passage of the anticommunist

Callahan Act. They fought the anticommunist Trucks Act that sought to regulate the party and Communist "fronts"—a passage aimed specifically at CRC. With Ernest Goodman on the case, this was fought all the way to the U.S. Supreme Court, where they lost, with Justices Black and Douglas in dissent. When an amendment was added to the state constitution defining subversion in an effort to cripple left activity, one paper went so far as to claim that CRC's opposition led to victory.[82]

The indictment of the Communist leaders saw increased attention paid to anticommunism. At CRC's statewide conference in 1949 declarations of support rang out. When the CP-Seventeen were charged, Raskin sent $1,100 for their defense. But problems mounted. When Matt Smith, president of the Mechanical Education Society of America sought out Walter Reuther about support of the CP-Eleven, the UAW leader reportedly told him "that he didn't want to talk about it on the phone"; he said he would go to Reuther's office but he was told "that it was too hot to touch that he didn't want to touch it." Similarly, according to Shore, the "reactionary red-baiting Reuther leadership here, prevented us from getting ANY labor opposition" to the state anticommunist bill. Reuther may have had reason to be intimidated. When Williams Albertson, Michigan Communist Party leader came to the CRC office, "five carloads (of FBI) came with him. . . . They boldly follow him everywhere he goes. . . . the crack-down is very soon." But Patterson was not accustomed to accepting the norm, state repression, as an excuse: "For some considerable time I have seen no reports on the work of CRC in the Michigan area. . . . Michigan has not met its responsibilities in the Steve Nelson case. . . . the weaknesses Michigan reflects are also to be found in Illinois, Ohio, and Wisconsin."[83]

If that were not enough, Detroit-CRC then had to deal with the indictment of the local Communist leadership pursuant to the Smith Act. Shore reached out to the American Jewish Congress affiliate: "[they] had contacted N.Y. National AJC office for advice and policy. Said he hoped that our national office had also called AJC to urge them to do something. . . . We are finding people of the above broad character concerned but each waiting for someone else to move first. This is characteristic of Detroit at this time." It was also characteristic of a good part of the nation. When they tried to pass out a flyer on the Smith Act and the Rosenbergs at the Hadassah convention in late 1952, "not only did [they] refuse to take any action but they called the cops and had the leaflet distributors chased away." This was at a time when the chapter was seeking to raise $40,000 for the local Smith Act case and they went about it with typical efficiency: "To date we have had one television broadcast [secured by the Progressive Party]. . . . pamphlets, flyers, etc. targeted." Growth in the face of difficulty was evidenced by the fact that in Detroit they were "not confronted with . . . liquidation tendencies. . . . two additional people have been added to the CRC staff." Indeed, their efficiency was such that not only did their bail fund aid "over fifty deportees free on bail ranging from one to five thousand dollars each" but also they were "$42,000 up on the local Smith Act people plus $20,000 on Bill (Sentner); and we have made loans to Pittsburgh on Smith Act bail there as well as having a large amount in the N.Y. Fund." This success was not unique to Detroit, as was indicated by Patterson, "the field is being narrowed in some respects by the growing attacks. Illinois is taking care of St. Louis; New Jersey has Sid Stein to take care of; the whole country was involved in the Pittsburgh cases and the New York cases." But Detroit's altruism had repercussions. In 1953 McPhaul had to tell Patterson, "Our sources for bail money are practically dried up." The Michigan Six, the Smith Act defendants, were shunted to prison even though CRC continued to raise a ruckus about Blacks in the crew, like Thomas Dennis, who was subjected to segregation in the Wayne County Jail. They pulled together a Committee to Keep McCarthyism Out of Michigan, but their reality belied the group's name.[84]

Their difficulties with Hadassah were replicated when the president and chairperson of the Jewish Community Council issued a "Warning [to their] . . . affiliates" not to be "duped" by the chapter. McPhaul and Co. received the ultimate compliment on their effectiveness when HUAC brought their traveling road show to Detroit in 1952. The *Detroit Times'* page-one photograph showed masses trying to jam their way into the hearings, many of whom were CRC supporters; for days the papers listed alleged Communist Party members and gave special attention to CRC ally Local 600. Dismissively, the *Times* spoke of "pro-Communist" CRC members who "marched under crudely lettered placards." Shore reflected on the ramifications of these events: "The 'unfriendly' witnesses gave them a very hard time. Coleman Young and Art were . . . really fighting them all the way. . . . [There were] 'Uncle Tom' statements from NAACP President Turner and Bishop Dade." CRC member Edith Van Horn was fired at Dodge, which led "to a walkout of 300 women. . . . But they too are becoming more and more insistent on getting answers to the 64 dollar question as a basis for continued support." This was the backwash from HUAC whose "objective [was to] terrorize the opposition into complete silence." A number of militant CRC members and supporters were sacked from the auto plants after HUAC's departure. Subsequently, the FBI proceeded to list CRC supporters like Ernest Goodman and Le Bron Simmons as Communists in an attempt to stampede them to the right. But unlike many chapters, Detroit had a counterintelligence operation of its own. They sent an ally to an American Legion testimonial for the stool pigeon Berniece Baldwin and maintained a file on her that included her marriage license, mortgage, divorce decrees, and other vital information; they also maintained a file on the apostate Richard O'Hair.[85]

The chapter in Michigan was also in the vanguard when it came to paying attention to issues involving youth and students. Nationally CRC maintained for a while a Youth and Student Division. Like Montgomery 1955, years before Berkeley 1964, CRC was laying the foundation for student protest. Academic freedom was a prime concern, and this question came dramatically to the fore in the person of James Zarichny of Michigan State University. In November 1946 the Student Council there refused to recognize the American Youth for Democracy chapter on campus. A few months later a FEPC rally was sponsored by twelve campus organizations and held on campus. AYD handed out flyers. Zarichny was placed on "strict disciplinary probation" as a result of his participation in this activity and was told that if he continued to work with AYD, which was viewed by some as a "Communist front," he would be suspended. On 1 July 1947 they suspended him. After the Lawyers' Guild intervened, a few weeks later, he was told he could return if he'd conform to prevailing dictates, but that fall he was not removed from the probation list. All hell broke loose in April 1948 when the president of the school announced at a session of the Michigan Senate that Zarichny was the only Communist on campus; he was subpoenaed and he declined to testify and was held in contempt. This was just the beginning of Zarichny's problems and the legal web that enveloped him kept CRC busy for years to come.[86]

This Michigan case was the centerpiece of a full CRC program aimed at youth and students. Unsurprisingly, Ellen Schrecker has concluded that college campuses, despite their role as centers of innovation and freethinking, were anticommunist too. CRC could well attest to this. Professors at the University of Washington were ousted for their political beliefs, an Oregon State University science teacher was harassed, and bills curbing academic freedom were introduced in Texas, New York, Illinois, and elsewhere. At their height in 1949, CRC could say without hubris that "this office has undoubtedly stimulated a good deal of activity," as evidenced by "numerous requests for information that we get from strangers." As late as 1952, one student leader, before buying a Coca-Cola machine for a student lounge, consulted CRC first about the company's "policy regarding Negroes."[87]

Although the Midwest was the main center of this activity, the East was not inactive. A student leader at Yale, William F. Buckley, was so put out with CRC activism that he wrote the Attorney General demanding that he start arresting and jailing them: "The Civil Rights Congress has asked me to write you to protest. . . . I want to urge you, with all possible sincerity, to be vigorous in your prosecution of these men and women." Under pressure, Yale cancelled a speech by Carl Marzani. This was mild compared to what happened at Dartmouth. A right-wing student beat a Progressive Party supporter to death in an unprovoked attack; he received a slap on the wrist in the form of a $500 fine and a suspended one-year sentence as a result. The culprit, Thomas Doxsee, led a gang of "12 fraternity men" who invaded the room of Raymond Cirotta; the killer, whose lawyer was vice-chairman of the state GOP, had argued with the victim previously in class about the Soviet Union; and Cirotta had committed the cardinal sin of singing "Joe Hill" in his room. CRC also defended Professor Dirk Struik, a Marxist under attack at M.I.T. because of his political beliefs.[88]

Then there was the case of Syracuse University student and ex-GI Irving Feiner, who made a speech on a street corner urging attendance at a meeting sponsored by the American Labor Party and the Young Progressives of America, at which Rogge was asked to speak on the subject of the Trenton Six. Police accused Feiner of maligning the city's mayor, the city itself, the U.S. president and the American Legion. He was convicted of disorderly conduct and promised parole if he would denounce his comrades. No way, was his curt response. He received the maximum sentence, thirty days in jail, and later he was expelled from school. He was in constant contact with the Youth and Student Division of CRC during this period, though division leader Doris Rashbaum complained that in news coverage the ACLU and Progressive Party were mentioned but CRC was "left completely out of the picture." This was not justifiable, for when Rogge was denied a permit to speak at a school building, it was CRC that he reached: "I feel this should be played up very big by the Youth and Student Division of CRC." And when the case that established critical free speech doctrine reached the U.S. Supreme Court, it was CRC alone that submitted an *amicus curiae* brief.[89]

Inevitably The City University of New York system was a hotbed of CRC support. In 1949 three members of the Karl Marx Society, one Black and two white, at Brooklyn College, were suspended from school for protesting the suspension of the society, which had invited Henry Winston to campus. CRC members and allies played a major role in the two-hour strike that was called in protest of these suspensions and the suspension of Student Council elections and the censorship of the school newspaper. During the same period, CRC was assailing Professor William Knickerbocker at City College, charging him with anti-Semitism, and Professor William Davis, charging him with being anti-Black. The beleaguered faculty members charged that Communists were in control of the unrest and strike that followed; their fears were not assuaged when it turned out that the students' attorney was CRC's own Emmanuel Bloch.[90]

When John Myers of the University of North Carolina faced a challenge to his academic freedom, he contacted CRC. Patterson suggested the "formation of a defense committee. . . . It would be well if the consolidation of such a committee took place at a meeting at which the question was aired." He told Myers to look at violations under the state and federal constitutions, send letters to the *New York Times* and *Washington Post,* and "force" liberal Senator Frank Graham "to take a position"; he also offered to send a "list of sympathetic contacts." UNC was also the site of the case of Sidney Shanker, also advised by CRC, who wore his Henry Wallace button openly and opposed local reactionaries; he then got a failing grade on his dissertation and was ousted from the English department. After CRC sympathizers at Talladega College reached CRC, they wrote the president of the University of

Alabama to protest: "the public meetings to be held in conjunction with the forthcoming Art Festival will be closed to Negro students and faculty members. . . . We demand that the University change its stand." The Talladega letter was sent "to about 175 individuals and organizations" asking that they protest also.[91]

Other than the Zarichny case, the major youth and student matter tackled by CRC involved Roosevelt Ward, prosecuted for draft evasion in a critical case that went to the U.S. Supreme Court. The case was seen as a political prosecution through and through. This twenty-one-year-old black administrative secretary of the Labor Youth League—a later-day analogue of Zarichny's AYD—was arrested in New York for extradition to Louisiana for failure to report for the draft as the war in Korea raged. He was arrested at the address he gave the draftboard, even though they said they couldn't find him to get the draft notice to him properly. Ward also had a Michigan connection and received support from that region because he attended the University of Michigan; he had been born in Louisiana and had attended Wilberforce College also. He was defended by Mary Kaufman and John Coe, who charged him $100 per day. Not because of this fee, but in order to provide experience and depth to a young Black lawyer, CRC assigned Alvin Jones to work with Coe. Powe was pleased with the "excellent job" of the two: "It is very important to see a white lawyer of your stature in a case of this importance working together with a young Negro lawyer and above all to find in the record that there was joint participation."[92]

There were other illustrative aspects of this case in addition to CRC seeking to retain a young Black lawyer of "tremendous promise." Though their critics accused them of "using" their clients and abusing cases for partisan gain, Coe's comments on this case are instructive:

Is it advisable to assume the defense openly as an attorney for the CRC or would it be better merely to be a lawyer retained by the Defendant in person? I am inclined to the latter view because it seems to me that he has an excellent moral defense, and if we can present him merely as a persecuted human being, without all of the political heat incident to a political trial we might get an acquittal.

Patterson also wanted a local lawyer like Jones, since "a lawyer at home, like a dog in his own dunghill, barks louder and more effectively before a jury." Equally, Patterson wasn't so wrapped up in the case at hand as to avoid chiding attorney John Coe for using a lower case "n" for Negro.[93]

Patterson agreed with Coe up to a point, but he knew they were not just a left-wing legal services program but a political organization: "I would however politicalize the case. It may be as you say 'an ordinary criminal case' but I do not think so. . . . Negro youth in particular should be made aware of this." Jones wanted to raise the question of Black exclusion from the jury, but again Coe objected, apologetically, "Perhaps my approach is legalistic."

Patterson was thinking in both a "legalistic" and political sense, for he had in mind the appeals process as well: "It may not serve us advantageously in this matter but it does become a guide for those who follow us." It turned out that the jury was mostly "clerks and bosses." The "capitalist press," as Coe put it, broadcast widely the case "with considerable emphasis upon the 'subversive' aspect thereof." He continued, "The jury stayed out for nearly an hour, and came back in for further instructions, the Negro woman with her handkerchief quite apparently in use." The guilty verdict came in after one hour. Patterson's political approach in retrospect was the sound approach, since politics, not facts nor law, motivated the prosecution—a fact recognized belatedly by Coe: "In my opinion no jury except one swayed by hysteria could possibly have found him guilty. I think they lied on their voir dire." This latter musing was a typical lawyer's last words, but the jailing of Ward was the ultimate result, even though CRC was able to win over the U.S. Supreme Court and the young Black man won on appeal.[94]

CRC was also involved in the case of the University of Washington professors who were purged and in the firing of Ralph Spitzer at Oregon State University, fired for following the ideas of the controversial Lysenko. But Michigan remained the heart of youth and student work because it continued to be a bulwark of support from labor. The defense of the leftist Zarichny was part of their overall anti-anticommunist thrust, for instance, their lobbying against the prosecution of the CP-Eleven, which brought together students from twelve states and twenty colleges to Washington. There was the connected campaign protesting the banning of AYD chapters at Queens College, Brooklyn College, Hunter College, San Francisco State College, and elsewhere in a manner prefiguring the Free Speech movement and student rebellions of the 1960s. Detroit was the scene of a fierce battle over the banning of Howard Fast's novel *Tom Paine* from school libraries. This was a prelude to a titanic struggle at the University of Michigan. In 1947 they had barred Eisler from speaking, but in 1952 the *Genocide* petition was the bone of contention. A debate on the question was barred from campus and a "furor [was] . . . created." A Trotskyite initiated the controversy and after pressure was generated by the Ann Arbor branch of CRC, the University of Michigan administration wanted to allow a non-CRC person, but a sympathizer, to present their view. Finally, the debate was held off campus at a Unitarian Church; in a "pouring rain" the hall was packed with "several hundred in the rain . . . trying to get in." Shore participated and the "consensus of opinion was that we wowed 'em." She was told by some "we won hands down." The next day the student legislature voted "unanimously" to alter the rules regulating campus speakers. This inspired the CRC branch to try to have other debates as an organizing tool, though the "biggest problem will be to get people to take the other side."[95]

The Zarichny case in Lansing helped to inspire the students in Ann Arbor. Part of the animus toward him was created because he insited on attending meetings with Communists like Carl Winter off campus. The staggering level of speaking engagements undertaken by him during a nationwide tour turned him into a virtual town crier of student protest. The Youth and Student Division of CRC published a pamphlet, "How to Organize Zarichny's Tour on Your Campus" that suggested that he speak to the editor of the student newspaper, speak at mass meetings, speak to veterans (he organized veterans at Michigan State), contact the NAACP and Black groups, and so forth. Spreading dissent in his wake, he spoke at the University of Chicago, Northwestern University, University of Wisconsin, the University of Minnesota, Oberlin, Western Reserve, Washington University of St. Louis, Vassar, Rutgers, Queens, and elsewhere. Student papers at Harvard and Minnesota ("World's Largest College Circulation") were among those covering the case. While the *Michigan Daily* supported him editorially and his right to speak on their campus, William F. Buckley, in the *Yale Daily News,* condemned him and CRC and urged forthwith passage of the Mundt-Nixon bill as an antidote to their actions. As elsewhere, Zarichny's visit to Minnesota raised hackles, just as Eisler's and Marzani's visits had previously. Students at the University of Oklahoma sent money and students at Antioch College protested directly to the Lansing administration.[96]

But there were problems. One CRC youth leader criticized Zarichny for his speech and for his "laconic manner," which did not facilitate organizing. One Madison student signalled that dirty tricks may have been played: "P.S. This letter was written over 10 days ago, but returned to me because of the incorrect address. Actually there was no incorrect address on it. Don't understand." Another Big Ten student in Bloomington, Indiana, had different concerns: "we are not as advanced or organized as effectively as some other schools. . . . the organization is opposed to the distribution of the leaflet campaign which you notified me you had on reserve for us. The fact that it emphasized Winters [sic] and not Zarichny was the cause. . . . The campaign will procede [sic] strictly on an academic freedom issue without the extraneous circumstances involving the indicted twelve. It was felt involving them might destroy the broad movement. . . . Don't ask me to explain the logic behind it all, because I can't." The conclusion could not be avoided that part of the reason for Zarichny's suspension was his attending an off-campus meeting sponsored by CRC featuring Carl Winter, no matter how much this rankled or bothered moderate students. According to one CRC youth leader, the YMCA implied that Zarichny was "being used. This must be answered! First, their own Program Paper on Civil Liberties on the campus should be quoted to them." Yet the dominant trend was represented by the comment that "we have received many requests for information . . . [many] unsolicited."[97]

The college administration in East Lansing was quite concerned about the dissemination of left-wing views, accelerated by the Zarichny case. They published privately an extraordinary document, "Michigan State College

Board of Examiners Basic College Inventory of Attitudes and Beliefs,'' which was smuggled out. It worriedly scrutinized in a primitive fashion views on Eastern Europe and progressive politics. The opposition was taking the case quite seriously, which might help to explain why Zarichny was having so much difficulty raising money for his court case. Glumly, he answered that CRC-Michigan was

> unable to give me a cent. The response from the unions is not too hopeful. Most of the larger locals are right-wing in Detroit. The left-wing locals are too broke. . . . I have become aware of what a poor organizer I am. . . . The CRC gave me a list of all the unions in Michigan from which they have been able to get any kind of support of even good resultions in the past year. This was a total of seventeen unions. . . . We wrote a letter to every union in the phone book. . . . Most unions and their exec boards out there met only once a month or once every two months. . . . I have spoken at only one union meeting.

The Detroit Lawyers Guild and CRC argued that the college had no right to inquire into his politics because of the protections of the First and Fifth Amendments, but the U.S. Supreme Court denied *certiorari* and their decision stood.[98]

St. Louis, a city that had known slavery, continued to possess a large Afro-American population, many of them recent migrants from Mississippi, and it had as well as substantial industrial base; both were major ingredients for a CRC presence that was not insubstantial. Most of the leaders of the chapter there were workers; many of the members were Black. In the late 1940s some of the principal issues issued they fought for included the refusal of the local bar association to admit Sidney Redmond, an activist Black lawyer, the "loyalty" firings of many postal and government workers (many of whom were Black), and the passage of Board Bill sixty-two, an antidiscrimination bill. For this legislation, the NAACP continued their national pattern in the Show-Me state by setting up a committee that did not "bar CRC but did not include it as a member organization . . . in the Committee." Despite the fact that in the Mound City there were "no full-time officers [and] . . . little liaison between the different city chapters . . . our method of work around issues is of a light brigade, spontaneous character." The CRC could flex its muscle when the situation called for it: "the Mayor again issued Negro History Week Proclamation at our request—sent it to us to release it to papers." The chapter also fought the good fight to have Marjorie Toliver, a Black woman, admitted to Harris Teachers College, which was predominantly white; in the usual "separate but equal" pattern, African-Americans were shunted to predominantly Black Stowe Teachers College, though it was not accredited, had a smaller library, and offered fewer courses. Black lawyers Robert Witherspoon and Redmond, who handled a number of CRC legal matters, fought the case. All this was taking place at a time when the chapter in St. Louis had a mere thirty members. But by 1952, when many chapters were swirling down the drain, their membership had jumped to between 175 and 200, according to the FBI, 75 percent of whom were "colored." In 1953, Dorothy Forest, the chapter leader, announced "CRC here is at last attaining a degree of stability and is steadily signing up new members."[99]

This rapt attention to questions of race distinguished the St. Louis chapter. In 1949 one of their key cases concerned a white St. Louis auto worker, twenty-four, who was harassed after he had invited a Black man and his wife and four kids into his home when he heard that one of the children had been bitten by a rat, "despite threats from white supremacist police, neighbors and employer elements, loss of his job . . ." Months later they had "smashed Jim Crow at Downtown dime stores' luncheon counters . . . and Dunkel's filling station at 10th and Brady has just hired a Negro filling station attendant after a city-wide boycott led by CRC." They they struck across the river in East St. Louis. The Majestic Theater denied admission to a number of Black and white CRC activists; not because they were Black, the theater claimed, but because they were red. In a trial on the charge of violating civil rights laws, a jury of eight whites and four Blacks was hung. Father Parker had come down from Chicago to lead the pickets, who faced a crowd of rednecks chanting, "kill the g-ddamn n-gg-rs and Jews"; then they attacked the picketers. But CRC won this campaign in the face of burning klan crosses, as schools and public accommodations were desegregated. The *St. Louis American,* the local Black paper, on 1 June 1950 carried a story on a special conference held in the office of Police Commissioner John English that was attended by CRC, the NAACP and "business men." The purpose of the meeting was to "consider charges made by [CRC]" that their pickets at the Majestic Theater "had been attacked and . . . police had done nothing." The result was that Mayor John T. Connors decided to "create a commission on human relations" to deal with discrimination and racism. East St. Louis by this time was well on its way to becoming a virtually all-Black northern metropolis, but with living conditions that rivaled in dilapidation those of any developing nation. CRC chapter chair, Ben Phillips, was a railroad worker who had enough local prominence to be one of two Black to run in the primary for the Board of Election commissioners in 1951. But by early 1952 it was being reported disconsolately, "We have no functioning CRC. The organization exists on paper. . . . [we] have held no meeting, socials or educational for four months. However, there is strong sentiment for CRC." Said chapter leader Eve Milton, CRC "will be built . . . when the women become involved."[100]

The FBI was quite to note that in St. Louis CRC had a "consistent policy . . . to have representatives contact the congregations of colored churches. . . . [the] representative is allowed to take up a special collection. . . . [a] religious vein has been injected into CRC meetings on numerous occasions." The chapter chair was a Black pastor who ultimately became an agency informant as the FBI turned a weakness into a strength. In any case 1950 saw further CRC advances along the anti-Jim Crow front. They organized a delegation "demanding an open hearing before the Board of Police Commissioners to protest recent cases of police brutality as well as police methods in general." This protest was ignited after a series of particularly egregious incidents, e.g., when a Black veteran, James Perry, was found dead in jail after a severe beating at the hands of police. In another victory CRC won the right of "public hearings before [the] Board of Police Commissioners in all cases involving police brutality"; this was a startling victory in that even today there are few if any police departments that have acceded to such hearings. CRC had organized a twenty-four-hour vigil, and had used leafleting and other tactics to win this fight and another that led to the desegregation of city swimming pools.[101]

These trends were continued throughout the so-called "silent fifties" by CRC in St. Louis. Their FEPC campaign received the support of the Metropolitan Church Federation, the "largest affiliation of Protestant churches" in the city. They demonstrated at the Board of Education against school segregation and protested vigorously the practice of the Adler Garment Company, which paid Black women less than white women and made them use the men's room; this action on their part prodded the union, the ILGWU, to intervene. Patterson asked his friend, the Black publisher Nathaniel Sweets, to investigate the case of Luther Jones, who bought a home in Wellston (a suburb of St. Louis) from Silverblatt Realty. He was harrassed by whites. The police chief asked him to leave home so he could apprehend the perpetrators when they showed up. He agreed reluctantly, but while he was gone, the Jones said the police chief raped his mother. Jones went to the police and FBI to no avail. The NAACP looked into the matter but dropped it. Patterson believed that Silverblatt was behind the whole thing by selling homes to blacks then harassing them away. The chapter also raised cain about literature circulated by Gerald L. K. Smith, some of which showed a Black ape kissing a white girl. They printed up en masse stamp-size stickers with the notation, "Jim Crow in St. Louis theaters Must Go." The CRC's defense of Black rights was so formidable that one of their leaders concluded "all politicians are very conscious of the CRC due to our having taken the fight for civil rights into the streets, in the form of mass delegations, into the churches and to the general public." The Black vote was becoming the "overwhelming balance of power" between the GOP and Democrats and increasingly CRC was influencing Blacks.[102]

Things were not going as well on the other side of the Mississippi. Chapter leader Ben Phillips was drafted and was in Arkansas facing a dishonorable discharge because he wouldn't sign a loyalty oath; "the worse thing that could happen to me" was his sober understatement. CRC was able to mobilize around the case of Bennie Truitt, who had stopped at a filling station in Brownsville, Tennessee, and was unable to use the restroom. He was driving to his home in Madison, Illinois. The white attendant tried to hit him with an iron pipe after a discussion about their Jim Crow policy. Truitt drew a pistol, then fled. He was caught by the police and his troubles were multiplied when it turned out that he was on parole. The chapter was also able to bring some of their forces to Springfield and about three hundred people, according to the FBI, "pushed their way" into the governor's inner office "where they demanded to know how [he] stood" on the Broyles anticommunist bill. Adlai Stevenson's demeanor went unreported by the FBI agent who had infiltrated and "heard and observed" all.[103]

Even though the East St. Louis forces played a role in beating back the Broyles legislation, St. Louis had as little luck as other parts of the country in repelling Smith Act prosecutions and organizing support for the victims. In 1949 they found that even the "VFW Post [Negro] cancelled the hall we had rented under great pressure by the FBI and VFW officers." They continued to try to work with the churches. But support here was ominous. "Rev. Obadiah Jones in his new position as minister to a church, got 50 letters on the question from his church on one Sunday"; this was the same Jones who became an informant for the FBI in his capacity as chapter chair. But his support was appreciated then, because "there aren't many at all who are willing to become associated with CRC at present—the scare has hit here, too."[104]

Before long they had to fight their own local Smith Act case when St. Louis Communist leaders were indicted, and they had problems in galvanizing support: "On the problem of lawyers—we have contacted over 40 so far on the basis I indicated in my last letter. . . . we have had no results." Grossman countered "I want to caution you that the issue is not just whether a lawyer can be got, but whether he can be got without fear at a nominal fee." Grossman traveled to St. Louis and termed his visit a "terrific boost" after engaging in discussions with a "prominent" local attorney John Raeburn, a member of a major local firm (Thomas Henning—junior and senior—were both politically prominent, were part of the firm) and had a "conference" with Patterson during his journey there; a "misunderstanding" arose over whether or not he'd work on the cases, but he did evince interest in a limited role. Ultimately Mary Kaufman rode to the rescue of the defendants, but that did not solve the similarly difficult issue of bail. Grossman sternly warned the St. Louis chapter, "You must begin this fight against the Government's program to bankrupt the whole left movement." High bail complicated further the getting of lawyers, since the money was basically coming from the same pocket. Perhaps looking ahead to an appeal on constitutional ground, Grossman added, "we are denied counsel if we can have attorneys only at the going rate." But the problem was now, not on appeal. Chapter leader Dorothy Forest revealed that "several of us did an exhaustive survey of what the pattern on bail really is in this District and of course it's considerably lower— since 1948 173 cases bonded at $500 and only 4 in 4 years at $10,000, the

highest bail set here and those for offenses carrying much larger penalties."
Eventually bail was reduced to $10,000 each, even though bail money was
still "slow." This did not allay the concerns of one supporter: "I was quite
disturbed over the lack of any realistic outlook for getting them out. I'm
afraid that locally there has developed some complacency, or rather a defeat-
ism. . . . I think the St. Louis people need help." [105]

This may have been an overly pessimistic assessment. The writer may have
forgotten the case of Jim Sage, arrested for collecting signatures on the
Stockholm Peace Appeal; CRC bailed him out, got him an attorney, who then
got him off with a fine. The chapter threw itself wholly into the local Smith
Act battle. One local leader said enthusiastically, "CRC has become more or
less engulfed by the defense committee" for the defendants. At the popular
"Veiled Prophet" parade, which originated as an antilabor orgy, they distributed ten thousand leaflets. At their urging, the *St. Louis Post-Dispatch* on
29 October 1952 protested against the "high bail" that had been set, while
weeks later the *St. Louis American* spoke similarly and raised the contradiction of the United States fighting communists although Blacks weren't free;
they likened James Byrnes to "President Malan of South Africa." They said
the defendants were not "undercover," but had been well-known in the
community for years. Patterson, perhaps recalling his own defense, stressed
involving the clergy. Thus, he said that great attention should be given to
releasing the Black defendant Marcus Murphy. Dutifully, chapter members
marched off to the NAACP, but the reception they got was not effusive.
Dorothy Forest spoke with "Dave Grant, a leading Negro Democrat who is
presently the NAACP attorney" in a raging school desegregation battle. But
he wouldn't help "because he has so many political enemies who would
welcome the chance to say, 'I always knew he was a Commie.' " [106]

The fact was that the government authorities were eager to put one CRC
leader in particular behind bars. William Sentner was president of District
Eight of the U.E. and a vice-president of the union. A bona fide working-class
intellectual, he had studied architecture at Washington University of St.
Louis and like William Z. Foster had spent time at sea. He was also a
Communist who was not reluctant to align his union and his party with CRC.
One scholar has noted how hard it was for the bosses to get workers to vote
out of office a Communist like Sentner, since he "delivered on the basic
economic questions." But the Taft-Hartley Act forced him to step down and
the Smith Act trial was the final blow. There was a St. Louis Emergency
Defense Committee coordinating Smith Act work, but they had problems
too: "It appears that the only persons we can get to endorse the Conference
[so far] are Negro leaders. . . . ACLU . . . may send observers but will take
no other part." In the spring of 1954, chapter activist Loretta Waxman
"spoke before the Negro Labor Council, the Associated Colored Women's
Club and Joint Council of Railroad and Freight Handlers. The results we

obtained were quite good." But optimism was tempered by the effort to deport Antonia Sentner, a leading member of the CRC Executive Board.[107]

At the same time that there were obstacles in the path of getting support for Communists, there was a much more positive response to the attempt to send delegates to Georgia on a mission to free Rosa Ingram. The St. Louis contingent was one of the largest and included Beatrice Allen, "who has close contact with both the Urban League, the NAACP and many of the leading lights in the Negro community." Waxman was self-critical despite the delegation's size because there were delays in mobilzing that reflected "white chauvinism and male supremacy." Terms like these, which became so prevalent years later in the United States, in the 1950s were mostly spoken in a critical or self-critical way by the left, not because the underlying phenomena did not exist, but because some chose to ignore or downplay its existence. From Pittsburgh to St. Louis, CRC was a major force in the industrial Midwest, knocking down the walls of Jim Crow, fighting for labor's rights, defending students and Communists. If this region was not the major seat of support for CRC, it surely came a close second. The only other region that could challenge its leadership was possibly the Far West.[108]

10

CRC in the Far West

One is tempted to put forward the typological paradigm that there can be no progressive national organization unless it has a base in the West, specifically in Southern California, the San Francisco Bay Area, and Seattle. Certainly, along with Detroit, these three areas produced the strongest chapters in the Civil Rights Congress. All three areas were suffused with postwar growth propelled in part by defense spending and home construction. All three were diverse ethnically. All three had a working class of diverse composition. But these were not the only areas of CRC strength. Denver, and to a lesser extent, Texas all had strong contingents, at least for a while. Like the organization itself, CRC in the West fell victim to vicious government repression.

There was little or scattered CRC activity in New Mexico, Utah, and Montana. With the region's substantial Chicano and Native American population and the vibrant Mine, Mill Workers union base, this may be deemed surprising. But according to activists in the self-proclaimed "Land of Enchantment," there were reasons explaining this result: "Don't expect anything fast here; as this is a peculiarly difficult area. . . . [there is] misinformation . . . and just straight fear. . . . If I had tried to work faster, there would not now be a CRC group forming." A year earlier in 1949 one CRC sympathizer in Albequerque posed one problem that CRC could have paid more attention to: "It would be wonderful if 'Deadly Parallel' could be put out in Spanish. One of the biggest handicaps in our work with the Mexican people is lack of material in their language." A hearty band of CRC'ers in Salt Lake City picketed the theater showing "Home of the Brave" in 1950 because of their placing Blacks in the balcony. The next year they defended John Henry Hudson, a Black man who killed his white wife and entered an involuntary manslaughter plea; this action may have been their *coup de grace* in the land of upright Mormonism. A correspondent in Great Falls, Montana, was told of the infinitesimal CRC presence there in 1951, "Although we have no organization to speak of in Montana, we do have a contact person."[1]

Arizona, principally Phoenix, presented a somewhat different picture. The fact that it had a larger Afro-American population may have accounted for this, even though Grossman had to chide chapter leader Yetta Land, lawyer and former ILD leader for not being more aggressive in recruiting them:

> I hope that you are really working at the question of poor attendance of your Negro members in membership meetings. It cannot simply be a question of transportation and early rising. In any event, you should minimize these factors by meeting, or meeting more often, in the Negro community; and by ending the meetings early enough for early rising workers. I am sure if you took affirmative steps to fully involve your Negro members in the leadership and activities of the organization you could report full participation of your Negro members. This is the experience elsewhere.

Apparently, Grossman's advice was followed, for before long there was a spurt in membership and this was during the difficult days of 1951. At one pro-McGee rally, "The overflow meeting was pronounced a huge success by all. . . . the enthusiasm at no point waned . . . 125 signed requests for more information on CRC and literature; 375 signed a mass telegram." All roads of advice did not lead to New York within the organization and it was natural for Arizona to call on L.A. for advice, as it did frequently. By late 1951, "attendance at mass meetings is 80 to 90% Negro [but] we find membership attendance is predominately [sic] white." Still that did not prevent the chapter from focusing on police brutality and pelting minstrel shows in Phoenix and Tucson; they launched a boycott of the racist T.V. shows "Amos and Andy" and "Beulah" and included their sponsor Proctor and Gamble in the boycott. In Tucson they were able to get a lawyer for a mentally ill man and bar his pending execution. As elsewhere, a principal issue was police violence. In Phoenix, police officers had a "notorious record of brutality especially against Negroes, Mexican-Americans and Indians, wholesale arrests on frame-up charges of vagrancy." Sometimes this right-wing violence tended to boomerang;

> We have been getting free radio publicity from a local facist (sic), who called for open attack and violence on our meetings. This he did a number of nights and furnished the address and time. . . . After his first harangue we had a hundred percent attendance. After his second harangue we had, in addition to a hundred percent attendance, two college students, who traveled from a suburban college to see and hear for themselves.

This sensitivity to fascist thought may have been provoked by visits there of people like Claudia Jones, Elizabeth Gurley Flynn, and Patterson; when the CRC leader arrived, three hundred people packed a two-hundred-seat church and twelve new members joined. But this 1951 visit was something of a swan song for CRC, for ultimately the Land of Goldwater ran them out of business.[2]

Oregon continued this negative pattern of islands of high spots in a sea of dismay. In 1949 after a CRC delegation visited the Immigration and Naturalization Service, they reduced bail for a Filipino activist, then freed him. At this point CRC had chapters in Portland, Astoria, and Albany, Oregon. They addressed the case of Professor Ralph Spitzer of Oregon State, dismissed for having written a letter to the *Chemical and Engineering News* in which he urged the suspension of judgment regarding the Lysenko genetics controversy. They launched a number of protests about Jim Crow in theaters, minstrel shows, and the like. But their biggest case concerned Theodore Jordan; in prison since 1933, he had been arrested for the alleged beating of a Southern Pacific Railroad steward. Torture led to his confession and an all-white jury sealed his conviction and sentenced him to be hung; pressure by the ILD led to a commutation of his sentence to life. After the demise of ILD, CRC's Prisoners Relief Committee took up the case, but then Alice Borden came along and said that her late husband, a key witness against Jordan, had confessed to the murder before his death. CRC intervened in full force. Their local attorney Irv Goodman got involved. Patterson was able to get the Marine Cooks Union to offer him a job, which would facilitate his release. Jordan was a fine writer and was like Wesley Robert Wells, another fabled CRC prisoner-client, in that regard. After CRC began to shine the spotlight, he became a trusty. "The hell I've endured through the years is over," was his premature analysis. Even though there were differences between CRC and him over strategy, Jordan realized that "This frame is expensive to the fascist framer and will cost even more before I am free." Finally, he was freed in May 1954, although it was unclear as to whether his prognostication proved prescient. The CRC chapter was hardly around long enough to savor this victory. They were constantly organizing and reorganizing. In January 1951 it was observed that "lack of membership meetings of CRC has resulted in too few people being involved in activities." By early 1952, John Daschbach was telling Patterson, "This was the first meeting Portland has had in over six months." Perhaps the key to all this was a FBI informant relating gleefully as 1953 dawned that the chapter was reorganizing "after a long period of inactivity because of internal strife."[3]

Ironically, Hawaii was one of the hotbeds of radicalism that became a hotbed of repression. The Hawaii Civil Liberties Committee was in existence for some time before it decided to affiliate with CRC in 1950. The *Honolulu Record* was a progressive newspaper that covered CRC activities and became a lightning rod attracting the reactionaries. After fourteen months of existence, in February 1949 they showed a hefty bank balance of $9,790.34. They conducted a vigorous antidiscrimination crusade aimed at public accommodations, worked actively for McGee, and avidly supported ILWU and the sugar strikers. The Smith Acts arrests of the Hawaii Seven were seen as involving peculiar "timing . . . with the final week of negotiations in [Hawaii's] great sugar industry [approaching]." This 1952 Smith Act trial, in which Telford Taylor participated, brought into being a new strategy with national impact:

> There has been a conclusion reached in New York, Pittsburgh, Seattle, St. Louis and Detroit that the expenditures for legal expenses in Smith Act trials must be severely curtailed. One simple reason for this is that there is not the money to maintain even a half or a third of the level of legal expenses maintained in the present Foley Square trial or the Los Angeles trial. Secondly, even if there were the money, it is regarded as incorrect to spend such a high proportion of the total that is spent for legal expenses, as distinguished from education, mass campaigning, etc. Consequently, the legal staffs are being built up on a very minimum level. Present plans are for a total of two attorneys in Pittsburgh, Seattle, St. Louis and Detroit.

This new edict applied especially to transcripts, "as expensive or more expensive than the attorneys. . . . it is the Government policy to deny defense in Smith Act cases, by so building up the expense of the defense that defendants are unable to meet it." The defense asked that either the government provide the transcripts or for the judge or the official trial reporter make them available. The Hawaii attorneys were warned that even if "you were so well fixed" to buy it, "you must have a responsibility to the other Smith Act cases and to the progressive movement to join in this fight." This advice was intentionally sent to Honolulu because their deep roots in the community and ties with the unions made them somewhat better off than defendants elsewhere. This also shows the role of the national office as the hub for Smith Act defense teams across the country. For example, in Hawaii a "witness named Muller" was scheduled to testify, and Grossman responded with alacrity "If he indicated that he had spent any substantial time in San Francisco, I would appreciate a picture of him if any is available, so that I can see if I have any information on him." But this massive, lengthy trial was also the death knell sounding for CRC and they were liquidated soon after it.[4]

The Lone Star state chapter of the Civil Rights Congress got off to a flying start. Its importance in the national organization is shown by the fact that there was a chapter as early as July 1946. It was formed in that month by 141 delegates from twenty-one cities. A state board of fifty people was formed that included the president of the state conference of NAACP branches, Oliver Sutton, the state director of the United Negro and Allied Veterans, Herman Wright of the Lawyers Guild, and many labor activists. A month later the *Houston Post* was telling its readers that at a five-hundred-strong NAACP rally, calling for a Klan ban, "Three white men were among the speakers" and speakers included "J. T. Kelley, youthful executive secretary of the Texas [CRC]." CRC at this time was "sharing an office, a typewriter and a mimeograph machine with the NAACP," a fact that raised ire among Association leaders in New York. On 5 August CRC and the NAACP sponsored a mass meeting on the "Georgia murders" and this was just one of many. That same year ties with the Latino community were solidified when CRC defended Humberto Silex. This Nicaraguan was a labor organizer for the Mine, Mill workers union and he had served as secretary of Local 509, as treasurer, and then as president, then as national representative for the whole union. In March 1946 a strike erupted at the American Smelting and Refining Company, a Phelps Dodge firm. The INS sought to arrest him while the strike was still on and deport him, even though he had served in the U.S. Army, had entered the United States "lawfully" and had six children born in the United States. A few years earlier they had tried to fire him for his union work and the National Labor Relations Board had him reinstated when Archibald Cox intervened on his behalf. CRC's defense of Silex solidified their ties with the important Mine, Mill Workers union as well.[5]

But after this promising statewide start, growth in the organization came to a screeching halt. In 1951 Waco was saying "the future of our small chapter here looked brighter than ever," but that proved as prescient as those predicting a boom on the eve of the Great Depression, for the Texas Attorney General was actively seeking to get them to register, pursuant to a state anticommunist law. In El Paso there were many meaty issues to attack e.g., anti-Chicano discrimination, particularly the slaying of José Morales by police in 1948. The city's ban on the use of sound trucks was also a target of CRC, but this chapter was not long for this world. The Dallas branch was monitored closely by the FBI. They were activated as a result of an immigration case involving Fred Estes of the Communist Party who had refused to testify at an INS hearing; they also handled the immigration case of José Estrada and José Cabello. Rev. R. H. J. Harris was chairman of the chapter and Augustine Estrada was treasurer. They were able to send a respectable integrated delegation to Mississippi in mid-1950 to lobby for McGee. They shared an office with the Progressive Party and carried a high profile for a while. But by late 1952 one of their leaders, the progressive attorney Sam Barbaria, was "suffering from a deep psychological disturbance." This reflected the intense pressure under which the chapter was operating. When their members went to Austin for a meeting, the FBI was able to give a detailed report of this November 1950 gathering—thirty-eight people present, half Black and half white, about four Chicanos—and the subject of the meeting was Jim Crow. By February 1951, the FBI agent on the scene was estatically bringing the glad tidings that there was no CRC office in Dallas at this time.[6]

For a while matters had proceeded swimmingly in Texas. Before the elections of 1946, CRC and their allies had had "speakers at practically every political meeting around Houston . . . on the general subject of voting." They were being recognized as a legitimate and powerful political force. In Waco the chapter was meeting in the offices of the Atlantic Life Insurance Building. In Port Arthur in 1947, CRC arranged for the release of two National Maritime Union members arrested for selling the *Daily Worker*. But the pendulum soon began to swing in the other direction. An informant for the FBI scornfully related that the CRC was operating "strictly as front for (the) Communist Party." CRC leader and progressive attorney Morris Bogdanow was kept busy. At the same time that he was running for state Attorney General on the Progressive Party ticket, he was defending in court those who had been charged with distributing Communist Party leaflets. James Green, state secretary of the party, was "picked up by the police, held overnight, pushed around and kicked, fingerprinted, grilled and maltreated." Yet the chapter was growing, with seventy at their last meeting at the "local YWCA."[7]

This pattern of growth in the face of difficulties continued. When Patterson tried to get statements from Houston attorneys on the Smith Act for a pamphlet, progressive lawyers Arthur Mandell and Herman Wright replied without enthusiasm, "Most of them refuse to even discuss it. Those who claim to be Liberals completely shy away from it." The inability to hold the center helped to bring on the McCarthyite onslaught, and Houston was a good example of this. Communists were being hit with "smear leaflets," and the picketing of an appearance by Tom Clark created mass consternation. But as of January 1950, Houston had "joined the list of chapters now issuing local news-letters," which reflected their growth. In that month they head-lined "CRC Delegates Attend State NAACP Meet" and a fundraising spaghetti dinner was held at the "Negro Elks Hall" in April. They received publicity over their handling of the contempt case against James Green, who refused to testify against Kurt and Steffi Wittenberg in deportation proceedings. The Wittenbergs had left Nazi Germany and came to the United States, but by July 1949 they wanted to return home to a developing socialist East Germany. The INS would not allow it. In the subsequent investigation, not only was the Communist Party subpoenaed, but so were CRC, the Young Progressives of America, the Progressive Party and the NAACP. Green was a particular target because of his party affiliation and background as a militant union member and activist in strikes. The NAACP and other allies were becoming apprehensive. The soon-to-be-celebrated desegregation plaintiff Herman Sweatt had been close to CRC; he spoke at the founding convention and joined in their resolutions against the white primary, segregated schools and so forth. But by the time of the war in Korea, most of these allies had fled in panic, as Bogdanow and Green related morosely.

no CRC work can be carried on here at the present time. Therefore . . . kindly discontinue all mailing to any Houston address until further notice from me personally. . . . CRC mail is snatched and any meetings held will be raided by police. . . . There are several unidentified spies within the organization who undoubtedly helped disrupt.

Though Patterson dissented vigorously, the locals thought CRC should liquidate, because "further meetings would be very dangerous for anybody who attended." The FBI declared happily in March 1952 that there had been no organized CRC activities in Houston since August 1950, right after the war commenced. In a perhaps connected development, CRC broke the news in April 1952 that so far that year there had been four "genocidal legal lynchings" of Blacks, with two having been executed for allegedly raping white women.[8]

CRC in Colorado faced problems similar to those of Texas, but they were able to hang on longer, at least in Denver. In the college town of Boulder there was an optimistic take-off. They zeroed in on discrimination at bowling alleys in 1948, established "flying squads" to investigate racial discrimination, and formed a newsletter for the "purpose of creating a means of communication . . . between all liberal organizations." But by October 1950, Robert Cook was explaining that the chapter had failed, for "two reasons":

> One was . . . a militant crusading zeal that won us before we had time or means to win friends. . . . A group of us felt that we should concentrate on local issues at first in an attempt to win some good will and confidence locally, before we launched any campaign for the Twelve or any other international issue.

They wanted to focus on "less discrimination in the hiring and serving of Negro and Spanish people . . . defense for two Negro boys framed for a manslaughter charge," etc. This was voted down and "shelved in favor of the New York cases for which we could arouse no local interest. . . . I have inquired all over town, but can find no one interested in reviving the chapter here." Most likely, this presumed local-national conflict was not so much the question as was a "liberal" approach that wilted in the face of increased repression. In any case after a promising start, the chapter did fade when confronted with a challenge from government authorities.[9]

The boom town of Denver, replete with rampant discrimination against national minorities, particularly Chicanos, provided more favorable conditions for CRC development. They attracted initial publicity when in October 1948 they marched into a half-empty hall where Tom Clark was speaking, sat down, then marched out. One of their early crusades also stirred interest in them. Gerald Winrod, a close ally of the fascist Gerald L. K. Smith, sued Communist leader Arthur Bary and others for slander after they had called him a fascist. A broad committee was set up that worked closely with the chapter. That same year they protested against the failure of the Denver University football coach to play a Black player whey they played Oklahoma A & M. They attacked head-on restrictive convenants: "We intend to encourage as many families as we can to move into 'white' districts and CRC will provide protection if needed." An outgrowth of this was their firm alliance with Blacks. They worked with the NAACP on matters like police brutality and their ranks were not lily-white: "Our membership is divided rather equally between Negro and white people." One of their main problems at this time, indicative of less-than-turbulent political waters, was a problem with the Progressive Party being reactivated and desiring to concentrate on civil rights, thereby stealing their thunder.[10]

These halcyon days continued through part of 1950. The NAACP, the Urban League, and National Association of Mexican-Americans supported the CRC petition drive for a local FEPC. Optimism was such that Denver saw itself as a regional center and made plans to start or breathe life into chapters in New Mexico, El Paso, Pueblo, Montana, Cour d'Alene, and a number of Utah towns. They called for a Patterson tour to push this drive so that "the organization will develop that much more quickly." It was not conceit that motivated their opinion that "Our reputation is beginning to spread." As part of Bill of Rights Week in late 1950, fifteen of their Black, white, and Chicano members dressed as minutemen with fife and drums and paraded through the streets during the "most crowded shopping hour before Christmas" with flags flying and banners blaring "repeal the McCarran Act." Chapter leader Nancy Kleinbord, another in a long line of female executive secretaries, said the "response was 100% favorable. . . . This is the first demonstrative action of CRC by itself." But already strains were beginning to manifest in strange ways. After Elizabeth Gurley Flynn and Arnold Johnson were sent to Denver to speak, Kleinbord plaintively inquired, "How is it that the only speakers we can get are those who must be announced as Communists? This puts the CRC exactly in the light that the red-baiters are looking for."[11]

In the spring of that fateful year Patterson had told her, "It has been our experience that police brutality cases always arouse the greatest of indignation and thereby offer very great possibilities for moving people into action." By Christmas they had such an issue, when a youth was gunned down by a police office. The chapter organized a delegation to meet with the major and district attorney. They sent a representative to the coroner's inquest, where the officer was found innocent in a snappy twenty minutes. But, in a sign of the times, "the city got the NAACP moving to red-bait" and two hours before a mass meeting planned at a Black church, the pastor pulled out. A Black mortician offered his facility, thus reinforcing the notion of the positive role often played by Black middle strata at this stage as they were more financially independent than others. Five hundred people jammed their way in. The D.A. managed to send two representatives to answer questions and a "Citizens Committee" with a youth affiliate was constituted with a CRC leader as treasurer. The united, mass struggle around this case was called by Patterson "in my opinion, the greatest civil rights victory of 1950." A trial of the officers was forced. But already other forces were working feverishly to undermine the newly found unity.[12]

The Red Scare was one of the opposition's most useful tools. Within weeks of the meeting at the mortician's, Kleinbord was despairing: "A few people have withdrawn from support and activity under terrific pressure, much of which is coming from the local NAACP . . . although many prominent people on the committee are members of the NAACP." At that same time the *Denver Post*'s page-one headline bellowed that John Blanks, a "Communist," said "he was instructed to write" the officer charged with the killing of the youth threatening to kill him; he said he had been directed by CRC to do so, which was alleged to have asked that he also write "Long live Russia" on the letter. Such a blatant red herring was stunning and shocking even in a era when dirty tricks were becoming the norm. CRC threatened a libel suit and called Blanks a "known psychopathic misfit" and said he had never been associated with the Civil Rights Congress. Correctly they pointed out that "This story attempts to cover up a civic scandal by diverting the public's attention. . . . The only thing 'red' about (CRC) . . . and the protest movement around the death of Charles Wilson III is the blood of the dead youth." But the damage had been done; many on the committee were not able to withstand the pressure. The upshot was predictable. The officer was acquitted and CRC wound up having to defend one of their members arrested in the court corridor in a frame-up, which bled their meager resources.[13]

In 1951 their momentum had been checked and the chapter was proceeding fitfully. The Pueblo NAACP invited them to speak and their reception was "excellent" by and large. Then they received an invitation to speak before the state conference of NAACP branches. One problem, according to Kleinbord, was some CRC members' "hatred of NAACP," which she called in a moment of understatement, "very unconstructive." Her view was to work with them "until they've completely exposed themselves." Her optimism was borne out when the state conference passed a resolution "unanimously" backing McGee and the redbaiting of CRC was answered by the pastor who served as state chairman who praised them, the left generally, and the Communists—no mean feat in early 1951.[14]

This negative and positive dialectic proceeded uninterrupted in this year. On the cases of the CP-Eleven and McGee, Kleinbord found that "Labor guys are wiring but did not want their names, so far anyway, on the amicus brief. . . . we have gotten such replies as . . . 'if the CRC wouldn't be the sponsor' and 'I'll sign, but not put down my union and title'. . . . and some rejections for 'security' reasons." When Patterson finally made it to Denver, CRC had to go to court in order to get the school board to rent them a space; they won. For a time, their chapter chairperson resigned, due to "health, differences in methods of work." For her part Kleinbord cited "white chauvinism," his "reformism," and his "seeking to make CRC acceptable." Ultimately they kissed and made up, but this discontent at the highest level could not be papered over. On the other hand, they sent a sizeable delegation to Richmond to lobby for the Martinsville Seven defendants and the impact of harsh Jim Crow on them was apparent to all: "We got even the most redbaiting ministers to say prayers. . . . on 4 February we tried to keep battle up all night with person-to-person phone calls." Weeks later they were meeting with the governor on a bill to deprive "subversives" of unemployment compensation. As a result of CRC pressure, the *Denver Post* condemned the bill and it was defeated. At the same time contrary trends were evident. There were continuing complaints of fear to sign their petitions and "rejections for 'security' reasons." The "Honorable Earl Mann," a longtime friend of Patterson, "due to pressures from the FBI . . . could not welcome him in Denver as before." The editor of a local Black paper agreed reluctantly to print one of their releases, while claiming he was "taking his 'life' in his hands doing it."[15]

The Treasury Department told them they could not be authorized as a nonprofit organization, even though they appeared to meet all the prerequisites. Actually, this setback for the chapter was in a sense a repetition of past times. In the early days of CRC in 1947 a right-wing religious paper, the *Western Voice,* redbaited them and their attorney furiously, while giving no quarter to the progressive weekly *Challenge,* which often went to bat for the Civil Rights Congress. Kleinbord herself was jailed for a while when Patricia Blau, Jane Rogers, and other left leaders were called before a grand jury in September 1948 and asked pointblank if they were Communists. But these early reversals hardly prepared them for the post-Korean barrage. They did not wilt immediately. Despite their checkered relationship with the NAACP, diplomatic ties with the National Mexican-American Association continued. During the summer of 1951, in a gesture redolent with symbolism, the chapter bested them in a softball game 27–18 even though they lent them players. After CRC "spadework" around "1st amendment" cases, an ACLU chapter was formed, illustrating directly how their presence and plowing of the ground led others to come along and plant seeds; while a Communist-led CRC would be frowned on, a liberal-led ACLU would not. The chapter was viewed so favorably by the national office that Grossman asked Kleinbord for a "50 word article . . . on how to break thru into the columns of a big city newspaper." Part of this success was their spirit of innovation, as shown by their 1776 foray through a shopping area at Christmas and their highlighting of the fact that McGee was executed on Truman's birthday.[16] But by 1952 turmoil in the chapter was apparent. Kleinbord had been replaced by another woman, Kathryn Bardwell. Patterson had another concern: "While composition is not the most vital factor I would like to know what proportion and who, are white." A few months later, that high-minded concern had become transmuted into another: "I do not know whether the Denver chapter is functioning at all." Bardwell informed him that "We have had to give up our office . . . [though] there is an active interested corps of about fifteen."[17]

But reports of the chapter's death were exaggerated. In 1954 their pamphlet "To Stop Police Brutality End Discrimination on Juries" was something of a runaway political bestseller. They demanded that Chicanos be included on juries, demanded a grand jury investigation of police brutality, and translated it all into Spanish in a pioneering move. They vehemently denounced a *Rocky Mountain News* series connecting Chicanos with Denver crime. Painstakingly they refuted the series point by point with statistics, photos, and analysis. The local Smith Act trial in 1954 also found them knee-deep in the muck of battle. Again the Chicano community was stirred by CRC. This was due in part to the indictment of Anna Correa Bary, wife of the Colorado Communist Party chairman and a leader in her own right, the "1st person of Mexican descent jailed under Smith Act. . . . highest bail for any Colorado woman . . . $25,000." Their literature on her case used cartoons effectively—a useful CRC tactic nationally—and spoke movingly of her father, Jesus Correa, who had helped to organize beet workers. Only thirty years old, she was a mother and member of Amalgamated Clothing Workers union. She was also a member of Local 21 of the United Packinghouse Workers. In a 1948 strike she with others, "lay down on the railroad tracks to prevent the company from moving . . . meat product." With all that, CRC faced its customary problems. They talked to 140 lawyers who refused to take the case and again Mary Kaufman rode to the rescue. Court-appointed lawyers that the defendants disdained didn't want "communism" to be involved in the case, though the Communists themselves believed that in a blatant political prosecution it would be foolhardy to ignore or downplay politics. In 1954 the CRC chapter's name had been changed to the Colorado Committee to Protect Civil Liberties, but this did not fool or deter the Subversive Activities Control Board who sought to get this CRC "front" to register. Many stool pigeons and infiltrators were called to testify and the liquidation of the organization didn't halt the inquisitors, who continued to chase them down in 1957.[18]

Just as rape cases animated the South and the Christoffel and Zarichny cases energized the Midwest and the Smith Act cases occupied the attention of the East, the cause célèbre for the West was the case of Black prisoner Wesley Robert Wells. His extended battle to be free and to escape an arduous sentence was a precursor of the fight twenty years down the road of George Jackson; in fact there were striking parallels between these individuals and their cases. Work with prisoners was a solemn obligation for CRC and they felt they could not shirk it.

Just as CRC criticized the disproportionate allotment of death penalty sentences to African-Americans, equally they criticized Black rates of imprisonment. The 1950 census showed that 10 percent of the nation's population was Black, but between 1930 and 1952, of the 3,219 men and women executed, 1,732 were Black and 1,449 white. Of the 365 executed for rape, 328 were Black; 1,386 whites and 1,381 Blacks had been executed for murder; of the 1953 executions in seventeen Southern states, 1,408 were Black, with Georgia leading with 298, followed by North Carolina with 252, and Texas with 230—all sites of CRC organizing. There was a similar disproportion when it came to imprisonments, with Black youths being special targets.

Almost all Black prisoners were under the age of thirty-four, with the greatest number between twenty-five and twenty-nine.[19]

There was obviously a need for CRC to attend systematically to the needs of this oppressed group. Their mission was not only to keep them out of jail, but not to forget them once they found themselves behind bars. In one poignant dialogue with a Black New Jersey prisoner, Patterson synthesized his views: "It is a terrible thing that men like you . . . are forced because of your color to spend the best part of your life behind prison bars. . . . Across my desk come tens of letters not only from men, but from women as well, whose conditions are similar to your own." Hence, CRC's Prisoners Relief Committee and Bulletin were established. They published stamps to be stuck on letters and elsewhere focusing on the cases of McGee, the CP-Eleven, Rosa Ingram with the notation, "Help Free Political Prisoners—Prisoners Relief Committee." They fought for "extra visits from families and friends, special mail privileges, special attention to diet and health. . . . [CRC] seeks to protect Negro prisoners in the Jim Crow prisons. It fights for parole and releases." When a prisoner needed sheet music for his trumpet, they responded. They had a holiday doll project with special Black dolls for the children of prisoners. Vito Marcantonio, chair of the committee, averred in December 1950 they had "been sending a monthly check to each political prisoner and his family on our list, year in and year out . . . [for] toys and clothing for the children" and soap, and shoes, for the inmates. This campaign was not viewed with equanimity by their opponents. The *Pittsburgh Press* joined a chorus in 1953 denouncing one of their pamphlets as "Communist propaganda" that had reached a "new low."[20]

From the early days of CRC, the needs of prisoners were a priority. This was part of the inheritance bequeathed them by the ILD. In 1946 they were responding to long letters from George Crawford in a Virginia prison, who like so many prisoners had time to set his thoughts down on paper at length. This could present a problem, as one CRC staffer informed him: "the one thing that grieves me is that I am not able to respond in like measure. We are so overtaxed here with work and times have become so difficult that we often must put off the important personal things." They did, however, tend to his requests, getting him a *Life* magazine subscription, suspenders, and a book on Joe Louis. Crawford, an Afro-American, had been convicted of murdering two white women in 1933 and sentenced to two life sentences in a trial described as unfair:

Crawford is only one of many prisoners to whom we send a monthly stipend for cigarettes and other incidental expenses. In addition we send similar monthly allowances to members of the families of many prisoners most of whom are Negros and others who were convicted for activities related to the building of the labor movement during the 1920s and early 1930s. There are 26 of these men who are serving sentences at the present time. . . . There are also monthly stipends being sent by us to the widows of the men killed in the Memorial Day Massacre.

CRC was like a big brother or sister to these prisoners. They had a drive to obtain *PM* subscriptions for them all and did such small but important tasks as repairing a razor blade sharpener and sending it back. They helped prisoners to find jobs upon their release, thus performing a task that should have been done by the state.[21]

Lack of resources did not always allow CRC to respond. In 1948 they were confronted with the case of Robert Denton. He had received the death penalty though he was alleged to be legally insane and would not have been convicted if he had been examined by psychiatrists. This Oklahoman had been jailed in 1934 at the age of nineteen. Though allegedly insane then, he was reputed to be sane in 1948 and owned a business. His brother said, "His business is a quite well known [music publishing house]. . . . His insanity is a statewide joke." According to his brother, Denton had "lost his citizenship, suffers daily financial loss because of claims that he is insane, yet he is unable to get a hearing before a jury on the latter issue, he has never had the legal protection accorded by statute to the insane, is now barred from mental examination or treatment. . . . The sanity issue is used to bar him from clemency hearing, of course, but has led to serious property entanglements and loss, as well. It is the only case of its kind in Oklahoma history." Despite this eloquent plea, Benjamin Goldring of CRC's legal committee was unable to help: "I have read the brief you forwarded to me. . . . We are unable to render any assistance in the case. We necessarily must limit ourselves to the broadest possible issues, and we are [at] present fully committed in pending legal cases." CRC had good intentions but it could not act as a legal services program, accepting every case that came through the door.[22]

But more typical was their response to Clyde Allen, "an old I.L.D. case," due for parole in 1950. They arranged for him to get the *New York Age* regularly. A CRC staffer inquired, "Do you smoke? Have you need for a few dollars? Please write and let us know." Allen's was the prototypical case that CRC handled. A Black man had been accused of hitting women over the head and raping them, and this Brooklynite had been accused unjustly of being the perpetrator. He was tried by an all-white jury and given twenty-five years. The public "was excluded from the trial and Allen was tried in private," said his proponents; they added, "[the record shows a] list of one hundred and thirty-three errors of law committed by the judge." When he was released finally, CRC found him a job. By 1951 the Prisoners Relief Committee was flying high, for the simple reason that there were so many political prisoners to service. A call went out when McGee's wife, Rosalee, was "threatened several times. . . . [she] is desperately in need of medical attention. She is suffering from an infected foot. . . . She hasn't worn a shoe in [some] time." While their opponents scored them for using and abusing clients like McGee,

CRC was quietly and effectively attending to their most profound and their most trivial needs and not reaping publicity dividends in the process. They appealed for shoes for Ingram's children, for "soap and shaving supplies" for Major Benton, and they obtained religious reading material for McGee. Finding jobs was a constant concern: "If you or your chapter, or your organization know an employer in your community willing to guarantee employment to a political prisoner, please write [CRC]." Little wonder Rosalee McGee gratefully exclaimed, "I want you to know that I feel that you did all that could be done to save McGee."[23]

Attending to prisoners' and their families' needs without attacking the underlying causes of their problems would have been quite unlike CRC. Jim Crow in prison, with Black prisoners consistently receiving the raw end of the bargain, was assailed frequently. In May 1950 CRC attorney Charles Garry, later the chief lawyer for the Blank Panthers, filed suit on behalf of CRC against Earl Warren and others, not only based on the U.S. and state constitutions but on the UN Charter, claiming discrimination against Black prisoners at San Quentin and Folsom prisons. Blacks were "forced to assemble for meals in lines separate from those of the white prisoners and are forced to eat separately." This prevented their "proper rehabilitation." Ben Davis filed a similar *mandamus* petition against the federal prison system's practice of segregation. Terre Haute, Indiana, where he was being held, had 1,200 inmates, 250 of them Black. The latter entered the mess hall separately, sat separately. Black prisoners whose behavior was "meritorious" and "exemplary" were not allowed the same privileges as whites who reached this status, e.g., access to the library, the recreation room, and daily showers after work. These pioneering suits were the cutting edge that ultimately sliced the cancer of Jim Crow from the prison system. Defending the reds was also viewed as a high priority. Maryland Communist and Smith Act defendant Philip Frankfeld had been imprisoned in Atlanta and in 1954 he was being harassed. He was "charged with attempting to proselyte [sic] Marxist ideology among fellow prisoners" and placed in "the 'hole.'" He had contracted an eye infection and Patterson demanded that a physician be allowed to examine him. But the result was that "he will only be able to distinguish light with his left eye and the use of the right eye may also be lost."[24]

CRC's politically humanitarian concern for the imprisoned was revealed in full relief in the case of Wesley Robert Wells. According to John Howard Lawson, "Wells is a hero of our time, not because there is anything spectacular . . . in his courage, but because it is so common, so rooted in the life and trials of his people." Certainly Wells was a cause célèbre in the state of California. Earl Warren and Goodwin Knight definitely would never forget him as they were the butt of many CRC petitions and demonstrations on his behalf. This Afro-American was one of three children born in Fort Worth. His mother died; he didn't remember his mother. He was sent to Denver to live with an uncle who was a preacher, then to Los Angeles to live with an aunt who had three children of her own and no husband. Six children were residing in two rooms. There was hunger. They lived near a swamp. This was a standard recipe for what followed. In 1921 when he was twelve he was sent to reform school for two years for stealing a car. By 1928 he was in San Quentin and in Folsom by 1931; in both prisons he faced racism, beatings, fights, and solitary confinement. He faced down the guards who had a quirky habit of shooting at prisoners and he was in solitary from August 1942 through March 1943; he was saved from execution a few times. The results on him were predictable: "I have been mean, hard and perhaps at one time or another, even savage. . . . I have scars on my person I will take to my grave that will testify to some of the brutal treatment I've received at the hands of both inmates and my prison keepers." As this passage demonstrates, Wells was a highly articulate and well-spoken prisoner and an excellent writer; his physically imposing presence made him even more impressive. But by the early 1950s, another prison beating had led to "permanent injury to my throat and larynx . . . the damage was irreparable."[25]

Wells was scheduled for execution on 27 January 1950, while CRC was in the midst of trying to save the lives of McGee, Washington, the Martinsville defendants, and others. He hadn't killed anyone, but while serving a life sentence, "he committed physical violence against a prison guard," i.e., he threw a cuspidor at him after being " 'stir crazy' . . . Jim Crow and prison terror had gotten him," though he was not allowed to testify about this at the trial. The Armenian-American lawyer, Charles Garry, who modestly called himself the "Streetfighter in the Courtroom" and a "People's Advocate," was on the case. Long close to the left, the Black Panther Party eventually was convinced by Patterson to become a client of Garry's. But it was Black Lawyer and eventual Circuit Court Judge Cecil Poole who hooked Garry up with Wells in 1949. Garry took a political approach to the case, believing that Wells had not been jailed for stealing or fights or for throwing a spittoon: "No, Wells was punished because he demanded equal treatment . . . because he refused to prostrate himself before prison officials, because he sought always to maintain his dignity, humanity, independence." But even the celebrated Garry was not beyond reproachful criticism. One L.A. CRC member was not too impressed with him. "Charles Garry, undoubtedly an intelligent lawyer . . . had the disrespect to come to the meeting unprepared. . . . he used profanity and insulted the religious people in the audience by his reference to 'God.' " Charlotta Bass was at this Wells rally, and she was criticized for her collection speech. Patterson was scored for only mentioning Wells twice and for focusing on McCarthy "Was [he] just using the name of Wells to get them to a meeting in defense of victims of the Smith Act." Yet this was virtually the sole dissenting voice, for most people there saw the effort that freed Wells as a model of the genre. He did not come out of jail until 1974, at which point CRC was no more than a misty memory in the minds of most and Wells himself was virtually broken by his harrowing prison experience; but for the CRC's crusade, however, he probably would have died in prison.[26]

The Wells case was a legal tangle that bounced around the U.S. court system like a pinball. State court, federal court, state court, back and forth it went. A key decision came in the October term of the California Supreme Court in 1953. Garry along with George and Barrington Parker argued forcefully in their brief that when in April 1947, Wells hit the guard, "[it] became a death penalty offense because the Adult Authority failed to fix Wells' sentence for a previous offense. Unfixed, the sentence was presumed to be for life, whereby the assault became a crime punishable by death. If fixed, it would not have been fixed at life. . . . If Wesley Robert Wells is executed, he will be the only person ever put to death . . . for an assault where no life was taken." Wells' fear for his safety was excluded from evidence, and the court held this to be an error, but it affirmed the conviction and death sentence by a four-to-three vote. The battle shifted to pressing the governor to commute this sentence. And the battle to get publicity became critical, along with obtaining mass support.[27]

But before they could get to this point, Wells' supporters had to exert tremendous pressure. Prominent southern California Black publisher Charlotta Bass was accurate in her assessment of the defense committee: "Perhaps the greatest concentration of people from all walks of life in the state of California—labor, the Negro people, civil libertarians, churches, women's clubs, youth organizations—joined in a great defense committee." Their impact was so far-reaching that even Walter Winchell in his nationwide broadcast felt constrained to speak positively about Wells. This year of 1950 was a key one for the prisoner, who wrote many of his own legal briefs and taught himself to play the trumpet in prison. In April Grossman informed Patterson that Governor Warren was receiving "3–4,000 signatures on petitions. . . . two or three times a week he gets a letter with a petition in it." This led to the usual problem: "(the NAACP) is both jealous of us and afraid of the 'reds.' " Indeed, despite the case's notoriety, they did not have to face a serious effort by the Association horning in in their typical manner. Also helpful was that Governor Warren was "very sensitive during the present election campaign: though . . . many people, including many Negro leaders, react against the case at first, because of Wells' criminal record." Still, *Ebony* joined Winchell in focusing on the case and Grossman "worked very closely" with the writer.[28]

This was the prelude to a CRC delegation that went to meet with Governor Warren. Composed of church, labor, and civic leaders, their numbers were so imposing that he would not allow all forty-five to enter his office. Undaunted by the rebuff, they demanded freedom for Wells and an end to segregation in prison. Nonplussed, the future famous civil libertarian asked CRC leader Ida Rothstein if she were a Communist. He asked in the form of a statement "isn't it true that [CRC] is a communist organization?" He then turned to the pastor, perhaps in search of divine guidance, and posed the same query. Apparently not satisfied with their response, he then charged that CRC was "merely using Wells as an instrument to try and commit sabotage of our courts and institutions." Not shaken by this tirade, the delegation continued calmly to press their point of view in this lengthy two-hour meeting. A similar occurrence took place when another CRC delegation, this time "90% trade unionist" went to see the warden of the prison. Among other things, Wells was being prevented from corresponding with certain individuals, in presumed contravention of his First Amendment rights, and he was being charged with being a "ringleader" of a supposed "riot" by thirteen inmates on death row. They demanded more exercise time, writing materials, and lights on after midnight. Wells was thankful: "it is really gratifying, in these trying days, to know that I have so many friends. . . . I appreciate your kind intentions and efforts." With defiance he alleged that if he were a "mad dog," as Warren had averred, then "I am the result of a cruel and inhuman system." All this lobbying paid off and Wells received a reprieve from death row. In June 1951 Grossman provided Garry with his analysis: "I should think that we should put enough pressure on Pat Brown so that he will not dare appeal the decision." He continued, "his case symbolized more than any other the jim crow in the prisons and establishes the responsibility of all departments of government for a jim crow policy." Despite Wells' heartfelt thanks they remained concerned about his attitude, "Is it perhaps that he has got the impression that all we do, is to save men from the electric chair, and having done so, we move on to other cases?" But Grossman need not have worried for Garry reassured him, "Frankly, Aubrey, of all the people he has had contact with he thinks more of you than of any other person."[29]

Wells was perspicacious enought to see who his friends were, for it is true that his defense committee made a quantum leap in effectiveness after Grossman returned to the West Coast in 1953. After organizing on a national and international scale in New York, California was somewhat mismatched against the hard-working lawyer cum organizer. At the same time an unnamed informant told Grossman that Wells had "dissatisfaction with Garry." That may have been true, but there was no doubt that one of the most formidable mobilizations of public opinion for any prisoner took place in California in the 1953–54 period. There were letters from "England, New Zealand, Sweden all pledging support." It was hard not to be impressed with Wells' case. He had gone to San Quentin as a teenager for possession of stolen clothing on an original sentence of one to three years. Movingly, Patterson stated "His body is covered with knife wounds inflicted by other prisoners seeking to 'curry official favor.' . . . He has spent a total of six years in solitary." The guard whom he hit with the cuspidor had been back at work for only a few days and was believed to have been skittishly provoking Wells, who thought he was trying to fulfill the court-imposed death sentence. Marcel Frym, a faculty member at the University of Southern California and

Director of Criminological Research at the Hackers Foundation for Psychiatric Research and Education in Beverly Hills, sent Governor Knight a lengthy letter disputing the efficacy of the death penalty, quoting numerous studies, and noting, "I do not usually respond to requests for intercession in cases of impending execution." The Black press joined in. The publisher of the *San Francisco Sun-Reporter* "promised" Patterson "favorable comment in his paper" and entree to the Elks, on whose Civil Liberties Committee he served. Judge A. A. Scott of the Superior Court in Los Angeles was so moved by articles in Bass' *California Eagle* "Championing the cause" of Wells that he moved into action: "I have written him that I will do all within my power to help him, in the hope that in my small way I can help to prevent a human tragedy."[30]

There were two important gatherings in 1953 that helped to galvanize such sentiment. In August there was a statewide meeting that led to the printing of a simple one-page leaflet for "factory gate distribution"; twenty-five thousand were designated for Los Angeles in the first run. Instructions were explicit: "Each area to seek advice from a white minister on how to move white churches. . . . Get a story in the Churchman, Catholic Worker, the Witness. . . . [Do a] state-wide mailing to all lawyers. . . . [issue] a special [Peoples World] supplement on Wells' case." This was followed by a late September meeting in Los Angeles. Legal issues were raised here. Wells was eligible for parole in 1944 but had been given "twenty-five years to life" sentence, an indeterminate sentence of the kind that became so infamous years later. Actions flowed from these meetings. In the Fillmore there were CRC "brigades" going to churches to get signatures on petitions. Forty Black attorneys, twenty-four Bay Area physicians, the ILWU, and others came out in support. In October Patterson spoke at Friendship Baptist Church in San Diego before a "large group." In this right-wing bastion, the church "received several calls protesting" his appearance.[31]

But a tidal wave had been unleashed that even the reactionaries found it difficult to stem. There was a setback that Patterson saw. In November 1953 the Supreme Court "refused to review the Wells case," following the elevation to chief justice of Earl Warren, who had persistently denied Wells' clemency plea when he was governor. Grossman was skeptical at first about church support: "generally speaking ministers do not have the organizational experience required to do the job [but] such a person would be better equipped to work in a broad kind of way than anyone that CRC could find or be able to convince." Jack Greenberg of the NAACP, after conducting what he termed an "on-the-spot examination," came to the conclusion that "the Wesley Roberts Wells case does not warrant NAACP intervention, in that no question of civil rights is presented in it." He did not grace his interlocutor with a definition of "civil rights." An aide made it clear that John Foster Dulles "has made it a practice not to intervene in matters which are not within the jurisdiction of the Department of State."[32]

This was all the storm before the calm. Over 50,000 signatures on petitions were presented to the governor. A newsletter on Wells was being issued regularly. In March 1954 Patterson instructed Grossman on which path to trod:

> I was wondering if in the clemency fight it was not time now for demonstrative actions such as picket lines around the state offices in San Francisco, Oakland, Los Angeles, and whenever else possible, perhaps being manned for 2 or 3 hours in the busy time of day. Some dramatic action will now be a logical step. The possibility of trucks with Wells' picture and the word free Wesley Robert Wells on the side being used on the streets. . . . I know I am bringing coals to Newcastle with these suggestions and yet, I am presumptuous enough to advance them.

CRC members moved to implement these proposals. It was suggested in activating unions to "be there before the meeting starts. . . . Remember: most unions start on time." They must have been early indeed for there were a number of notable successes with workers and others. Fifty trade unions, 575 California attorneys, 500 ministers, several hundred doctors, and others endorsed Wells' call. This included Dan Del Carlo of the San Francisco Building Trades Council, carpenters in Mill Valley, unions in Britain, New Zealand, and other parts of the Commonwealth. George Christopher, soon to be mayor of San Francisco and then president of the Board of Supervisors endorsed the defense effort. But even his weighty support was outweighed by that of labor. UAW and USWA locals, UE and ILWU locals were joined by the San José NAACP and other Association chapters in Marin County and Monrovia; eleven newspapers, including virtually all the Black ones and others like the "Valley Jewish News" joined in.[33]

This press support, and particularly the press coverage, proved critical in shaping public opinion about the case. The *San Francisco Chronicle* observed slyly that "the world political situation has given him propaganda value in some quarters" but praised Wells personally for becoming a "chess expert," while pointing out that the law that led to his increased sentence after tossing the cuspidor at the guard required "malice aforethought," which he clearly did not have. In an editorial they noted that this law, Section 4500 of the California Penal Code, was "enacted in hysteria some years ago. . . . This draconian law should be re-examined. . . . It can fairly be said that he was deliberately and designedly entrapped—we do not think the word too strong—into committing his offense." They couldn't resist however bashing the Communists "ever eager for a 'martyr' to exploit." The *Los Angeles Mirror* told their readers that two thousand people had signed a letter to the governor asking that he spare Wells' life. The *Bay Area Journal* lamented the convolution that had sent the case three times to the California Supreme Court and twice to the U.S. Supreme Court. The *Seattle Daily Times* and the *Pittsburgh Courier* were among the papers joining the stampede. Papers in

Paris and Rome covered the case and the speech by Josephine Baker at a large meeting in the French capital received maximum publicity. This latter incident caused Patterson to remark, "It is my opinion that 'WRW' will be saved but the credit will go to Walter Winchell nationally and that he will be projected as a great savior of the Negro people. Do not forget that the Josephine Baker suit against him is scheduled to begin in March. This is a very interesting phenomenon and has a direct relation to his activity."[34]

According to acting CRC-SF secretary Frances Schermerhorn, both the *Los Angeles Tribune* and the *Peoples World* "made hay on the Wells case so far as circulation is concerned." She contended that the *Chronicle's* support was motivated by partisan politics in that they were opposed to the Hearst press and its support for a Democratic candidate for governor. Whatever the case, Wells received clemency in 1954 on the recommendation of Governor Goodwin Knight. And this was the direct result of a massive campaign launched by CRC in California that made him a household name.[35]

Southern California, an area experiencing rapid and dislocating postwar growth, was a bastion of support for Wells and CRC. However, this strength did not include San Diego, then as now a right-wing and military stronghold with heavy anti-Chicano discrimination. The CRC chapter there did innovative work in the area of bilingualism. They put out a large English-Spanish flyer designed to inform people about their rights: "Attention Mexican Workers—These Are Your Rights. . . . Do Not Talk . . . Do Not Sign . . . Do Not Consent [to voluntary deportation]. . . . Demand An Interpreter. . . . Demand To See a Search Warrant. . . . Demand To See A Warrant For Your Arrest. . . . Demand The Right To Notify Your Family, A Friend or a Lawyer. . . . If You Do Not Have a Lawyer [call CRC]. . . . Demand Bail . . . Demand a Hearing." This was obviously designed to foil the INS raids that were terrorizing the Spanish-speaking community. There were overtures made to the Black community also. They interceded on behalf of Henry, "leader of local Muslim of Islam cult [sic]," charged with assault on a police officer. They came to the aid of Emory Collier, a thirty-four-year-old Black man who had been convicted of rape and assault by an all-white jury of four women and eight men. When the "crime" took place, there was evidence showing he was elsewhere. One of the alleged victims changed her story identifying him. The racism whipped up was thick: "The authorities attempted to harass white persons attending the trial by pointing them out to a photographer." CRC also worked closely with the Rosenberg Committee but generally in the organizational constellation, their star shone dimly. Again part of the reason may have been government repression. FBI reporters were present at their meetings: "The first CRC open meeting was held in San Diego on 25 February 1949 and was attended by approximately 150 persons. The pattern of the meeting was to 'ridicule' every one who was opposed to the Communists or who attempted to link the Communist program with that of the labor unions."[36]

Naturally the opposite was true for the home of stars, Los Angeles. A substantial Black population had developed there, consisting mostly of migrants from the southwest and they flocked to the factories that dotted the landscape. From the founding of CRC in 1946 the Los Angeles chapter was one of its strongest units. They had strong working-class leadership. On their board at various times were representatives of the ILWU, the Food, Tobacco and Allied Workers union, the United Furniture Workers union, UAW. The veteran labor leader Wyndham Mortimer served as chairman of their labor committee. Also important for a place that encompassed Hollywood, the chapter attracted the requisite number of prominent personalities, which helped to attract the nonprominent. Their sponsors in 1946 included Artie Shaw, Lena Horne, Dalton Trumbo, John Garfield, Gregory Peck, Frank Sinatra, and others. They were also blessed with sound leadership in Emil Freed, Marguerite Robinson and Anne Shore. Freed was a graduate of Manual Arts High School and the University of Southern California in 1923. An electrical engineer by training, he was also an inventor of some note. He was a member of the International Association of Machinists, Local 311, the NAACP (CRC and the Association picketed Sears jointly over the issue of job discrimination), the National Association of Mexican-Americans and the National Jewish Welfare Board; in 1948 he participated in the "Blood for Israel" campaign. Obviously ecumenical in spirit, he was arrested and jailed in the late 1940s because of his militance on the picket line during a Hollywood strike. His mass contacts were exhibited then and he received hundreds of letters of all kinds; forty-two on May Day of 1949 alone. Averill Berman, a studio labor chief, expressed the view of many workers: "We were talking about people who made a real, unselfish contribution to the labor movement and your name naturally came up."[37]

Freed's influence was reflected in the fact that the chapter had not only a trade union division but a transit workers committee, garment workers committee, and so forth. La Rue McCormack, who had served eight long years as executive director of ILD, was CRC's labor coordinator in the area. Like other CRC chapters, in Los Angeles CRC was not derelict in attending to Blacks' rights. Margie Robinson, chapter organizational secretary, took Patterson's words to heart:

> He who has the leadership of the Negro people for equal rights, has the leadership of the whole American movement for constitutional liberties, civil and human rights. . . . there is no problem, no issue, no project . . . that takes priority over the Negro question.

It was this typical Pattersonian statement that some saw as denigrating or ignoring labor, but he did not agree. In any case the chapter was not bereft of victories in cases of extradition (Joseph Brocks, Lester Tate, Dott Turner), frame-ups (Bucky Walker, Joseph White, Sam Walker), police brutality (Alvin Jones, Rubio). This success was reflected in members and dollars. In 1951 when repression was keen they had about a thousand members and that number showed up for an affair honoring Patterson. In December 1948 alone they took in $4,037.21. Because of such support they exerted wide influence. It was not surprising, for example, that the Southern California Civil Liberties Union was more to the left than the ACLU nationally—and remains so; their top lawyer, A. L. Wirin, worked closely with CRC attorneys.[38]

The lawyers panel of the chapter was probably the best in the organization. One conference they held brought together thirty-five attorneys, of whom thirty-three signed cards "to join up . . . The Conference was chaired by a leading member of the Bar . . ." and an executive committee of eleven people was formed. These industrious lawyers built a brief bank, did "research work, trial of cases," motions. This was at a time when "all members of our panel know that the Civil Rights Congress is on the Attorney General's list of alleged 'subversive organizations.'" CRC lawyers like Ben Margolis, Fred Steinmetz, John McTernan were not only progressive politically but were some of the top litigators in the nation. They did not escape the gaze of the FBI, which took note in 1950 of their record: ninety-eight cases tried, thirty-three won, three lost, the rest in process. This total included twenty-five "Mexican" cases, fourteen Black, twenty-one "political minority" cases as the three biggest categories. By March 1952 CRC's bail fund had already secured freedom for fifty-one foreign-born persons from the clutches of the INS and was assisting hundreds of victims of police brutality.[39]

There were certain problems between the Los Angeles chapter and the national office. When Patterson became national leader in 1948, he agreed that "the connection between the national CRC and the local chapter is hazy and unproductive." Anne Shore was displeased with staffing in New York: "I notice that we are presented with a new addition to the staff of CRC . . . without any opportunity to discuss the question. . . . this method of administration is one of the causes for our difficulties in working as a national organization." But Los Angeles operatives were consoled by the coming of the new Patterson regime: "how much I appreciate your letters. What a difference! This is the first time in my two and a half years with CRC that I've ever gotten an answer to a letter of mine. . . . It is wonderful to get some real political leadership." Despite this euphoria, while still in California Grossman was hesitant about the capability of Milt Wolff and about the high turnover: "the leading personnel of CRC has [sic] been changed at least as frequently as French cabinets. . . . We cannot follow ILD experience." The chapter had its own difficulties, however, in organizing members: "The problem appears to be how to keep them activated in between hot cases."[40]

These Los Angeles members were grouped in about a score of local branches and this division meant they had to concentrate on local, citywide, statewide, and national cases. Since this was California, there were CRC "folk singers," and productions of plays and cultural activities playing a crucial role in the chapter's life; they sponsored films on race prejudice and an "authentic Indian dance film." They held observances of Negro History week regularly. They pledged to defend anyone ousted from public housing because of membership in an organization on the Attorney General's list. They held six-week classes on issues like the Bill of Rights, *Brown v. Board of Education,* the history of civil rights struggles, etc. They held annual carnivals. And like chapters nationally, they encountered the hot breath of reaction. In 1952 when they put together a demonstration about the Rosenbergs, eight marines harassed them with anti-Semitism, broke their placards, and "molested" women.[41]

Los Angeles participated fully in national campaigns, which was facilitated by the production of numerous leaflets and publications. Genocide petition sales were respectable and the trip of Bessie Mitchell to Los Angeles was a big hit. Over $400 was raised for the defense of the Trenton Six: "We reached many new forces. . . . The case has now become one of major importance to the city [though] . . . we did not reach enough of the more conservative channels, such as our Negro churches." During her stay in Los Angeles, Shore actually demanded a national program from Patterson, contending that its absence "tends to limit the program to the Coast."[42]

There were enough citywide cases to keep the Los Angeles chapter busy and the Wells case was the leading state case, along with the Smith Act prosecution of California Communists. Like San Diego, members in Los Angeles were sensitive to the question of bilingualism and printed a number of publications in Spanish. The Jean Fields case was one local issue of importance. Her husband departed leaving her with two children. Years later he came back and absconded with them. The judge ruled against her petition because of her views on peace (in Korea) and civil rights. Her defense committee charged "this is the first time in the history of the United States that a parent has lost children for expression of a political belief." The court didn't like the fact that her boy liked Jackie Robinson and Larry Doby and objected to segregation. In 1953 the son of movie mogul Daryl Zanuck and two others "raided a party held in the home of an Indian family in Palm Springs, on reservation property, broke up the party and severely beat one of the guests." Richard Zanuck and his hoodlum friends were released while the Native Americans were arrested. CRC helped raise $1000 for their bail and one of their attorneys handled the case.[43]

While other chapters faced problems of demise, Los Angeles faced the problem of growth. In 1950 they were cautioned "about splitting up into separate chapters too rapidly before solid base is established. Instead, if practical, have local committees with responsibility to report to master Exec. until time is ripe to set up separate chapters. Coordinate work with sympathetic groups. . . . Encourage joint affairs with other organizations." As for dues, 25 percent went to the branch and 75 percent to the Los Angeles chapter. Each branch was encouraged to have its own slogan. Los Angeles was like other chapters in its attention to race. In 1947 they were holding an "open meeting" on "very real problems" of Japanese-Americans, e.g., "escheat of their homes and farms, obstacles to naturalization," FEPC, anti-lynch legislation, anti-poll tax efforts, the case of Ferdinand Smith, were constant concerns. Paul Robeson was a frequent fundraiser for Los Angeles, as in his 1948 concert at the Second Baptist Church. There were similar problems also: "When Negro and white of the opposite sex are seen driving in cars they are stopped by police, questioned and searched. . . . Mexican and Negro workers are stopped on the street without cause, searched and arrested on trumped-up charges." They blamed the L.A. Merchants and Manufacturers Association for not stopping this outrage. The chapter worked closely with the National Mexican-American Association on issues of police brutality and won quite a few.[44]

It was *de rigueur* at chapter functions to show antiracist films like the War Department's World War II film "Don't Be a Sucker." In 1952 the East Hollywood unit of CRC held an extraordinary conference "to examine and study the problem of white chauvinism, to exchange ideas and experiences." While so many whites were encouraging Blacks to "go slow" or prating about the deep roots of Jim Crow, CRC was fearlessly confronting racism. In this predominantly white area they were concerned about the lack of Black participation in their activities. In a harbinger of a battle decades in the future, they underscored "ending the practice of Negroes being the last hired and the first fired." They vowed to escalate the crusade to end discrimination in housing in East Hollywood, and to encourage the hiring of Black teachers at local schools and libraries. These noble notions were followed up when the *Los Angeles Examiner* began to blame "rat-packs" and "pachucos" for a crime wave. CRC asked their local City Councilwoman to "take a stand against the recent press attacks" on Chicano youths: "if these youths were given proper recreational facilities, they would not get into difficulties."[45]

In Long Beach, the major issues were defending those arrested for circulating the Stockholm Peace Appeal and the integration of the Cabrillo Housing Project. Riverside prepared detailed information on the privilege against self-incrimination for the use of city activists. A brouhaha erupted there in August 1951 when Sgt. Lawrence Walker, a twenty-year-old Afro-American in a "frame-up . . . perpetrated by the local sheriff, FBI agents and the judge" was convicted of murder. Margaret Chance, the "lone Negro juror," exposed the situation. Nine Black and white soldiers testified he was twenty-three miles from the scene of the crime. But a white jury foreman, without waiting for the jury's deliberation, proclaimed him guilty, then after the jury's deliberation, ten voted yes on his guilt.

During the trial, FBI agents threatened soldiers at Walker's airfield who sought to testify for him. . . . Mrs. Chance also reported that the white jurors threatened that if she did not vote with him then there would never be another Negro on A Riverside County jury. . . . She finally assented to finding the innocent Negro soldier "guilty" when she was assured that Walker would get a life sentence.

Walker was alleged to have killed a white couple and to have raped the wife, even though ballistic experts said that the bullets could not have come from his gun. Their protest was taken to the doorstep of the governor. But the response of the State Legislative Committee on Un-American Activities to a CRC inquiry preordained the governmental response: "It is one of the largest front organizations in the United States . . . one which is so much an integral part of the Communist party . . . that it can barely qualify as a front organization anymore."[46]

The drive against deportations and extraditions was another expression of CRC's attention to the race question. This was done through the publishing of a English-Spanish pamphlet, "Stop the Deportation Drive . . . Know your Rights." One of their major cases concerned the Korean intellectual David Hyun who the INS wanted to send back to the none-too-tender clutches of the U.S. puppet regime in Seoul. They sought unsuccessfully to block the extradition of Eugene Backstrom, a forty-one-year-old Black laborer, who had been serving a life sentence in Mississippi for stealing food. They did win the case of Lester Tate, a Black shop steward, who they "saved from extradition to a Virginia chain gang." The case was brought to their attention by the Mine, Mill Workers union and they jointly raised $5,000 and got former state Attorney General and Lawyers Guild leader Robert Kenny to represent him. After mass pressure, Governor Warren refused extradition and the chapter bragged about their "20th Century Underground Railroad." Ben Margolis and John McTernan won the extradition case of Sylvester Middlebrooks, wanted by Georgia at the district court level, and spared him more inhumane treatment on a chain gang. But the court's opinion was ominous: "A vocal and disloyal group in the country continually seizes upon alleged violation of right of Negros, not for the purpose of honestly assisting the Negro, but for the purpose of allowing this group to proclaim itself as the protector of Negro rights. . . . The untreated wound becomes an ulcer and the ignored grievance a cause." Taking the cue, CRC's victory was reversed at the circuit court level, despite the legal labor of Nanette Dembitz, Loren Miller, and A. L. Wirin. Yet even with this defeat, the upshot was a familiar scenario from the other CRC losses, i.e., the law was expanded to protect human rights, this time in the area of extradition.[47]

Because of the strength of CRC in the area and the concomitant influence of Communists, an anticommunist drive was inevitable and it became a chapter concern of the first magnitude. In late 1950 they held a well-attended Bill of Rights week in the form of "open air meetings, teas, parties, street corner mobilizations, etc." But Grossman was not impressed and complained about their slighting of "Foley Square and the Smith Act" during this affair: "If one of our best chapters . . . is guilty of this neglect what can we expect of our others?" The national office was also critical of their neglect of the Martinsville Seven petition, but in reply Robinson explained "Our people are now circulating both Gilbert and Wells petitions and circulating leaflets on Bill of Rights Week and the McCarran Act." New York's worry about their parochialism was not assuaged when Shifra Meyers, administrative secretary, requested "more details on Paul Washington now that the stay has been granted. . . . No one in the office even remembered what the case was about." Yet, perhaps reflecting its substantial Jewish membership, the chapter had the Rosenberg case on the agenda constantly. It also had its hands full dealing with local malevolence e.g., the case of Joseph White, a nineteen-year-old Black man "picked up at random [and] charged with rape," even though the medical report showed no rape and he was elsewhere at the time anyway. Despite their having a relatively healthy bank balance and the assistance of moneyed contributors like Alan Deutsch, Patterson was concerned about "tendencies toward liquidation" in what he termed "one of the most effective mass organizations" in the Far West.[48]

But given the anticommunist backlash that hit the area, the chapter did a good job just surviving. The attack on the film community in 1947 affected many of their supporters, John Howard Lawson and Dalton Trumbo most notably. Hard on the heels of this disaster was the effort made in Los Angeles County to have employees swear they were not members of scores of organizations, including CRC, if they wanted to maintain their employment. CRC, the Lawyers Guild, and the Southern California Civil Liberties Union fought this ordinance all the way to the U.S. Supreme Court—and lost. Evidently the justices were not persuaded by the briefs submitted by Samuel Neuberger for CRC, Loren Miller for the Lawyers Guild, nor by the argument made by A. L. Wirin and John McTernan. Justice Frankfurter wrote the opinion holding that employees' efforts to bar enforcement of the "loyalty" program was not ripe, pleading wanly, "This is not what is invidiously called a technical rule." The Board of Public Works of Los Angeles won a similar case in the high court. CRC also lost the case of *California v. Henry Steinberg,* involving a Communist Party registration ordinance. And on 25 October 1948 ten people were served with subpoenas for a federal grand jury and asked if they were Communists; they wouldn't talk and by June 1949, twenty-one had been jailed.[49]

The California Smith Act indictments hit the region with a bruising punch. Fourteen paid informers had been used against the fourteen defendants and the intelligence gleaned by the FBI was not helpful to the fortunes of CRC. The defendants were arrested 26 July 1951 and a press release and leaflet were gotten out immediately. A meeting was held with over fifty attorneys, labor leaders, and the like to discuss the fightback. Then all the CRC chapters—Hollywood, Santa Monica, San Pedro, Long Beach, Tubman, Eastside, Central Avenue (Isiah Nixon), East Hollywood, Echo Park, West

Jefferson (Frederick Douglass) and the Valley—sponsored meetings on the implications of these arrests; the Valley had the largest attendance with 150 people. Resolutions were passed and sent to Truman. A mass meeting was held at the Embassy Auditorium and 1,200 people were present. A petition was circulated throughout the region. People named Smith were recruited to protest the Smith Act. A separate lawyers meeting of fifty was held with representatives from the ACLU, the NAACP, the NLG, and so forth. They resolved to place an ad in the *Los Angeles Times*. Fifteen of them agreed to speak publicly against the Smith Act. Full-page ads were placed in the *Valley Times* and the *B'Nai B'rith Messenger*. A delegation visited the U.S. Attorney and demanded lower bail for the defendants. At the bail hearing, five hundred of their supporters packed the courtroom. At an 5 August mass meeting of 1,500 in the Embassy Auditorium, $1,600 was collected for the defense, August 11 a picket line was thrown up and 8,000 leaflets were distributed and 500 people were present "from 7 months to 70 years of age." Days later, they picketed a speech of the U.S. Attorney. The CRC's staff of five was the spark behind all this, including the formation of the California Emergency Defense Committee, formally in charge of the case. This staffing pattern was a bit deceptive, since, for example, Dorothy Mayr, who served as membership secretary, was a "wage earner, up at 6:00 A.M. and not free to carry on CRC activity until 7:00 P.M."[50]

When the stunning victories came in the *Stack* and *Yates* decisions, a great deal of the credit could be laid at the feet of CRC. The national office was in close contact with their local colleagues. It was Grossman's idea to call for the lawyers meeting and to organize them along the pattern of those appearing "in court" and those who "do research." He forwarded "legal memos prepared in New York" for the CP-Eleven trial and a copy of the Foley Square record to Ben Margolis, along with "all the motions." Unlike other regions, A. L. Wirin, who worked with the Southern California CLU (SCCLU) and Leo Branton, who was close to the NAACP, were both involved in various stages of the defense. The chapter was innovative in sponsoring house meetings on the case; Congressmen were visited, "shop gate distributions" were made, "letters to editors" were sent, publications were produced.[51]

The accomplishments of the local chapter are even more stunning when the repressive atmosphere in which they organized is taken into account. After all, this was the home of the John Birch Society, of Orange County reaction, and popular right-wing politicians like Sam Yorty. A typical situation occurred when a Democratic Party club planned a meeting to protest the Marshall Plan. The American Legion "ordered" them not to hold it, but they proceeded anyway; at that point the meeting was disrupted forcefully. CRC supported the lawsuit brought by the Democrats in which plaintiffs invoked the Reconstruction anti-Klan Act in seeking relief. The District Court dismissed the suit, the Circuit Court reversed that decision and they were in turn reversed by the U.S. Supreme Court in a decision in which Justice Jackson inadvertently demonstrated the importance of historians by citing Claude Bowers' inaccurate *The Tragic Era* in demonstrating how bad Reconstruction legislation was. Wirin and Loren Miller argued this case and were able to get Arthur Goldberg of the CIO and Thurgood Marshall to file *amicus curiae* briefs.[52]

Buoyed by this victory, apparently reaction felt this was a signal for them to act in any way they pleased. In 1952 Los Angeles was rocked by a series of anti-Black and anti-Jewish and anti-Chicano bombings. Two Black homes on Dunsmuir Road were bombed, along with a Chicano home on Presidio Drive. Others were threatened with bombing in this reaction to residential desegregation. The NAACP, the Progressive Party, the County Central Democratic Committee, the Emma Lazarus Federation of Jewish Women, the clergy, all joined CRC in a ringing protest. Police brutality in the area gave Los Angeles a well-deserved national reputation that cries about a "Red Plot" aimed at protesters could not drown out.[53]

CRC in Southern California also had to grapple with constant surveillance by the FBI. Their files show detailed reports of CRC meetings, rallies, demonstrations, and the like. When CRC began to show its opposition to the Communist Control Act, an informant was at a meeting where Ben Margolis "delivered his usual analysis"; this person reported on the size of the crowd and provided the names of those he knew. At another meeting he added glumly, "The only person I recognized at this meeting was Bob Large, a rail roadman." The Los Angeles Committee to Secure Justice in the Rosenberg Case, in which CRC planed a pivotal role, also received the constant watching of the FBI. Apparently this was not sufficient for they inveigled David Brown, a "Communist trade unionist in the East" who moved West in 1948, to become their agent after he had become a CRC leader. He received five dollars for each report "up to a maximum of $50 a month." Kim Hunter won an Academy Award in 1952, but after it was discovered, among other things, that she "supported a CRC petition . . . calling for a new trial for McGee," she was blacklisted and was "offered no more parts . . . for . . . three years." Kim Chernin, the daughter of CRC leader Rose Chernin, has written tearfully on the pressures placed on her as a child growing up in Southern California when classmates teased and hounded her and her mother was jailed. Aligning with CRC during this tumultuous era was in itself a courageous act, which makes the fact that they were able to maintain a high level of activity and membership throughout CRC's history that much more impressive.[54]

The San Francisco Bay Area was not far behind Los Angeles in accomplishments, and given the smaller population CRC was dealing with there, their impact might have been less diluted and greater overall; certainly they had a much smaller Black population to deal with, a general prerequisite for CRC growth. They took the lead in the Wells' victory. When important rules were established in this case concerning the insanity defense, legal presumptions, state of mind, this chapter could claim a large share of the credit. Their tenaciousness caused Supreme Court Justice Robert Jackson to explode in exasperation: "Pages full of numbers fail to indicate what the states must contend with as vividly as the history of particular litigation. The *Wells* litigation in California is an object lesson in conflict." He went on to complain of CRC's litigiousness, but they were not moved. Before he moved to New York in 1949, Aubrey Grossman was West Coast Director of CRC based in the Bay Area. He had left his law practice in the mid-forties to become a full-time political operative. The strength of CRC in the West was due in no small part to his skills. As Patterson made Black rights a CRC priority nationally, Grossman felt that "if CRC is to be built in the Southwest (and West), in fact if the progressive movement is to be built, we must break through in the Mexican community." He spoke of the "opportunity . . . necessity and the obligation" presented by the "drive to deport 250,000 Mexicans" in 1949. At his initiative, a campaign took off aimed at the Attorney General, which included delegations to see local immigration officials, special appeals to unions, "bringing of a test case (and) injunction, a conference," pamphlets. As was his wont, he saw labor as being the key and saw this immigration drive as a shameless move to split the unions. He chided both Phoenix and Tucson—which at the time had ninety and eighty members respectively—for their failures in this area, even though they had "prestige" for their "fight around a civil rights law" in the state. San Diego was congratulated for having a Chicano executive secretary, but more had to be done everywhere.[55]

From his San Francisco office, Grossman reported to Patterson on problems faced in the immediate area and region:

we are trying to resolve the question of how we can concentrate on one or two campaigns, so that we can really produce results, when there are three, four or more non-local campaigns of importance as well as at least one local campaign. We haven't yet found the answer to this question.

He termed the CP-Eleven "our most important case," but carped about the lack of a "coordinated national program . . . national petition or national resolution," which meant that chapters "don't feel their little petition or resolution is added to similar actions elsewhere until it becomes something big and powerful." The national office was so taken by the cogency of Grossman's argument that he was invited to implement these ideas in New York. San Francisco's loss was New York's and the national organization's gain.[56]

The East Bay was a particularly vibrant area of CRC growth. Not coincidentally, the year the chapter arose, 1946, was the year of the stormy Oakland general strike. The growing black population, whipsawed by high prices and spreading unemployment, was increasingly attracted to CRC's message. The leadership of the chapter was the odd couple of Decca Truehaft, of clipped

English diction and privileged British background, and Hursel Alexander. He was born in 1914 on an Omaha Indian reservation. His father was an ex-slave and his mother was Scotch-Irish. He was a farmworker, then vice-president of an Omaha local of the Amalgamated Meatcutters Union in the 1930s; later he participated in the Salinas lettuce strike, organized Teamster Local 630, and was a shipyard worker in San Pedro. An inveterate unionist, he was also an ILWU member, a NMU member, and an organizer for the Food, Tobacco and Allied Workers union. "Forced underground" during part of the McCarthyite period, he demonstrated the continuity of CRC by surfacing in the 1970s as president of Local 1108 in the American Federation of State, County, and Municipal Employees. Truehaft, or Jessica Mitford to use her other name, gushed about his value to CRC:

> Under Hursel's guiding hand, the East Bay CRC was transformed from a small, sterile committee of aging, foreign born whites into a dynamic, predominantly black organization with some five hundred active dues-paying members—this at a time when the NAACP chapter in Oakland could muster no more than fifty.

The "executive committee" of the chapter had about twenty members and "was largely made up of non-Communists. . . . Our president was a black member of the Laborer's Union." She did see a problem, which Grossman had alluded to, of conflict between local and national cases. Many members were recruited on the basis of a local question like police misconduct and were often hard-pressed to see their connection with a national case. She praised Patterson for working this through with the chapter and suggested fighting for what the local board desired. She noted how their "broad contacts" allowed them to mobilize "out of all proportion to our size."[57]

As Mitford observed, by late 1955, "CRC [was] in shambles. . . . [it] had become the special target of a massive FBI sweep . . . visiting every member's place of work." The claim that the FBI "had infiltrated the organization to such an extent that it was believed they made up the majority of the membership" was inaccurate, but it reflected the turbulence brewing. Oakland and the Bay Area generally had the added burden of contending with the Hearst press. But the fact that Huey Newton, founder of the Black Panther Party in their former stronghold of West Oakland, recalled hearing and being inspired by their defense efforts when he was a small child showed that their existence was not without meaning.[58]

This was far from the mind of the Oakland activists of CRC in the forties. They had at this point a popularly received radio program where the issues of the day were tackled. This program, "Civil Rights in the News" on KTIM, was a sounding board for their growing campaign against police misconduct. As a result of CRC pressure, the State Commission on Crime and Correction held a police brutality hearing. "The first time in the history of the state of California and . . . in the nation . . . where such a hearing takes place" was

Alexander's proud claim. State Assemblymen Augustus Hawkins, W. N. Rumford, John Moss, and Harlan Hagan were present at the 1949 hearing and also participating were CRC's customary allies, The Progressive Party, The Communist Party, CIO, ILWU. Detailed reports on the cases were issued and the press coverage was heavy. Bertram Edises, CRC's General Counsel, presented proposals that were thought then to be premature, but which in large part were implemented subsequently, e.g., bonding all police and revoking the bonds if they engaged in misconduct, establishing a state law fixing minimum qualifications for police and "compulsory on-the-job training" of police in "race relations." CRC was instrumental in bringing the hearing to Oakland and keeping the police department under close scrutiny. They would read the papers, seek out cases, talk to victims, get them to file a complaint, and back it up with a mass campaign. According to Truehaft, this led to a membership jump "from 40 in the beginning of 1949 to over 500 [by early 1950]."[59]

Oakland-CRC's crusade against police brutality was seen as a model worthy of national emulation by the New York office and steps were taken to disseminate the "secret" of their success across the country. The same held true for their successful effort to save the life of Jerry Newson. This eighteen-year-old Black youth was involved in a robbery in Oakland where one Black and one white were killed in a drugstore. He conceded that the robbery had involved himself, but he denied that he had played a role in the murders. "CRC had a weekly radio program over station KTIM. The story of the Newson case was told over and over." Newson was on death row and "every Negro in Oakland knew that if Jerry Newson's skin had been white, he never would have been convicted. . . . The verdict was the greatest single topic of conversation in West Oakland. Hundreds of persons, especially Negro women, flocked to the Civil Rights Congress offices to see what they could do." Bert Edises and Bob Truehaft, the husband of Decca, fought the case through the California courts until the verdict was reversed in the Supreme Court.[60]

As with the police brutality campaign, Oakland prepared a memo in this case for national distribution so that other chapters could emulate their defense efforts. Between November 1949 and June 1950, they had total expenses of $1,348.56 with the largest amount having been turned in by Newson's family, but with the ILWU and a local church close behind. To publish a popular pamphlet on the case, they borrowed $800 to pay the printer. They gave a "meet the authors party" with a two-hour program of "songs, speeches, skits" and four hundred copies of the pamphlet were sold that night alone. Three weeks later the debt was paid as orders for 23,200 copies flooded the office. West Oakland stores sold them over the counter with no commission. The Marine Cooks bought one hundred. In Vallejo, where CRC was the "the only progressive organization with a local headquarters," CRC was so successful in raising this question of Newson that the

City Council moved to pass a "little Mundt" bill "directed specifically at" CRC. After the high court reversal, Newson had two more trials ending in hung juries; 250,000 leaflets were put out and 10,000 copies of the booklet on him were sold. Black lawyer Terry Francois aided CRC in providing him with "free legal defense," but he was forced to spend fifteen years in prison, though normally first offense robberies led to two-to-three-year sentences.[61]

Vallejo was also the scene around this same time of the case of Charles Williams. Mrs. Coleen Marlatt told police that two Black males had entered her home, demanded money, and hit her. Allegedly one was dark, heavy-set and about twenty-five; the other was about nineteen, light-skinned with long sideburns. Two weeks later Charles Williams, not yet eighteen, married father of one, was arrested "simply because he was a young Negro with sideburns," identified by Marlatt though he was not light; after he changed clothes she did not recognize him. On the day in question he was at home with his wife at a card party with friends. Marlatt was accused of having "persecution feelings." After the "crime" she alleged that he walked up and down the street in front of her home, sat behind her in a movie theater, "leered" and "laughed at her"; she didn't try to apprehend him, though she was with her husband during this latter "incident." The only evidence against Williams was Marlatt's testimony, but it was sufficient to convince the all-white jury.[62]

Despite this setback, 1950 was the take-off point for CRC there, just as other chapters were crashing. Not only the Newson case but the police brutality hearings were responsible. It was revealed that police lay in wait at taverns for Blacks on paydays, then rolled and beat them. Alexander said that there was "very little red-baiting" because so "many community leaders" were involved, thus proving once again that breadth was the antidote to repression. The three-day session even brought in the NAACP "due to the tremendous amount of pressure"; and the "excellent coverage by the press was due primarily to the fact that we furnished them nightly with press releases." Alexander added that a new chapter was forming in Alameda with the "majority of the people" working at the Naval Air station where they had just been helped by CRC to win a loyalty case. By early 1951, Patterson was relating to Truehaft how a "friend . . . who is a great political leader on the West side of Berkeley and nationally said that [CRC] in Berkeley was now larger than any progressive political party there."[63]

The Bay Area, after all, was Patterson's home and he had a special interest in progress there. Truehaft and he were frequent correspondents and he provided detailed suggestions as to what path they should follow. They planned in the summer of 1950 a conference on "Negro Rights"; he suggested that they address job issues, particularly job discrimination: "We should not, however, attempt ourselves to become the driving force in the field." Peace was to be stressed and the defense of Communists, and he cautioned "my letter imposes tremendous responsibilities upon you. . . . this is unfortunately true. You will do, however, only what you can." This conference led directly to a campaign against Jim Crow hiring practices at a local hospital. CRC was progressing so rapidly that Patterson felt their image was lingering behind; he urged them to get "printed letterhead" since "mimeographed letterhead . . . is not worthy of the high position CRC occupies in that area." Patterson added the ultimate compliment, "let me commend you on the splendid job you are doing out there, on the cadres you are building."[64]

The chapter could also be the butt of national office criticism. Grossman brought Truehaft up short by telling her "[although] all your criticisms of me and the National Office are correct . . . My criticism is that the East Bay still seems to spend 99% of its time and energy on local cases, thereby distorting what is a proper proportion of local to national importance." She conceded that while there was "much discussion" on the CP-Eleven case, "many of the new [members] have not thus far been involved in this struggle." Their struggles *were* mostly local. They were stopping the Board of Education from sponsoring minstrel shows; afterward, when CRC called to get a room in McClymonds High School for Negro History Week, the secretary asked them about the content of their material since they had to be "extremely careful" about Black topics and avoid "derogatory" material about Blacks. This victory had a wide impact, but the chapter's inattention to national issues nagged. Wanly Truehaft claimed that "you don't hear about" their victories in that field and, in any case, "we are pushed by our membership into mainly local activities . . . to some extent." While Truehaft continued to object to what she felt were too many directives from New York requiring quick action, Grossman riposted on the CP-Eleven case, "your chapter has always, with rare exceptions, participated less than we have a right to expect on issues so important." Patterson gently prodded, "I think you have the greatest organization in the apparatus [but the CP-Eleven] fight takes precedence over all others."[65]

There seemed to be an interesting triangle existing between Patterson, Truehaft, and Grossman. While she ingratiated herself with Patterson, her relationship with his colleague deteriorated. Warming up for her subsequent successful writing career, she told Grossman at one point, "I almost started this letter by saying 'I wish to God you'd go underground again' but wouldn't bring myself to say these hard and cruel words. . . . This isn't New York where you can shove people around and get away with it." Responded Grossman, "if I were not a gentlemen, I'd say 'keep your pants on.'" These personal differences did not prevent them from making progress on a number of fronts. In early 1952 the chapter garnered maximum publicity from picketing the Alpha Kappa Phi fraternity at the College of the Pacific when they displayed a Confederate flag. At first, "all the radio stations . . . carried the story," and they were friendly but "changed [their] tune completely and said we were nothing but a Communist front."[66]

This lack of personal cordiality combined with an oncoming rush of political repression made for a difficult situation after a while. Early in 1953 Truehaft acknowledged that "terrible inroads are being made on our membership because" of the Attorney General's listing; "it really is *the* major obstacle to recruiting." Later she told Patterson "Our members have been under terrific attacks by the authorities. Following your tour last year, the persons who sponsored your meetings were subjected to all kinds of pressures. Therefore . . . the kind of follow-up we had planned was not possible." She continued to claim that "some pressing local issue" always seemed to prevent their taking up national issues, noting the "one-sidedness of our work, based for the most part on one section of the community."[67]

At this juncture Patterson became more hostile. He criticized one of their pamphlets as "vague . . . we are not tailist rather leaders . . ." He knocked one of their brochures: "You have not linked any of the national issues with the local issues. . . . The ground you have lost can be recovered." He admitted that "It has always been extremely difficult for us to mount more than one campaign . . . [yet] you have rarely made an inseparable part of such campaigns the building of CRC, . . . as your membership dues indicate." Truehaft had grumbled that "the number of active members has dropped consistently, until now there are only a small number" who were active. They had twenty to forty hardcore activists and a debt of $500. Yet she resisted a merger with the San Francisco branch as not "practical or beneficial" because "distances are too great." There were four branches in the East Bay. Richmond, for example, had "5 or 6 active people" and since they were on the branch executive and two were on the chapter board executive, it was possible for them to "attend as many as 6 CRC meetings a month." There were sixty-five members in Richmond and fifty in Oakland and the same was true there and for the other two branches. Hence, activists who "feel they have to attend all these meetings . . . become demoralized." It was a prescription for burnout. Grossman was not sufficiently convinced to resist criticizing their pamphlet because it stressed the "exclusion of Negroes" instead of "workers from juries." Patterson was more pointed and harsh: "What is the weakness with you out there as I see it. The failure to trust people. To give them work to do. To let them make mistakes if they will and not [adopt] a superior know-it-all air as you criticize them." Truehaft, a transplanted Briton of aristocratic background, was particularly vulnerable to such a charge.[68]

While these internal conflicts were raging, political progress continued to be made. The chapter was able to send $1,000 to the national office, loaned by a friend who "has a restaurant in West Oakland." There was a Teenage Defense Committee formed for a youth charged with a juvenile offense and the distribution of leaflets in "all East Bay high schools" and with picketing. In response to a police shooting in Richmond, a petition was circulated, a delegation was sent to the City Council, NAACP leaders participated and they filed a $200,000 damage suit. They launched their project on jury discrimination with the exclusion of Blacks and workers from juries as the focal point: "We have discussed the plan with several [conservative] plaintiff's attorneys who lose huge sums because of inadequate damages' granted by present juries. They have guardedly expressed interest, some even promised finances for the printing."[69]

The chapter was not so sufficiently demobilized as to be unable to fight back when the HUAC traveling road show came to town. Eighty people were subpoenaed in late 1953, including a number from CRC and labor. "Negro people are a prime target of these hearings" was the chapter's solemn declaration. But HUAC was cowed by the fierce reaction the hearings generated. Truehaft concluded, "I can't remember any previous time when unity . . . reached such a high point." The Un-Americans wound up funding the progressives inadvertently; thirty people under subpoena were never called, including Truehaft, even though they still received the witness fee: "$45 in my case, first money I've earned in a long time," was her sprightly reply. Buoyantly she continued, "I have to get back to the children who have been sadly neglected during the hearings. . . . Their teachers took a swell position, said they were on your side!"[70]

Across the Bay, CRC was also relatively strong. By 1948 they had a bail fund of about $60,000, and a membership of five hundred. They were able to collect ten thousand signatures on Rosa Ingram petitions and sent $1,000 to her family. Their relationship with the ILWU was particularly close and the union printed up much of their literature, including 25,000 leaflets on repressive legislation in 1951; like Oakland they had ties to small businesses as well. The heart and soul of the chapter was embodied in chapter secretary, Ida Rothstein, a Russian emigré who came to the United States at the age of eleven, became a U.S. citizen by marriage in 1922, and was an active ILWU member who also happened to have been a participant in the fabled Gastonia strike. In 1951 on the day she was supposed to visit the governor about Wells, she was arrested for the purpose of deportation. In one of the more chilling incidents of the plethora there are to choose from, she was killed by a speeding auto in January 1954: "She was carrying material on the Wells case when the accident occurred."[71]

Although the Smith Act cases and the case of Harry Bridges were two of their most pressing concerns, they found time for other matters in San Francisco. By 1951 they had 810 members, 170 added in the first five months alone, which was striking, given that Los Angeles with a much greater population had about the same size chapter. Attendance was described as "weak," however, although the chapter was good in non-meeting work like circulating petitions or "special requests for funds and letters." They did not have the problem of parochialism faced by Los Angeles and Oakland. In fact Rothstein lamented "some of our work in the various cases has fallen off because of our concentration in the McGee case. . . . our members and branches were so involved in the McGee case that little work was done on anything else." Though relatively satisfied with their performance, Patterson saw room for improvement. He counseled that they "learn from the Negro church. . . . it establishes all kinds of committees," which kept the membership involved, unlike the chapter. When Patterson returned home in 1951 there was a tumultuous reception for the native son. It attracted one of the biggest crowds the chapter had ever had and "thirty-six members . . . were recruited." Still, he remained convinced that "growth and development in San Francisco seemed exceedingly slow and . . . we [do] not enjoy the closest contact with friends and supporters of the struggle for democracy." He was quite critical of their efforts outside the city on the peninsula and recommended a "Stakhanovite" corrective movement; he scored the "failure to draw into the leadership . . . a Negro force." Patterson was a hard man to satisfy when it came to the struggle against racist and political repression.[72]

The Australian-American longshore leader Harry Bridges had been an object of scorn for governmental authorities ever since he led the bloody San Francisco general strike of 1934. They tried to deport him in the late thirties and during the forties. He became a naturalized citizen in 1945, but this did not abate the government's hunger for revenge. In early 1950 the government moved to jail him for perjury, claiming that he had lied when he swore he wasn't a red during naturalization procedings. Grossman was a longtime colleague of Bridges and he saw this case as an opportunity to rectify what he perceived to be a major CRC weakness, its inattention to labor. Actually it was an open secret that what motivated the government's belated interest was the fact that the salty union chief addressed a union meeting in opposition to a resolution that would have fully endorsed a U.S. intervention in Korea and a number of powerful U.S. Senators took offense. In any event the CRC organizational secretary quickly joined Carol King and Vincent Hallinan in the legal defense of Bridges.[73]

Perhaps because of the repeated attempts to isolate him by associating him with the cursed reds, Bridges was at times reluctant to be seen being too cozy with them or with organizations led by them. It was not until the spring of 1950 that Grossman was able to confide to Patterson, "it looks as if Bridges and his co-defendants learned the really hard way, and are now ready to cooperate with CRC and do a real defense campaign job." At various stages in his court battle, the longshore leader was able to attract Dalton Trumbo, Leo Huberman, and Philip Murray to write pamphlets on his behalf. CRC sent out an "Action Letter" to all the chapters and it was naturally implemented most thoroughly in San Francisco:

Your job is to coordinate your work with the unions in your area. . . . you must go to the community and inspire immediate protests. Demands should go to Attorney General James McGranery that he agree to a rehearing of the case in the Court of Appeals, or if that fails a hearing in the

Supreme Court. Special appeals can be made to minority groups pointing out that this union maintains and fights for full integration of its Negro, Japanese, Hawaiian and Mexican members—into its industry and into its union. No union has a better record on this question.

In his weekly column Arthur McPhaul in Detroit observed that many of the union's top officers were Black, they had a FEPC clause, fought for the advance of "Negro women" and had "the highest average pay rate of any industrial union in the world." When the U.S. Supreme Court in a *per curiam* judgment finally decided to grant Bridges justice, no small thanks was due to CRC for the role they had played in his defense.[74]

Bridges was not the only labor ally of CRC that came under fire. Marine Cooks union leader Hugh Bryson was indicted and tried in 1953. Patterson gave precise instruction to Rothstein on how to proceed: "there ought to be a working-class jury set up to watch the trial very carefully. . . . watch for . . . the rigged jury which is now characteristic. . . . The trial should be watched for denial of pre-trial motions, use of which procedure indicates most clearly the frame-up character of the trial. The absence in the main of Negro and working-class elements on the jury should be noted." They were not able to prevent Bryson being forced to leave the union nor the destruction of the union itself. Bertram Edises, an Oakland lawyer who traversed the bay, did not have to suffer the fate of defrocked CRC lawyers like Maurice Braverman and Abe Isserman when he was accused of being a member of the Communist Party, because the strength of the Bay Area chapters helped to sway the anticommunists.[75]

The contrasting examples of Bryson and Edises reflected the chapter's success and lack of it in confronting the anticommunist upsurge in the region. CRC-SF had influential sponsors like Dr. Carlton Goodlett, the publisher of the local Black paper the *Sun-Reporter,* and lawyers like Charles Garry and Benjamin Dreyfus. Not only were there problems with antagonists, but even allies rebelled from time to time. In the midst of combating the anticommunists, CRC received a discouraging word from ILWU: "We will be unable to use, at all, the Civil Rights Congress cartoon folder on the Smith Act, directed to labor. The omission of any reference to Jack Hall and the ILWU not only makes it ineffective for West Coast distribution, but politically wrong."[76]

These roadblocks did not cause CRC to swerve sharply away from its goal. When Judge Harold Medina of Foley Square infamy came to San Francisco to speak at the Press Club, the chapter threw up a "very effective picket line . . . organized in only two days. . . . all the radio stations reported [it]. . . . They also mentioned CRC. . . . the *Chronicle,* the *News* and even the *Call-Bulletin* gave an account. . . . The Chronicle even quoted our leaflet. All this without our spending one cent!" This was a mere prelude to their adamant defense of the Bay Area Communists, like Albert Lima, who were soon to be indicted. They played a key role in the Emergency Defense Committee set up to defend these Smith Act victims and sponsored full-page ads in the local newspapers proclaiming defiantly "We are not afraid to Sign Our Names" to petitions defending Communists.[77]

The so-called "Harboring Case" was an offshoot of the Smith Act prosecutions that took up much of the chapter's time. Four defendants—Carl Ross, Shirley Kremen, Sam Coleman, and Patricia Blau—were indicted for "aiding" Smith Act defendants Bob Thompson and Sid Stein and thus were seen as accessories after the fact to their conviction; harboring only carried a six-months sentence, but accessory called for two-and-a-half years; this despite the fact that the "crime" took place in 1945, while the alleged accessory acts were in 1953. A conspiracy charge was also thrown in for good measure. Kremen was only twenty-one and was the "youngest Smith Act victim"; Ross was former state secretary of the Communist Party in Minnesota and was sufficiently popular to get fifteen thousand votes on a "peace platform" in 1949. With the Communists having made a collective decision to send part of their leadership "underground" and to provide the concomitant aid they would require, this indictment was seen as heightening an already relentless pursuit.[78]

The San Francisco chapter provided a pamphlet "intended to be used to provide material for speakers, articles, leaflets and letters to the editors of union and other journals." They formulated model resolutions, solicited funds, sent observers to the trial, organized house parties, and sent speakers to rallies. They pointed out that at one time Frederick Douglass himself had been a "fugitive" needing help and pointed out that this altruistic act could mean eight-and-a-half years in jail altogether; when the Attorney General tried to amend Title 18 S1071 of the U.S. Code on harboring a criminal to increase the penalty, the level of fear was increased. A "Trial Bulletin" was published regularly and Coleman reported happily "We are also working on a recording, on tape or on long-playing records. . . . [we] have broken through at our first union and have a good chance of appearing before some others." But this optimism was shattered when an all-white jury was selected and no Blacks were on the panel. All except Blau were convicted in the spring of 1954.[79]

Smith Act prosecutions also dogged Washington State. Like so many other CRC units, after a while CRC there was spending more time defending itself than any other force. But the fact that Washington's was one of the few CRC chapters to oppose its own liquidation signals that it was unique indeed. Part of this uniqueness was due to the nature of the leader there, John Daschbach. Born in Spokane in 1913, he was a former minor league pitcher, an "outstanding" football player, and a determined tennis buff. He had a degree from the University of Washington in political science and had toiled on the railroads and in the shipyards. By 1952 CRC had about five hundred members in the state, and they held public meetings in the organization's name monthly in Seattle and bimonthly elsewhere; their newsletter the *Liberator* went to eleven hundred people in the state. They were active in Spokane, Seattle, Anacortres, Sedro-Woolley, Everett, Olympia Aberdeen, Bellingham, and Tacoma. The bulk of their membership was in Seattle, which had 350 members—seventy-five Black; correspondingly, there were only twenty-seven CRC'ers in Spokane at that time. It was not difficult to understand how a red-led organization could be so popular during the dog days of 1952. They could and did point to their victories—saving Wells' life, forcing the federal government to say they would enforce Reconstruction anti-Jim Crow laws, drawing up anti–Jim Crow laws in nearby Portland, forcing a prosecutor in Tacoma to abandon a "psychiatric frame-up" of a Black veteran—all of which were persuasive. In Spokane, all churches and pastors, all Superior Court judges, "Negro leaders," attorneys, unions, libraries and newspapers received their literature.[80]

One of the early crusades of the chapter involved the effort to save the jobs of the sacked University of Washington teachers, fired on anticommunist grounds. Among other things, they filed an *amicus curiae* brief in the Supreme Court of the state signed by sixteen union leaders, with decided support from the Woodworkers union. This labor thrust continued when they aided the Metaline Miners Defense Committee during their eleven-month strike beginning in 1948. And like most CRC chapters, they were on line with the national thrust toward Black liberation. After applying concerted pressure, they "won a pledge from the State Director of Public Institutions that no blackface minstrel shows will take place in any institutions under his direction." The harrowing film "South Africa Uncensored" was shown in public meetings at a time when most people in the United States had never heard of the term "apartheid." After the chapter contacted the mayor, the city of Aberdeen proclaimed its first observance of Negro History Week in the mostly white town. They enticed the University of Washington and its law school to purchase the "Genocide" petition. The Seattle, Everett, Aberdeen, and Spokane chapters donated copies of the petition to the libraries. But after a furor was raised, the Seattle library decided to reject the book, "in absolute contradiction to their own Library Bill of Rights," said Daschbach: "Our Everett chapter sold a copy to a lawyer there who grew up with Lie in Norway. This attorney . . . agreed to write to Lie and demand action by the U.N." Still, it seemed like stopping minstrel shows was one of their main activities, which was paradoxical, maybe, in a state with such a small Black population. CRC's role in halting this cultural form should be underscored, particularly in an era when shows like "Amos and Andy" were having a resurgence of popularity. After their meeting with the State Director they had a "victory against the proposed minstrel show in the Monroe Reform School; the Sedro-Woolley chapter also stopped another one in the local high school."[81]

The Spokane chapter was deemed to have the "best Negro composition in the state." This went hand in hand with labor composition, for its secretary was an "AFL carpenter who is going to town." Everett also had a "fine trade union composition in its executive." Patterson regarded the Seattle chapter "as one of the best in the country." These accolades were tested fully when Paul Robeson came to town in 1952. An attempt was made to bar Robeson from the Seattle Civic Auditorium, after the contract had been signed: "The leading Negro ministers led prayers for Mr. Robeson. White ministers protested to the newspapers and the mayor. The Kings County Democratic convention went on record 731–1 for Paul Robeson's right to sing." Yet a protracted legal and political battle ensued:

> the fight for the Civic Auditorium for Paul's concert here on May 20th was won yesterday . . . though he was not here in person. It was Paul's wonderful leadership and reputation which dominated everything. It was Paul who brought together the people—Negro and white—who filled the courtroom to overflow every day of the three-day trial. It was Paul who by his leadership . . . prevented the appearance of any Uncle Tom—except a coerced Negro police officer, who was visibly ashamed of his role on the witness stand and whose testimony was turned around in favor of Paul. Pat: Paul's standing was of such an overwhelming nature that another Negro police-officer who was in the audience passed our counsel a note. . . That showed most dramatically the profound roots of Paul in the Negro community . . . capped by a Dimitrov-like stand by the local (NNLC v.p.)— James McDaniels (also a CRC member).

Robeson also found time to perform before forty thousand people at the Blaine Peace Arch at the Canadian border. This was after he was barred from attending the Mine, Mill Workers convention in Vancouver. But the newspapers did not consider this rebuff to the red scare worth reporting.[82]

The local *Peoples World* reporter Terry Pettus may have been inspired by this gross omission when he suggested the idea of a project on how the right was undermining the press; he listed a score or more of journalists and editors of the left and foreign-language press who were under siege. Pettus himself was "appealing five-year Smith Act and three-year 'contempt' sentences." His publication on the press in 1954 "reached . . . to the other continents. People in Europe are getting that news around, and undoubtedly when Dulles gets to Geneva he will see one for the first time. The labor press of British Columbia is re-running the material." The *Liberator*, the state's CRC journal, made much of a startling incident when two FBI agents called on ILWU official Jack Hall in Hawaii and asked if he would be a stool pigeon; if so, the Smith Act charges would be dropped against him. Unbeknownst to them, the whole conversation was being taped and later the union broadcast it. "The tape recording caught the agents hooting and jeering at the notion that Jack Hall and the other indicted Hawaiians were " 'conspiring to advocate the overthrow of the government.' " Yet, the press ignored this by and large. CRC–Washington had come to the conclusion that other chapters had arrived at, i.e. that the words "free press" were being given a novel interpretation during this era.[83]

Another aspect of repression also caught their attention. A campaign was launched against the state's anticommunist bill, the "Powell Padlock Bill," which was designed to prevent the left from using schools as meeting places and was the local equivalent of the Smith and McCarran Acts. A campaign was launched against the Tule Lake "concentration camp," which was designed to house leftists and other dissidents in times of "national emergency" and was all too eerily reminiscent of the recent experience of Japanese-Americans. Snohomish County-CRC initiated a postcard campaign against the camp aimed at Senator Warren Magnuson; twenty-five thousand copies of the related and startling *Peoples World* supplement were distributed. Daschbach concluded, "A letter-writing campaign to Washington State Congressman is under way and they don't like the heat."[84]

At a time when so many were hunkering down or sitting out this repressive period, the CRC chapter was often the most organized if not the only force fighting back militantly. And in relatively small lakes like Washington, CRC could be a big fish indeed. It was CRC that was responsible for reviving the Lawyers Guild chapter there in 1952. They worked to place Initiative 183 on the ballot concerning civil rights. During Bill of Rights Week in December 1952, they "won editorials in the Aberdeen and Bellingham press and Sedro. . . . the Washington State Superintendent of Education adopted our suggestion and sent a memo to all School Directors in the state urging special attention to display, lectures, special observances, etc. on December 15." Weeks later CRC continued their upward swing: "5 picket lines in the past weeks, reaching thousands of people. . . . Radio broadcasts over Western Washington . . . A delegation in this week called on the Chief Justice of the state Supreme Court. . . . I've been constantly on the move speaking on the Rosenberg case and Northwest Smith Act." In Aberdeen CRC circulated detailed questionnaires to those running for office and issued recommendations. Daschbach also proudly noted that in North Washington "every chapter is headed by women." At this juncture they were sponsoring regional and citywide meetings on issues of the day from a progressive perspective hard to ferret out in the doldrums of 1953. In Bellingham they had a session on the "crisis in foreign policy," hitting Korea, Formosa, and other issues. Another focus was on the "Eisenhower depression," considering "how the issues of civil rights ties right into this, with the Rosenberg case at the very apex." After meetings, the "Public Relations Committee" of each chapter targeted for lobbying Catholic priests, AFL business agents, Protestant ministers and other opinion molders.[85]

It was undeniably accurate to say that CRC in Washington state put the "Rosenberg case at the very apex." In this critical year of 1953 they organized a "steady and systematic series of visits to ministers, priests, union officers . . . and to hit an average of one visit every two days for the coming six weeks before the Rosenberg case [reaches] the Supreme Court again. . . . with the Rosenberg Committee we assisted in organizing, has held seven picket lines in the past six weeks." All CRC chapters in the state were directed to picket. They saw this case as the tip of the proverbial iceberg of repression and they were correct in a sense they may not have recognized. Without their knowledge, the FBI had obtained somehow the names of contributors to their local bail fund, along with the entire mailing list of the chapter. They were also still smarting from the murder of one of their supporters, Laura Law, by Ralph Hall, formerly business manager of the *Peoples World,* "last seen in Seattle in July 1950." The act of this "traitor, enemy of the Working Class and pervert" sent chills cascading throughout the chapter. Moreover, even the aftermath of the Robeson victory saw the firing of Jack Kinzel, a radio announcer, and Vincent Davis, a tailor, after they had testified. And there was the case of Margaret Donaldson, who, in a local manifestation of a national issue, attempted to divorce her husband for "cruelty and excess drinking." But because she was a Communist and CRC supporter, he absconded with her child. This followed the case of sending a businessman to a mental hospital for "observation" on allegation that he was giving funds to communists. Donaldson, a former staff organizer for the Office and Professional Workers union won her case on appeal when her ex-spouse's divorce decree was set aside. Still a clear message was being communicated statewide.[86]

CRC had an early experience with repression at the University of Washington when Professor Herbert Phillips of the Philosophy Department and five others answered (but not in a way deemed responsive or satisfactory) questions posed by a state committee investigating "communism." CRC helped to form the Committee to Abolish the Cantwell Committee. Their defense of the "Seattle Six" included organizing a 2,500-strong rally on the University of Washington campus in the spring of 1949. Yet this case could well be considered a defeat that whetted the appetite of some for subsequent Smith Act prosecutions. At the outset, Phillips and Professor Joe Butterworth of the English Department both said that they had been Communists since 1935, but three other professors only acknowledged former memberships and one denied any tie to the party whatsoever. There was concern about this last professor and the three others, but the two reds were bounced out altogether. This despite an incredible number of donations for their defense and the support of people like John Bunzel and Syvilla Fort.[87]

Thus the chapter was ready and in gear when the McCarran Act was being considered in 1950. "CRC has called about 3 dozen Democratic candidates sounding the alarm and asking what they can do to straighten out the top men on their ticket—Magnuson and Mitchell. Been quite a bit of heat generated on this. . . . a chain telephone campaign has been organized . . . similar programs of action . . . in nine other cities of Washington." Their Smith Act brochure was judged by Patterson as "the finest that has yet appeared in the country" and without hesitation he told Daschbach, "You are doing a magnificient job."[88]

Others apparently did not think so, for the local CRC leader was jailed after having refused to answer "who are the members of the District Committee of the Communist Party" and he was indicted under the Smith Act. CRC fought back. There was a King County Trade Union Committee to Repeal the Smith Act and the Northwest Citizens Defense Committee won the lowering of bail from $200,000 to $50,000; in filing eight pre-trial motions for dismissal, forty thousand pages were prepared and mimeoed in a week. There was a clear impact on the fortunes of the chapter after their leader was put on trial in 1953; to cite an example, their publications became less attractive and in a sense less informative; obviously also their organizing for other causes fell off. Patterson maintained an intense interest in the trial, for not only was Daschbach a CRC leader but he was a comrade as well. Moreover, "Patterson's name came up" in the trial regularly, especially when "the stool pigeon [Paul] Crouch was cross-examined." Patterson disgustedly called the indictment "like the dropping of an atomic bomb upon the Bill of Rights." More concretely, "no membership fees [came] in during the trial."[89]

As the trial progressed, Patterson continued to follow it closely and to proffer advice: "We should not allow any fascist activity to take place in the community . . . without using it as the basis for a motion for a mistrial on the grounds that it must be calculated to influence the jury and to prevent due process of law. Several of these motions have been made in Pittsburgh." But this advice came too late. One defendant, Bill Pennock, who as a result of the trial and the accompanying commotion "had been harried and nervous," accidentally took too many sleeping pills, allegedly, and died, although "there are a number of big and unanswered questions." This graduate of the University of Washington was *magna cum laude* and Phi Beta Kappa; he had been elected to the state legislature four times. Then another defendant, Barbara Hartle, decided to switch sides and become an agent of the state in return for a reduced sentence. The judge, Harry McCain, was well known to Daschbach. This ex-Senator had written CRC many times "on the McCarran Act"; these letter showed "that he is psychologically incapable of being a fair and impartial judge." But the besieged remaining defendants could take heart from the large attendance at Pennock's funeral. One thousand people attended. "The undertaker and cops were overheard saying that the line of cars going to the cemetery was the longest they have ever seen. . . . People came from Montana, Idaho, Oregon, California and every city in Washington."[90]

There were other problems. The defendants had a "serious problem" with the Northwest Citizens Defense Committee, which had been organized specifically to handle this defense. The situation became so extreme that they were thinking of obtaining "a court order fobidding them to act in our name in any way." Daschbach felt that they were negligent in defense, despite the fact that "all funds go through their hands." Patterson was conciliatory: "We should start thinking of bringing the defense committee and the CRC together. The opposition to ad hoc committees expressed at the conference was sharp indeed." Their lawyer John Cauglan was considered quite competent, but even he had to be thinking about an indictment for allegedly stating falsely at one time that he was not a Communist.[91]

The Black defendant, Paul Bowen, had his own special problems: He was defending himself but didn't think that he had a fool for a client. Patterson advised him to go on the offensive; not to "defend: but to go forward as a complainant." He told him to make a special appeal to the "Negro Juror" on the issue of the oppression of Blacks: "You should make much of this." Similar advice was given to the others standing trial. If a "Negro . . . trade unionist . . . or a language group member" testifies, then "get out a special leaflet" addressed to the "group to which he or she belongs and show how the testimony not only is harmful to the defendants but how it worsens the conditions of the group to which the witness belongs. . . . This special approach . . . has been very effective." But all this proved to be for naught. Daschbach and Bowen were convicted, while the labor leader, Karly Larsen, was acquitted—which had to be considered a major victory nonetheless. There were complaints about the "outrageous sentences and the extortionate bail," which was complicated by the fact that "the bondsmen in Seattle refuse to deal with us." The national office could only offer advice and not money at this point, since already they were "concerned with bail for the Pittsburgh . . . San Francisco . . . Cleveland . . . and Detroit defendants [also] St Louis." This political form of triage left Seattle to fend for itself. Besides New York State was suing CRC for $23,500 over the bail fund. There were further mixed results. Professor Phillips received a "savage 3 year sentence for being an expert witness" at the Smith Act trial. But on the bright side he was defended by Philip Burton, a local Black attorney and NAACP leader, on appeal. Perhaps this promising factor contributed to the CRC chapter's virtual isolation in opposition when the vote was taken to liquidate the national organization in 1956.[92]

11

The Demise of the Civil Rights Congress

It cannot be said that CRC went gently into that good night of liquidation, but rather it raged and raged against the dark dying of the light. At their national Leadership Conference in New York in December 1955, Patterson did allow a moment for balefulness when he lamented already in the past tense, "We of CRC spoke out but our voices no longer reached many thousands"; yet he was quick to add that the organization was "still a must." Candidly he acknowledged that state repression was forcing them out of existence. They owed $2,000 on the fight to free him from prison in his latest scrap and they were locked in battle against the Joint Legislative Committee of New York. The prosecution by the Subversive Activities Control Board was costing a handsome $400 per week. The *amicus curiae* for Steve Nelson would cost $3,000. Administrative costs alone were $2,000 per month. This was at a time when a number of past contributors had been scared off for various reasons, e.g., the revealing of the names of those who gave to the bail fund. But all was not pessimism, and Patterson projected a "mass national conference on civil liberties" and "a program for 1956." Yet by January 1956 the Civil Rights Congress was just a sweet historical memory. The Pittsburgh chapter reflected the feelings of many chapters when it declared, "This decision is made unwillingly and under strong protest." They blamed the "McCarran Internal Security Act of 1950" which would mean giving the government "names and addresses of all members, all financial accounts, and a list of all printing and duplicating facilities. . . . Members could become liable to arrest and prosecution under the Smith Act." The angry consideration of the recent lynching of Emmet Till in Mississippi convinced the chapters that there was still a need for CRC and for an organized struggle against racist and political repression, but liquidation was voted overwhelmingly nonetheless.[1]

There were three linked legal/political battles that directly drove CRC out of business. One involved New York State, the other involved the IRS, and another concerned the SACB. These powerful adversaries enacted a crushing pincers movement that crushed and strangled the organization. Early in 1955 the state began hearings on "charitable and philanthropic" agencies and racketeering. The committee proceeded to impound CRC's records and audit everything. There was controversy about an alleged "Three Hundred Thousand Dollars" collected in the Trenton case and only "Six Thousand Dollars spent." Rogge testified and called for "some form of remedial legislation" to protect contributors to funds raised for civil rights. The *New York Times* reporter said, "The all-day hearing was marked by anger and comedy and weighed down by long speeches." Mildred Blauvelt, a city detective who joined a Communist club in Brooklyn claimed that the party ordered its members in 1949 to use CRC petitions to solicit money from the public. Read into the record was testimony by Len Goldsmith, who alleged that Patterson had been chosen to head CRC at a meeting in Communist headquarters in New York in 1948. As for the CRC leader, he spoke angrily and eloquently on behalf of the thirty plus chapters. But the legislative leaders were not predisposed to hear him or read CRC's statement to the press for that matter: "The attempt to destroy CRC takes several different forms. One is to impair its reputation as an honorable people's organization. Another is the imprisonment of its leadership. A third is to find some technicality on which to prosecute the organization itself."[2]

While they were trying to extinguish this blaze, they found themselves fighting on another front. In October 1954 Patterson was subpoenaed to turn over CRC records. The next month he was brought before District Court Judge Edward Weinfeld. Assistant U.S. Attorney Richard Owen made a motion citing Patterson for criminal contempt, even though he had been given neither notice of the action nor a right to a hearing or a motion. Early in the year the Internal Revenue Service began an audit of CRC and spent twenty days burrowing through the office. They requested a list of contributors for 1950, 1951, and 1952. In an affidavit Patterson claimed that the list did not exist. Until 1953 CRC was at 23 West 26th Street, then they moved. Seventeen cartons were stored with the Supreme Delivery Service of 10 East 17th Street. He said he wasn't sure of their contents, though certain receipt books may have been there. But in May 1954 the Supreme Delivery Service informed him that all seventeen cartons had been tossed out. In any case, he had never sent in the alleged receipt books because he did not keep the books for the organization. His story was not believed. He was hit with contempt charges and served ninety days in Danbury Prison. Then he was hit with another subpoena asking for the 1953 contributors' list upon his release. This resulted in another sentence over his arguments against self-incrimination, over the sufficiency of the evidence and the propriety of summary contempt charges and the fact that he had been willing to give the court a detailed statement of the organization's income. This led to a legal battle that led to the U.S. Supreme Court and back. Finally in early 1955 the Circuit Court held that the evidence was insufficient to establish that Patterson possessed the records or even that they existed. Like his lawyer Milton Friedman, Patterson was jubilant about this victory, but he had to wonder if CRC was truly becoming a physician that spent most of its time healing itself.[3]

There was definitely a concerted public campaign against his jailing. J. A. Rogers in the *Pittsburgh Courier* echoed the feelings of many in the Black press when he condemned Patterson's jailing and the horrible conditions in Danbury Prison, where not only Blacks but Jews as well were segregated. CRC's Prisoners' Relief Committee quickly shifted to focus on their leader. Du Bois cried out against the "injustice" done to Patterson "because he refuses to be a stool pigeon." He observed that Howard Fast, Richard Morford, Edward Barsky, and Alphaeus Hunton "also preferred prison rather than surrender to government persecution the names of those persons who have contributed to the work of the organization which they served." The NAACP was silent, but soon they were to face similar efforts by the State of Alabama to drive them out of business. Charlotta Bass, the legendary Black publisher born in Rhode Island, who was a student at Brown, Columbia, and UCLA and a transplanted Californian rallied pastors to support "a native Californian . . . Rev. B. V. Douglas, Rev. McNeil and Rev. Stephen Frichtman [sic] join me in asking if you are willing to arrange a mass meeting in your church." From prison Patterson shot out missives across the nation, giving poignant advice to his fourteen-year-old daughter and providing adivce on how to fight his case. Evidentiary of his support during these trying times was the fact that he received 1,400 Christmas cards there. The Executive Board of the ILWU called for support for him. When he was freed, the *Daily Worker* headlined triumphantly, "Patterson Says His Release Proves Victories Can Be Won." At a victory party at Harlem's Smalls Paradise attended by four hundred cheering supporters, he repeated this defiant message.[4]

As if that were not enough to be fighting furiously on these two fronts, there was also another linked do-or-die struggle with the SACB. Their petition ordered CRC to register as a "Communist Front" and suffer all the untoward consequences of that. They claimed the CRC was "substantially directed, dominated and controlled" by the reds and pointed to the alleged overlapping leadership of the two and to their mutual support; they also cited their identical views on such questions as "atomic weapons," loyalty oaths, HUAC, the Rosenbergs, and NATO and this convergence was seen as especially decisive and in turn was a warning to any organization that happened to adopt progressive positions. By mid-1955 Patterson saw the writing on the wall: "It is too much to expect a favorable finding. Twenty-two witnesses were produced by the government; all of them paid informers and agents of the FBI. The Schneider woman in whose house we slept in San Diego happened to be one of the scum that they produced." He also told Emil Freed that the hearing brought out that Los Angeles "has been a point of concentration" for FBI monitoring of CRC.[5]

There was quite a line-up trooping to the stand to testify. Professional stool pigeons like Berniece Baldwin (formerly of CRC–Detroit), Matt Cvetic (formerly of CRC–Pittsburgh), Bella Dodd (formerly of CRC–NY), Rev. Obidiah Jones, (formerly of CRC–St. Louis), Anita Bell Schneider (formerly of CRC–San Diego), and others were just a few of the big guns wheeled out. Patterson could have been excused a touch of nostalgia as these faces from the past whizzed by. There were reversals too. David Brown of Los Angeles, who had been on the FBI payroll as CRC leader, testified for CRC, as did Rosalie McGee. Patterson objected to their counsels' "insulting attitude" toward her, which led to his being termed "that creature." Brown claimed that Goldsmith told him that he had to be an informer against his will because he was "in business" and subject to pressure. Patterson was questioned closely at the hearing about his ties to the reds and answered with sarcasm dripping, "What are you trying to do, implicate me in some criminal proceedings?"[6]

CRC was faced with the task of refuting the testimony of a gaggle of stool pigeons alleging that Communists helped in setting up CRC chapters and the like. But some of their words could be questioned; for example, one averred that there was an identity of membership between the reds and CRC "from 1944 to 1953" in Dayton, Ohio. There was much worry and attention paid to CRC's impact on Blacks and their role in defense of the Rosenbergs. They pooh-poohed any impending dissolution of CRC, because ILD had dissolved itself too, only to arise phoenix-like in another form. In their motion for relief, CRC blasted the "disorderly" and "disrespectful" attitude of the prosecution toward Ms. McGee, which they said merited a mistrial. They denied flatly that they were "established and organized under the direction of the Communist Party," and pointed to their origin as an amalgamation of ILD, NNC, and NCFL. The bail fund, they retorted, was not just created for the benefit of the reds: "[it] originated in connection with a threatened National Maritime Union strike in 1946 and set up to help with any arrests in civil rights cases which might arise in connection with that strike." They pointed to their subsequent aid to Fletcher Mills, to the Greek seamen, and many others. The Feds were kind enough to transfer Patterson from prison in New York to Washington so he could testify.[7]

In jail because of the tax case brought by Internal Revenue, grilled by the SACB, Patterson also had to confront the state hearing that was coming to a head. With mock credulity one State Senator asked how CRC could claim that they had no list of contributors, but that after their investigation was launched, they managed to send out an appeal for funds to some identifiable individuals. It was claimed that in 1946 the national and New York chapters raised over a million dollars, but Patterson countered that 80 percent of the receipts for CRC contributions were made out to "anonymous" or "friends" because of donors being "fearful of your persecution." Coming back to haunt them over the Trenton Six case, Clifford Moore of the NAACP said that they had spent $90,000, the ACLU $80,000, hence "There was no need for another organization" like CRC to raise funds for the defendants' defense. Robeson said that though he sang frequently to raise money for CRC, he didn't know how much. He did call Patterson one of the "greatest of men, known throughout the world." Hammett pleaded the Fifth Amendment when asked if he were a Communist. Piped the *New York World Telegram*, "Mystery writer Dashiell Hammett didn't live up to his detective characters today." Supposedly he averred that he didn't know how much was raised and was quoted as saying: "I don't know. I got a bad memory for names and people." It was quite a spectacle and was meant to be. An editorial in the *New York World Telegram* captured the view of the legislators who intended to pass laws to penalize and drive CRC out of business when they called CRC, Joint Anti-Fascist Refugee Board, Committee for the Protection of the Foreign Born, etc. "phony charities."[8]

The Civil Rights Congress went down fighting. When the Un-Americans came to New York in August 1955, Patterson was not afraid to say, "Let's show Rep. Walter and his un-American committee that New York City wants no part of him." He called for a picket line at the hearing. But CRC went down nevertheless. Even after the liquidation they faced the problem of the "government's possible right to hold CRC members responsible for the [tax] obligation" of the organization. SACB continued their hot pursuit after CRC's liquidation as well. In 1962 Attorney General Robert Kennedy was still after CRC, as "[four] paid informants" testified against Patterson at a hearing concerning CRC; they doubted its dissolution, despite overwhelming evidence. Not until weeks before the death of President Kennedy did the Justice Department formally drop this case against an organization they called a "Communist front." But the hounding of members continued. During the reign of Nixon, the renamed House Committee on Internal Security worriedly noted that Patterson was at the Emergency Conference to Defend the Right of the Black Panthers to Exist, which took place in Chicago in March 1970; worse, both he and Grossman were on the Continuations Committee.[9]

Yet, the legacy they left continued. Their early anti-anticommunism was vindicated during the Vietnam War. Their anti–Jim Crow crusade paved the way for the gains of the 1960s. Their tactics, like "freedom rides," continue to be emulated.[10] The notion that the Communist Party was directed by Moscow has been au courant in certain circles. The fact that this same thesis has been used to discredit and destabilize movements from Vietnam to South Africa should not be ignored either. Still, it is a shame that one is compelled to aver that there is absolutely no evidence that CRC, an alleged "Communist front," was directed from the Kremlin. The kind of stinking racism and hysterical Nazi-like anticommunism that feverishly gripped this nation was more than sufficient to spur the courage in the face of great odds that characterized the Civil Rights Congress.

Notes

Introduction

1. *New York Times,* 31 August 1947; Roger Baldwin to Robert Morss Lovett, 23 October 1947, vol. 20, American Civil Liberties Union Papers (hereinafter cited as ACLU Papers); *New York World-Telegram,* 10 August 1951.

2. *Application of Middlebrooks,* 88 F. Supp. 943 (1950), 188 F2d 308 (1951); *Lancaster v. Hammond,* 194 Md. 462 (1949); *Stack v. Boyle,* 342 U.S. 1 (1951); *Blau v. U.S.,* 340 U.S. 322 (1950); *Rogers v. U.S.,* 340 U.S. 367 (1950); *Marshall v. U.S.,* 85 U.S. App. D.C. 184 (1949), 176 F2d 473 (1949); *McPhaul v. U.S.,* 364 U.S. 372 (1960); *Hughes et al. v. Superior Court for Contra Costa County,* 339 U.S. 460 (1949). Despite a reasoned dissent by the immortal Roger Traynor and Jesse Carter, the California Supreme Court did not uphold petitioners right to picket (198 P2d 885 [1948]). In a curious precursor of the bogus claim of "reverse discrimination" that reverberated in the courts years later, Justice Felix Frankfurter agreed with the enjoining of the picketing, since the action violated California antidiscrimination law because it would force hiring on the basis of race; cf.also 198 P2d 885 (1948).

3. Sylvia Brown to William Patterson, 1 February 1955, box 9, folder 39, William Patterson Papers; William Patterson to Arthur Wallander, 17 August 1948, reel 35, box 60, M79, Civil Rights Congress Paper (hereinafter cited as CRC Papers); *National Lawyers Guild v. FBI,* 100-1945-Sub A-1345, National Lawyers Guild Papers; Anthony Marro, "FBI Break-in Policy," in Athan Theoharis, ed., *Beyond the Hiss Case: The FBI, Congress and the Cold War* (Philadelphia: Temple University Press, 1982), 78–128, 98; *New York Herald Tribune,* 27 April 1952.

4. Brochure, reel 50, box 88, R1, CRC Papers; "Les" to "Pat," undated, reel 35, box 59, M60, CRC Papers. In addition to the cases, organizational matters (23 items, 110 inches), political analyses (9 items, 74 inches), fund drives (13 items, 42 inches), membership (8 items, 45 inches), international solidarity cases (8 items, 28 inches) also were featured prominently. Interestingly, some have criticized CRC for not giving enough attention to CP cases.

5. Arthur Kinoy, *Rights on Trial: The Odyssey of a People's Lawyer* (Cambridge: Harvard University Press, 1983), 73, 83, 86.

6. *Time,* 14 May 1951; *Life,* 21 May 1951; *Miller v. State,* 41 So. 2d 375 (1949); *Taylor v. State,* 32 So. 2d 659 (1947); *Patton v. Mississsippi,* 41 So. 2d 55 (1949).

7. 328 U.S. 373 (1946).

8. *People v. Newson,* 37 C2d 34 (1951); *People v. Wells,* 202 P2d 53 (1949).

9. 138 F2d 173 (1943); 320 U.S. 790 (1943).

10. *Daily Worker,* 14 August 1949; *Daily Worker,* 16 August 1941.

11. File, reel 3, box 4, A63, CRC Papers; Jessica Mitford, *A Fine Old Conflict* (New York: Knopf, 1977), 128–29, 133.

12. *Hollywood Life,* 13 July 1951 and 30 March 1951; "National Committee to Oust Bilbo," reel 38, box 64, N75, CRC Papers. Symptomatic of the impact of Cold War repression is Garson Kanin's 1952 note to CRC: "I do not know whether or not you list my name as a member or as a sponsor of your organization. In the event that you do, I hereby request that it be withdrawn at once" (Garson Kanin to CRC, 23 June 1952, reel 35, box 59, M66, CRC Papers). George Marshall to Thelma Dale, 16 September 1947, reel 24, box 41, J41, CRC Papers: a HUAC report listed Robinson and Rockwell Kent as sponsors for the purposes of "intimidation," according to Marshall. Also involved with the veterans were Walter Bernstein, Millard Lampell, Bill Mauldin, Pete Seeger, Jose Ferrer, E. Y. Harburg, J. Raymond Jones, Albert Maltz et al. (Circular, 13 May 1946, reel 48, box 74, P136, CRC Papers). Involved in the L.A. effort as well were Ben Margolis, Carlton Moss, Earl Robinson, Lester Cole, Lena Horne, NAACP leader H. Claude Hudson, et al. (Circular, October 1946, reel 45, box 77, P11, CRC Papers). David Caute, *The Great Fear: The Anti-Communist Purge under Truman and Eisenhower* (New York: Simon & Schuster 1979), 525.

13. Fundraising letter from Canada Lee, July 1949, reel 6, box A204, CRC Papers. Alice Childress served as cochair of the Artists Exhibition and Sale for CRC (Circular, ca. 1951, reel 56, box 99, V138, CRC Papers). The N.Y. chapter had an "Entertainment and Advertising Arts" branch ("Civil Rights Action Bulletin," 18 December 1951, reel 56, box 99, V142, CRC Papers). Childress also served with Ollie Harrington and George Murphy at a conference at Harlem's Hotel Theresa sponsored by the Provisional Harlem Committee to Repeal the Smith Act (19 September 1951, reel 29, box 49, J185, CRC Papers). In addition to W. C. Handy, taking part in this "Sing to Kill Jim Crow" performance were Lee Hays, Sonny Terry, Brownie, McGhee, and Dock Reese, "straight from a Texas Prison farm" (Circular, 15 September 1946, reel 21, box 35, G40, CRC Papers). The Asadata Dafora dancers "will dance the Rise of African Civilization and their disruption." William Marshall "will portray Nat Turner" and the "Loyal Gospel Singers" also performed (*Daily Worker,* 31 March 1952). William Patterson to William Nunn, 23 May 1951, reel 34, box 58, M36, CRC Papers; Decca Truehaft to William Patterson, 30 July 1951, reel 45, box 77, P8, CRC Papers. Elizabeth Catlett did a beautiful woodcut of Patterson ripping a Klansman away from a little Black boy with the notation that the CRC leader was "now in prison for defending civil liberties" (Woodcutt, box 14, folder 64, *William Patterson Paper*). William Patterson to Lena Horne, 5 October 1948, reel 34, box 58, M54, CRC Papers; Patterson was also close to Langston Hughes, and his wife Louise Thompson was one of the bard's closest friends (William Patterson to "Dear Lang," 10 February 1952, reel 34, box 58, M55, CRC Papers). As is apparent from this brief recitation, the subject of the left's influence and close ties with the world of artists is worthy of further study.

14. Frazier McCann, cousin of heiress Barbara Hutton, and allegedly the possessor of a $15 million inheritance was said to be the culprit (*New York World-Telegram,* 4 August 1951). *Newsweek,* 10 July 1950; *New York Herald-Tribune,* 16 December 1951. Reid's columns in the *Sunday Trib* were a major source of misinformation and disinformation during this period. He wrote frequently on alleged Communist assassination techniques, bombmaking techniques, etc. Naturally, he began by stating, "This information comes from sources which cannot be revealed but in which this newspaper has full confidence" (*New York Herald-Tribune,* 13 May 1951). The column was taken over eventually by Herbert Philbrick and his coauthor Newton Fulbright (*New York Herald-Tribune,* 18 May 1952). Cf. also *New York Herald-Tribune,* 1 July 1951, 8 July 1951. J. Edgar Hoover, *J. Edgar Hoover on Communism* (New York: Random House, 1969), 125, 127.

15. Speech by William Patterson at Fur & Leather Workers Convention, undated, reel 26, box 44, J89, CRC Papers; William Patterson to Rabbi Mauskopf, 19 August 1952, reel 35, box 59, M74, CRC Papers; Walter White of the NAACP termed the National Committee to Defend Negro Leadership a " 'Communist front' and [warned] NAACP brances to shun it." Ted Poston

in the *New York Post,* 8 October 1952 made a similar allegation concerning this organization that included W. E. B. Du Bois, Paul Robeson, Rev. Charles Hill, Charlotta Bass; National Committee to Defend Negro Leadership to "Dear Editor," 1 November 1952, reel 68, #614, W. E. B. Du Bois Papers; Willard Townsend to J. Finley Wilson, 2 February 1949, reel 36, box 60, M101, CRC Papers; Roger Keeran, *The Communist Party and the Auto Workers Unions* (Bloomington: Indiana University Press, 1980), 11.

16. Philip S. Foner, *Paul Robeson Speaks* (Secaucus, N.J.: Citadel, 1974) 24; Caute, *The Great Fear,* 178; Michael Belknap, *Cold War Political Justice: The Smith Act, the Communist Party and American Civil Liberties* (Westport, Conn.: Greenwood Press, 1977), 58,60.

17. William A. Nolan, *Communism versus the Negro* (Chicago: Regnery, 1951), 87, 89; Thomas Brooks, *Walls Come Tumbling Down: A History of the Civil Rights Movement, 1940–1970* (Englewood Cliffs, N.J.: Prentice-Hall, 1974); Diane Johnson, *Dashiell Hammett: A Life* (New York: Random House, 1983); Robert Zangrando, *The NAACP Crusade against Lynching, 1900–1950* (Philadelphia: Temple University Press, 1980); Irving Howe and Lewis Coser, *The American Communist Party: A Critical History, 1919–1957* (Boston: DaCapo, 1957); Nathan Glazer, *The Social Basis of American Communism* (New York: Harcourt Brace, 1961): Joseph Starobin, *American Communism in Crisis, 1943–1957* (Cambridge: Harvard University Press, 1972); Jane Sanders, *Cold War on the Campus: Academic Freedom at the University of Washington, 1946–1964* (Seattle: University of Washington Press, 1979): Mary Sperling McAuliffe, *Crisis of the Left: Cold War Politics and American Liberals, 1947–1954* (Amherst: University of Massachusetts Press, 1978).

18. Elizabeth Gurley Flynn, "The Militant Traditions of Labor Defense Inspire Our Fight Today," *Political Affairs* 30 (February 1951): 124–32, 128; Mitford, *Fine Old Conflict,* 116; Henry Williams, *Black Response to the American Left, 1917–1929* (Princeton: Princeton University Press, 1973), i; 315; Henry Winston, "The Meaning of Industrial Concentration," *Political Affairs* 31 (July 1952): 27–36: "Undoubtedly, our Party generally enjoys greater influence and support among the Negro people than among any other group. This has been shown on innumerable occasions. But it is also true that there exists a very wide gap between this general support and influence and the numerical growth and stability of our Party in the Negro community. (Blacks) rightfully demand of us more than of anyone else." The apostate Phillip Abbott Luce agreed, though in a different sense: "All American Communists, regardless of their particular theoretical persuasion are adamant in their belief that the Negro people are the essential catalyst for the projected revolutionary situation in the United States" (Phillip Abbott Luce, *Road to Revolution: Communist Guerrilla Warfare in the USA* [San Diego, Calif.: Viewpoint, 1967], 45).

19. Pettis Perry, "Certain Prime Aspects of the Negro Question," *Political Affairs* 30 (October 1951): 11; Bob Thompson, "Strengthen the Struggle against White Chauvinism," *Political Affairs* 28 (June 1949): 15; William Z. Foster, "Notes on the Struggle for Negro Rights," *Political Affairs,* 34 (May 1955): 38. Just as Afro-Americans tended to be the most vehement opponents of Cold War foreign policy, CRC leader Nat Ross in the party's theoretical journal pointed out that "In Congress, the main Dixiecrat leaders have been among the most vociferous supporters of the Truman Doctrine, the Marshall Plan, The North Atlantic Pact, and other major aspects of the bipartisan war policy" (Nat Ross, "The Dixiecrat Fascist Menace," *Political Affairs* 28 [July 1949]: 35). J. Edgar Hoover also perceived this tendency of Blacks and reds to coalesce (Hoover, *Hoover on Communism,* 131).

20. William Patterson to Les Davis, 18 February 1952, reel 46, box 80, P64, CRC Papers; I. F. Stone, *The Truman Era* (New York: Random House, 1953), 134. Sherrill served as editor of the paper *Garvey's Voice.* Patterson scored him for skirting the issue of U.S. domination of the United Nations in an article: "All this you hide for some reason known only to yourself. You do not identify the black people of Africa with the colored peoples of Malaya, Indonesia, Korea and China. It is too late for black men 'to go it alone'" (William Patterson to William Sherrill, 8 August 1951, reel 34, box 58, M36, CRC Papers). In his typical poetic style, Patterson averred,

"Peace between my country and the Soviet Union is the guarantee of human freedom. American-Soviet friendship means freedom as well as peace" (William Patterson to Holland Roberts, 8 August 1952, reel 34, box 57, MIA, CRC Papers).

21. "Jim Crow-Courts" file, undated, reel 6, box 9, A 161, CRC Papers. A random selection from this file contains the following: Arkansas State Supreme Court upholds legislation restricting primaries to whites (*New York Times*, 27 June 1946); nine farmers fined $200 each for killing Blacks, (*New York Times*, 10 December 1946); Black preacher convicted by all-white jury after clash with the police in which he was beaten (*New York Times*, 1 May 1947); Greenville, South Carolina, jury acquits all defendants on all counts in lynching of twenty-four-year-old Black (*New York Times*, 22 May 1947); two whites acquitted of slaying Black after jury deliberates twenty-seven minutes (*Afro-American*, 27 March 1948); fourteen-year-old Black gets thirty years for second-degree burglary in North Carolina (*Afro-American*, 3 April 1948); Twenty-three-year-old white gets 2–5 years for raping twelve-year-old Black girl in Brunswick, Georgia (*Daily Worker*, 30 July 1951). One careful student concluded that CRC's evaluation of the press was not peculiar: "A significant part of the world—possibly even a majority of nations—disliked the American press for one reason or another and with greater or lesser intensity" (Margaret Ann Blanchard, "American First, Newspapermen Second? The Conflict between Patriotism and Freedom of the Press during the Cold War, 1946–1952" [Ph.D. diss., University of North Carolina, 1981]). Anthony Lake Newberry, "Without Urgency of Aaardor: The South's Middle-of-the-Road Liberals and Civil Rights" (Ph.D. diss., Ohio University, 1982). Patterson followed the Black press carefully. William Patterson to Albert Hart, 11 May 1950, reel 34, box 58, M36, CRC Papers: "I follow the Negro press very closely, reading even the smaller papers and especially those that come from the deep South." Cf. also P. L. Prattis to William Patterson, 5 April 1950, reel 34, Box 58, M36, CRC Papers; Vicki Lynn Rutz, "AUCAPAWA, Chicanos and the California Food Processing Industry, 1937–1950 (Ph.D. diss., Stanford University, 1982).

22. Nanette Dembitz, "Congressional Investigation of Newspapermen, Authors, and Others in the Opinion Field—Its Legality under the First Amendment," *Minnesota Law Review* 40 (April 1956): 517; see Comment, "Communism and the First Amendment: The Membership Clause of the Smith Act," *Northwestern Law Review* 52 (September–October, 1957): 527–42. This bit of scholarship relied heavily on Herbert Philbrick and included this observation: "The fact that most 'front' organizations are completely under Communist control, in spite of the fact that only a small percentage of their members are Communists, is a tribute to the Communist discipline. All 'fronts' are propaganda and to recruit new members."

23. William Patterson statement, 17 March 1954, reel 5, box 8, A142, CRC Papers.

24. William Patterson to Marvin Karp, 11 September 1951, reel 11, box 18, A352, CRC Papers; Keynote Address, National Leadership Conference, 19–20 February 1955, reel 26, box 44, J90, CRC Papers; "Draft Report," 10–12 June 1950, National Board Meeting, reel 24, box 41, J43, CRC Papers. William Patterson to Nadya Schwartz, 12 May 1954, reel 47, box 81, P80, CRC Papers.

25. William Patterson to Irving Anderson, 25 January 1950, reel 34, box 57, MIA, CRC Papers; Keynote Address, National Leadership Conference, 19–20 February 1955, reel 26, box 44, J90, CRC Papers; William Patterson to CRC Chapters, 2 October 1950, reel 4, box 6, A83, CRC Papers.

26. "Someone whom I didn't know wandered into our August meeting, took an active part in the discussion on *We Charge Genocide*. After the meeting I approached him and asked him to join the CRC. His reply was, 'I thought I belonged to all these organizations'" (Alma Foley [CRC-Mn.] to Aubrey Grossman, 8 September 1952, reel 48, box 83, P110, CRC Papers).

27. In 1954 Patterson was repeating a similar refrain: "I think you ought also to move slowly in injecting other fundamental issues in a major way into your activities but always keeping clearly in mind that the Ben Davis case must be linked with Robert Welsey Wells as must also the Rosa Lee Ingram matter. The Davis case is now the most important but in terms of timing the Wells matter now occupies the center of the stage" (William Patterson to Lucille King, 4 March 1954, reel 5, box 8, A142, CRC Papers). "Tasks and Perspectives," 21 March 1950, reel 39, box

66, N113, CRC Papers; William Patterson to Frank Spector, 26 July 1955, reel 15, box 24, B34, CRC Papers. CRC pamphlets included, inter alia, "The Cold War Murder: The Frame-up against Ethel and Julius Rosenburg"; "Musmanno Isn't Loading Coal—Just Baloney" re: Pittsburgh Smith Act case; "What Is Meant by Subversive" re: Communist Steve Nelson: "The Heat Is On" re: Smith Act and McCarran Act; "The Bill of Rights: How Safe Are You?"; "The Reign of Witches: The Struggle against the Alien & Sedition Laws," an obvious parallel to the Smith Act; "Not guilty! The Case of Claude Lightfoot"; "The Crimes of Claude Lightfoot and Junius Scales"; "The Right to Speak for Peace": Can Americans Tolerate Prison for Ideas?"; "McCarthy in the Courts" again, re: Nelson, "Ideas behind Bars." This selected list is not inclusive insofar as it omits pamphlets concerning leading Black cases, but it does show that CRC was far from inactive in working on red cases.

28. "Reminiscences of George Schuyler," Columbia University Oral History, no. 431, vol. 3, p. 433; William O'Neill, *A Better World: The Great Schism: Stalinism and the American Intellectuals* (New York: Simon & Schuster, 1982); Mari Jo Buhle, ed., *Women and the American Left: A Guide to Sources* (Boston: Greenwood Press, 1983), 146; Bernard Johnpoll, *The Impossible Dream: The Rise and Demise of the American Left* (Westport, Conn.: Greenwood Press, 1982), 328; Robert Clayton Pierce, "Liberals and the Cold War: Union for Democratic Action and Americans for Democratic Action, 1940–1949" (Ph.D. diss., University of Wisconsin, 1979), 142–43, 147, 395; Kenneth Waltzer, "The American Labor Party: Third Party Politics in New Deal-Cold War New York, 1936–1954" (Ph.D. diss., Harvard University, 1977). Like too many "left" historians Waltzer relies unduly on apostates for evidence (e.g. p. 434) and downplays repression as an element in the left's decline. For example, after alleging that the ALP "never itself became an object of direct governmental repression" (p. 458) he says sentences later: "ALP campaigns were disrupted, ALP candidates were harassed and ALP members were hounded . . . it was standard practice to copy names from ALP petitions for subsequent investigations." Leo K. Adler and Thomas Paterson, "Red Facism: The Merger of Nazi Germany and Soviet Russia in the American Image of Totalitarianism," *American Historical Review* 75 (April 1970): 1046–64; Don Parson, "Los Angeles' 'Headline-Happy Housing War,' " *Southern California Quarterly* 65 (Fall 1983): 251–85; Charles Eagles, *Jonathan Daniels and Race Relations: The Evolution of a Southern Liberal* (Knoxville: University of Tennessee Press, 1982), 127. Cf. also *Pittsburgh Courier,* 13 September 1947 column by George Schuyler where he blasts CRC as a "notorious Communist front" and similarly attacks Benjamin Mays, Mary McLeod Bethune, et al. for their association. As shall be seen, such pressure caused such figures to move away from this particular popular front and correspondingly weakened the opposition to conservative maneuvers. For further reflection on such issues, cf. John Salmond, "Vanguard of the Civil Rights Movement: The Post New Deal Career of Aubrey Willis Williams," *The Historian* 44 (November 1981): 51–68.

29. Interview, Aubrey Grossman, 28 May 1984: Douglas Ayer, "American Liberalism and British Socialism in a Cold War World, 1945–1951" (Ph.D. diss., Stanford University, 1983).

Chapter 1. Germinating and Ripening

1. Folder, Yergan meeting, 12 January 1946, box 57, Papers of Civil Rights Congress of Michigan (hereafter denoted as CRC-Mich.). Present at this discussion concerning the formation of CRC were many ILD officials; present, inter alia, were Louis Colman, Fred Field, Hulan Jack, Jack Raskin; folder, national correspondence 1947, statement of the merger of NNC with CRC, Chicago, 22–23 November, 1947—signed by Thelma Dale, Ernest Thompson, Doxey Wilkerson, George Marshall, Louis Colman, Joseph Cadden, et al., *CRC-Mich Papers;* John Streator, "The National Negro Congress, 1936–47" (Ph.D. diss., University of Cincinnati, 1981). Streator scores Wilson Record, Harold Cruse, and Harvard Sitkoff for their characterizations of NNC (cf. chap. 1). Randolph attempted to exclude whites from his movement, which roiled relations with NNC: he also attempted to bar both the Communists and the CIO, and was opposed to any

discussion of a third party. Mary Church Terrell, William Pickens of the NAACP, and Benjamin Mays were among the Black leaders with ties to NNC. Concludes Streator, "The domestic thrust of the Cold War was particularly important for the NNC, in that the NNC combined each of the main targets of the building repression, Blacks, labor and Communists" (cf. 185, 315, 337, 355). Note that the former NNC office at 307 Lenox Avenue in Harlem became the CRC office (Thelma Dale to TWU, et al., 31 December 1947, reel 33, box 70, folder 30, Papers of National Negro Congress [hereafter denoted as NNC Papers]).

2. Rosalie Berry (of City Councilman Benjamin Davis' office) to Daniel Hard, 30 October 1945, box 4, reel 3, A64, CRC Papers; Louis Burnham to Esther Jackson, ca. 1946, folder, "Staff-Burnham Personal," "Thursday afternoon," Southern Negro Youth Congress Papers; CRC press release, 8 June 1950, reel 30, box 66, N131, CRC Papers (note that Marhsall was formerly assistant editor of the *Encyclopedia of Social Sciences*); *George Marshall v. USA* (Petition for Reconsideration of Determination Denying Petitioner's Application for a Writ of Certiorari to the Court of Appeals for the District of Columbia Circuit), October 1949. On 10 April 1950 the High Court denied the appeal of Marshall's attorney Osmond Fraenkel. Relying on another CRC case, *Christoffel v. U.S.*, 338 US 84, Fraenkel challenged the quorum of HUAC as a basis for overturning the verdict against Marshall. The CRC did not abandon their leader upon his jailing; Patterson wrote both the *Times* and the *Herald Tribune* complaining about "the attitude of prison authorities toward you" (William Patterson to George Marshall, 8 June 1950, reel 2, box 1, A-5, CRC Papers). Nevertheless, symptomatic of prevailing anti-CRC prejudice, Patterson was forced to write Marshall at the federal prison in Ashland, Kentucky, reassuring him: "There are some who seem to think that we have tried to make a martyr of you. This is not so" (Patterson to George Marshall, 28 July 1950, reel 6, box 10, A204, CRC Papers).

3. Minutes of Executive Board of National Federation for Constitutional Liberties, 11 November 1946, file NCFL, Southern Negro Youth Congress Papers; Introduction, reel 1, CRC Papers; Roger Baldwin to members of ACLU Board, 4 April 1946, vol. 2715, 27–28 April 1946, reel 38, box 64, N66 CRC Papers. Congressman Hugh De Lacy also spoke at the founding, as did Bill Patterson, who was then serving as legislative director of the Communist Party of Illinois. Of the delegates and visitors, 67 from the South, 258 from the Midwest, 35 from the East, and 7 from the West were from 20 national organizations, 119 AFL and CIO unions, 26 Black, 21 civic and political action, 20 women's, 21 national minority, and 18 civil rights organizations. A Continuations Committee of 85 was elected; the Robert Marshall Foundation provided $21,500 to CRC's initial kitty, the largest amount of the $51,272.49 total income. The registration fee, perhaps as a result, was a mere $2. George Marshall to Thelma Dale, 16 September 1947, reel 24, Box 41, J41, CRC Papers; inevitably, Marshall's keynote speech stressed protection of labor and minority rights and gathering reaction; Cicero Hughes, "Toward a Black United Front: The National Negro Congress Movement" (Ph.D. diss., Ohio University, 1982).

4. Minutes of meeting of Continuations Committee, 11 May 1946, reel 27, box 45, J110, CRC Papers; Acceptances on CRC Board, undated, reel 39, box 66, N101, CRC Papers. Decisions of CRC Resident Board Meeting, 9 August 1952, reel 27, box 45, J110, CRC Papers. Note that Harry Ward also served as a chair of CRC.

5. William Patterson to Mary McLeod Bethune, 15 September 1948, reel 10, box 16, A324, CRC Papers.

6. Benjamin Mays to Milton Kaufman, 23 October 1946; Milton Kaufman to Benjamin Mays, 17 October 1946; Benjamin Mays to Milton Kaufman, 10 October 1946; and George Marshall to Benjamin Mays, 20 September 1947, reel 39, box 66, N101, CRC Papers.

7. George Marshall to Executive Committee, 29 September 1947, folder, national CRC Correspondence, box 7, CRC-Mich, papers; Minutes of CRC Executive Committee, 25 September 1948, reel 38, box 64, N69, CRC Papers; minutes of Executive Committee meeting, 5 August 1947, reel 24, box 41, J41, CRC Papers; George Marshall to Helen Benner, 14 Feburary 1949, reel 45, box 77, P27, CRC Papers; William Patterson to Maia James, 31 March 1949, reel 46, box 79, P40, CRC Papers.

8. *Daily Worker*, 28 December 1950.

9. Minutes of Legal Committee meeting, 14 November 1946, reel 8, box 13, A268, CRC

Papers; "Memorandum on Ralph Powe Tour," undated, reel 10, box 16, A314, CRC Papers; Samuel Neuberger and David Scribner also served on the Legal Committee. Samuel Rosenwein served as CRC General Counsel.

10. *Daily Worker,* 27 February 1955. In this article Patterson talks of the attempt to deport him in the 1930s. Records of his birth were destroyed in the earthquake and fire of 1906: ". . . luckily, a witness to my birth was found"; "Alumni News," vol. 5, no. 4, Larkspur, California, July 1971, folder 54, box 14, William Patterson Papers; Geraldine Segal, *Blacks in the Law: Philadelphia and the Nation* (Philadelphia: University of Pennsylvania Press, 1983); William Patterson to Edwin Burrows, 7 September 1948, reel 35, box 60, M80, CRC Papers; William Patterson to Margie Robinson, 25 July 1953, reel 45, box 77, P15, CRC Papers, (February 1951): 5–10, passim; Brief Biography of William Patterson, 2 June 1954, reel 19, box 30, F1, CRC Papers.

11. Brief Biography.

12. Brief Biography.

13. William Patterson to E. D. Alston, 17 July 1951, reel 4, box 4, A67, CRC Papers; William Patterson to Albert Hart, 11 May 1950, reel 34, box 58, M36, CRC Papers; Brief Biography.

14. William Patterson to Dr. M. Abowitz, 5 February 1951, reel 34, box 57, MIA, CRC Papers; *Daily Worker,* 14 July 1977.

15. Passport of William Patterson, folder 67, box 14, William Patterson Papers; income tax returns, folder 8, box 1, William Patterson Papers; William Patterson to Alexander Trachenberg, 26 April 1950, reel 28, box 47, J157, CRC Papers; files of William Patterson, undated, reel 29, box 48, J161, CRC Papers; William Patterson to Miriam Schultz, 22 December 1953, reel 49, box 85, P175, CRC Papers.

16. Harvey Klehr, *Communist Cadre: The Social Background of the American Communist Elite,* (Stanford, Calif.: Stanford University Press, 1978), 67, 60; Mark D. Naison, "The Communist Party in Harlem: 1928–1936" (Ph.D. diss., Columbia University, 1975), 269; John Graves, "Reaction of Some Negroes to Communism" (Ph.D. diss., Teachers College, Columbia University, 1955).

17. Raymond Pace Alexander to William Patterson and Louise Thompson, 4 January 1951, box 2, folder 1, William Patterson Papers; William Patterson to Earl Dickerson, 17 July 1952, reel 34, box 57, M31, CRC Papers; James Ford to William Patterson, 2 February 1949, reel 34, box 58, M40, CRC Papers; Charlotte Armstrong to William Patterson, 21 August 1951, reel 34, box 57, M12, CRC Papers; *Time,* 14 August 1950; *Amsterdam News,* 9 February 1952; Adelle Jackson to William Patterson, 17 July 1953, reel 35, box 60, M91, CRC Papers; Bella Dodd, *School of Darkness* (New York: P. J. Kenedy, 1954), 186; Howard Fast to William Patterson, 30 December 1952, reel 34, box 58, M40, CRC Papers; circular, ca. 1954, reel 34, box 58, M38, CRC Papers; Jack Dyhr to John Daschbach, 4 February 1951, box 4, folder 26, John Daschbach Papers.

18. William Patterson to Louise Patterson, 18 May 1951, reel 19, box 30, F14, CRC Papers; William Patterson to Ruth, Bob, and Agnes Jane Patterson, 21 May 1949, reel 35, box 60, M82, CRC Papers.

19. Speech by William Patterson, ca. 1951, reel 28, box 47, J157, CRC Papers; William Patterson to Joan and Charles Intrator, 16 February 1952, reel 35, box 59, M56, CRC Papers.

20. *Freedom,* August 1951, 1; *National Lawyers Guild, et al. v. Federal Bureau of Investigation, et al.,* 100-10769, 3 November 1953; 10769-923, 2 December 1953; 10769-1028, 24 March 1954; 100-10769-1036, 22 June 1955. Patterson alleged, "Last summer I entered Canada twice without any trouble." (*Toronto Evening Telegram,* 18 December 1947). Perhaps this was a result of increasingly frigid political climes. *Toronto Daily Star,* 18 December 1948; Civil Rights Union bulletin, ca. 1949, reel 37, box 63, M33, CRC Papers.

21. Report to the National Executive Board—Civil Rights—The State of the Nation by William Patterson, ca. late 1949, reel 27, box 10, J110, CRC Papers; Len Goldsmith to William Patterson, 22 September 1948, reel 34, box 58, M52, CRC Papers: "A personal word of caution. I suggest that you watch the tone of some of your letters." William Patterson to Len Goldsmith, 30 September 1948, reel 34, box 58, M52, CRC Papers: "I think your letter is a little subjective. No

one seeks to ignore the fact that you are a national officer and a leading one, and I don't think you will ignore the fact either." George Marshall to CRC National Board, chapter secretaries, 1 June 1950, reel 38, box 64, N55, CRC Papers: "I think that there has been too great a tendency to work in a sectarian way, both in terms of contacts made and phraseology used. I think we must be much more imaginative and flexible than most of us have been of late. . . . I think we must learn to be much more flexible, imaginative and daring in our approach to organizations and individuals, and to learn to meet them half way . . ."; minutes of special meeting of CRC Board, 7 August 1950, reel 38, box 64, N61, CRC Papers.

22. John Holton to Aubrey Grossman, July 1952; Aubrey Grossman to John Holton, 15 July 1952, reel 49, box 85, P159, CRC Papers.

23. William Patterson to Arthur McPhaul, 28 July 1953, reel 47, box 82, P95, CRC Papers.

24. Louis Colman to Milt Kaufman, 15 August 1946, reel 48, box 84, P134, CRC Papers; report on organization, 6 November 1948, reel 39, box 66, N104, CRC Papers.

25. Report of Chicago Chapter Secretaries Conference by William Patterson and Aubrey Grossman, 1 May 1952, reel 47, box 82, P94, CRC Papers (cf. also William Patterson to Arthur McPhaul, 5 May 1952); background on Freedom Crusade, 18 November 1949, reel 27, box 45, J112, CRC Papers; press release, 4 September 1951, reel 49, box 85, P169, CRC Papers.

26. Chapter income report, ca. 1949, Civil Rights Congress Papers of the Tamiment Institute (hereafter referred to CRC-Tamiment); undated list of CRC chapters, reel 41, box 70, N243, CRC Papers; CRC bulletin, 20 November 1948, vol. 1, no. 4, reel 8, box 13, A259, CRC Papers: new chapters "all formed during the past two weeks" in Bridgeport, Hartford, New Haven, Pasadena, San Diego, Colorado Springs. In Cleveland, "Making excellent use of city newspapers through articles on CRC, letters to the editors, etc.; circular re: chapters, 19 May 1947, reel 39, box 66, N104, CRC Papers. Report on membership, ca. 1952, reel 23, box 40, J27, CRC Papers: in the East Bay the branch executives and membership met twice monthly and the chapter board every two weeks; in Southern California 12 branches (East L.A. "Negro," West Adams "mixed," Bay Cities "mixed," Echo Park "Mexican," etc.); in San Diego 16 paid-up members, 50 not paid-up, 100 on mailing list with the executive meeting every other week. In Illinois 8 functioning chapters with 5 dormant or reorganizing; in Wisconsin 100 paid-up with 250 in arrears and 3 chapters (Milwaukee, Racine, and Barron Country—first two meet regularly, Barron irregularly); William Patterson to Len Goldsmith, ca. 1948, reel 42, box 73, N299, CRC Papers.

27. CRC circular, undated, reel 17, box 28, Dd2, CRC Papers; CRC mailing lists, undated, reel 41, box 70, N239, CRC Papers; "Pointers for Building Civil Rights Congress Chapters and Carrying Out Chapter Activities," undated, reel 3, box 4, A51, CRC Papers (ca. 1951).

28. Aubrey Grossman to "Dear Friends," 21 June 1952; and "To All State Organizations, Chapter . . ." etc., 2 August 1952 and 28 August 1952, reel 24, box 41, J46, CRC Papers; "Membership Drive Bulletin," 26 August 1950, reel 27, box 45, J110, CRC Papers.

29. Les Davis to William Patterson, undated, reel 35, box 59, M60, CRC Papers; "Chapter Bulletin," vol. 2, no. 29, 17 September 1951, reel 10, box 16, A328, CRC Papers.

30. Draft of minutes of National Emergency Conference on Civil Rights, 19 July 1948, reel 24, box 41, J39, CRC Papers (51 from 13 states were present); Chicago Chapter Secretaries Conference, 21 June 1949, reel 42, box 73, N300, CRC Papers (17 chapters were represented); "Summary of National Conference of the Civil Rights Congress . . ." 12–24 June 1954, reel 24, box 41, J43, CRC Papers.

31. CRC "Chapter Bulletins," 1950–1954, reel 23, box 40, J18–25, CRC Papers.

32. Ibid.

33. "Chapter Bulletin," vol. 2, no. 4, 22 January 1951, reel 8, box 13, A259, CRC Papers.

34. Undated report, reel 38, box 63, N51, CRC Papers; Anne Shore to Marguerite Robinson, box 3, folder, Correspondence 1954–55, CRC-Mich. Papers; William Patterson to Maia James, 16 September 1949, reel 3, box 4, A62, CRC Papers: Patterson let the Denver chapter know of upcoming conventions in their town and to get pamphlets there; similar letters were sent to L.A. and San Francisco chapters.

35. Report of National Executive Secretary, Proceedings—CRC National Board, Chicago, 7–10 July 1952, reel 38, box 65, N86, CRC Papers.

36. "Abridged Report of National Organizational Secretary for Meeting of National Board," 7 July 1952, reel 38, box 64, N74, CRC Papers.

37. *Washington Legislative Bulletin,* 17 February 1949, box 7, folder, National Correspondence 1949, CRC-Mich, Papers; organizational letter, 24 June 1949, box 1, folder 1, John Daschbach Papers: *Censored News,* ca. 1948, reel 28, box 47, J143, CRC Papers; *Civil Rights Congress Tells What to Do if Approached by FBI Agent,* undated, reel 24, box 41, J44, CRC Papers; *Civil Rights News, Peoples Champion, Pittsburgh Freedom News,* ca. 1951, reel 24, box 41, J45, CRC Papers; Anne Shore to National Office, 11 July 1951, reel 47, box 82, P93, CRC Papers; *Let Freedom Ring,* vol. 1, no. 1. November 1953, reel 49, box 85, P170, CRC Papers; action letter, 6 January 1946, reel 24, box 41, J41, CRC Papers; requests for literature, reel 35, box 59, M69, CRC Papers.

38. Circular, 10 July 1948, box 3, folder, Dance 1948, CRC-Mich. Papers; flyer, box 3, folder, "Picnic-1950," CRC-Mich. Papers; "The Plot against the People," box 5, folder 7, Naomi Benson papers; pamphlet, box 3, folder 3, John Daschbach Papers.

39. Minutes of Executive Committee meeting, 5 August 1947, reel 24, box 41, J41, CRC Papers; national balance sheet, 1 May–31 December 1946, box 7, folder, National Correspondence, 1946, CRC-Mich. Papers; Bernard Ames to CRC, 5 November 1948, reel 40, box 69, N193, CRC Papers; Executive Board meeting, 28 June 1946, reel 38, box 64, N66, CRC Papers.

40. Membership report, ca. 1949, reel 38, box 64, N64, CRC Papers; balance sheet, 1949, reel 38, box 64, N71, CRC Papers; Virginia to Emil Freed, ca. September 1949, Emil Freed Papers; *Baltimore Afro-American,* 17 September 1949; Edith Rosenberg to "All CRC Districts and Chapters," 21 August 1952, reel 24, box 41, J46, CRC Papers; Freedom Fund News, 30 June 1951, no. 1. reel 24, box 41, J44, CRC Papers; "Civil Rights Fund-Action Bulletin," 17 January 1951, reel 7, box 10, A234, CRC Papers; Aubrey Grossman and William Patterson to "All Chapters," 28 September 1952, reel 24, box 41, J46, CRC Papers.

41. Robert Truehaft to Aubrey Grossman, 6 July 1951, reel 45, box 77, P8, CRC Papers; G. Randolph Erskine to CRC, 30 July 1952, reel 34, box 57, MIA, CRC Papers; Benjamin Asia to CRC, 26 July 1948, reel 34, box 57, MIA, CRC Papers; Moses Weinman to Ralph Powe, 27 June 1950, reel 3, box 4, A63, CRC Papers.

42. Aubrey Grossman to Anne Shore, 15 July 1950, reel 47, box 82, P92, CRC Papers; Aubrey Grossman to Frederick Field, 9 June 1952, reel 34, box 58, M41, CRC Papers; Frederick Field to Aubrey Grossman, 28 May 1952, reel 34, box 58, M41, CRC Papers; D. Quailey to CRC, 15 February 1952, reel 34, box 58, M41, CRC Papers; CRC lease, 1 February 1953–31 January 1955, box 9, folder 60, William Patterson Papers; John Holton to Aubrey Grossman, 26 July 1952, reel 49, box 85, P159, CRC Papers; circular, 15 April 1954, box 3, folder, Correspondence 1954–55, CRC-Mich. Papers.

43. Interview with Aubrey Grossman, 28 May 1984, in possession of author; report of the National Executive Secretary to the Leadership Conference of the Civil Rights Congress, 12–14 June 1954, St. Louis, reel 38, box 65, N86, CRC Papers.

44. Speech by William Patterson at CRC National Leadership Conference, 19–20 February 1955, box 1, folder 7, John Daschbach Papers; minutes of National Convention of CRC, 6 January 1956, reel 42, box 72, N274, CRC Papers; *New York Post,* 15 December 1955; *Daily Worker,* 19 July 1956, 23 July 1956; William Patterson, "And New Witch-Hunt against Pensioners," *Jewish Life,* March 1956, reel 50, box 87, Q25, CRC Papers; Leon Katzen to "Dear Friend," 8 March 1956, reel 51, box 90, S59, CRC Papers.

Chapter 2. Racism and Political Repression

1. Interview with Aubrey Grossman, 4 December 1983, in possession of author.

2. William Patterson to chapter secretaries, 15 May 1950, reel 40, box 69, N190, CRC

Papers; William Patterson to Oakley Johnson, 14 April 1949, reel 2, box 4, folder 17, Oakley Johnson Papers: interestingly Patterson supported the demand for more Black police but doubted that it would mean less brutal treatment.

3. William Patterson to Harry Ward, 13 June 1955, reel 15, box 24, B34, CRC Papers.

4. Statement by William Patterson to Senate Judiciary Committee, ca. 1949, reel 39, box 66, N121, CRC Papers; William Patterson to Mrs. Andrew Simkins, 18 November 1952, reel 6, box 10, A199, CRC Papers; Don Carleton, "A Crisis of Rapid Change: The Red Scare in Houston, 1949–1955," in F. A. Rosales and B. J. Kaplan, eds., *Houston: A 20th Century Urban Frontier* (Port Washington, N.Y.: Kennikat, 1983), 139–59.

5. CRC Pledge, ca. 1948, reel 9, box 15, A309, CRC Papers.

6. Report of East Hollywood Conference, 29 June 1952, box 2, CRC-L.A. Papers; Aubrey Grossman to Detroit, L.A., and St. Louis chapters, 10 December 1952, reel 24, box 41, J48, CRC Papers; William Patterson to *Daily Worker,* December 1948, reel 34, box 57, M25, CRC Papers.

7. Sophie Goff to William Patterson, 12 August 1949, reel 2, box 4, folder 17, Oakley Johnson Papers; William Patterson to James Aronson, 3 January 1950, reel 3, box 4, folder 19, Oakley Johnson Papers.

8. Steven Lawson, *Black Ballots: Voting Rights in the South, 1944–1969* (New York: Columbia University Press, 1976), 104 (how such a book could devote so little space to CRC is symptomatic of the larger problem of historiography of the civil rights movement); circular, undated, reel 38, box 64, N75, CRC Papers; circular, undated, box 1, General Correspondence 1946, CRC-L.A. Papers; "Action Bulletin," 16 September 1946, CRC-Tamiment Papers; minutes of CRC Board meeting, 25 January 1947, box 7, file, National Correspondence, 1947, CRC-Mich. Papers; "You Can Oust Bilbo" poster, undated, reel 25, box 43, J72, CRC Papers; Board of Directors meeting minutes, 28 June 1946 and Executive Committee meeting minutes, 18 December 1946, reel 39, box 66, N110, CRC Papers. Charles Pope Smith, "Theodore G. Bilbo's Senatorial Career. The Final Years: 1941–47" (Ph.D. diss., University of Southern Mississippi, 1983); CRC petition on Columbia, ca. 1946, reel 29, box 60, folder 8, National Negro Congress Papers.

9. Norman Wilson to CRC, 14 December 1946, box 5, folder, "Threat Letters," CRC-Mich. Papers: "You want a damned Black N-g-er to get hold in this country . . . [CRC] is truly in respect for the N-g-er Race . . ."; Rev. Charles Hamilton to CRC, 19 December 1947, reel 48, box 83, P116, CRC Papers.

10. George Marshall to Tom Clark, 21 August 1946, box 62, Folder, "Georgia Mass Lynchings," CRC-Mich. Papers; *Michigan Chronicle* 3 August 1946.

11. Report on police brutality, undated, reel 42, box 73, N309, 310, CRC Papers; "Lobby to End Lynching," 6 February 1948, reel 40, box 68, N178, reel 41, box 71, N252, CRC Papers; press releases, 20 July 1948, 27 July 1951, 7 September 1951, reel 6, box 9, A172, CRC Papers; statement on Till lynching, ca. 1955, reel 27, box 45, J105, CRC Papers.

12. CRC memorandum, "Civil Liberties in 1947–48: An Analysis of Purposes and Methods for the Civil Rights Congress," reel 6, box 9, A188, CRC Papers; minutes of Executive Committee meeting, 10 September 1947, reel 24, box 41, J41, CRC Papers; "Action Letter" 15 April 1947, 15 May 1947, 22 January 1947, reel 24, box 41, J41, CRC Papers.

13. Joseph Cadden to C. Wayland Brooks, 17 March 1948, reel 15, box 25, B39, CRC Papers; circular, ca. 1946–47, reel 47, box 82, P97, CRC Papers; report of proceedings, CRC National Conference in Chicago, 21–23 November 1947, reel 26, box 43, J102, CRC Papers; Leon Weiner to William Patterson, 23 May 1949, reel 2, box 4, folder 17, Oakley Johnson Papers.

14. Aubrey Grossman to C. H. Talbot, 19 June 1951, reel 47, box 81, P77, CRC Papers; CRC press release, ca. 1951, reel 18, box 27, C22, CRC Papers; series of Patterson statements on *Brown* decision, reel 29, box 48, J163, CRC Papers; Clyde Jackson to Aubrey Grossman, 29 March 1951, reel 35, box 60, M88, CRC Papers.

15. Evelyn Murov to Ralph Powe, 19 September 1949, reel 13, box 22, A425, CRC Papers.

16. "Summary, Annual Report of Secretary of Lawyers Panel for Civil Rights," 27 April 1950, reel 6, box 9, A182, CRC Papers.

17. Frank Davis to William Patterson, 19 November 1948, reel 34, box 57, M27, CRC Papers.

18. Arthur McPhaul to Abner Green, 14 March 1952, box 65, Folder, Defense Committee for Negro Leadership, CRC-Mich. Papers; Doxey Wilkerson to Arthur McPhaul, 2 April 1952; and Arthur McPhaul to Doxey Wilkerson, 7 April 1952, box 65, Folder, Defense Committee for Negro Leadership, CRC-Mich. Papers.

19. Len Goldsmith to L. G. Dutton, 13 December 1948, reel 10, box 16, A321, CRC Papers; *Daily Worker,* 24 April 1949; Russell Coppock to CRC, 14 August 1949, reel 48, box 83, P125, CRC Papers; *State v. Katz,* 241 Iowa 115 (1949); unnamed newspaper from Des Moines, Iowa, 15 December 1949, reel 47, box 81, P76, CRC Papers; Edna Griffin and John Bibbs to CRC, 11 December 1949, reel 47, box 81, P76, CRC Papers.

20. Edna Griffin to William Patterson, 5 October 1949, reel 47, box 81, P76, CRC Papers; Elizabeth Wright to Milt Wolf, 13 June 1949, reel 47, box 81, P76, CRC Papers; Charles Howard to William Patterson, 22 February 1950, box 9, folder 37, William Patterson Papers; Robert Goostree, "The Iowa Civil Rights Statute: A Problem of Enforcement," *Iowa Law Review* (Fall 1952): 242–48.

21. *Tuscon Daily Citizen,* 5 April 1949; report, ca. 1952, reel 48, box 84, P156, CRC Papers.

22. Discrimination forms, box 65, folder, Discrimination, Local, 1950–1952, CRC-Mich. Papers; *Liberator,* March 1949, reel 38, box 64, N18, CRC Papers; *Liberator,* January 1949, reel 8, box 13, A261, CRC Papers; Ralph Shapiro to Ralph Powe, 27 September 1949, reel 5, box 7, A122, CRC Papers; Hillis Hooper to Ida Rothstein, 11 October 1951, reel 45, box 77, P24, CRC Papers; press release, 25 January 1954, box 66, Folder, "Discrimination-1954," CRC-Mich. Papers; Beulah Whitby to Arthur McPhaul, 25 February 1954, box 66, Folder, "Discrimination 1954," CRC-Mich. Papers.

23. Cedric Belfrage, *The American Inquisition, 1945–1960* (Indianapolis, Ind.: Bobbs-Merrill, 1973), 141; Oakley Johnson, "The New Orleans Story," December 1965, box 2, folder 55, William Patterson Papers; *Louisiana Weekly,* 5 June 1948; *City of New Orleans v. Joseph Mouledos et al.,* no. 129, 943, Criminal District Court, Parish of New Orleans, State of Louisiana; *Louisiana Weekly,* 26 November 1949; *Daily Worker,* 24 April 1949; *New Orleans Times-Picayune,* 3 November 1949; William Patterson to Oakley Johnson, 23 April 1951, reel 35, box 60, M88, CRC Papers.

24. C. L. R. James to Walter White, 24 September 1952, box 210, NAACP Papers; Lene Koch, "Anti-Communism in the American Labor Movements; Reflections on the Communist Expulsion in 1949–1950," *American Studies in Scandinavia* 14 (Winter 1981): 93–110.

25. W. C. Turmaine to Anne Shore, 17 December 1948, box 1, CRC-L.A. Papers; John Gose to CRC, undated, box 1, CRC Papers.

26. William Patterson to Arthur Hollander, 17 August 1948, reel 35, box 60, M79, CRC Papers; David Rein to George Marshall, 4 November 1948, Bail Fund-Case records, Robert Dunn Papers.

27. *New York Herald Tribune,* 27 April 1952; William Patterson to Mr. and Mrs. R. L. Caulder, 12 August 1952, reel 34, box 57, M12, CRC Papers; William Patterson to Robert Bush, 16 April 1954, reel 34, box 57, M9, CRC Papers; William Patterson to Lu Ping, 15 April 1954, reel 34, box 57, M8, CRC Papers; *Daily Worker,* 14 April 1955.

28. Nadya Schwartz to William Patterson, 7 August 1953, reel 47, box 81, P80, CRC Papers.

29. *St. Louis Argus,* 12 March 1954; *U.S. v. James Forest,* no. 27236, U.S. District Court for Eastern District of Missouri.

30. Circular, ca. 1955, reel 25, box 43, J77, CRC Papers; *Daily Worker,* 3 March 1955, 24 March 1955.

31. Press release, ca. 1955, reel 2, box 2, A26, CRC Papers.

32. William Patterson to David McKay, 2 February 1955, box 9, folder 47, William Patterson Papers; Sylvia Brown to William Patterson, 1 February 1955, box 9, folder 39, William Patterson

Papers; Civil Liberties docket, *Brownell v. CRC*, 106–53, Subversive Activities Control Board, reel 2, box 4, A49, CRC Papers. Ben Margolis to Gerald Horne, 4 April 1984, in possession of author.

33. Press release, 13 October 1955, reel 5, box 7, A136, CRC Papers.

34. U.S. Congress, House, Committee on Un-American Activities, hearings. Testimony of Walter S. Steel regarding Communist Activities in the U.S. 80th Congress. 1st Session on HR 1884 and HR 2122, 21 July 1947 (Washington, D.C.: G.P.O.); U.S. Congress, House, Committee on Un-American Activities, *Report on Civil Rights Congress as a Communist Front Organization*, 80th Congress, 2d session, 27–29, 31 May 1948 (Washington, D.C.: G.P.O.); "Guide to Subversive Organizations and Publications," 3 March 1951, reel 29, box 48, J176, CRC Papers.

35. U.S. Congress, House, Committee on Un-American Activities, Exposé of the Communist Party of Western Pennsylvania. Based upon Testimony of Matthew Cvetic. 81st Congress, 2d session, 21–23 February 1950 and 13–14, 24 March 1950 (Washington, D.C.: G.P.O.), 1293, 1303.

36. U.S. Congress, House, Committee on Un-American Activities, hearings. Investigation of Communist Activities in the Pacific Northwest Area. Part 10 (Portland). 83d Congress, 2d session, 19 June 1954, testimony of Robert Wishart Canon; U.S. Congress, House, Committee on Un-American Activities, hearings. Investigation of Communist Activities in the San Diego, California Area. 84th Congress, 1st session, 5–6 July 1955; *Detroit Free Press*, 15 February 1955; press release, 1 October 1948, reel 6, box 9, A167, CRC Papers.

37. *National Lawyers Guild v. FBI*, DOJ file 146-1-16-241, FBI document serial no. 100-7321, 100-31535-1B-27-20, 100-31535, 100-1945-Sub A-1345, 100-26851A. National Lawyers Guild Papers.

38. *National Lawyers Guild v. FBI*, DOJ file 146-1-16-241, FBI document serial no. 100-7321, 100021340, section 56, 100-26851, 100-26851A, NY-100-10769-870; Anthony Marro, "FBI Break-in Policy," in Athan Theoharis, ed., *Beyond the Hiss Case: The FBI, Congress and the Cold War* (Philadelphia: Temple University Press, 1982), 78-128, 98.

39. *People's Whirl*, ca. 1951, box 3, folder 24, Daschbach Papers.

40. Postcards, reports, box 3, folder 24, Daschbach Papers.

41. John Daschbach to Winfield King, 20 June 1950, box 3, folder 24, Daschbach Papers; "Art" to John Daschbach, 17 June 1950, box 3, folder 24, Daschbach Papers; John Daschbach to Gazzetta Italiana, 2 August 1951, box 3, folder 24, Daschbach Papers.

42. *Pittsburgh Courier*, 5 May 1951; circular, ca. 1952, box 4, folder, "Steering Committee, 1952–55," CRC-Mich. Papers; Anne Shore to Aubrey Grossman, 26 February 1952, reel 47, box 82, P104, CRC Papers; Anne Shore to Aubrey Grossman, 26 February 1952, reel 47, box 82, P104, CRC Papers.

43. Circular, ca. 1953, box 3, folder, "Garden Party Case—1953," CRC-Mich. Papers; *Detroit Free Press*, 28 July 1953; *Detroit News*, 12 August 1953; Arthur McPhaul to Paul Robeson, 13 March 1953, box 3, folder, "Correspondence 1953," CRC-Mich. Papers.

44. Anne Shore to William Patterson, 6 November 1953, reel 47, box 83, P95, CRC papers; Arthur McPhaul to Aubrey Grossman, 15 January 1953, reel 47, box 83, P95, CRC Papers; Arthur McPhaul to Aubrey Grossman, ca. 1953, reel 47, box 83, P93, CRC Papers.

45. William Patterson to Ruth, Bob, and Agnes Jane Patterson, 21 May 1949, reel 35, box 60, M82, CRC Papers; "Marge and Roger" to Emil Freed, 26 September 1949, Emil Freed Papers: U.S. Congress, Senate, Committee on the Judiciary, hearings before the Subcommittee to Investigate the Administration of the Internal Security Act and Other Internal Security Laws on Communist Underground Printing Facilities and Illegal Propaganda. 83d Congress, 1st session, 6, 13, 31 March, 10 April–28 May, 11 June, 11 July 1953; *Orloff v. Willoughby*, 345 US 83 (1952).

46. U.S. Congress, House, Committee on the Un-American Activities, hearings. Communist Infiltration of Hollywood Motion Picture Industry—Part 2, 17, 23–25 April, 1–18 May 1951; Eric Bentley, ed., *Thirty Years of Treason: Excerpts from Hearings before the House Committee on Un-American Activities, 1938–1968* (New York: Viking, 1971), 533–43; U.S. Congress, House, Committee on Un-American Activities. Investigation of Communist Activities in the New York

City Area—Part 1. 83d Congress, 1st session, 4 May 1953; David Caute, *The Fellow-Travellers: A Postscript to the Enlightenment* (New York: MacMillan, 1973); U.S. Congress, House, Committee on Un-American Activities, hearings on Communism in the Detroit Area—Part 1. 82d Congress, 2d session, 25–29 May 1952, p. 2886; Amiri Baraka, *The Autobiography of LeRoi Jones* (New York: Freundlich, 1984), 122.

Chapter 3. Against His Will

1. Jessie Guzman to William Patterson, 28 February 1951, reel 9, box 14, A280, CRC Papers; Memorandum from Bella Abzug, 28 February 1951, reel 6, box 10, A201, CRC papers.

2. Willie McGee to CRC, 17 August 1948, reel 6, box 10, A206, CRC Papers; Willie McGee to William Patterson, 17 November 1948, reel 6, box 10, A206, CRC Papers; Willie McGee to William Patterson, 27 April 1951, reel 20, box 27, C21, CRC Papers.

3. Bessie McGee to William Patterson, 18 June 1949; Rosa McGee to William Patterson, 1 August 1950; William Patterson to Willie McGee, 22 November 1950; William Patterson to Willie McGee, 13 November 1950; William McGee to William Patterson, 29 September 1948, reel 6, box 10, A206, CRC Papers. Milton Kaufman to Bessie McGee, 15 October 1946, reel 6, box 10, A206, CRC Papers.

4. *New York Post,* 8 May 1951; undated news articles, reel 12, box 26, C4, CRC Papers; Anthony Lake Newberry, "Without Urgency or Ardor: The South's Middle-of-the-Road Liberals and Civil Rights, 1945–1960" (Ph.D. diss., Ohio University, 1982), 199, 195–96, 124–5.

5. Decca Truehaft to William and Louise Patterson, 17 May 1975, box 2, folder 81, William Patterson Papers; *Afro-American,* 5 August 1950, 24 March 1951, 21 May 1955; *Pittsburgh Courier,* 5 August 1950, 19 May 1951, 4 October 1952; *Amsterdam News,* 29 July 1950, 10 February 1951, 24 March 1951, 12 May 1951, 19 May 1951.

6. Carl Rowan, *South of Freedom* (New York: Knopf, 1954), 186–87, 175.

7. James Jackson, "The Effect of the War Economy on the South," *Political Affairs* 30 (February 1951): 116; William Patterson to John Abt, George Murphy, Louis Burnham, 21 July 1950, reel 6, box 10, A204, CRC Papers; Frederick Cropp to Lottie Gordon, 24 February 1950, reel 51, box 90, S38, CRC Papers.

8. Copy of affidavit by Willie McGee, 3 February 1951, reel 6, box 10, A201, CRC papers; "Recorded Interview in Jackson, Mississippi on 30 June 1952 with Mr. Dixon Pyle, Defense Attorney in the Second McGee Trial," reel 7, box 11, A222, CRC Papers; "Recorded Interview in Laurel, Mississippi on 26 June 1952 with Rev. G. D. Tucker, Mrs. Troy Hawkins' Pastor," reel 7, box 11, A223, CRC papers.

9. Affidavit of Rosalee McGee, 6 July 1950, reel 6, box 10, A201, CRC papers.

10. "Fact Sheet" on Willie McGee case, 22 May 1950, reel 6, box 10, A205, CRC Papers.

11. Affidavit by Louis Burnham, 14 April 1948, File, "Willie McGee Case," SNYC Papers.

12. George Marshall to Louis Burnham, 13 December 1945, reel 51, box 90, S37, CRC Papers; "The Willie McGee Fact Sheet," undated, reel 7, box 11, A216, CRC Papers; interview with Dan Breland, 30 June 1952, reel 7, box 11, A219, CRC Papers; "Recorded Interview in Jackson, Mississippi on 2 July 1952 with John Poole, Defense Attorney in the Third McGee trial," reel 7, box 10, A221, CRC Papers.

13. Breland interview, 30 June 1952, reel 7, box 11, A219, CRC Papers.

14. "Recorded interview in Hattiesburg, Mississippi on July 3, 1952 with Mr. London, Defense Attorney associated with Mr. John Poole in the Third McGee trial," reel 7, box 11, A220, CRC Papers.

15. "Fact Sheet" on Willie McGee case, 22 May 1950, reel 6, box 10, A205, CRC Papers.

16. Aubrey Grossman to Dick Gladstein, 10 April 1951, reel 6, box 10, A204, CRC Papers; *McGee v. Mississippi,* 337 US 922, 338 US 805, 330 US 958, 340 US 921, 340 US 905, 40 S. 2d 160 (1951).

17. Pyle interview; London interview.

18. Abe Isserman to Mortiner Wolff, 21 February 1946, reel 6, box 10, A205, CRC Papers; Harriet Bourlog to Aubrey Grossman, undated, reel 6, box 10, A204, CRC Papers.

19. *NLG v. FBI,* Report on Bella Abzug and McGee case, 1 May 1951; other reports, 13 May 1951, 14 March 1951, 2 November 1951, 100-358684, memo from Royal J. Untreiner, 18 December 1947, JK 100-6-vol. 3, NLG Papers.

20. SAC Mobile to Director FBI, 7 April 1951, 100-358684, vols. 1 and 2, NLG Papers.

21. Bella Abzug to CRC, 6 February 1951, Bella Abzug to CRC, 24 May 1951, Bella Abzug to CRC, 1 August 1951, reel 6, box 20, A205, CRC Papers; Aubrey Grossman to Bella Abzug, 19 December 1951, reel 6, box 9, A182, CRC Papers; William Patterson to Bella Abzug, 18 May 1951, reel 19, box 30, F12, CRC Papers.

22. William Patterson to Jennings Perry, 8 July 1950, reel 6, box 10, A204, CRC Papers.

23. Arthur McPhaul to William Patterson, 17 May 1951, reel 47, box 82, P93, CRC Papers; William Patterson to William Nunn, 23 May 1951, reel 34, box 58, M36, CRC Papers.

24. Oakley Johnson to Dr. John Dombrowski, 7 July 1950, reel 6, box 10, A204, CRC papers; Oakley Johnson to Bishop G. Bromley Oxnam, 7 July 1950, reel 6, box 10, A204, CRC Papers; William Patterson to John Garfield, 15 July 1950, reel 6, box 10, A204, CRC Papers; William Patterson to workers' leaders, 20 July 1950, reel 6, box 10, A204, CRC papers; Aubrey Grossman, 14 March 1951, reel 6, box 10, A204, CRC Papers.

25. Aubrey Grossman to William Patterson, 29 March 1951, reel 7, box 11, A210, CRC Papers.

26. *Daily Compass,* 28 July 1950; *Daily Compass,* 3 August 1950, 4 August 1950, 6 August 1950, 8 August 1950, 9 August 1950, 10 August 1950, 14 August 1950, 7 September 1950; *Daily Worker,* 7 August 1950; *Daily News,* 2 August 1950; CRC report on McGee rally in Times Square, July 1950, reel 53, box 93, V33, CRC Papers.

27. Les Davis to Aubrey Grossman, 19 August 1950, reel 46, box 80, P62, CRC Papers; Les Davis to William Patterson, 19 July 1950, reel 46, box 80, P62, CRC Papers; press release, 13 February 1951, reel 7, box 11, A233, CRC Papers.

28. "A Program of Action to Save Willie McGee," 22 February 1951, reel 7, box 11, A215, CRC Papers.

29. "Chapter Bulletin," 19 March 1951, reel 10, box 16, A328, CRC Papers.

30. "Information to Assist Delegates in Seeing Members of Congress," undated, reel 7, box 10, A224, CRC Papers; Emmanuel Celler to Attorney General McGrath, 26 April 1951, reel 6, box 10, A204, CRC Papers; Nancy to Aubrey Grossman, 4 April 1951, reel 6, box 10, A204, CRC Papers.

31. William Patterson to Telepress, undated, reel 6, box 10, A204, CRC Papers; *The Nation,* 3–10 September 1983, p. 172, press releases, undated and 13 March 1951, reel 7, box 11, A215, CRC Papers.

32. William Patterson to contemporary writers, 2 September 1948, reel 34, box 57, M25, CRC Papers; *Memphis Commercial Appeal,* 27 March 1951.

33. *Daily Worker,* 25 June 1950; press release, 13 May 1950, reel 51, box 90, S38, CRC Papers; Belfrage, *The American Inquisition, 1945–1960,* 142; press release, 26 April 1951, reel 43, box 73, N312, CRC Papers; statement by William Patterson, 29 May 1951, reel 43, box 73, N312, CRC Papers; CRC Statement, 1 June 1951, reel 43, box 73, N312, CRC Papers; Bella Abzug and John Coe to Tom Elliston, 2 May 1951, reel 6, box 10, A208, CRC Papers; report on trade union delegation, 4 May 1951, reel 43, box 73, N312, CRC Papers; CRC statement, 4 May 1951, reel 43, box 73, N312, CRC Papers; William Patterson to Telepress, 4 April 1951, reel 43, box 73, N312, CRC Papers.

34. Leo Margolin to Alan Reitman, ca. 1951, vol. 56, 1951, American Civil Liberties Union Papers; Alan Reitman to Roger Baldwin, 29 Jun 1951, vol. 56, 1951, ACLU Papers; Roger Baldwin to Alan Reitman, ca. 1951, vol. 56, 1951, ACLU Papers.

35. Memo from Paris office of American Jewish Committee, 18 May 1951, vol. 56, 1951, ACLU Papers.

36. Herbert Levy to Victor Gollancz, 21 July 1950, vol. 56, 1951, ACLU Papers.

37. William Patterson to Telepress, 26 April 1951, reel 43, box 73, N312, CRC Papers.

38. George Blake, "The Trade Union Movement and the McGee Case," *Political Affairs* 30 (August 1951): 23; James Carey to Isidore Rosenberg, undated, reel 6, box 10, A204, CRC Papers.

39. "Program of Action for Trade Unions to Save the Life of Willie McGee," 2 March 1951, reel 7, box 11, A215, CRC Papers; Aubrey Grossman to John Daschbach, 16 April 1951, reel 6, box 10, A204, CRC Papers; Nat Ross to U.E., Local 430 and UOPWA, 20 July 1950 and 28 July 1950, reel 6, box 10, A205, CRC Papers; Nat Ross to Shipyard Workers, Local 22, 24 July 1950, reel 6, box 10, A205, CRC Papers.

40. Report on Detroit McGee Activity, ca. 1951, box 63, folder, "Willie McGee Clipping, 1948–1951," CRC-Mich. Papers; *Pittsburgh Courier,* 21 April 1951; McGee resolution, box 63, folder, Willie McGee Correspondence 1951, CRC-Mich. Papers.

41. William Patterson to "All Chapter Secretaries," 19 March 1951, reel 4, box 4, A68, CRC Papers; Aubrey Grossman to Rev. R. H. Harris, et al., 12 July 1950, reel 6, box 10, A204, CRC Papers; press release, 21 October 1952, reel 43, box 74, N320, CRC Papers.

42. Forrest Jackson to Abe Isserman, 23 February 1946, reel 6, box 10, A208, CRC Papers; CRC to Benjamin Dreyfus and Francis McTernan, 16 July 1946, reel 6, box 10, A209, CRC Papers.

43. Laurent Frantz to Milton Kaufman, 23 September 1946, reel 6, box 20, A206, CRC Papers; Laurent Frantz to "Milt," 21 January 1947, reel 48, box 83, P116, CRC Papers.

44. *Jackson Daily News,* 20 July 1950; Aubrey Grossman to "All Chapters with Cars Leaving for Jackson, Mississippi," 20 July 1950, reel 6, box 10, A204, CRC Papers; William Patterson to James Wechsler, Ralph Matthews, Hodding Carter, Frank Kelly, J. Howard McGrath, 21 July 1950, reel 6, box 10, A204, CRC Papers.

45. *South Bend Tribune,* 27 July 1950; *St. Louis American,* 3 August 1950; report, 16 August 1950, file no. 100-13556, New Orleans, FBI.

46. Affidavit of Dorothy Bushnell Cole, 16 October 1950, reel 7, box 11, A215, CRC Papers.

47. Report on women's delegation, 18 March 1951, reel 6, box 10, A205, CRC Papers; *Jackson Daily News,* 17 March 1951; Aubrey Grossman to Mary Kalb, 2 May 1951, reel 6, box 10, A204, CRC Papers.

48. Decca Truehaft to Aubrey Grossman, 11 June 1951, reel 45, box 77, P7, CRC Papers; Decca Truehaft to William Patterson, undated, reel 45, box 77, P8, CRC Papers; William Patterson to Decca Truehaft, 7 April 1951, reel 45, box 77, P8, CRC Papers.

49. *Jackson Daily News,* 17 January 1951, 18 January 1951, 15 January 1951.

50. Anne Braden to Aubrey Grossman, 3 May 1951, reel 6, box 10, A204, CRC Papers.

51. Aubrey Grossman to Jack Dhyr, 2 May 1951; William Patterson to J. Pius Barber, 18 August 1950; and Rae Gwynn to CRC, 5 May 1949, reel 6, box 10, A204, CRC Papers.

52. Aubrey Grossman to Louis Goldblatt, ca. 1951, reel 6, box 10, A204, CRC Papers; *New York Times,* 6 May 1951; *Daily Compass,* 7 May 1951; *Peoples World,* 7 May 1951.

53. "The Reminiscences of Anne Braden," July 1979, #1275, PRCQ, Columbia University Oral History.

54. "Civil Rights Champion," reel 7, box 11, A217, CRC Papers; Bessie McGee to CRC, undated, reel 51, box 90, S40, CRC Papers; *New York Times,* 8 May 1951; *New York Times,* 6 November 1951; *New York Times,* 18 January 1951; *New York Times,* 8 May 1951; *Daily Compass,* 9 May 1951; *Droit et Liberté,* 4–10 May 1951; Carl Rowan, *South of Freedom* (New York: Knopf, 1954), 191; *Arkansas State Press,* 25 May 1951; *Daily Worker,* 16 April 1951.

55. *Daily Worker,* 28 May 1951; *Willett Hawkins v. Freedom of the Press Co., Inc., John Gates and George Lohr,* U.S. District Court, Southern District of New York, reel 5, box 7, A111, CRC Papers; "Recorded Interview in Jackson, Mississippi on June 30, 1952, with Mr. Dixon Pyle, Defense Attorney in the Second McGeen Trial," reel 7, box 11, A222, CRC Papers; *Daily Worker,* 28 July 1952.

56. Aubrey Grossman to B. F. Logan, 8 June 1951, reel 34, box 58, M36, CRC Papers; Ralph Bunche to Aubrey Grossman, 13 January 1952, reel 6, box 10, A205, CRC Papers; "Monthly

Report," 26 May 1952, reel 10, box 16, A328, CRC Papers; press release, 12 May 1952, reel 7, box 11, A213, CRC Papers; press release, 29 May 1952, reel 15, box 27, C21, CRC Papers; press release, 17 April 1952, reel 15, box 27, C21, CRC Papers.

57. William Patterson to Al-Tony Gilmore, 19 August 1975, box 2, folder 45, William Patterson Papers; William Patterson to Dorothy Cole, 17 May 1951, reel 46, box 80, P63, CRC Papers; William Patterson to Decca Truehaft, 29 May 1975, box 2, folder 81, William Patterson Papers; Patterson's comments about Truehaft's *A Fine Old Conflict* are also revealing: ". . . I am not happy with it." he criticizes her for not allowing him to comment beforehand on certain chapters and stated that he did not consider the book "a positive contribution." Truehaft, CRC leader in Oakland, joined the Communist Party in 1943 and left in 1958. William Patterson to Decca Truehaft, 9 September 1977, box 2, folder 81, William Patterson Papers. Robert Nemiroff, "From These Roots: Lorraine Hansberry and the South," *Southern Exposure* 12 (September–October 1984): 32–36; Those seeking to engage in further research on the McGee case should contact the Clerk, Supreme Court of Mississippi, Carroll Gartin Building, Jackson, Ms. 39201; Circuit Clerk, Jones County, Second District, Laurel, Ms. 39440 (File no. 1173, 1268); Mississippi State Library, P.O. Box 1040, Jackson, Mississippi 39205; also Mississippi Department of Archives.

Chapter 4. Defending Communists; Fighting Anticommunism

1. Claude Lightfoot, "The Struggle to End the Cold War at Home," *Political Affairs* 34 (September 1955): 36; *Crisis* 62 (December 1955): 620; Lloyd Brown, *Stand Up for Freedom: The Negro People vs. the Smith Act* (New York: New Century, 1952), 101. During the same time, Lightfoot was told by a Black Illinois State Senator that in order to get a civil rights bill, he was told he had to support an anticommunist bill (Claude Lightfoot, *Chicago Slums to World Politics: Autobiography of Claude M. Lightfoot* [New York: New Outlook, 1986], 119).

2. David Jacob Group, "The Legal Repression of the American Communist Party, 1946–1961: A Study in the Legitimation of Coercion" (Ph.D. diss., University of Massachusetts, 1979), 85; CRC statement, 7 December 1950, reel 43, box 74, N326, CRC Papers; statement by George Marshall on the Cole Bill, 6 November 1948, reel 39, box 67, N150, CRC Papers; U.S. Congress, House, Committee on Un-American Activities, report on Hawaii Civil Liberties Committee: A Communist Front, 23 June 1950; U.S. Congress, Senate, permanent Subcommittee on Investigation of the Committee on Government Operations, Communist Party Activities, Western Pennsylvania, 18 June 1953, vol. 122, p. 7, 13499, reel 3, box 4, A58, CRC Papers; U.S. Congress, Senate, Committee on the Judiciary, hearing before the Subcommittee to Investigate the Administration of the Internal Security Act and Other Internal Security Laws, 83d Congress, 2d session, 22 June 1954. Here *Daily Worker* reporter Abner Green was queried at length about CRC (p. 30).

3. Michael Belknap, *Cold War Political Justice: The Smith Act, the Communist Party and American Civil Liberties* (Westport, Conn.: Greenwood Press, 1977), 58, 60, 172; Alex Deutsch to CRC, 31 July 1952, reel 34, box 57, M27, CRC Papers.

4. Undated statement by William Patterson, reel 28, box 47, J156, CRC Papers.

5. Ibid.

6. Elizabeth Gurley Flynn, "The Militant Traditions of Labor Defense Inspire Our Fight Today," *Political Affairs* 30 (February 1951): 126, 128.

7. William Patterson to Yetta Land, 17 October 1951, reel 45, box 77, P2, CRC Papers; Yetta Land to William Patterson, 13 September 1951, reel 45, box 77, P2, CRC Papers; William Patterson to Yetta Land, 26 September 1951, reel 45, box 77, P2, CRC Papers; Conference Program, 11 October 1947, reel 24, box 41, J41, CRC Papers; *New York Times,* 22 July 1948; *Daily Worker,* 22 July 1948; Conference Program, 16–17 July 1949, reel 2, box 1, A12, CRC Papers. Other sponsors were Earl Dickerson, Thomas Emerson, Robert Kenny, Linus Pauling, Percy Green, Albert Maltz, Vito Marcantonio, Clifford Odets, Paul Robeson, I. F. Stone, Mary

Church Terrell, Melville Herskovits et al.; press release, 28 June 1950, reel 6, box 9, A181, CRC Papers. On the program at Madison Square Garden were Patterson, Earl Conrad, Ring Lardner, Jr., Vincent Hallinan, Ben Gold, Gus Hall, Gale Sondergaard, Ferdinand Smith, Paul Robeson, Vito Marcantonio, Albert Kahn, Richard Morford, Abe Lederman (suspended New York City teacher) and the wives of political prisoners (Edith Marzani, Peggy Dennis, Betty Fast et al.) Telegrams were sent to Truman (re: Smith Act defendants), Gov. John Battle of Virginia and Gov. Fielding Wright of Mississippi (re: Martinsville 7 and Willie McGee respectively).

8. Henry Wallace, "America's Thought Police," reel 59, box 104, W99, CRC Papers; "Speaker's Outline: The Smith Act," reel 10, box 16, A328, CRC Papers; comic book, reel 4, box 5, A80, CRC Papers; *Daily Compass,* 22 February 1951. Printed here was an open letter to Chief Justice Fred Vinson from Howard Fast calling for voiding of the Smith Act.

9. "Smith Act Trial Reports," 10 April 1952, reel 14, box 23, B21, CRC Papers; memo from Sarah Lesser, undated, box 5, folder 10, Daschbach Papers; minutes of CEDC meeting, 15 July 1952, reel 57, box 101, W14, CRC Papers; memo on CEDC, ca. 1952, reel 57, box 57, W14, CRC Papers; Smith Act News, 20 September 1951, reel 29, box 48, J164, CRC Papers.

10. Sam Kantner to Clifford McVoy, 1 April 1953, reel 57, box 101, W14, CRC Papers; "In the Matter of the Proposed Designation of the Citizens Emergency Defense Conference Pursuant to Executive Order No. 10450," reel 57, box 101, W16, CRC Papers; CEDC to Warren Olney, III, 13 November 1953, reel 57, box 101, W16, CRC Papers.

11. *The Nation,* 12 July 1947; circular from CRC, 24 July 1947, reel 24, box 41, J41, CRC Papers; Joseph Cadden to Virginia Dodge, 12 August 1947, reel 48, box 83, P107, CRC Papers; *Marzani v. U.S.,* 335 US 895 (1948).

12. William Patterson to "Dear Friend," undated, reel 4, box 6, A99, CRC Papers; minutes of CRC meeting on Eisler case, 20 November 1948, reel 4, box 6, A99, CRC Papers.

13. *Detroit Times,* 16, December 1947; *Daily Worker,* 11 December 1947; *Detroit News,* 27 October 1947; Harry Ward to Max Yergan, 19 February 1947, reel 24, box 41, J41, CRC Papers; undated latter to Harry Truman, reel 4, box 6, A99, CRC Papers; Gerhart Eisler to David Rein, 19 August 1948, reel 4, box 6, A99, CRC Papers; "Reversible Errors in Both Eisler Convictions," 10 July 1949, reel 4, box 6, A99, CRC Papers; Attorney George Bragdon, a retired government attorney with twenty-five years experience in the field penned an incredibly detailed five-page single-spaced memo on the legal issues of the case (Memo, 27 June 1949, reel 4, box 6, A99, CRC Papers). Gerhart Eisler to William Patterson, 5 February 1949, reel 3, box 3, N34, CRC Papers; U.S. Congress, House, Committee on Un-American Activities, "The Shameful Years: Thirty Years of Soviet Espionage in the United States," 82d Congress, 2d session, 1952. A section on Eisler and CRC appears at pp. 42–45; *Eisler v. U.S.,* 337 US 912 (1949), 338 US 883 (1949), 170 F2d 273 (1948), 83 U.S. App. D.C. 315 (1948).

14. Group, *Legal Repression,* 97, 101, 105, 110.

15. "Loyalty and Private Employment: The Right of Employers to Discharge Suspected Subversives," *Yale Law Journal* 54 (May 1953): 954–84; *CRC v. Tom Clark et al.,* U.S. District Court, reel 3, box 4, A51, CRC Papers; Al Tanz to William Patterson et al., 24 January 1949, reel 6, box 9, A188, CRC Papers; newsclipping, undated, reel 6, box 9, A189, CRC Papers; U.S. Congress, House, Committee on Un-American Activities, report on Civil Rights Congress as a Communist front organization. Investigation of Un-American Activities in the United States. 80th Congress, 1st session, 2 September 1947.

16. Grace Stewart to William Patterson, 24 December 1948, reel 34, box 57, M25, CRC Papers; press release, 5 December 1947; Joseph Cadden to Harry Truman, 10 December 1947; and John Rogge to William Patterson, 1 September 1949, box 9, folder 43, 12 August 1949, William Patterson papers; George Marshall to Secretary of War et al., 2 July 1946, reel 34, box 57, M22, CRC Papers; William Patterson to Joe Clark, 7 October 1948, reel 34, box 57, M25, CRC Papers.

17. Minutes of emergency meeting of Executive Committee, 19 March 1947, reel 24, box 41, J41, CRC Papers; minutes of emergency conference of CRC Chapter Executives, 30 June–1 July 1947, reel 24, box 41, J41, CRC Papers.

18. *Daily Worker,* 23 May 1947; "The Case of Eugene Dennis," reel 4, box 6, A82, CRC Papers; *Eugene Dennis et al. v. USA,* draft of amicus brief by Black lawyers, reel 4, box 5, A79, CRC Papers; F. B. Morris, "58 Years of Congressional Perjury," reel 19, box 30, F16, CRC Papers; *Dennis v. U.S.,* 84 US App. D.C. 31, (171) F2d 986 (1948), 339 US 162 (1949).

19. Press release, 20 July 1948, reel 3, box 3, A37, CRC Papers.

20. *Daily Workers,* 22 August 1948; *Daily Worker,* 29 August 1948.

21. *Daily Worker,* 22 July 1948; *San Francisco Chronicle,* 12 October 1948; press release, 22 September 1948, reel 38, box 63, N53, CRC Papers; circular, ca. 1948, reel 59, box 104, W99, CRC Papers.

22. William Patterson to Dr. K. J. Benes, 24 November 1948, reel 3, box 3, A34, CRC Papers; *Daily Worker,* 10 October 1948; H. Neumann to CRC, 27 March 1950, reel 3, box 3, A31, CRC Papers; Miscellaneous, reel 3, box 3, A31, CRC Papers; *Peoples Voice,* 29 October 1948; Friedrich Schlotterbeck to William Patterson, 1 November 1948, reel 3, box 3, A34, CRC Papers.

23. "$64 Questions—For All Americans," reel 3, box 3, A37, CRC Papers; "What Are the Facts in the Case of the Twelve Indicted Communist Leaders?" reel 3, box 3, A32, CRC Papers; "Campaign against the Frame-up of the Communist Leaders—Speaker's Notes," reel 3, box 3, A35, CRC Papers. "The opening remarks of the speaker should relate the cases under discussion to the problems of the people making up the audience"; George Marion to William Patterson, 26 November 1949, reel 3, box 3, A33, CRC Papers; "Maroon Quill," 20 November 1948, reel 23, box 39, J17, CRC Papers.

24. Plan for CP-11 campaign, September 1948, reel 20, box 34, G30, CRC Papers; William Patterson to Felix Spielman, 1 April 1949, reel 3, box 3, A33, CRC Papers; Felix Spielman to William Patterson, 31 March 1949, reel 21, box 36, G56, CRC Papers; report by Elizabeth Gurley Flynn, 7 April 1949, reel 21, box 36, G56, CRC Papers; press release, 29 March 1949, reel 20, box 34, G29, CRC Papers. Eugene Dennis termed Strong's $1000 donation "tainted."

25. Plan for CP-11 campaign, September 1948, reel 20, box 34, G30, CRC Papers. The relationship with the CP-11 was far from being one-sided: "Every action taken during this campaign must have as one of its goals the recruiting of members into the CRC." *Daily Worker,* 17 January 1949; *Cleveland Plain Dealer,* 28 October 1948; *Cleveland News,* 25 October 1948; Patterson also sought to mobilize the chapters after Communist leader Bob Thompson's seven-year-old daughter was molested by right-wingers. William Patterson to CRC chapter, 22 November 1948, reel 20, box 34, G30, CRC Papers; Harrison Parker to William Patterson, 8 November 1949, reel 34, box 57, M16, CRC Papers.

26. Newspaper clipping, 9 September 1949, reel 20, box 34, G26, CRC Papers; William Patterson to "All Chapter Secretaries," 19 June 1950, reel 27, box 45, J110, CRC Papers.

27. Memo to CRC chapters, 11 September 1950, reel 43, box 74, N327, CRC Papers; William Patterson to CRC chapters, 19 August 1950, reel 43, box 74, N327, CRC Papers; memo to "all chapter secretaries," 22 November 1950, reel 43, box 74, N327, CRC Papers.

28. Arnold Johnson to chapter secretaries, 11 December 1950, reel 35, box 60, M85, CRC Papers; *New York Times,* 22 June 1951; undated memo from Aubrey Grossman, reel 14, box 23, B17, CRC Papers; "Dennis v. U.S.," box 39, folder 14, box 33, folder 12, box 43, folder 15, Felix Frankfurter Papers.

29. Undated flyer, reel 14, box 23, B2, CRC Papers; Detroit CRC release, 1 December 1952, reel 14, box 23, B2, CRC Papers; Aubrey Grossman to Ernest Goodman, 26 November 1952; Anne Shore to Aubrey Grossman, 7 October 1952; and William Patterson to Ernest Goodman, 30 September 1952, reel 14, box 23, B5, CRC Papers.

30. Union resolutions, reel 20, box 32, G4, CRC Papers; Conrad Komorowski to William Patterson, 21 September 1949, reel 19, box 30, F4, CRC Papers; press release, 17 August 1951, reel 27, box 45, J110, CRC Papers.

31. CRC fact sheet, ca. 1950, reel 20, box 33, G12, CRC Papers; William Patterson to Si Gerson, 25 July 1949, reel 20, box 33, G12, CRC Papers; CRC statement, 9 August 1950, reel 20, box 34, G27, CRC Papers; William Patterson to Irving Dillard, 23 April 1952, reel 34, box 58,

M37, CRC Papers; "The American Negro in the Communist Party," 22 December 1954, HUAC report, NAACP Papers.

32. "The Case of the 11 Communist Leaders," May 1951, reel 20, box 33, G23, CRC Papers; "Deadly Parallel," reel 8, box 13, A262, CRC Papers; CRC billboard, reel 52, box 92, U3, CRC Papers.

33. Undated memo from Louise Jeffers on "Ben David Freedom Committee (Provisional)," reel 4, box 5, A80, CRC Papers; brochure and attached petition calling for Ben Davis' freedom, reel 4, box 5, A80, CRC Papers; *Daily Worker,* 13 August 1951; Lloyd Brown, *Stand Up for Freedom: The Negro People vs. the Smith Act,* 10; "Memorandum with Respect to the Content of the Scope of a Petition for a Re-hearing and Supporting Brief on Behalf of Benjamin J. Davis, Jr.," reel 4, box 5, A80, CRC Papers.

34. *Daily Worker,* 15 August 1955; William Patterson to R. L. Witherspoon, 19 April 1954, 27 April 1954, 7 May 1954, 21 May 1954, reel 4, box 5, A78, CRC papers; R. L. Witherspoon to William Patterson, 21 April 1954, reel 4, box 5, A78, CRC Papers; William Patterson to Hope Stevens, 11 March 1954, reel 4, box 5, A78, CRC Papers; William Patterson to Edward J. D'Antignac, 21 September 1953, reel 4, box 5, A78, CRC Papers; William Patterson to Edward J. D'Antignac, 4 February 1954, reel 4, box 5, A78, CRC Papers.

35. William Patterson to Walter Aiken, 11 March 1954, reel 4, box 5, A78, CRC Papers; William Patterson to A. T. Walden, 15 March 1954, reel 4, box 5, A78, CRC Papers; William Patterson to A. T. Walden, 15 March 1954, reel 4, box 5, A78, CRC Papers.

36. William Patterson to Dr. C. B. Powell, 5 September 1952, reel 34, box 57, MIA, CRC Papers; William Patterson to Carl Murphy, 22 September 1953, reel 4, box 5, A78, CRC Papers; William Patterson to Carl Murphy, 4 March 1954, reel 4, box 5, A78, CRC Papers. Patterson had to correct some of Murphy's reportage, reminding him that in refusing to squeal on his associates, Davis did not invoke the Fifth Amendment; Murphy also labored under the popular misconception that Davis had been convicted of conspiring to overthrow the government by force and violence. At that point Davis was serving the third year of a five-year term; William Patterson to Carl Murphy, 13 November 1954, reel 5, box 8, A143, CRC Papers.

37. William Patterson to Hope Stevens, 10 September 1953, reel 4, box 5, A78, CRC Papers; Harry Sacher to J. Howard McGrath, 16 October 1951, reel 4, box 5, A80, CRC Papers; CRC National Office to CRC-Philadelphia, 21 June 1953, reel 4, box 5, A78, CRC Papers.

38. Muriel Symington, 14 August 1953, reel 4, box 5, A78, CRC Papers; William Patterson to James Bennett, 11 August 1953, reel 4, box 5, A78, CRC papers; press release, ca. 1955, reel 4, box 5, A80, CRC Papers; *Afro-American,* 17 July 1954; press release, 18 February 1954, reel 4, box 5, A80, CRC Papers; press release, 17 June 1954, reel 4, box 5, A80, CRC Papers.

39. William Patterson to Willard Ranson, 16 March 1954, reel 4, box 5, A78, CRC Papers; William Patterson to Willard Ransom, 2 April 1954, reel 4, box 5, A78, CRC Papers; William Patterson to Willard Ransom, 25 March 1954, 29 June 1954, reel 4, box 5, A78, CRC Papers; affidavit of James Bennett, ca. 1955, reel 4, box 5, A79, CRC Papers; press release, 28 March 1955, reel 4, box 5, A79, CRC Papers.

40. *Cooper et al. v. Hutchinson,* 88 F. Supp.774, 184 F.2d 119 (1950); *Braverman v. Bar of Association of Baltimore,* 209 Md. 328 (1956), 352 US 830 (1956); *Hallinan v. U.S.,* 182 F2d 880 (1950), 341 US 952 (1950); Conference Working Group, "The Independence of the Bar," *Lawyers Guild Review* 13 (Winter 1953): 161, 162; *Schlesinger Petition,* 367 Pa. 476 (1951), 478.

41. Aubrey Grossman to Richard Gladstein, 28 June 1951, reel 45, box 77, P26, CRC Papers; Aubrey Grossman to Joe Forer, 20 September 1951, reel 14, box 23, B12, CRC Papers; Aubrey Grossman to John McTernan, 17 September 1951, reel 14, box 23, B12, CRC papers; Aubrey Grossman to John Coe, 10 August 1951, reel 14, box 23, B12, CRC Papers.

42. Aubrey Grossman to William Patterson, 22 January 1950, reel 11, box 17, A345, CRC Papers; *Peoples World,* 12 December 1952; memoranda, ca. 1952–53, folders 5, 18, 19, box 5, Daschbach Papers.

43. "Lawyers under Fire," November 1952, reel 50, box 88, R11, CRC Papers; "To All

Chapters," from national office-CRC, 14 November 1950, reel 43, box 74, N327, CRC papers; *Daily Compass,* 6 February 1950; CRC flyer, ca. 1950, reel 14, box 23, B17, CRC Papers. I. F. Stone added, "Every sophisticated person in Washington knows the affair [i.e., prosecution of CP-11-GH] was timed to strike a blow against the Wallace movement lest it take too many votes from the Democrats in the 1948 election. . . . A concerted campaign to intimidate independent members of the bar is under way"; Prof. Thomas Emerson to Lawyers Defense Committee, 17 February 1950, reel 59, box 104, W89, CRC Papers; *New York Post,* 6 July 1952.

44. Harold Ickes to Harold Cammer, 2 August 1951, reel 5, box 7, A135, CRC Papers.

45. Royal France, *My Native Grounds: The Autobiography of Royal W. France* (New York: Cameron, 1957), 97.

46. "Notes of Meeting on Foley Square Lawyers," 25 October 1951, reel 5, box 7, A108, CRC Papers; "Argument to the Jury of Richard Gladstein in the New York Communist Trial," CRC-SF pamphlet, reel 3, box 4, A57, CRC Papers; memorandum on Harry Sacher's disbarment and Isserman's suspension of practice for 2 years by National Lawyers Guild NYC chapter, reel 9, box 14, A275, CRC Papers; *Sacher et al. v. U.S.,* 342 US 858 (1951), 343 US 1 (1951), 341 US 952 (1950), 182 F2d 416 (1950); *In Re Isserman,* 345 US 286 (1952), 9 NJ 269 (1952), 87A2d 903, 88 A2d (1952); *Sacher v. Association of Bar of City of New York,* 346 US 894 (1953) Certioari granted. Note that Telford Taylor, prominent New York lawyer, agreed to serve as counsel in this case (*In Re Isserman* 347 US 388 [1953], Per Curiam, disbarment reversed, *In Re Disbarment of Isserman,* 348 U.S. 1 (1959), earlier decision reversed).

47. Aubrey Grossman to Lewis Moroze, 21 November 1951, reel 11, box 17, A345, CRC Papers; Aubrey Grossman to D. N. Pritt, 5 December 1951, reel 11, box 17, A345, CRC Papers; Ralph Powe to Milton Freedman and Harry Sacher, 2 November 1951; and George Crockett to Aubrey Grossman, 30 October 1951, reel 6, box 9, A177, CRC Papers.

48. Memorandum, 4 August 1949, box 27, folder, Crockett Committee—1949, CRC-Mich. Papers; *Pittsburgh Courier,* 28 January 1950.

49. Esther Jackson to "Dear Member," 29 November 1949, reel 20, box 34, G24, CRC Papers; *NLG v. FBI,* file of George Crockett, HQ 100-367743, vol. 1. DE 100-14857.

50. "Smith Act News," 20 September 1951, reel 11, box 18, A54, CRC Papers; "Summary Proceedings—National Meeting of Families Committee of Smith Act Victims," 26–27 February 1952, reel 19, box 30, F20, CRC Papers; ["United Summer Appeal for Children," 25 June 1953, reel 28, box 47, J150, CRC Papers.]

51. "United Summer Appeal for Children," 25 June 1953, reel 28, box 47, J150, CRC Papers; Doxey Wilkerson to W. E. B. Du Bois, 10 September 1948, reel 3, box 3, A38, CRC Papers; Du Bois address, 17 December 1953, reel 4, box 5, A80, CRC Papers; Du Bois petition to Trgve Lie, Carlos Romulo, Eleanor Roosevelt, Lester Pearson, ca. 1950, reel 65, #360 Du Bois Papers; Du Bois to Pierre Cot, Vaclaw Navratil, et al., 4 March 1954, reel 70, #526, Du Bois Papers; W. E. B. Du Bois to Celia Zitron, 17 June 1954, reel 70, #871, Du Bois Papers.

52. William Patterson to Rev. Sandy Ray, 24 June 1950, reel 2, box 1, A5, CRC Papers; pamphlet on amnesty for Smith Act prisoners, ca. 1953, reel 24, box 41, J48, CRC Papers; "National Committee to Win Amnesty for Smith Act Victims," stationery, ca. 1953, reel 9, box 14, A272, CRC Papers; circular, ca. 1953, reel 57, box 100, W9, CRC Papers; circulars, ca. 1953, reel 23, box 39, J10, 11, 12, CRC Papers.

53. Thomas Emerson, "An Essay on Freedom of Political Expression Today," *Lawyers Guild Review* 11 (Winter 1951): 12, 13, 14; "A Fact Sheet on the McCarran Act," ca. 1949, reel 6, box 10, A195, CRC Papers; Patrick McCarran, "The Internal Security Act of 1950," *University of Pittsburgh Law Review* 12 (Summer 1951): 512; Jerome Edwards, *Pat McCarran: Political Boss of Nevada,* (Reno: University of Nevada Press, 1982).

54. "Provisional Committee for Democratic Rights to Defeat Thomas-Rankin Committee on Un-American Legislation," ca. 1948, reel 28, box 46, J133, CRC Papers; National Committee to Defeat the Mundt Bill, ca. 1948, reel 28, box 46, J133, CRC Papers; National Non-Partisan Mass Delegation to Washington, 2 June 1948, reel 28, box 46, J133, CRC Papers; pamphlet by National Committee to Defeat the Mundt Bill, ca. 1949, reel 42, box 71, N266, CRC Papers.

55. Testimony of Len Goldsmith before Judiciary Committee of U.S. Senate, 28 May 1948, reel 28, box 46, J133, CRC Papers; statement to Subcommittee of Senate Judiciary Committee, on S.1194 and S.1196 by Thomas Buchanan, ca. 1949, reel 40, box 68, N158, CRC Papers; William Patterson to Senator Pat McCarran, 28 April 1949, reel 34, box 57, M24, CRC Papers; Joseph Cadden to George Marshall, 1 June 1948, reel 38, box 64, N55, CRC Papers; William Lawrence to all Executive Board members, 8 July 1948, reel 38, box 64, N55, CRC Papers; Lon Devere Marlowe, III, "The Roots of McCarthyism: The House of Representatives and Internal Security Legislation, 1945–1950" (Ph.D. diss., University of Georgia, 1981); William Patterson to "Dear Friend," 25 October 1950, reel 35, box 60, M88, CRC Papers; Aubrey Grossmen to Ben Margolis, 16 October 1950, reel 35, box 60, M88, CRC Papers; press release, 27 October 1950, reel 43, box 74, N317, CRC Papers; "Memo on Court Test of McCarran Bill," ca. 1950, reel 6, box 10, A192, CRC Papers.

56. List of Congresspersons who voted for and against McCarran Bill, 1951, reel 6, box 10, A194, CRC Papers; John Abt, "The People vs. McCarthysim—The Case against the McCarran Act," 24 October 1953, reel 6, box 10, A196, CRC papers; "People's Conference in Washington to Repeal the McCarran Act," 7–8 March 1954, reel 25, box 44, J91, CRC Papers (cf. also reel 29, box 48, J161 and reel 6, box 10, A195, 197).

57. Press releases, 7 October 1953, 19 October 1953, 22 February 1954, reel 6, box 10, A195, CRC Papers; Charles Metzner to Aubrey Grossman, 4 March 1954, reel 6, box 10, A192, CRC Papers; William Patterson to Louis Graham, 3 April 1954; and Louis Graham to William Patterson, 15 April 1954, reel 19, box 31, F31, CRC Papers; "Data on Communist Control Act of 1954 (Public Law 637)," ca. 1954, reel 3, box 4, A56, CRC Papers; *New York Times,* 21 August 1954; *St. Louis Dispatch,* 21 August 1954.

58. Bob Silberstein to William Patterson, 5 January 1954, reel 19, box 31, F31, CRC Papers; *New York Times,* 9 December 1954; *New York Times,* 10 December 1954; Harold Josephson, "Ex-Communists in Crossfire: A Cold War Debate," *The Historian* 44 (November 1981): 69–84. On Smith Act prosecutions, Robert Mollan, "Smith Act Prosecutions: The Effect of the *Dennis* and *Yates* Decisions," *University of Pittsburgh Law Review* 26 (June 1965): 705–48. This article provides an adequate listing of the various Smith Act prosecutions across the country along with a mildly critical analysis of the legal travesty involved. Cf. also *Doran v. U.S.,* 181 F2d. 489 (1950), appeals from judgments for civil contempt for refusing to answer questions from a federal grand jury in L.A. on the CP. CRC joined the United Steel workers of America and Carey William as amicus. CRC lawyers Ben Margolis and John McTernan were counsel; *Kasinowitz v. U.S.,* 181 F2d 632 (1950). This involved criminal contempt and a sentence of one year for refusing to answer questions before the grand jury. CRC leader Maurice Braverman was indicted under the Smith Act here. In support of his motion for severance, he has amicus filed, signed by over 200 attorneys. Yet, Braverman claimed "he has been unable to obtain the services of one or more members of the Bar to defend him in this case although he has made considerable effect to obtain such professional service." Cf. 198 F2d 679 (1952); *Thompson v. U.S.,* 348 US 841 (cert. denied) (1954), 214 F2d 545 (1954); *Scales v. U.S.,* 227 F2d 581 (1955); *Lightfoot v. U.S.,* 228 F2d 861 (1956). Attorneys for the Black Red were George Crockett, John Abt, and Pearl Hart; *Kremen v. U.S.,* 231 F2d 155, 353 US 346 (1956); *Sentner et al. v. U.S.,* 348 US 935 (1954); *Frankfeld v. U.S.,* 198 F2d 679, cert. denied 344 US 922; *Stein v. U.S.,* 231 F2d 109; *Yates et al. v. U.S.,* 225 F2d 146 (1955). This California Smith Act case had Leo Branton, Ben Margolis, Ben Dreyfus, and A. L. Wirin serving as counsel; *U.S. v. Fujimoto,* 102 F. Supp. 890 (1952). This was a Hawaii Smith Act case.

Chapter 5. A Northern Scottsboro

1. "Fact Sheet on the Case of the Trenton Six," 21 December 1949, reel 8, box 13, A257, CRC Papers.
2. Ibid.

3. Ibid.

4. O. John Rogge, *Our Vanishing Civil Liberties* (New York: Gaer, 1949), 255, 259; William Patterson to Margie Woody, 27 September 1949, reel 12, box 20, A385, CRC Papers; *State of New Jersey v. Ralph Cooper et al.,* 20 vols., (Princeton, 1954); NAACP press release, 26 November 1952, reel 8, box 13, A257, CRC Papers.

5. *Cooper et al. v. Hutchinson,* U.S. District Court, 1949, reel 212, box 20, A392, CRC Papers; *State v. Cooper et al.,* 2 NJ 540, 67 A2d 298 (1949).

6. *Cooper et al. v. Hutchinson,* 184 F2d 119 (1950), 88 F Supp 774 (1949); *Cooper et al. v. Hutchinson,* no. 1036-49, petition of Mercer County Bar Association, reel 12, box 20, A385, CRC Papers.

7. Press release, 25 July 1950, reel 12, box 20, A392, CRC Papers; press release, 4 January 1950, reel 12, box 20, A380, CRC Papers.

8. File on ACLU, reel 23, box 39, J4, CRC Papers; Keynote address by William Patterson, 19–20 February 1955, National Leadership Conference, reel 26, box 44, J90, CRC papers; Donald McCoy and Richard T. Ruetten, *Quest and Response: Minority Rights and the Truman Administration* (Lawrence: University of Kansas Press, 1973).

9. Amicus brief of ACLU on CP-11 cases, ca. 1950, reel 3, box 3, A35, CRC Papers; Clifford Rorster to Allan Knight Chalmers, 5 October 1948; and Roger Baldwin to Dean John Day, 12 May 1948, "National Committee," vol. 20, no. 6, ACLU Papers; Roger Baldwin to Charles Houston, 20 May 1948; and Charles Houston to Roger Baldwin, 21 June 1948, "National Committee," vol. 20, no. 2, ACLU Papers.

10. Corliss Lamont to Norman Thomas, 27 December 1948, 25 February 1947; Norman Thomas to Corliss Lamont, 1 October 1952, 26 February 1947, box 119, ACLU, Norman Thomas Papers; Stephen Mark Cens, "Paranoia bordering on Resignation: Norman Thomas and the American Socialist Party" (Ph.D. diss., University of Oaklahoma, 1982), 252; Norman Thomas to Roger Baldwin, 12 September 1947; Norman Thomas to Ernest Angell, 18 September 1951, box 119, ACLU, Norman Thomas Papers.

11. Junius Scales to CRC, 21 February 1949, reel 34, box 57, M24, CRC Papers; William Patterson to *Daily Compass,* 29 September 1949, box 9, folder 43, William Patterson Papers.

12. William Patterson to Elizabeth Allen, 14 December 1949, reel 35, box 59, M71, CRC Papers; Elizabeth Allen to William Patterson, 19 November 1948, reel 35, box 59, M71, CRC Papers.

13. William Patterson to Patrick Malin, 13 April 1951, reel 20, box 32, G1, CRC Papers; William Patterson to ACLU, 20 July 1951, reel 37, box 62, N4, CRC Papers; Aubrey Grossman to Decca Truehaft, 10 October 1950, reel 45, box 77, P6, CRC Papers; William Patterson to Anne Shore, 3 July 1953, reel 47, box 82, P95, CRC Papers.

14. Walter White to Norman Thomas, 3 November 1951, box 119, ACLU, Norman Thomas Papers.

15. Hoover, *J. Edgar Hoover on Communism,* 131; Pettis Perry, "Next Stage in the Struggle for Negro Rights," *Political Affairs* 28 (October 1949): 36, 45; Edward E. Strong, "On the 40th Anniversary of the NAACP," *Political Affairs* 29 (February 1950): 24, 25, 30, 32.

16. Doxey Wilkerson, "The 46th Annual Convention of the NAACP," *Political Affairs* 34 (August 1955): 6 10–11, 13, 15; Frederick Hastings and Charles P. Mann, "For a Mass Policy in Negro Freedom's Cause," *Political Affairs* 34 (March 1955): 22, 26.

17. Len Goldsmith to William Patterson, 22 September 1948, reel 34, box 58, M52, CRC Papers; minutes of Board of Directors meeting, 28 June 1946, reel 38, box 64, N66, CRC Papers. The CRC conference in Houston was attended by 141 from 25 cities; the president of the "Young Democrats" presided. "Negro reprentation very broad . . . State Board of 50 was set up . . ."; Thurgood Marshall to J. Edgar Hoover, 2 January 1948, box 274, NAACP Papers; Lulu White to Thurgood Marshall, 8 December 1947, box 274, NAACP Papers.

18. Walter White to Don Petit, 29 April 1949; Don Jones to Dan Byrd, 31 May 1949; Daniel Byrd to William Patterson, 12 March 1949, box 189, NAACP Papers; Lulu White, the CRC and

NAACP leader, scored Walter White for including her name in a release scoring CRC. Lulu White to Walter White, 26 January 1949, box 189, NAACP Papers; Roy Wilkins to Charles Howard, 3 November 1949, box 445, NAACP Papers; Gloster Current to J. O. Gilliam, 8 September 1952, box 494, NAACP Papers.

19. Announcement, 22 April 1948, reel 4, box 6, A102, CRC Papers; undated press release, reel 18, box 27, C22, CRC Papers; Lou Kalb to William Patterson, 25 December 1950, reel 19, box 30, F18, CRC Papers; press release, 28 March 1952, reel 18, box 27, C21, CRC Papers; press release, 27 February 1952, reel 18, box 27, C22, CRC Papers.

20. *Jackson Advocate,* 29 June 1950; Edgar T. Rouzeau, 2 April 1952, reel 35, box 59, M62, CRC Papers; Aubrey Grossman to Herbert Aptheker, 13 November 1950, reel 35, box 60, M84, CRC Papers.

21. Walter White to Edward Scheidt, 15 December 1950, box 274, NAACP Papers; Walter White to J. Edgar Hoover, 13 June 1951, box 274, NAACP Papers; Clarence Mitchell to J. Edgar Hoover, 17 August 1953, box 274, NAACP Papers.

22. Irving Kristol to Paul Lehmann, 21 January 1953, box 182, NAACP Papers; Walter White to James Imbrie, 27 January 1953, box 182, NAACP Papers; *Seattle Post-Intelligencer,* 18 February 1955; *Seattle Times,* 18 February 1955.

23. Roy Wilkins to NAACP Branches, 18 October 1949, NAACP Papers; *Crisis* (August–September 1951): 475–76.

24. John Starks to William Patterson, 11 July 1950, reel 48, box 83, P119, CRC Papers; Margie Robinson to William Patterson, 5 September 1951, reel 45, box 77, P15, CRC Papers.

25. *Pittsburgh Courier,* 7 July 1951; *Michigan Chronicle,* 21 April 1951; *Pittsburgh Courier,* 30 June 1951; article by Arthur McPhaul, box 11, folder, "Civil Rights" 1952, CRC-Mich. Papers; The Jewish Community Council warned its affiliates not "to be duped" into supporting CRC (*Detroit News,* 2 August 1950, *Detroit Times,* 2 August 1950). Mayor Cobo accused CRC of attempting to provoke incidents among Blacks and police after their campaign against police terror got underway (*Detroit Free Press,* 14 October 1951).

26. Franklin Williams, 19 March 1954, box 210, NAACP Papers; *Crisis* (May 1954): 296.

27. Address by Walter White, 1 July 1951, reel 42, box 72, N269, CRC Papers; Walter White, *How Far the Promised Land?* (New York: Viking, 1955) 10–11, 4–5, passim; Herbert Hill, "The Communist Party—Enemy of Negro Equality," *Crisis* 58 (June–July 1951): 424; Herbert Delany to William Hastie, 31 October 1952; William Ming to Thurgood Marshall, 13 January 1953; Marshall to Ming, 19 January 1953, 100-5, William Hastie Papers.

28. Kenneth O'Reilly, *Hoover and the Un-Americans: The FBI, HUAC and the Red Menace* (Philadelphia: Temple University Press, 1983), 172; Pettis Perry, "Lessons of the Civil Rights Mobilization," *Political Affairs* 29 (March 1950): 63; Roy Wilkins to Carlton Goodlet, 20 April 1949, box 189, NAACP Papers; Thurgood Marshall to Roy Wilkins, 16 November 1949, box 189, NAACP Papers.

29. Len Goldsmith to William Patterson, 17 February 1949, reel 34, box 58, M52, CRC Papers; William Patterson to Roy Wilkins, 29 November 1949, reel 42, box 72, N268, CRC Papers.

30. William Patterson to CRC chapters, 3 February 1950, reel 9, box 14, A280, CRC Papers; William Patterson to Walter White, 15 February 1952, reel 42, box 72, N268, CRC Papers.

31. William Patterson to NAACP, 14 November 1949, reel 3, box 4, A51, CRC Papers; *Washington Afro-American,* 23 February 1952; William Patterson to "all District Leaders," McPhaul, 23 April 1952, reel 47, box 45, J114, CRC Papers.

32. Press release, 18 August 1949, reel 39, box 66, N121, CRC Papers; William Patterson to Henry Lee Moon, 10 June 1951, reel 134, box 58, M36, CRC Papers; Henry Lee Moon to William Patterson, 13 June 1951, reel 34, box 58, M36, CRC Papers; CRC newsletter, 26 August 1949, reel 27, box 45, J114, CRC Papers.

33. William Patterson to Chris Bates, 16 July 1951, reel 34, box 58, M36, CRC Papers; William Patterson to George Ross, 9 December 1949, reel 34, box 58, M35, CRC Papers; press

release, 10 January 1952, reel 8, box 13, A270, CRC Papers; Angie Dickerson to public relations director of Florida A&M, 4 February 1952, reel 34, box 57, MIA, CRC Papers; William Patterson to NAACP, 22 March 1955, reel 15, box 24, B34, CRC Papers.

34. Statement by Charles Houston, 2 February 1950, reel 59, box 104, W91, CRC Papers; Genna Rae McNeil, *Groundwork: Charles Hamilton Houston and the Struggle for Civil Rights* (Philadelphia: University of Pennsylvania Press, 1983), 181, passim; William Patterson to Thurgood Marshall, 22 January 1954, reel 19, box 31, F31, CRC Papers; press release, 29 November 1948, reel 41, box 71, N251, CRC Papers; *California Eagle,* December 1948, reel 36, box 61, M140, CRC Papers; Roy Wilkins to Cleveland Robinson, 25 February 1953, box 210, NAACP Papers.

35. On 23 December 1946 Leslie Perry of the NAACP chaired a meeting on civil rights participated in by CRC, NLG, Southern Conference on Human Welfare, etc. Discussed, inter alia, was the Oust Bilbo case ("The Consent of the Governed: An Analysis of Some Aspects of the Report of the President's Committee on Civil Rights," ca. 1947, reel 43, box 73, N316, CRC Papers). William Patterson to CRC chapters, 21 September 1948, reel 40, box 68, N180A, CRC Papers: said Patterson about the DuBois case, "This is one way of building your membership of reaching into your Negro community . . . [reach] as many Negro leaders in your community as possible." William Patterson to Richard Morford, 26 January 1950, reel 40, box 69, N185, CRC Papers: "I regard the betrayal of FEPC as the most vicious, cynical and arrogant affront to the American people . . ." Urged by Patterson, Morford of the Council on American-Soviet Friendship conceded to Roy Wilkins that he hoped it was not a "hindrance" for him to have sent a telegram supporting FEPC to Congress, since now "affiliation with [CRC] cuts one off from cooperative effort with the rest of you in the FEPC fight"; McGee lists, ca. 1950, reel 7, box 11, A212, CRC Papers; William Patterson to Robert Silberstein, 3 July 1951, reel 3, box 4, A52, CRC Papers: a similar letter on the Clarendon case was sent to Attorney Thomas Jones, National Bar Association and the Harlem Bar Association, uring them to analyze the case closely. He told Laurent Frantz that Jim Crow was said by Judge Parker to be a policy for all times, not just the present, which signified that "gradualism" of the NAACP was a fraud. William to Laurent Frantz, 11 July 1951, reel 3, box 4, A52, CRC Papers; William Patterson to George Hays, 21 May 1954, reel 4, box 5, A78, CRC Papers; William Patterson to Maurice Braverman, 15 October 1952, reel 47, box 81, P80, CRC Papers; press release, 15 February 1952, reel 15, box 27, C22, CRC Papers: here Patterson called on "NAACP leaders" to unify behind Walter Irvin, sentenced to death in Florida.

36. Prof. Fred Rodell to William Patterson, 12 October 1951, reel 24, box 41, J46, CRC Papers; William Patterson to Fred Rodell, 17 October 1951, reel 24, box 41, J46, CRC Papers; *Beauharnais v. Illinois,* 343 U.S. 250 (1951); Prof. Fred Rodell to William Patterson, 25 October 1951, reel 36, box 61, M112, CRC Papers; William Patterson to Prof. Fred Rodell, 13 November 1951, reel 36, box 61, M112, CRC Papers; CRC's relations with the *Nation* magazine were not always close and chummy. Alleged Patterson, "There are those . . . on the Nation, who are not aware that in their articles [which] are critical of reaction's program, they are not dealing with isolated instances but with an action program which has as its ultimate aim fascism and war" (William Patterson to Alan Max, 23 June 1952, reel 34, box 57, M29, CRC Papers). Future legal scholar Maurice Rosenberg, then editor-in-chief of the *Columbia Law Review,* praised the CRC: "On behalf of the Note on Constitutional limitations on the Un-American Activities Committee which appears in the April issue of the Review. Your memorandum was extremely useful in this work" (Maurice Rosenberg to Benjamin Goldring, 16 April 1947, reel 3, box 4, A65, CRC Papers).

37. Patrick Malin to Board, 9 August 1951, box 119, ACLU, Norman Thomas Papers; Robert Bush to Clifford Forster, 18 November 1948; Solomon Golat to Clifford Forster, 17 January 1949; Clifford Forster to Solomon Golat, 27 January 1949; and Solomon Golat to Clifford Forster, 29 January 1949, vol. 58, 1953, ACLU Papers; for an inkling of the massive press coverage that helped change the ACLU's mind, cf. e.g., *National Guardian* 21 November

1949; *New York Age*, 2 April 1949; *New Republic*, 1 May 1949; *Philadelphia Bulletin*, 22 July 1950.

38. Herbert Levy to Morris Ernst, 8 March 1949; Herbert Levy to Daniel Heller, 21 March 1949; William Patterson to ACLU, 24 March 1949; and Herbert Levy to Fleming James, 6 April 1949, vol. 28, 1953, ACLU Papers; William Patterson to Roger Baldwin, 21 June 1949; and Herbert Levy to George Thomas, 7 December 1950, vol. 58, 1953, ACLU Papers; the intense interest of Gladys Chang, president of the Sarah Lawrence College student body, was typical of the pressure that helped change the union's mind. She met with the NAACP, wrote the Urban League, *New York Times, New York Post, Pittsburgh Courier,* etc. before reaching the Union (Gladys Chang to ACLU, 23 March 1949, vol. 58, 1953, ACLU Papers).

39. Imogene Johnson to William Patterson, 11 April 1949, reel 46, box 80, P59, CRC Papers; Arthur Price to William Patterson, 2 May 1949, reel 46, box 80, P59, CRC Papers. Comparing the Trenton 6 campaign to another simultaneous effort, Price added, "The campaign on the 12 has lagged miserably;" thus indicating that the docket of CRC was heavier than imagined and it may have been easier or more politic to organize around the Black cases than the red; Thurgood Marshall to William Patterson, 25 February 1949, reel 12, box 21, A399, CRC Papers; William Patterson to Thurgood Marshall, 28 February 1949, reel 12, box 21, A399, CRC Papers.

40. William Patterson to MIC, 8 March 1951, reel 46, box 79, P42, CRC Papers; William Patterson to James Imbrie, 25 April 1951, reel 12, box 20, A380, CRC Papers; Harold Ridenour to Dr. Edward Corwin, 20 April 1951, reel 12, box 20, A380, CRC Papers.

41. William Patterson to Max Lerner, 8 May 1951, reel 34, box 58, M36, CRC Papers; "Labor Reports," May 1951, reel 12, box 20, A378, CRC Papers; as early as February 1947, CRC-NJ was complaining of being "not . . . able to get cooperation from the NAACP in any activity" ("Sarah" to Milt Kemnitz, 7 February 1947, reel 48, box 83, P128, CRC Papers).

42. O. John Rogge to William Patterson, 2 August 1950, reel 3, box 3, A42, CRC Papers; W. E. B. Du Bois to William Patterson, 8 February 1952, reel 6, box 9, A182, CRC Papers: in seeking information on why and when Rogge left the Trenton 6 case, he inquired, "Did it have anything to do with the exclusion of New York lawyers?"

43. Press release, 4 January 1950, reel 8, box 13, A257, CRC Papers; press release, 14 June 1951, reel 12, box 21, A395, CRC Papers; "Stella" to William Patterson, undated, reel 12, box 20, A379, CRC Papers; press release, 4 December 1952, reel 12, box 20, A387, CRC Papers; "Petition to Governor Alfred E. Driscoll for the Removal of Prosecutor Volpe," reel 12, box 20, A387, CRC Papers; statement of Lewis Moroze, 22 February 1953, reel 51, box 90, S52, CRC Papers.

44. Henry Winston to "Dear Comrades," 17 March 1949, reel 21, box 35, G33, CRC Papers; William Patterson to "Dear Friend," 30 March 1949, reel 21, box 35, G33, CRC Papers.

45. "CBS Views the Press," #94, 19 March 1949, reel 12, box 20, A390, CRC Papers; "Justice and the Negro," broadcast no. 96, ABC, 14 February 1949, reel 12, box 21, A397, CRC Papers; *New York Herald Tribune*, 18 December 1949; William Patterson to Ogden Reid, 27 December 1949, reel 34, box 58, M35, CRC Papers; William Patterson to editor of *Trenton Times*, 25 December 1949, reel 34, box 58, M35, CRC Papers; *Trenton Times*, 22 November 1949; William Patterson to Barry Gray, 18 February 1952, reel 34, box 58, M49, CRC Papers; *The Reporter*, ACLU Papers. The ACLU Papers contain figuratively tons of clippings on the Trenton Six case, indicating their intense interest in the matter.

46. *Freedom*, November 1950; Letters from Dashiell Hammett, 1 March 1949, reel 12, box 2, A400, A401, CRC Papers; *Daily Worker*, 22 July 1949; *Philadelphia Tribune*, 24 July 1949; letters from Clifford Odets, 22 April 1949, 15 July 1949, 3 June 1949, reel 12, box 22, A380, CRC Papers; Eleanor Roosevelt to Bessie Mitchell, 28 April 1949, reel 12, box 20, A379, CRC Papers.

47. Statement of protest, 12 January 1949, reel 12, box 20, A378, CRC Papers; statement of protest, 11 August 1949, 12 February 1951, reel 12, box 20, A378, CRC Papers; Aubrey Grossman to Harry Truman, 6 March 1951, reel 12, box 20, A378, CRC Papers; Therese Thompson to John Rogge, 27 April 1949, reel 12, box 20 A379, CRC Papers; press release, 10

May 1949, reel 12, box 20, A392, CRC Papers.

48. Report on Trenton 6 by Will Hayett, 18 January 1951, reel 12, box 20, A378, CRC Papers; Aubrey Grossman to union representatives, 28 May 1951, reel 12, box 20, CRC Papers; William Patterson to James Ibrie, 20 June 1951, reel 12, box 20, A378, CRC Papers. William Patterson to Abe Pomerantz, 4 August 1949, reel 3, box 4, A66, CRC Papers.

49. Press release, 19 May 1949, reel 31, box 50, J205, CRC Papers; *New York Times,* 24 May 1949; Rashbaum wrote to the missions of Denmark, Guatemala, Australia, Belgium, Byelorussia, Chile, Egypt, India, Panama, China, Lebanon, France, Britain, USSR, Ukraine, Iran, and Yugoslavia. Patterson wrote to the representatives to the UN Human Rights Commission, including Uruguay, Guatemala, Australia, Belgium, Byelorussia, Chile Egypt, India, Panama, China, Lebanon, France, Britain, USSR, Ukraine, Iran, and Yugoslavia (William Patterson to Commission representatives, 26 April 1949, reel 12, box 20, A381, CRC Papers). William Patterson to Claude Dennery, 25 November 1949, reel 12, box 20, A381, CRC Papers.

50. Charles Doyle to Sol Oaklander, 9 March 1949, reel 12, box 21, A399, CRC Papers; Charles Doyle to Nick De Maria, Michael De Cicco, et al. 9 March 1949, reel 12, box 21, A399, CRC Papers.

51. Social Service Employees Union to William Patterson, 30 June 1949, reel 12, box 21, A399, CRC Papers; Grant Oakes, president of United Farm Equipment and Metal Workers to Charles Doyle, 9 March 1949, reel 12, box 21, A399, CRC Papers: He sent a list of "District Presidents"; Ewart Guinier, Secretary-treasurer of the Office and Progressional Workers Union, to UPOWU field workers, 6 April 1949, reel 12, box 21, A399, CRC Papers; he also wrote governor Alfred Driscoll of New Jersey protesting, 24 March 1949; Louis Slocum, executive secretary Eastern Division of National Farmers Union, to Alfred Driscoll, 16 December 1949, reel 12, box 21, A399, CRC Papers; Robert Cummings, International Fishermen and Allied Workers, to Alfred Driscoll, 28 April 1949, Arthur Osman, president of Wholesale and Warehouse Workers, Local 65, 1 June 1949, to Alfred Driscoll, Lyndon Henry, Chair, Anti-discrimination Committee-International Fur & Leather Workers, to Local Affiliates, 16 May 1949 (urges protest), reel 12, box 21, A399, CRC Papers; William Patterson to Regina Boyd, El Paso branch of Southern Conference of Human Welfare, 15 August 1949, reel 12, box 21, A399, CRC Papers; gives thanks for "contribution"; Thomas Quinn, UE, to CRC, 6 June 1949, reel 12, box 21, A399, CRC Papers: sends several "petitions and a check."

52. William Patterson to Aubrey Grossman, 15 March 1949, reel 45, box 77, P25, CRC Papers; flyer, undated, reel 48, box 84, P142, CRC Papers; press release, 23 November 1949, reel 7, box 11, A216, CRC Papers.

53. Arthur Brown to Felix Kusman, 21 September 1948, reel 48, box 83, P128, CRC Papers; pamphlet, ca. 1949, reel 48, box 83, P129, CRC Papers; Jersey Justice, March 1948, Civil Rights, April 1948, reel 48, box 83, P129, CRC Papers.

54. John Reynolds, president of Local 208, UAW, to CRC, 20 May 1949, box 63, folder, Trenton 6, 1949–1952, CRC-Mich. Papers; many Detroit churches gave money; *New York Times,* 28 November 1951, *Nation,* 21 July 1951. Many clippings are in these files. Newsletter, 30 September 1949, reel 27, box 48, J107, CRC Papers; Isabelle Goldfarb to William Patterson, August 1951, reel 34, box 57, M1A, CRC Papers.

Chapter 6. The Man Who Cried Genocide

1. *Pittsburgh Courier,* 12 August 1950; William Patterson fact sheet, ca. 1951, reel 19, box 30, F19, CRC Papers.

2. *USA v. William Patterson,* in U.S. District Court of Washington, D.C., Crim. No. 1787-50, reel 19, box 30, F19, CRC Papers; *Congressional Record,* 6 April 1951, p. 3507; U.S. Congress, House, Select Committee on Lobbying Activities, 81st Congress, 2d session, created pursuant to House Resolution 298. "Lobbying, Direct and Indirect," part 9 of hearings before

the committee, 3–4 August 1950; CRC showed receipts of $36,546.65 on 1946 and expenditures of $28,352.42; $92,332.06 vs. $103,603.25 in 1947. They deposited $214,829.23 in the bank in 1948; $87,959.77 in 1949; $44,767.98 in 1950 with the bulk of deposits over $500. At that time Cadden was receiving a salary of $3,380 per year; Tom Buchanan to William Patterson, 19 February 1949, reel 10, box 16, A324, CRC Papers; Tom Buchanan to George Marshall, 25 January 1950, reel 19, box 30, F10, CRC Papers.

3. Abe Isserman to William Patterson, Aubrey Grossman, and Ralph Powe, 5 January 1951, reel 19, box 30, F17, CRC Papers; Abe Isserman to Ralph Powe, 14 March 1951, reel 4, box 4, A68, CRC Papers.

4. George Crockett to Abe Isserman, 12 February 1951, reel 19, box 30, F19, CRC Papers; William Patterson to Gene Holmes, 3 February 1951, reel 19, box 30, F12, CRC Papers.

5. Laurent Frantz to Ralph Powe, 2 February 1951, reel 19, box 30, F19, CRC Papers; William Patterson to Gene Holmes, 3 February 1951, reel 19, box 30, F12, CRC Papers.

6. George Crockett to William Patterson, 28 December 1950, reel 19, box 30, F12, CRC Papers; William Patterson to George Crockett, 26 December 1950, reel 19, box 30, F12, CRC Papers.

7. Affidavits and motions, *U.S. v. Patterson,* reel 19, box 30, F12, CRC Papers.

8. "Breakdown of Defense," undated, reel 19, box 30, F10, CRC Papers; *Denver Star,* 14 April 1951.

9. *U.S. v. Patterson,* transcript of proceedings, p. 11, reel 19, box 30, F7, CRC Papers; Ralph Powe to Margaret Griffin, 2 March 1951, reel 19, box 30, F19, CRC Papers; undated Patterson memo, reel 19, box 30, F17, CRC Papers; Stetson Kennedy to William Patterson, 10 March 1953, box 2, folder 1, William Patterson Papers; *Daily Worker,* 12 April 1951; press release, 16 April 1951, reel 19, box 30, F2, CRC Papers; press release, 11 April 1952, box 27, C21, CRC-Mich. Papers; NAM v. McGrath, 103 Fed. Supp. 510 (1951); *U.S. v. Patterson,* 92 US App. D.C. 222, 206 F2d 433 (1951); Ralph Powe to George Parker et al., 15 December 1951, reel 10, box 17, A335, CRC Papers; William Patterson to Agenes Aans, 13 July 1951, reel 34, box 57, M1A, CRC Papers; *Daily Worker,* 4 January 1951; William Patterson to Ted Thackeray, 27 March 1952, box 57, reel 34, M28, CRC Papers. Patterson said here that pressure from the Baptists and "18 Negro Bishops of the AME Zion Church" helped free him more than did the *NAM* decision; *Tulsa Black Dispatch,* 26 August 1950; *Arizona Sun,* 4 January 1951; Clyde Jackson to William Patterson, 23 January 1951, reel 34, box 58, M36, CRC Papers; *New York Age,* 12 August 1950. Their editorial blasted Lanham. The *Afro-American* carried ¼-page ads from the Patterson Defense Committee.

10. Press release, undated, box 27, C21, CRC-Mich. Papers; Roscoe Dunjee to William Patterson, 26 December 1950, reel 34, box 57, M33, CRC Papers; Roscoe Dunjee to William Patterson Defense Committee, 18 April 1951, reel 34, box 57, M10, CRC Papers; William Patterson to Roscoe Dunjee, 20 May 1952, reel 34, box 57, M10, CRC papers; William Patterson to Roscoe Dunjee, 21 July 1952, 3 July 1952, reel 34, box 57, M10, CRC Papers. This latter letter was about doing articles on the NAACP convention; William Patterson to Roscoe Dunjee, 23 June 1951, reel 34, box 58, M36, CRC Papers. Here Patterson urged his friend to publish articles on the CP-11 case; Congressman Lanham died in 1957 after his car was hit at a rail crossing (*New York Times,* 11 November 1957).

11. William Patterson to Carl Murphy, 23 June 1951, reel 34, box 58, M36, CRC Papers; William Patterson to William Walker, 28 September 1958, reel 34, box 58, M33, CRC Papers; Ted Hallock to William Patterson, 30 January 1951, reel 34, box 58, M55, CRC Papers; William Patterson to Ida Rothstein, 27 December 1950, reel 45, box 77, P27, CRC Papers.

12. William Patterson to Angie Dickerson, 18 May 1951, reel 19, box 30, F14, CRC Papers; Herbert Levy to Alan Reitman, 23 April 1951, vol. 20, 1952, ACLU Papers.

13. William Patterson tour, January 1951, reel 19, box 30, F18, CRC Papers; William Patterson to Aubrey Grossman, 10 January 1951, reel 19, box 30, F18, CRC Papers.

14. William Patterson to Aubrey Grossman, 10 January 1951, reel 19, box 30, F18, CRC Papers; *Oregon Journal,* 23 January 1951; Eve Milton to Aubrey Grossman, 9 February 1951,

reel 19, box 30, F18, CRC Papers; Irving Goodman to William Patterson, 24 January 1951, reel 19, box 30, F18, CRC Papers; unsigned letter to Aubrey Grossman, 29 January 1951, reel 19, box 30, F18, CRC Papers.

15. Radio Reports, Inc. (N.Y.), "Texts of Broadcasts AM, FM, TV," 30 December 1951, box 9, folder 37, William Patterson Papers; undated *Life* magazine article, ca. 1951, box 210, NAACP Papers; *Los Angeles Times*, 11 January 1951; Vito Marcantonio, *I Vote My Conscience: Debates, Speeches, and Writings* (New York: Memorial, 1956), 442.

16. Undated press release, ca. 1951, box 27, C21, CRC-Mich. Papers. The National Baptist Convention represented 2.5 million. Rev. R. L. Turner to William Patterson, 22 March 1952, reel 19, box 30, F11, CRC Papers; L. W. Goebel to Ollie Harrington, 2 April 1951, reel 19, box 30, F11, CRC Papers; D. V. Jemison to Angie Dickerson, 6 May 1952, reel 35, box 60, M90, CRC Papers; Prof. W. J. Fizpatrick to Defense Committee, 29 March 1951, reel 35, box 60, M88, CRC Papers; W. C. Dabney to Aubrey Grossman, undated, reel 19, box 30, F11, CRC Papers; letter from Eslanda Goode Robeson, 10 August 1950, reel 19, box 30, F11, CRC Papers; A. J. Elrod to Ollie Harrington, undated, reel 19, box 30, F11, CRC Papers; William Patterson to Rev. J. Henry Patten, 2 October 1951, reel 19, box 30, F11, CRC Papers; Arthur Huff Eauset to Ollie Harrington, 2 April 1951, reel 19, box 30, F11, CRC Papers; drawings by Charles White and Hugo Gellert, ca. 1951, reel 19, box 30, F26, CRC Papers; letter from Thomas Mann, 26 March 1952, reel 19, box 30, F26, CRC Papers; W. Africa Students Committee (Charles U.) to Patterson, 11 April 1951, reel 34, box 58, M46.

17. William Patterson and Aubrey Grossman to all chapters, ca. 1952, reel 19, box 30, F11, CRC Papers; Angie Dickerson to Rev. John Sanders, 12 March 1952, reel 19, box 30, F11, CRC papers; *Daily Worker,* 30 April 1951; *Daily Worker,* 1 February 1952; *Daily worker,* 14 August 1950, *New York Times,* 5 August 1950, *New York Times,* 31 August 1950, *Daily Worker,* 3 September 1950; emblematic of the cultural component of CRC, a "Ballad for William Patterson" was prepared; George Crockett to William Patterson, 6 November 1951, reel 34, box 57, M12, CRC Papers; CRC also prepared buttons and posters in support of their leader. In addition to the religious delegation, a trade union delegation also met with officials of the Justice Department, including the Attorney General.

18. Press release, 26 May 1952, box 27, C21, CRC-Mich. papers; Aubrey Grossman to Ralph Powe, 8 December 1952, reel 19, box 30, F11, CRC Papers; *Toronto Globe & Mail,* 29 June 1948, 30 June 1948; *Toronto Star,* 30 June 1948; *Toronto Telegram* 30 June 1948. The visit by Dr. Harry Ward to Canada was covered adequately by the Toronto press; William Patterson to Thomas Roberts, 5 October 1951, reel 34, box 58, M42, CRC Papers: "As you know, however, I am denied entree into Canada and cannot be there"; statement from Canadian Communists calling for support of CP-11, December 1948, reel 3, box 3, A31, CRC Papers; Isabel Smaller, Sudbury Ladies Auxiliary, Local 117-Ontario, to CRC, reel 34, box 58, M45, CRC Papers. She sends $10. Thomas Roberts to Aubrey Grossman, ca. 1952, reel 45, box 79, P36, CRC Papers; Thomas Roberts to Gov. John Fine, 31 July 1952, reel 45, box 79, P36, CRC Papers; Thomas Roberts to Aubrey Grossman, 6 October 1950, reel 6, box 9, A182, CRC Papers; Aubrey Grossman to Thomas Roberts, 18 October 1950, reel 6, box 9, A182, CRC Papers.

19. Aubrey Grossman to Thomas Roberts, 18 October 1950, reel 6, box 9, A182, CRC Papers.

20. Ibid.

21. Abraham Pena to William Patterson, 22 March 1951, reel 35, box 60, M89, CRC Papers; Abraham Pena to CRC, 12 July 1951, reel 6, box 9, A180, CRC Papers; Abraham Pena to CRC, 24 August 1951, reel 34, box 58, M42, CRC Papers; press release, 20 July 1955, reel 10, box 17, A333, CRC Papers; William Albertson to "Dear Friend," 2 September 1955, reel 27, box 45, J111, CRC Papers.

22. William Patterson to General Fulgencio Batista, 10 August 1953, reel 34, box 57, M9, CRC Papers; William Patterson to John Foster Dulles, 10 August 1953, reel 34, box 57, M9, CRC Papers; Robert Woodward to William Patterson, 1 September 1953, reel 35, box 60, M89, CRC Papers; William Patterson to Nelson Davis, 10 September 1953, reel 47, box 82, P95, CRC Papers; Saul Cascallar Carrasco to William Patterson, 25 January 1949, reel 35, box 59, M71,

CRC Papers; Gerardo Pisarello to CRC, 19 September 1952, reel 4, box 4, A70, CRC papers; William Patterson to "Dear Friend," 7 September 1955, reel 15, box 24, B35, CRC Papers; William Patterson to Telepress, 16 May 1951, reel 43, box 73, N313, CRC Papers; William Patterson and Oakley Johnson manuscript, ca. 1955, box 6, folder 148, William Patterson Papers; Greetings on 8th anniversary from Movement Contre le Racisme, L'Antisemitisme et pour La Paix (Paris), Confederacion de Trabajadores de America Latina (Mexico) from Vincente Toledano, World Federation of Trade Unions, D. N. Pritt, et al., ca. 1954, reel 34, box 58, M38, CRC Papers; William Patterson Statement, undated, reel 29, box 48, J175, CRC Papers; Ferdinand Smith to William Patterson, 12 February 1954, box 2, folder 74, William Patterson Papers. By 1958 Smith was president of the Jamaica Federation of Trade Unions, signifying the continuity and lingering influence of the left and CRC allies in the post-1956 era.

23. William Patterson and Aubrey Grossman to West African Civil Rights Congress, 9 April 1953, reel 34, box 57, M3, CRC Papers; S. T. Addico to CRC, 30 November 1953; Turkson-Ocran and Amaefule Nkoro to "Comrades," 27 March 1953; Olatunji A. Fabiyi to William Patterson, 27 February 1952, reel 34, box 57, 58, M3, 26, 40, CRC Papers; William Patterson to Bankole Akpata, 17 November 1950, reel 35, box 60, M88, CRC Papers; press release, 1 April 1952, reel 15, box 27, C21, CRC Papers; William Patterson to ANC, 26 September 1952, reel 34, box 58, M44, CRC Papers; Sam Kahn to Elizabeth Gurley Flynn, 19 February 1951, reel 10, box 16, A322, CRC Papers.

24. William Patterson to Prime Minister U Nu, 21 October 1955, box 2, folder 18, William Patterson Papers; Hla Kyway to CRC, 15 November 1954, reel 34, box 57, M8, CRC Papers; press release, 15 April 1952, reel 15, box 27, C21, CRC Papers; undated memo, reel 4, box 4, A70, CRC Papers; William Patterson, "The Fight against Racism: The Monumental Contributions of Bandung And Geneva," box 1, folder 7, Daschbach Papers; William Patterson to Roscoe Dunjee, 9 June 1955, reel 15, box 24, box 34, CRC Papers; Calvin Holder, "Racism toward Black African Diplomats during the Kennedy Administration," *Journal of Black Studies* 14 (September 1983): 31–48; press release, 14 February 1952, reel 15, box 27, C22, CRC Papers. "U.S. Negro History Week . . . observed in Asia, Africa and Europe."

25. William Patterson to Martin Popper, 31 August 1948, reel 3, box 3, A38, CRC Papers; William Patterson to I. A. Bonner, 10 July 1950, reel 3, box 3, A31, CRC Papers; Mavis Hill to William Patterson, 7 September 1948, reel 3, box 3, A38, CRC Papers; Elizabeth Allen to William Patterson, 1 July 1955, reel 15, box 24, B34, CRC Papers; undated press release, reel 15, box 27, C21, CRC Papers; CRC statement to French Consul in New York, undated, reel 4, box 6, A96, CRC Papers; William Patterson to Telepress, 4 June 1951, reel 43, box 73, N312, CRC Papers.

26. Abe Pomerantz to William Patterson, 11 August 1949, reel 3, box 4, A66, CRC Papers; CRC Chapter Bulletin, 18 April 1953, box 11, folder, National CRC, CRC-Mich. Papers; William Patterson to Bea Johnson, 27 May 1952, reel 34, box 58, M45, CRC Papers.

27. Harry Haywood, "A Mighty Weapon in the Fight against Genocide," *Political Affairs* 31 (January 1952): 60; *New York Times,* 14 December 1951.

28. Documentation of Genocide Petition, 1951, reel 15, box 26, C4, CRC Papers; William Patterson et al., eds., *We Charge Genocide: The Historic Petition to the United Nations for Relief from a Crime of the United States Government against the Negro People* (New York: International, 1951).

29. William Patterson to Leon Josephson, 29 November 1951, reel 35, box 59, M62, CRC Papers; *New York Times,* 9 August 1973; *Daily World,* 10 August 1973; William Patterson to Richard Boyer, 26 November 1951, reel 14, box 23, B20, CRC Papers; William Patterson to Mordecai Johnson, 20 May 1952, reel 35, box 59, M62, CRC Papers; Oakley Johnson to William Patterson, 30 July 1951, reel 35, box 59, M65, CRC Papers. Johnson also spent money out of his own pocket to fund the petition, including $207.40 for calls and telegrams.

30. William Patterson to Olive Weaver, 13 June 1955, reel 15, box 24, B14, CRC Papers; Paula Gidings, *When and Where I Enter: The Impact of Black Women on Race and Sex in America* (New York: Morrow, 1984), 90, 92; William Patterson to William Z. Foster, 16 November 1951, reel 34, box 57, M12, CRC Papers.

31. William L. Patterson, *The Man Who Cried Genocide* (New York: International, 1971), 175.

32. "In Defense of Human Rights," 10 May 1950, reel 8, box 13, A262, CRC Papers; *The Black Panther*, 21 March 1970; Black Panther Party Petition on Genocide, ca. 1970, box 10, folders 104–7, William Patterson Papers.

33. *Daily Worker*, 2 December 1951; Patterson, *The Man Who Cried Genocide*, 201, 196; *New York Times*, 18 December 1951. Lemkin taught at Yale, Duke, and Rutgers. Of Polish descent, he developed the term genocide in 1933 in response to the tragedy that was befalling the Jewish people. About South Africa he was obtuse enough to say, "The Boers had a paternalistic attitude toward the natives and generally did not treat them too badly" ("South Africa," box 50, p. 50, Raphael Lemkin Papers). Accession sheet and "Newspaper Radio" file, 20 April 1950, Frederic Nelson to Ralph Post, Lemkin Papers; "Nazi Conspiracy and Aggression—Volume 1— Office of United States Chief Counsel for Prosecution of Axis Criminality," 1946, box 14, folder 19, William Patterson Papers; *New York Times*, 8 January 1952.

34. Subversive Activities Control Board exhibit, reel 21, box 36, G53, CRC Papers; price list for "We Charge Genocide," ca. 1951, reel 10, box 17, A335, CRC Papers; chapter quotas for sales, 20 May 1952, reel 24, box 41, J46, CRC Papers; "Campaign for the Sale of 'We Charge Genocide'" 10 December 1951, reel 15, box 26, C25, CRC Papers; William Patterson to Angie Dickerson et al., 27 November 1951, reel 15, box 27, C25, CRC Papers.

35. Press release, 28 February 1952, reel 55, box 96, V102, CRC Papers; Beulah Richardson play *Genocide*, ca. 1952, reel 15, box 27, C29, CRC Papers.

36. Press release, 17 April 1952, reel 41, box 27, C21, CRC Papers; *New Statesman* and *Nation*, 2 February 1952; *Chicago Tribune*, 22 December 1951; *Los Angeles Herald*, 31 January 1952; press release, 20 November 1951, reel 41, box 27, C25, CRC Papers; *Trenton Times*, 25 September 1952; *MCS Voice*, 11 April 1952, reel 41, box 69, N204, CRC Papers.

37. *New York Times*, 25 November 1951; William Patterson to *New York Times*, 25 November 1951, reel 34, box 56, CRC Papers; *Chicago Tribune*, 22 December 1952; Lester Davis to editor of *Chicago Tribune*, 31 December 1952, reel 34, box 57, M12, CRC Papers; transcript of interview with Angie Dickerson on WHBI radio, Newark, 25 November 1951, reel 24, box 41, J46, CRC Papers.

38. J. Finley Wilson to William Patterson, 15 November 1951, box 26, C11, CRC Papers; Stephen Frichtman to CRC, 13 December 1951, Box 26, C11, CRC Papers; Paul Robeson review, ca. 1952, box 26, C11, CRC Papers; Prominent Chicago attorney Richard Westbrooks called the book "one of the best prepared publications I have had the honor to read . . . careful research and sagacity" (Richard Westbrooks to CRC, 11 December 1951, box 26, C11, CRC Papers). Charles Fielding to CRC, 1 December 1951, reel 34, box 58, M40, CRC Papers; Edith Allen to William Patterson, 28 November 1951, reel 34, box 57, M27, CRC Papers; William Patterson to Felix Frankfurter, 26 November 1951, reel 34, box 58, M40, CRC Papers; "Two Harvard Law Students" to CRC, 7 February 1952, reel 34, box 58, M55, CRC Papers; William Patterson to Pettis Perry, 26 November 1951, reel 34, box 57, M12, CRC Papers; on the 10th anniversary meeting of the UN in San Francisco, CRC presented copies of the petition to each nation. Press release, 24 June 1955, reel 45, box 77, P10, CRC Papers; Hugh Bryson to William Patterson, 25 April 1952, reel 34, box 57, M30, CRC Papers; Angie Dickerson wrote a series of letters promoting the petition among church figures. Angie Dickerson letters, ca. 1952, reel 34, box 57, M30, CRC Papers; *Daily Worker*, 21 January 1952; *Daily Worker*, 20 February 1952.

39. Through Robeson's good offices, Patterson attempted to obtain the assistance of Nehru of India. At the meeting in Paris Patterson charged that the US was trying to stall distribution of petitions at the UN session. *Daily Worker*, 3 January 1952; press release, box 27, C25, 17 December 1951, CRC papers; William Patterson to Les Davis, 29 November 1951, reel 46, box 80, P63, CRC Papers; statement by William Patterson at General Assembly, box 27, C25, CRC Papers.

40. *New York Herald Tribune*, 1 January 1952; article from John Pittman, 24 November 1950, reel 29, box 48, J158, CRC Papers; *New York World Telegram*, 8 January 1952.

41. *Droit et Liberté*, 11 January 1952, box 9, folder 88, William Patterson Papers. This Paris weekly was typical of the French press in that it carried a front page laudatory article on the petition; undated Patterson statement, ca. 1951, William Patterson to Louise Thompson, undated, box 9, folder 87, William Patterson Papers; William Patterson, "We Charge Genocide," *Political Affairs* (May 1966): 32–41; *Amsterdam News*, 2 February 1952; William Patterson to Richard Wright, 28 January 1952, reel 34, box 58, M45, CRC Papers.

42. J. Saunders Redding, "Report from India," Autumn 1953, reel 25, box 43, J72, CRC Papers; J. Sounders Reading, *An American in India* (Indianapolis, Ind.: Bobbs-Merrill, 1954), 169, 218.

43. Press release, 29 January 1952, box 27, C21, CRC Papers; *New York Times*, 24 January 1952; press release, 26 January 1952, box 27, C21, CRC Papers.

44. William Mandel to William Patterson, 7 November 1951, reel 35, box 59, M61, CRC Papers; William Mandel to William Patterson, 16 November 1951, reel 35, box 59, M61, CRC Papers.

45. Plan of work for "Genocide," August 1952, reel 39, box 65, N98, CRC Papers; Aubrey Grossman to Anne Shore, 18 December 1951, reel 47, box 82, CRC Papers; undated speech by William Patterson at Fur and Leather Workers Convention, reel 26, box 44, J89, CRC Papers; translated article from *Yiddish Daily*, ca. December 1951, reel 25, box 43, J73, CRC Papers; Lester Davis to William Patterson, 25 November 1951, reel 46, box 80, P63, CRC Papers; circular on "Labor Symposium on 'We Charge Genocide'" 10 January 1952, reel 43, box 74, N321, CRC Papers; Aubrey Grossman to Arvella Greatorex, 26 March 1952, reel 49, box 86, P194, CRC Papers.

46. William Patterson, "The Battle for Civil Rights Today," *Political Affairs* 37 (Febraury 1958): 1–15; James Rosenberg to Roger Baldwin, 21 September 1949, vol. 26, 1949, ACLU Papers; statement by Roger Baldwin, 1952, vol. 52, ACLU Papers; William Patterson to Roger Baldwin, 21 November 1951, reel 34, box 57, M4, CRC Papers; undated memo from Elizabeth Lawson, box 27, C25, CRC Papers; S. J. Res. 1, 83d Congress, 1st session; Bert Lockwood, Jr., "The United Nations Charter and U.S. Civil Rights Litigation: 1946–1955," *Iowa Law Review* 5 (1984): 901–56.

47. John Daschbach to Shifra Meyers, 20 January 1951, box 2, Washington State, CRC-LA Papers; William Patterson to chapter secretaries, 15 May 1950, reel 28, box 47, J156, CRC Papers; *New Orleans Courier*, 3 March 1951.

48. William Patterson to Thomas Richardson, 20 July 1951, reel 34, box 57, M6, CRC Papers; minutes of "Initial Meeting of the Committee on Organization and Coordination," 23 July 1951, reel 34, box 57, M6, CRC Papers.

49. Bill to Carol King, 10 July 1944, reel 3, box 4, A64, CRC Papers: ". . . the fellow in question had a good record in Spain. . . . However, he is very bombastic and erratic . . . he probably was indiscreet in his conduct and gave them an opening . . . at the time we didn't think anything could be done about it, as there were many examples of discrimination against 'premature' anti-fascists. . . . He is a nice fellow but tends to exaggerate, so be sure you have the facts in the case"; Clyde Harris to Admiral J. Tuassig, 11 May 1941, reel 5, box 7, A130, CRC Papers. CRC wrote the Lawyers Guild, the prestigious law firm Covington & Burling, and a law professor at Columbia seeking help for Harris. Benjamin Goldring to C. A. Horsky, 16 November 1947, to Prof. Albert Jacobs, 22 January 1947, reel 5, box 7, A130, CRC Papers. Harris was fired after eleven years with no notice. Belatedly he was seeking reinstatement and back pay. The last "left" meeting attended by him was in 1936 or 1937 where a nephew of General Pershing and son of an ambassador was speaking. Benjamin Goldring to Clyde Harris, 19 December 1946, reel 5, box 7, A130, CRC Papers; Ernest Goodman to Jack Raskin, 7 August 1947, Box 64, Lemas Woods Correspondence 1947, 1948–49, CRC-Mich. Papers; *San Francisco Chronicle*, 9 August 1947; *Jewish News*, 11 July 1947; *PM*, 22 July 1947, 8 August 1947, 30 July 1947, 29 July 1947, 28 October 1946, 24 October 1946, *Michigan Chronicle*, 7 June 1947; Dorothy Burnham to Ben Goldring, 5 March 1947, reel 3, box 4, A65, CRC Papers.

50. Lee Epstein to Ralph Powe, 3 December 1947, reel 10, box 16, A324, CRC Papers.

51. John Martyn to Peter Knemp, 6 April 1948, reel 3, box 4, A65, CRC Papers; Peter Knemp to John Martyn, 11 May 1948, reel 3, box 4, A65, CRC Papers; Ralph Powe to Judge William Hueston, 21 October 1948, reel 10, box 16, A322, CRC Papers.

52. *Daily Compass,* 23 February 1951.

53. *Gilbert v. U.S.* (JAGJ-CM343472), reel 5, box 7, A116, CRC Papers; *Daily Worker,* 14 January 1951.

54. Judson Ruch to Morris Greenbaum, 20 August 1951, reel 5, box 7, A114, CRC Papers; Morris Greenbaum to William Patterson, 24 August 1951, reel 5, box 7, A114, CRC Papers.

55. William Patterson to Kay Gilbert, 15 August 1951, reel 5, box 7, A114, CRC Papers.

56. "Committee of 100" pamphlet, ca. 1951, reel 5, box 7, A114, CRC Papers; William Patterson to Kay Gilbert, 17 September 1952, reel 5, box 7, A114, CRC Papers; Leon Gilbert to Morris Greenbaum, undated, reel 5, box 7, A114, CRC Papers.

57. William Patterson to Kay Gilbert, 5 March 1951, reel 5, box 7, A114, CRC Papers; William Patterson to Kay Gilbert, 1 December 1950, reel 5, box 7, A114, CRC Papers; John Holton to Kay Gilbert, 5 January 1951, reel 5, box 7, A114, CRC Papers; Leon Gilbert to William Patterson, 22 January 1950, reel 5, box 7, A114, CRC Papers; *Pittsburgh Courier,* 30 September 1950.

58. Col. C. Robert Bard to William Patterson, undated, reel 5, box 7, A114, CRC Papers; John Starks to Leon Gilbert, undated, reel 5, box 7, A114, CRC Papers; flyer on Ben Davis appearance, 27 January 1951, reel 5, box 7, A114, CRC Papers; William Patterson to Morris Greenbaum, 15 August 1951, reel 5, box 7, A114, CRC Papers; protesters of the plight of Gilbert included the Marine Cooks and Stewards, American Labor Party, Harlem Trade Union Council, both Pennsylvania Senators, American Legion, Veterans of Foreign Wars, Jewish War Veterans, etc.; William Patterson to Morris Greenbaum, 10 August 1951, reel 5, box 7, A114, CRC Papers; Kay Gilbert to CRC, 22 January 1951, reel 5, box 7, A114, CRC Papers; Leon Gilbert to William Patterson, reel 19, box 30, F17, CRC Papers. "I wish to extend my heartfelt thanks to you and the entire Civil Rights Congress for coming to my assistance in my time of need. . . . Without such help I am sure that the persons who have now condemned me to this present sentence would have been satisfied to see my executed"; *U.S. v. Gilbert,* 4 Ct. Martial Repts, 131 (1952). Insane at the time of offense, sentence set aside.

59. *Pittsburgh Courier,* 30 September 1950; *Michigan Chronicle,* 2 December 1950; *Michigan Chronicle,* 2 December 1950; *Pittsburgh Courier,* 7 June 1952; "Leon Gilbert-1951-52 Clippings," box 62, folder, Gilbert, CRC-Mich. Papers; Kay Gilbert to John Holton, 2 February 1955, box 9, folder 39, William Patterson Papers.

60. Ralph Powe to Martin A. Martin, 5 September 1951, reel 4, box 4, A67, CRC Papers; William Patterson to Dept. of Defense, 28 November 1955, reel 9, box 15, A308, CRC Papers; William Patterson to dept. of Defense, 22 January 1954, reel 9, box 15, A308, CRC Papers; M. F. White to Ben Phillips, 11 June 1954, reel 19, box 31, F31, CRC Papers.

Chapter 7. I Will Not Live in Peace with Jim Crow

1. *New York Times Magazine,* 28 October 1951; William Patterson to editor of *New York Times Magazine,* 30 October 1951; William Patterson to editor *New York Times,* 1 November 1949, reel 34, box 57, M35, CRC Papers.

2. William Patterson to Harold Flowers, 23 April 1952, reel 7, box 11, A235, CRC Papers; *Maxwell v. Arkansas,* 343 US 929 (1951), 243 SW2d 377 (1951), 219 Ark 513 (1951); William Patterson to *Arkansas State Press,* 18 May 1953, 15 June 1953, reel 34, box 57, M1A, CRC Papers.

3. *State v. Major Benton,* Supreme Court of North Carolina, 13th district, fall term, CRC amicus brief, reel 17, box 12, A244, CRC Papers; Major Benton File, ca. 1946, reel 2, box A14 CRC Papers.

4. *Carolina Times,* 23 November 1946; *Durham Herald,* 28 November 1946; *Carolina*

Times, 14 November 1946; *New York Age,* 14 December 1946; *Raleigh News and Observer,* 20 November 1946; *Daily Worker,* 21 May 1946, 19 May 1946, 20 May 1946; press release, 30 October 1951, reel 45, box 45, J111, CRC Papers.

5. Laurent Frantz to Milt Kaufman, 19 June 1946, reel 51, box 89, S15, CRC Papers; Laurent Frantz to Milt Kaufman, 24 June 1946, reel 51, box 89, S15, CRC Papers.

6. Laurent Frantz to Milt Kaufman, 10 July 1946, reel 51, box 89, S12, CRC Papers; Milt Kaufman to A. T. Spaulding, 22 May 1946, reel 51, box 89, S15, CRC Papers; press release, ca. May 1946, reel 51, box 89, S15, CRC Papers; H. G. Dunston, "The Black Struggle for Equality in Winston-Salem, North Carolina: 1947–77" (Ph.D. diss., Duke University, 1981).

7. Laurent Frantz to Ben Goldring, 11 November 1946, reel 51, box 89, S10, CRC Papers; Benjamin Goldring to W. R. Jones, 13 November 1946, reel 51, box 89, S10, CRC Papers; Laurent Frantz to Milt Kaufman, 20 November 1946, reel 51, box 89, S10, CRC Papers.

8. Rev. L. W. Wertz to CRC, 12 April 1947, reel 51, box 89, S12, CRC Papers; R. O. Everett to Benjamin Goldring, 14 April 1947, reel 51, box 89, S12, CRC Papers.

9. Rev. L. W. Wertz to Ralph Powe, 21 April 1947, reel 51, box 89, S12, CRC Papers; Ralph Powe to L. W. Wertz, 18 April 1947, reel 51, box 89, S12, CRC Papers; R. O. Everett to Ralph Powe, 29 April 1947, reel 51, box 89, S10, CRC Papers.

10. W. R. Jones to Ben Goldring, 21 April 1947, reel 51, box 89, S12, CRC Papers; Benjamin Goldring to R. O. Everett, 17 April 1947, reel 51, box 89, S12, CRC Papers; Rev. L. W. Wertz to Milt Kaufman, 17 June 1946, reel 51, box 89, S10, CRC Papers.

11. *Daily Worker,* 14 June 1951.

12. Hosea Price to Ralph Powe, 2 September 1950, reel 10, box 16, A322, CRC Papers; Velma Hopkins to Ralph Powe, 12 September 1950, reel 10, box 16, A322, CRC Papers; *Brown v. North Carolina,* 233 NC 202, 63 SE2nd 99 (1951), 341 US 943, cert. denied (1951), *Brown v. Allen,* 344 US 443 (1951).

13. Press release, 12 June 1951, 2 April 1952, reel 2, box 2, A25, CRC Papers.

14. Leon Straus to William Umstead, 12 March 1953, reel 9, box 15, A293, CRC Papers; *Speller v. Allen, Brown v. Allen* 192 F2d 477 (1951), *State v. Speller,* 47 SE2d 537 (1948); Robert Black to Ralph Powe, 24 July 1950, reel 2, box 2, A25, CRC Papers; *Daniels et al. v. Allen,* 192 F2d 763 (1951), 342 US 941, cert. granted, (1952).

15. William Patterson to John Hunt, 1 August 1949, reel 4, box 5, A77, CRC Papers; Defense Committee flyer, undated, reel 4, box 5, A77, CRC Papers.

16. *Durham Morning Herald,* 19 July 1949; open letter to Governor Scott, 20 July 1949, reel 4, box 5, A77, CRC Papers.

17. William Patterson to John Hunt, 12 August 1949, reel 4, box 5, A77, CRC Papers; William Patterson to Daniels Defense Committee, 28 July 1952, reel 8, box 15, A293, CRC Papers; William Patterson to Peoples Defense Committee, 24 December 1953, reel 8, box 15, A293, CRC Papers; William Patterson to C. A. Simmons, 13 October 1949, C. A. Simmons to Paul Robeson, 10 October 1949, reel 4, box 5, A77, CRC Papers; E. L. Rankin to Leon Straus, 30 March 1953, reel 4, box 5, A77, CRC Papers; financial statement, 29 July–1 January 1954, reel 4, box 5, A77, CRC Papers.

18. *Carolina Times,* 25 February 1950; Defense Committee pamphlet, undated, reel 4, box 5, A77, CRC Papers; undated newsletter, reel 4, box 5, A77, CRC Papers; flyer, 6 November 1953, reel 4, box 5, A77, CRC Papers.

19. Patricia Sullivan, "Gideon's Southern Soldiers: New Deal Politics and Civil Rights Reform, 1932–1948" (Ph.D. diss., Emory University, 1983), 198; letter from William Patterson, 22 April 1955, reel 11, box 18, A347, CRC Papers; *Scales v. U.S.,* 227 F2d 581 (1955), 350 US 992 (1956); William Patterson to Andrew Simpkins, 18 November 1952, reel 6, box 10, A100, CRC Papers; *Watlkins et al. v. North Carolina,* 43 SE2d 82, 227 NC 560 (1947), 332 US 841 (1947).

20. William Lawrence to Theresa Kanter, 11 May 1948, reel 46, box 80, P53, CRC Papers; Bella Fisher to William Lawrence, 26 July 1948, reel 46, box 80, P53, CRC Papers; Bella Fisher to Len Goldsmith, 16 December 1948, reel 46, box 80, P53, CRC Papers; Felix Kusman to Bella Fisher, 22 September 1948, reel 46, box 80, P53, CRC Papers. CRC had an embryo of a chapter

in Tampa with Louis Ornetz of the Tobacco Workers as principal contact; Matilda Graff to Leon, 24 March 1949, reel 46, box 80, P53, CRC Papers; *Miami Daily News,* 16 March 1949; after the attack by the *Daily News* "several of our leading members either resigned or were frightened off." Alfred Neufeld to William Patterson, 12 May 1949, reel 46, box 80, P53, CRC Papers; Bobby Graff to William Patterson, 9 July 1949, reel 46, box 80, p53, CRC Papers; *Miami Daily News,* 7 February 1954.

21. Len Goldsmith to William Patterson, ca. 1948–49, reel 34, box 58, M52, CRC Papers; *Miami Daily News,* 6 March 1949; Leon Goldsmith, 10 January 1949, box 9, folder 36, William Patterson Papers.

22. Milton Wolff to Jim Nemo, 3 March 1950, reel 46, box 80, P53, CRC Papers; Bobby Graff to William Patterson, 4 May 1950, reel 46, box 80, P53, CRC Papers; Bobby Graff to William Patterson, 30 June 1952, reel 46, box 80, P53, CRC Papers; Bobby Graff to William Patterson, 20 November 1950, reel 35, box 60, M87, CRC Papers.

23. Bobby Graff to William Patterson, 20 November 1950, reel 35, box 60, M87, CRC Papers; Bobby Graff to Aubrey Grossman, 6 May 1952, reel 46, box 80, P53, CRC Papers. Though the chapter was defunct, Graff still forwarded $115.

24. NAACP press release, 8 November 1951, reel 5, box 7, 124, CRC Papers; Ewart Guinier to "Dear Brother," reel 5, box 7, 107, CRC Papers; Telepress article, 29 October 1951, reel 5, box 7, 107, CRC Papers.

25. Telepress article, 29 October 1951, reel 5, box 7, 107, CRC Papers; *Shepherd et al. v. Fla.,* 341 US 50 (1950), Franklin Williams and Bob Carter argued this case with Marshall on the brief. Ultimately Jack Greenberg and Alex Ackerman joined the case. The high court took note of the fact that "Negroes were removed from the community to prevent their being lynched" and the National Guard was called out. *Irvin v. Florida,* 346 US 927 (1954), cert. denied, 6, 348 VS 866 (1954).

26. *Daily Worker, 11 November 1951; press release, 14 November 1951, reel 5, box 7, A124, CRC Papers; New York Post,* 19 November 1951, 13 November 1951; *Daily Worker,* 9 November 1951; *New York Times,* 8 November 1951, 9 November 1951.

27. *St. Louis American,* 15 November 1951.

28. Ibid.; *National Guardian,* 14 November 1951; *Daily Compass,* 13 November 1951; *Florida Times Union,* 9 November 1951, *New York Post,* 19 November 1951, 16 November 1951, *New York Age,* 17 November 1951; *St. Petersburgh Times,* 8 November 1951; *Daily Worker,* 12 November 1951; *Time,* 19 November 1951.

29. William Patterson to Bobby Graff, 19 August 1949, reel 46, box 80, P53, CRC Papers; Bobby Graff to William Patterson, 17 August 1949, reel 46, box 80, P53, CRC Papers; William Patterson to Bobby Graff, 13 August 1949, reel 46, box 80, P53, CRC Papers; William Patterson to Bobby Graff, 14 December 1949, reel 46, box 80, P53, CRC Papers; Bobby Graff to William Patterson, 12 December 1949, reel 46, box 80, P53, CRC Papers.

30. Myron Marks to William Patterson, 17 October 1951, reel 4, box 4, A70, CRC Papers; Lucinda Finley to William Patterson, undated, reel 6, box 8, A166, CRC Papers; James Aronson to William Patterson, 22 September 1952, reel 4, box 4, A70, CRC Papers; chapter bulletin, 15 February 1952, box 10, folder, National CRC chapter bulletin, January–May 1952, CRC-Mich. Papers.

31. CRC to Dorothy Burnham, 15 November 1945, reel 4, box 4, A101, CRC Papers; press release, 2 September 1950, reel 37, box 63, N38, CRC Papers; press release, 18 October 1950, reel 4, box 4, A101, CRC Papers; *St. Louis American,* 27 July 1950; Asbury Howard, 7 August 1952, reel 4, box 4, A70, CRC Papers; William Patterson to Asbury Howard, 4 August 1952, reel 4, box 4, A70, CRC Papers; Solicitor of Juvenile and Domestic Relations Court, 6 August 1952, reel 4, box 4, A70, CRC Papers; Rev. J. H. Petty to Aubrey Grossman, 12 June 1951, reel 45, box 77, P1, CRC Papers.

32. *Memphis Commercial Appeal,* 19 August 1946; *Jackson Daily News,* 25 August 1946; *Jackson Advocate,* 7 September 1946; *Jackson Daily News,* 25 August 1946; *Jackson Advocate,* 24 August 1946; *Peoples Voice,* 9 November 1946; *Jackson Clarion-Ledger,* 20 August 1946.

33. *Craft v. Mississippi,* testimony of Albert Craft, reel 4, box 5, A73, CRC Papers.

34. Milton Kaufman to Dixon Pyles, 13 February 1947, 15 February 1947, reel 4, box 4, A73, CRC Papers; Ralph Powe to Dixon Pyles, 5 August 1947, reel 4, box 5, A73, CRC Papers; Dixon Pyles to Milton Kaufman, 7 August 1947, reel 4, box 5, A73, CRC Papers; Dixon Pyles to Milton Kaufman, 11 August 1947, reel 4, box 5, A73, CRC Papers.

35. Ralph Powe to Dixon Pyles, 25 July 1947, reel 4, box 5, A74, CRC Papers; *Mississippi v. Craft,* in the Circuit Court of Smith County, Mississippi, October 1946, reel 4, box 5, A74, CRC Papers; Stanley Kutler, *The American Inquisition: Justice and Injustice in the Cold War* (New York: Hill & Wang, 1982): William Patterson to Oakley Johnson, 2 June 1950, reel 3, box 4, folder 19, Oakley Johnson Papers.

36. *Daily Worker,* 14 September 1955; *Daily Worker,* 14 October 1955.

37. *Louisiana Weekly,* 5 June 1948; *Louisiana Weekly,* 26 November 1949; Oakley Johnson, "The New Orleans Story," *Centennial Review* 12 (Spring 1968): 194–219; *City of New Orleans v. Joseph Mouledos et al.,* no. 129, 943, Criminal District Court, Parish of New Orleans: *Wilson v. La.,* reel 13, box 22, A423, CRC Papers.

38. Report, 28 April 1950, file no. 100-13556, New Orleans, FBI; *Daily Worker,* 24 April 1949; *New Orleans Times-Picayune,* 3 November 1949; Oakley Johnson to William Patterson, 13 May 1970, box 2, folder 55, William Patterson Papers; Seymour Linfield to Mary Borders, 21 February 1949, box 9, folder 36, William Patterson Papers; Leon Weiner to William Patterson, 7 May 1949, box 9, folder 36, William Patterson Papers; Leon Weiner to William Patterson, 23 May 1949, box 9, folder 36, William Patterson Papers; *Pittsburgh Courier,* 2 July 1949.

39. *Wilson v. La.,* reel 13, box 22, A423, CRC Papers, *Pittsburgh Courier,* 28 July 1951; 340 US 864 (1951).

40. Press release, 14 July 1952, reel 12, box 21, A410, CRC Papers; *Louisiana Weekly,* 18 July 1952; *Pittsburgh Courier,* 19 July 1952; *Daily Worker,* 20 July 1951; Oakley Johnson to William Patterson, 14 April 1950, reel 3, box 4, folder 19, Oakley Johnson Papers.

41. Oakley Johnson to Aubrey Grossman, 10 September 1950, reel 3, box 4, A63, CRC Papers; press release, 29 June 1951, reel 10, box 16, A320, CRC Papers; Oakley Johnson to Aubrey Grossman, 10 September 1950, reel 35, box 60, M85, CRC Papers; Grossman responded in kind: ". . . if it must be one or the other and it seems to me it must be, your energy must be given to the mass campaign instead of to the legal. . . . I do not care what legal steps are taken by what lawyers, the legal points cannot be won without a mass campaign." Aubrey Grossman to Oakley Johnson, 11 September 1950, reel 35, box 60, M85, CRC Papers; Oakley Johnson to William Patterson, 30 May 1950, 8 May 1950, reel 3, box 4, folder 19, Oakley Johnson Papers.

42. Oakley Johnson to William Patterson, August 1954, reel 1, box 13, A259, CRC Papers; press release, 29 January 1952, box 27, C22, CRC Papers; William Hastie to Oakley Johnson, 14 September 1951, reel 2, box 2, folder 169, Oakley Johnson Papers.

43. *Pittsburgh Courier,* 26 July 1952; Velma Washington to William Patterson, undated, reel 12, box 21, A410, CRC Papers; William Patterson to Velma Washington, 24 July 1952, reel 12, box 21, A410, CRC Papers; *Washington v. La.,* 340 US 856 (1952) Victor Rabinowitz argued this case at this level; *State v. Jugger, Washington et al.* 47 So. 2d 46 (1952); *State v. Wilson,* 37 So. 2d 804, 214 La. 317 (1948); 46 So. 738, 217 La. 470, 340 US 864, 341 US 901, 934, 217 La. 470 (1950), 341 US 901; *Arkansas State Press,* 30 December 1949; *California Eagle,* 29 December 1949; *National Guardian,* 26 December 1949, 2 January 1950.

44. *State v. Honeycutt,* 44 So. 2d 313, 216 La. 610 (1950), 49 So. 2d 610, 218 La. 362 (1950); *Honeycutt v. Gilbeau,* reel 5. box 7, A132, CRC Papers; Oakley Johnson to Alvin Jones, 9 December 1954, reel 9, box 15, A311, CRC Papers; *L.A. Daily News,* 4 December 1954.

45. Oakley Johnson to Louis Brown, 20 November 1949; Oakley Johnson to William Patterson, 21 November 1949, reel 3, box 4, folder 19; Oakley Johnson to Milt Wolf, 11 December 1949, reel 4, box 4, folder 19; Oakley Johnson to Milt Wolf, 11 December 1949, reel 4, box 4, folder 19; Oakley Johnson to William Patterson, 4 May 1950, reel 3. box 4, folder 19; Sophie Goff to William Patterson, 1 September 1949, reel 2, box 4, folder 17; Oakley Johnson to William Patterson, 30 May 1950, reel 3, box 4, folder 19; William Patterson to Oakley Johnson, 19

January 1950, reel 3, box 4, folder 19; Mayor de Lesseps Morrison to A. A. O'Brien, undated, reel 3, box 4, folder 19, Oakley Johnson Papers.

46. Oakley Johnson to William Patterson, 16 April 1949, reel 2, box 4, folder 17; Oakley Johnson to William Patterson, 20 May 1951, reel 4, box 5, folder 25; Oakley Johnson to William Patterson, 4 June 1951, reel 3, box 4, folder 19; statement by Oakley Johnson, April 1952, reel 1, box 2, folder 13; Oakley Johnson Papers; *Pittsburgh Courier,* 19 May 1951.

47. Anne Braden to William Patterson, 21 May 1952, reel 47, box 81, P78, CRC Papers; J. Benjamin Horton, Jr., to CRC, 29 November 1948, reel 34, box 58, M54, CRC Papers.

48. The FBI was present at early CRC meetings in Atlanta (Report by Nicholas Purchia, 13 January 1949, file no. 100-4014, FBI). On 3 June 1949 Purchia reported that the chapter was "presently inactive" (cf. also *Atlanta Daily World,* 10 February 1949). Leon Weiner to CRC, 15 March 1949, box 9, folder 36, William Patterson Papers; *Miami Daily News;* 6 March 1949; Leon Weiner to Len Goldsmith, 31 January 1949, box 9, folder 36, William Patterson Papers. Weiner was also involved in the controversial case concerning Senator Glen Taylor, Progressive Party vice-presidential candidate arrested after speaking before a desegregated audience in Birmingham; Louis Burnham was involved on behalf of SNYC; Larkin Marshall to William Patterson, 19 April 1951, reel 35, box 60, M88, CRC Papers; Milton Wolf to William Patterson, 2 February, ca. 1950, reel 46, box 80, P56, CRC Papers.

49. Larkin Marshall to William Patterson, 18 April 1950, reel 46, box 80, P56, CRC Papers; William Patterson to Larkin Marshall, 23 April 1951, reel 46, box 80, P56, CRC Papers.

50. *Daily Worker,* 19 February 1950; Milton Wolf to Larkin Marshall, 3 March 1950, reel 46, box 80, P56, CRC Papers; flyer on Claybon case, ca. 1951, reel 3, box 4, A53, CRC Papers; Abe Weisburd to CRC, 30 July 1952, reel 3, box 4, A53, CRC Papers; William Patterson to Louis Jones, undated, reel 6, box 9, A168, CRC Papers; Larkin Marshall to William Patterson, 27 June 1950, reel 43, box 74, N322, CRC Papers; Numan Bartley, *The Creation of Modern Georgia* (Athens: University of Georgia Press, 1983), 187–89.

51. William Patterson to Victoria Garvin, 24 March 1954, reel 5, box 8, A142, CRC Papers; memo from Maude Katz, undated, reel 5, box 8, A150, CRC Papers; Maude White Katz, "Learning from History: The Ingram Case of the 1940's," *Freedomways* 19 (1979): 82–86.

52. Oakley Johnson, "The Case of the Ingram Family," undated, Women's Committee for Equal Justice, "The Case of Mrs. Ingram," undated, reel 5, box 8, A148, CRC Papers; Dorothy Coles to CRC, 30 March 1948, reel 5, box 8, A148, CRC Papers.

53. "The Case of Mrs. Ingram," March 1948, reel 5, box 8, A148, CRC Papers.

54. Note, "Group Action in Fight for Civil Liberties," *Yale Law Journal* 58 (Fall 1949): 474–98, 584; Walter White to "Gentlemen," 22 April 1948, box 8, A146, CRC Papers; William Patterson to R. Hanson, 18 November 1949, reel 5, box 8, A146, CRC Papers; William Patterson, Ingram Case—Outline of Activities in Atlanta, 14 August 1951, box 9, folder 67, William Patterson Papers; *Ingram v. State,* 48 S.E. 2d 891 (1949); *N.Y. Post,* 8 March 1948; *Ellaville Sun,* 30 January 1948.

55. William Lawrence to Marva Bovingdan, 28 May 1948, reel 5, box A146, CRC Papers; William Patterson to Joseph Cadden, 5 April 1948, reel 5, A146, CRC Papers; *Morgan v. Virginia,* 328 US 373 (1946), *Taylor v. Commonwealth,* 187 Va. 214, 46 SE2d 384, (1948).

56. Geneva Ruskin to Ralph Powe, 7 August 1951, reel 5, box 8, A146, CRC Papers; Rosa Lee Ingram to Ralph Powe, 8 August 1951, reel 5, box 8, A146, CRC Papers; William Patterson to Larkin Marshall, 15 August 1951, reel 5, box 8, A146, CRC Papers.

57. Mary Kanable to Eleanor Roosevelt, 26 December 1949, reel 5, box 8, A152, CRC Papers; Eleanor Roosevelt to Herman Katzen, 6 May 1949, reel 5, box 8, A145, CRC Papers; *California Eagle,* 13 October 1949; *Afro-American,* 20 August 1949; *Pittsburgh Courier,* 1 October 1949; *Ingram v. State,* 204, Ga. 164 (1948).

58. Release, NCFIF, 6 April 1950, reel 5, box 8, A144, CRC Papers; *Philadelphia Tribune,* 8 May 1954; Harry Raymond, "The Ingrams Shall Not Die," March 1948, reel 5, box 8, A148, CRC Papers; William Patterson and Aubrey Grossman to chapters, 18 September 1951, reel 38, box 64, N61, CRC Papers.

59. William Patterson to Heloise Moorhead, 10 February 1949, reel 36, box 61, M141, CRC Papers; Gene Weltfish to William Patterson, 19 February 1949, reel 36, box 61, M141, CRC Papers; William Patterson to Gene Weltfish, 23 February 1949, reel 36, box 61, M141, CRC Papers.

60. Mary Church Terrell to William Patterson, undated, reel 5, box 8, A142, CRC Papers; William Patterson to Mary Church Terrell, 9 March 1954, reel 5, box 8, A142, CRC Papers; Muriel Symington to Carl Murphy, William Patterson to Rebecca Styles Taylor, 3 March 1954, reel 5, box 8, A142, CRC Papers; William Patterson to Mary Church Terrell, 24 March 1954, reel 5, box 8, A142, CRC Papers; William Patterson to Halois Robinson, 24 March 1954, reel 5, box 8, A142, CRC Papers; Beverly Washington Jones, "Quest for Equality: The Life of Mary Eliza Church Terrell 1863–1954" (Ph.D. diss., University of North Carolina, 1980). Symptomatic of the misinformation disseminated on CRC, this writer claims that the Ingrams were free in 1950 (p. 131). She does observe correctly that the sit-ins in Washington, D.C., against Jim Crow "paved the way" for Montgomery and involved CRC members and allies like Joseph Forer (p. 135).

61. Maude White Katz to *New York Times,* 25 July 1949, reel 5, box 8, A144, CRC Papers; Mrs. C. Jones to Mary Church Terrell, 13 May 1954, reel 5, box 8, A141, CRC Papers; Halois Robinson to Ida Henderson, 8 May 1954, reel 5, box 8, A141, CRC Papers; Ida Henderson to Mary Church Terrell, 4 May 1954, reel 5, box 8, A141, CRC Papers; William Patterson to CRC chapters, undated, reel 5, box 8, A141, CRC Papers.

62. Margaret Gibbons to Angie Dickerson, 5 January 1952, reel 5, box 8, A145, CRC Papers; undated press release, reel 5, box 8, A145, CRC Papers; K. R. Reid to Maude White Katz, 25 July 1949, reel 5, box 8, A145, CRC Papers; William Patterson to Viola Brown, 28 June 1945, reel 5, box 8, A141, CRC Papers; Halois Robinson to Prof. Louise Pettibone Smith, 3 June 1954, reel 5, box 8, A141, CRC Papers; M. A. Barnett to Elaine Ross, 7 May 1954, reel 5, box 8, A141, CRC Papers.

63. WCEJ, "A Report from Georgia," ca. 1954, reel 5, box 8, A149, CRC Papers; *Pittsburgh Courier,* 1 October 1949; *California Eagle,* 13 October 1949, 20 October 1949; *Daily Worker,* 4 April 1949, 14 February 1948, 16 February 1948, 28 February 1948, 22, 24 February 1948, 6 March 1948, 4, 11 April 1949, 4 May 1948, 15 June 1948; *Pittsburgh Courier,* 13 March 1948, 6 March 1948, 13 March 1948, 15 May 1948, 24 July 1948, 16 October 1948, 16 April 1949, 22 January 1949, 1 July 1950; *New York Post,* 31 March 1949.

64. *Daily Worker,* 11 January 1953; *Afro-American,* 16 April 1949; *Freedom,* May 1952; *Atlantic Constitution,* 19 December 1953; Phyllis Berger, 9 January 1954, reel 5, box 8, A143, CRC Papers; "Mar. Alex" to William Patterson, 13 December 1953, reel 5, box 8, A143, CRC Papers. William Patterson to Governor Talmadge, 23 December 1952, reel 5, box 8, A152, CRC Papers; Governor Talmadge to William Patterson, 24 December 1952, reel 5, box 8, A152, CRC Papers.

65. Halois Robinson to Edna Griffin, 22 January 1954, reel 5, box 8, A143, CRC Papers; Halois Robinson to Mamie Reese, 14 January 1954, reel 5, box 8, A143, CRC Papers; M. C. Terrell to J. A. Rogers, 5 March 1954, reel 5, box 8, A152, CRC Papers. "New York Report: Funds on Ingram Case," undated, reel 5, box 8, A152, CRC Papers.

66. WCEJ press release, 12 March 1954, reel 5, box 8, A142, CRC Papers; Maxwell Rabb to M. C. Terrell, 1 June 1954, reel 5, box 8, A145, CRC Papers; William Patterson to Angie Dickerson, undated, reel 5, box 8, A151, CRC Papers; William Patterson to M. C. Terrell, 27 February 1954, reel 5, box 8, A142, CRC Papers; Rebecca St. Taylor to M. C. Terrell, reel 5, box 8, A142, CRC Papers.

67. Wilson Record, *The Negro and the Communist Party* (Chapel Hill: University of North Carolina Press, 1951), 258, 262. Record couples this with a withering and scurrilous attack on Patterson and CRC, 254–62; John Holton to William Patterson, 15 September 1952, reel 49, box 85, P160, CRC Papers; *Philadelphia Tribune,* 8 May 1954; John Holton to William Patterson, undated, reel 5, box 8, A142, CRC Papers.

68. Esther Jackson to Maude White Katz, 16 November 1949, box 62, folder, "Rosa Ingram

Case, 1947–54," CRC-Mich. Papers. This file contains voluminous clippings, along with an adjacent one; Elizabeth Wroton to CRC, 14 April 1948, reel 5, box 8, A146, CRC Papers; Leon Straus to Rosa Lee Ingram, 12 April 1950, reel 5, box 8, CRC Papers; R. L. Ingram mailing lists, undated, reel 5, box 8, A138, CRC Papers.

69. *Daily Worker,* 21 July 1949; *Daily Worker,* 15 March 1948; *New York Post,* 22 December 1948. James Ford and Claudia Jones were at an 18 March 1948 delegation to Justice on the case; in May 1949 Truman refused to meet with them; in November 1949 they met with Justice again; M. C. Terrell to Rebecca Styles Taylor, 27 February 1954, reel 5, box 8, A142, CRC Papers. Regarding Ben Davis, she said: "I am particularly interested in the release of 'Little Ben.' His voice is woefully needed at this hour. You know I was a dear friend of his father. . . . It is not popularly known that no person who ever sat in that Council brought more civil rights legislation to its forum. I believe that he is where he is because of the great fight. . . . There are times when I feel like a young woman again in the throes of this wonderful fight"; Rev. John Saunders to CRC, 30 April 1954, reel 5, box 8, A154, CRC Papers.

70. Mary Kalb to William Patterson, 3 August 1951; William Patterson to Mary Kalb, 6 August 1951; CRC press release, 6 August 1951; William Patterson to Mary Kalb, 14 August 1951; Mary Kalb to William Patterson, 10 August 1951; reel 10, box 17, A337, CRC Papers.

71. *Afro-American,* 21 January 1950; Wm. Anderson to WP, 9/30/51, reel 34, box 57, M1A, CRC Papers; *New York Times,* 23 August 1952; *Daily Worker,* 20 August 1952; *Compass,* 20 August 1952; press release, 14 August 1952, reel 6, box 9, A157, CRC Papers.

72. Senora Lawson to Aubrey Grossman, 8 September 1952, reel 6, box 9, A157, CRC Papers; "Urgent Action Letter re: Case of Albert Jackson, Jr." to CRC, 18 August 1952, reel 6, box 9, A157, CRC Papers.

73. *Hampton et al. v. Smith,* reel 7, box 11, A230, CRC Papers; William Patterson to Bishop W. J. Walls, 1 June 1950, reel 43, box 74, N328, CRC Papers.

74. "The Case of the Martinville Seven—Fact Sheet," reel 7, box 11, A227, CRC Papers; Robert Harris, research paper on the Martinsville 7, 21 August 1964, box 9, folder 90, William Patterson Papers.

75. Josephine Grayson to William Patterson, 20 August 1951, reel 34, box 58, M49, CRC Papers; William Patterson to Josephine Grayso, 27 August 1951, reel 34, box 58, M49, CRC Papers; Floyd Joyner to William Patterson, 8 December 1950, reel 7, box 11, A227, CRC Papers; William Patterson to Floyd Joyner, William Patterson to Mary Kalb, 11 December 1950, reel 7, box 11, A227, CRC Papers.

76. Harris, *Nation,* 3 March 1951.

77. William Patterson to Tom Buchanan, 21 June 1949, reel 46, box 80, P50, CRC Papers; William Patterson statement, 12 June 1949, reel 7, box 11, A232, CRC Papers; *Times Dispatch,* 13 June 1949, reel 7, box 11, A228, CRC Papers; undated article, *News Leader,* 14 June 1949, *Times Dispatch,* 14 June 1949, reel 7, box 11, A228, CRC Papers; *Daily Worker,* 25 June 1950; *Louisiana Weekly,* 21 May 1949; *Hampton et al. v. Commonwealth,* 190 Va. 531 (1950), 339 US 989 (1950), 340 US 914 (1950) cert. denied.

78. William Patterson to Roy Wilkins, 7 June 1950, press release, 14 March 1950, reel 7, box 11, A232, CRC Papers; William Patterson to Walter White, undated telegram, reel 6, box 10, A204, CRC Papers.

79. Martin A. Martin, 6 October 1950, reel 6, box 9, A180, CRC Papers; Anne Shore to Aubrey Grossman and William Patterson, 11 November 1950, reel 47, box 82, P92, CRC Papers.

80. *Nation,* 20 February 1951; Earl Dickerson to Nation, 25 July 1952, reel 34, box 57, M31, CRC Papers; *Time,* 12 February 1951; *New Republic,* 29 January 1951; *Christian Century,* 21 February 1951; William Patterson to Whitelaw Reid, 1 February 1951, reel 34, box 58, M36, CRC Papers; *Nation,* 27 January 1951; *Daily Worker,* 6 July 1949, 15 October 1950, 3 January 1951, 14 January 1951, 23 July 1950, 1 February 1951, 31 May 1949, 15 June 1950, 27 July 1950, 14 July 1950, 2 February 1951, 3 August 1950, 27 July 1950, 12 June 1950, 17 June 1950; naturally the *Worker*'s coverage was more sympathetic and accurate; *Time,* 12 February 1951; *New York*

Times, 14 March 1950, 11 October 1950, 6 February 1951; *Guardian,* 7 February 1951; *Sepia Record,* August 1954.

81. *Coker v. Georgia,* 433 U.S. 584 (1977); the most recent exhaustive examination of the death penalty concludes, "state imposed executions for rape may have become the counterpart to lynching." The success of the antilynch movement, it could be argued, forced the racists to move into "legal" channels to enforce their diktat in the face of a militant postwar upsurge by Afro-Americans. William Bowers et al., *Legal Homicide: Death as a Punishment in America, 1864–1982* (Boston: Northeastern University Press, 1984), 79; Robert Frederick Burk, "Symbolic Equality: The Eisenhower Administration and Black Civil Rights, 1953–1961 (Ph.D. diss., University of Wisconsin, 1982); Jacquelyn Dowd Hall, "'The Mind That Burns in Each Body': Women, Rape and Racial Violence," 328–49 in Ann Snitow, et al., *Powers of Desire: The Politics of Sexuality* (New York: Monthly Review Press, 1983). The controversial equation of Black men-white women and rape had been taken up for years and is being taken up afresh again today; petitions, ca. 1951, reel 7, box 11, A231, CRC Papers; William Patterson to pastors, 8 January 1951, reel 7, box 11, A229, CRC Papers; "Sol" to Elaine Ross, 4 January 1951, reel 7, box 11, A229, CRC Papers.

82. Anne Shore to William Patterson and Aubrey Grossman, 11 November 1950, box 62, folder M-7, 1950–51, CRC-Mich. Papers; Anne Shore to Aubrey Grossman, 17 November 1950, reel 47, box 82, P92, CRC Papers.

83. "Membership Builder Article," December 1950, reel 27, box 45, J110, CRC Papers; Arthur McPhaul to James Smith, 14 November 1950, box 62, folder M-7, 1950–51, CRC Papers; *Beacon,* February 1951, box 62, folder M-7 miscellaneous, CRC-Mich. Papers.

84. "Action Bulletin," no. 3, Harlem chapter, ca. 1950, reel 56, box 98, V128, CRC Papers; Walter Lowenfels to William Patterson, 2 October 1971, box 2, folder 57, William Patterson Papers; "Chapter Bulletin," vol. 2, 19 March 1951, reel 10, box 16, A328, CRC Papers; Billy Strachan to CRC, 1 August 1951, William Patterson to NCASP, 22 November 1948, Aubrey Grossman to MCRAPP, 23 February 1951, Association of Polish Jurists to William Patterson, 29 September 1950, Bankole Akpata to CRC, 2 February 1951, Americo de Carvalho to CRC, 8 March 1951, Amaefuke Ikoro to CRC, 17 October 1950, reel 34, box 58, M46, CRC Papers.

85. Press release, ca. November 1950, reel 7, box 11, A227, CRC Papers.

86. "Civil Rights Action Bulletin," 1 November 1950, reel 7, box 11, A227, CRC Papers; Aubrey Grossman to Rosalee Etta Safford McGee, 6 January 1951; excerpts from interview with Rosalee McGee including affidavit, 17 May 1951, reel 6, box 10, A207, CRC Papers; "Proposed Rules for Delegation," ca. 1951, reel 7, box 11, A233, CRC Papers.

87. Aubrey Grossman to chapter secretaries, 9 January 1951, reel 7, box 11, A229, CRC Papers; participating unions from Detroit included Plymouth Local 51, Fleetwood Local 15, De Soto Local 227, Cadillac Local 22, Bohn Aluminum Local 208, Dodge Local 3, Fur and Leather Local 38, Packinghouse Local 69; Shore later claimed that this was an inflated estimate. Release, 18 January 1951, Anne Shore to Aubrey Grossman, 19 January 1951, box 62, folder M-7, 1950–51, CRC-Mich. Papers; Arthur McPhaul to Mary Kalb, 17 January 1950, box 62, folder M-7, 1950–51, CRC-Mich. Papers.

88. Press release, 15 January 1951, 29 January 1951, reel 7, box 11, A233, CRC Papers; D. V. Jemison to William Patterson, 15 January 1951, reel 7, box 11, A233, CRC Papers; press release, 26 August 1950, reel 7, box 11, A233, CRC Papers. "1044 Polish organizations and groups ranging from trade unions to summer camp colonies" protested; Anne Shore report on Virginia trip, February 1951, box 62, folder M-7, 1950–51, CRC-Mich. Papers.

89. William Mandel to Gerald Horne, 20 June 1984 (in possession of author).

90. Press release, 2 February 1951, reel 7, box 11, A233, CRC Papers; William Mandel report, 10 February 1951, reel 7, box 11, A233, CRC Papers.

91. *Freedom,* February 1951; press release, undated, reel 7, box 11, A233, CRC Papers.

92. Press release, 5 February 1951, reel 7, box 11, A233, CRC Papers; *Richmond News-Leader,* 1 February 1951; press release, 13 February 1951, reel 7, box 11, A233, CRC Papers;

William Patterson to pastors in Chicago, Florida, Michigan, Louisiana, etc., 29 March 1951, reel 7, box 11, A228, CRC Papers; Aubrey Grossman to Frank Render, 27 February 1951, reel 7, box 10, A228, CRC Papers; Anne Shore to Marguerite Robinson, ca. 1951, box 62, folder M-7, 1950–51, CRC-Mich. Papers; *Jewish Life,* April 1951, box 9, folder 90, William Patterson Papers; fourteen years later James Grayson, son of one of the executed men, was found guilty himself of murder, *Afro-American,* 21 December 1965.

Chapter 8. Pulling the Worm from the Apple

1. William Lawrence to Ralph Powe, 23 May 1949, reel 53, box 93, V9, CRC Papers; *Feiner v. New York,* 91 NE 2d 316 (1950), 300 US 391, 339 US 962, 340 US 315 (1950).
2. W. E. B. Du Bois to George Marshall, 15 September 1950, reel 64, #1058, W. E. B. Du Bois Papers; circular, reel 56, box 99, V138, CRC Papers; auditor's statement, 13 September 1946, reel 48, box 84, P136, CRC Papers; results of Emergency Fund Drive, 8 March 1951, reel 56, box 98, V116, CRC Papers. Amounts garnered by various chapters give a view of relative strength in the city. Manhattan—West Side, $585; Chelsea, $325; Village, $300; Harlem, $207; East Side, $635; Washington Heights, $124; Manhattan County, $65; East Harlem, $50; Musicians, $18.50; ILD, $246 (there was a special chapter of the International Labor Defense). Bronx—West Bronx, $319; Allerton, $205; Mosholu Parkway, $10. Brooklyn—Brooklyn Heights, $399; Shorefront, $260; Brownsville, $260; Flatbush, $86; Hospital, $111 (this was part of CRC's concentration on organizing at work-sites). Queens—Sunnyside, $745; Laurelton, $275; Jamaica, $305; Flushing, $110; Rockaway, $16. In addition to raffles and the like, other tactics to raise money included sustainers, personal solicitations for large gifts, affairs at summer resorts, and a special approach to unions, Blacks, businesses, etc. In 1952 there was another fundraising endeavor; the quotas for each chapter again reflects the relative strength of CRC in the city. Brooklyn—Brooklyn Heights, $500; Brighton Beach, $350; Coney Island, $250; Crown Heights, $350; Brownsville, $250; Fort Greene, $25; Bedford Styvesant, $50; Bath Beach, $250; Queens—Sunnyside, $100; Jamaica, $50; Laurelton, $50; Flushing, $100; Rockaway, $50; Bornx—Allerton, $200; Kingsbridge, $50; Parkchester, $25; Burnside, $25; Prospect, $25; Manhattan—Harlem, $50, Washington Heights, $50; East Side, $50; Park West, $50; Upper West Side, $100; West Midtown, $100; Lincoln Square, $25; East Harlem, $25, Chelsea, $250; Greenwich Village, $100; Yorkville, $50; East Midtown, $25. Perhaps because Brooklyn was seen as falling down on the job during the last drive, its quota was upped. "Civil Rights Action Bulletin," 14 February 1952, reel 54, box 95, V68, CRC Papers.
3. *Daily Worker,* 9 May 1946; minutes of meeting of Board, 24 June 1946; minutes of meeting of Organizing Committee, 6 June 1946; program, 15 May 1946; conference, 11 October 1947; reel 48, box 84, P135, CRC Papers.
4. Executive Secretary's Informational Report, 6 June 1946, reel 48, box 84, P135, CRC Papers; circular, ca. 1949, reel 48, box 84, P142, CRC Papers; "Community Notes," Greenwich Village CRC, 25 January 1947, CRC-Tamiment Papers; minutes of meeting of Executive Council of CRC-NY, 30 July 1947, reel 48, box 84, P136, CRC Papers.
5. "List of cases handled by Lawyers Committee of Civil Rights Congress of New York . . .", ca. 1947, reel 10, box 16, A318, CRC Papers; memo by attorneys Hope Stevens, Mildred Roth, Bennett D. Brown, 13 February 1951, reel 4, box 5, A81, CRC Papers; press release, 24 July 1950, reel 2, box 1, A9, CRC Papers; Melbourne Mitchell to Ralph Powe, undated, reel 14, box 4, A69, CRC Papers.
6. William Patterson to Rev. Eliot White, 1 November 1949, reel 34, box 57, M15, CRC Papers; minutes of National Board meeting, 11 June 1950, reel 38, box 65, N91, CRC Papers; flyer, 28 October 1951, reel 48, box 84, P137, CRC Papers; Francis Henry Touchet, "The Social Gospel and the Cold War: The Melish Case," pamphlet, reel 7, box 11, A236, undated, CRC Papers; William Patterson to Les Davis, 16 October 1951, reel 46, box 80, P63, CRC Papers; W. J. Walls to William Patterson, 14 September 1953, reel 19, box 31, F31, CRC Papers.

7. Flyer, undated, reel 8, box 13, A267, CRC Papers; *Compass,* 15 August 1952, 13 August 1952; *Afro-American,* 3 May 1952; *Brunswick News,* February 1952; *Compass,* 10 August 1952; *New Jersey Home News,* 7 June 1952; *Daily Worker,* 13 July 1955; *Daily Worker,* 17 October 1955.

8. Circular, undated, reel 37, box 62, N8, CRC Papers; press release from "Committee to Act against the McCarran and Walter Bills," ca. 1952, reel 34, box 57, M12, CRC Papers; report by Harriet Barron, National Conference of Defense Committee, 18–20 June 1954, reel 6, box 10, A197, CRC Papers; Carol King and Ann Fagan Ginger, "The McCarran Act and the Immigration Laws," *Lawyers Guild Review* 11 (Summer 1951): 133.

9. *Daily Worker,* 19 Mary 1949; *National Guardian,* 23 May 1949; *New York Times,* 19 May 1949; Hans Friestadt to William Patterson, 2 June 1949, reel 5, box 7, A112, CRC Papers; flyer, ca. 1951, William Patterson letter, 21 November 1952, reel 13, box 22, A426, CRC Papers; *National Guardian,* 11 September 1952; "Order of Parole under Supervision" 22 October 1952, reel 13, box 22, A426, CRC Papers.

10. *Daily Worker,* 18 October 1955; *Daily Worker,* 11 May 1955; *Daily Worker,* 4 April 1955; schedule of deportation hearings, ca. 1955, reel 2, box 1, A3, CRC Papers.

11. *New York Times,* 8 May 1950; *Daily Worker,* 5 May 1950; *Compass,* 7 May 1950; Nat Ross to Maximillian Ross, 8 May 1950, reel 53, box 94, V45, CRC Papers; flyer, undated, reel 8, box 13, A267, CRC Papers; summary of findings and decisions of the Conference for Civil and Human Rights, 25 June 1949, reel 9, box 15, A290, CRC Papers. Hammett gave the welcoming address. Rogge and Bob Thompson spoke. Others participating including Guinier, Jesus Colon, Patterson, Weltfish, Philip Morrison, Doris Peterson, Thomas Emerson, Fast, Melish, Irving Potash, Langston Hughes, Anton Refregier, et al.

12. *New York Times,* 10 August 1948, 18 November 1949, 24 November 1949, 30 November 1949, 2 December 1949, 5 January 1950, 6 November 1950, 12 January 1950, 20 February 1950, 10 March 1950, *New York Star,* 11 August 1948, 14 September, 9 December 1948, *Compass,* 21 November 1949, 27 November 1949, 4 December 1949, 11 December 1949, 6 November 1950, 27 January 1950, 20 February 1950, 5 March 1950, 8 March 1950, 9 March 1950, 9 April 1950, *Daily Worker,* 2 August 1950; Touchet, 271; Nat Ross to John Di Leonardo, ca. 1952, Nat Ross to Herman Stichman, 21 March 1952, Knickerbocker Village Tenants Association memo, March 1952, reel 53, box 94, V44, CRC Papers; press release, ca. 1950, reel 53, box 93, V10, CRC Papers.

13. "CRC May Day Bulletin," May 1952, reel 23, box 39, J15, CRC Papers; "CRC-NY Chapter Guide," August 1946, reel 48, box 84, P136, CRC Papers.

14. CRC-NY newsletter, 20 June 1946, release, 11 December 1947, reel 48, box 84, P136, CRC Papers; CRC-NY pamphlet, ca. 1949, reel 8, box 13, A267, CRC Papers; flyer, ca. 1949, reel 53, box 94, V56, CRC Papers; *Compass,* 6 November 1949; *New York Times,* 4 November 1949, *Compass,* 4 November 1949, *Compass,* 1 December 1949.

15. Memo, undated, reel 53, box 93, V33, CRC Papers; petition, undated, CRC-Tamiment Papers.

16. "Hoodlum Violence against a Political Party," January 1948–November 1948, reel 53, box 93, V33, CRC Papers.

17. "Memorandum on Some Typical Examples of Police Violence and Other Political Violations of Civil Rights," undated, reel 53, box 93, V33, CRC Papers.

18. Alice Stapleton to Jesus Colon, 25 July 1950, reel 53, box 94, V39, CRC Papers.

19. Civil Rights News, April 1950, reel 48, box 84, P136, CRC Papers; CRC-NY pamphlet, ca. 1951, reel 4, box 6, A88, CRC Papers.

20. Press release, 24 January 1949, reel 53, box 93, V11, CRC Papers; press release, 9 April 1952, 24 April 1952, 17 June 1952, reel 53, box 93, V2, CRC Papers; *New York World Telegram and Sun,* 11 June 1952; *Amsterdam News,* 14 June 1952; Rev. Frank Glenn White to Rudolph Halley, undated, reel 53, box 93, V2, CRC Papers; circular, undated, reel 2, box 1, A13, CRC Papers; petition to the Honorable Thomas Dewey . . .," 22 April 1952, reel 8, box 13, A258, CRC Papers.

21. *Amsterdam News,* 5 July 1952; *National Guardian,* 22 May 1952; *Oaklahoma Black Dispatch,* 31 May 1952; release, ca. 1952, reel 53, box 93, V4, CRC Papers.

22. Press release, 9 April 1950, reel 53, box 94, V55, CRC Papers; Civil Rights Action bulletin, 27 May 1952, reel 54, box 95, V68, CRC Papers; press release, 1 October 1952, reel 55, box 96, V102, CRC Papers.

23. Philip S. Foner, *Paul Robeson Speaks,* 543, 544; James Rorty and Winifred Rauschenbush, "The Lessons of the Peekskill Riots: What Happened and Why," *Commentary* 15 (October 1950): 309–23.

24. Undated article, box 10, folder 16, William Patterson Papers; Foner, *Robeson,* 283–85.

25. William Lawrence to Paul Robeson, 4 February 1949, reel 53, box 94, V61, CRC Papers; *Afro-American,* 8 October 1949; Though eager to comply, George Bernard Shaw replied circuitously to "Paul" when asked to campaign on behalf of CRC clients; "If you connect my name and reputation with your meeting, and invite me to speak for you in the USA, as Wallace's silly committee did at the presidential election, you will gain perhaps two thousand adherents, ten of them Negro, and lose two million. The rest will ask (if they ask or care anything at all) 'who the hell is Bernard Shaw?' In the U.S.A. an enormous majority of those who know that I exist, know me as an Irish foreigner, a Red Communist, a friend and agent of Stalin, an atheist, and in literature, a joker who thinks himself a better playwright than Shakespeare and made a reputation by calling black white. Keep me out of it; and do not waste your time courting the handful of people whose votes you are sure of already. Play for Republican votes and episcopal support all the time, and when you get a big meeting of all sorts, don't talk politics, but sing 'Old Man River.' Always your sincere friend . . ." George Bernard Shaw to Paul Robeson, 13 June 1950, reel 38, box 64, N70, CRC Papers; *Freedom,* January 1951, February 1951, March 1951.

26. *Philadelphia Tribune,* 24 July 1949; statement of Negro delegates, 16–17 July 1949, reel 27, box 45, J110, CRC Papers; Ronald Smith, "The Paul Robeson-Jackie Robinson Saga and a Political Collision," *Journal of Sport History* 6 (Summer 1979): 5–27; *Robeson v. John Foster Dulles,* ca. 1956, reel 43, box 74, N340, CRC Papers; William Patterson to Frank Spector, 14 September 1955, box 9, folder 49, William Patterson Papers.

27. Milton Kaufman to Dean Leon Green, 8 May 1947; Milton Kaufman to Rev. L. J. Tignor, 6 May 1947; Julius Crane to Peoria Mayor, 28 May 1947; and Mary Sweat to Milton Kaufman, 26 April 1947, reel 15, box 25, B45, CRC Papers; William Patterson to Bobby Graff, 4 October 1949, reel 46, box 80, P53, CRC Papers.

28. *New York Mirror,* 3 September 1949; *New York Times,* 8 September 1949; affidavit of Pete Seeger, Albert Spivey, Leo Stark, Irving Warman, Anita Payne, Seymour Gladstone, Harold Taylor, Nina Phillips, Starr Koss, September 1949, reel 9, box 15, A299, CRC Papers; press release, 28 August 1949, CRC newsletter, 5 September 1949, reel 9, box 15, A305, CRC Papers.

29. *Pittsburgh Courier,* 10 September 1949; *New York Sun,* 9 September 1949; *New York World Telegram,* 8 September 1949; *New York Times,* 17 October 1949; *Daily Worker,* 29 August 1949; *New York Age,* 17 September 1949; *Afro-American,* 17 September 1949; *Christian Science Monitor,* 8 December 1949; *Daily Worker,* 8 December 1949; William Patterson to W. E. B. Du Bois, 2 April 1952, reel 4, box 6, A95, CRC Papers; William Patterson to Bess Dlugin and Clarence Parker, 30 August 1949; reel 19, box 30, F4, CRC Papers; Albert Maltz from William Patterson, 26 April 1951, William Patterson to fellow organizations in Canada and U.K., reel 34, box 58, M42, CRC Papers; CRC-NY report, 27 September 1949, reel 9, box 15, A302, CRC Papers.

30. Grand Jury investigation, 1949, reel 11, box 18, A357, CRC Papers; *Robeson v. Fanelli,* 94 F. Supp. 62 (1950); Ralph Powe to CRC lawyers, 15 August 1949, reel 3, box 4, A65, CRC Papers; George Marshall to Howard McGrath, 5 October 1949, Bella Abzug to William Lawrence, 14 December 1949, reel 9, box 15, A304, CRC Papers; *Time,* 5 September 1949; Leon Straus to Adjutant General-Army, 11 January 1950, reel 9, box 15, A304, CRC Papers. He was discharged "under other than honorable conditions as 2nd Lieutenant, Infantry Reserve and from commission as 2nd Lt., U.S. Army for role in Peekskill." He read of it in the newspaper.

31. Report by CRC-NY, September 1949, reel 9, box 15, A302, CRC Papers; Roy Wilkins to

Thomas Dewey, 29 August 1949, box 445, NAACP Papers; William Read to Roy Wilkins, 9 September 1949; James Wechsler to Roger Baldwin, 8 December 1949; and Patrick M. Malin to Roy Wilkins, 18 August 1950, box 445, NAACP Papers; *Crisis* (October 1949): 265.

32. *New York Herald Tribune,* 20 April 1952; *New York Herald Tribune,* 7 October 1951; action bulletin, 14 November 1950, reel 56, box 98, V128, CRC Papers; press release, 31 July 1952, CRC-Tamiment Papers; undated article by William Patterson, reel 15, box 24, B34, CRC Papers; *Daily Worker,* 6 August 1952; proposals of the CRC before the Platform Committee of the Democratic National Convention, 8 July 1948, reel 6, box 9, A188, CRC Papers; "An Open Letter to the Delegates to the Republican National Convention," 9 July 1952, reel 28, box 47, J157, CRC Papers.

33. *Daily Worker,* 25 June 1951; Arnold Johnson to chapter secretaries, ca. 1950, reel 58, box 102, W45, CRC Papers; defendants included Elizabeth Gurley Flynn, Pettis Perry, Claudia Jones, Alexander Bittelman, Alexander Trachtenberg, V. J. Jerome, Al Lannon, Sid Stein, Israel Amter, Fred Fine, Louis Weinstock, Arnold Johnson, Betty Gannett, Jacob Mindel, William Weinstone, George Charney, Si Gerson, Isadore Begun, and Marion Bachrach, *U.S.A. v. Elizabeth Gurley Flynn et al.,* reel 3, box 4, A57, CRC Papers; *Flynn et al. v. U.S.,* 216 F2d 354 (1954). James Jackson and Wm. Norman were sought.

34. Civil Rights News, April 1950, reel 56, box 98, V117, CRC Papers; press release, 8 March 1951, reel 4, box 4, A68, CRC Papers; Dashiell Hammett to W. E. B. Du Bois, 18 March 1952, reel 68, #144, Du Bois Papers; fact sheet, ca. 1951, reel 6, box 9, A160, CRC Papers; press release, ca. 1951, box 27, C22, CRC Papers; undated press release, box 27, C21, CRC Papers; Mary Kaufman memo, 2 March 1955, reel 7, box 11, A238, CRC Papers; flyer of National Committee to Defend Negro Leadership, 11 January 1953, reel 69, #1042, Du Bois Papers.

35. William Patterson to Myles Lane, 25 November 1952, reel 14, box 23, B15, CRC Papers; William Patterson to Hugh Bryson, Ben Gold, J. Pius Barbour, 5 December 1952; William Patterson to *Daily Worker,* 2 December 1952, press release, 25 November 1952, News in Brief-Berlin, 11 Febraury 1953, reel 14, box 23, B15, CRC Papers; circular, undated, Action Letter to chapters, 20 June 1951, "Publisher on Trial: A Symposium; The Case of Alexander Trachtenberg," reel 14, box 23, B16, CRC Papers.

36. *New York Herald Tribune,* 11 July 1951; Abner Green affidavit, 13 November 1949, Bail Fund case records, Robert Dunn Papers; *Detroit Times,* 14 August 1951; William Patterson to E. D. Alston, 17 July 1951, reel 4, box 4, A67, CRC Papers.

37. Affidavit in Support of Defendants, ca. 1951, reel 2, box 1, A10, CRC Papers; *Daily Worker,* 1 July 1951, 10 July 1951, 12 July 1951, 1 July 1952; *New York Times,* 15 February 1952, 6 May 1952, 15 March 1953; *New York Post,* 5 May 1952.

38. *New York Post,* 5 May 1952; Frederick V. Field, *From Right to Left: An Autobiography* (Westport, Conn.: Lawrence Hill, 1983), 224, passim; *Newsweek,* 15 May 1950; *Saturday Evening Post,* 9 September 1950; *Life,* 31 July 1950; Richard Layman, *Shadow Man: The Life of Dashiell Hammett* (New York: Harcourt Brace, 1981), 206, 213, 222; "The Case of Dashiell Hammett" (film), KQED-San Francisco, 1982; Richard Moody, *Lillian Hellman: Playwright* (New York: Knopf, 1972), 233; Katherine Lederer, *Lillian Hellman,* (Boston: Twayne, 1979); Lillian Hellman, *An Unfinished Woman: A Memoir* (Boston: Little Brown, 1979), 261.

39. Balance sheets, 31 December 1948, 1 June 1950, "Bail Fund-Financial Records," Robert Dunn Papers; Robert Dunn to "Dear Friend," 26 September 1949, box 9, folder 53, William Patterson Papers; liquidation records, "Bail Fund-Financial Records, Robert Dunn Papers; Bail Fund case records, 18 October 1950, Robert Dunn Papers; Lou Diskin to Robert Dunn, 4 April 1950, "Bail Fund-Case Records," Robert Dunn Papers; Abner Green to Sam Barbaria, 8 March 1950, "Bail Fund-Case Records," Robert Dunn Papers; Robert Dunn to Fred Field, 4 November 1949, "Bail Fund-Case Records," Robert Dunn Papers.

40. Robert Dunn to "Dear Friend," 26 September 1949, Bail Fund forms, Robert Dunn Papers; *NLG v. FBI,* H.Q. 100-358684, memo, 5 August 1952, NLG Papers; Aubrey Grossman to Tassia Freed, 30 July 1952, reel 34, box 58, M40, CRC Papers.

41. Abner Green to William Patterson, 21 August 1951, William Patterson to Abner Green,

24 August 1951, reel 34, box 57, M10, CRC Papers; William Patterson to Dashiell Hammett, 24 July 1951, reel 34, box 58, M55, CRC Papers; *Field et al. v. U.S.* 193 F2d 86, 342 U.S. 894 (1951).

42. *New York Herald Tribune,* 22 July 1951; William Patterson to editor, *New York Times,* 11 August 1951, reel 34, box 58, M36, CRC Papers; *Compass,* 25 November 1951; copy of full-page ad, 25 November 1951, reel 8, box 13, A261, CRC Papers; *New York Herald Tribune,* 10 August 1951; *New York World Telegram,* 9 August 1951; *New York Journal American,* 3 August 1951; *New York Herald Tribune,* 2 August 1951, 1 August 1951, 31 July 1951, 28 July 1951, 26 July 1951, 25 July 1951, 10 July 1951, 7 July 1951, 6 July 1951; *New York Daily News,* 24 July 1951, 15 July 1951, 7 July 1951; *New York World Telegram,* 24 July 1951, 14 July 1951; *New York Journal American,* 24 July 1951, 15 July 1951, 11 July 1951, 10 July 1951.

43. Mary Kaufman to Leo Linder, 7 April 1952, liquidation correspondence, Robert Dunn Papers; Grace Hutchins to Frederick Greenman, 12 November 1952, liquidation correspondence, Robert Dunn Papers.

44. Sam Barbaria to Abner Green, 13 August 1953; Grace Hutchins to Sam Barbaria, 25 August 1953; Sam Barbaria to Grace Hutchins, 27 August 1953; and Robert Dunn to Sam Barbaria, 28 October 1953, liquidation correspondence, Robert Dunn Papers.

45. Frederick Greenman to "Dear Sir or Madam," 16 July 1953, Bail Fund forms, Robert Dunn Papers; Fred Greenman to Grace Hutchins, 9 November 1954, liquidation correspondence, Robert Dunn Papers; Victor Rabinowitz to Robert Dunn, May 1956; Robert Dunn to Victor Rabinowitz, 31 May 1956, Robert Dunn Papers; Henry Caron to David Rein, 19 December 1952; Davin Rein to Leo Linder, 2 November 1953, liquidation correspondence, Robert Dunn Papers.

46. Leo Linder to Floyd Wilkins, 15 September 1953, liquidation correspondence, Robert Dunn Papers; Grace Hutchins memo, 13 December 1953, liquidation correspondence, Robert Dunn Papers; *New York Times,* 14 June 1956; *Daily Worker,* 7 April 1953, 8 April 1953, 13 March 1953; *New York Post,* 9 March 1953; Leo Linder to Grace Hutchins, 19 September 1960, liquidation correspondence, Robert Dunn Papers.

47. Ronald Radosh and Joyce Milton, *The Rosenberg File: A Search for Truth* (New York: Holt, Rinehart, 1983), 330; William Patterson to Emily Alman, 31 December 1952, reel 10, box 17, A339, CRC Papers.

48. Robert and Michael Meeropol, *We Are Your Sons: The Legacy of Ethel and Julius Rosenberg* (Boston: Houghton, Mifflin, 1975), 201; James Ford to "Comrade Patterson," 29 June 1955, reel 15, box 24, B34, CRC Papers; Robert Charles Cotthell, "Wielding the Pen as a Sword: The Radical Journalist, I. F. Stone" (Ph.D. diss., University of Oklahoma, 1983). Stone's weakness on the case was evidentiary of the problem faced by CRC (p. 226).

49. Roy Wilkins to Ben Bell, 14 August 1952, box 210, NAACP Papers; Ben Bell to Roy Wilkins, 20 August 1952, box 210, NAACP Papers; memos and mailings, ca. 1952, box 211, NAACP Papers; William Patterson to David Dubinsky, 3 December 1952, reel 10, box 17, A339, CRC Papers.

50. Aubrey Grossman to Anne Shore, 22 January 1953, reel 47, box 82, P95, CRC Papers; Aubrey Grossman to Maurice Travis, 9 December 1952, reel 10, box 17, A339, CRC Papers.

51. Circular, undated, reel 8, box 13, A257, CRC Papers; William Patterson to David Alman, 25 November 1952, reel 10, box 17, A339, David Alman to William Patterson, 26 August 1952, CRC Papers; pamphlet by Richard Boyer, ca. 1952, reel 24, box 41, J48, CRC Papers.

52. Meeropols, *Sons,* 55–56; Ethel and Julius Rosenberg, *The Testament of Ethel and Julius Rosenberg* (New York: Jero, 1954); Muriel Symington to William Patterson, 7 December 1952, reel 10, box 17, A339, CRC Papers; *New York Herald Tribune,* 22 December 1952. J. H. Healey to M. Brock, 4 December 1952, reel 54, box 95, V65, CRC Papers.

53. Boyer, *Murder,* 7; press release, 8 May 1952, box 27, C21, CRC Papers; Irene Paull to William Patterson, ca. April 1952, reel 48, box 83, P110, CRC Papers.

54. William Patterson, "The Rosenberg Case and the Negro People," ca. 1952, reel 10, box 17, A339, CRC Papers; Jo Granat to Paul Robeson, 15 December 1952, reel 10, box 17, A339, CRC papers; press release, 26 May 1952, box 27, C21, CRC Papers; memo from Herbert Levy, 2

May 1952, reel 10, box 17, A339, CRC Papers; akin to how working on the Rosenberg case motivated Irene Paull, it along with the rest of its explosive docket had an impact on CRC as well. It was at this time, in August 1952, when CRC's Resident Board "resolved to instruct the officers to work as speedily to bring a woman into one of the national offices." Months earlier Patterson had commented at length on a closely related question: ". . . this movement of Negro women must not be a divisive movement in any way. It is of course subordinated to the major struggle in America. . . . It cannot be in opposition to that movement [of workers] . . . It is subordinate to the Negro liberation struggle and by virtue of the fact that within that struggle the oppression of the Negro woman is the greatest" and will sweep up broad forces "even some who are right of center. . . . Secondly it must not be a separatist movement . . ." Ethel Rosenberg, along with Rosa Lee Ingram, Claudia Jones, Betty Gannett, Elizabeth Gurley Flynn, et al. were among the many female political prisoners defended by CRC, and through this defense their consciousness on the question of male supremacy and women's equality became more acute; John McManus to William Patterson, 18 December 1952, reel 10, box 17, A339, CRC Papers.

55. *Le Monde,* 20 June 1953; MCLRLPP to CRC, 6 November 1952; DRC to CRC, 15 October 1952; I. Mitchell to William Patterson, 19 October 1952; D. N. Pritt to William Patterson, 8 June 1953; and Cath. Vazlin to William Patterson, 14 October 1952, reel 10, box 17, A340, CRC Papers.

56. William Patterson to Ida Rothstein, 22 June 1953, Ida Rothstein to William Patterson, 19 June 1953, reel 45, box 79, P28, CRC Papers; David Alman to William Patterson, 10 March 1952, John Daschbach to Aubrey Grossman, 30 December 1952, Aubrey Grossman to Abe Weisburd, 30 December 1952, reel 10, box 17, A339, CRC Papers; press release, 7 November 1953, reel 10, box 17, A339, CRC Papers; press release, 16 May 1952, reel 10, box 17, A339, CRC Papers.

57. Ida Rothstein to William Patterson, 2 January 1953, reel 45, box 79, P28, CRC Papers; Frances Schermerhorn to William Patterson, reel 45, box 79, P29, CRC Papers; Frances Schermerhorn to William Patterson, 20 April 1954, reel 45, box 79, P29, CRC Papers; Walter Stack to William Patterson, 24 March 1954, reel 45, box 79, P29, CRC Papers; Anne Shore to William Patterson, 8 June 1953, reel 47, box 82, P95, CRC Papers; memo from J. Z. Zucker, 19 November 1952, reel 10, box 17, A339, CRC papers; flyer, ca. 1952, reel 43, box 74, N322, CRC Papers; William Patterson, "Some Lessons of the Rosenbergs Struggle," ca. 1953, reel 10, box 17, A339, CRC Papers. *Rosenberg et al. v. U.S.,* 345 US 989, 346 US 271 (1953).

58. Interview with Lewis Moroze, 16 August 1983 (in possession of author); Rev. Harry Pine of Trenton and Joseph Squires of UE were the chapter's first chairs. *Daily Worker,* 12 December 1948.

59. CRC was able to pressure the prosecutor in the case of the Hartford 4 on breach of the peace to enter a nolle plea (Report, 9 March 1951, File No. 100-11179, FBI). Part of the weakness of CRC was magnified when NAACP leader Herbert Hill came to a Black church in Hartford and blasted the Congress (*Hartford Courant,* 18 August 1951). Mrs. Sidney Stein to William Patterson, 23 September 1955, reel 32, box 53, K43, CRC Papers; Bert McLeech to Regina Frankfeld, 21 January 1955, reel 3, box 4, A61, CRC Papers; *Commonwealth v. Hood,* 334 Mass. 76 (1955); brief for defendant, ca. 1955, reel 5, box 7, A134, CRC Papers.

60. Henry Cooperstock to Len Goldsmith, 17 November 1948; Len Goldsmith to Henry Cooperstock, 18 November 1948, 4 January 1949; Henry Cooperstock to Len Goldsmith, 7 February 1949; Henry Cooperstock to William Patterson, 1 July 1949, reel 47, box 81, P84, CRC Papers; Henry Cooperstock to CRC, 4 December 1948, reel 47, box 81, P85, CRC Papers.

61. "Bill of Rights Sentinel," 7 June 1954, reel 47, box 81, P85, CRC Papers.

62. Bertha Reynolds to Len Goldsmith, 3 January 1949; Bertha Reynolds to Milt Wolff, 25 April 1949, reel 47, box 81, P86, CRC Papers.

63. Edmund Izzo to William Patterson, 24 October 1951, reel 35, box 59, M56, CRC Papers; Edna Brown, undated, reel 47, box 81, P83, CRC Papers; *Boston Globe,* 28 October 1948; *Boston Herald,* 28 October 1948; Steve Savides to William Patterson, 2 October 1948; William Patterson to Henry Cooperstock, 14 October 1948; and flyer, 18 November 1948, reel 47, box 81, P84, CRC Papers; report, 4 April, 21 October 1949; 4 May 1950, file no. 100-17847, FBI.

64. Income statement, 1951, reel 49, box 85, P166, CRC Papers; income statement, 1952, reel 49, box 85, P163, CRC Papers; J. S. Zucker to William Patterson, 20 July 1950, report from CRC-Philadelphia, 17 July 1950, reel 49, box 85, P157, CRC Papers.

65. Washington Thorton to William Patterson, 25 August 1952, reel 49, box 86, P183, CRC Papers; John Holton to J. Henry Patten, 11 September 1952, reel 49, box 85, P160, CRC Papers; Rev. S. A. Amos to J.S. Zucker, 23 November 1952, reel 49, box 86, P182, CRC Papers.

66. Undated *Pittsburgh Courier* article, undated *Philadelphia Tribune* article, reel 49, box 85, P157, CRC Papers; Saul Waldbaum and Harry Levitan of CRC freed Harold Allen, nineteen-year-old Black, charged with "inciting a riot" after "successful picketing" of South Philadelphia Woolworth's on jobs; it involved CRC, CP, YPA, and "all the local Negro weeklies"; *Philadelphia Afro-American*, 11 February 1950; *Philadelphia Inquirer*, 30 July 1945; *Philadelphia Inquirer*, 27 February 1955; J. S. Zucker to Walter Annenberg, 2 March 1955, reel 49, box 85, P157, CRC Papers; the chapter was highly active in the McGee defense, and when Rosalee McGee visited the city the trip was used to recruit scores of new members. John Holton to Aubrey Grossman, 9 September 1952, reel 49, box 85, P160, CRC Papers.

67. Fred Richard Zimring, "Academic Freedom and the Cold War: The Dismissal of Barrows Dunham from Temple University, A Case Study" (Ph.D. diss., Columbia Teachers College, 1981), 415; *Philadelphia Inquirer*, 14 August 1953; "Emergency Conference to Defeat the Philadelphia Smith Act-Frame-Up," 5 August 1953, reel 29, box 48, J165, CRC Papers; Ralph Powe to Jack Zucker, 10 January 1951, reel 10, box 16, A323, CRC Papers; flyer, Fall 1952, reel 13, box 22, A424, CRC Papers. Eric Winston was a metallurgist arrested for not stating alleged CP membership in a security questionnaire for his employer, SKF Industries; the chapter took on the case; report, 17 February 1950, file no. 10-31535, FBI.

68. Ralph Powe to Irving Backman, 4 December 1951, reel 4, box 4, A67, CRC Papers; *Pittsburgh Courier*, 7 May 1949. Byard Jenkins, nineteen years old, was convicted of murdering Kathryn Meller, a local white author. He was sentenced to death in the electric chair. Later a white gravedigger confessed to the crime, but after talking to the police he said he was "drunk" and recanted though his brother-in-law continued to maintain that he was guilty. Ten members of Jenkins' jury asked that the original verdict be reversed. Jenkins had worked with a white iceman and delivered ice to the victim. A panel of three judges reversed and ordered a new trial; at this trial on 14 January 1950 he was convicted but this time received life; flyer, ca. 1949, reel 3, box 4, A62, CRC Papers; "Fact on the Fletcher Mills Case," ca. 1950, reel 7, box 11, A239, CRC Papers; *Afro-American*, 20 May 1950; *Philadelphia Tribune*, 13 May 1950; *Pittsburgh Courier*, 20 May 1950; *Detroit News*, 28 December 1945; *Michigan Chronicle*, 8 December 1945, 22 December 1945; *Detroit Free press*, 15 December 1945; "Prospectus on Campaign to Reach 100,000 People to Save the Life of Fletcher Mills," 19 May 1952, reel 7, box 11, A240, CRC Papers; J. S. Zucker to Ralph Powe, 30 October 1950, reel 7, box 12, A242, CRC Papers; William Patterson to Gerber and Galfind, 24 June 1949, reel 7, box 12, A242, CRC Papers.

69. Flyer, ca. 1952, reel 7, box 11, A239, CRC Papers; Aubrey William to David Levinson, 19 April 1951, reel 7, box 12, A240, CRC Papers.

70. Non-Sectarian Anti-Nazi League to Champion Human Rights, Inc. to Ralph Powe, 23 March 1950, reel 7, box 12, A242, CRC Papers; John Holton to William Patterson, 4 May 1953, reel 49, box 85, P161, CRC Papers; *U.S. ex. rel. Mills. v. Reing*, 191 F2d 297 (1951).

71. Albert Gerber to William Patterson, 10 September 1949, reel 7, box 12, A240, CRC Papers; J. s. Zucker to Ralph Powe, 30 October 1950, reel 7, box 12, A242, CRC Papers; Albert Gerber to William Patterson, 4 November 1949, reel 7, box 12, A242, CRC Papers; Ralph Powe to John Holton, undated, reel 9, box 16, A320, CRC Papers.

72. John Holton to William Patterson, 14 May 1953, reel 49, box 85, P161, CRC Papers; William Patterson to John Holton, 4 September 1953, reel 49, box 85, P161, CRC Papers; William Patterson to John Zucker, 11 January 1954, reel 49, box 85, P162, CRC Papers; William Patterson to John Holton, 21 November 1952, reel 49, box 85, P174, CRC Papers.

73. William Patterson to Baltimore Committee to Defeat the Smith Act, 1 October 1952, reel 14, box 23, B9, CRC Papers; William Patterson to Bea Kantor, 1 February 1950, reel 47, box 81,

P80, CRC Papers. With pride the FBI reported prematurely in 1951 about the Baltimore chapter: "It has recently been partially inactive due to public recognition as a CP front organization" (Report, 16 June 1951, file no. 100-12312, FBI).

74. *Baltimore Sun*, 10 September 1948; *Boyer et al. v. Garrett et al.*, 88 F Supp 353 (1949), 183 F2d 582 (1950), 340 US 912 (1950).

75. Foner, *Robeson*, p. 547, n. 9; *Lancaster v. Hammond*, 194 MD. 462 (1949); *Lancaster v. Hall Hammond*, ca. 1949, reel 9, box 15, A294, CRC Papers; Buchman's brief for the Marine Cooks compared the Ober Law to a similar piece of Nazi legislation, section by section; Louis Shub to William Patterson, 1 November 1949, reel 9, box 15, A294, CRC Papers; Ralph Powe to Maurice Braverman, 15 November 1949, reel 9, box 15, A294, CRC Papers; *Shub v. Simpson*, 196 Md. 177 (1950).

76. *Gerende v. Board of Supervisors of Elections of Baltimore*, 341 US 56 (1950); *Reid v. Md.*, 87 A227, 344 US 848 (1952); *Hammond v. Frankfeld*, 194 Md. 487 (1949); Nadya Schwartz to Aubrey Grossman, 18 November 1952, reel 47, box 81, P82, CRC Papers; *U.S. v. Frankfeld et al.*, ca. 1950, reel 47, box 81, P82, CRC Papers; William Patterson to Nadya Schwartz, 27 February 1953, reel 47, box 81, P80, CRC Papers.

77. Thomas Buchanan to CRC, 28 December 1948, undated press release, Tom Buchanan to William Patterson et al., 24 January 1949, Tom Buchanan to William Patterson, 20 September 1948, Tom Buchanan to William Patterson, 31 January 1949, reel 46, box 80, CRC Papers; *Washington Post*, 6 August 1948; *Washington Star*, 6 August 1948; *Washington Times-Herald*, 6 August 1948.

78. Press release, 18 November 1948; Tom Buchanan to William Patterson, 31 January 1949; Tom Buchanan to William Patterson, 11 October 1948; Tom Buchanan to Robert Barrett, 5 October 1948; Tom Buchanan to William Patterson, 30 November 1948; and Tom Buchanan to William Patterson, 20 September 1948, reel 46, box 80, P48, CRC Papers; *Daily Worker*, 7 October 1948.

79. Thomas Buchanan to Ralph Powe, 13 April 1949, reel 6, box 9, A188, CRC Papers.

80. Tom Buchanan to Milton Wolff, 14 September 1949, reel 46, box 80, P49, CRC Papers; Tom Buchanan to William Patterson, 20 June 1949, reel 46, box 80, P49, CRC Papers; Tom Buchanan to William Patterson, 27 April 1949, reel 46, box 80, P49, CRC Papers; *Washington Times-Herald*, 19 May 1949, Tom Buchanan to "Dear Friends," 22 February 1950, reel 46, box 80, P49, CRC Papers; Tom Buchanan to William Patterson, 7 March 1949, reel 46, box 80, P49, CRC Papers.

81. "Washington Legislative Bulletin," 2 February 1949, reel 43, box 74, N323, CRC Papers; William Patterson to Tom Buchanan, 27 December 1949; and Tom Buchanan to William Patterson, 24 February 1950, reel 46, box 50, P51, CRC Papers; *Washington Star*, 21 December 1949, transcripts of radio broadcasts, undated, reel 46, box 50, P51, CRC Papers; Tom Buchanan to William Patterson, 22 February 1949, reel 46, box 80, P49, CRC Papers.

82. William Patterson to Tom Buchanan, 21 June 1949, reel 46, box 80, P50, CRC Papers; William Patterson to Muriel Paul, 18 May 1950, reel 46, box P50, CRC Papers; "The Case of Marie Richardson Harris: The Victim of a Modern Witch Hunt," ca. 1951, reel 10, box 17, A334, CRC Papers.

83. Lynwood Cundiff to William Patterson, 27 June 1952, reel 10, box 17, A334, CRC Papers.

Chapter 9. Working-Class Heroes and Heroines

1. Statement by Miriam Schultze, ca. 1953, reel 6, box 10, A194, CRC Papers; circular, ca. 1948–49, Hilda Marcusson to "Dear Friends," September 1949, reel 49, box 85, 179, CRC Papers; *Commonwealth ex. rel. Roth v. Musmanno*, 364 pa. 359 (1950). The Roth case raised the critical question of whether a Communist could be barred from a grand jury. She was summoned to the judge's chambers where stool-pigeon Matt Cvetic accused her of being a Communist; she

was disqualified; *Albert Appeal,* 372 Pa. 2d. 13 (1952); Ken Lawless, "Continental Imprison-ment": Rockwell Kent and the Passport Controversy," *Antioch Review,* 38 (Summer 1980): 304–12.

2. Mirian Schultz to Joe Cadden, 29 December 1947, reel 49, box 85, P172, CRC Papers; *Pittsburgh Press,* 6 April 1949; *Pittsburgh Press,* 9 February 1948; John Holton to William Patterson, 18 December 1952, reel 49, box 85, P160, CRC Papers; Evelyn Abelson to William Patterson, 15 September 1952, reel 49, box 85, P160, CRC Papers.

3. Report by FBI, 13 August 1950, 100-8849; *Daily Worker,* 25 January 1950; *NLG v. FBI,* informer files, 19 September 1949, 5 January 1953, 100-9091, NLG Papers; *NLG v. FBI,* informer files, 24 July 1953, PG-115 S, 5 January 1950, PG 115, file 66-2542, NLG Papers.

4. Draft of Nelson pamphlet, ca. 1955, reel 9, box 14, A282, CRC Papers; pamphlet undated, reel 9, box 14, A284, CRC Papers; *Nation,* 6 February 1954.

5. Abe Isserman to Leon Josephson, 10 January 1950, reel 9, box 14, A281, CRC Papers, Basil Pollitt to Ralph Powe, 17 January 1951, reel 9, box 14, A281, CRC Papers; Basil Pollitt, 10 January 1951, reel 9, box 14, A281, CRC Papers; Basil Pollitt to William Patterson, 12 April 1951, reel 35, box 60, M88, CRC Papers.

6. J. S. Zucker to William Patterson, 17 March 1953; J. S. Zucker to William Patterson 25 March 1953; and William Patterson to Walter Lowenfels, 28 August 1953, reel 49, box 85, P161, CRC Papers; *Catholic Worker,* September 1952; CRC pamphlets, reel 49, box 85, P177, CRC Papers; undated article, reel 42, box 71, N203, CRC Papers; memorandum and order, ca. 1953, reel 4, box 5, A79, CRC Papers; *Daily worker,* 22 June 1955, *U.S. v. Mensorosh et al.,* 116 FSupp 345, 223 F2d 449 (1955). Powe, Frank Donner, and Thomas McBride were the attorneys at this level.

7. *Pa. v. Nelson,* 350 US 497 (1950); Steve Nelson, James Barrett, Rob Buck, *Steve Nelson: American Radical* (Pittsburgh: University of Pittsburgh Press, 1981); Steve Nelson, *The 13th Juror; The Inside Story of My Trial* (New York: International 1955); Mirian Schultz to William Patterson, 27 April 1953, reel 49, box 85, P175, CRC Papers; William Patterson to Jo Norstrand, 18 May 1953, reel 49, box 86, P216, CRC Papers; William Patterson to Mirian Schultz, 10 June 1953, reel 49, box 85, P175, CRC Papers; Mirian Schultz to William Patterson, 21 July 1953; and William Patterson to Mirian Schultz, 7 August 1953, reel 49, box 85, P175, CRC Papers.

8. Steven Nelson to Aubrey Grossman, 27 February 1952, reel 9, box 14, A284, CRC Papers; William Patterson to Arnold Johnson, undated, reel 9, box 14, A284, CRC Papers; William Patterson to Pa.-CRC, 6 October 1952, reel 49, box 85, P185, CRC Papers; *Pittsburgh Post-Gazette,* 29 April 1955; James Dolsen, *Bucking the Ruling Class: Jim Dolsen's Story* (New York: International 1984).

9. FBI file no. 100-7660, 24 March 1949, by S. A. Charles Le Clair; Milt Kemnitz to Frieda Katz, 23 December 1946; Milt Kaufman to Frieda Katz, 17 January 1947, and statement by Executive Board of Cleveland Industrial Union Council, reel 48, box 84, P153, CRC Papers; *Cleveland Plain Dealer,* 13 June 1946.

10. Violet Tarcai to Milton Kemnitz, 6 March 1947; and Joseph Cadden to Sam Handelman, 30 September 1947, reel 48, box 84, P153, CRC Papers; flyer, ca. 1948, reel 48, box 84, P155, CRC Papers; Ann Brumbaugh to CRC, 17 January 1947, reel 48, box 84, P153, CRC Papers; statement of William Patterson, 20 October 1949, reel 23, box 40, J32, CRC Papers.

11. *Cleveland News,* 19 November 1950; *Cleveland Plain Dealer,* 8 March 1948, 6 February 1948, 8 November 1948; *Cleveland News,* 6 November 1948, *Cleveland Plain Dealer,* 15 December 1948, 12 September 1951, *Cleveland Press,* 14 November 1951.

12. Elsie Zazrivy to CRC, 27 October 1950, reel 48, box 84, P148, CRC Papers; Frieda Katz to William Patterson, 22 December 1952, reel 48, box 84, P149, CRC Papers; Aubrey Grossman to Frieda Katz, 21 August 1952, reel 48, box 84, P149, CRC Papers.

13. Ohio Bill of Rights Conference Bulletin, 1 August 1952, reel 48, box 84, P149, CRC Papers, *Cleveland Call and Post,* 26 July 1952; Frieda Katz to Aubrey Grossman, 7 February 1952, reel 48, box 84, P149, CRC Papers.

14. *NLG v. FBI,* informers' files, 18 April 1952, serial 140 of 66 35, Sub. 264 SA, 23 January

1952, 66 35, Sub 264, Sub A NLG Papers; Frieda Katz to William Patterson, 7 May 1953; and Frieda Katz to William Patterson, 4 June 1953, reel 48, box 84, P149, CRC Papers.

15. Circular, 6 October 1953, reel 42, box 71, N263, CRC Papers; *Hamshall v. Ohio,* 117 NE 24 606 (1954), 348 US 842, cert. denied. (1954).

16. Frieda Katz to William Patterson, 21 July 1953, reel 48, box 84, P149, CRC Papers; open letter 26 March 1954, reel 48, box 84, P151, CRC Papers; flyer, ca. 1954, reel 48, P155, CRC Papers; the chapter also fought a case involving $25,000 bail for leading Communist Hyman Lumer for a minor traffic violation. The ACLU also became involved. Circular, ca. 1955, reel 9, box 15, A295, CRC Papers.

17. Katherine Hyndman to CRC 21 May 1949; and Katherine Hyndman to William Patterson, 19 November 1949, reel 47, box 81, P74, CRC Papers.

18. Katherine Hyndman to Milt Wolff, 14 November 1949, reel 47, box 81, P74, CRC Papers.

19. Katherine Hyndman to William Patterson, 19 May 1950, reel 47, box 81, P74, CRC Papers.

20. Ibid.

21. Katherine Hyndman to Milt Wolff, 14 November 1949; and Katherine Hyndman to William Patterson, 19 May 1950, 21 June 1950, reel 47, box 81, P74, CRC Papers.

22. William Patterson to Katherine Hyndman, 22 May 1950, reel 47, box 81, P74, CRC Papers.

23. *Gary Post-Tribune,* 7 August 1950; *Gary Post-Tribune,* 5 November 1949; Katherine Hyndman to William Patterson, 9 August 1950, reel 47, box 81, P74, CRC Papers; *Gary Post-Tribune,* 5 November 1949.

24. Katherine Hyndman to Aubrey Grossman, 14 November 1951; and Katherine Hyndman to Aubrey Grossman, reel 47, box 81, P74, CRC Papers. Herein Hyndman also reported that they were unable to have a meeting for Mrs. McGee though "it hurts to have to write this." She promised though that "what forces we are able to muster: would work in the Progressive Party campaign"; Katherine Hyndman to Aubrey Grossman, 11 August 1952, reel 47, box 81, P74, CRC Papers.

25. Katherine Hyndman to Milt Wolf, 25 January 1950, reel 47, box 81, P74, CRC Papers; "Public Relations Report" by Will Hayett, June 1950, reel 38, box 65, N92, CRC Papers. Hayett also said that "today practically everything we send to the Negro press—on all our campaigns—is used," thus indicating their broad impact especially among Blacks; Josephine Bush to Aubrey Grossman, 1 June 1951, reel 47, box 81, P75, CRC Papers; *Indianapolis News,* 2 February 1949; Edna Cochran to William Patterson, 7 April 1949, reel 47, box 81, P75, CRC Papers; Shirley Dubin to Aubrey Grossman, 1 October 1952, reel 47, box 81, P74, CRC Papers; *New York Mirror,* 3 September 1949.

26. Alfred Wagenknecht from William Patterson, 8 September 1948; Alfred Wagenknecht to William Patterson, 14 September 1948; Alfred Wagenknecht to William Patterson, 14 September 1948; and Martin Kennelly to Rev. Clarence Parker, 4 December 1948, reel 46, box 80, P58, CRC Papers.

27. William Patterson to Clarence Parker, 24 June 1949; William Patterson to Ed Starr, 7 June 1949; William Patterson to Arthur Price, 11 July 1949; Milton Wolff to Arthur Price, 2 August 1949; and William Patterson to Arthur Price, 13 August 1949, reel 46, box 80, P58, CRC Papers.

28. Alfred Wagenknecht to William Patterson, 20 December 1948, reel 46, box 80, P58, CRC Papers; Conrad Komorowski to William Patterson, 21 July 1949, reel 46, box 80, P58, CRC Papers, report from Arthur Price, 11 August 1949, reel 46, box 80, P60, CRC Papers; Conrad Komorowski to Milt Wolf, 24 October 1949; Conrad Komorowski to Milt Wolf, 10 October 1949; Milt Wolf to Conrad Komorowski, 18 November 1949; and Conrad Komorowski to Milt Wolf, 21 November 1949, reel 46, box 80, P60, CRC Papers. Indicative of Robeson's importance to CRC was the fact that when he spoke at one gathering, 110 new members joined.

29. Milt Wolf to Conrad Komorowski, 16 December 1949, reel 46, box 80, P60, CRC Papers; *Daily Worker,* 27 July 1949; circular, March 1949, reel 38, box 64, N75, CRC Papers.

30. Les Davis to Aubrey Grossman, 5 January 1950, reel 46, box 80, P60, CRC Papers; press release, 7 February 1950, reel 8, box 13, A257, CRC Papers; Dorothy Cole to Milt Wolf, 21 April 1950; Les Davis to William Patterson, 11 April 1950, reel 46, box 80, P60, CRC Papers.

31. William Patterson to Father Clarence Parker, 8 April 1950, reel 46, box 80, P61, CRC Papers; Les Davis to William Patterson, 11 May 1950, reel 46, box 80, P62, CRC Papers; Les Davis to William Patterson, 19 July 1950, reel 46, box 80, P62, CRC Papers.

32. Father Clarence Parker, to William Patterson, 18 May 1950; and Les Davis to William Patterson, reel 46, box 80, P62, CRC Papers.

33. William Patterson to Father Clarence Parker, 9 February 1950; William Patterson to Father Clarence Parker, 5 April 1950; Conrad Komorowski to William Patterson, 4 April 1950, reel 46, box 80, P61, CRC Papers. Ruling-class concern with progressive clerics like Father Parker is reflected in two recent biographies: Eugene Link, *Labor Religion Prophet: The Life and Times of Harry Ward* (Boulder, Colo.: Westview, 1984); Robert Moats Miller, *Harry Emerson Fosdick: Preacher, Pastor, Prophet* (New York: Oxford, 1985).

34. Conrad Komorowski to Milt Wolf, 23 January 1950, reel 46, box 80, P61, CRC Papers.

35. Arthur Price to William Patterson, reel 46, box 80, P61, CRC Papers; William Patterson to Arthur Price, 2 March 1950, reel 46, box 80, P61, CRC Papers. Les Davis to Aubrey Grossman, 16 October 1950; and Clarence Parker to Aubrey Grossman, 3 November 1950, reel 46, box 80, P62, CRC Papers; Les Davis to Aubrey Grossman, 3 November 1950, reel 46, box 80, P63, CRC Papers.

36. Theresa Hendrickson to Aubrey Grossman, 20 September 1950, reel 47, box 81, P73, CRC Papers; *Waukegan News Sun,* 5 June 1948; Les Davis to William Patterson, 23 May 1951, reel 46, box 80, P63, CRC Papers; William Patterson to CRC Chicago, 30 July 1951; and Les Davis to Aubrey Grossman, 12 June 1951, reel 46, box 80, P61, CRC Papers; William Patterson to Les Davis, 5 June 1951, reel 46, box 80, P63, CRC Papers.

37. William Patterson to Les Davis, 15 November 1951, reel 46, box 80, P63, CRC Papers; William Patterson to Les Davis, 29 November 1951, reel 46, box 80, P63, CRC Papers.

38. Undated CRC-Chicago newsletter, reel 47, box 81, P68, CRC Papers; undated CRC-Chicago release, reel 47, box 81, P69, CRC Papers; flyer, ca. 1950, reel 47, box 81, P68, CRC Papers; *Daily Worker,* 30 July 1952; "The Bulwark," (CRC-Chicago newsletter), 8 May 1952, reel 47, box 81, P65, CRC Papers; *Daily Worker,* 17 July 1952; "Civil Rights Guardian," (CRC-Illinois newsletter), ca. 1952, reel 47, box 81, P69, CRC Papers; William Patterson to Arthur McPhaul, 23 April 1952, reel 47, box 82, P94, CRC Papers; William Patterson to Les Davis, 29 April 1952; William Patterson to Les Davis, 26 May 1952; and William Patterson to Les Davis, 2 December 1952, reel 46, box 80, P64, CRC Papers.

39. Emily Freedman to William Patterson, 3 November 1952; and Les Davis to William Patterson, 18 December 1952, reel 46, box 80, P64, CRC Papers.

40. Press release, 18 February 1952, reel 46, box 80, P68, CRC Papers; Les Davis to Aubrey Grossman, 13 September 1952, reel 46, box 80, P64, CRC Papers; Otto Wangerin to William Patterson, 28 March, 1954, reel 47, box 81, P66, CRC Papers; William Patterson to Anne Shore, 3 July 1953, reel 47, box 81, P65, CRC Papers; "I have just come from a very splendid demonstration before the Cuban representative to the United Nations. Something of a similar character would be prepared before the Cuban consulate, if there is one, in Chicago"; *U.S. v. Konovsky,* 202 F2d 721 (1953).

41. U.S. Congress, House Un-American Activities Committee, hearings on Legislation to Outlaw Certain Un-American and Subversive Activities, 81st Congress, 2d session, 1950; Milt Wolf to Clarence Parker, 21 March 1950; and Clarence Parker to Milt Wolf, 31 March 1950, reel 46, box 80, P61, CRC Papers; William Patterson to Arthur Price, 25 October 1948, reel 46, box 80, P58, CRC Papers; flyer, ca. 1955, reel 12, box 21, A411, CRC Papers; "Fact Sheet in the Case of Claude Lightfoot," ca. 1955, reel 6, box 9, A183, CRC Papers; press release, 3 October 1954, reel 6, box 9, A186, CRC Papers; *Chicago Sun-Times,* 27 November 1954; press release, 19 September 1955, reel 6, box 9, A186, CRC Papers; *Chicago Daily News,* 18 December 1954.

42. CRC to Abertine Warren, 24 June 1946, reel 49, box 86, P214, CRC Papers; *Milwaukee Journal,* 30 May 1946, 9 May 1947; Karl Sewitz to editor, *Milwaukee Journal,* 11 May 1947, reel 49, box 86, P217k, CRC Papers; "The Issues," ca. 1950, reel 49, box 86, P218, CRC papers; James Selcraig, *The Red Scare in the Midwest, 1945–1955: A State and Local Study* (Ann Arbor, Mich.: UMI Press 1982), 89; undated *Milwaukee Journal* and a Barron County newspaper, ca. 1949, reel 49, box 86, P213, CRC Papers; "Civil Rights Champion," 2 January 1951, March 1952, reel 49, box 86, P219, CRC Papers.

43. William Patterson to Josephine Norstrand, 12 August 1953, reel 49, box 86, P215, CRC Papers; Josephine Norstrand to William Patterson, 15 August 1953, reel 49, box 86, P215, CRC Papers.

44. William Patterson to Jo Norstrand, 28 March 1952; Jo Norstrand to William Patterson, 1 May 1953; William Patterson to Jo Norstrand, 4 May 1953; and Jo Norstrand to William Patterson, 11 June 1953, "Membership Drive Report Form," 2 October 1952, reel 49, box 86, P215, CRC Papers.

45. John Gilman to William Patterson, 26 May 1954; and William Patterson to John Gilman, 4 February 1954, reel 49, box 86, P216, CRC Papers.

46. "Summary Report of Activity in Milwaukee," ca. 1954, reel 49, box 86, P218, CRC Papers; Herman Olson to editor, *Rice Lake Chronotype,* 7 March 1951, reel 49, box 86, P218, CRC Papers.

47. Ted Livingston to Perry Love, ca. 1954, reel 49, box 86, P216, CRC Papers; John Gilman to William Patterson, 28 January 1954, reel 49, box 86, P216, CRC Papers; *Milwaukee Journal,* 4 February 1954, 7 January 1954; CRC bulletin, March 1954, reel 49, box 86, P216, CRC Papers.

48. Aubrey Grossman to William Patterson, 3 July 1949, reel 37, box 63, N42, CRC papers; Aubrey Grossman to Shirley Dubin, 7 June 1951, reel 47, box 81, P75, CRC Papers; William Green to Milt Kaufman, 26 June 1947, box 48, folder, Christoffel and Rogge 1948, CRC-Mich. Papers.

49. Poster-sized cartoon panels on labor's take in Smith Act, undated, reel 25, box 43, J84, CRC Papers; "Civil Rights Bulletin," ca. 1951, reel 23, box 39, J15, CRC Papers; Labor Advisory Committee to CRC, 21 June 1951, reel 6, box 9, A173, CRC Papers; U.S. Congress, House, Committee on Un-American Activities, 82d Congress, 2d Session, 13–16 October 1952, Communist Activities in the Philadelphia Area, circular, 19 September 1952, reel 38, box 64, N74, CRC papers; *U.S. ex.rel. Doyle v. Shaughnessy,* 112 FSupp 143 (1953); *U.S. ex.rel. Doyle v. INS,* 169 F2d 753 (198).

50. Michael Francis Urmann, "Rank and File Communists and the CIO" (Ph.D. diss., University of Utah, 1981); Philip Foner and Ronald Lewis, eds., *The Black Worker from the Founding of the CIO to the ALF-CIO Merger, 1936–1955* (Philadelphia: Temple University Press, 1983), 538, 579, 555; after the formation of the NNLC a number of CIO and AF of L unions, sufficiently challenged, moved to form a similar committee, thus indicating how the left prodded the center toward progress. *New York Times,* 2 March 1952; flyer, 2 March 1951; Leon Strauss to CRC, 18 September 1952; William Patterson to Maurice Travis, 5 September 1951; Albert Pezzati to CRC, 13 March 1951; C. D. Smotherman to CRC, 15 August 1951; Aubrey Grossman to Maurice Travis, 8 October 1952; William Patterson to Rod Holmgren, 21 November 1951; Aubrey Grossman to Maurice Travis, 18 August 1952; and Maurice Travis to William Patterson, 29 September 1952, reel 35, box 59, M57, CRC Papers.

51. Undated pamphlet, reel 6, box 10, A196, CRC Papers; *Emspak v. U.S.,* 349 US 190 (1954); briefs and affadavits on UE case, undated, reel 6, box 9, A190, CRC Papers; file on 12–15 June 1949 meeting, reel 2, box 1, A11, CRC Papers.

52. Appeal of Watson, 105 A2d 576, cert. denied 348 Us 879 (1954); *Adler v. Board of Education,* 342 US 485, 301 NY 476, 95 NE2d 806 (1952); *Thompson et al. v. Wallin et al.,* 301 NY 476, 342 US 801 (1951); Bertram Washington to Joseph Cadden, 6 October 1947, reel 35, box 59, M72, CRC Papers; William Lawrence to Edward Pogorsky, 31 December 1948; Abraham Janko to Edward Pogorsky, 5 October 1947; V. C. Burke to Edward Pogorsky, 15 December

1948; and Herbert Fabrican to Edward Pogorsky, 1 December 1948, reel 9, box 15, A310, CRC Papers; Clarence Emery to CRC, 27 October 1948, reel 10, box 16, A323, CRC Papers; William Patterson to Clarence Emery, 28 October 1948; undated memo to NLG, ACLU, et al., reel 10, box 16, A323, CRC Papers; Ben Goldring to Alexander Bourgerie, 11 March 1947, reel 5, box 7, A118, CRC Papers.

53. Memo on the Christoffel case, undated, reel 3, box 3, A39, CRC Papers; *Milwaukee Sentinel,* 30 March 1948; World Federation of Trade Unions press release, 26 April 1950; and Federated Press articles, 21 February 1950, 15 February 1950, reel 3, box 3, A42, CRC Papers.

54. William Patterson to John Rogge, 28 July 1950, reel 3, box 3, A39, CRC Papers.

55. *New York Times,* 12 May 1951; John Rogge to Harold Christoffel, 10 July 1951, 13 August 1951, 18 September 1951, 4 October 1951, 11 October 1951, 18 October 1951; and John Rogge to William Patterson, 2 August 1950, reel 3, box 3, A42, CRC Papers; John Rogge to Harold Christoffel, 22 October 1951, reel 3, box 3, A42, CRC Papers; William Patterson to Harold Christoffel, 30 October 1951, reel 3, box 3, A40, CRC Papers.

56. Emil Mazey to John Rogge, 26 March 1948; Emil Mazey to Robert Buse, 6 April 1948; and Robert Buse to Walter Reuther, 8 March 1948, reel 3, box 3, A42, CRC Papers; undated fact sheet on case, reel 3, box 3, A41, CRC Papers.

57. Harold Christoffel to William Patterson, 2 February 1953, reel 39, box 3, A40, CRC Papers.

58. William Patterson to Lottie Gordon, April 1950, reel 3, box 3, A40, CRC Papers.

59. *U.S. v. Bryan,* 339 US 323 (1949); *U.S. v. Fleichman,* 339 US 349 (1949); *JAFRC v. McGrath,* 339 US 910 (1949); *Christoffel v. U.S.,* 338 US 84 (1948); David Scribner to Harold Christoffel, 2 September 1952, reel 3, box 3, A39, CRC Papers. Other lawyers involved in the Christoffel case included Arthur Kinoy, David Rein, Ernest Goodman, Mary Kaufman, and Joe Forer.

60. David Scribner to Harold Christoffel, 9 January 1953, reel 3, box 3, A40, CRC Papers; *Christoffel v. USA,* no. 10568, 28 November 1952, reel 3, box 3, A40, CRC Papers. The advice given by Grossman to Christoffel demonstrated that he did not see support of labor as a one-way street: "In my opinion, the possibilities of success on your case will be greatly enhanced if you will tie it in with other cases; for example, Martinsville, I consider it of the greatest importance that you go to as many unions as possible in Wisconsin, or anywhere in the Middle West and speak on the Martinsville case. I believe you should speak along with Mrs. Grayson when she is in your area and I think you should be part of the delegation going to Virginia. In fact I think this last is a 'must' " (Aubrey Grossman to Harold Christoffel, 10 January 1951, reel 3, box 3, A39, CRC Papers).

61. John Earl Haynes, "Liberals, Communists and the Popular Front in Minnesota: The Struggle to Control the Political Direction of the Labor Movement and Organized Liberalism" (Ph.D. diss., University of Minnesota, 1978), 753, 54, 812; John Haynes, "Communists and Anti-Communists in the Northern Minnesota CIO, 1936–49," *Upper Midwest History* 1 (1981): 55–73; pamphlet by CRC-Mn., undated, and circular, undated, reel 48, box 83, P114, CRC Papers; Irene Paull to Len Goldsmith, August 1948; Irene Paull to Len Goldsmith, undated; William Patterson to Irene Paull, 23 February 1950; and Irene Paull to William Patterson, 8 March 1950, reel 48, box 83, P108, CRC Papers.

62. Irene Paull to William Patterson, 21 March 1950, reel 48, box 83, P109, CRC papers; Irene Paull to William Patterson, ca. April 1950, reel 48, box 83, P109, CRC papers; Irene Paull to William Patterson, 2 June 1951; Alma Foley to CRC, 2 June 1951; and Irene Paull to Aubrey Grossman, 9 March 1951, reel 48, box 83, P110, CRC Papers.

63. Irene Paull to Aubrey Grossman, 9 March 1951, reel 48, box 83, P110, CRC Papers. As early as 1949, Paull admitted that the chapter was "actually going to pot because I work eight hours a day earning a living . . . frankly, I think the national office puts out too much material without knowing if the chapters can take care of it. . . . The national puts out loads of expensive leaflets much of it repetitious." Paull could not only be self-critical but critical as well. Irene Paull

to Milt Wolff, ca. 1949, reel 48, box 83, P108, CRC Papers; Irene Paull to William Patterson, ca. 1951, reel 48, box 83, P110, CRC Papers; Irene Paull to William Patterson, ca. 1951, reel 48, box 83, P110, CRC Papers; Alma Foley to Aubrey Grossman, 31 November 1952, reel 48, box 83, P110, CRC Papers.

64. Elmer Bormanto to CRC, 22 November 1953, reel 48, box 83, P110, CRC Papers; Paull's burnout was not a peculiar case within the nation or chapter. By early 1953 Borman was acknowledging that "I have a chronic [sic] case of sinus and . . . I have such headaches and am getting very nervous and irritable. . . ." Working in a movement under siege was not easy (Elmer Borman to William Patterson, 27 January 1954, reel 48, box 83, P111, CRC Papers). "Annual Activities Report," 195455, reel 48, box 83, P114, CRC Papers; minutes of Annual Meeting, 6 March 1955, reel 48, box 83, P114, CRC Papers.

65. *Daily Worker,* 9 October 1949; Anne Shore to Milt Kemnitz, 13 May 1947, reel 47, box 82, P89, CRC Papers; letter from Sam Sage, 12 July 1946, reel 47, box 82, P89, CRC Papers; CRC-Michigan to "Milt," 16 January 1947, reel 47, box 82, P89, CRC Papers.

66. Anne Shore to Aubrey Grossman, 10 July 1950, reel 47, box 82, P92, CRC Papers; Milt Kaufman to Jack Raskin, 21 August 1946, box 7, folder, National Correspondence 1946, CRC-Mich. Papers; William Patterson to Jack Raskin, 8 April 1949, reel 47, box 82, P91, CRC Papers; William Lawrence to Jack Raskin, 1 July 1948, reel 47, box 82, P90, CRC Papers; Dudley W. Buffa, *Union Power and American Democracy: The UAW and the Democratic Party, 1935–1972* (Ann Arbor, Mich.: UMI Press, 1984).

67. William Patterson to Jack Raskin, 4 November 1948; William Patterson to Jack Raskin, 22 November 1948; and Jack Raskin to William Patterson, 15 December 1948, reel 47, box 82, P90, CRC Papers; Anne Shore to William Patterson, 29 January 1949, reel 47, box 82, P91, CRC Papers; William Patterson to Jack Raskin, 9 November 1949, reel 47, box 82, P91, CRC Papers; William Patterson to Jack Raskin, 3 May 1950, reel 47, box 82, P92, CRC Papers.

68. Undated press release, reel 47, box 82, P100, CRC Papers; *Detroit Free Press,* 25 April 1950; *Detroit Times,* 26 February 1952; *Detroit Times,* 25 February 1952; fact sheet, McPhaul-Grossman case, ca. 1952, reel 7, box 11, A225, CRC Papers; *McPhaul v. U.S.,* 364 US 372 (1960).

69. William Patterson to Anne Shore and Art McPhaul, 28 June 1951; and Anne Shore to Aubrey Grossman, 5 April 1951, reel 47, box 82, P93, CRC Papers.

70. Jack Raskin to William Patterson and Milt Wolff, 23 November 1949, reel 47, box 82, P91, CRC Papers; Jack Raskin to William Patterson, 9 May 1950, reel 47, box 82, P92, CRC Papers; William Patterson to Jack Raskin, 17 May 1950, reel 47, box 82, P92, CRC Papers; Anne Shore to William Patterson, 22 September 1953, reel 47, box 82, P95, CRC Papers; Anne Shore to "Dear Friend," 8 January 1953, reel 47, box 82, P100, CRC Papers.

71. Fact sheet, ca. 1950, Haywood Patterson to Aubrey Grossman, 4 September 1950, reel 9, box 15, A298, CRC Papers; *Time,* 10 July 1950; *Detroit News,* 27 June 1950; Anne Shore to William Patterson, undated, box 63, folder, Haywood Patterson, 1950–52, CRC-Mich. Papers; press release, 25 August 1952, box 63, folder, Haywood Patterson Extradition, 1950–52, CRC-Mich. Papers; Aubrey Grossman to Anne Shore, 3 July 1950, reel 47, box 82, P92, CRC Papers; various news articles, ca. 1950–52, box 63, folder, Haywood Patterson clippings, CRC-Mich. Papers; Louis Machetta to Patterson Defense Committee, 10 July 1950, box 63, Folder, Haywood Patterson Extradition, 1950–52, CRC-Mich. Papers; Haywood Patterson and Earl Conrad, *Scottsboro Boy* (New York: Doubleday, 1950). William Patterson was given thanks for helping in producing this book.

72. Jack Raskin to Booth Radio, 28 February 1948, box 48, Folder, Harold Christoffel and John Rogge, 1948, CRC-Mich. Papers; *Detroit Times,* 22 August 1948, Arthur McPhaul to Carl Winter, 16 August 1951, box 2, folder, Correspondence—August–December 1951, CRC-Mich. Papers.

73. Report by Arthur McPhaul to National Executive Board of CRC, undated, box 5, folder, "Reports, 1953–54," CRC-Mich. Papers.

74. Letter from Anne Shore, 25 February 1953, box 3, folder, Dinners, 1949–54, CRC-Mich.

Papers; CRC publication, box 57, file, Labor Defender—1953, CRC-Mich. Papers; Anne Shore to Aubrey Grossman, 27 February 1951, box 7, folder, National Correspondence, January–June 1951, CRC-Mich. Papers.

75. Nadine Baxter to Aubrey Grossman, 13 June 1952, box 7, folder, National Correspondence, January–June 1952, CRC-Mich. Papers; minutes of Board of Directors meeting of CRC, 25 January 1947, reel 24, box 41, J41, CRC papers; *Afro-American*, 26 July 1947; memo to all CRC chapters, 17 June 1947, box 61, folder, Anti-Lynching 1946–48, CRC-Mich. Papers; undated press release, box 61, folder, Anti-Lynching 1946–48, CRC-Mich. Papers; *Detroit Free Press*, 12 June 1948; *Detroit Times*, 11 June 1948.

76. CRC telegram on Gordy case, 6 December 1950; and CRC to Aubrey Grossman, 28 December 1950, reel 5, box 7, A120, CRC Papers; Arthur McPhaul to *Detroit News* editor, 12 January 1951, box 72, folder, Horace White, CRC-Mich. Papers.

77. *Detroit Free Press*, 22 November 1951, 21 November 1950, 22 November 1950, 27 November 1950, 24 November 1950; *Detroit News*, 23 November 1950; *Detroit Times*, 20 November 1950; Edward Turner to Esther Gordy, 20 December 1950, box 62, folder, Charles Gordy Case, 1950–51, CRC-Mich. Papers; *Michigan Chronicle*, 2 December 1950, 9 December 1950, 16 June 1951, 19 May 1951, 26 May 1951, 9 December 1950.

78. CRC to Aubrey Grossman, 28 December 1950, reel 5, box 7, A120, CRC Papers.

79. Arthur McPhaul to Mayor Albert Cobo, 12 December 1950; and flyer, ca. 1950, box 62, folder, Charles Gordy Case, 1950–51, CRC-Mich. Papers; *Daily Worker*, 9 January 1951.

80. Anne Shore to James Wilson, 2 April 1952; and memo from Local 600, undated, box 62, folder, James Henderson Case, 1951–53, CRC-Mich. Papers; *Labor Defender*, February 1953, reel 42, box 71, N263, CRC Papers.

81. Anne Shore to Aubrey Grossman and William Patterson, 9 August 1950, reel 47, box 82, P92, CRC Papers.

82. Press release, 6 October 1947, reel 47, box 82, P97, CRC Papers; minutes of Executive Committee meeting, 8 October 1947, reel 39, box 66, N110, CRC Papers; *Albertson et al. v. Millard*, 106 FSupp 635, 345 US 242 (1952).

83. Newspaper article, 8 November 1950, box 26, folder, Constitutional Amendment—1950, CRC-Mich. Papers; Jack Raskin to Elizabeth Gurley Flynn, 17 February 1950, 6 May 1950, box 2, folder, CRC Correspondence, January–April 1949, and folder, State CRC Conference, 1949, CRC-Mich. Papers; Arthur McPhaul to William Patterson, 11 July 1951, reel 47, box 82, P63, CRC Papers; Anne Shore to William Patterson, 13 September 1950; and Art McPhaul to William Patterson, 9 August 1951, reel 47, box 82, P93, CRC Papers; William Patterson to Arthur McPhaul, 1 December 1952, reel 47, box 82, P94, CRC Papers.

84. Anne Shore to Aubrey Grossman, 22 June 1951, reel 47, box 82, P62, CRC Papers; Art McPhaul to Aubrey Grossman, 30 October 1952, reel 47, box 82, P94, CRC Papers; Art McPhaul to William Patterson, reel 47, box 82, P94, CRC Papers; Anne Shore to William Patterson, 22 September 1953; William Patterson to Anne Shore, 24 September 1953; and Art McPhaul to William Patterson, 13 October 1953, reel 47, box 82, P65, CRC Papers; *Daily Worker*, 3 October 1953, circular, 25 January 1954, reel 47, box 82, P99, CRC Papers; Jack Raskin and Anne Shore to Dr. Shmarya Kleinman and Harry Yukkoff, 3 August 1950, reel 47, box 82, P100, CRC Papers.

85. *Detroit Times*, 26 February 1952, 25 February 1952; Anne Shore to Aubrey Grossman, 3 March 1952, reel 47, box 82, P94, CRC Papers; memo, 100-7321, Sec. 8, DE 100-2760, *NLG v. FBI*, NLG Papers; folder, Berniece Baldwin—biography 1952, box 83, CRC-Mich. Papers.

86. Case of James Zarichny, 12 November 1946, reel 13, box 22, A427, CRC Papers.

87. Ellen Schrecker, "Academic Freedom and the Cold War," *Antioch Review* 38 (Summer 1980): 313–27; memo, 31 March 1949, "Fact Sheet on Academic Freedom," April 1949, reel 31, box 50, J205, CRC Papers; pamphlet, undated, reel 5, box 6, A104, CRC Papers; organizing memo, 2 June 1949; and memo, undated, reel 42, box 73, N300, CRC Papers; Conrad Komorowski to Doris Rashbaum, 18 August 1949, reel 27, box 46, J128, CRC Papers; *New York Times*, 7 July 1949; *New York Times*, 12 June 1949; *Compass*, 9 June 1949; Doris Rashbaum to

Dr. Ephraim, 17 June 1949, reel 9, box A274, CRC Papers; J. Wunderlich to CRC, 31 January 1952, reel 34, box 58, M34, CRC Papers.

88. William Buckley to Tom Clark, 10 February 1949; and S. Y. Wilson to Marcia Freedman, 5 March 1949, reel 13, box 22, A430, CRC Papers; *Daily Worker,* 2 June 1949; Telepress article, 17 September 1951, reel 6, box 9, A170, CRC Papers.

89. Undated memo, Ralph to Doris, 14 September 1949, reel 5, box 6, A104, CRC Papers; *Feiner v. New York,* 340 US 315 (1951).

90. *Brooklyn Vanguard,* 20 May 1949, reel 2, box 2, A24, CRC Papers; *New York Times,* 12 April 1949, "CCNY Knickerbocker and Davis—Bulletins, 1949," reel 3, box 4, A47, CRC Papers.

91. William Patterson to John Myers, 22 November 1949; and William Patterson to T. O. Thackrey, 27 December 1949, reel 34, box 57, M2, CRC Papers; Marcia Freedman to Dr. John Gallalee, 18 April 1949, reel 11, box 18, A373, CRC Papers.

92. "The Case of Roosevelt Ward," 2 June 1951; John Coe to CRC, 12 September 1951; John Coe to William Patterson, 3 September 1951; and Ralph Powe to John Coe, 25 April 1952, CRC Papers; law student-members of the Lawyers Guild filed an amicus in Ward's behalf. Thomas Roberts to Mark Lane, 21 April 1952, reel 12, box 21, A407, CRC Papers.

93. William Patterson to John Coe, 17 July 1951; John Coe to William Patterson, 19 July 1951; and William Patterson to John Coe, 2 August 1951, reel 12, box 21, A407, CRC Papers.

94. William Patterson to John Coe, 2 August 1951, reel 12, box 21, A407, CRC Papers; *Ward v. U.S.,* 195 F2d 441, 344 US 924 (1952); pamphlet on Roosevelt Ward, undated, reel 10, box 16, A320, CRC Papers; John Coe to William Patterson, 1 August 1941, reel 12, box 21, A407, CRC Papers; John Coe to William Patterson, 12 September 1951, reel 12, box 21, A407, CRC Papers.

95. Aubrey Grossman to William Patterson, 20 March 1949, reel 45, box 77, P25, CRC Papers; Marcia Freedman to Frank Patterson, 13 April 1949, reel 9, box 15, A296, CRC Papers; Paul Robeson, Jr. et al. to "Dear Friend," 19 November 1948; press release, 8 December 1946; and press release, 15 December 1948, reel 31, box 50, J205, CRC Papers; pamphlet, "Whither Education in the USA?" July 1949, reel 23, box 39, J2, CRC Papers; *Detroit News,* 17 March 1947, 26 April 1947; *New York Times,* 20 February 1947; *Detroit News,* 17 March 1947, 26 April 1947; *New York Times,* 20 February 1947; *Daily Worker,* 27 February 1947; *Detroit News,* 13 December 1947; Aubrey Grossman to Paul Graubard, 31 January 1952, reel 47, box 82, P88, CRC Papers; Anne Shore to William Patterson, 2 June 1952, reel 47, box 82, P94, CRC Papers; Arthur McPhaul to Malcolm Rivkin, 8 April 1952, box 72, folder, "We Charge Genocide" 1951–52, CRC-Mich. Papers; *Detroit News,* 21 May 1952; *Michigan Daily,* 21 May 1952.

96. Undated CRC pamphlet, reel 13, box 22, A432, CRC Papers; *Detroit Free Press,* 22 December 1948 (they backed Zarichny's ouster); *Daily Texan,* 4 February 1949; *Michigan Daily,* 2 March 1949; *New York Post,* 24 March 1949; *Daily Cardinal,* 8 February 1948; *Michigan Daily,* 9 March 1949, 12 March 1949, 6 March 1949; *The Observation Post,* 12 January 1949; *Yale Daily News,* 19 February 1949; *New York Post,* 2 January 1949; *Observation Post,* 22 March 1949; *Minnesota Daily,* 24 February 1949; *Harvard Crimson,* 17 March 1949; *Daily Worker,* 30 August 1949; Gary Paul Henrickson, "Minnesota in the McCarthy Period, 1946–54" (Ph.D. diss., University of Minnesota, 1981), 64, 65; Maurice Ogden to Marcia Freedman, 15 January 1949; and Lewis Kleinkopf to Marcia Freedman, 18 January 1949, reel 13, box 22, A429, CRC Papers.

97. Jackie James to Marcia Freedman, 18 April 1949; Mark Berman to Marcia Freedman, undated; Perry Rosenstein to Marcia Freedman, 16 January 1949; and Marcia Freedman to Marvin Gladstone, 8 April 1949, reel 13, box 22, A429, A430, CRC Papers; Heln Cohn to James Zarichny, 7 February 1949, reel 13, box 22, A430, CRC Papers.

98. "Michigan State College Board of Examiners Basic College Inventory of Attitudes and Beliefs," ca. 1949, reel 7, box 11, A237, CRC Papers; James Zarichny to Marcia Freedman, undated, reel 13, box 22, A430, CRC Papers; "In the Matter of James Zarichny, Alleged Contemnor," undated, reel 13, box 22, A431, CRC Papers; *Zarichny v. State Board of Agriculture et al.,* 338 US 816 (1949), cert. denied.

99. Ray Koch to William Patterson, 1 February 1949; Ray Koch to William Patterson, 16

January 1950; and John Starks to Aubrey Grossman, 17 August 1950, reel 48, box 83, P118, P119, CRC Papers; press release, 18 November 1949, reel 43, box 74, N323, CRC Papers; *State ex. rel. Toliver v. Board of Education,* 360 Mo. 671 (1950); *NLG. v. FBI,* St. Louis, 100-7318, 7 February 1952, NLG Papers; Dorothy Forest to William Patterson, 26 May 1953, reel 48, box 83, P111, CRC Papers.

100. Dorothy Forest to William Patterson, 26 May 1953, reel 48, box 83, P111, CRC Papers; flyer, ca. 1950, reel 47, box 81, P72, CRC Papers; *East St. Louis Journal,* 10 January 1951; *Daily Worker,* 30 April 1950; *St. Louis American,* 1 June 1950; David Milton to William Patterson, 22 March 1952; and Eve Milton to Angie Dickerson, 15 January 1952, reel 47, box 81, P72, CRC Papers.

101. *NLG v. FBI,* St. Louis, 100-7318, 29 June 1950, NLG Papers; John Starks to "Dear Friend," ca. 1950, St. Louis CRC Highlights of 1950, reel 48, box 83, P119, CRC Papers.

102. Loretta Waxman to William Patterson, 9 December 1953, reel 48, box 83, P119, CRC Papers; "Civil Rights News," September 1952, reel 48, box 83, P120, CRC Papers; William Patterson to Nathaniel Sweets, 27 May 1952, reel 4, box 4, A70, CRC Papers; William Patterson to Loretta Waxman, 15 September 1953, reel 48, box 83, P119, CRC Papers; Loretta Waxman to William Patterson, 30 March 1953, reel 48, box 83, P119, CRC Papers; Ray Koch to Will Hayett, 25 January 1950, reel 48, box 83, P120, CRC Papers.

103. Ben Phillips to CRC, 13 December 1953, reel 48, box 83, P122, CRC Papers; FBI, file no. 100-7264, 31 March 1950; FBI, file no. 100-7264, 8 August 1949.

104. Ray Koch to William Patterson, 16 November 1949; and Bess Dlugin to William Patterson, 26 March 1949, reel 48, box 83, P118, CRC Papers.

105. Dorothy Forest to Aubrey Grossman, 21 November 1952; Aubrey Grossman to Dorothy Forest, 22 October 1952; and Dorothy Forest to Aubrey Grossman, 19 October 1952, reel 14, box 23, B7, CRC Papers; John Raeburn to William Patterson, 13 November 1952, reel 14, box 23, B7, CRC Papers; ibid.; Dorothy Forest to Aubrey Grossman, 26 October 1952, reel 14, box 23, B7, CRC Papers; Carl Hirsch to William Patterson, 18 November 1952, reel 14, box 23, B7, CRC Papers.

106. St. Louis-CRC "Bulletin," ca. 1950, reel 48, box 83, P120, CRC Papers; *St. Louis American,* 11 December 1952; *St. Louis Post Dispatch,* 29 October 1952; John Starks to William Patterson, 12 October 1952, reel 14, box 23, B7, CRC Papers; William Patterson to Dorothy Forest, 17 November 1952, reel 14, box 23, B7, CRC Papers; Dorothy Forest to Aubrey Grossman, 3 December 1952, reel 14, box 23, B7, CRC Papers.

107. Ronald Johnson, "Organized Labor's Postwar Red Scare: The U.E. in St. Louis," *North Dakota Quarterly* 48 (Winter 1980): 28–39; U.S. Congress, House, Committee on Un-American Activities, hearings regarding Communist Infiltration of Labor Unions—Part 1 (Local 601, UE), 81st Congress, 1st session, 9–11 August 1949, p. 676; Brockman Schumacher to William Patterson, 15 July 1953, reel 48, box 83, P122, CRC Papers; Loretta Waxman to William Patterson, 29 May 1954, reel 48, box 83, P123, CRC Papers.

108. Loretta Waxman to William Patterson, 11 January 1954, reel 48, box 83, P122, CRC Papers.

Chapter 10. CRC in the Far West

1. Alzira Albaugh to Aubrey Grossman, 28 November 1950, reel 48, box 83, P131, CRC Papers; Dorothy Mohr to William Patterson, 9 October 1949, reel 48, box 83, P131, CRC Papers; reports, 1 March 1950, 7 March 1951, Salt Lake City Utah, 100-7409, FBI; William Patterson to R. F. Watters, 3 October 1951, reel 48, box 83, P1234, CRC Papers.

2. Aubrey Grossman to Yetta Land, undated, reel 6, box 10, A204, CRC Papers; Yetta Land to Aubrey Grossman, 23 April 1951; Yetta Land to Emil Freed, 12 October 1951; Phoenix CRC bulletin, August 1951; Yetta Land to CRC, 23 January 1951; William Patterson to Yetta Land, 13

March 1952; and report to Patterson meeting, 8 January 1951, reel 45, box 77, P2, CRC Papers; bulletin, August 1951, box 2, CRC-L.A. Papers.

3. CRC-Oregon Newsletter, 1 September 1949, January 1950, reel 48, box 84, P156, CRC Papers; *National Guardian,* 24 October 1951, fact sheet on the Theodore Jordan case, undated; Theodore Jordan to William Patterson, 4 August 1952; Irvin Goodman to William Patterson, 11 August 1952; William Patterson to Hugh Bryson, 11 August 1952; and Theodore Jordan to William Patterson, 27 September 1952, reel 6, box 9, A169, CRC Papers; *Oregonian,* 25 May 1954; John Daschbach to William Patterson, 30 January 1952, reel 49, box 86, P200, CRC Papers; Newsletter, 8 January 1951, reel 48, box 84, P156, CRC Papers; report, 11 December 1952, 100-345092.

4. The FBI monitored Hawaii progressives closely. Report by Wade E. Knapp, 30 September 1948, file no. 100-4905, 100-357983, FBI, *Hawaii Herald,* 11 May 1949; *Honolulu Star Bulletin,* 3 May 1949; *Hawaii Times,* 14 September 1948. One of HCLC's key cases involved the firing of John and Aiko Reinecke from their teaching posts on the grounds that they were Communists. By early 1950 the FBI was happily reporting on CRC, "dwindling active membership . . . now less than twenty." They were being refused use of meeting spaces by the YMCA, public library, etc. (file no. 100-4905, 27 February 1950, FBI). Aubrey Grossman to Myer Symonds, 29 October 1952, reel 14, box 23, B12, CRC Papers; Aubrey Grossman to Claude White, 16 October 1950, undated flyer, reel 46, box 80, P57, CRC Papers; Hawaii CRC bulletin, 12 June 1951, 22 July 1952, reel 46, box 80, P57, CRC Papers: *Honolulu Record,* 26 June 1952, William Patterson to Kunyi Ariyoshi, 5 January 1952, reel 14, box 23, B12, CRC Papers; Myer Symonds to Aubrey Grossman, 14 November 1952, reel 14, box 23, B12, CRC Papers. The local attorneys acceded to Grossman's request about the transcripts.

5. *Tri-County Herald,* 19 July 1946, *Houston Post,* 6 August 1946. Report from J. T. Kelly, 12 August 1946; and J. T. Kelly to Milt Kaufman, 25 July 1946, reel 49, box 86, P191, CRC Papers; *American Smelting Refining Co. v. NLRB,* 128 F2d 345 (1942).

6. R. D. Dixon to Aubrey Grossman, 19 April 1951, reel 49, box 86, P193, CRC Papers; Aubrey Grossman to R. D. Dixon, 13 April 1951, reel 35, box 60, M88, CRC Papers; *Peoples World,* 24 September 1948; *Dallas Morning News,* 13 November 1949, 30 January 1950; William Patterson to Rev. R. H. Harris, 6 August 1952; and William Patterson to Irene Barbaria, 31 December 1952, reel 49, box 86, CRC Papers; CRC Newsletter, 1 March 1950, box 5, folder 32, John Daschbach Papers; report, 8 November 1950, San Antonio, 100-7205, FBI; report, 26 February 1951, Dallas 100-7980, FBI.

7. J. T. Kelly to Mary Kaufman, 12 August 1946, reel 49, box 86, P191, CRC Papers; Morris Bogdanow to CRC, 27 October 1948; and James Green to William Patterson, 27 October 1948, reel 10, box 16, A323, CRC Papers; press release, 12 December 1947, box 8, folder, National CRC Release—1947, CRC-Mich. Papers.

8. Arthur Mandell and Herman Wright, 1 October 1948, reel 11, box 18, A353, CRC Papers; *Waco Tribune-Herald,* 10 April 1949; *Houston Chronicle,* 14 April 1949; *Houston Post,* 10 April 1949; CRC Newsletter, 19 January 1950, reel 8, box 13, A257, CRC Papers; CRC Newsletter, 13 January 1950, flyer, 28 April 1950, newsletter, 8 March 1950, reel 49, box 86, P190, CRC Papers; press release, 6 June 1946, reel 49, box 86, P190, CRC Papers; Morris Bodganow to William Patterson, 19 July 1950; and William Patterson to Jack Green, 21 August 1950, reel 35, box 60, M86, M87, CRC Papers; report, 7 March 1952, file nos. 10-7645, 106-345092, FBI; release, 15 April 1952, box 27, C21, CRC Papers: M. D. Rhinehart, "A Lesson in Unity: The Houston Municipal Workers' Strike of 1946," *Houston Review* 12 (Fall 1982): 137–53.

9. Civil Rights Newsletter, 17 December 1948, reel 46, box 79, P39, CRC Papers; Robert Cook to Aubrey Grossman, 20 October 1950, reel 35, box 60, M85, CRC Papers.

10. Article, 19 October 1948, reel 52, box 92, W10, CRC Papers; L. R. La Vallee to George Marshall, undated; Maia James to John Baker, 25 October 1948; and Maia James to William Patterson, 30 June 1949, reel 46, box 79, P40, CRC Papers; Maia James to William Patterson, 27

March 1950, reel 46, box 79, P41, CRC Papers; Nancy Kleinbord to William Patterson, 18 May 1950, reel 46, box 79, P41, CRC Papers.

11. *Statesman,* 6 May 1950; Nancy Kleinbord to William Patterson, 4 August 1950, reel 46, box 79, P41, CRC Papers; Nancy Kleinbord to Aubrey Grossman, 8 December 1950, reel 46, box 79, CRC Papers; Nancy Kleinbord to Aubrey Grossman, 15 November 1950, reel 46, box 79, P41, CRC Papers.

12. William Patterson to Nancy Kleinbord, 17 May 1950, reel 46, box 79, P41, CRC Papers; Nancy Kleinbord to Aubrey Grossman, 23 December 1950; and William Patterson to Nancy Kleinbord, 27 December 1950, reel 46, box 79, P41, CRC Papers.

13. Nancy Kleinbord to Aubrey Grossman, 6 January 1951; and CRC press Releases, 5 January 1951, 30 March 1951, reel 46, box 79, P41, CRC Papers; *Denver Post,* 5 January 1951; *Rocky Mountain News,* 6 January 1951.

14. Nancy Kleinbord to Aubrey Grossman and William Patterson, 14 February 1951; and Nancy Kleinbord to Aubrey Grossman, 7 March 1951, reel 46, box 79, P42, CRC Papers.

15. Nancy Kleinbord Wertheimer to William Patterson, 18 June 1951; and Nancy Kleinbord Wertheimer to Aubrey Grossman, 3 June 1951, reel 46, box 79, P46, CRC Papers; Nancy Kleinbord to Aubrey Grossman and William Patterson, 14 February 1951; Nancy Kleinbord to Aubrey Grossman, 9 April 1951; Nancy Kleinbord to Aubrey Grossman, 3 March 1951; and Nancy Kleinbord to Aubrey Grossman, 28 February 1951, reel 46, box 79, P42, CRC Papers; *Denver Post,* 4 March 1951; *Rocky Mountain News,* 3 March 1951; "In the District Court and for the City and County of Denver and State of Colorado," Civil Action #75074, division 4, *CRC v. School District, no. 1.,* judgment and order, Judge William Black, 26 January 1951.

16. Nancy Kleinbord to William Patterson, 10 August 1951, reel 46, box 79, P42, CRC Papers; *Western Voice,* 1 December 1947; *Challenge,* 31 December 1946; *Blau v. U.S.,* 340 US 332 (1950), *Rogers v. US.,* 340 US 367 (1950); Nancy Kleinbord to William Patterson, 28 June 1951; and Aubrey Grossman to Nancy Kleinbord Wertheimer, 13 August 1951, reel 46, box 79, P42, CRC Papers.

17. William Patterson to H. H. Robnett, 1 February 1952; William Patterson to H. H. Robnett, 29 May 1952; Kathryn Bardwell to Aubrey Grossman, 8 June 1952; and Kathryn Bardwell to William Patterson, 23 June 1952, reel 46, box 79, P42, CRC Papers.

18. Pamphlet, ca. 1954, reel 4, box 6, A86, CRC Papers; *Rocky Mountain News,* 1 February 1954; flyer, 1 July 1954, reel 4, box 6, A86, CRC Papers; Denver Smith Act Trial Report, 2 May 1955, reel 4, box 6, A96, CRC Papers; Denver Smith Act Trial Report, 2 May 1955, reel 4, box 6, A86, CRC Papers; *U.S. v. Bary et al.,* District Court, No. 14163, reel 4, box 6, A94, CRC Papers.

19. Flyer, ca. 1953, reel 8, box 13, A264, CRC Papers.

20. William Patterson to Clarence Hill, 18 May 1953, reel 5, box 7, A131, CRC Papers; Prisoners Relief Bulletin, ca. 1950, reel 50, box 88, R16, CRC Papers; Prisoners Relief Bulletin, April 1950, reel 51, box 89, S1, CRC Papers; Prisoners Relief Bulletin, October 1950, January 1952, reel 51, box 89, S1, CRC Papers; Vito Marcantonio to "Dear Friend," December 1950, reel 50, box 88, R17, CRC Papers; *Pittsburgh Press,* 15 December 1953.

21. Mary Pond to George Crawford, 10 September 1946; Milt Kaufman to George Crawford, 31 March 1947; and Joseph Cadden to Max Lerner, 16 October 1947, reel 4, box 5, A76, CRC Papers; Milton Kaufman to George Crawford, 28 August 1947, reel 4, box 5, A76, CRC Papers; Ralph Powe to Mrs. L. C. Akins, 6 January 1948, reel 2, box 1, A1, CRC Papers.

22. William Denton to Milton Kaufman, 28 October 1946; and Benjamin Goldring to Robert Denton, 25 November 1948, reel 4, box 6, A85, CRC Papers.

23. William Lawrence to Ralph Powe, 28 March 1950; and William Lawrence to Clyde Allen, 28 March 1950, reel 2, box 1, A2, CRC Papers; Prisoners Relief Bulletin, October 1951, reel 8, box 13, A261, CRC Papers.

24. *Pittsburgh Courier,* 11 November 1950; *CRC v. Earl Warren,* ca. 1950, reel 3, box 4, A51, CRC Papers; *Ben Davis v. Brownell et al.,* ca. 1953, box 63, folder, Ben Davis, CRC-Mich. Papers; *Ben Davis v. Brownell et al.,* ca. 1953, reel 4, box 5, A79, CRC Papers. Ralph Powe

drafted this petition; William Patterson to James Bennett, 19 January 1954, reel 5, box 7, A110, CRC Papers.

25. "Letters from the Death House," ca. 1953, Pele DeLappe Papers; "My Name Is Wesley Robert Wells," ca. 1951, DeLappe Papers.

26. Press release, 11 January 1950, reel 10, box 316, A328, CRC Papers; *Berkeley Barb,* 20 December 1968; Charles Garry and Art Goldberg, *Streetfighter in the Courtroom: The People's Advocate* (New York: Dutton, 1977), 24, 35; Barbara Kaplan to CRC-LA, ca. 1953, box 1, General Correspondence, 1953–55, CRC-LA Papers.

27. *People v. Wells,* 68 CA.2d 476 (1945); *People v. Wells,* 33 Ca.2d 330 (1949); *In re Wells,* 35 Cal.2d 889 (1950), *Ex Parte Wells,* 90 FSupp. 855 (1950), 99 FSupp 330 (1950), 201 Fed.2d 503 (1953); *Wells v. California,* October term 1953, petition for cert. writ, reel 13, box 22, A416, CRC Papers: Aubrey Grossman to Ralph Powe, 26 September 1950, reel 10, box 16, A322, CRC Papers; *Freedom,* August 1951; *Freedom,* February 1954; Aubrey Grossman to W. R. Wells, 17 July 1950, reel 13, box 22, A414, CRC Papers.

28. Charlotta Bass, *Forty Years: Memoirs from the Pages of a Newspaper* (Los Angeles: Bass, 1960), 180; *New York Daily Mirror,* 10 February 1950; Aubrey Grossman to William Patterson, 8 April 1950, reel 45, box 79, P27, CRC Papers.

29. "My Name Is Wesley Robert Wells"; Report on Warren delegation, 16 October 1950, reel 45, box 79, P34, CRC Papers; Ida Rothstein to Aubrey Grossman, 20 October 1950, reel 45, box 79, P27, CRC Papers; W. R. Wells to Ida Rothstein, 14 October 1950, reel 45, box 79, P27, CRC Papers; Aubrey Grossman to Charles Garry, 27 June 1951; W. R. Wells to Charles Garry, 3 December 1950; and W. R. Wells to Charles Garry, 3 December 1950, reel 13, box 22, A414, CRC Papers.

30. Letter to Aubrey Grossman, undated, reel 13, box 22, A414, CRC Papers; letter, 11 December 1953, reel 45, box 79, P28, CRC Papers; William Patterson to Publication, 10 November 1953, reel 13, box 22, A414, CRC Papers; Marcel Frym to Gov. Knight, 8 December 1953, reel 13, box 22, A414, CRC Papers; William Patterson to Ida Rothstein, 29 June 1953, reel 45, box 79, P28, CRC Papers; Judge A. A. Scott to Robert Ellis, 16 November 1953, reel 50, box 87, Q6, CRC Papers. *California Eagle* publisher Charlotta Bass was on Wells' defense committee.

31. Minutes of statewide meeting, 22–23 August 1953, reel 13, box 22, A414, CRC Papers; CRC Call to Work Conference: To Save the Life of Wesley Robert Wells, 12 September 1953, reel 45, box 77, P19, CRC Papers; Ida Rothstein to William Patterson, 17 September 1953, reel 45, box 79, P27, CRC Papers; information on Wells defense, newspaper of the San Francisco Building and Construction Trades Council, 29 January 1954, reel 50, box 87, Q6, CRC Papers; *San Diego Lighthouse,* 10 October 1953.

32. William Patterson to Carl Murphy, 10 November 1953, reel 13, box 22, A414, CRC Papers; Aubrey Grossman to Charles Garry, 23 March 1953, reel 13, box 22, A414, CRC Papers; Jack Greenberg to Louis Bradley, 30 March 1954; and John Hanes to Louis Bradley, 30 March 1954, reel 13, box 22, A413, CRC Papers.

33. William Patterson to Aubrey Grossman, 22 March 1954, reel 14, box 22, A414, CRC Papers; "Suggestions to Speakers," ca. 1954, reel 13, box 22, A419, CRC Papers; pamphlet on Wells, ca. 1954, CRC-Tamiment Papers; partial list of WRW supporters, ca. 1954, reel 50, box 87, Q6, CRC Papers.

34. *San Francisco News,* 1 June 1954; *San Francisco Chronicle,* 19 March 1954, 21 March 1954; *Los Angeles Mirror,* 8 March 1954; *Peoples World,* 19 March 1954; *San Francisco Chronicle,* 29 January 1954; *Los Angeles Tribune,* 22 January 1954; *Bay Area Journal,* 23 January 1954; *National Guardian,* 7 December 1953; *Seattle Daily Times,* 15 February 1954; *Pittsburgh Courier,* 3 October 1953, William Patterson to Aubrey Grossman, 23 February 1954, reel 13, box 22, A414, CRC Papers.

35. Frances Schermerhorn to William Patterson, 27 April 1954, reel 45, box 79, P29, CRC Papers; Frances Schermerhorn to William Patterson, 22 March 1954, reel 45, box 79, P29, CRC

Papers; statement, 4 May 1954, reel 51, box 90, S62, CRC Papers.

36. Flyer, undated, reel 8, box 13, A267, CRC Papers; report, file no. 100-2572, 19 February 1951, FBI; *San Diego Lighthouse,* 29 March 1952. CRC grouped the Collier story with an incident involving a Lawton, Oklahoma, white woman, wife of a soldier, who said she was gagged and raped by a Black; later she identified one of four Blacks following an intensive "manhunt"; he was arrested, but a white farmer for whom the man worked said he was working at the time, "police then began to feel a little fishy about the woman's tale." She was examined by a doctor and the whole story turned out to be a hoax. (*Oklahoma City Black Dispatch,* 21 December 1950, reel 7, box 12, A251, CRC Papers). FBI report, 25 March 1953, 100-80675.

37. Minutes of Provisional Committee of CRC-LA, 11 July 1946, reel 45, box 77, P16, CRC Papers. The focus at this early meeting was on restrictive covenants, police brutality, and strikers' aid and defense; sponsors of CRC-LA, October 1946, reel 45, box 77, P11, CRC Papers; Averill Berman to Emil Freed, 29 August 1949; Frieda Rapoport to Emil Freed, 26 January 1949; and Frank Alexander to Emil Freed, 3 May 1949, Emil Freed Papers.

38. L.A. chapter bulletin, 11 May 1949, box 1, CRC-L.A. Papers; William Patterson to Margie Robinson, 17 November 1949, reel 45, box 77, P13, CRC Papers; list of chapter victories, ca. 1954, box 2, CRC-L.A. Papers; circular, ca. 1951, box 1, CRC-L.A. Papers; financial report to CRC-L.A. Executive Board, 5 January 1949, reel 45, box 77, P22, CRC Papers; Jerold Simmons, "The Origins of the Campaign to Abolish HUAC, 1956–61; The California Connection," *Southern California Quarterly* 64 (Summer 1982): 141–57, 149. This article also illustrates the continuity of CRC members continuing the antirepression struggle after 1956.

39. "Memoradnum on Formation of Legal Panel of Los Angeles Civil Rights Congress," ca. 1948, reel 3, box 4, A66, CRC Papers; report, 9 November 1950, file no. 100-23717 FBI; CRC bulletin, March 1952, file no. 100-23717, FBI.

40. William Patterson to Anne Shore, 15 April 1948; Anne Shore to Joseph Cadden, 6 April 1948; W. S. to Anne Shore, 17 August 1948; and Aubrey Grossman to William Patterson, 28 March 1949, reel 45, box 77, P13, CRC Papers; flyer, 17 July 1953; flyer, undated, "Practical Training Course in Defense Work," ca. 1954; flyer, ca. 1953; and press release, November 1952, reel 45, box 77, P18, P19, P20, CRC Papers.

41. Flyer, undated, CRC Papers.

42. Anne Shore and Margie Robinson to William Patterson and Milt Wolff, 29 September 1949, reel 45, box 77, P12, CRC Papers.

43. "Your Rights in Case of Arrest," undated, reel 38, box 64, N75, CRC Papers; "The Jean Fields Case," undated, reel 5, box 7, A106, CRC Papers; chapter bulletin, February–March 1953, box 1, CRC-L.A. Papers.

44. Membership plan, ca. 1950, box 1, General Correspondence 1950, CRC-L.A. Papers; William Bidner and Lory Titelman to Kenneth MacGowan, 21 August 1947, box 1, General Correspondence—1947, CRC-L.A. Papers; William Bidner to "Dear Friend," 16 February 1948, box 1, General Correspondence—1948, CRC-L.A. Papers; "Civil Rights Congress—Tells the Story," ca. 1951, CRC-Tamiment Papers.

45. Flyer, undated, reel 45, box 77, P21, CRC Papers; conference minutes, 29 June 1952, box 2, East Hollywood chapter, CRC-L.A. Papers; Paulette Frishkoff, 20 January 1954, box 2, East Hollywood chapter, CRC-L.A. Papers.

46. Long Beach Bulletin, 21 August 1950, box 2, CRC-L.A. Papers; pamphlet, undated, reel 3, box 3, A28, CRC Papers; statement, 16 August 1951, reel 12, box 21, A405, CRC Papers; *Valley Sun,* 24 September 1953, box 2, Elsinore chapter, CRC-L.A. Papers.

47. Newsletter, 19 January 1950, reel 8, box 13, A257, CRC Papers; "Report on Extradition Fight and Lester Tate Victory," box 66, Extradition Material, 1950–53, CRC-Mich. Papers; *Peoples World,* 7 May 1951; *Application of Middlebrooks,* 88 FSupp 943 (1950), 948, 188 F2d 308 (1951); chapter leader Shifra Meyers asked Patterson in 1952 to look into the Niels McCullough case. He was shipped from reform school in Mississippi to Vernor, Alabama, jail "for execution under a false name" (Shifra Meyers to William Patterson, 1 August 1952, reel 6, box 10, A200,

CRC Papers). *David Hyun v. Landon,* 186 F2d 190 (1950); "Stop the Deportation Drive . . . Know Your Rights," reel 40, box 68, N174, CRC Papers; *In Re Eugene Backstrom,* 98 Ca. 2d 220 (1950).

48. Margie Robinson to William Patterson, 11 December 1950; Aubrey Grossman to Margie Robinson, 13 December 1950; Shifra Meyers to Aubrey Grossman, 29 June 1951; and Aubrey Grossman to Margie Robinson, 20 August 1951, reel 45, box 77, P14, CRC Papers; William Patterson to Margie Robinson, 15 April 1953; and Margie Robinson to "Dear Friend," 22 June 1953, reel 45, box 77, P18, CRC Papers.

49. *Parker v. L.A. County,* 338 US 327 (1949); *Garner et al. v. Board of Public Works of L.A. et al.,* 341 US 716 (1950); *People of State of California v. Henry Steinberg,* reel 10, box 17, A332, CRC Papers; pamphlet of L.A. grand jury, ca. 1949, reel 45, box 77, P20, CRC Papers; *Kaisinowitz et al. v. U.S.,* 181 F2d 632, cert. denied, 340 US 920; *Alexander v. U.S.,* 181 F2d 480 (1950), *Doran v. U.S.,* 181 F2d 489 (1950); *Alexander et al. v. U.S.,* 173 F2d 865 (1949).

50. Margie Robinson and Emil Freed to Aubrey Grossman, 30 August 1951, reel 45, box 77, P14, CRC Papers; Dorothy Mayr to Aubrey Grossman, 11 December 1952, reel 45, box 77, P15, CRC Papers; press release, 24 October 1951, reel 57, box 100, W13, CRC Papers; chapter leaders meeting, 30 September 1952, reel 45, box 77, P20, CRC Papers.

51. Aubrey Grossman to Fred Steinmetz, 22 June 1951, reel 45, box 77, P14, CRC Papers; ibid.; CEDC publication, ca. 1954, reel 42, box 71, N263, CRC Papers.

52. *Collins et al. v. Hardyman et al.,* 341 US 651 (1950), 80 FSupp 501 (1948), 183 F2d 303 (1950).

53. Press release, 17 March 1952, box 27, C22, CRC Papers; bulletin of Frederick Douglass chapter, May 1952, box 1, Frederick Couglass Chapter, 1948–53, CRC-L.A. Papers; *New York Times,* 16 March 1953.

54. Report, 29 November 1954, 9 February 1955, file no. 100-23717, FBI; report, 19 October 1954, file no. 100-23717, FBI, *NLG v. FBI,* NLG Papers; David Caute, *The Great Fear: The Anti-Communist Purge under Truman and Eisenhower,* 120, 525; Kim Chernin, *In My Mother's House: A Daughter's Story* (New York: Ticknor & Fields, 1983).

55. *Wells v. California,* 338 US 836, cert. denied (1949); *People v. Wells,* 202 P2d. 53 (1969); *Brown v. Allen,* 344 US 443 (1952), p. 537, f.n.11; *Peoples World,* 31 December 1948; *Peoples World,* 20 June 1949. Here Grossman also explained CRC's lack of support for James Kutcher, the legless Trotskyite, who was supported by the American Legion. Ruth Fischer, also a Trotskyite, testified against Eisler, and the *Militant,* their newspaper, praised her. *Los Angeles Daily News,* 9 July 1948; and Aubrey Grossman to William Patterson, 21 May 1949, reel 45, box 77, P24, CRC Papers.

56. Aubrey Grossman to William Patterson, 20 March 1949, reel 45, box 77, P25, CRC Papers.

57. Philip Wolman, "The Oakland General Strike of 1946," *Southern California Quarterly* 57 (Summer 1975): 147–73; "Hursel Alexander: Early Recollections, ca. 1976, box 14, folder 34, William Patterson Papers. Jessica Mitford, *A Fine Old Conflict,* 107.

58. Mitford, *A Fine Old Conflict,* 255.

59. Hursel Alexander to William Patterson, 16 December 1949; and Hursel Alexander to William Patterson, reel 45, box 77, P7, CRC Papers; "Report on Police Brutality," ca. 1950; Bertram Edises statement, 5 January 1950; and Decca Truehaft to "Dear Friend," 31 March 1950, reel 45, box 77, P8, CRC Papers; radio transcript, ca. 1949, reel 45, box 77, P11, CRC Papers; *San Francisco Sun-Reporter,* 14 January 1950.

60. "The Jerry Newson Story," by Buddy Green and Steve Murdock, ca. 1950, reel 8, box 13, A262, CRC Papers; *People v. Newson,* 37 Ca2d. 34 (1951).

61. Financial statement of Jerry Newson Defense Committee, ca. 1950, reel 45, box 77, P8, CRC Papers; "How We Published and Sold the 'Jerry Newson Story,'" ca. 1950, reel 45, box 77, P10, CRC Papers.

62. "Facts in the Case of Charles Williams," 27 July 1950, reel 8, box 13, A257, CRC Papers.

63. Hursel Alexander to William Patterson, 12 November 1950, reel 45, box 77, P7, CRC Papers; Hursel Alexander to William Patterson, 17 November 1949; and William Patterson to Decca Truhaft, 10 March 1951, reel 45, box 77, P7, CRC Papers.

64. William Patterson to Decca Truehaft, 18 July 1950; fact sheet on Jim Crow Hirin at Permanente Foundation Hospital, ca. 1950; and William Patterson to Decca Truehaft, 17 May 1951, reel 45, box 77, P6, CRC Papers. Though Patterson was a frequent correspondent, Truehaft could not get enough of hearing from him: "Why don't you guys write? I haven't had a letter from you or Pat for months . . . it becomes such a one-way road because I never hear from the National Office anymore" (Decca Truehaft to William Patterson, 11 April 1952, reel 45, box 77, P6, CRC Papers).

65. Aubrey Grossman to Decca Truehaft, 4 December 1950; Decca Truehaft to William Patterson, undated; Decca Truehaft to Aubrey Grossman, 7 December 1950; Decca Truehaft to Aubrey Grossman, 11 June 1951; Aubrey Grossman to Decca Truehaft, 27 June 1951; and William Patterson to Decca Truehaft, 27 June 1951, reel 45, box 77, P6, CRC Papers.

66. Decca Truehaft to Aubrey Grossman, 28 August 1951; and Aubrey Grossman to Decca Truehaft, 30 August 1951, reel 19, box 30, F5, CRC Papers; *Oakland Tribune,* 3 January 1952; Decca Truehaft to Aubrey Grossman, January 1952, reel 45, box 77, P5, CRC Papers.

67. Decca Truehaft to William Patterson, 19 February 1953; and Decca Truehaft to William Patterson, 6 August 1953, reel 45, box 77, P5, CRC Papers.

68. William Patterson to Decca Truehaft, 19 September 1953; and William Patterson to Decca Truehaft, 20 November 1953, reel 45, box 77, P5, CRC Papers; Decca Truehaft to William Patterson, 6 August 1953, reel 45, box 77, P5, CRC Papers; Decca Truehaft to William Patterson, 13 August 1953, reel 45, box 77, P5, CRC Papers; William Patterson to Decca Truehaft, 15 August 1953, reel 45, box 77, P5, CRC Papers.

69. Decca Truehaft to William Patterson, 19 February 1953; Mary Green to William Patterson, 9 April 1953; and Decca Truehaft to William Patterson, 22 June 1953, reel 45, box 77, P5, CRC Papers.

70. Decca Truehaft to William Patterson, 23 November 1953; Decca Truehaft to William Patterson, 7 December 1953; and undated flyer, reel 45, box 77, P5, CRC Papers.

71. Report on CRC-S.F., ca. 1947, reel 45, box 77, P21, CRC Papers; Ida Rothstein to CRC, 27 August 1951, reel 19, box 30, F5, CRC Papers; statement of Ida Rothstein on her arrest, 11 January 1951, reel 45, box 77, P25, CRC Papers; chapter bulletin, February 1954, reel 45, box 79, P29, CRC Papers.

72. Ida Rothstein to Aubrey Grossman, 19 May 1951; William Patterson to Ida Rothstein, 5 February 1951; Ida Rothstein to Aubrey Grossman, 23 January 1951; and William Patterson to Ida Rothstein, 15 November 1951, reel 45, box 77, P25, CRC Papers.

73. Press release of Bridges-Robertson-Schmidt Defense Committee, 15 September 1951, reel 2, box 2, A21, CRC Papers; William Patterson to Harry Bridges, 31 May 1949, reel 2, box 2, A16, CRC Papers; *New York Times,* 8 January 1950.

74. Aubrey Grossman to William Patterson, 8 April 1950, reel 45, box 77, P27, CRC Papers; circular, undated, reel 2, box 2, A22, CRC Papers; "Action Letter on Bridges Cases," 12 September 1952, reel 2, box 2, A21, CRC Papers; article by Arthur McPhaul 12 December 1952, reel 2, box 2, A21, CRC Papers; *Bridges et al. v. U.S.,* 345 US 904, 199 F2d 845, 345, US 979 (1952).

75. William Patterson to Ida Rothstein, 4 May 1953, reel 45, box 79, P29, CRC Papers; Edward Robert Long, "Loyalty Oaths in California, 1947–1952: The Politics of Anti-Communism" (Ph.D. diss., University of California-San Diego, 1981), 132.

76. Press release, 8 May 1950, reel 6, box 9, A181, CRC Papers; NAACP flyer, undated, reel 45, box 79, P29, CRC Papers; Iris Noble to CRC, 10 October 1952, reel 34, box 57, M13, CRC Papers.

77. Ida Rothstein to William Patterson, 14 February 1950, reel 45, box 77, P27, CRC Papers; circular, undated, reel 3, box 3, A29, CRC Papers; *Oakland Tribune,* 16 December 1951.

78. CRC-SF pamphlet, ca. 1954, reel 15, box 7, A129, CRC Papers.

79. Ibid.; undated appeal from William Patterson; Sam Coleman to William Patterson, undated; press release, 27 May 1954; and undated William Patterson appeal, reel 15, box 7, A129, CRC Papers; press release, 3 May 1954, trial bulletin, 12 May 1954, reel 45, box 79, P29, CRC Papers.

80. Undated flyer, reel 42, box 71, N263, CRC Papers; Questionaire, ca. 1952, box 1, folder 1, Daschbach Papers; "Memorandum of Discussion with Seattle Executive Board, 25 December 1952," reel 49, box 86, P203, CRC Papers; Arthur Mulase, 11 May 1952, reel 49, box 86, P200, CRC Papers; *New Republic,* 20 February 1951; list, ca. 1952, box 2, folder 1, Daschbach Papers.

81. Circular, 1949, box 2, folder 6, Daschbach Papers; John Daschbach to Metaline Miners Defense Committee, 27 March 1949, box 4, folder 7, Daschbach Papers; John Daschbach to William Patterson, 21 February 1952, reel 49, box 86, P200, CRC Papers; John Daschbach to CRC, 17 June 1952, reel 49, box 86, P200, CRC Papers; CRC Action Letter, 21 February 1950, reel 49, box 86, P203, CRC Papers; John Daschbach to William Patterson, 30 January 1952, reel 49, box 86, P200, CRC Papers; John Daschbach to William Patterson, 10 April 1952, reel 49, box 86, P200, CRC Papers: Jerry Lembcke and William Tattam, *One Union in Wood: A Political History of the International Woodworkers of America* (New York: International, 1984).

82. Lembcke and Tattam, *One Union in Wood; Washington Liberator,* May 1952, reel 49, box 86, P208, CRC Papers; John Daschbach to William Patterson, 8 May 1952, reel 49, box 86, P200, CRC Papers.

83. Terry Pettus to William Patterson, 2 March 1954, reel 49, box 86, P202, CRC Papers; John Daschbach to William Patterson, 22 March 1954, reel 49, box 86, P202, CRC Papers; *Washington Liberator,* February 1952, reel 49, box 86, P200, CRC Papers.

84. *North End Bulletin,* 25 October 1954, reel 49, box 86, P200, CRC Papers; *Peoples World,* May 1952 extra; John Daschbach to William Patterson, 8 May 1952, reel 49, box 86, P200, CRC Papers; John Daschbach to William Patterson, 10 April 1952, reel 49, box 86, P200, CRC Papers.

85. John Daschbach to William Patterson, 10 April 1952, reel 49, box 86, P200, CRC Papers; John Daschbach to CRC, 17 June 1952, reel 49, box 86, P200, CRC Papers; John Daschbach to Aubrey Grossman, 10 January 1953, reel 49, box 86, P201, CRC Papers; John Daschbach to Aubrey Grossman, 13 February 1953, reel 49, box 86, P201, CRC Papers; *Aberdeen Daily World,* 15 December 1952; [John Daschbach to William Patterson, 27 February 1953, reel 49, box 86, P201, CRC Papers.]

86. John Daschbach to William Patterson, 27 February 1953, reel 49, box 86, P201, CRC Papers; report, 13 January 1950, file no. 100-18270, FBI; circular, undated, box 1, folder 3, Daschbach Papers; *Liberator,* April 1952, reel 49, box 86, P200, CRC Papers; report, ca. 1950, box 3, folder 5, Daschbach Papers; *Seattle Post-Intelligencer,* 25 May 1951.

87. Pamphlet, ca. 1949, reel 49, box 86, P205, CRC Papers; Ted Astley to CRC, 13 May 1949, report on "Washington and Oregon Academic Freedom Cases," ca. 1949, reel 49, box 86, P206, CRC Papers; report, ca. 1949, box 5, folder 1, folder 3, Daschbach Papers.

88. John Daschbach to CRC, 29 August 1950; William Patterson to John Daschbach, 30 August 1951; and John Daschbach to William Patterson, 28 August 1951, reel 49, box 86, P199, CRC Papers; William Patterson to John Daschbach, 16 December 1952, reel 49, box 86, P200, CRC Papers.

89. Newsletter, ca. 1953, reel 59, box 103, W68, CRC Papers; flyer, ca. 1953, box 5, folder 30, Daschbach Papers; John Daschbach to William Patterson, 26 May 1953; William Patterson to John Daschbach, 2 June 1953; and William Patterson to John Daschbach, 7 August 1953, reel 49, box 86, P201, CRC Papers.

90. William Patterson to John Daschbach, 8 August 1953, reel 49, box 86, P201, CRC Papers; John Daschbach to William Patterson, 11 August 1953; and William Patterson to John Daschbach, 14 August 1953, reel 49, box 86, P201, CRC Papers.

91. John Daschbach to William Patterson, 24 March 1954; and William Patterson to John Daschbach, 16 June 1954, reel 49, box 86, P202, CRC Papers.

92. William Patterson to Paul Bowen, 20 August 1953, reel 49, box 86, P201, CRC Papers; William Patterson to John Daschbach, 20 April 1953, reel 49, box 86, P201, CRC Papers; Eleanor

Nelson to William Patterson, 31 October 1953; William Patterson to Eleanor Nelson, 24 November 1953; and John Daschbach to William Patterson, 22 March 1954, reel 49, box 86, P201, CRC Papers; statement by Irv Goodman before Ninth Circuit, 13 July 1956, box 5, folder 11, Daschbach Papers.

Chapter 11. The Demise of the Civil Rights Congress

1. National Leadership Conference, keynote address, report of deliberations, 19–20 January 1955, New York City, CRC-Tamiment Papers; statement on dissolution of the Pittsburgh Civil Rights Congress, 7 January 1956, CRC-Tamiment Papers.

2. CRC press release, 4 March 1955, reel 8, box 13, A259, CRC Papers; *New York Times,* 24 February 1955, 25 February 1955; *Daily Worker,* 27 January 1955; "Minutes of Private Hearing of Joint Legislative Committee on Charitable and Philanthropic Agencies and Organizations," 15 November 1954, reel 11, box 18, A368, CRC Papers. Patterson was disappointed in the *Pittsburgh Courier,* which published an editorial supporting the state investigation (William Patterson to W. Beverly Carter, 9 April 1955, reel 15, box 24, CRC Papers).

3. Summary of legal issues in the case of William Patterson, ca. 1954, reel 19, box 31, F33, CRC Papers; "In the Matter of the Tax Liability of Civil Rights Congress for the Years 1950, 1951, 1952," ca. 1954, reel 19, box 31, F40, CRC papers; *Patterson v. U.S.,* 125 FSupp 881, 219 F2d 659 (1955); *Patterson v. U.S.,* 75 S. CT. 256 (1954); *In the Matter of the Application of William Patterson,* 125 FSupp 881 (1954), *In the Matter of the Tax Liability of Civil Rights Congress,* 124 FSupp 68 (1954); *Patterson v. U.S.,* 124 FSupp 68 (1954).

4. *Pittsburgh Courier,* 20 November 1954; Prisoners Relief Bulletin, September 1954, reel 19, box 31, F34, CRC Papers; statement by Du Bois, 2 July 1954, reel 70, #517, Du Bois Papers; Louise Patterson to W. E. B. Du Bois, 21 July 1954, reel 70, #917, Du Bois Papers; Charlotta Bass to "Dear Pastor," 29 October 1954, folder 14, Charlotta Bass papers; Patterson letters from prison, ca. 1954, box 4, folder 3, William Patterson Papers; Louise Patterson to Mary Church Terrell, 20 July 1954; and William Patterson to Louis Burnham, 1 February 1955, reel 19, box 30, F11, CRC Papers; *Daily Worker,* 2 February 1955, 7 February 1955, 24 January 1955, 14 February 1955.

5. SACB petition, ca. 1955, reel 11, box 18, A360, CRC Papers; William Patterson to Emil Freed, 13 June 1955, reel 15, box 24, B34, CRC Papers.

6. *Herbert Brownell, Jr., v. CRC,* 1 SACB 564 (1955); *Daily Worker,* 8 May 1955; *New York Times,* 10 May 1955; *Daily Worker,* 24 May 1955; press release, 5 may 1955, reel 11, box 18, A360, CRC Papers.

7. *Herbert Brownell, Jr., v. CRC,* 1 SACB 564 (1955), pp. 596, 618, 630; CRC motion for relief, ca. 1955, reel 11, box 18, A361, CRC Papers.

8. *New York Times,* 29 March 1955; *New York Herald Tribune,* 22 February 1955; *Daily Worker,* 28 February 1955, *Daily Worker,* 24 February 1955; *New York Times,* 9 March 1955, *New York World Telegram,* 23 February 1955.

9. *Daily Worker,* 12 August 1955; *Daily Worker,* 6 July 1955; Milt Friedman to William Patterson, 7 December 1956, box 9, folder 40, William Patterson Papers. Du Bois was reluctant to testify for CRC before the SACB finding it "neither necessary nor logical" (W. E. B. Du Bois to William Patterson, 25 March 1955, reel 71, #290, Du Bois Papers). *Patterson v. SACB,* 322 F2d 395 (1963); U.S. Congress House, Committee on Internal Security, 91st Congress, 2d session, 6–8, 13–15 October, 17 November 1970.

10. But cf. e.g., August Meier and Elliot Rudwick, "The First Freedom Ride," *Phylon* 30 (1969): 213–22.

Bibliographic Note

As the notes indicate amply, the heart of this study is imbedded firmly in the Civil Rights Congress Papers (CRC Papers) located at the Schomburg Library in Harlem. The CRC collection at Wayne State University in Detroit (CRC-Mich.) is similarly full and has considerable information on the chapter's active predecessor, which sheds great light on the union battles of the 1930s and other monumental fights now unfortunately forgotten. The Southern California Library for Social Studies and Research, little known but a necessary stop for those seeking to understand the history of the U.S. left, has a CRC collection (CRC-L.A.); the Emil Freed Papers there not only are revelatory about CRC activity but also about California radicalism generally.

The William Patterson Papers at Howard University has to be deemed one of the most significant collections pertaining to the important intersection of Afro-America and the U.S. left. Those who posit a break between the so-called Old Left and New Left apparently are not familiar with the influence of Patterson and other Communists on the Black Panther party. (The fact that Charles Garry, noted CRC counsel, went on from this training to serve as the BPP's chief counsel is evidence of this "continuity.") Similarly, those who posit the Communist Party of the United States as a quiescent, pliant tool of the Soviet Union apparently have not examined the Patterson collection either. If they had, they might have concluded that these two entities are more like an old and loving married couple who have their disagreements from time to time but agree on the fundamentals and see no reason to broadcast said disagreements to neighbors—especially hostile ones.

Like the Emil Freed Papers, the Oakley Johnson Papers at the Schomburg, the John Daschbach Papers at the University of Washington-Seattle, and the Robert Dunn Papers at the University of Oregon contain significant amounts of information on the CRC but also reveal much about Euro-American Communists and leftists generally and how they fought racism specifically. New York University's Tamiment Institute has a small but adequate CRC collection (CRC-Tamiment) and other related important collections, for example, the papers of Elizabeth Gurley Flynn and Pete Cacchione.

The papers of Felix Franfurter and the papers of William Hastie, both at Harvard Law School, have only selected nuggets on CRC. The American Civil Liberties Union Papers at Princeton University are voluminous; it is long past time for these to be distilled into a comprehensive study. Like the ACLU Papers, the NAACP Papers and the Arthur Spingarn Papers, both at the Library of Congress, must be examined in order to understand reform and radicalism in the United States in the twentieth century. A fortiori this hold true for the papers of W. E. B. Du Bois at the University of Massachusetts-Amherst. The papers of Norman Thomas and the papers of Raphael Lemkin are located at the New York Public Library; critical re-evaluation of both of these vastly overrated figures are long overdue.

The papers of Ben Davis are soon to be at the Schomburg and will form the basis for my forthcoming biography of this leading Black Communist. The papers of Pele De Lappe are not yet at any library, but selected items were made available to me by her former colleague at the Communist weekly *People's World,* Mark Allen.

The papers of the National Lawyers Guild (NLG Papers) are located primarily at the Martin Luther King Center in Atlanta. Through the intervention of Ann Mari Buitrago and the massive discovery order obtained by the celebrated New York City law firm of Victor Rabinowitz, Leonard Boudin et al. in their unfortunately neglected lawsuit against the FBI on behalf of NLG (i.e., neglected by the press and the historians), I was able to view critical documents pertaining to illegal government interference in constitutionally protected CRC activity.

In addition to the Freedom of Information Act, close reading of the *Daily Worker* is a must in a study of this type, along with *Political Affairs.* Neither can judicial opinions be overlooked; nor can the Black press be neglected by any who would attempt to understand the fortunes of the U.S. left. The newspapers are many, but the *Afro-American* chain controlled by the heralded Murphy clan of Baltimore can be seen as a bellwether and weathervane.

Index